KINGS OF THE Bs

TODD McCARTHY is a graduate of Stanford University, where he was film critic and entertainment editor of the *Stanford Daily* for four years. He has covered film festivals in Cannes, San Francisco, London, Atlanta, and Edinburgh and has interviewed dozens of film personalities while writing for such publications as the *Chicago Daily News,* the *San Francisco Chronicle, The Boston Phoenix, Los Angeles Free Press, Hyde Parker, Film Society Review, Chaparral,* and the *San Francisco Fault.* He has also made three prize-winning short films, one of which, *Mimi,* was the first film of former Playmate and current B movie star Claudia Jennings.

CHARLES FLYNN is a graduate of the University of Chicago, where he edited and designed *Focus!* magazine. He has published film criticism in the University of Chicago *Maroon,* the *Chicago Sun-Times,* the *Chicago Daily News, Midwest,* the *Chicago Reader, Film Society Review, Hyde Parker,* and *The Journal of Popular Culture.* He has also appeared as film critic on WLS-TV, WBBM, and WLTD radio in Chicago, and has lectured about film at Lake Forest College, the University of Wisconsin, De Paul University, and Michigan State University. He has directed 16 mm. educational films about James Joyce (1971), Thoreau (1972), and the Pre-Raphaelites (1973).

E. P. DUTTON & CO., INC.
NEW YORK
1975

KINGS OF THE Bs

WORKING WITHIN THE HOLLYWOOD SYSTEM

An Anthology of Film History and Criticism

EDITED BY
TODD McCARTHY
AND
CHARLES FLYNN

Published simultaneously in Canada by Clarke, Irwin & Company Limited,
Toronto and Vancouver.

ISBN 0-525-47378-5 (DP)   ISBN 0-525-14090-5 (Cloth)
Library of Congress Catalog Card Number: 74-10478

Designed by The Etheredges

TO THE CLARK THEATRE

(1948–1970)

To paraphrase the final line of Edgar G. Ulmer's

Ruthless,

"IT WASN'T JUST A THEATRE . . .

IT WAS A WAY OF LIFE."

ACKNOWLEDGMENTS

For their contributions to the preparation of this volume, the editors would like to thank Robert Altman, Barbara Bernstein, Eddie Brandt, John Cawelti, Jack Friend, Sam and Christa Fuller, Harry Horner, Ruth Lewton, Daniel F. McCarthy, Art Murphy, Robert Newman, Shirley Ulmer, Mae Woods, and the staff of the Academy of Motion Picture Arts and Sciences Library.

.Special thanks are extended to John Mong, Linda May Strawn, and all of our interviewees, who were invariably gracious and generous with their time.

CONTENTS

FILMS

INTERVIEWS

FILMOGRAPHIES

THE CONTRIBUTORS

INTRODUCTION

Eventually we must talk of everything if there is enough time and space and printer's ink.—ANDREW SARRIS, *The American Cinema*

The genesis of this book, as of many great but as yet unmade films, can be traced to many Friday nights of drinking at a bar on the North Side of Chicago. Charles Flynn and I, along with a variable number of other film enthusiasts, discussed film, film, and more film, and would invariably get around to the previous Wednesday's edition of *Variety*, where, in the obituary section on the last inside page, the deaths of two or three more artists important to us were inevitably reported. Yes, the cinema would continue somehow, but the world was growing smaller and less distinguished. These artists to whom we'd toast farewell weekly (whose work, fortunately, we can continue to enjoy) cannot be replaced; an era was, and is, dying.

In the late 1960s and now in the 1970s, many critics have rightly complained about the enforced inactivity of such indisputably talented directors as Orson Welles, Jean Renoir, Samuel Fuller, and Nicholas Ray. These, like Buster Keaton, D. W. Griffith, Josef von Sternberg, and Erich

xi

von Stroheim before them, are the truly tragic cases because of the awesome waste caused by their nonproductivity. Directors such as Alfred Hitchcock, John Huston, and Joseph L. Mankiewicz may have revived themselves somewhat over the last couple of years, but even BBS couldn't see its way clear to giving Orson Welles the kind of money it passed out to such unproven commodities as Henry Jaglom and Jack Nicholson.

Our original thought, then, was to record and collect the testaments of the ignored and/or forgotten among Hollywood's elder statesmen (though neglected within the industry, people like Welles and Fuller have no trouble attracting scholars and critics). In accord with Henri Langlois' policy at the Cinémathèque Française, that every film ever made deserves to be saved because of the constantly changing perspective of history, we determined to reach back (some might say down) into film history as far as possible, to disregard temporarily the upper crust, to let qualitative considerations, by and large, surface where they may, perhaps to illuminate the business side of the art form for a change, and, hopefully, partially to fill a gap in film history, to study the American B (and C and Z) movie.

During the relatively few years of Charles's and my involvement in the critic/interview game, we had discovered one fact that altered our course somewhat. It is unfortunate but true that many people of advancing years do not remember the past with unfailing accuracy or clarity (there are many wonderful exceptions, of course!). Some, such as William Wyler, often choose to remember whatever the given interviewer remembers. Howard Hawks has remarked that many film critics know more about his work than he does. Others, such as Raoul Walsh and Fritz Lang, have been confronted with the same questions so many times that their answers, however amusing and fascinating, often come in the form of anecdotes, polished and perhaps revised over the years. And then there was John Ford, who delighted in tongue-twisting his interrogators. These men and their contemporaries, of course, comprise a breed of genuine originals and are among the great characters of Hollywood, but we realized that a book composed completely of interviews would not entirely fulfill our intentions.

Almost as quickly as we abandoned the idea of a predominantly interview-oriented book, we greatly modified our directorial bias in approaching our work. This is not to say that we have had second thoughts about the director as *the* film artist (Edgar G. Ulmer is the ultimate proof that distinctive and personal direction can emerge at any level of filmmaking), but we found that, especially at grade B and lower levels, the work of a given producer and even of a studio head can sometimes prove as consistent and interesting as that of many directors. Hence the significant amount of material on such figures as Sam Katzman, Val Lewton, Joe Solomon, Samuel Z. Arkoff, Steve Broidy, and producers/directors Russ Meyer, Roger Corman, William Castle, Arthur Lubin, Herschell Gordon Lewis, and Albert Zugsmith. Sadly, several men with whom we were especially anxious to talk, such as Katzman and Robert Siodmak, died while the project was still in the planning stages, which further redirected our activities.

Another factor that caused our study to deal with the present and recent past as well as the ignored personalities of earlier times was *Positif* editor Michel Ciment's call for young, modern critics not to repeat their predecessors' mistake of neglecting contemporary talents. Granted, the past must continue to be researched and mined for its rewards, but let's not overlook the Sirks, Rays, and Loseys of today.

We have elected to break down our book into five basic sections. Charles Flynn's essay, "The Schlock/Kitsch/Hack Movies" and our analysis of the economics of B movies were written expressly for this volume and, hopefully, explain the whys and hows of the field. The sections entitled "People" and "Films" are self-explanatory and, if nothing else, assert that some of these unknown or disreputable films have been seen and even appreciated by people with, we feel, discerning minds and active critical faculties. Our original list of possible subjects for the interview section ran to about forty names, but the sensibilities displayed by the individuals we finally settled upon may still represent something of a cross-section of the sensibilities that have controlled a great number of the American films ever made. The reader and scholar, as always, can draw their own conclusions.

The directorial filmography section at the end of the book is something we felt needed to be done and we also felt that it was highly appropriate to the concerns of the book. Three hundred and twenty-five is obviously an arbitrary number and we can't have escaped missing someone here or there, but most of the names are there. The names that are *not* there are those that can be found almost anywhere these days—Chaplin, Hawks, Cukor, Wilder, Welles, and even such a luminary of the B movie as Samuel Fuller. In short, the directors left out are those who are currently monopolizing the attention of the film-book industry. And the collection of photographs goes at least part of the way toward proving that, yes, there really is someone named H. Bruce Humberstone.

TODD McCARTHY

APPROACHES

THE SCHLOCK/KITSCH/HACK MOVIES (1974)

CHARLES FLYNN

Art is born of constraint and dies of freedom.—ANDRÉ GIDE

We're out to save the Hollywood film industry.—DENNIS HOPPER

Don't knock it if you haven't tried it.—LEE VAN CLEEF TO PRESTON FOSTER
IN PHIL KARLSON's *Kansas City Confidential* (1955)

> *O Watch for this remote*
> *But very self of Byron and of me,*
> *Blown empty on the white cliffs of the mind,*
> *A dispossessed His Lordship writing you*
> *A message in a bottle dropped at sea.*—LAWRENCE DURRELL, "BYRON"

My life is a B movie . . . the typical American success story is a B movie.

3

The most brilliant example of that is our new Secretary of State, Mr. Kis-
singer.—KIRK DOUGLAS ON THE *Dick Cavett Show* (ABC), OCTOBER 4, 1973

It reminds me of a movie I saw last month out by Lake Pontchartrain. Linda
and I went out to a theater in a new suburb. It was evident that somebody
had miscalculated, for the suburb had quit growing and here was the theater,
a pink stucco cube, sitting out in a field all by itself. A strong wind whipped
the waves against the seawall; even inside you could hear the racket. The
movie was about a man who had lost his memory in an accident and as a
result lost everything: his family, his friends, his money. He found himself a
stranger in a strange city. Here he had to make a fresh start, find a new
place to live, a new job, a new girl. It was supposed to be a tragedy.
—WALKER PERCY, *The Moviegoer* (1962)

I: "THE AUTHOR IS TRYING TO SAY . . ."

The first movies, if we can believe the accounts of their creators (Edison,
Muybridge, Lumière, Dickson, *et al.*), were made with absolutely no artistic
intentions. The simple miracle of a moving photographic image was more
than sufficient for the first cinema audiences.

Perhaps the biggest analytical problem confronting film criticism today—as always—is the fallacy of intention: judging a work on the basis of
the (apparent) intentions of its maker(s), and not on the intrinsic merits of
the work itself.

The New Criticism has pretty thoroughly demolished the criterion of
intention (cf. D. H. Lawrence, "Trust the tale, not the teller."). Good intentions, after all, are the materials with which, we understand, the road to hell
is paved. But the brainwashing we all received from our high-school English
teachers over *Death of a Salesman* or *The Red Pony* or *The Old Man and
the Sea* dies hard.

Historically, the fallacy of intention was introduced into movies as they
gradually became subject to old-fashioned literary-style criticism. (The
movies themselves, with highfalutin literary adaptations like D. W. Griffith's
Enoch Arden [1911] and Victor Seastrom's *Scarlet Letter* [1928] in the
silent era and later with the Thalberg/Goldwyn/Selznick "quality" cycle—
David Copperfield [1935], *Romeo and Juliet* [1936], *The Good Earth*
[1937], *Pride and Prejudice* [1940]—unfortunately promoted the concept of
movies-as-literature to generations of moviegoers and critics.)

With the words of our high-school English teachers still ringing in our
subconscious—if not in our ears—we implicitly apply the standard of inten-

tion, which we rationally admit is false. "The author is trying to say" insidiously becomes "The author *meant*" as we interpreters subtly force works to conform to our expectations of them. We devise our interpretation first and our rationale afterward.

The failure of academic film criticism—from which neither movies nor criticism may ever recover—is its implicit acceptance of the standard of intention. College English professors, who wouldn't think of criticizing Fielding or Dickens for their lack of "serious" intentions, praise Ingmar Bergman and Stanley Kubrick movies for their seriousness of moral purpose.

And even *auteur* criticism, which has turned our thinking around to some degree, can leave the impression that there are no American directors left to unearth. Ten years ago, Andrew Sarris felt the scathing wrath of Pauline Kael when he dared to propose in print that John Ford, Howard Hawks, Alfred Hitchcock, and Orson Welles are great film directors. A little later, the *Movie* group of critics resurrected Vincente Minnelli, Nicholas Ray, Frank Tashlin, Otto Preminger, and Richard Brooks. We now have book-length critical studies of Samuel Fuller, George Cukor, Joseph Losey, and Arthur Penn (as well as of such peripheral figures as Rouben Mamoulian and John Frankenheimer). Serious film journals devote entire issues to the films of Douglas Sirk and Frank Borzage.

The battle for visually oriented criticism in this country has been won. (Or, as I put it a couple of years ago at an academic gathering, *la guerre est finie*.) There is no point in prolonging the battle for the benefit of the John Simons and Stanley Kauffmanns.

The emerging trend is to assimilate "underground" Manny Farber–style criticism into the Academic Establishment. This, obviously, harms underground criticism far more than it harms academic criticism. Our critics and academics already see the same films, teach the same classes, and write the same books over and over again. The danger, and it is already happening, is that the "superstars" get all the critical attention. This happens in all academic fields, especially in the humanities. Everyone wants to "do" someone like Velázquez or Faulkner. The superstars of film history are already pretty well established: Renoir, Ford, Welles, Griffith, a few others. So we get book after book on the heavyweights.

Nothing could be further from the world of intentional/literary criticism and academic film studies than the schlock/kitsch/hack movies, as we have chosen to call them. One thing all these films have in common—perhaps the *only* thing—is their utter disreputability. Many of them were made by now-vanished minor studios with names like Republic, Monogram, PRC,

Eagle-Lion. Others are still ground out today by outfits like American-International Pictures, Cinemation, and Fanfare Pictures.

The disreputability that we ascribe to the s/k/h movies proceeds from their subject matter (more on this later), their bargain-basement budgets, and their single-minded purpose: to make money. Only one out of every eight films released today ever returns a profit. We can safely say that a far larger percentage of the s/k/h movies ultimately rewarded their makers.

Consistently praising works obviously designed to make money is quite at odds with intentional criticism. After all, what motive is lower than the profit motive? There is a strain of this anticapitalist thinking running through most academic film criticism: extended critiques of Ingmar Bergman, for example, seldom fail to mention in glowing terms that Bergman's films are funded by a division of the Swedish government, "so they don't have to make money." (And, come to think of it, we cannot recall ever seeing or hearing the slightest criticism or comment on the Swedish government in any of Ingmar's films. *Honi soit qui mal y pense.*)

Hand in hand with these two indictments of the s/k/h movies—their lack of "serious" motives and their mercenary intentions—is a third and even more telling observation: At least ninety-nine percent of the films we shall be discussing are genre films. They are formulaic. They are Westerns, gangster flicks, horror and sci-fi movies, teenpix. Almost all of the s/k/h movies fit into some generic pigeonhole. And, as we all know, genre movies are "unoriginal." They have conventions that must be observed—the Good Guy, the Happy Ending, the Mad Scientist. We demand of artists as Jean Cocteau (rightly) did: "Astonish me." Just another Western, too often, doesn't seem to turn the trick. William Beaudine, a s/k/h director if ever there was one, made the ultimate comment on the subject late one night in 1938 as he was rushing to complete a now-forgotten Monogram Western to meet a release schedule: "You mean someone out there is actually waiting to see *this*?"

II: THE INSTRUMENTS OF DARKNESS

So far we have defined the s/k/h movies in terms of (*a*) budget (low), (*b*) intention (mercenary), and (*c*) generic/formulaic structure. These are three reliable signs. Today, we might find that such movies as *The Third Man* (1950), *High Noon* (1952), and *Ben Hur* (1959) are kitsch, but they are neither schlock nor were they made by hacks (whatever other unkindnesses we might visit upon their directors).

There are sociological justifications for the s/k/h movies: the panorama of American life they present to us is both more compelling and more accurate than that of their Oscar-winning counterparts. The whole teen-movie phenomenon, for example, from the Sam Katzman and Albert Zugsmith productions of the 1950s through the Roger Corman/AIP cycle of the late 1960s, is a fascinating mirror of the gradual acceleration of Kid Kulture (see "The Truth About Teen Movies" by Richard Staehling, p. 220). In fifteen years, we have progressed from the planetarium of *Rebel Without a Cause* (1955) to Altamont and Kent State.

But ultimately, a critic must present an aesthetic justification (or explanation, at least) for the works he praises. "Greatness" is a relative matter in art. The works of William Shakespeare were generally out of favor from about 1675 to 1825. In all the one hundred years of the eighteenth century, the academy today finds but one great English poet—Pope. And most people would be doing well indeed if they could name ten truly "great" painters in the whole history of art.

So judgments of greatness, and even of artistic worth, are not to be made hastily. Even the establishment critics are gradually coming round to the view that such certified Rotha/Griffith/Grierson "classics" as *All Quiet on the Western Front* (1930), *I Am a Fugitive from a Chain Gang* (1932), *Mrs. Miniver* (1942), *The Best Years of Our Lives* (1946), *Odd Man Out* (1947), and *High Noon* look feeble at best as we move into the 1970s.

We predict that such 1960s "classics" as *West Side Story* (1961), *Lawrence of Arabia* (1962), *Tom Jones* (1963), *Dr. Strangelove* (1963), *Hud* (1963), *The Pawnbroker* (1965), *A Man for All Seasons* (1966), *The Graduate* (1967), *Easy Rider* (1969), and *Midnight Cowboy* (1969) will wear just as badly as their 1930s and 1940s cousins. (These films, indeed, are already kitsch, in the truest sense of the word.)

The point is simply that the judgments of the moment are often wrong. The movies we are speaking of as s/k/h movies may not all be worth seeing, but they are all worth saving. The challenge is to resurrect forgotten artists without being obscurantist; to celebrate little glories in minor movies without being disproportionate; to praise odd genres and artists without being perverse.

The purpose here is not to argue that *The Amazing Colossal Man* (1957) is a better movie than *Citizen Kane* (1941). The purpose is simply to assert the existence of Bert Gordon's film.

This isn't necessarily as simple as it sounds. One of the central problems with the study of the s/k/h movies is just finding out whether they exist. Many of the most disreputable films never even show up on television, and, at the moment, there is no central film index (although the activities of the American Film Institute may correct this). Another problem is cultural resistance. And here is where we reencounter the matter of genre.

As many people believe, all films in a single genre *are* more or less the same. This is both the great fascination and the great weakness of genre films. What genres embody is no less than a set of cultural myths that we like to see reenacted over and over again.

Claude Lévi-Strauss goes even further in his extensive work on the function of myth in society. In *Structural Anthropology*, Lévi-Strauss refers to the "unconscious nature of collective phenomena." The myths we celebrate are not social, but universal (not Universal), nonrational, messages. These myths are modified by the kind of culture in which we live, but their essential *structural* characteristics are the same in all cultures, whether the myths are spoken, written, or enacted.

These myths, which genres embody, are collective dreams. The form of the myth contains the encoded "message" that is the basic element of the myth. One form of "entertainment" that Lévi-Strauss discovered in several disparate societies (China, American Indian, twelfth-century Europe) was the "instrument of terror"—a strange sort of musical instrument that emitted unworldly sounds as part of a death ritual. (In European society, the death ritual was part of the Christian rites connected with Good Friday and Easter.) Our horror movies are an equivalent "instrument of terror." (See the interviews with William Castle and Herschell G. Lewis.)

We can draw a couple of conclusions from Lévi-Strauss's theories.[1] Genre films operate on audience expectations. There is very close to a one-to-one relationship between a genre movie (i.e. a s/k/h movie) and its audience. This is why s/k/h movies mirror changes in society far more closely and more accurately than their more prestigious counterparts. The audience comes to a genre movie to see the myth acted out. There is a compulsion to see the myth in its purest form.

This leads to the second conclusion: Genres operate as cultural shorthand. When we want to know about a movie, we generally ask two questions: "Who's in it?"[2] and "What's it about?" The answer to the second question can be as simple as "It's a Western" or "It's a horror movie" or even "It's an Elvis Presley movie," and we are satisfied.

[1] Mostly contained in the three-volume *Mythologiques* (Paris: Librairie Plon, 1964–1968).

[2] The intellectual may ask "Who directed it?" No one ever asks all three.

When we say that the world of the s/k/h "road" movies of the 1940s
(Edgar Ulmer's *Detour* [1945], Nicholas Ray's *They Live by Night* [1949],
Joseph Lewis' *Gun Crazy* [1949] is a world that our experience confirms,
we are responding to the universality of the myths these movies draw on.
These movies make "statements," if you will, about twentieth-century
American life in general. Obviously, these three films can be understood,
enjoyed, and appreciated by a far larger audience than that for which they
were originally designed.

So far, we have spoken of the interest that the *common* elements of films
in a single genre hold for us. It is easier to analyze the *variables* (and that,
indeed, is what the bulk of this book is devoted to). Look at two films from
the same genre:

TITLE:	*The Big House*	*The Criminal Code*
GENRE:	Prison movie	Prison movie
YEAR:	1930	1931
STUDIO:	M-G-M	Columbia
DIRECTOR:	George Hill	Howard Hawks
CAST:	Wallace Beery,	Walter Huston,
	Robert Montgomery,	Boris Karloff,
	others	others

First a note of caution: what follows is a *general* analysis of two genre
films. Arguably, neither film is a B movie in the strict sense (although *The
Criminal Code* comes close), and certainly neither director is insignificant.

But, were it not for the near-superstar reputation of Howard Hawks,
both films might qualify as perfect s/k/h movies. (George Hill, who committed suicide in 1934, should not be confused with the still-extant George
Roy Hill.)

It is somewhat irrelevant to this analysis, but most true connoisseurs
of prison films maintain that the genre did not reach its apex until the late
1930s and the early 1940s with Warners films like *Each Dawn I Die* (1939)
and *Castle on the Hudson* (1940). The two films in question, though, are
certainly among the best prison films.

We can analyze the films along a "grid" system: the common structural
element is genre. This, in turn, dictates plot, locale, and a few stock
characters.

Within this framework, one can see a whole range of variables. Visual style—including all the nuances of cutting, framing, lighting, and move-ment—is primary. Although *Min and Bill* (1930) and *The Secret Six* (1931) have their proponents, few would dispute Hawks's general superiority to Hill as a director. (We could be accused of unfairness in comparing a director who has made forty-three films in every genre over a forty-year period with one whose major output for the sound period was six films, but let us remember that Hill's departure from the film industry was voluntary.)

Certainly, we find *The Criminal Code* visually more meaningful than *The Big House.* Unfortunately *The Criminal Code* is burdened with an atrocious screenplay, as well as Columbia's Poverty-Row production values. So, on the basis of script and studio, *The Big House* has a definite edge. Again, the performances of Wallace Beery and Robert Montgomery in *The Big House* are excellent, whereas *The Criminal Code* labors under the burden of two of the worst leading players of the 1930s: Phillips Holmes and Constance Cummings. Boris Karloff's performance is extraordinary, and Walter Huston's is very good, but on balance, *The Criminal Code* suffers from its acting as well as from its screenplay.

So where do we come out on the total analysis? The voters of the august Academy of Motion Picture Arts and Sciences bestowed no less than three Oscars on *The Big House,* and none on Hawks's film the next year. That alone is a clue to critical direction. The virtues of *The Big House* are apparent to just about any viewer: script, acting, M-G-M production gloss. To appreciate *The Criminal Code,* the viewer must first wade through the deficiencies of script, acting, and production. He must, in effect, "read" the film almost as if it were in code.

Under any kind of conventional standards, *The Big House* is probably a "better" film than *The Criminal Code.* All the elements that went into it, including the direction, are reasonably decent. *The Criminal Code* has some things that are very good and some things that are very bad. Thus, the conventional critic, seeking balance and proper relationship of parts to the whole work, will opt for *The Big House.* The generic critic may find *The Criminal Code* one of the high points of Hawks's art.

The matter of variable elements within genre films leads to a paren-thetical note here: a certain film may be a "purer" example of a genre than another, whereas the film that is an inferior *genre* film may be a better film unto itself. The critic's preference here, as in all matters, is ultimately a matter of taste. Auteur critics who don't particularly like Westerns study Westerns by directors like Ford, Hawks, and Walsh because of their di-rectors, not because they are Westerns. On the other hand, critics doing generic studies of the Western will sit through miles of Western footage by insignificant directors.

The variables in genre films—small though they may seem at first glance—are the chinks in the apparently seamless armor of so many of the s/k/h films. If one watches two or three sci-fi films, one will probably not notice any great differences in quality. If one watches, say, five hundred sci-fi films, one will be aware of vast differences in quality. The mere decision to analyze a work or a group of works implies an evaluation. We spend time on those works that interest us.

To summarize what we have said so far, criticism of generic/formulaic films can work in two ways: (*a*) to isolate common, structural elements, Lévi-Strauss's "universal myths," or (*b*) to evaluate genre films individually, by concentrating on the variables within the basic genre structure. Both forms of criticism can be either aesthetic or sociopolitical.

The new wave of black-oriented films (*Shaft, Super Fly, Blacula, Slaughter, Black Caesar, Trouble Man, The Mack,* all 1970–1973) are the nearest contemporary equivalent to the s/k/h movies of yesteryear: cheaply-made, turned out in great quantity and at great speed, carefully geared to audience expectations. The titles of the black films are the giveaways of their aims; they're deliciously explicit, almost ludicrously direct (in contrast, could anyone figure out what *They Only Kill Their Masters* [1973] or *The King of Marvin Gardens* [1973] were about?).

Serious critical evaluation of the s/k/h movies elevates them to the equivalent of the Pop art of the 1960s (especially the works of Claes Oldenburg). The s/k/h movies seem to *obliterate* content (to use Susan Sontag's words). They seem positively to *wallow* in idiocy. (We shall not speak here of the idiocy of highly thought-of films like *Carnal Knowledge* [1971] and *A Clockwork Orange* [1971]; their idiocy is of a far more deadly variety.)

III: "SO WHAT *WAS* THE AUTHOR TRYING TO SAY?"

Look again at the lines from Durrell's "Byron" at the beginning of this essay. These lines could summarize the tragedy of the director in the classical Hollywood cinema. From the invention of the movies (Edison may well have been the first film director) through the early days of the silents, the director was the undisputed Lordship of the movies. Then, one day, movies became a business. The directors were dispossessed; their former business partners, the moneymen, became the bosses; and the director became an employee. Many of our greatest directors—Griffith, von Stroheim, von Sternberg, Welles—floundered on these reefs and were broken. The parallel with Byron is not inapt. The Hollywood movie director is the most Romantic artist of our age. What we are really speaking of, whether in auteur criticism or in generic criticism, is deciphering the cryptic, seemingly one-dimensional movies, the messages we find in the "bottles dropped at sea."

This, of course, is criticism at its most intellectual. The ultimate aesthetic value of the s/k/h movies has little to do with another level of our response: we like movies, I think, in which we can identify with the world the movie creates.

Hollywood is so fraught with social, psychological, historical, and mythical implications that we cannot completely separate our response to a classical Hollywood movie from our response to Hollywood-as-object.

Bernardo Bertolucci's *Before the Revolution* pays homage—through references to Jean-Luc Godard's *A Woman Is a Woman*—to the Hawks/Minnelli tradition of Hollywood cinema. In 1964, only a European director could maintain such a charmingly innocent notion of Tinseltown; today, we wonder whether anyone can. Perhaps the ultimate step in cinematic corruption will be achieved, say, around 1984 (if not before), when a young University of Southern California graduate director places in his first feature a homage to the pre-Brando Bertolucci.

Significantly, the s/k/h movies run defiantly counter to the prevailing trend (disintegration) of American cinema. From the artistic stability and integrity of Griffith's *Broken Blossoms* (1919), von Sternberg's *The Last Command* (1928), von Stroheim's *The Wedding March* (1928), Chaplin's *The Circus* (1928), and Vidor's *The Crowd* (1928), American movies have gradually become self-parodistic and self-conscious. The history of the American cinema is the history of a loss of innocence. The s/k/h movies represent a fragment of that lost innocence. They are part of an earlier way of life.

Finally, we go to the movies for great experiences, not for great ideas. Our aesthetic response to a movie is inevitably linked to our movie experiences. And, for quite a while, the s/k/h movies *were* America's movie experiences.

Obviously, today's moviegoer may find it difficult to develop a taste for the s/k/h movie. But these movies constituted the preponderance of Hollywood's output for so long that they are not only a part of movie history, but also of American cultural history.

THE ECONOMIC IMPERATIVE: WHY WAS THE B MOVIE NECESSARY? (1974)

CHARLES FLYNN and
TODD McCARTHY

For many years, supporting films have been sheer rubbish because exhibitors attach little importance to anything but the main picture . . . One of the most progressive steps that could take place in the industry would be the abolition of the double-feature bill and the substitution of a well-balanced programme. This would automatically rid us of that dubious import, the Hollywood "B" picture.—PAUL ROTHA, *The Film Till Now* (1949)

A "B" movie is a movie in which the sets shake when an actor slams a door. —ANON.

We just about owned Monogram.—HUNTZ HALL (ONE OF THE BOWERY BOYS)

Some five thousand full-length theatrical motion pictures were produced and released in the United States between 1930 and 1939 and an additional four thousand were made between 1940 and 1949.

13

The sheer volume of Hollywood's output in these two decades is paralleled in few other art forms. And, like the flourishing of painting in fifteenth-century Florence or the glory of the novel in Victorian England, the Golden Age of the movies was the product of some very definite economic circumstances.

For one thing, the Golden Age was, qualitatively, far from "golden." A very small proportion of the films produced in the 1930s and the 1940s is remembered today. We still see the star vehicles and the personal works of the great directors (Ford, Hawks, Walsh, Cukor, McCarey, *et al.*), but the overwhelming proportion of Hollywood films of the 1930s and 1940s were strictly workhorses: films designed to pay the rent and light bills.

This, indeed, implies a financial analysis that may be beyond the scope of this essay or even of this book. The definitive financial history of Hollywood has yet to be written, and this essay is hardly even a beginning. For one thing, our emphasis is almost exclusively on the studios that made B movies.

The group of disparate B studios was collectively called "The B-Hive" and "Gower Gulch." They thrived between 1935 and 1950. Today, film historians remember them as Poverty Row. Most of their products have been long forgotten; few of them appear even on television or at university film societies. And certainly few admirers of Jean-Luc Godard's *Breathless* (1959) have more than the foggiest notion of what Monogram Pictures (to which the film is jokingly dedicated) was.

A few of Poverty Row's directors have been resurrected, most notably Edgar G. Ulmer. But its organizing principles remain obscure.

Most people think of B movies (Ulmer's *Detour* [1946], for example) simply as low-budget films with formulaic plots.

Others may knowledgeably observe that the B movie was the movie on the lower half of the double bill.

These definitions are both correct—but perhaps incomplete.

The reason the Bs were the way they were (and why they existed at all) was the system of exhibition of films in the United States in the 1930s and 1940s.

THE DOUBLE BILL

From 1935 to about 1950, the American moviegoing audience expected a double bill of two complete features every time it attended the movies.

Added to this would be cartoons, a newsreel, and several trailers (previews of coming attractions, so named because they "trailed" the main feature and were often physically spliced onto its last reel).

It was the Depression-era moviegoer who first insisted on a complete three-hour-plus program for his or her money, and the practice is a logical outgrowth of the Depression state of mind. That more than a few movie-goers often failed to sit through the entire program is beside the point.

By 1932, many American theatres had started to present double bills, and by the end of 1935, the practice had proved so popular that eighty-five percent of the theatres in this country were presenting double bills. Only the most elegant first-run theatres in the major cities stuck to single features.

There had certainly been low-budget features before the arrival of the double bill, but, as we shall see, it was the double bill that made the Bs a necessity.

DISTRIBUTION: A DIGRESSION

As the double-bill era dawned, the system of movie distribution was very different from today's (and very profitable for the studios, while it lasted)

Five of the major studios (RKO, M-G-M, Twentieth Century-Fox Warner Brothers, and Paramount) owned large chains of theatres. Thus they controlled the means of exhibition as well as production and distribution. These five *vertically integrated* studios (in business terminology) controlled their products every step of the way, from creation through marketing to end use.

In a historic antitrust decision in 1948,[1] the Supreme Court decided that this type of vertical integration violated the antitrust laws, and ordered the five companies in question to sell off their theatres (see table 1).

It gradually became apparent that the studios had been making a great deal of money on their theatres and very little on production and distribution, but that is another story.

The separation of exhibition from production/distribution took time nearly five years. In order, this is how the studios divested themselves o their theatres:

[1] Written by Associate Justice William O. Douglas.

TABLE 1

December 31, 1949:	Paramount splits into Paramount Pictures Corporation and United Paramount Theatres.
December 31, 1950:	Radio-Keith-Orpheum Corporation (RKO) splits into RKO Pictures Corporation and RKO Theaters Corporation.
February 6, 1952:	M-G-M sells its theatres to Loews, Inc.
September 27, 1952:	Twentieth Century-Fox sells its theatres to National Theaters, Inc.
February 28, 1953:	Warner Brothers theatres acquired by newly formed Stanley Warner Corporation; WB stock splits two-for-one.

Until the divestiture order, a large part of the movie industry enjoyed *guaranteed* distribution. RKO films were booked into RKO theatres, Paramount films were booked into Paramount theatres, and so on. Each studio knew how many theatres it controlled and could rely on.

The studios knew, too, that they had what amounted to a guaranteed audience. Movie attendance[2] had reached seventy-five million weekly by the end of the 1930s, had continued to climb during the war, and had finally peaked at an astounding one hundred million weekly—two-thirds of the total American population—in 1946. Two years later, weekly attendance had slipped to eighty-five million and had begun the long slide to forty million in 1957, finally bottoming out at about twenty million in the late 1960s and early 1970s.

Due largely to an almost complete lack of alternate sources of entertainment (except for radio, an equally vital but formally different medium), there was an overwhelming demand for movies in the 1930s and 1940s.

The guaranteed audience meant guaranteed bookings, and vice versa.

ENTER THE B MOVIE

The enviable position of the studios in relation to their audience and the

[2] Measured in number of *tickets* sold weekly, not the actual number of people attending.

The very high mortality rate among these infant studios is not surprising when we consider that a completely new industry (producing B pictures) was being born. It was a case of survival of the fittest, and one must admire the sheer determination of the many people who chose to start movie companies in the very depths of the Great Depression.

By 1934, it was clear that the two leading B studios were Monogram, which had been founded by W. Ray Johnston in 1930, and Mascot, which Nat Levine had started in 1929. Mascot was a major source of serials and Monogram had a well-balanced B production program. By 1934, Monogram was producing thirty-six films a year.

It so happened that both firms were in debt to Consolidated Film Laboratories, a film-processing laboratory that handled many Bs. CFL's owner, Herbert J. Yates, had decided that he wanted to run a movie studio. So he foreclosed on Monogram and Mascot and merged them into Republic Pictures (a name borrowed from a previous Yates lab) early in 1935.

Levine apparently was happy with this arrangement, and Mascot-style serials produced by Levine soon became a Republic staple. But after a couple of years, Johnston and his partner Trem Carr realized that they weren't getting along with the domineering Yates; so they left Republic and resurrected Monogram during 1936 and 1937. Johnston had been president of Republic, but was clearly subordinate to Yates, who was chairman of the board. In 1937, Levine became Republic's president, a position that he, like Johnston, held for less than two years.

By the end of 1937, the new Monogram had released twenty films. And [a] new "major minor" had appeared on the scene: Grand National. It was [fo]unded early in 1936 by Edward Alperson, a former film-exchange man[ag]er, who had managed to sign up James Cagney during one of the actor's [peri]odic quarrels with Warners. Cagney appeared in John Blystone's *Great [Guy]* (1937), Grand National's one notable release. The firm did grind out [quit]e a few forgettable pictures in its three-year history; it went bankrupt in [1940] after investing $900,000 in a Victor Schertzinger musical, *Something to [Sing] About*. Alperson shared Yates's and Johnston's ambitions; it was his [finan]cial mismanagement that sank Grand National.

[A]round the time of the Grand National collapse, another film-exchange [mana]ger, Ben Judell, decided to form a studio to produce Bs and took over [for]mer Grand National studios. After running through several names [Progr]essive Pictures, Producers Distributing Corporation, Sigmund Neu[mann Pro]ductions) and a financial crisis (early in 1940, Judell's states' rights [licens]ees had to help the studio out of debt in order to obtain needed

theatres, coupled with the double bill, put the studios in something of a dilemma. They were more than willing to supply the top-of-the-bill drawing cards, the class features with big names like Gable, Cagney, Bogart, Tracy, Harlow, Davis, Crawford; but by and large, the major studios had neither the inclination nor the resources to supply the second feature. This was especially true in the 1940s, when rising production costs led the majors to abandon program pictures altogether.

It was clear that the top (or A) feature would garner the lion's share of the box-office take. Thanks to the guaranteed distribution, there was practically no risk in producing the second (or B) feature, but there were only modest profits. So the major studios found little or no financial reason for producing the B feature.

The reason for this was a system the major studios had developed in which the A feature played with a percentage of the box-office take going to the producer/distributor, and the exhibitor taking the rest. (In the case of the integrated companies, this was more or less a bookkeeping exercise since all the money eventually found its way into the same till, but the production and exhibition divisions of these companies were managed separately.) The split might be 60/40—60 percent to the distributor, 40 percent to the theatre. For an extremely popular film, the split might go to 80/20 or even 90/10.[3]

It is obvious why the studios didn't double bill two first-class pictures together. Why blow your wad on one throw, when you can extract two admissions for two films?

In contrast to the A picture's percentage deal, the bottom-half picture played for a flat (fixed) rental. Since the rental wasn't based on attendance or popularity, the producer could predict with great accuracy how much he would take in on each B picture. But the potential of spectacular gains on a smash hit was missing. That is why the major studios largely eschewed producing such films. However, there was little downside risk. A studio could produce a B for, say, $75,000 or $80,000 and clear $10,000 or $15,000 profit.

And, seeing that someone could make such a fairly certain profit supplying nothing but cheaply produced hour-long genre films for the bottom of the double bill, Republic, Monogram, and many other studios stepped in to garner the minuscule profits that the majors shunned.

[3] Even today, exhibitors can be heard to howl loud and long when the studios extract 90/10 deals for blockbusters like *The Godfather* (1972) and *The Exorcist* (1973).

A DIGRESSION: THE STATES' RIGHTS SYSTEM

Many of the B studios, financially unable to set up a national system of company-owned distribution exchanges, farmed out the releasing of their product to independent distributors under the states' rights system.

Under this arrangement, a form of franchising, a studio sold the right to distribute its films on a territorial basis. Monogram in the 1930s, for example, might sell its films in the Southeast to a distributor in Atlanta, in the Midwest to a Chicago distributor, and so on.

The states' rights distributors were known as *franchisees*. A single firm, of course, could handle product from several studios, and most did.

Monogram and Republic studios eventually set up exchanges of their own in major cities, but almost all the other B studios used the states' rights system. It was the most economical method of distribution, because it required no outright advance investment by the producer for distribution (other than the cost of producing the film in the first place). Of course, the states' rights franchisees received a percentage of each film's income for their efforts.

In the 1930s, a leading states' rights outfit was First Division, which handled Monogram, Chesterfield, and Invincible studios. In the 1940s, Astor Pictures and Cavalcade Films were two of the more important independent distributors.

Even today, many independent producers, such as Russ Meyer and Roger Corman's New World Pictures, use the states' rights system. And there are still quite a few thriving states' rights distributors, such as Chicago's Jack Gilbreth and Atlanta's Jack Vaughan.

THE B STUDIOS

In addition to the five fully integrated majors, there were three other "semimajors." Columbia and Universal (Universal-International from 1946 to 1964) were producer/distributors; United Artists distributed only.

Then came the B studios. The two most important were Republic and Monogram. They both lasted from the mid-1930s into the 1950s. (And, indeed, they merged for a little over a year, from 1935 to 1936.) The products of these two studios epitomized the classical Hollywood B studio.

In addition to Monogram and Republic, small B studios proliferated just after the introduction of sound. There was a shake-out, with many studios going under, as the Depression bottomed out from 1932 to 1934. The situation gradually stabilized, and, by 1937, the three most important B studios were Republic, Monogram, and Grand National. The B phenomenon of the 1940s was Producers Releasing Corporation (PRC), but it was gone by 1947. The 1950s saw the end of Republic and Monogram and the formation of American-International Pictures. In the 1960s, a new wave of B-cum-exploitation outfits, including Cinemation, Fanfare, and Crown International, evolved.

One of the earliest of the second-rung studios was Tiffany, known as Tiffany-Stahl in the silent era (director John M. Stahl was also the studio's part owner and head of production . . . a very nice situation for a director!). Tiffany-Stahl's chief asset at that time was Mae Murray. Its product, mainly airy high-society pictures like Stahl's *Husbands and Lov* (1924), would certainly have passed for A later on.

By 1931, however, Stahl had departed for Universal. Tiffany shift emphasis (due to the increased production costs necessitated by sour inexpensive Westerns, often with Phil Rosen or Al Rogell directing; the fall of 1932, Tiffany was in dire financial straits.

Sono Art–World Wide, another Poverty Row studio, bought remaining features as the Tiffany firm closed its doors. The same Sono Art–World Wide within a year. Twentieth Century-Fox Sono Art–World Wide, which had been founded just three years

Many other obscure studios were casualties of the 1932 Majestic, operated by an ambitious producer named Larry Da in 1935, after three years in business. Its one notable rele Strayer's *The Vampire Bat* (1933).

Chesterfield, founded in 1928, and Invincible, founded office and studio space as well as financial connections. specialized in action and mystery melodramas; they folded

Producer Ralph M. Like released his productions Pictures and Mayfair Pictures names; both firms disapp larly, producer M. H. Hoffman released under the names; he dropped both in 1934 to become a Mo went, with Monogram, to Republic in 1935.

Victory Pictures (Sam Katzman's first enter Ambassador-Conn (Maurice Conn)—the pattern over in the early 1930s. There were literally doze with impressive corporate names, that lasted tv disappeared.

product), Judell finally arrived at a name he could live with: Producers Releasing Corporation.

PRC, which even owned some theatres, was the major competition for Republic and Monogram throughout the 1940s. It produced several types of pictures: Westerns, war films, mysteries, musicals, even a couple of serials. (Monogram, it should be noted, avoided the serial field altogether.)

By the end of the 1940s, demand for Bs had dropped. PRC, always a marginal operation, was in trouble. In 1947, PRC was absorbed by Eagle-Lion, a distribution company owned by England's J. Arthur Rank. And so the PRC name disappeared. Four years later, United Artists bought out Eagle-Lion. Arthur Krim, Eagle-Lion president, became president of UA. Like Sono Art–World Wide, PRC was ultimately absorbed into a major . . . a rare occurrence.

THE MEN BEHIND THE SCENES

Few of the producers and executives associated with B studios appear to have been men of great vision or artistic ambition. Most were doubtlessly motivated by a desire for profit. Their objective was to produce pure entertainment as cheaply as possible and to earn a tidy profit.

Herbert J. Yates is something of an exception. A former tobacco-marketing executive with American Tobacco and Liggett & Myers, he had been in the film-lab business since the World War I era. In the late 1940s and early 1950s, Yates seemed consciously to be aiming Republic at major status. Unfortunately, this move came years too late—the contraction had started. And Allan Dwan, a regular Republic director, has suggested[4] that Yates was afraid to risk tying up too much money in important productions, thus denying Republic the possibility of making large profits. Republic collapsed in 1959, but Yates's lab survives today as Consolidated Film Industries.

Yates (who died in 1966 at the age of eighty-six) was an aggressive and commanding man. Always Republic's chairman and principal stockholder, Yates also took over the company's presidency in 1938, after running through several unsatisfactory candidates for the job.

W. Ray Johnston, founder of Monogram, and his partner, production executive Trem Carr, were also ambitious men. They headed up Monogram's operations until 1945, when Steve Broidy, the company's general

---

[4] In Peter Bogdanovich, *Allan Dwan: The Last Pioneer* (New York: Praeger Publishers, 1971).

sales manager, was elected president. (Broidy held the position for twenty years.) Carr died in 1946, but Johnston stayed on as chairman into the 1950s.

Leon Fromkess is the name most often associated with PRC; he was its executive producer from 1942 to 1945 when director Edgar G. Ulmer was active at the studio.

Equally industrious in their day were the King brothers (né Maurice, Frank, and Herman Kozinski), who made an impressive string of hits, mostly topical crime thrillers, for PRC and Monogram, culminating in Monogram's *Dillinger* (1945).

Sam Katzman produced just about every type of B, from serials for Victory, to Westerns for Monogram, to teenpix for Allied Artists, AIP, and Columbia.

Many B producers chose to specialize even further. Among the most prolific producers of B Westerns were A. C. Lyles (Republic), Harry Sherman, and Harry Joe Brown (Columbia). William Howard Pine and William C. Thomas (known as "The Dollar Bills") produced war and detective Bs for several studios. Edward Small (producer of many Dwan films) and Al Zimbalist (Don Siegel's *Baby Face Nelson,* 1957) specialized in action.

Applying the B approach at the majors were Brian Foy (Warners), Sol C. Siegel (Paramount), Ben Stoloff (Fox), and Sol Wurtzel (Fox).

The men who financed and produced the Bs had picked their niche, and they knew B production inside out.

PRODUCTION AND FINANCE

The B studios displayed endless imagination in their budget-cutting techniques. Inexpensive—and often inexpressive—acting, minimal sets, hack scripts, truncated shooting schedules, all were standard practices.

Most B studio front offices reviewed scripts with a fine-tooth comb to eliminate bits of time-consuming business. A script called for the actor to light a cigarette in mid-scene? A fumble would call for a retake; the actor entered with the cigarette lit. In fact, as often as not, the scene would begin with our cigarette-puffing hero already in the room! (Why waste the time, and risk a retake, by having him open the door?)

This elimination of stage business, of entrances and exits, gives most Bs a strange, almost cryptic air of flatness and unreality. The best of the B directors (Ulmer, Karlson, Dwan, Lewis, Ripley, Tourneur) developed a kind of visual shorthand to turn these minimal resources into expressive devices.

Edgar Ulmer's *Detour* (1946, PRC), probably the greatest B ever made, has a cast of only two actors (Tom Neal and Ann Savage), one minimal hotel-room set (a bed and a window), and a back-projection screen displaying an endlessly moving highway scene.

Few B studios had any qualms about reusing footage from earlier productions, especially for such expensive-to-stage scenes as chases, fights, battles, and natural disasters. And many Bs are liberally sprinkled with stock footage.

Indeed, perhaps the most audacious use ever of stock footage occurs in Ulmer's *Girls in Chains* (1943, PRC), a classic women's prison picture, incidentally. A murder scene supposedly takes place late at night atop a dam. The actors involved play the scene in medium shot, with appropriately dim lighting, on a minimal set representing the catwalk atop the dam. This scene is *intercut* with stock footage of Hoover Dam, shot at high noon (take that, Alain Resnais)!

Republic serials were routinely rereleased under different titles. All in all, Republic made sixty-six serials in its twenty-two years, and most of them were seen more than once. The twelve-episode *The Phantom Rider* became *Ghost Riders of the West;* the fifteen-episode *Secret Service in Darkest Africa* became *Manhunt in the African Jungle.* (Spencer Gordon Bennet directed both, or all four, assisted by Fred Brannon on *The Phantom Rider.*) This trick was used more than once with features, too.

On another level, the director was under great pressure at a B studio. Budgets and schedules (important at every studio) were observed as Holy Writ. After all, a day or two over schedule, a thousand or two over budget could spell the difference between profit and loss for a B. At an M-G-M, a speedy, slapdash director like W. S. ("One-Take Woody") Van Dyke was an oddity, a house joke. At a Monogram or a PRC, the second and third takes were extravagances.

In fact one PRC director, Sam Newfield (whose brother Sigmund Neufeld was PRC's executive producer), was so prolific that even PRC was embarrassed to have his name on so many of its releases. So Newfield used two aliases, "Peter Stewart" and "Sherman Scott"[5] in rotation with his real name on his PRC films.

[5] Don Miller, *B Movies* (New York: Curtis Books, Inc., 1973), pp. 202–203.

THREE STUDIOS

1. MONOGRAM. Monogram illustrates how thin a financial tightrope the B studios walked. In the decade between 1940 and 1949, Monogram released a total of 402 pictures, an average of just over 40 a year. The highest number was 53 in 1940; the lowest was 29 in 1945 and in 1947. If one excludes 1949 (in which the studio sustained a loss of over $1,100,000), Monogram's average profit per film was a minuscule $1,932.12. In 1947, Monogram's best year, it averaged a $12,996.38 profit per film. The next two years, Monogram lost money (see table 2).

Series pictures[6] were Monogram's stock-in-trade (as were Westerns for Republic). The company took over the Charlie Chan series from Fox in the early 1940s. Monogram also produced the Bowery Boys, Mr. Wong, Cisco Kid, and Bomba the Jungle Boy films. (The last series was the first production venture of Walter Mirisch, who has since gone on to far bigger things, like *West Side Story* [1961] and *In the Heat of the Night* [1967].)

In 1947, Monogram started releasing some of its films under the banner of its wholly-owned subsidiary Allied Artists, in hopes of finding new audiences for its more expensive product. Presumably, this was among those who didn't normally attend Monogram films. During this period, most Monogram budgets fell within the $90,000 to $1,000,000 range, but the first AA production, *It Happened on Fifth Avenue*, was budgeted at over $1,700,000, with director Roy del Ruth receiving $75,000 down payment as his fee, against ten percent of the world gross. The film turned out to be highly successful.

The B studios were always thinly capitalized: that is, their physical assets, cash on hand, and borrowing power were never very great. So they had no financial cushion on which to fall back in bad times. A few lean months and that was usually it. At the end of 1949, for example, Monogram (certainly one of the two most successful independents at that time) had a total net worth of about $7,000,000. By contrast, Loew's, the holding company for M-G-M and its theatres, had total assets of $230,000,000.[7]

---

[6] *Series pictures:* features with continuing characters are, of course, different from multi-episode *serials*.

[7] At the end of 1972, Loew's (without M-G-M, no less) reported total assets of $1,260,000,000; Allied Artists, the successor to Monogram, had assets of about $2,000,000.

theatres, coupled with the double bill, put the studios in something of a dilemma. They were more than willing to supply the top-of-the-bill drawing cards, the class features with big names like Gable, Cagney, Bogart, Tracy, Harlow, Davis, Crawford; but by and large, the major studios had neither the inclination nor the resources to supply the second feature. This was especially true in the 1940s, when rising production costs led the majors to abandon program pictures altogether.

It was clear that the top (or A) feature would garner the lion's share of the box-office take. Thanks to the guaranteed distribution, there was practically no risk in producing the second (or B) feature, but there were only modest profits. So the major studios found little or no financial reason for producing the B feature.

The reason for this was a system the major studios had developed in which the A feature played with a percentage of the box-office take going to the producer/distributor, and the exhibitor taking the rest. (In the case of the integrated companies, this was more or less a bookkeeping exercise since all the money eventually found its way into the same till, but the production and exhibition divisions of these companies were managed separately.) The split might be 60/40—60 percent to the distributor, 40 percent to the theatre. For an extremely popular film, the split might go to 80/20 or even 90/10.[3]

It is obvious why the studios didn't double bill two first-class pictures together. Why blow your wad on one throw, when you can extract two admissions for two films?

In contrast to the A picture's percentage deal, the bottom-half picture played for a flat (fixed) rental. Since the rental wasn't based on attendance or popularity, the producer could predict with great accuracy how much he would take in on each B picture. But the potential of spectacular gains on a smash hit was missing. That is why the major studios largely eschewed producing such films. However, there was little downside risk. A studio could produce a B for, say, $75,000 or $80,000 and clear $10,000 or $15,000 profit.

And, seeing that someone could make such a fairly certain profit supplying nothing but cheaply produced hour-long genre films for the bottom of the double bill, Republic, Monogram, and many other studios stepped in to garner the minuscule profits that the majors shunned.

---

[3] Even today, exhibitors can be heard to howl loud and long when the studios extract 90/10 deals for blockbusters like *The Godfather* (1972) and *The Exorcist* (1973).

Many of the B studios, financially unable to set up a national system of company-owned distribution exchanges, farmed out the releasing of their product to independent distributors under the states' rights system.

Under this arrangement, a form of franchising, a studio sold the right to distribute its films on a territorial basis. Monogram in the 1930s, for example, might sell its films in the Southeast to a distributor in Atlanta, in the Midwest to a Chicago distributor, and so on.

The states' rights distributors were known as *franchisees*. A single firm, of course, could handle product from several studios, and most did.

Monogram and Republic studios eventually set up exchanges of their own in major cities, but almost all the other B studios used the states' rights system. It was the most economical method of distribution, because it required no outright advance investment by the producer for distribution (other than the cost of producing the film in the first place). Of course, the states' rights franchisees received a percentage of each film's income for their efforts.

In the 1930s, a leading states' rights outfit was First Division, which handled Monogram, Chesterfield, and Invincible studios. In the 1940s, Astor Pictures and Cavalcade Films were two of the more important independent distributors.

Even today, many independent producers, such as Russ Meyer and Roger Corman's New World Pictures, use the states' rights system. And there are still quite a few thriving states' rights distributors, such as Chicago's Jack Gilbreth and Atlanta's Jack Vaughan.

THE B STUDIOS

In addition to the five fully integrated majors, there were three other "semimajors." Columbia and Universal (Universal-International from 1946 to 1964) were producer/distributors; United Artists distributed only.

Then came the B studios. The two most important were Republic and Monogram. They both lasted from the mid-1930s into the 1950s. (And, indeed, they merged for a little over a year, from 1935 to 1936.) The products of these two studios epitomized the classical Hollywood B studio.

In addition to Monogram and Republic, small B studios proliferated just after the introduction of sound. There was a shake-out, with many studios going under, as the Depression bottomed out from 1932 to 1934. The situation gradually stabilized, and, by 1937, the three most important B studios were Republic, Monogram, and Grand National. The B phenomenon of the 1940s was Producers Releasing Corporation (PRC), but it was gone by 1947. The 1950s saw the end of Republic and Monogram and the formation of American-International Pictures. In the 1960s, a new wave of B-cum-exploitation outfits, including Cinemation, Fanfare, and Crown International, evolved.

One of the earliest of the second-rung studios was Tiffany, known as Tiffany-Stahl in the silent era (director John M. Stahl was also the studio's part owner and head of production . . . a very nice situation for a director!). Tiffany-Stahl's chief asset at that time was Mae Murray. Its product, mainly airy high-society pictures like Stahl's *Husbands and Lovers* (1924), would certainly have passed for A later on.

By 1931, however, Stahl had departed for Universal. Tiffany shifted its emphasis (due to the increased production costs necessitated by sound) to inexpensive Westerns, often with Phil Rosen or Al Rogell directing; but by the fall of 1932, Tiffany was in dire financial straits.

Sono Art–World Wide, another Poverty Row studio, bought Tiffany's remaining features as the Tiffany firm closed its doors. The same fate befell Sono Art–World Wide within a year. Twentieth Century-Fox bought out Sono Art–World Wide, which had been founded just three years before.

Many other obscure studios were casualties of the 1932 to 1934 era. Majestic, operated by an ambitious producer named Larry Darmour, folded in 1935, after three years in business. Its one notable release was Frank Strayer's *The Vampire Bat* (1933).

Chesterfield, founded in 1928, and Invincible, founded in 1932, shared office and studio space as well as financial connections. Both companies specialized in action and mystery melodramas; they folded in 1936.

Producer Ralph M. Like released his productions under the Action Pictures and Mayfair Pictures names; both firms disappeared in 1933. Similarly, producer M. H. Hoffman released under the Allied and Liberty names; he dropped both in 1934 to become a Monogram producer, and went, with Monogram, to Republic in 1935.

Victory Pictures (Sam Katzman's first enterprise), Puritan Pictures, Ambassador-Conn (Maurice Conn)—the pattern repeats itself over and over in the early 1930s. There were literally dozens of tiny studios, usually with impressive corporate names, that lasted two or three years and then disappeared.

The very high mortality rate among these infant studios is not surprising when we consider that a completely new industry (producing B pictures) was being born. It was a case of survival of the fittest, and one must admire the sheer determination of the many people who chose to start movie companies in the very depths of the Great Depression.

By 1934, it was clear that the two leading B studios were Monogram, which had been founded by W. Ray Johnston in 1930, and Mascot, which Nat Levine had started in 1929. Mascot was a major source of serials and Monogram had a well-balanced B production program. By 1934, Monogram was producing thirty-six films a year.

It so happened that both firms were in debt to Consolidated Film Laboratories, a film-processing laboratory that handled many Bs. CFL's owner, Herbert J. Yates, had decided that he wanted to run a movie studio. So he foreclosed on Monogram and Mascot and merged them into Republic Pictures (a name borrowed from a previous Yates lab) early in 1935.

Levine apparently was happy with this arrangement, and Mascot-style serials produced by Levine soon became a Republic staple. But after a couple of years, Johnston and his partner Trem Carr realized that they weren't getting along with the domineering Yates; so they left Republic and resurrected Monogram during 1936 and 1937. Johnston had been president of Republic, but was clearly subordinate to Yates, who was chairman of the board. In 1937, Levine became Republic's president, a position that he, like Johnston, held for less than two years.

By the end of 1937, the new Monogram had released twenty films. And a new "major minor" had appeared on the scene: Grand National. It was founded early in 1936 by Edward Alperson, a former film-exchange manager, who had managed to sign up James Cagney during one of the actor's periodic quarrels with Warners. Cagney appeared in John Blystone's *Great Guy* (1937), Grand National's one notable release. The firm did grind out quite a few forgettable pictures in its three-year history; it went bankrupt in 1939 after investing $900,000 in a Victor Schertzinger musical, *Something to Sing About*. Alperson shared Yates's and Johnston's ambitions; it was his financial mismanagement that sank Grand National.

Around the time of the Grand National collapse, another film-exchange manager, Ben Judell, decided to form a studio to produce Bs and took over the former Grand National studios. After running through several names (Progressive Pictures, Producers Distributing Corporation, Sigmund Neufeld Productions) and a financial crisis (early in 1940, Judell's states' rights franchisees had to help the studio out of debt in order to obtain needed product), Judell finally arrived at a name he could live with: Producers Releasing Corporation.

PRC, which even owned some theatres, was the major competition for Republic and Monogram throughout the 1940s. It produced several types of pictures: Westerns, war films, mysteries, musicals, even a couple of serials. (Monogram, it should be noted, avoided the serial field altogether.)

By the end of the 1940s, demand for Bs had dropped. PRC, always a marginal operation, was in trouble. In 1947, PRC was absorbed by Eagle-Lion, a distribution company owned by England's J. Arthur Rank. And so the PRC name disappeared. Four years later, United Artists bought out Eagle-Lion. Arthur Krim, Eagle-Lion president, became president of UA. Like Sono Art–World Wide, PRC was ultimately absorbed into a major . . . a rare occurrence.

THE MEN BEHIND THE SCENES

Few of the producers and executives associated with B studios appear to have been men of great vision or artistic ambition. Most were doubtlessly motivated by a desire for profit. Their objective was to produce pure entertainment as cheaply as possible and to earn a tidy profit.

Herbert J. Yates is something of an exception. A former tobacco-marketing executive with American Tobacco and Liggett & Myers, he had been in the film-lab business since the World War I era. In the late 1940s and early 1950s, Yates seemed consciously to be aiming Republic at major status. Unfortunately, this move came years too late—the contraction had started. And Allan Dwan, a regular Republic director, has suggested[4] that Yates was afraid to risk tying up too much money in important productions, thus denying Republic the possibility of making large profits. Republic collapsed in 1959, but Yates's lab survives today as Consolidated Film Industries.

Yates (who died in 1966 at the age of eighty-six) was an aggressive and commanding man. Always Republic's chairman and principal stockholder, Yates also took over the company's presidency in 1938, after running through several unsatisfactory candidates for the job.

W. Ray Johnston, founder of Monogram, and his partner, production executive Trem Carr, were also ambitious men. They headed up Monogram's operations until 1945, when Steve Broidy, the company's general

[4] In Peter Bogdanovich, *Allan Dwan: The Last Pioneer* (New York: Praeger Publishers, 1971).

sales manager, was elected president. (Broidy held the position for twenty years.) Carr died in 1946, but Johnston stayed on as chairman into the 1950s.

Leon Fromkess is the name most often associated with PRC; he was its executive producer from 1942 to 1945 when director Edgar G. Ulmer was active at the studio.

Equally industrious in their day were the King brothers (né Maurice, Frank, and Herman Kozinski), who made an impressive string of hits, mostly topical crime thrillers, for PRC and Monogram, culminating in Monogram's *Dillinger* (1945).

Sam Katzman produced just about every type of B, from serials for Victory, to Westerns for Monogram, to teenpix for Allied Artists, AIP, and Columbia.

Many B producers chose to specialize even further. Among the most prolific producers of B Westerns were A. C. Lyles (Republic), Harry Sherman, and Harry Joe Brown (Columbia). William Howard Pine and William C. Thomas (known as "The Dollar Bills") produced war and detective Bs for several studios. Edward Small (producer of many Dwan films) and Al Zimbalist (Don Siegel's *Baby Face Nelson,* 1957) specialized in action.

Applying the B approach at the majors were Brian Foy (Warners), Sol C. Siegel (Paramount), Ben Stoloff (Fox), and Sol Wurtzel (Fox).

The men who financed and produced the Bs had picked their niche, and they knew B production inside out.

PRODUCTION AND FINANCE

The B studios displayed endless imagination in their budget-cutting techniques. Inexpensive—and often inexpressive—acting, minimal sets, hack scripts, truncated shooting schedules, all were standard practices.

Most B studio front offices reviewed scripts with a fine-tooth comb to eliminate bits of time-consuming business. A script called for the actor to light a cigarette in mid-scene? A fumble would call for a retake; the actor entered with the cigarette lit. In fact, as often as not, the scene would begin with our cigarette-puffing hero already in the room! (Why waste the time, and risk a retake, by having him open the door?)

This elimination of stage business, of entrances and exits, gives most Bs a strange, almost cryptic air of flatness and unreality. The best of the B directors (Ulmer, Karlson, Dwan, Lewis, Ripley, Tourneur) developed a kind of visual shorthand to turn these minimal resources into expressive devices.

Edgar Ulmer's *Detour* (1946, PRC), probably the greatest B ever made, has a cast of only two actors (Tom Neal and Ann Savage), one minimal hotel-room set (a bed and a window), and a back-projection screen displaying an endlessly moving highway scene.

Few B studios had any qualms about reusing footage from earlier productions, especially for such expensive-to-stage scenes as chases, fights, battles, and natural disasters. And many Bs are liberally sprinkled with stock footage.

Indeed, perhaps the most audacious use ever of stock footage occurs in Ulmer's *Girls in Chains* (1943, PRC), a classic women's prison picture, incidentally. A murder scene supposedly takes place late at night atop a dam. The actors involved play the scene in medium shot, with appropriately dim lighting, on a minimal set representing the catwalk atop the dam. This scene is *intercut* with stock footage of Hoover Dam, shot at high noon (take that, Alain Resnais)!

Republic serials were routinely rereleased under different titles. All in all, Republic made sixty-six serials in its twenty-two years, and most of them were seen more than once. The twelve-episode *The Phantom Rider* became *Ghost Riders of the West;* the fifteen-episode *Secret Service in Darkest Africa* became *Manhunt in the African Jungle.* (Spencer Gordon Bennet directed both, or all four, assisted by Fred Brannon on *The Phantom Rider.*) This trick was used more than once with features, too.

On another level, the director was under great pressure at a B studio. Budgets and schedules (important at every studio) were observed as Holy Writ. After all, a day or two over schedule, a thousand or two over budget could spell the difference between profit and loss for a B. At an M-G-M, a speedy, slapdash director like W. S. ("One-Take Woody") Van Dyke was an oddity, a house joke. At a Monogram or a PRC, the second and third takes were extravagances.

In fact one PRC director, Sam Newfield (whose brother Sigmund Neufeld was PRC's executive producer), was so prolific that even PRC was embarrassed to have his name on so many of its releases. So Newfield used two aliases, "Peter Stewart" and "Sherman Scott"[5] in rotation with his real name on his PRC films.

[5] Don Miller, *B Movies* (New York: Curtis Books, Inc., 1973), pp. 202–203.

THREE STUDIOS

1. MONOGRAM. Monogram illustrates how thin a financial tightrope the B studios walked. In the decade between 1940 and 1949, Monogram released a total of 402 pictures, an average of just over 40 a year. The highest number was 53 in 1940; the lowest was 29 in 1945 and in 1947. If one excludes 1949 (in which the studio sustained a loss of over $1,100,000), Monogram's average profit per film was a minuscule $1,932.12. In 1947, Monogram's best year, it averaged a $12,996.38 profit per film. The next two years, Monogram lost money (see table 2).

Series pictures[6] were Monogram's stock-in-trade (as were Westerns for Republic). The company took over the Charlie Chan series from Fox in the early 1940s. Monogram also produced the Bowery Boys, Mr. Wong, Cisco Kid, and Bomba the Jungle Boy films. (The last series was the first production venture of Walter Mirisch, who has since gone on to far bigger things, like *West Side Story* [1961] and *In the Heat of the Night* [1967].)

In 1947, Monogram started releasing some of its films under the banner of its wholly-owned subsidiary Allied Artists, in hopes of finding new audiences for its more expensive product. Presumably, this was among those who didn't normally attend Monogram films. During this period, most Monogram budgets fell within the $90,000 to $1,000,000 range, but the first AA production, *It Happened on Fifth Avenue*, was budgeted at over $1,700,000, with director Roy del Ruth receiving $75,000 down payment as his fee, against ten percent of the world gross. The film turned out to be highly successful.

The B studios were always thinly capitalized: that is, their physical assets, cash on hand, and borrowing power were never very great. So they had no financial cushion on which to fall back in bad times. A few lean months and that was usually it. At the end of 1949, for example, Monogram (certainly one of the two most successful independents at that time) had a total net worth of about $7,000,000. By contrast, Loew's, the holding company for M-G-M and its theatres, had total assets of $230,000,000.[7]

---

[6] *Series pictures:* features with continuing characters are, of course, different from multi-episode *serials.*

[7] At the end of 1972, Loew's (without M-G-M, no less) reported total assets of $1,260,000,000; Allied Artists, the successor to Monogram, had assets of about $2,000,000.

TABLE 2

MONOGRAM INCOME AND PROFIT, 1940–1949

Year	Gross Film Rentals	Net Profit/ (Loss)
1949	$10,177,868	$(1,108,433)
1948	9,030,906	(497,696)
1947	8,100,205	376,895
1946	6,235,228	397,474
1945	4,807,446	165,161
1944	4,300,627	177,833
1943	2,567,186	99,144
1942	2,186,092	157,103
1941	2,030,459	10,897
1940	1,945,875	(179,656)

2. THE REPUBLIC OF YATES. The largest and most stable of the B studios was unquestionably Herbert Yates's Republic. But even Republic was never able to break out of the financial straitjacket of flat-rental B bookings that, in effect, imposed a ceiling on its profit per film. Production costs rose, but income was more or less fixed, creating a squeeze on profit margins.

By the mid-1940s, Yates had devised a production system that he hoped would solve this problem. It didn't, but it provides a fascinating insight into B production methods.

Yates neatly organized Republic's product into four categories: films were classified as Jubilee, Anniversary, Deluxe, or Premiere grade.

"Jubilee" pictures were almost exclusively Westerns, Republic's mainstay, shot in seven days on $50,000 budgets. Typical of these in 1950 and 1951 were Fred Brannon's *Night Riders of Montana,* budgeted at $55,200, and Phil Ford's *Dakota Kid,* budgeted at $52,471. Republic usually cranked out two Jubilees a month, normally shooting one the first week and another the third week of every month.

A step up were the "Anniversary" pictures, with fourteen- and fifteen-day schedules and budgets in the $175,000 to $200,000 range. Again in 1950 and 1951, such Anniversaries as William Witney's *In Old Amarillo* ($184,686) and William Beaudine's *Havana Rose* ($183,744) were produced.

REPUBLIC PRODUCTIONS, INC.

SUMMARY OF DETAIL BUDGET

DIRECTOR **Phil Ford**

EST. NO. DAYS **7**

NEGATIVE FOOTAGE **23,000**

FORM 30- 2M REV. 7-48

PRODUCTION NO. **6027 "THE DAKOTA KID"**

DATE **January 3, 1951**

BUDGET DEPT. NO.	CLASSIFICATION	BUDGET
1.	STORY—Pg. 2	1,800
2.	STAFF—Pg. 2	4,960
3.	CAST, BITS & EXTRAS—Pg. 3	8,761
4.	SET CONSTRUCTION & MAINTENANCE—Pg. 4	1,451
5.	SET OPERATIONS—Pg. 4	1,993
6.	SET DRESSING & PROPS—Pg. 5	1,299
7.	WARDROBE—Pg. 5	1,091
8.	MAKEUP & HAIRDRESS—Pg. 6	491
9.	LIGHTING—Pg. 6	1,641
10.	CAMERA—Pg. 7	1,532
11.	SOUND—Pg. 7	3,304
12.	MUSIC—Pg. 8	1,920
13.	SPECIAL EQUIPMENT—LIVESTOCK, WRANGLERS & TRAINERS—Pg. 9	950
14.	TRANSPORTATION—Pg. 9	635
15.	LOCATION—Pg. 10	240
16.	SPECIAL EFFECTS—Pg. 10	355
17.	MINIATURES—Pg. 11	
18.	INSERTS—Pg. 11	163
19.	TRICK OR MATTE SHOTS—Pg. 12	
20.	PROCESS AND STOCK SHOTS—Pg. 12	317
21.	FILM—Pg. 13	1,907
22.	LABORATORY—Pg. 13	2,142
23.	TITLES & OPTICALS—Pg. 13	820
24.	FILM EDITING—Pg. 14	1,834
25.	FOREIGN VERSION—Pg. 14	
26.	TESTS—Pg. 14	
27.	NON-PRODUCTIVE SALARIES & EXPENSES—Pg. 15	12,865
	TOTAL	52,471

Vice-President _____

Producer in Charge ////////_____

Associate Producer _____

Sec. and Treas. Flat Charges Only _____

Production Manager _____

A Republic "Jubilee" budget—Phil Ford's *The Dakota Kid*.

REPUBLIC PRODUCTIONS, INC.

SUMMARY OF DETAIL BUDGET

DIRECTOR **Wm. Beaudine**

EST. NO. DAYS **14 days**

NEGATIVE FOOTAGE **45,000**
FORM 35- 2M REV. 7-48

PRODUCTION NO. **1911 "HAVANA ROSE"**

DATE **February 24, 1951**

BUDGET DEPT. NO.	CLASSIFICATION	BUDGET
1.	STORY—Pg. 2	10,334
2.	STAFF—Pg. 2	12,587
3.	CAST, BITS & EXTRAS—Pg. 3	28,776
4.	SET CONSTRUCTION & MAINTENANCE—Pg. 4	14,546
5.	SET OPERATIONS—Pg. 4	4,817
6.	SET DRESSING & PROPS—Pg. 5	5,775
7.	WARDROBE—Pg. 5	4,804
8.	MAKEUP & HAIRDRESS—Pg. 6	2,409
9.	LIGHTING—Pg. 6	5,763
10.	CAMERA—Pg. 7	2,885
11.	SOUND—Pg. 7	7,662
12.	MUSIC—Pg. 8	15,204
13.	SPECIAL EQUIPMENT—LIVESTOCK, WRANGLERS & TRAINERS Pg. 9	400
14.	TRANSPORTATION—Pg. 9	454
15.	LOCATION—Pg. 10	185
16.	SPECIAL EFFECTS—Pg. 10	440
17.	MINIATURES—Pg. 11	
18.	INSERTS—Pg. 11	212
19.	TRICK OR MATTE SHOTS—Pg. 12	
20.	PROCESS AND STOCK SHOTS—Pg. 12	847
21.	FILM—Pg. 13	4,725
22.	LABORATORY—Pg. 13	6,732
23.	TITLES & OPTICALS—Pg. 13	1,655
24.	FILM EDITING—Pg. 14	4,560
25.	FOREIGN VERSION—Pg. 14	
26.	TESTS—Pg. 14	
27.	NON-PRODUCTIVE SALARIES & EXPENSES—Pg. 15	47,972
	TOTAL	183,744

Vice-President

Producer in Charge ~~XXXXXXXXXXXXXXXXXXXXXX~~

Associate Producer

Sec. and Treas. Flat Charges Only

Production Manager

A Republic "Anniversary" budget—William Beaudine's *Havana Rose*.

REPUBLIC PRODUCTIONS, INC.

SUMMARY OF DETAIL BUDGET

DIRECTOR **Joseph Kane**   PRODUCTION NO. **1910 "Fighting U.S. Coast Guard'**

EST. NO. DAYS **22 - 4 P.P. - 2 Hol-1Male**   DATE **December 12, 1950**

NEGATIVE FOOTAGE **55,000**

FORM 33 2M REV. 7-48

BUDGET DEPT. NO.	CLASSIFICATION	BUDGET
1.	STORY—Pg. 2	12,173
2.	STAFF—Pg. 2	32,980
3.	CAST, BITS & EXTRAS—Pg. 3	114,236
4.	SET CONSTRUCTION & MAINTENANCE—Pg. 4	41,439
5.	SET OPERATIONS—Pg. 4	10,647
6.	SET DRESSING & PROPS—Pg. 5	14,221
7.	WARDROBE—Pg. 5	20,138
8.	MAKEUP & HAIRDRESS—Pg. 6	3,286
9.	LIGHTING—Pg. 6	10,747
10.	CAMERA—Pg. 7	8,909
11.	SOUND—Pg. 7	9,446
12.	MUSIC—Pg. 8	28,027
13.	SPECIAL EQUIPMENT—LIVESTOCK, WRANGLERS & TRAINERS Pg. 9	1,315
14.	TRANSPORTATION—Pg. 9	5,749
15.	LOCATION—Pg. 10	8,534
16.	SPECIAL EFFECTS—Pg. 10	5,970
17.	MINIATURES—Pg. 11	
18.	INSERTS—Pg. 11	359
19.	TRICK OR MATTE SHOTS—Pg. 12	
20.	PROCESS AND STOCK SHOTS—Pg. 12	6,161
21.	FILM—Pg. 13	5,242
22.	LABORATORY—Pg. 13	5,890
23.	TITLES & OPTICALS—Pg. 13	1,905
24.	FILM EDITING—Pg. 14	7,585
25.	FOREIGN VERSION—Pg. 14	
26.	TESTS—Pg. 14	
27.	NON-PRODUCTIVE SALARIES & EXPENSES—Pg. 15	177,150
	TOTAL	532,111

Vice-President_____

Product in Charge / / / / / / / /

Associate Producer_____

Sec. and Treas. Flat Charges Only _____

Production Manager_____

A Joseph Kane "Deluxe" budget—*Fighting U.S. Coast Guard.*

REPUBLIC PRODUCTIONS, INC.

SUMMARY OF DETAIL BUDGET

DIRECTOR **John Ford**   PRODUCTION NO. **1799 - "Rio Bravo"**

EST. NO. DAYS **32 (30. - 1 Holiday-1Travel)** DATE **June 14, 1950**

NEGATIVE FOOTAGE **80,000**

FORM 35- 2M REV. 7-46

BUDGET DEPT. NO.	CLASSIFICATION	BUDGET
1.	STORY—Pg. 2	25,450
2.	STAFF—Pg. 2	214,825
3.	CAST, BITS & EXTRAS—Pg. 3	318,433
4.	SET CONSTRUCTION & MAINTENANCE—Pg. 4	51,364
5.	SET OPERATIONS—Pg. 4	12,699
6.	SET DRESSING & PROPS—Pg. 5	38,993
7.	WARDROBE—Pg. 5	27,146
8.	MAKEUP & HAIRDRESS—Pg. 6	7,315
9.	LIGHTING—Pg. 6	8,986
10.	CAMERA—Pg. 7	15,071
11.	SOUND—Pg. 7	13,683
12.	MUSIC—Pg. 8	47,572
13.	SPECIAL EQUIPMENT—LIVESTOCK, WRANGLERS & TRAINERS—Pg. 9	49,601
14.	TRANSPORTATION—Pg. 9	56,166
15.	LOCATION—Pg. 10	68,474
16.	SPECIAL EFFECTS—Pg. 10	12,040
17.	MINIATURES—Pg. 11	
18.	INSERTS—Pg. 11	
19.	TRICK OR MATTE SHOTS—Pg. 12	
20.	PROCESS AND STOCK SHOTS—Pg. 12	227
21.	FILM—Pg. 13	5,595
22.	LABORATORY—Pg. 13	6,178
23.	TITLES & OPTICALS—Pg. 13	1,950
24.	FILM EDITING—Pg. 14	12,400
25.	FOREIGN VERSION—Pg. 14	
26.	TESTS—Pg. 14	1,500
27.	NON-PRODUCTIVE SALARIES & EXPENSES—Pg. 15	219,811
	TOTAL	1,214,899

Vice-President _____

Producer in Charge _____

Associate Producer _____

Sec. and Treas. _{Flat Charges Only} _____

Production Manager _____

A John Ford budget at Republic. *Rio Grande*'s original title, *Rio Bravo*, was, of course, used by Howard Hawks for his 1959 masterpiece.

By 1950, Joseph Kane[8] had become Republic's top house director. He was directing "Deluxe" pictures, with twenty-two-day schedules and budgets around the $500,000 mark. Among these were Kane's *The Black Hills* (1950), budgeted at $414,674, and *Fighting U.S. Coast Guard* (1951), budgeted at $532,111.

(Between 1940 and 1949, general production costs rose sixty percent, so we can project that in the early 1940s, a Jubilee cost around $30,000, an Anniversary around $120,000, and a Deluxe around $300,000.)

When directors such as John Ford, Fritz Lang, and Frank Borzage checked into the Republic lot, their projects were designated "Premiere" pictures. These were Republic's top-of-the-line pictures, designed to compete with major-studio productions for playing time in the best theatres. Yates also hoped that the Premieres would enhance Republic's public image. Beginning in the late 1940s, Republic attempted to produce at least two or three Premieres a year.

Ford's *Rio Grande* (1950), for example, the first of his three Republic films, had a thirty-two-day schedule and a budget of $1,214,899.

Similarly, Republic invested $849,452 and thirty-one days in Borzage's *Moonrise* (1948); this included a $100,000 salary for the director. Lang's *Secret Beyond the Door* (1949) was shot in thirty-three days on a $615,065 budget.

Edward Ludwig's *Wake of the Red Witch* (1948), with John Wayne and extensive tank and special-effects work, also fell into the Premiere class. Shooting took thirty-nine days, plus an extra fifteen days of tank work. (In the 1940s, Republic's miniature and tank department, headed by Theodore and Howard Lydecker, was widely regarded as the finest in Hollywood.) *Wake* was budgeted at $1,200,343, including over $50,000 for miniature and tank work.

Other Republic Premiere pictures were Orson Welles's *Macbeth* (1948), Allan Dwan's *Sands of Iwo Jima* (1949), Lewis Milestone's *The Red Pony* (1949), Ford's *The Quiet Man* (1952), which won Oscars for direction and cinematography, and Ben Hecht's *Spectre of the Rose* (1946).

The last, on every count the oddest film ever made, was Republic's first venture into "art." It epitomizes, in some strange way, Yates's impulse toward greatness; an impulse that was never purposefully directed or channeled. It is entirely likely that Mr. Yates produced *Spectre of the Rose* simply because he didn't understand it at all!

[8] See interview, pp. 313–324.

Obviously, the more expensive films were expected to bring in higher grosses. But into the early 1950s, Republic's low-budget Westerns were the company's bread and butter. Jubilee and Anniversary pictures usually grossed $500,000 each; they were the backbone of the company's profitability.

By 1957, it was quite clear that Yates's system wasn't working. A combination of audience shrinkage, television, high production costs, and a boycott against Republic by the Screen Actors Guild (over Yates's refusal to pay residuals for Republic films sold to television) was killing the studio.

As a last-ditch measure, Yates resorted to producing a few Westerns on 1940s budgets of $150,000 each. Joe Kane was briefly lured back from directing in television to helm *Duel at Apache Wells*, *Last Stagecoach West*, and *Gunfire at Indian Gap*, all made for Republic's 1957/58 season.

It was all to no avail, of course, for these prototypical Republic films were exactly what the public was now seeing free on television.

Republic was trapped and Herbert Yates knew it. Between 1935 (its first year in business) and 1939, Republic's annual gross income from film rentals stayed in a range between $8,000,000 and $9,600,000. Its net profit stayed in a narrow range between $500,000 and $1,000,000 a year, which it was never to transcend.

In the 1940s, Republic's annual grosses (for the fiscal year ending October 31) grew impressively: from $7,235,335 in 1940 to $28,086,597 in 1949. Much of the growth, however, is attributable to the sixty percent increase in the average ticket price in the same period, from $.25 (1940) to $.40 (1949).

In the same decade, Republic's profits actually *declined* by eighteen percent, from $590,031 in 1940 to $486,579 in 1949. This reflects (*a*) increased production costs; (*b*) the beginning of a decline in audience acceptance of Republic product; and (*c*) Yates's introduction of the more expensive Premiere pictures.

Republic's grosses actually made it to over $42,000,000 in 1956. But then Republic lost over $1,000,000 in 1957 and, again, in 1958.

On April 1, 1958, the aging Yates told Republic's annual stockholders' meeting that Republic was "trying to get out of the motion picture business by July 1, 1958." (What new business the company planned to enter wasn't clear.)

Indeed, Republic releases had dropped from an average of forty per year in the 1940s, to twenty-seven in 1957, to fourteen in 1958. Republic released four pictures in 1959, including a French import *OSS 117 Is Not Dead.*

In January 1959, Republic released its last picture. Fittingly, it was a B Western, Albert C. Gannaway's *Plunderers of Painted Flats,* which ran seventy-seven minutes in black-and-white.

In May 1959, the Republic studio, Yates's ultimate monument to himself and his ambitions, was leased to Lippert Pictures. Shortly thereafter it was sold to CBS and is now CBS Studio City. Yates resigned from Republic on July 31, 1959, and the firm went out of business.

All that remains now of Republic is Herbert Yates's lab, Consolidated Film Industries.

TABLE 3

REPUBLIC PICTURES, INC.

FINANCIAL DATA FOR YEAR ENDING OCTOBER 31:

Year	Gross Revenues	Net Profit/ (Loss)
1958	$33,464,482	$(1,487,337)
1957	37,899,826	(1,362,420)
1956	42,236,306	758,401
1955	39,621,099	919,034
1954	37,962,359	804,202
1953	37,265,035	679,217
1952	33,085,511	759,604
1951	33,409,613	646,404
1950	30,310,748	760,574
1949	28,086,597	486,579
1948	27,072,636	(349,990)
1947	29,581,911	570,200
1946	24,315,593	1,097,940
1945	10,016,142	572,040
1944	11,137,125	561,719
1943	9,465,338	578,339
1942	6,700,358	504,351
1941	6,256,335	513,451
1940	7,235,335	590,031

(SOURCE: *Motion Picture Almanac,* 1941–1959)

3. RKO AND CITIZEN HUGHES. The decline and fall of RKO is almost a paradigm of the history of the studios in the 1940s and 1950s. The studio that made *Citizen Kane* (1941), the Astaire-Rogers musicals, and Val Lewton's elegant cycle of thrillers also made its share of routine Bs. As one of the five integrated majors, RKO owned a network of theatres as well as the production and distribution machinery.

RKO's financial and managerial history is the most checkered of any major studio's. Between 1929 and 1955, RKO experienced eight distinct regimes, in contrast with the relatively stable, continuous management at Warner Brothers, M-G-M, and Columbia.

Between 1943 and 1947, RKO averaged an annual profit of between $5,000,000 and $7,000,000 (except in the postwar boom year of 1946, in which its profit reached $12,000,000). The value of RKO's assets (its studio, theatres, and finished films) almost doubled between 1943 and 1947, from $69,000,000 to $114,000,000.

The downhill slide began in 1948. In May of that year, Howard Hughes bought the company from financier Floyd Odlum[9] for $8,825,690. The Supreme Court antitrust decision came that same month. RKO lost $5,600,000 in 1948, $4,200,000 in 1949, and $5,800,000 in 1950. At the end of 1950, RKO Theaters, Inc., was spun off from the parent company.

The combination of (a) Hughes's highly erratic management, (b) the loss of the theatres, (c) the dwindling audience, and (d) higher production costs all contributed to the losses.

In 1952, Hughes sold RKO, but then changed his mind and regained control (at a considerable profit) when the background of the buyers was questioned and Hughes balked at giving them credit.

The losses continued. Finally, in June 1955, Hughes sold RKO to The General Tire & Rubber Co. One year later, RKO ceased to exist as a separate company. In 1958, Desilu Productions acquired the studio itself.

Mitchell Leisen's *The Girl Most Likely* (1957) was the last film RKO made. (Completed after the General Tire take-over, the film was sold to Universal-International for distribution.) *The Girl Most Likely* was a remake of a 1941 RKO film (Garson Kanin's *Tom, Dick, and Harry*), because RKO lacked even the funds to purchase new story properties.

Leisen shot *The Girl Most Likely* in the spring of 1956; the experience

---

[9] Odlum's outrageously original technique for taking over asset-rich companies, especially mutual funds, is too complicated to explain here, but it should be a part of any history of American business.

was an eerie one. Leisen has described[10] how each RKO department shut down after it had finished its work for his film. When the costumes were completed, the costume department closed. When the sets were finished, the set-design department closed. This rather depressing process continued until the film was finished—and so was RKO.

TODAY'S BS

MONOGRAM AND ALLIED ARTISTS. On November 11, 1953, Monogram metamorphosed into Allied Artists. For more than a decade, under the leadership of Steve Broidy, the company cranked out an erratic mixture of sci-fi, horror, and teenpix, including several Roger Corman, Albert Zugsmith, and Sam Katzman efforts. Like Republic, AA also tried its hand at "class" productions, with such films as William Wyler's *Friendly Persuasion* (1955) and Billy Wilder's *Love in the Afternoon* (1957), but this phase didn't last long.

Production was halted between 1965 and 1969, during which time AA simply distributed such imports as Sidney Furie's *The Leather Boys* (1963), Joseph Losey's *King and Country* (1964), Luis Buñuel's *Belle de Jour* (1967), Claude Chabrol's *La Femme Infidèle* (1969), and Claude Lelouch's phenomenally successful *A Man and a Woman* (1966).

AA made a comeback with Bob Fosse's *Cabaret* (1972) and Franklin Schaffner's $13,000,000 *Papillon* (1973). Light-years away from Monogram's Tailspin Tommy series and its 1940s slogan ("Monogram's GREAT EIGHT . . . UP with the NEW MONOGRAM"), AA is still a thinly capitalized, hit-or-miss operation. At the end of 1973, AA stock could be picked up on the American Stock Exchange for around $3.00 a share. There were few takers.

THE "EXPLOITATION" ERA. What we have been discussing up until now could be called the "classical" B period. There were definite rules of the game. There was a definite demand for Bs.

Since the mid-1950s, we have been in what might be called the "Exploitation" B period (although many contemporary producers wish to avoid the B designation altogether). These films are usually low-budget and they are usually formulaic; but they aren't designed for the bottom of the bill any-

[10] In David Chierichetti, *Hollywood Director* (New York: Curtis Books, Inc., 1973).

more—or for double bills at all. And the distribution rules are out the window, too.

There is still money to be made in inexpensive exploitation films, of course. Today's B movies, call them what you will, usually attempt to cash in on social phenomena: rock 'n roll (the Katzman/Zugsmith beat/twist cycle), youth in revolt (from *The Wild One*, 1954 to *The Wild Angels*, 1966), youth at play (the Zugsmith college series; the Asher/AIP beach-party series), drugs (*The Trip*, 1967; Richard Rush's *Psych-Out*, 1968; *et al.*), sexual liberation (from Russ Meyer to today's 16 mm. hard-core pornography), black pride and awareness (*Shaft*, 1971; *Super Fly*, 1972; *Cleopatra Jones*, 1973). The list could go on.

Beginning in 1955, Roger Corman started producing and directing topical science-fiction films. The earliest were budgeted between $18,000 and $70,000. Corman's budgets escalated up to the $250,000–$350,000 area as he moved into the early 1960s Poe cycle, but his net profit dropped from $100,000 per film to less than $30,000 per film.

After a fling with the majors (Fox and UA), Corman formed his own production company in 1970, New World Pictures. He is back on the super-low-budget ($200,000 and under) exploitation beat.

Like many earlier independents, Corman releases his New World pictures through a combination of company-owned exchanges and states' rights franchisees. But unlike the management at Monogram/Allied Artists in the late 1940s, Corman doesn't seem worried about public confusion over his corporate image. He has no qualms about releasing a *Cries and Whispers* and a *Women in Cages* in the same year (1973) under the same New World banner. Tight financial controls and careful budgeting have kept New World above water—and profitable.

Russ Meyer, through his Eve Productions, has made millions on nudies and sex pictures. He, too, stumbled when he tried to go big-time at Fox in 1970, although his first Fox film, *Beyond the Valley of the Dolls*, grossed $10,000,000 on a production cost of $900,000. But the subsequent *The Seven Minutes* (1971) and his independent *Blacksnake!* (1973) did disappointing business. Early in 1974, Meyer concluded a two-picture deal with AIP. The first picture, reportedly budgeted under $250,000, is *The Supervixens*.

The B field is still financially unstable as we move through the 1970s. Recently, Joe Solomon's Fanfare Corporation and Jerry Gross's Cinemation Industries have tumbled into near-insolvency after early hits (Fanfare's *Hell's Angels on Wheels*, 1968 and Cinemation's *Sweet Sweetback*, 1971).

Only American-International Pictures, after twenty years in existence, has carved out a stable niche in the schlock/exploitation field. The ingredients have been sharp and stable management (Samuel Z. Arkoff has run the company since its inception, and his partner James Nicholson was with AIP until shortly before his death in 1972) and a sufficiently large and diversified list of releases (usually twenty to thirty films per year, without fail).

AIP (American Releasing in 1954 and 1955) has had annual gross revenues in the $21,000,000 to $28,000,000 area during the early 1970s. AIP's profit for the fiscal year ending March 1, 1972, was $271,000. By March 1, 1973, the figure had grown to $744,000—about what Monogram and Republic were earning on comparable grosses in the late 1940s and early 1950s.

The reason for frequent failures in today's B production companies is the same as it was in the 1930s and 1940s: thin capitalization. The smaller studios have always lived from hand to mouth, mortgaging the present and the future in hopes that last month's picture will pay for this month's. Such businesses have few sources to turn to for working capital.

A monumental credit crunch developed from 1968 to 1970 when the major studios had so much of their capital ($1,200,000,000 at one point) tied up in a few massively budgeted spectaculars. The banks turned off the lending spigot (with a little help from the Federal Reserve Board, which had turned off the spigot to the banks) and, lacking capital for day-to-day operations, more than one major came wrenchingly close to bankruptcy.

THE MAJORS. Recently, a couple of major studios have attempted to institute a "two-tier" production policy: making, each year, a limited number of high-class A-grade "art" pictures by prestige filmmakers (Robert Altman, Arthur Penn, Peter Bogdanovich, et al.) as flyers, and a continuous flow of B-style junk to pay the rent.

James Aubrey tried this first, during his 1969 to 1973 M-G-M reign. Unfortunately, "Jungle Jim" and his production chief Daniel Melnick turned out the junk and forgot the art.

M-G-M potboilers like Soylent Green, Shaft, Kansas City Bomber, and House of Dark Shadows (all 1971–1973) turned in modest profits, but most of the studio's 1970–1973 profits were the result of cost-cutting and of selling off assets (such as old props and costumes).

Art Murphy pointed out rather acidly in Variety[11] that, of M-G-M's $9,267,000 profit in fiscal 1973 (9/1/72–8/31/73), ninety-nine percent was

[11] December 12, 1973.

derived from the nonrecurring sale of assets, tax write-offs, and a change in accounting methods. *One* percent came from the company's operations (including its films, film lab, and music publishing operation; M-G-M subsequently sold everything but the lab to United Artists).

In June 1973, Aubrey told *Business Week*[12] that M-G-M had no intention of withdrawing from films. Less than three months later, he changed his mind: MGM closed its distribution system and announced that it would produce four or five "special" films a year. The practicability of such a program, of course, remains to be seen.

Concurrent with this decision, Aubrey announced his resignation as M-G-M's president.

More recently, floundering Columbia Pictures, reeling from the disastrous *Lost Horizon* (1973) and a general lack of successful films, announced plans, late in 1973, for its own two-tier production system.

Starting in 1974, Columbia planned to produce a few high-quality $2,000,000 to $3,000,000 films a year, plus several "AIP-type" films in the $600,000 to $800,000 budget range. Columbia hired former AIP production chief Lawrence Gordon to oversee the latter. So the first step has been taken to return Columbia to its origins as a producer of B movies.

Columbia is caught in a trap that has downed more than one studio: its outstanding bank loans are staggeringly high ($150,000,000 at the end of 1973); interest costs alone run to $17,000,000 a year—a sum that in itself could finance several fairly elaborate films.[13]

Late in 1973, Columbia's new president Alan J. Hirschfield admitted that Columbia's fourteen banks had suggested that the studio "might do a better job" in the future. Hence the new production plan.

This recurring pattern of studio rises and falls is parodied in Tay Garnett's *Stand-In* (1937), in which a stuffy New York banker (Leslie Howard) takes over a bankrupt studio in hopes of pulling it into the black. The studio is populated with the likes of Humphrey Bogart, Joan Blondell, and Jack Carson. *Stand-In* is a comedy. Of course.

---

[12] June 23, 1973.

[13] It is a little complicated to explain, but such a high level of debt in relation to the size of a company diminishes—and ultimately destroys—the value of the stockholders' ownership equity in the company. And, indeed, Columbia's stockholders watched their stock drop from $30.00 a share in 1971 to $2.00 a share at the end of 1973.

	THE 1920s and BEFORE	THE 1930s	THE 1940s
AIP			
COLUMBIA	1924: CBC Film Sales Corp. becomes Columbia Pictures Corp.	1932: Harry Cohn replaces Joe Brandt as president and remains chief of production; Jack Cohn, v.-p.	1942–1944: Sidney Buchman, v.-p.—assistant head of production
M-G-M	1924: Metro-Goldwyn-Mayer formed, with Louis B. Mayer, v.-p. and general manager; Irving Thalberg, supervisor of production; and Nicholas Schenck, president of parent company, Loew's, Inc.	1936: Thalberg dies	1948–1956: Dore Schary, v.-p. in charge of production
MONOGRAM/ ALLIED ARTISTS	1924: W. Ray Johnston forms Rayart Pictures	1930: Johnston and Trem Carr convert Rayart into Monogram Pictures 1936: Johnston and Carr revive Monogram	Nov. 1945: S. Steve Broidy becomes president of Monogram; Johnston, chairman of board 1946: Allied Artists Productions formed as wholly owned subsidiary of Monogram; Broidy, president
REPUBLIC		1935: Herbert J. Yates merges Monogram and Mascot to form Republic Pictures; Yates, chairman of board; W. Ray Johnston, president 1936: Johnston and Carr leave Republic 1937: Levine becomes president; then replaced by Yates	
MASCOT	1929: Nat Levine forms Mascot Pictures		
PARAMOUNT		1930: Paramount Famous Lasky Corp. becomes Paramount Public Corp.; Adolf Zukor, president 1930–1937: Succession of studio heads: B. P. Schulberg, Emanuel Cohn, Ernst Lubitsch, Henry Merzbrun, William LeBaron 1935: Company name changed to Paramount Pictures, Inc.; Barney Balaban, president;	1949: Paramount splits into Paramount Pictures Corp. and United Paramount Theatres

RKO	Keith-Albee-Orpheum theatre circuit, creating RKO Radio Pictures Nov. 1931: David O. Selznick becomes chief studio executive Dec. 1932: Merian C. Cooper becomes chief studio executive 1935: Floyd B. Odlum takes control of RKO; appoints Samuel Briskin v.-p. in charge of production 1937: George Schaefer becomes president of RKO Radio Pictures; Pandro S. Berman named v.-p. in charge of production	1942: Ned Depinet replaces Schaefer; Charles M. Koerner becomes v.-p. in charge of production 1943: Odlum becomes chairman of RKO Corp. board 1946: Koerner dies; N. Peter Rathvon becomes president of RKO Radio Pictures; Dore Schary, v.-p. in charge of production 1948: Howard Hughes buys controlling interest in RKO from Odlum and assumes title, managing director in charge of productions; Depinet appointed president of RKO Corp.
FOX	1915: William Fox founds Fox Film Corporation 1930: William Fox resigns as company president 1931: Fox forced out of directorship	
20TH CENTURY	1933: Darryl F. Zanuck and Joseph M. Schenck form 20th Century Pictures 1935: Merge to form 20th Century-Fox Film Corporation; Schenck, chairman; Sidney R. Kent, president; Zanuck, head of production	1942: Kent dies; Spyros P. Skouras becomes president 1942–1943: William Goetz, head of production 1942–1944: Wendell L. Willkie, chairman of board; position then abandoned 1943: Zanuck returns as head of production; Schenck returns as executive production head
PRC	1938: Ben Judell forms Progressive Pictures Corporation 1939: PPC becomes Producers Distributing Corporation	1940: Financial crisis; Mar.: PDC becomes Sigmund Neufeld Productions; Nov.: SNP becomes Producers Releasing Corporation Apr. 1946: Eagle-Lion Studios new name for PRC Studios Aug. 1947: PRC completely absorbed by Eagle-Lion, with Arthur Krim president
UNITED ARTISTS	1919: UA founded by Charles Chaplin, D. W. Griffith, Mary Pickford, Douglas Fairbanks	
UNIVERSAL	1912: Carl Laemmle forms Universal Pictures Corporation 1935–1938: New management as Laemmle retires; J. Cheever Cowdin, chairman of board; Nate Blumberg, president; Cliff Work, head of production	1946: Merger with International Pictures Corporation (i.e. William Goetz and Leo Spitz who take charge of production); Universal-International name adopted
WARNER BROTHERS	1923: Warner Brothers Pictures, Inc., formed 1928: Warner Bros. purchases First National studios; Harry M. Warner, president; Jack L. Warner, v.-p. in charge of production	

continued

	THE 1950s	THE 1960s	THE 1970s
AIP	1954: Formed as American Releasing Corp. by Samuel Z. Arkoff and James Nicholson 1956: Reincorporated as American-International Pictures		1972: Nicholson resigns to join 20th Century-Fox as a producer 1974: AIP takes over distribution arm of Cinerama Releasing Corp.
COLUMBIA	1952–1956: Jerry Wald, a v.-p. and executive producer 1956: Jack Cohn dies; Abe Schneider succeeds as head of East Coast office 1958: Harry Cohn dies; Abe Schneider becomes president; Leo Jaffe, 1st v.-p.; Samuel J. Briskin, West Coast v.-p.	1961: Sol A. Schwartz replaces Briskin 1963–1968: M. J. (Mike) Frankovich, v.-p. in charge of global production 1968–1969: Robert M. Weitman, v.-p. in charge of studio 1968–1969: Columbia Pictures becomes division of Columbia Pictures Industries, Inc.; A. Schneider, chairman; Jaffe, president of CPI; Stanley Schneider, president of Columbia Pictures division	1973: Schneider regime replaced by Alan J. Hirschfield, president of CPI, David Begelman, president of Columbia Pictures division, and Herbert Allen; Peter Guber becomes v.-p. in charge of worldwide production
M-G-M	1951: Mayer forced to resign as head of studio 1952: M-G-M sells its theatres to Loew's, Inc. 1955: Schenck becomes chairman of board; Arthur M. Loew becomes president of Loew's 1956: Schenck resigns; Loew becomes chairman; Joseph R. Vogel, president of Loew's; Benjamin Thau, head of studio 1958: Sol C. Siegel becomes head of studio	1960: Company name changed from Loew's, Inc., to Metro-Goldwyn-Mayer, Inc. 1962: Robert M. Weitman becomes head of studio 1963: Robert H. O'Brien elected president of M-G-M; Vogel, chairman of board 1967: Weitman resigns; replaced by Clark Ramsay Jan. 1969: Louis F. Polk, Jr., elected president; O'Brien becomes chairman of board, retires in May Apr. 1969: Herbert F. Solow appointed v.-p. in charge of production Oct. 1969: Kirk Kerkorian takes control; James Aubrey becomes M-G-M president	Jan. 1971: Solow leaves; post of v.-p. in charge of production abolished Feb. 1972: Daniel Melnick appointed v.-p. of production Sept. 1973: M-G-M cuts distribution arm Oct. 1973: Aubrey resigns; Frank E. Rosenfelt becomes president Nov. 1973: United Artists buys M-G-M film library and distribution arm
ALLIED ARTISTS/ MONOGRAM	1953: Name changed to Allied Artists Pictures Corp.; Monogram name dropped	1962: Claude A. Giroux becomes chairman of board Feb. 1965: Production stopped; Broidy resigns; Giroux becomes president 1967: Roger W. Hurlock becomes president; Emanuel L. Wolf, chairman of board 1968: Production resumes 1969: Wolf also assumes presidency	
REPUBLIC	1959: Last Republic picture released spring 1959; studio leased July 1959; Yates resigns		
MASCOT			
PARAMOUNT	1959: Jacob M. Karp becomes studio head	June 1964: George Weltner named president; Balaban elected chairman of board; Zukor made chairman emeritus Sept. 1964: Howard W. Koch becomes studio head Oct.–Nov. 1966: Paramount merged with Gulf & Western Industries, Inc., with G & W the surviving corporation and Paramount a subsidiary with own management; Charles G. Bluhdorn, chairman of G & W board; Robert Evans, v.-p. in charge of production; Bernard Donnenfeld, administrative v.-p. of studio	July 1970: Stanley Jaffe named president of Paramount; Bluhdorn remains chairman of board May 1971: Frank Yablans elected president of Paramount Oct. 1974: Barry Diller becomes chairman of board and chief executive officer of Paramount Jan. 1975: Yablans resigns

RKO	1955: Hughes sells RKO to General Teleradio division of General Tire & Rubber Co. 1956: RKO Studios become Desilu Studios 1959: Company name changed to RKO General, Inc.		
20TH CENTURY FOX	1952: 20th Century-Fox sells its theatres to National Theatres Corp. 1956: Zanuck resigns; replaced, in succession, by Buddy Adler, Robert Goldstein, Peter Levathes Mar. 1969: Skouras retires; D. F. Zanuck becomes chairman of board; R. D. Zanuck becomes president	1962: Skouras becomes chairman of board; D. F. Zanuck becomes president; Richard D. Zanuck becomes head of production	Dec. 1970: R. D. Zanuck resigns Mar. 1971: Dennis C. Stanfill elected president June 1971: William T. Gossett replaces D. F. Zanuck as chairman of board; D. F. Z. becomes chairman emeritus Sept. 1971: Stanfill becomes chairman of board; Gordon Stulberg becomes president; Dec. 1974: Stulberg resigns
PRC	Jan. 1950: Film Classics merged with Eagle-Lion Feb. 1951: Eagle-Lion merged into UA; Arthur Krim becomes UA president		
UNITED ARTISTS	Jan. 1952: Krim group buys 50% of UA stock (including Fairbanks estate's 25%); Robert S. Benjamin becomes chairman of board Feb. 1955: Krim group buys Chaplin's 25% Feb. 1956: Krim group buys Pickford's 25%; has 100% control of UA Apr. 1957: UA goes public	May 1967: Transamerica Corporation (primarily an insurance company) buys all UA stock	1974: UA now wholly owned subsidiary of Transamerica; Krim, chairman of Transamerica; Benjamin, co-chairman
UNIVERSAL	1950: Cowdin resigns Nov. 1951: Decca Records acquires 28% of Universal stock Apr. 1952: Goetz and Blumberg sell their Universal stock to Decca; Decca now has control July 1952: Milton R. Rackmil, president of Decca, also becomes president of Universal Pictures; Blumberg, chairman of board 1953: Edward Muhl becomes v.-p. in charge of production	June 1962: MCA talent agency converted to holding company for Universal and Decca; talent agency and Universal-International name gradually dropped 1966: Universal becomes subsidiary of MCA, Inc.; Jules Stein, chairman of MCA; Lew Wasserman, president of MCA	1973: Henry H. Martin replaces Rackmil as Universal president; Muhl resigns
WARNER BROTHERS	Feb. 1953: Stanley Warner Corporation formed to acquire WB theatres; WB stock split in two July 1956: Harry and Albert Warner sell their shares; Jack Warner becomes president of WB	1967: Seven Arts Productions, Ltd., buys controlling interest in WB from Jack Warner; company name changed to Warner Bros.–Seven Arts, Ltd.; Eliot Hyman becomes chairman of board of WB-7A; Jack Warner, vice-chairman; Benjamin Kalmenson, president; M. Kenneth Hyman, v.-p. in charge of worldwide production 1969: Warner Bros., Inc., becomes subsidiary of Kinney Services, Inc., with Steve Ross chairman of parent company; Seven Arts name dropped; Jack Warner resigns; Ted Ashley becomes chairman and chief executive officer of WB, Inc.; John Calley becomes v.-p. in charge of world production	1971: Parent company name changed to Warner Communications, Inc., with Ross chairman 1972: Frank Wells becomes president of WB, Inc.; Richard Shepherd appointed executive v.-p. for production 1973: Company name changed to Warner Communications, Inc., Ashley, chairman; Steve Ross, president of parent company; Frank Wells, president of subsidiary WB 1974: Ashley becomes co-chairman of board with Wells who becomes chief executive officer; Calley becomes WB president, remaining as production head; Shepherd resigns; Robert H. Solo named executive v.-p. for production

CONCLUSION: THE RISE AND FALL OF THE B MOVIE

What made the B movie and high-volume movie production possible was the guaranteed sale of eighty million to one hundred million tickets a week. The audience was loyal, enthusiastic, and, by and large, undiscriminating. Its movies were provided through a system of exchanges and theatres that the major studios owned outright.

And indeed, so great was the demand for movies (and so few and far between were alternate types of entertainment) that certain studios survived producing nothing but second features.

The antitrust theatre divestiture and the rise of television occurred at the same moment: the end of the 1940s. The theatrical film industry, which thrived during times of scarcity and deprivation (the Great Depression and World War II), saw eighty percent of its market disappear in a little over twenty years. So ended the classical double bill and the B movie.

The Bs were always an economically marginal product, but the traditional B movie probably vanished as much for social reasons as for economic ones. The audience for the B movie was lower middle class. The upward social mobility of the 1950s and the transition of the dominant social group in America to middle middle and upper middle class coincided with the end of the conventional double bill. The new middle class moved on to more sophisticated leisure activities and lost its taste for the simplistic entertainment that the Bs provided (which could be found on television, anyway).

It is no accident that the predominant audience for B-type films in the 1950s and 1960s was the teen-age market. Perhaps this group escaped, or rebelled against, the social imperatives that drove their parents away from the movies.

Going beyond even this, the best of the Bs seem uniquely products of the *Zeitgeist* of the 1940s. The most memorable B images are of postwar urban America. Monogram's sparse expressionistic sets and PRC's generic, unchanging city-street set seem to sum up that brief time between World War II and the Korean War.

It may be the Korea-A-bomb-McCarthy era, as much as anything else, that drove the audience inward, to isolate itself with television. Certainly the two most compelling dramatic events of the early 1950s were not to be found on movie screens but on television: the Senate's MacArthur dismissal hearings (1951) and the Senate's Army-McCarthy hearings (1954).

And it was in the 1950s that David Riesman discovered *The Lonely*

Crowd (1950) and William Whyte isolated *The Organization Man* (1956). The American mind had changed and so, inevitably, did American movies.

However, the B movies and the B studios should always be remembered as the ultimate expression of that brief time when Hollywood was truly a movie factory. The best of the Bs are genuine art and the worst of the Bs are genuine junk, but most of the Bs do nothing more than epitomize the dictum that a movie is a movie, nothing more and nothing less.

BLAME THE AUDIENCE* (1952)

MANNY FARBER

While Hollywood, after all, still makes the best *motion* films, its 1952 products make me want to give Los Angeles back to the Conquistadores. Bad films have piled up faster than they can be reviewed, and the good ones (*Don't Bother to Knock, Something to Live For, The Lusty Men, My Son John, The Turning Point, Clash by Night*) succeed only as pale reminders of a rougher era that pretty well ended with the 1930s. The people who yell murder at the whole Hollywood business will blame the current blight on censorship, the star system, regimentation, the cloak-and-suit types who run the industry, the dependence of scriptwriters on a small group of myths, television, the hounding of the Un-American Activities Committee, and what I shall laughingly call montageless editing.

There is plenty of justification for trying to find what is causing this plague, and I point my thumb accusingly at the audience, the worst in history. The present crowd of moviegoers, particularly the long-haired and intellectual brethren, is a negative one, lacking a workable set of values or a sense of the basic character of the medium, so that it would surprise me if any honest talent in Hollywood had the heart to make good pictures for it.

Their taste for preciously styled, upper-case effects and brittle sophistication has encouraged Hollywood to turn out some of the most smartly tooled artworks of the times—films like *Sunset Boulevard* (1950) and *The Bad and the Beautiful* (1953), stunning mixtures of mannerism, smooth construction, and cleverly camouflaged hot air. While I find these royal creations pretty good entertainment, I keep telling myself that the audience's craving for costly illusion (overacting, overscoring, overlighting, overmoralizing) may produce total confusion in Hollywood. The industry is still turning out movies that are supposed to be moderately naturalistic, but it must grow puzzled at having to make plain simple facts appear as special and delectable as the audience demands. So what we have to deal with now is a spectator who has Tiffany-styled aesthetics and tastes in craftsmanship, and whose idea of good movies is based on an assortment of swell attitudes.

If some stern yearner makes a movie full of bias for the underdog, or a clever actor crowds his role with affectations picked out of real life, or the scriptwriter sets up innumerable situations wherein the camera can ponder over clocks, discarded cigar bands, and assorted bric-a-brac, the audience responds as though it were in the climate of high art.

Faced with such an audience—half Tory and half culture bug—Griffith, with his practical genius, or Sennett, with his uninhibited improvising talents, would probably have passed up moviemaking for something more virile and exciting.

The reason movies are bad lies is this audience's failure to appreciate, much less fight for, films like the unspectacular, unpolished B, worked out by a few people with belief and skill in their art, who capture the unworked-over immediacy of life before it has been cooled by "art." These artists are liberated from such burdens as having to recoup a large investment, or keeping a star's personality intact before the public; they can experiment with inventive new ideas instead of hewing to the old surefire box-office formula.

Such pictures are often made under "sleeper" conditions (sometimes even the studio hotshots didn't know they were being made), and depend, for their box-office success, on word-of-mouth approval instead of "colossal" ads. But since there is no longer an audience response to fresh filmic trends, this type of movie is being replaced, by most of the big Hollywood factories, with low-budget jobs that emulate prodigious spectacles, foreign-film sentiments, or best-seller novels, until you can no longer tell a B from an A.

In the past, when the audience made underground hits of modest B films, Val Lewton would take a group of young newcomers who delighted in being creative without being fashionably intellectual, put them to work on a pulp story of voodooists or grave robbers, and they would turn $214,000 into warm charm and interesting technique that got seen because people, rather than press agents, built its reputation. After 1940, a Lewton, a Preston Sturges, a Sam Fuller, an Allan Dwan, or a Budd Boetticher found his best stride in a culture-free atmosphere that allowed a director to waste his and the audience's time, and then lost himself in the culture-conscious conditions of large-scale work.

The low budget appears to economize the mind of a director, forcing him into a nice balance between language and what is seen. Given more money and reputation actors, Sam Fuller's episodic, spastically slow and fast film would probably dissolve into mouthy arrogance, where characters would be constantly defining and apologizing for the class separation that obsesses Fuller, and burying in words the skepticism and energy that he locates in his 1949 to 1952 low budgets. The structure that Fuller invented in *I Shot Jesse James* (1949) depends on close-ups of large faces and gestures, combustive characters in close face-to-face confrontations where they seem bewitched with each other but where each one is actually in a private, lightly witty rumination about the wondrous information that springs up from being professionals pursuing highly perfected skills. In *The Steel Helmet* (1950), the weight of too many explanations about race-class-position seems to make leaden Fuller's work, drives him into a pretentious strain that is not apparent in the totally silent *Jesse James* opening.

Sturges' turning point occurs in *Hail the Conquering Hero* (1944), when he begins patronizing, caricaturing his small-towners with patriotic sentimentality. The Eddie Bracken hero—no energy, desiring isolation, trying to free himself from responsibility—is a depressing symbol suggesting the spiritual difficulties Sturges must have been working under, trying to psych himself into doing culture-conscious work. The last good Sturges occurs in *Sullivan's Travels* (1942), which is not low budget, but its best sections—the hobo material, rudimentary slapstick, an expensive cross-country bus trying to stay with a kid's homemade motor tank, Veronica Lake's alertness within leisure—are elemental B handling.

In 1943, William Castle, the director of the Monogram melodrama

When Strangers Marry, could experiment with a couple of amateurs (Robert Mitchum and Kim Hunter), try out a then new Hollywood idea of shooting without studio lights in the sort of off-Broadway rented room where time seems to stand still for years and the only city sounds come through a postage-stamp opening on the air well. The movie was a hit with perceptive moviegoers, made a fair profit, and prepared audiences for two new stars and some of the uninvented-looking cinema later made famous in *Open City.* All this was possible because Castle wasn't driven to cater to clichéd tastes.

Once, intellectual moviegoers performed their function as press agents for movies that came from the Hollywood underground. But, somewhere along the line, the audience got on the wrong track. The greatest contributing cause was that their tastes had been nurtured by a kind of snobbism on the part of most of the leading film reviewers. Critics hold an eminent position, which permits control of movie practice in one period by what they discerned, concealed, praised, or kicked around in the preceding semester of moviemaking. I suggest that the best way to improve the audiences' notion of good movies would be for these critics to stop leading them to believe there is a new "classic" to be discovered every three weeks among vast-scaled "prestige" productions. And, when they spot a good B, to stop writing as if they'd found a "freak" product.

BEATITUDES OF B PICTURES* (1974)

ANDREW SARRIS

Let us now praise the B picture. But what is it exactly? Or, rather, what was it? In this age of inflation and instant insights, there is nothing on the screen that we can point to and say: This is a B picture. A Z movie, perhaps, but not a B picture. There is too much ambition at one end, too little craftsmanship at the other, and the bottom has fallen out of the middle. Nor is there today any genre lowly enough to be dismissed out of hand by the critical establishment. Kung-fu, porn (soft-core and hard-core), Damon and Pythias squad-car serenades, revisionist Westerns, regressive Disneys, black-power fantasies: all have their sociological and even stylistic rationales. The snobberies that afflicted supposedly serious film criticism in the 1930s, 1940s, and 1950s have now been superseded by an open-mindedness that errs on the side of credulity. Another problem today in finding a B picture is that the notion of the A picture is more nebulous than ever, and you can't have B pictures without A pictures. Indeed, with the predetermined double feature's disappearance, it is less and less often that one hears the once familiar refrain: "I liked the second feature better than the main one." Nowadays a double feature is more likely to consist of two failed A pictures, with the older one on the bottom of the bill.

Still, we are beginning to define the conditions that bred the B picture even as we bemoan the absence of these conditions. The B picture trudged out from Hollywood in the 1930s, 1940s, and 1950s. Silent movies tended to be major and minor rather than A or B, and comedy shorts and pulp Westerns didn't really count at any time as Bs. From the point of view of the American moviegoer, the cheapest, tawdriest, silliest foreign-language film was still too exotic to qualify as a B movie. The B picture was thus almost by definition a product of the Hollywood studio system. The B picture was usually in black and white, the feeling being that color was both too expensive and too immodest for a true B. Of course, color became so commonplace in the 1950s and 1960s that the black-and-white requirement went by the board. So much so, in fact, that the black and white used for *The Last Picture Show* (1971) seemed pretentiously archaic and A-picture-ish all the way.

There are at least two ways of looking fondly at any given B picture. One is the way of the trivia hound, and the other is the way of the treasure hunter. Whereas the trivia hound loves all B pictures simply because they are B pictures, the treasure hunter loves only certain B pictures because they have somehow overcome the onus of having started out as B pictures. Thus, the trivia hound tends to be encyclopedic, and the treasure hunter tends to be selective. By necessity, the treasure hunter must share some of the zeal of the trivia hound, but the trivia hound need not recognize the aesthetic restrictions of the treasure hunter. I would tend to classify myself as a treasure hunter with a touch of the trivia hound. Hence, I cannot embrace all the B-ness of B pictures. Nor do I consider all genres equal.

Musicals and comedies, for example, seldom surmount the ritualized format of the Bs. Indeed, the big curse of the Bs as a class of movies is a dreary tendency toward facetiousness without wit or humor. Nothing is more depressing about a bad movie than its bad jokes or its failed musical numbers or its unimaginative slapstick. Thus, a disproportionate number of fondly remembered B pictures fall into the general category of the *film noir*. Somehow even mediocrity can become majestic when it is coupled with death, which is to say that if only good movies can teach us how to live, even bad movies can teach us how to die.

But are we talking about really good movies, or merely good moments in bad movies? Even *King Kong* (1933) isn't much good until the last half hour; and it isn't great until the last ten minutes. Not that *King Kong* qualifies as a B picture, *Son of Kong* (1933) qualifies, but not *Kong* itself. One might say that *King Kong* is the heroic night before, and *Son of Kong* the hung over morning after. But I've always had a soft spot in my heart for the ratty fatalism of *Son of Kong*. In its depressing way, the last tramp-steamer two-shot of Robert Armstrong and Helen Mack on their way to no place in particular is every bit as memorable as Kong's last anguished expression atop the Empire State Building. Still, we can stipulate that the progression from an original to a sequel is often from A to B, not always, but almost always. *Dead End* (1937) is an A, but the Dead End Kids and East Side Kids series run from B to Z. The Warner Oland Charlie Chans are either A or high B, the Sidney Toler Chans are all B. *What a Life!* (1939) with Jackie Cooper as Henry Aldrich (and a Brackett and Wilder screenplay) is not only an A, but also one of the most sadistic studies of American adolescence in any medium. Andy Hardy was always A, and Blondie was always B, although both were fantastically profitable. *The Bride of Frankenstein* (1935) and *The Son of Frankenstein* (1939), however, were every bit as ambitious as the original *Frankenstein* (1931). *The Curse of the Cat People* (1944) was even more literary although less mythic than *The Cat People* (1942). Not so the sequels to *Tarzan, the Ape Man* (the 1931 version with Johnny Weissmuller and Maureen O'Sullivan) and *Planet of the Apes* (1968). There sequelitis was more interesting sociologically than stylistically.

If, as the late Robert Warshow once suggested, the faces, bodies, and personalities of players constitute the linguistic tropes of the cinema, then Helen Chandler's mere presence in a Mayfair special entitled *Alimony Madness* (1933) is its own justification. Mayfair, Tiffany, Republic, Monogram, PRC, Eagle-Lion: these are corporate names to conjure with in any discussion of B pictures. Almost everything they turned out was B or lower. Republic is a spectacular case in point. From 1941 to 1958, a Miss Vera Hruba Ralston, the wife and perennial protégée of Republic's President, Herbert Yates, made twenty-six indescribably inane pictures, all for Republic, a feat of conjugal devotion (on her husband's part) romantically credited with dispatching Republic into receivership. Paradoxically, Republic participated during this period in several very arty (though inexpensive) auteurist productions: John Ford's *Rio Grande* (1950), *The Quiet Man* (1952), and *The Sun Shines Bright* (1954); Ben Hecht's *Spectre of the Rose* (1946); Fritz Lang's *House by the River* (1950); Nicholas Ray's *Johnny Guitar* (1954); and Orson Welles's *Macbeth* (1948), none of which fits into the campy category of Vera Hruba Ralston, and none of which qualifies as a B picture.

Nor is the ideal B picture simply a "sleeper" that catches on with audiences. *It Happened One Night* (1934), *Casablanca* (1942), *Going My Way* (1944), *Sitting Pretty* (1933), *A Letter to Three Wives* (1949), and even *Easy Rider* (1969) were all authentic sleepers in their time, but either their casts were too prominent, or their aspirations were too fully articulated, or both. The late James Agee described *Double Indemnity* (1944) as "trash," but that didn't make it a B picture. In New York and other cosmopolitan centers in America, the run and ruck of Westerns tend to be so unfashionable that they seem to qualify as Bs in retrospect. Nonetheless it is difficult to consider expansive spectacle on a wide screen and in color as a B picture no matter how unfashionable it may be otherwise. Even a black-and-white, wide-screen Western like Sam Fuller's *Forty Guns* (1957) seems somewhat too elaborate to be considered a B, despite Barbara Stanwyck's working at a lower salary, not to mention the mere presence of Barry Sullivan in the lead role. Barry Sullivan was a born B picture actor, and a damned good one, so good, in fact, that he usually lifts up Bs in quality, if not in prestige. *The Gangster* (1947) is his greatest vehicle, and it is worth watching just for the pleasure of his understated authority setting up the histrionics of Akim Tamiroff and Joan Lorring. In A pictures, Barry Sullivan could never have been anything more than a leading man, and usually a secondary leading man. But in Bs Barry Sullivan could be a tragic hero.

The last thing I want to do, however, is to restrict the range of the B picture. Nor do I wish to dictate the conditions under which it can be discussed. It's much more fun, and perhaps more useful too, to throw out some recollections of a lifetime of moviegoing. One can never say the last word on this haunting subject. Not only are there too many memories to begin with, but also more and more are being reconstructed each day through revivals.

Black Angel (1946): Dan Duryea falls in love with June Vincent, who is obsessed with saving her unfaithful dullard of a husband from the electric chair. A very erotic movie for the 1940s. Peter Lorre and Freddie Steele are especially fascinating as underworld characters, Lorre lecherously and Steele sadistically, and the girl voluptuously masochistic in their midst. Roy William Neill, who directed the best of the Basil Rathbone–Nigel Bruce Sherlock Holmes pictures, may have had something to do with the edgy elegance of the production, and Cornell Woolrich (the literary source of Hitchcock's *Rear Window*) supplied the original story. But mainly, I think, it is Duryea, who takes the opportunity in a B picture to pull a switch on the ratty villains he played in the As.

Wicked Woman (1953): This B comes closer to camp than almost anything else I can think of in a favorable way, but its sordidness is somehow delicious. I don't remember anymore whether the girl was Beverly Michaels or Cleo Moore,[1] but she was one of these two Hugo-Haas-type blonde floozies of the 1950s, and the movie's one indelible image is that of porcine Percy Helton's kissing his way desperately up her arm, all the while squeaking out expressions of endearment. There is something so marvelously indefatigable about Helton as an actor that he makes most left-wing movies about underdogs seem about as egalitarian as the novels of Disraeli.

Detour (1946): Edgar G. Ulmer directed Tom Neal and Ann Savage in this most despairing and most claustrophobic of all B pictures. *Detour* is not so much an example of a B that rises unexpectedly in class (like *Blondie's Blessed Event* [1942] in the Blondie series) as of a poetic conceit from Poverty Row. Unfortunately, since Ulmer's canonization as a cult favorite, his legitimate successes—*The Black Cat* (1934), *Bluebeard* (1944), *Ruthless* (1948), and *The Naked Dawn* (1955)—make him too prominent for this article. Similarly, Joseph H. Lewis, lately the subject of directorial retrospectives, can no longer be cited solely for *Gun Crazy* (1950), a lyrical meditation on a gun-crazed couple several years before *Bonnie and Clyde* (1967), and several years more before *Badlands* (1974).

Rendezvous with Annie (1946): I liked this movie long before I ever knew it was directed by Allan Dwan, or even who Allan Dwan was supposed to be. What I remember most vividly is Eddie Albert's sharing a cake during the London blitz with Sir C. Aubrey Smith. I enjoyed *Brewster's Millions* (1945), which Dwan also directed, and which looms as large in his later legend as the anti-McCarthy Western *Silver Lode* (1954), which he directed, with Dan Duryea as a villain.

When Strangers Marry (1944): Kim Hunter, Dean Jagger, and Robert Mitchum in a not-bad William Castle imitation of Alfred Hitchcock. The

---

[1] It was Beverly Michaels—Ed.

three leads give the film an A gloss, but the most memorable sound in the film is the rollicking, yet rasping laugh of a small, rotund, cherubic character actor named Dick Elliott. His laugh is one of the most explosively distinctive expressions of mirth on the edge of malignancy in the entire history of the sound film, and yet I doubt that there are any more than a handful of moviegoers and trivia hounds who can identify the name with the face, or even recall the face. No matter. He shall serve as my personal proxy for all the other unsung and unremembered favorites of other moviegoers. Dick Elliott has a small part in *Mr. Smith Goes to Washington* (1939), but I would never have noticed him if it hadn't been for his extraordinary eruptions in *Vogues of 1938* and *So This Is New York* (1948). In the latter film, Elliott heckles Dona Drake's hapless first-night performance as a maid in an atrocious play written by Bill Williams. Elliott's gusto in reading fairly ordinary insult lines transforms these lines into the roaring sounds of comic opera. But it is in *Vogues of 1938* that Elliott's unique gift serves to fashion one of the most imaginative jokes in the history of the cinema. We first see Elliott at an out-of-town tryout box-office window. Twirling an outsize cigar, he asks for his usual house seats. The show's producer (Warner Baxter) asks the ticket seller about the freeloader with the big cigar and he is told that Elliott is notorious in New Haven for always guessing wrong on shows that later open on Broadway. If he likes a show, it is bound to be a flop. At the intermission, Baxter nervously follows Elliott into the lobby. At first Elliott chuckles quietly to himself, but the bubbling merriment is beginning to spill over his face like lava from a live volcano, and the explosion is not long in coming. As the relatively grim members of the audience look on disapprovingly, Elliott begins to go into convulsions. The last damning peals of laughter occur off screen as Baxter goes to the telephone to make arrangements to close the show out of town. The sound of Elliott's laughter is one of the comic coups of the 1930s, and an example of the many unrecorded glories of the movies from A to B. I could go on and on, but you get the picture. It is my hope that books like this will help illuminate the still-dark corners of the medium. Perhaps if we all pool our memories without shame or snobbery, we can see to it yet that nothing of merit in the movies is ever completely forgotten or completely undiscovered.

WHAT'S SO HOT ABOUT GOING TO THE MOVIES

Some Free Association on the Nature of B Movies,
Trivia, and the Film Experience* (1974)

CLIVE T. MILLER

Most B movies of the 1940s are awful. If you haven't seen them, you might be fooled by the warm evaluations they're given in film-history books.

Movie historians, in particular, tend to work from assumptions which their readers are not always aware of. It's not that the historians mean to be esoteric. On the contrary, they assume that their knowledge is not unique but is, rather, personal history shared by all. Hence the profound concentration on "trivia." But only outsiders refer to that painstaking accumulation of facts as trivia. Insiders call it scholarship.

A friend of mine, a professor of nineteenth-century English literature, recently made a special trip to Wessex to see the chair Thomas Hardy used to sit in when he wrote his novels. When she returned, my wife offered to sell her my chair at a reasonable price, but she wasn't amused or interested.

Part of the difference, of course, is that she knows my flesh but she never knew Hardy's. So the only tangible way she can get to "know" him personally is through the objects and places that were attached to him. There's no enrichment of life's values when a Ph.D. thesis on a minor writer's abominable poetry is encouraged as worthy scholarship while a treatise on the dimensions and texture and comfort of Thomas Hardy's seat is dismissed as trivial!

What's so surprising about a widower giving away all his wife's clothes to Goodwill Industries and then spending a large portion of his life's savings at the M-G-M auction buying Vera-Ellen's old toe shoes?

I've never heard anyone who loves movies refer to the little-known facts about them as trivia. I've met people who have told me that they "just *love* movie trivia," but inevitably it turns out that they don't love *movies.* Anyone of normal modesty, sensitivity, self-perception would be astounded and thrilled to read a collection of minute details of his public accomplishments, and, reading, grow bewildered, even appalled. If your work has commitment, you can't separate your public life from your private life that easily. The next time we come across an old diary or scrapbook of ours, a school yearbook, a group picture from camp, should we dismiss the contents as trivia—those entries with their soulless dates and forgotten activities, the movie and record reviews we wrote, the endless lists, the inscriptions from friends whose faces we can't recall, those faces of friends whose names we don't even recognize on the roll-call caption? I insist that even if life is trivial, like any work of art, its details are not!

And they are important beyond the pure psychological satisfaction of putting an order to chaos. Out of embarrassment, however, we might be eager to bury the details of our own self. They're trivial compared to the image of ourself that each of us holds.

But nothing in the life of Charles Coburn, for example, could have been as important and satisfying as the details of his death. He died, aged eighty-four, at 2:00 P.M., August 30, 1961, of heart failure while recovering from minor throat surgery at Lenox Hill Hospital in New York City. Just before surgery he had been appearing in Indianapolis summer stock in *You Can't Take It with You.* At his bedside was his second wife, Mrs. Winifred Jean Clements Natzka, whom he had married two years before. She carried out his instructions, had him cremated, and saw to the scattering of his ashes— at the base of Edwin Booth's statue in Gramercy Park and at the foot of a tree planted there in memory of his first wife, Ivah Wills (she died in 1937—their romance had been one of the most famous of America's great love stories, for thirty years they addressed each other as Orlando and Rosalind); on the outdoor stage of Union College in Schenectady, New York (in the summer of 1935, he and Ivah had founded the Mohawk Drama Festival there); on the graves of his mother, father, and sister in Savannah, Georgia; and, according to his will, "along the Mohawk Trail from the highest peak between Albany, New York, and Fitchburg, Massachusetts." Charles Coburn, you see, was a rather large man and had a very grand vision.

The reason people get hooked on movie details or on B movies in general or on, say, movie serials has nothing to do with the quality of either those films or those details, any more than getting hooked on rock 'n' roll or baseball has anything to do with the quality of the individual songs or games. Unlike the Ph.D. candidate forced to illuminate the works of a minor writer, the lover of B movies never attempts to raise them up to the level of high art or to analyze them by applying high art's standards.

That isn't to say that movie freaks don't exercise discriminatory taste. It's quite unlike getting hooked on minor literature. Mystery novel addicts often feel uncomfortable with high literature, and people who read spy novels often don't want to put in the work it takes to enjoy a better book. Addicts of subliterature don't really like reading, just as those executives who attend the World Series and never go to any other games don't like baseball. So, too, Rodgers and Hammerstein shows exist for people who don't like musicals—i.e., stories at the service of song and dance. (Stories, they feel, are more important, more "serious," than singing and dancing. In those somber Rodgers and Hammerstein shows and, to a large extent, in Gene Kelly movies the singing and dancing, no matter how exuberant, sentimentally and pretentiously support the plot.)

On the other hand, when it comes to film classics, a person hooked on B movies is usually more perceptive about the true nature of those classics than the "pure" critical analyst is, and, in the profoundest way, he appreciates them more, too.

For one thing, he approaches the movies with different expectations. Of course, we're always using a sliding scale of values, although often unconsciously, when expressing our preferences. The enjoyment of living depends on such flexibility. And B isn't a grade, after all. To give trash that high a rank, you'd be more than generous—you'd have to be an imbecile. B simply designates the movie's position on a double bill, like the A and B sides of a single record. But in movies, the A picture gets more than heavy promotion.

Throughout its creation, its production values are infinitely higher than the B picture's, which are based on hardly any budget at all.

So just as you approach a newspaper differently from a novel, and one kind of novel differently from the next, you approach a B movie with other demands. I suppose, if you want to break down the appeal, acting and action (or the *suggestion* of action) are the two most important B-movie components, set within the framework of a familiar story and familiar characterizations. The art of the acting (or whatever quality there is in it that evokes our sympathetic response) and the purity of the action, in good B movies, manage to overcome the clichés of the story line and of the dialogue, as well as the caricatures of people. At the same time, the very familiarity of things gives the movie mythic qualities, as long as the film's suspense and realization of aims don't depend on our constantly being surprised by the predictable. Often, we not only accept the clichés but demand them, according to the picture's form: horror, mystery, Western, gangster, musical (although musicals were usually so expensive to make that there were few good B ones, mostly bad A ones—aesthetically, all the difference in the world).

It doesn't take naïveté to feel suspense at a Western showdown; but you'd have to be a nincompoop to be wondering whether the good guy or the bad guy is going to win. If you had never once seen a Western, you'd still know the outcome from what goes before, from watching your general fears and desires given external shape and structure.

An anthropologist friend of mine, when exploring the Panamanian jungles, came upon a group of Indians seated in front of a gigantic movie screen in a clearing, watching *Top Hat*. Another anthropologist had gotten there first. (Although I prefer the notion of God finding a new chosen people and deciding to celebrate by showing them *Top Hat*.) The Indians were mesmerized. Can Fred Astaire and Ginger Rogers and the charming, elegant white world they inhabit be part of *everyone's* preconscious?

B movies, it's true, exploited every dumb formula. The jokes were stupid (the Chief Inspector, holding a bag but ignorant of what's inside, saying, "If I could only get my hands on those jewels . . .") and the characterizations were heavy. But at least B pictures did not often try to do things they couldn't accomplish. Perhaps what makes them so appealing is their very unself-consciousness, even self-effacement. It's hard enough telling which studios they came from, much less who directed them. They don't impose their mediocrity on anyone. They simply exist, like white bread. If they did try anything audacious, it was not with intellectual pretentiousness, but merely an outrageous action or an unusual plot twist. It didn't always come off, but the attempt itself could be visually exciting or emotionally stimulating enough to satisfy you with the possibility, the suggestion rather than the achievement.

Sometimes a B picture got a reputation beyond itself, such as *The Mask of Dimitrios* (1944). If you know of its reputation, you're bound to be disappointed when seeing it. You'll wind up concentrating on its deficiencies and dishonesties instead of its small successes. But perhaps *The Mask of Dimitrios* is too talky to be a first-rate B picture anyway. I prefer *Three Strangers* (1946).[1]

Sometimes a picture got an A production that ultimately spoiled it, such as *Nightmare Alley* (1947) and perhaps even *White Heat* (1949). When that happened, the actors sometimes found themselves out of their depth.

But when the B movies' repertory companies were at their best, working quickly and efficiently, the audience's film experience was joyous.

If anything, being a movie freak is like being a rabid baseball fan: The true baseball fanatic goes to the ball park whether or not he knows ahead of time that the game's going to stink or that the home team's going to lose. Sure, he gets a special delight out of momentary tension or an expert play. But it's the quality of the *experience* of attending the ball game that counts. And the B movie fan loves the experience of going to the movies. Only in his case, he's like an early Mets fan: for him, the home team always loses.

The film experience is not at all like the literary experience. Virtually no film offers the profound intellectual satisfactions that an undiffused attack by a single artist can. Nor does it offer, while in progress, time for reflection (except in rare cases, such as *L'Avventura* [1960] and *Death in Venice* [1972]), whereas a book affords us time to pause and meditate upon it and upon the reading experience itself, to analyze the book and to savor the experience. As a matter of fact, a movie will cheat in every way possible to manipulate our emotions and distort our intellectual judgment, through background music, startling editing, abrupt changes of pace, visceral photo-

---

[1] Unfortunately, UA/16, the 16 mm. distributor of pre-1950 Warner Bros. movies, intends to milk inflated reputations for all they're worth. The rental cost of *The Mask of Dimitrios,* and of *Three Strangers* as well, is the same as that of *The Maltese Falcon* (1941) and *Casablanca* (1943). Obviously, as you increase the expectations, you increase the disappointment. But most 16 mm. distributors (except for independents) hardly care if they burn away future film buffs. Given the industry's current unstable economic position and the rapidity of electronic inventions, who knows who will have the movies' reissue rights or the ability to screen them a year or ten from now?

graphic effects, not to mention withheld information and our own trained responses to familiar actors. So the film experience is not like the subliterary experience either, for it achieves its superficial satisfactions more successfully. It not only realizes its world visually, but it also realizes its dramatic intentions with more immediacy, more urgency, and greater lasting effect.

The film experience depends on and plays upon our deep personal involvement—and not just because it assaults several senses at once. We select a book or a record in keeping with whatever mood we're in. And we select a movie that way, too. But if the book or the record doesn't fully satisfy us or if we find it's not what we expected, we can always put it down and pick up another, come back to it when we're ready for it. With a movie, we're stuck. And our own reaction to the movie is affected by everything we bring into the theatre with us—including our bills and our friends and our headache. Anything in a movie, whether it is as big as the set or as small as a gesture, can cause some irrational, deeply personal response.

At home, with our literature and music and in control of our solitude, we can isolate the art. And with most art, our perception of the work changes as we change over the years. But with movies, the changes take place from day to day, from one viewing to the next. Not only does a theatrical movie look different seeing it the second time on television, it also looks different seeing it the second time in a theatre!

Of course, I'm not suggesting that film is a lower art form than literature, even though few films are profound, integral works of art. There are things beyond the works themselves that coalesce to make the experience a profound and satisfying one. Much of the tension and force of the experience comes from its dual nature: the individual, lonely solitariness of viewing a movie—among hundreds of other spectators; the individual, unique rapport that we each establish with the movie—at the same time that everyone else is establishing a different one. And there are other things to stir us: the electricity generated by sitting among hundreds watching the same event; the black hall itself, which gives us an acute sense of privacy and safety through which, in turn, we retain a certain cherished anonymity and a heightened awareness of our self-identity. The canned life becomes an immediate experience, closer to music than to literature, closer still to dream.

Yes, if any analogy must be made, it must be to pornography: film as wet dream.

Ah, the excess of the experience! The enormity of those figures that feed our fantasy, their savage power: King Kong leering down on us; the love goddesses, with their extravagant makeup, bending over; the Westerner walking toward us at the showdown, all leather and metal, as the camera eye aims up from the boots and spurs to the crotch and gun. We get hooked on movies at puberty, or never . . . while we stuff ourselves sucking Popsicles, chocolate melting in our fists, shredded coconut between our fingers, popcorn between our teeth, the melted butter ceaselessly dripping down our chins.

To hell with necking! And never mind the detailed disappointments. The mythic proportions of the Hollywood movie stories, especially the most active forms, the gangster and Western and musical forms (all peculiarly American)—those human configurations of our amorphous hidden desires— hold the same sort of illicit excitement and anticipation that pornography does. Going to the movies is like buying pornography in a cellophane wrapper. If you really want to love Hollywood movies, you have to look at each one as a long, extended preview of coming attractions that never arrives.

PEOPLE

ROGER CORMAN: THE SCHLEMIEL AS OUTLAW* (1974)

CHRIS MORRIS

Roger Corman is the American director whose work is probably most often described as "faceless." Throughout his early career in the mid- and late-1950s and early 1960s at Allied Artists and American-International Pictures, Corman toiled to produce "the quickies"—the cheap sci-fi extravaganzas rushed through small studios on small budgets to fill the "selected outlying theatres."

Corman's work has often been dismissed with ease by most critics as a lowbrow derivative of the dying Hollywood studio system, which demands raw "product" devoid of any personal stamp or unique vision. Indeed, Corman's reputation in Hollywood rests on his cheaply made and extremely lucrative series of Edgar Allan Poe "adaptations" that were produced in the early 1960s as vehicles for Vincent Price.

Critics who attack Corman's filmology for its seeming vacuity are evidently overlooking two of his late 1950s productions that, although shot on minuscule budgets at breakneck speed, display an astonishing, even prodigious, exploration of black humor, coupled with a personal theme that reappears in many of Corman's other films.

A Bucket of Blood (1959) and *The Little Shop of Horrors* (1960) must rate as two of the strangest anomalies ever produced in Hollywood. Corman states that *Bucket* was shot in five days, and *Little Shop* was filmed in two. Both run under an hour and ten minutes.

The above production figures smack of the "product" mentality, but the films are plotted in such an unusual, nay irrational, manner that the chances for audience understanding and appreciation were marginal at best.

The two films are virtually identical in plot and character development; Corman's frequent collaborator Charles B. Griffith scripted both. They are identical in another fashion: they work most poorly on their own purported level, as horror films. Both *A Bucket of Blood* and *The Little Shop of Horrors* function primarily as social satire of the most violent sort. A particularly apt, though not readily apparent, comparison would be the English feature *Kind Hearts and Coronets* (1949), which is thematically quite similar.

The conflict in both films is between WASP society and the archetypical unassimilated Jewish schlemiel. Corman visualizes his Jewish protagonists as slight, quiet (though prone to monologizing), and inarticulate. Both are unsuccessful and trapped in menial positions under a cretinous, materialistic, and tyrannous boss. Despite their position, they still dream of material success in the profession on the margins of which they work and the affection of their "secret loves."

Both protagonists arrive at the same conclusion as the bourgeois English hero of *Kind Hearts and Coronets*: if success through the normal societal channels appears impossible, then it is worth killing for it. This particular view of outlawry as a function of ethnic group and (subordinately) class background reappears tangentially in Corman's other films, but it predominates the action in *A Bucket of Blood* and *The Little Shop of Horrors*.

A Bucket of Blood is a rather inept modernization of Guy de Maupassant's short story "The Horla" (which was made by AIP into *Diary of a Madman* [1963] with Vincent Price as a result of the success of the Poe/Corman spin-offs). Its greatest sucess is as a satire of the then-burgeoning

Long Beach beatnik coffeehouse scene, which in 1959 was getting a lot of space in the national newsmagazines.

The "hero" of this grisly success story is Walter Paisley (Corman stalwart Dick Miller doing a very curious Jerry Lewis imitation), a bus boy in a Long Beach coffeehouse run by a ruthless art hustler named Leonard (Antony Carbone). There beat poet Max Brock (Julian Burton) lords it over the assembled junkies and culture vultures with the funniest mock-beat poesy since *High School Confidential* (1959) ("All is art . . . the rest is graham crackers"). Young and voluptuous Carla (Barboura Morris) has a thing for poets, and Walter, enamored of the lithe Carla, wants desperately to attract her by breaking into the art game.

Walter decides to take up sculpture, much to the distaste of his yenta landlady. Despite the chanting of inspirational verses:

> *Either a canvas is a canvas . . . or it's a painting*
> *Either a rock is a rock . . . or it's sculpture*
> *Either a sound is a sound . . . or it's music*

Walter's work doesn't advance beyond the Playdoh stage of composition. In a fit of artistic high dudgeon, he throws his putty knife, neatly spearing his pet cat. After a moment of remorse, he hits on the idea of covering his cat with clay to hide the damage, and voila!—instant Henry Moore.

Walter exhibits his thus-disguised pet at the coffeehouse the next day and becomes the immediate rage of the beat crowd. One "hip chick" is so impressed that she impulsively lays a nickle bag of heroin on hapless Walter, who is immediately cornered by the local narc, cleverly disguised in argyles and letter sweater. Walter accidentally snuffs the narc and immortalizes him. The next day he introduces his new piece *Murdered Man* to Leonard and Carla, the latter showing an increasing sexual interest.

Walter is feted at the coffeehouse for his artistic achievements, but all is not well; the heat is on for new masterworks. In order to provide his adoring audience with new art objects and maintain his social position, he disposes of an obnoxious cultural groupie and a workman, and comes up overnight with pieces that would take artist George Segal at least a year to complete.

Understanding that Walter is a big drawing card—even the junkies have stopped nodding—Leonard gives Walter a public exhibition at the coffeehouse. On the night of the opening, Carla rebuffs Walter's advances. She discovers the true nature of his artwork and he offers to immortalize her. A chase through a lumber yard ensues, Carla eludes the mad "artist,"

and Walter is finally cornered in his apartment. There he creates his ultimate work of art: he covers himself with clay and hangs himself.

The Little Shop of Horrors deals with the same themes and motifs as *A
Bucket of Blood,* but it has a special flavor lacking in its predecessor. The
film is set on the Lower East Side of New York; the parodies of Jewish
characters (particularly Mel Welles's turn as the Shylock-like florist Mushnik) crystallize a theme that might get lost in the broad monster-movie
shenanigans.

Again, we find schemiel figure Seymour Krelboin (Jonathan Haze,
again borrowing from Jerry Lewis) working as a toady for the greedy florist
Mushnik, under the thumb of his yenta landlady, and hopelessly in love
with Mushnik's retarded Jewish princess daughter Audrey (Jackie Joseph).

Seymour is saddened by the impending death of a mysterious young
plant in the shop. One night as he tends the withering sapling, the novice
florist cuts his finger and discovers that the weed has been wasting away for
want of its natural food—blood. The plant immediately livens up, grunting,
groaning, and slurping with glee. The next day, the assembled citizenry
applaud the miraculous recovery of the plant.

Loath to surrender his newborn celebrity because of the plant's demise
due to lack of sustenance, Seymour squeezes as much hemoglobin as he can
from his own body and agonizes over a suitable substitute. One night he
fortuitously happens upon the body of a bum killed in the convenient
nearby railway yards and feeds the remains to the ravenous fern. It blooms
incredibly, becoming in the process a sort of surrogate Jewish mother,
besieging Seymour with screams and pleas—"FEEEEEEED me—I'm
HUNNNgreee!"

As a result of these leafy torments, Seymour begins to exterminate his
neighbors to placate the ravenous plant. And as the green carnivore continues to develop, Seymour wins the admiration of his fame-starved boss
and the affections of the boss's daughter, after whom he names his creature
(yes, Audrey, Jr.).

A horticultural magazine expresses an interest in photographing the
rare plant. Mushnik holds an exhibition to celebrate the event. At an inop-
portune moment, the fern's enormous flowers bloom, exposing the terrified
faces of Seymour's victims. Another wild chase ensues, this time through a
tire graveyard. Seymour runs into the shop as a last resort, and, surrounded
and trapped, feeds himself to his hungry pet.

Absurd? Certainly. No audience could be expected to take either *A*

Bucket of Blood or *The Little Shop of Horrors* seriously as horror films. They are, instead, social comedies of the blackest order. Although the comedy is certainly grosser than anything in the pages of Bruce Jay Friedman, the intent is certainly humor rather than horrific titillation.

Both films speak from a consistent moral vantage point; both represent a social situation in which an immobile man happens by chance upon a destructive attitude that will advance him upward. Once the character's initial innocence is lost, he becomes merely a rapacious social animal who is unwilling to sacrifice his position, with the sacrifice of his vestigial humanity being the result. Ultimately, the protagonist meets his downfall at the hands of his own chosen instrument of destruction—Walter in the clay that molded his fame, Seymour in the plant that nourished his renown.

As already noted, both films have an ethnic locus. Both Walter and Seymour are lower-middle-class Jews with social yearnings. They are little more than the schlemiels of Yiddish stage shows with murderous instincts. Does this homicidal position reflect a wish fulfillment on Corman's part? His background is uncertain, but it would seem that a satire of Jewish social climbing of the most ruthless sort was intended.

This point of view is evident in its most interesting version in, surprisingly, *The St. Valentine's Day Massacre* (1967). Although George Segal (the archetypical *Yiddische kopf* of Hollywood) is portraying German gangster Frank Guesenberg in the film, he ultimately gives one of the few delineations of the Jewish gangster on film—a quirky (and quite inauthentic) hybrid of Meyer Lansky and James Cagney.

There is a masterful scene, which simultaneously reveals Corman's ethnoparodistic intent and plays a joke upon the Cagney-Mae Clarke grapefruit scene in *The Public Enemy*, in which tired and horny Segal is roughed up and finally KO'd with a lamp by his Harlowesque mistress. It is at the same time a wonderful puncturing of the tough guy gangster cliché and a truly Semitic look at thugdom.

Corman treats the theme of social ascension by assassination without the ethnic-racial overtones in other films. *Von Richthofen and Brown* (1971) is nothing if not the story of an anonymous character (Brown, an unknown Canadian pilot) who gains the spotlight by killing a celebrity (the German air ace). The maintenance of the social order and the achievement of the benefits of society through the use of extermination are often tangential (if not central) themes in the Poe films. And there is the ludicrous *The Wasp Woman* (1959), in which a WASP cosmetics manufacturer turns herself into an honest-to-God wasp in the pursuit of fame, fortune, and the perfect perfume scent.

A *Bucket of Blood* and *The Little Shop of Horrors* remain superior achievements in this particular thematic exploration. When dealing with this level of filmmaking, the dangers of assuming too academic an air are obvious; in the end, both are relentlessly funny and utterly mad murder comedies that can be enjoyed in the simplest of terms. For the more enthusiastic viewer of Corman's films, there are pleasures galore.

Either way, Roger Corman has given us two dark, dark social comedies that refuse to take themselves seriously at all. They may make you wonder about that nebbish that you mistreated all the way through high school.

Sam Katzman

SAM KATZMAN: JUNGLE SAM, OR, THE RETURN OF "POETIC JUSTICE, I'D SAY"* (1969)

RICHARD THOMPSON

SAM KATZMAN'S JERRY
PRODUCING; FOUR LEAF
MOVES ON NEW PATH

HOLLYWOOD, April 29—*Angel, Angel Down We Go* is the first pic in what is described as a new direction for Four Leaf Productions, Sam Katzman's production company with son Jerry acting as producer on this particular film.

Following a long list of exploitation films ranging from *Get Yourself a College Girl* to *Hootenanny Hoot*, Katzman is turning to pics with "depth and a point of view." "The day of the exploitation picture is gone. We learned that with *Riot on Sunset Strip*," son Jerry said. "We learned that people are no longer interested in headlines. There is so much sensationalism on TV it doesn't work anymore."

Angel will be released in June by American-International and the producers say it will serve a purpose for them as well as Four Leaf. "AIP is trying to go much more highbrow. They have made a fortune, but this is a business of money as well as art. This will be one of the first pictures in an effort to change their image."

The pic, the first for Jerry as producer, returns to the screen Jennifer Jones who "plays the mother of an 18-year-old fat girl born in the slums of Santa Monica who winds up marrying one of the richest men in the world." Jordan Christopher and Roddy McDowall complete cast. Film is in wrap-up stage with a second pic being prepped for production by Jerry. *Jeremy Rabbit, the Secret Avenger* will be directed by Robert Thom who did *Angel.* "Here again I want to say something about society. It deals with a court reporter who concentrates on tax evasion to get the Mafia."—*Variety*, April 29, 1969

Sam Katzman is one of the cultural technicians who made the 1950s what they were. Also the 1940s and the 1960s, but mainly the 1950s. Of the more than one hundred and four movies Katzman has made, none has lost money—a record shared with Jerry Lewis and few others. His 1940s training in Buster Crabbe serials made him, in the 1950s, one of the few producers in Hollywood with the qualifications and the vision to make *Rock Around the Clock* (1956). Arguably, Katzman is a necessary precedent for the Mothers of Invention.

No particular quality of Katzman's musical fadflicks claims immortality: their significance lies in their existence, all over the country, at drive-ins and nabes, when they were needed. I mean, who wanted to take his chick to see Mario Lanza? What we needed and got was teenpix, sketches of a world of our own, where adults were not indulgently tolerated in all their stupidity. No, better yet, they were totally irrelevant, except when they made the means of cultural production available to our screen surrogates by holding out record contracts or letting us drag on the harness racing track. American-International Pictures, kid-kult titan of the sicksties, has cleaned up by shrewdly applying Katzman's methods (sometimes with a little more surreal pizzazz than Jungle Sam, viz. the surf-boarding gorilla in *Bikini Beach*, 1964). It is also said that Katzman created the term *beatnik*, a freebie term like *hippy*, *rock 'n' roll*, even *teen-ager*, which the media grab and turn into basic English key words to cover everything unique, deviant, weird, and upsetting—and hence somehow valid and pertinent as critique—that kids do or are.

An ex-production exec of Katzman's remembers that one day, taping over-dubbing for a fad musical, one of the engineers was giving the pickup drummer static about his buddy, the grubby, out-of-it bass player. The drummer kept explaining to the engineer that his buddy was "just beat, Nick." Sam loved the word, and took it without realizing that the engineer's name was Nick.

Cahiers du Cinéma, in its review of American producers, covers Katzman:

KATZMAN Sam: Born July 7, 1901 in New York. 24–31: worked for Fox, First National, and Cosmopolitan. He created the Jungle Jim series, which won for him the nicknames "Gorilla" and "Jungle Sam Katzman."

PRINCIPAL FILMS (Restrained choice):[1] 1942: *Spotlight Scandals.* 1944: *Voodoo Man.* 1946: *Freddie Steps Out.* 1951: *Last of the Buccaneers.* 1952: *The Golden Hawk, California Conquest, Brave Warrior.* 1953: *Siren of Bagdad.* 1956: *Rock Around the Clock, Earth vs. the Flying Saucers, Rumble on the Docks, The Werewolf.* 1957: *Don't Knock the Rock, Utah Blaine, The Man Who Turned to Stone, Zombies of Mora-Tau, The Giant Claw, Calypso Heat Wave, The Night the World Exploded, The Tiajuana Story, Escape from San Quentin.* 1958: *Crash Landing, Going Steady, The World Was His Jury, Life Begins at 17.* 1959: *The Last Blitzkrieg, Juke Box Rhythm, The Flying Fontaines.* 1960: *The Enemy General, The Wizard of Bagdad.* 1961: *The Pirates of Tortuga.* 1962: *Don't Knock the Twist, Let's Twist Again.*
    Deserves to be cited as the most prolific of all producers. His films (science-fiction, crime thrillers, Westerns) beat all records for speed of shooting, modesty of budget, and artistic nullity. Socio-musicologists are excited by his study of the evolution of modern dance, from *Rock Around the Clock* to *Hootenanny Hoot,* including *Calypso Heat Wave* and *Don't Knock the Twist,* not to mention the deafening *Mambo Boom.* We await, with impatience but without much hope, *Don't Knock the Shake-It-Out-Baby.—Cahiers du Cinéma,* No. 150–151 (December 1964–January 1965)

More recently, Katzman gave us *The Love-Ins* and *Hot Rods to Hell* (both 1967).
    The only logical certainties in Katzman's musical fad pix are: You'll hear a lot of music; see some dancing; and the kids will surmount whatever yakety-yak adult difficulties they encounter. Beyond these guarantees, there

---

[1] What is *Cahiers* hiding?

is no logical argument, no rational narrative, no causal sequence of events. Sam brought to the musical fad pic the same cavalier attitude toward plotting he developed into non-sequiturial art in such works as the Thunda, King of the Congo serial. Katzman makes ideal drive-in fare, because you can look up at any point and comprehend it without prior knowledge of the plot line. In Thunda, there is a boulder that, when struck with one of the Rock people's stone axes, throws off scratchy lightning, but also magnetizes people to another boulder down the trail. No explanatory con glosses this in the film (Katzman, the soul of brevity): it is simply the meeting of the worlds of magic and empirical science. If we know that a phenomenon occurs and we can reproduce it, it becomes ours even if it is magic (see Esther the chimpanzee and the invention of B-4 in Howard Hawks's *Monkey Business* [1952] for a high art application of this principle). It is something like the tribal position we are sliding into—how does that go again about the little beam of light passing through the film to the photo-electric cell and making sound?

> One report has it that he bought the term *beatnik* from Allen Ginsberg for an undisclosed but substantial amount of money with the comment, "I don't really understand what it's all about, but it's bound to be good business."

Although it is impossible for the serious scholar to view all of Katzman's films (besides which he'd leave after ten minutes, or else cease being a serious scholar), it seems from available information that any mass-culture talent that moves from *Spotlight Scandals, Voodoo Man,* and *Freddie Steps Out* in the 1940s to *The Wizard of Bagdad, The Pirates of Tortuga,* and *Don't Knock the Twist* in the 1960s is simply not following a progressive career of aesthetic growth through evaluation, synthesis, and reevaluation.

> A studio flack described it this way: "You really hadda be there. All the creative people on the picture were in conference, and they wanted to know what Sam was going to call the weird kids. Somebody said hippies, Sam said no; somebody said freaks, Sam said no. Then he leaned back for a minute, quiet, then said, 'It's gotta be something special: a word like the old country, a word with a beat. That's it! We'll call them . . . *beatniks!*'"

Tom Wolfe still wishes he'd covered that story.

Sam's art is intuitive and associative. When he needs something, he reaches into the teeming gumbo of his semiconscious, filled with the flotsam of one hundred and four pictures and God knows how many serials, and plucks something out, undigested, unpolished, still wriggling, which plugs into the movie as a component. As close to automatic writing as the arts or technology have come, probably; it certainly makes the Marx Brothers' well-ordered anti-logic seem calculated. It is at this point that Katzman begins to confound any practical criticism. Standard ideas of harmony, propriety, and unique generic properties have no relation to the work of a reflexive, fragmented plumber-poet like Katzman. And if his career does not move linearly from one triumph to another, certainly all his works coexist in a trans-planar time warp of common triumph. The magnitude of this triumph is increased slightly every time another Katzman movie comes out: once again Sam has beaten the ridiculous-ass adult game and wrought, out of damn near nothing, let's face it, another prototypical drive-in flick (really, Roger Corman is such a serious, ambitious, artistic director, always involving us in those long-term forms and developments and such).

> No mystery about it, man, he got it from the extras on the set. All of us were beat then, you know, and picking up a little side bread from the studios. That was when Sputnik went up and Shorty, you know, the poet, he said we must all be beatniks now cause we were usually higher than that anyhow. Katzman said, "Put it in the picture."

But all this doesn't mean that Katzman movies are always the same; anyway, it forces us to examine what we mean by "same." His work in the 1950s is a direct extension of his work in serials. In serials, Jungle Sam was the master of stock footage and the king of anachronism and blithe, internalized actions of murky motivation. He probably chose the serial as a form for self-expression because it had characteristics that satisfied his personal concept of drama. The serial, a form explored by Dickens, Dostoevsky, Chandler, and many lesser popular artists, is unlike either the novel or the feature film. It introduces an extended time factor; that is, the serial goes on for weeks or months, rather than being over in one showing or reading. This gives the serialist a chance to insinuate himself and his characters into the life of the audience by his ubiquitous nature alone: the feature changes every week but Thunda runs all summer. It's the same principle that sustains Walt Kelly, Al Capp, and all the comic-strip artists. Also, the serial demands and produces, by its very nature, the multiclimax: a climax every week, but a climax that breeds anticipation of the next installment. Indeed, it is only part of a climax, and yet not an anticlimax: that's what starts each new episode. This economical form has no room for extensive character delineation or subtle, detailed plots. Minute detail or complex logic is too easily forgotten and consumes too much recapitulation time. Katzman has chosen a form whose tragic or comic possibilities are limited by convention: he must provide ten minutes of material that seems relevant and linear but rarely is; the principals must be separated from each other and provided with their own parallel plot lines; and whenever resolution seems possible, another cliff-hanger situation must be provided, one that is functionally open-ended but doesn't appear to be. At some point near the end of the budget and schedule, all the villains are dumped off a cliff, all the good characters are gathered into the same scene, and the action is wrapped up with some quick moralizing. Despite their lack of pretensions, serials are still some kind of folk art, a reflection of American life; for four decades they were, if not the opium, the television of the people. Katzman was an intuitive master of that quicksilver dramatic form that audiences accepted as more concrete and more climactic, more complete than it really was—like a boned chicken.

> Sam once beat a major Hollywood producer in a big-money Scrabble game by playing seven letters at once to spell *beatnik*. The producer challenged, Sam assured him it was a word in common usage, and that his latest picture had the word in the title. The next day on the set Sam changed the covers on all the shooting scripts just before the producer came to visit. He liked the word enough; he used it in the picture and it caught on.

His approach to feature films suggests that he sees his more recent filmmaking as an extended serial on the subject of pop culture, sustained by the cliff-hangers of fads milked to death, with the next chapters revitalized by the next craze. Considered organically this way, Katzman's career is far more interesting in its response to change than the careers of most major filmmakers. Anyway, the sequence of films that included those titles listed earlier and finished up with such late-1960s titles as *For Singles Only* and *The Young Runaways* (both 1968) is obviously not a body of work based on flights of fancy or wandering imagination. Katzman's serial work gave him the reflexes to make a picture and release it before a fad played out, and probably contributed the eye for the satisfyingly weird with which he picked the mass idiocies he would immortalize. He did not, of course, invent any of the musical rages. But he did take the fad from the contained universe of the radio/phono/jukebox (where does the music come from inside that little box?) and fuse it with an appropriately accurate yet romanticized life-style that perfectly filled out the dimensions of teen-age movie watching.

In performing this creative fusion, of course, as early as possible in the course of a fad, Katzman increased the impact of whatever music was involved: if his movies didn't innovate, they sure popularized. The proper stars of these films were the fads (you didn't pay to see Johnny Desmond when you went to *Calypso Heat Wave*), and their BO evaporated fast once the trend peaked. One key to Katzman's supersonic response to emerging fads, and perhaps the essence of Katzman's oeuvre, was the adaptation from serials of a continuous all-purpose world matrix that lends equal credibility to anything that happens within it, and that allows anything to happen without dramatic strain. This world, this crazy Katzmanian ambience, stretches from his serials through all his features and lies there behind all the really zany, evanescently aging Happenings with all the impassive calm of the Okeefenokee in *Pogo*. William Asher, progenitor of the Beach Party series, developed this lesson to its movie limit: he created a continuing world, like that of the Western, specific but general, that could be used over and over again without any variation of background or situation: only plot events changed. Katzman's forms achieved that type of inevitability, but Asher brought it even further into ritual details.

> Invent it? Sure he invented it. How? Who knows how he gets his stuff? It's enough to know that it was the right time, the right place, all the forces were in line for the word, circumstances cried out for it. So Sam, almost acting as interpreter for all these aligned forces, with quiet greatness like Gary Cooper saying "Draw," Sam says, "Here it is: *beatnik*."

Where will it all end? Where is it all going? The one really proper conclusion to the career of Jungle Sam, the mind-corrupter who stood there at the interface of Camp and Pop throwing off resonances madly as he spun the coaxial accelerator into the image of Bill Haley (before him, only the most visionary of Dadaists; snapping at his heels, the ravening monster AIP), the only possible escape from this mind-jellying cycle (Will Sam Escape? Can the Mind-Warp Hold AIP Captive in Inter-static Space? See Chapter IV—The Reuben Effect) is for Zappa to do the biopic, *The Sam Katzman Story*.[2] What if Katzman put up the $300,000 The Mothers claim they need for *Uncle Meat*? What a flick. Katzman might even *be* Uncle Meat—what does a guy who wanders around with a mind full of what

---

[2] It should be noted that, long before *Payday* (1973), Katzman did *Your Cheatin' Heart* (1965), the Hank Williams biopic that established so many conventions/clichés for country and western characters.

Katzman's mind is full of—sitting out there in his Hollywood home—really think about?

Back to specifics. The use of stock footage in Thunda, King of the Congo made it Eisensteinianly clear that the monkeys felt Buster Crabbe's antics were staged solely for their simian amusement. At the end of the serial, after the Rock people and the Cave people, after the philosopher-king stuff, and after the magic/science explorations and the who's-got-who, and after the line drawn down the middle of the entire African continent to illustrate the Commie plot: "Divide and conquer," after all that and more, the old guy looks at the Commies' crashed plane and lets go the film's final line, for Katzman I hope, "Poetic justice, I'd say."

N.B.: Sam Katzman died in August 1973.

Joseph H. Lewis

JOSEPH H. LEWIS: TOURIST IN THE ASYLUM* (1974)

MYRON MEISEL

The most striking quality of Joseph H. Lewis' direction is its invariable appositeness, its projection of an operating intelligence through even the most trivial of circumstances. It is almost as easy to overrate his early, ludicrously ephemeral work as it is to underrate it. *The Invisible Ghost* (1941), *The Mad Doctor of Market Street* (1942), and *The Boss of Hangtown Mesa* (1942) are only arguably related to art, yet, given the intractable awfulness of the goings-on, Lewis manipulates his camera and scissors with startling integrity.

Take the climax of *The Mad Doctor*, with its subjuvenile dialogue about what course of action a group of people in danger ought to take. Lewis quite unexceptionally breaks the scene into combinations of one-shots, two-shots, and three-shots, which are nonetheless so minutely measured that each shot, juxtaposed in modulated rhythm to the preceding shot and to the one to follow, advances the exposition with precision and delicacy. The dreadful lines function as verbal cues for a highly complex visual definition of altering alliances and trusts, culminating in a fundamental unity of purpose among the cardboard characters. It is nothing that would not be taken for granted in a good, well-directed film, but to find such an appreciation of the minute implications of the more pedestrian aspects of technique operating on such unprepossessing material commands an attention all its own. *The Mad Doctor of Market Street* has virtues beyond the merely apt: Richard Thompson has pointed out its affinities with Edgar Ulmer's "perversely minimal" *Club Havana* (1946) and the "compulsively catatonic" movies of Luis Buñuel. The moronic repetitions and zombie performances function as a metronome that beats lugubrious cadences for the film's implacable visual staging, with characters marching into the empty single set from off-frame as if to commence their appointed hours upon it. Most of Lewis' more direct horror-film effects are vitiated by the gargantuan cheapness of the production values, and he scores less by underlining the deficiencies of his project than by realizing its genre requirements. The film is hardly terrifying, but on any other level than the dramatic, it is a desultory marvel.

The earlier *Invisible Ghost* makes a more likely candidate for mainstream genre honors, although its greater conventionality produces a less interesting movie. Here the virtues and flaws are substantially those one might expect from a creditable Universal entry of the period; but coming from Monogram, they might be regarded as no mean feat. Lewis exhibits more fluidity of style than is customary on this level. Unlike *Mad Doctor, Invisible Ghost* attempts to realize the hypnotic qualities of its scenario, employing dollies into depth through amenably menacing corridors and audacious crosscutting that conveys the magnetism of Bela Lugosi's stare.

The Boss of Hangtown Mesa, a workmanlike job on a most conventional Western (Johnny Mack Brown rides, Fuzzy Knight sings), contains notable shots that antedate some in John Ford's *My Darling Clementine* (1946)—limpid vistas and crisp glimpses of movement—lacking the forceful thematic resonance of Ford, surely, yet, on a lesser plane, still satisfying. Essentially ordinary, the film proceeds with a narrative organization superior to the usual on this level of filmmaking; again Lewis does not transcend his material, but rather invests his own direction with a solicitude that stands out against the emotional sloppiness of a low-budget oater.

Lewis' erratic track record in this early period includes the expected complement of duds: the relentlessly worthless Bowery Boys films (*Boys of the City*, 1940; *That Gang of Mine*, 1940; *Pride of the Bowery*, 1941); the listless, indistinguishable *The Silver Bullet* (1942); and the pedestrian *The Falcon in San Francisco* (1945). Yet even in a film as patently badly directed as most of *Secrets of a Co-ed* (1942) is, one sequence reveals a courage of technique that dwarfs the poverty of the rest of the picture. In a courtroom scene rife with bogus drama, Lewis does the entire sequence in a magnificent ten-minute crane shot that would be startling in any film, let alone one made on a six-day schedule. It is a bit of brilliance without purpose that cannot redeem a valueless film. Yet the shot, which is clearly a dry run for the imaginative daring of the later single-take robbery sequence in *Gun Crazy* (1949), suggests a developing talent hungry for a meaningful assignment.

Minstrel Man (1944), with sets designed by the inimitable Ulmer, might have been it, with its story of a song-and-dance man who deserts his infant daughter because of grief over her mother's death; but the sentimentality of Benny Fields and an inadequate script sank the film despite some savvy staging of musical numbers by Lewis (a handy apprenticeship for *The Jolson Story* [1946], where he served as director for the musical sequences).

Instead, Lewis emerged with the success of *My Name Is Julia Ross* (1945), an ambitious baroque exercise that excited critics and audiences alike. Although of programmer length, the film was clearly budgeted beyond the normal restrictions attendant on a sixty-five-minute running time, and Lewis responded with flourish to his expanded resources. The virtuosity displayed in *Secrets of a Co-ed* here serves the devious purposes of suspense direction, and since Lewis is working with creditable performers (Nina Foch, George Macready, and Dame May Whitty), for the first time in his career a sense of personal relationships comes through with some success. The film, extraordinary as it is, is not nearly so rich a work as his next film, *So Dark the Night* (1946), and it suffers from formal deficiencies that are more the fault of an overly contrived script than of Lewis' very fastidious, deliberate direction. Lewis' penchant for shooting through foreground bric-a-brac makes an extensive debut, and the competition between self-conscious awareness and calculated artistry ends in something of a draw. I prefer to consider *Julia Ross* a prelude to the complete achievement of the subsequent *So Dark the Night*, which reveals Lewis at last as a filmmaker of astonishing complexity.

So Dark the Night illustrates the developing Lewis style at its most metaphorically controlled, and it presents in the most direct fashion the preoccupations of this deviously effacing artist. From this point on, although he would continue to helm his share of clinkers, Lewis fully assumes his most congenial creative role, wending his way through permutations of obsession with the bemused decency of a tourist in an asylum. Approaching his absurd low-budget project with conviction, he honed his style to a lucid edge: Lewis displays a keen instinct for the visual essence of a scene, arraying his players and placing his camera with terse pertinence.

So Dark the Night comes on like a Simenonized *La Règle du Jeu* (1939). Decked out like a French studio production, the film applies Ophulsian-style camera movements to the less exalted purposes of the whodunit. Stephen Geray plays the first distinctive Lewis hero, a man precariously balanced on the edge of control. The film introduces two essential Lewis motifs: the plot structure of hunter and hunted; and the progressive discovery of the inseparability of individual identity from social action. In *So Dark the Night*, these two key elements are fused—the murderer that the detective uncovers is revealed as his undiscovered self. In this sense, the film is Lewis' most abstract thematically, although without the overschematization that mars an ambitious, underrealized work like *Cry of the Hunted* (1953).

From the opening, the film shows complete visual control. From an extreme close-up of a phone, cut to a close-up of the Parisian prefect of police and a cutaway to an oblique high angle of the scene, now established, shot through the rotating blades of an overhead fan. The conversation immediately asserts Geray's integrity ("He would arrest his own mother if he were convinced of her guilt"); but the master detective needs a vacation badly, and Lewis economically sets up city-country oppositions, notably presenting Geray's entrance into the town from the viewpoint of how the town sees him, and not the other way around. Lewis wants us to observe Geray from the outside, the better to share his subjective revelations later. Lewis sets up a telling high-angle shot of Geray's entrance by intercutting a short shot of a woman peering out of a window, always covering his extreme shots by logically establishing them as some individual's point of view. Thus, he rarely editorializes as an omniscient director, but rather lets his technique make its points through participants in the scene.

Geray meets a fresh young girl at the inn, with whom he begins to fall in love. She is taken by him and by the more exciting life he as a Parisian represents. When her sweetheart since childhood enters, Lewis dollies in fast to his face, paralleling Geray's own perception of his entrance. Later he shoots a love scene between Geray and the girl with their backs to the camera, as it discreetly tracks into a close enough position so that over-the-shoulder crosscutting becomes viable. But most importantly, when the subject of marriage is seriously broached, Lewis pans up from an idyllic contemplation of Geray's image in the murky pond to Geray himself, the first of many such images emphasizing the separation within Geray between a submerged murderous identity and a gentle, sympathetic character. It is only the challenge of marriage to a much younger woman that forces the hidden identity out into the open.

Lewis also perceptively uses point-of-view shots from interiors looking outward to designate separations between characters. On several stunning occasions, from an outside position looking at a group of people, he dollies back through a window to reveal others observing them from the inside, thus interposing the physical separation of the set's walls rather than using the less obtrusive temporal device of cutting. In this manner, whoever is being observed (whether the girl, or the boyfriend, or Geray) is directly related to the view others are taking of them, whereas a cut would simply establish the fact of observation without implying a relation between an objective (the camera as observer) and a subjective (the camera as a person's point of view) apprehension of the character. In another film, such technical flourish might be merely that, but in the rarefied context of the plot's abnormal psychology, such technique elevates the visual expression, if not to poetry, then, to a highly poeticized prose.

When the boyfriend threatens Geray ("You'll never really have her"), Lewis puts tinkling bells on the music track over Geray's close-up, an aural motif for the gradual emergence of his killer-self. When the news of his fiancée's death is brought to him by the town humpback, Lewis modulates his lighting to place ripples on Geray's face, ostensibly from the slats in the bridge overhead. The affinity of this image with that of the pond reflection in the earlier scene at the same location further develops the visual link between Geray's repressed realization and images of himself reflected in water, mirrors, and the like.

The extraordinary scene in which Geray discovers the body of the boyfriend exemplifies much of the film's visual method. The camera is placed inside the stable where the body lies. It pans up to the open door, and we see the principals outside, in deep focus. Far back in the frame, the girl's father discovers the clue that indicates the body is in the barn. As the characters approach the barn entrance, the camera pulls back with their motion, and it stops, as they do, just short of the entranceway. Then reverse to outside the barn, forcefully producing the palpable sense of poising before forbidden territory that we ought not to enter. Geray does not enter the barn. He theorizes, as the now subjectively expressive camera tracks away from him, pulling farther back from the entranceway. Geray turns to face the camera, his back now to the barn, and he discovers the footprint of the murderer. He does not recognize it as his own. Baffled over his inability to track down the culprit, he later agonizes with unconscious irony, "He does not *seem* to exist, yet he *does* exist."

Lewis also displays his penchant for objects in hard focus in the foreground while the action takes place farther back in the frame. The death of the girl's mother is evoked through the metaphor of a dripping faucet and a steaming teapot, our view of them obscured by the clutter of various other kitchen objects.

All of these visual devices converge in the stunningly designed climax, in which the complex motifs of framing, objects in the foreground, reprised bells on the sound track, deep focus, mirror images, and ratcheted light are orchestrated to the theme of realization. One shot, perhaps the only justifiable camera-in-fireplace shot in cinema, lets us see the placid, respectable Geray imagistically burned up as his submerged character emerges. From this expressionistic vantage, we suddenly are absorbed into Geray's viewpoint, as he sees through the window from the identical angle from which he had been perceived upon entering the town. There is, at last, a consonance between Geray's perception of himself and an "objective" (i.e., from an outside point of view) perception of his true, divided spirit. He recollects his arrival at the village through cutting that conveys a feeling of looking from the "inside out," and when Geray beholds his image reflected in the window, now representing the memory of the character that the murderous personality has taken over, he smashes the glass. With this gesture he not only catches the criminal (to the end, vindicating his social role as the finest detective in France), but he simultaneously destroys the image of the now "false," respectable self.

The scene might have simply appeared a virtuoso baroque passage without the very precise buildup of all its composite visual and aural symbols. Because of the reverberations that have accreted over the course of the film, these symbols, as good symbols should, interact with a cumulating richness that would have been impossible to express in any other fashion. Thus, *So Dark the Night* succeeds as a matchless stylistic exercise, marking it as the first major film in the Lewis canon.

The Undercover Man (1949), a police-procedural film with a semi-documentary patina, like Anthony Mann's work in the period (*T-Men,* 1947), adds substantial elements of *film noir* to the common blend of urban location shooting, emphasis on naturalistic detail, and homage paid to the virtues of dogged persistence. Lewis' aggressive camera produces striking, forceful action sequences with ample imaginative wrinkles to sustain the novelty necessary to a successful *noir* project in which personal reinterpretation is required to keep a repetitive genre fresh. Lewis employs the standard paraphernalia of short, taciturn dialogue exchanges, sharp action montage, characterization by physical gesture and type, as well as towing the familiar Columbia anti-Populist line on individual responsibility (more meaningful than usual, perhaps due to the participation of Robert Rossen, who took it all personally). The most vivid *noir*-styled sequence involves the killing of the bookkeeper Rocco while he is meeting with his little girl in his neighborhood, a bravura scene of high-pitched emotional intensity implicating trash cans, shopping carts, and crowds of people in the queasy mortal terror of a harrowing, panicky tracking shot. All in all, a classic example of the genre.

And yet Lewis shoots the scene as one of a derelict father returning to his home to swell with pride over his beloved daughter. The camera stays on him and the girl as he spots the danger off screen. Then, he suddenly pushes the girl away as the tension builds before exploding into the high-powered track. The emphasis falls on the little girl frantically running after her "Papa," screaming for him, and the scene fades out on her shocked, blank face as she looks at his dead body. Whereas a director with typical *noir* concerns might shoot a scene in this fashion for shock effect or visceral impact, Lewis takes pains to underline that it is the love of the father and the daughter, and not the killing, that is the essence of the scene. The force of the scene is a function of that intensity of emotional commitment; it is not an end in itself, achieved by the manipulation of that intensity.

Beneath its surface affectations of *film noir,* then, *The Undercover Man* runs emotionally counter to the usual preoccupations of the form. The dramatic center of the film involves the efforts of agent-accountant Glenn Ford to reconcile his vocation with his marriage, to discharge both his responsibilities to his family and his obligations to society through his job. The long, dangerous months in cramped offices leave no room for visits with his wife (Nina Foch), and Ford finds his family threatened as a result of his endeavors to bring the mob to heel. Lewis delicately probes the Ford-Foch relationship in terms of their need for mutual support and love, linking this need to larger social concerns.

For Lewis, all men, even the worst of them, have a need for love, and the desire to preserve love relationships and, most particularly, family ties is what makes people willing to fight for an orderly society. Potential witnesses in *The Undercover Man* may sincerely wish to remain uninvolved, but when they see that the security of their emotional lives may be threatened by their silence, they are capable of great moral courage. For all the script's talk of individual responsibility as the critical element in controlling crime, meaningful action in the film is always propounded within the context of family bonds.

Even the sharp, crooked attorney (Barry Kelley) is depicted in his home playing with his children in a scene in which Ford intrudes on his domestic peace in order to harass him, and his annoyance at the intrusion is unmistakable. Later on, Kelley intimates to Ford that his family is largely the rationale for his shady activities.

Lewis best illustrates his theme in two extraordinary scenes that were each improvised in a single take with three cameras (certainly an unusual procedure for a low-budget film). In one, Ford and Foch sit under a tree and discuss his intention to quit his job because of the danger to her and the children, a scene remarkable for its spontaneous tact and unmediated emotional validity. In another, more declamatory, scene, Rocco's mother and his daughter make a speech to Foch and Ford about wanting to help men such as he make the world free from gangsters and intimidation (they are turning over the mob's account books). Lewis makes the shopworn didacticism of the statement genuinely moving by composing a master shot that arrays the several generations spatially in a line of succession, expressing the passing of responsibility through the family unit in order to maintain the social order. The line gives a standard confrontation scene a true purpose and concurrently demonstrates to Ford and Foch the unavoidable relation between their bond and Ford's chosen work. Although it occurs only two-thirds of the way through the film, the sequence provides the indisputable emotional climax, linking responsibility to one's loved ones with responsibility to the law, implying that the need to love underlies the need for an orderly society. From then on, we know, for once, *why* a man must do what he has to do.

In a way, the harsh stresses of Lewis' technique might seem at odds with the gentleness of his theme. When Ford and Foch first meet his colleagues in his office, Lewis uses Wellesian-style shots that maintain a single plane in deep focus to establish both the tension of their impending separation and the persistent nature of their bond (Foch is lit strongly, filling up the left foreground and dominating the frame, while Ford and his buddies are sharp in the back). Similarly, when Ford and Kelley attempt to walk out of a trap in an alley, Lewis segues from their generalized point of view to strenuously framed point-of-view shots of the anonymous assailants, ending with Kelley's body thrust assertively forward in front of the attacking automobile. Throughout the film directorial calculation mixes with behavioral spontaneity (some head-shots in real locations inescapably suggest Jean Renoir).

Such a contrast marks a director unattuned to ironies, and for all its conviction, *The Undercover Man* utterly lacks the intellectual ardor of a film like Chaplin's *Monsieur Verdoux* (1947), to which it is thematically related. Lewis' forte does not lie in argument, and he cannot reconcile the *noir* determinism of his style with his brief for family ties as the root of social responsibility. It's a case of a personal credo elaborated through the emotional texture of a genre film, with unstressed juxtapositions discreetly made under the cover of imaginative turbulence. It therefore qualifies as a highly effective, personal work by a minor artist.

Gun Crazy (1949), on the other hand, establishes conclusively that the minor artist is nonetheless a major talent. It hurtles along with the mad energy of its protagonists, the personification of "youth run wild," the drive of vitality run amok. Unwavering intelligence with forms of mania has always been a hallmark of Lewis; here he deals with its most unbridled exemplar, without sacrificing any directorial sensibleness. Few films are more singularly preoccupied with externals to the exclusion of attention to interior states. In *Gun Crazy*, there are no interior states to be ignored. No psychological explanations are implied—John Dall is merely an intelligent, gentle man who (sigh) "just likes guns." This makes for good visceral cinema, wherein characters express themselves exclusively through their actions, and it is particularly appropriate to a central relationship such as the one between Dall and Peggy Cummins: their competition at marksmanship and their robberies become their means of expressing their feelings toward one another. Lewis again centers his narrative around sexual tensions; he has said that he wanted to show that "their love for each other was more fatal than their love for guns." Freed of the analytical baggage of abnormal psychology, Lewis fashions a direct cinema in which action and emotion are inseparable.

Admirable and exciting as his results are, they are not all to the good. The lack of psychological depth inhibits our identification with the protagonists, although Lewis achieves formidable audience sympathy with his shallowly amoral heroes. Since their feelings are only communicated through action, their relationship can be complex but never subtle. This is hardly Lewis' fault: these are flaws inherent in much of the more dispassionate action cinema (Robert Siodmak, Henry Hathaway, and Jacques Tourneur, as compared to Samuel Fuller, Phil Karlson, or Anthony Mann). Yet they do limit his achievement. Of the four great renditions of the "Bonnie and Clyde" tale (Fritz Lang's *You Only Live Once*, 1937; Nicholas Ray's *They Live by Night*, 1949; and Arthur Penn's, 1967), Lewis' is paradoxically the most impressive and the least important. In choosing to render the story down to its leanest elements, Lewis achieves unique originality at a slightly lower level of profundity.

Lewis achieved sequences in *Gun Crazy* that were unprecedented in American film. His famous single-take bank robbery reconciled budget problems and dramatic impact with imaginative flair. The location shooting gives the film a feel totally out of keeping with its period, and much of the staging and framing antedates the Jean-Luc Godard of *Vivre sa Vie* (1962) and *Bande à part* (1964). The freshness of Lewis' direction closely parallels the giddy elation of his lovers, as he daringly attempts "impossible" shots and stunningly brings them off. The robbery of the Armour Meat Packing Plant, covering no less than six locations, is organized with exemplary narrative lucidity, enabling Lewis to let the whole operation go surprisingly awry and to have the audience recognize the slipups as immediately as the participants. We experience their exhilaration and tension and rush of bravado as they do. *Gun Crazy* entices the audience into the dizziness of irresponsibility.

The film opens with a young boy breaking in a shop window to steal a gun and falling in a puddle. The camera pans with the gun as it slides from his hand to rest at the feet of a cop. In a world going too fast, Lewis repeatedly reminds us, people tend to trip. Later, Cummins will slip and lose some of the money during the Armour robbery; she will trip when they are discovered on their night on the town and leave her coat behind; they both fall repeatedly during their final flight into the swamps. It isn't easy to keep your balance when you're crazy over guns.

The youthful Dall is shown to be a kid of amazing sensitivity to life, suffering, in extreme close-up, when he cannot bring himself to shoot a mountain lion despite the exhortations of his comrades. When the adult Dall returns after a hitch in the Army, he is introduced through a bough of bottles hard in the foreground, which he picks off one by one to reveal his figure, in deep focus, far away. His existence is defined by his ability with firearms. When he goes to the county fair and sees Cummins performing her act, he cannot resist the sheer fun of challenging her to a "duel."

The character of Cummins is treated entirely in terms of her physical effects. Carrying the implicit concept of woman as other to a stylistic extreme, Lewis rigorously avoids any shots from her point of view. When Dall puts on the crown of matches in the duel, we see Cummins shooting at him, and when they switch places, we switch camera position, too, still watching through his eyes as he shoots at Cummins. Throughout, we look *at* Cummins, never *with* her. Her consciousness may be apprehended through her actions but it is never shared.

There is only one, perhaps significant, exception. When, in the Armour robbery, Cummins pauses needlessly to shoot her officious supervisor, we cut from her face in delicious anticipation to her point of view of the victim being killed. This is the first killing in the film and it precipitates the mechanism of the couple's undoing. Dall had steadfastly refused Cummins' requests that he kill pursuing cops, shooting away their tires instead. In this action she finally triumphs over his residual moral inhibitions and his last resistance to the force of their shared, mad love.

Lewis employs a lot of standard B movie devices, more than his wont, using inserts of objects (such as FBI teletypes or shot-away ornamental balls) for transitions, and short-take tableaux setups for cumulative short-hand when he wishes to convey a series of minor holdups. Lewis compensates for the bare, unparticularized sets by alternating flexible compositions in deep focus with an inordinate number of tight close-ups. A deep-focus scene of testiness in a greasy spoon is followed by a prolonged moral argument in a barren hotel room, culminating in the singular crosscutting of one-shots of Dall and Cummins, *both* in right-profile close-up as they bicker. Many such scenes are staged with the characters facing away from each other or from the camera. In this way the tensions of the relationship in turgid circumstances are communicated in the same direct way as the release is conveyed during the action scenes—by embroiling the audience in the actions that stand in for the characters' emotions.

Contrasts with the other "Bonnie and Clyde" films are instructive. In *They Live by Night,* the couple risks a night out because of their deep desire to live like "normal people," but the forces of normal society just won't let them alone. In the comparable sequence in *Gun Crazy,* the couple go out for the sheer daring of it, as one more jolt to sustain their relationship. Their own incaution gives them away. Similarly, when Bonnie and

Clyde visit home, the scene is a nostalgic idyll, concocted only to be shattered by the mother's clear thinking. No such clear thinking burdens Dall and Cummins as they eventually flee back to his sister's place. When they go there, it isn't because of some fatalistic apprehension of impending disaster (as with Faye Dunaway's Bonnie), but because, quite simply, their jig is up, their crazy passion has faltered, there is no place else left to go. When the car stalls in the penultimate chase, Lewis' two frontal close-ups emphasize that their *amour fou* has lost its sustaining energy.

Discovered by his childhood friends (now a sheriff and a reporter), Dall flees into the white fog of the swamp with Cummins, the first of many Lewis swamp climaxes (*A Lady Without Passport, Cry of the Hunted,* and *Desperate Search*). Lewis envelops his characters in mist, heads bobbing in and out of it, emerging always in extreme close-up whether in one- or two-shot. When Cummins readies herself to kill his childhood friends, Dall shoots her. She is the only person he has ever killed. The odd, weak man puts an end to all this madness. It's not a moving moment so much as a satisfyingly reasonable one, our involvement with consuming passion perfunctorily curtailed. Cummins, the embodiment of irresponsible gratification, is summarily destroyed as reason and morality dawn on Dall, for whom it is also too late. It's not much of a tragic climax, rather more like the finish of a roller-coaster ride.

Perhaps the loveliest of Lewis' neglected works, *A Lady Without Passport* (1950), might have been an ideal Samuel Fuller project; it is about a muscle-headed undercover agent out to smash an alien-smuggling ring. The community of corruption in Havana, refugees exploited by unscrupulous "importers," has the kind of tepid atmosphere in which Fuller might exult. Lewis captures the sweat, but his characters melt when exposed to protracted emotion. The hard-boiled agent begins to empathize deeply with the plight of the displaced persons, and when he meets concentration camp victim Hedy Lamarr, now driven to an ignoble existence, he finds himself contracting a serious case of romantic love. No Fuller character would suddenly pull up short and write out his resignation, giving as his reason the simple declaration: "I am in love."

Lewis braves his way through the stickier aspects of the plot with a similar deadpan earnestness that ends up far more moving than laughable. Both Lamarr and John Hodiak give what are easily the best performances of indifferent careers, and Lewis' virtuosity is in some ways more in evidence here than in *Gun Crazy*. The long-take opening is even more astounding than its counterpart in the earlier film. Here, we are tracking behind an automobile moving slowly through a crowded daytime street and we swing around to a side view as the car halts. Some dialogue with a pedestrian follows, and, as the car pulls away, the camera moves around to a frontal view, looking into the windshield. Then, through the rear window, in extreme deep focus, we see the pedestrian meeting with a fatal accident.

Throughout Lewis exhibits an uncanny ability to make his long shots count as if they were close-ups, selecting revealing angles and editing in long shots where reaction shots would generally be. Limber camera movements set up startling, offhanded shots, as he tracks back to position for a telling cut or dollies in closer to get inside a café. Above all, Lewis' command of interlocked point-of-view shots creates complexity where there might otherwise be artiness. Lamarr, after an innuendo-laden exchange with heavy George Macready, walks away and up the stairs with her back to the following camera. As she reaches the top of the landing, without turning round, she pauses, and the camera pans down directly to Macready, who walks over to the stairs and follows. The camera remains stationary as Macready climbs the steps, having switched points of view within a single shot. Equally impressive is Lewis' handling of a nightclub act. The camera enters the room on a cut away from Hodiak (impersonating a Czech wheeler-dealer). The dancer is consistently contained by low-angle setups or dominated by the unyielding presence of the grand piano maintained in the foreground by Lewis' crane, with the music setting the emotional outlines of the framing (including some effective cutting in counterbeat to the drums).

Some of the silly intrigue is nonetheless complicated and Lewis' stress on the burgeoning love affair between Hodiak and Lamarr makes it all seem very important. Lewis doesn't use his love interest as an excuse to slough off the plotting; instead, he elucidates the story line with methodical visual organization and then charges it with the edgy softness of the distrustful, vulnerable lovers. Unfortunately, the script is ill-constructed: the last third of the picture is an extended chase, good enough in its own right but only tenuously integrated with the earlier action and a far too conventional resolution of the conflicts to be satisfying. Still, the moral issues posed by Hodiak's conflicting duties (to his job and to Lamarr, as well as to preserve the lives of the smuggled aliens) are not shirked and are given a full dramatic development, although not with a complexity worthy of the issues. One imaginative piece of direction presents Hodiak sitting in his office, sick over the decisions of his superiors in the manhunt that might endanger innocent lives. Lewis cuts from an angle off to the side of the discouraged Hodiak to the same angle slightly farther away. It's almost imperceptible, but, between one shot and another, Hodiak's companions in the office are placed just barely outside the frame, underlining the individual moral anxiety of the character in a compassionate way.

Lewis' next two films, although full of interesting elements, rank as distinct disappointments. *Retreat Hell!* (1952) concerns a draftee officer who feels he cannot lead because of his overweening commitment to his wife and family, a notion to which Lewis might be unusually sympathetic. Yet the story ignores the implications of the situation, and the film is a conventional combat tale. *Desperate Search* (1952) is more interesting. A pair of acrimonious divorced parents attempt to locate their children who are lost in the Canadian wilderness. The tensions between the ex-wife, who is a flyer, and the husband's second wife, who is not, lead to conflicts similar to those at the end of *A Lady Without Passport,* concerning the moral implications of personal involvement in a procedural operation. Lewis attempts a classic contrast between the innocence of the children's adaptation to nature and the waspish tensions among the adults that is shallowly effective, but he also draws startling parallels between the sexual problems of the adults and the behavior of the children—an outrageous idea that never gets off the ground. Again as in *Passport,* Lewis shies away from just what a director like Fuller or Ulmer might respond to. He hasn't any sympathy with outrageousness for its own sake; as in *Gun Crazy,* he can observe it, even draw us into it, but he remains detached, rarely violating the underlying exigencies of his melodramas.

Lewis comes close to confronting the outrageous in *Cry of the Hunted* (1953), a very personal work that is so abrasively overwrought that it makes little sense. The film is organized entirely as a chase—an escaped convict being hunted down in the mud of his native bayou by a California prison official. Both men are odd, sympathetic characters, drawn to each other by a personal bond so obscure in its detailed moral accounting as to be nearly incomprehensible. The film finds two-shots in the unlikeliest situations, including a prison cell fistfight in which the careening heads never fall out of tight medium close-up. Once again passion asserts itself over rationality: the convict explains why he headed straight for home, with the cryptic, "Memories and desires mean more than freedom." The escape scene, as the convict flees on a San Francisco cable car after he emerges from a tunnel, makes for a striking long-held shot that organizes light textures, space, and movement to evoke the confusion and elation of flight. For all the obtuse variations of "I've got you and now you owe me," ad infinitum, its immediacy and freakish intensity suggest the director's strong emotional involvement in the material, which invests such cinematic bombast with noteworthy sincerity and conviction.

But in many ways, *Cry of the Hunted* denotes a turning point in Lewis' career. His films from here on grow more resolutely male-oriented, and his delicacy in dealing with relationships accordingly disappears. If anything, his films grow more eccentric in substance and quirky in method, while forfeiting his gentle touch with hard material that had set him apart from his other comrades working in the mainstream of B films.

The Big Combo (1955) provides the bridge between Lewis, the man of tactful compassion, and the Lewis of the four last Westerns, a man considering varieties of passion itself.

From the moment Jean Wallace tries to elude her gun-carrying chaperones by fleeing down darkened alleys shot from long, low angles, we know that *The Big Combo* fits snugly in the *noir* mold. The contributions of writer Philip Yordan and cameraman John Alton inescapably stamp this film as Lewis' most classical exploit in the genre. The harshness of the characterizations evidenced in *Cry of the Hunted* is under firmer control here; unfortunately, the corresponding humanizing touches are not. Instead of the softness that had come to be associated with the Lewis hero, we have simply the weakness of uncontained neurosis. Cop Cornel Wilde is out to get gangster Richard Conte, and, except for the hunter-hunted structure, it would be impossible to speculate who is the more socially undesirable. Both are obsessive haters; Conte goes so far as to proclaim it the secret of his success. Wilde's mania about bagging Conte isn't simply a zealous pursuit of duty—Wallace, allegedly a classy society dame, has left Wilde to take up with Conte, and Wilde continues to hound her with sick devotion. The motivations are a trifle unclear, but Wilde's single-mindedness seems to have gotten to her. Conte may be vile, but at least he has outside interests. Wilde, as his heedless treatment of a doting chorine reveals, is incapable of any kind of love.

Wilde's tenacity sweeps aside petty questions of morality or propriety: when informed that Conte has been arrested a dozen times and was always acquitted, he beefs to his boss, who is trying to cool him, that "it's unnatural to be so innocent." Conte in his way is equally absolutist: "First is first, and second is nothing." He is very sensitive to matters of status.

What gives *The Big Combo* distinction beyond being an original, superbly realized genre piece is Lewis' revulsion at much of the behavior in the film, a distaste not conveyed by a criticism of the form (as Robert Aldrich does in *Kiss Me Deadly*, 1955—Lewis is too conscientious a genre craftsman and too passive an artistic temperament to assay such an exercise) but instead by establishing his values through finely attuned visual symbols, as he had in *So Dark the Night*.

The key is his treatment of Wallace. Superficially, she seems an undercharacterized woman typical of *films noirs* of the period, after the 1940s' model had sported a rich array of highly individual types. (Not a little of it probably derives from her inadequacies as an actress.) Lewis continually enshrouds her in light, setting her eerily aglow amid the blackness of the concentrated *maudit* style. Lewis characteristically employed close-ups as motifs, generally to chronicle a slow progression into awareness (e.g., Dall and Geray), but here Wallace's inexpressiveness transforms her statically beautiful face into an object of feeling without a personality, a repository of passion and submission in some ways comparable to Robert Bresson's Balthazar (in *Au Hasard Balthazar*, 1965). This is underlined by the condescending tone taken by Conte when he complains about the color of her gown: "You should wear white. I like you in white. You have twelve white dresses . . . A woman dresses to please a man." She suffers this and worse from Wilde, who makes her the brunt of the most nasty accusations because of her association with Conte. Her iconic significance is made most explicit when Conte makes love to her, kissing her ears and neck and dropping out of the shot as we stare intently at the impassive absorption of her inscrutable face, bathed in quivering light.

This beacon of light transmutes itself from a passive quality into an assertive gesture when Wallace punctuates the climactic shoot-out by turning the sharp beam of a spotlight on Conte, preventing his getaway. Wilde, meanwhile, has finally realized (through the rather hoary device of the death of the chorine who adores him—she is assassinated in his place as she waits for him in his apartment) that he has been reprehensibly oblivious to the feelings of the people around him and that he has been morally responsible for the grim consequences of his obsessions. His moral insularity has been in fact tantamount to the immoral. Wilde must recognize with grief that he is capable of feelings other than revenge and vindictiveness. "Nobody knows how another person feels," Wallace had pleaded to him in one of his heedless rages of intolerance. Depicting the first positive steps either character has taken toward a natural love relationship, the film accepts this somewhat unlikely possibility as a sufficiently upbeat resolution.

The value Lewis places on emotional sensitivity figures in the film's famous set piece, the two scenes where Brian Donlevy's hearing aid figures in the action. Robert Mundy has noted how Lewis effectively manages to underplay the violence both times by objectively shooting a torture scene in which the hearing aid is placed in Wilde's ear with the volume screaming into his brain (i.e., we see Wilde writhing in agony but hear the dialogue normally), and then by subjectively shooting Donlevy's death scene without the aid (we see the bursts of machine-gun fire without hearing anything). But equally pertinent is Lewis' refusal to share Wilde's consciousness in the earlier scene and his desire to share the unnaturalistic sensations of the deaf Donlevy's apprehension of impending death. Lewis further gives highly sympathetic shticks to the many minor characters who are exposed to danger through Wilde's insensitivity to their fates, which ensures that our sympathy remains withheld from Wilde. These include several ethnic bits that Lewis and his players breathe into life despite the conventional schematic attitudinizing of the writing. The most impressive contrast to the ruthless solipsism of Wilde and Conte is the deep mutual affection displayed by a pair of hired killers, a devotion of which the protagonists are sadly incapable.

It is virtually a cliché of the criticism of *film noir* to hail a director for creating a consistent vision of the world, however perversely bleak and dark the urban image depicted might be. Lewis, on the contrary, takes care *not* to suggest that all this murky ambience constitutes any vision of the world at large, although his apprehension of this stylized piece of it is certainly admirable in its unwavering integrity of vision. Instead, Lewis inserts startling open-air linkage shots that indicate the presence of a normal world existing completely beyond this seamy underlife (contrast Anthony Mann, who could shoot high noon as if it were midnight). Again, Lewis' style stresses the conventions of the form while his attitude stays unimplicated in the material itself. He insists on preserving his reasonableness for all his fascination with dementia.

With his last spate of Westerns, however, Lewis turns about to examine just this quality of reason amid chaos, querying whether it is possible to remain a reasonable being when confronted with encroaching darkness. In these films, Lewis flirts with despair, finding it both inevitable and vanquishable. He comes close to defining a central theme to which his work had been tending throughout his career—the conflict between the exigencies of survival in a tough world dominated by a capacity for evil and the impulse of man toward the best that is in him; to reconcile the necessity to be tough and the need to draw back from the battle and seek emotional peace. One gathers that these last few films are in many ways Lewis' most personal; unfortunately, largely due to formal deficiencies in the scripts and inadequate performances, they are for the most part (with the exception of *The Halliday Brand*) not among his best realized. Somewhat more rhetorical in form, less satisfying as drama, they are also intractable, fascinating works characterized by Lewis' expanding scope of visual control. All of them have an overlay of weirdness, both calculated and inadvertent, but none is without portions that move more deeply than most previous instances in the Lewis canon. Whereas before there was beauty in action, in leanness, in delicacy of touch, in poetic harmony, and in matter-of-fact audacity, now the communicated feeling reaches us more directly, less disguised by conventional gestures, often too inchoate to be successful art but nonetheless genuinely affecting. When considered in light of the themes of his earlier films, the last Westerns convey a greater moral urgency, just as they lend a retroactive fervor to the less explicitly personal earlier work.

The Randolph Scott character in *A Lawless Street* (1955) scrupulously maintains a public image of hard-bitten toughness, an impression that he "isn't human," in order to preserve a shallow, peaceable private existence making idle small talk and enjoying his vittles. His desire for isolation from his social role as sheriff is neatly expressed when he locks himself into his own jail cell, in order to get a "peaceful sleep." Of course, a sheriff cannot maintain any such separation between his public and private self when, underneath the town's surface respectability, there resides an impulse to chaos and disturbance that can be summoned up by conspiring forces of corruption.

Lewis uses very complex camera movements to tie Scott in with the happenings in the street: the opening shot, under the credits, is an impressive vertical crane downward to meet a revenge-seeking gunman riding into town, beginning with him in long-shot and ending with him reaching the camera's position. Subsequently, the camera duplicates the same effect, this time horizontally: it tracks from Scott conversing with a gambler, picking up a stage coming into town, and gradually meeting it as it pulls up. A similar pattern of repetition emerges when Lewis backtracks through a barbershop window with Scott as he enters, continuing the dialogue in a single take (with the operator adjusting the framing as necessary). When a killer looks for Scott at the shop, the track back as he enters doesn't penetrate the window but picks him up from a position already inside, and a cut is employed instead of the continuous movement to bring the character into the room.

These moves visually belie Scott's insistence that he can live his life on two separate levels, publicly tough and privately vulnerable. His every action, even one so personal as getting a shave, is followed up by action in the public sphere. The false character of this separation is directly challenged when the stage brings in Angela Lansbury, a music-hall star who was married to Scott years ago, unbeknownst to anyone in the town. The romantic subplot, including an extramarital affair of the town heavy (interested in Lansbury) with the rich man's wife, is notably unconvincing and banal, except as it relates to Scott's recognition of the single nature of his conflicting impulses.

In his efforts to prevent the town's take-over by the heavy, Scott is brutally beaten on several occasions, yet he refuses to reveal his "humanness" in public (Lansbury does catch him in a vulnerable moment in the privacy of the jail, with his friend Dr. Wallace Ford, as she watches him from behind a windowpane). Finally, he is apparently "killed" in a gunfight, only to "rise from the dead" literally and turn the very flaming barrels used by the evildoers to burn and destroy against them. In the interim, Lewis treats us to provocative images suggesting the underlying disorder latent in civilized society, nearly up to similar moments in Ford's *Two Rode Together* (1961), were they not marred by some clumsy handling of extras and, of course, the comparatively shallow context in which the scene functions. The town clearly has eagerly awaited a pretext to break down its tenuous order and to express repressed impulses for destruction. In this chaotic situation, Lewis contends that a man like Scott must translate his desire for peace into active terms and fight with quasi-supernatural force in order to prevail, a development from his position in *The Undercover Man*.

The idea itself is not terribly compelling, but one shot exemplifies the stunning artistic realization Lewis gives his theme. Lansbury is nearly trampled by a runaway horse race in the streets, a graphic representation of Scott's capacity for feeling directly threatened by the lawlessness of the public beast emergent. Lewis stages this action in a single shot, declining to cut for emotional emphasis, as he well might have, in order to preserve instead the directness of his representation. Scott's private passions are thus not merely affected by what is happening in the street; they are *in* the street and in mortal danger there. *A Lawless Street* implies that abstract distinctions in the way one lives are meaningless in the face of the chaos underlying human society. Its force is somewhat vitiated by a pedestrian screenplay with some lamentable lines, and the action is not particularly profound on the level to which Lewis takes it. Still, the film frames its position almost exclusively in visual terms, no small achievement, and it does represent a more personal rendition of a thematic motif familiar from earlier Lewis opuses, earning the film a standing beyond that to which its B movie limitations might otherwise relegate it.

The Seventh Cavalry (1956), although achieving far less as a whole, accomplishes some passages so potently melancholic that no familiarity with Lewis' work can prepare a viewer for them. The film opens shortly after the Custer massacre and concentrates on the effects the defeat has on the main body of the Seventh Cavalry. Randolph Scott plays an officer, dispatched by Custer to report back to the fort on the eve of the battle at the Little Big Horn, who must overcome the guilt he feels at being a survivor. The first surge of revulsion the unthinking mourners feel toward him as he bears the shocking news carries a charge we have hardly been readied for, and Lewis' compositions, with characters facing away from each other (Antonioni-style) and shot full-figure in low-keyed stage lighting (not unlike Joseph LaShelle's camera work on Ford's Seven Women, 1966), communicate the internal anguish of all concerned through striking surfaces. The thought of Carl Dreyer in the sagebrush does not seem ridiculous during these sequences. Remarkable pickup shots of Scott and his troops inspecting the carnage very nearly sustain this tone, but the working out of the themes is disappointingly routine, and most of the direction is merely straightforward in customary fluid fashion. The ending, with Scott successfully negotiating a passive victory over an Indian encirclement, runs daringly counter to the active vindication that we expect the genre to insist upon. The Seventh Cavalry remains Lewis' most tantalizing film, rich in unresolved emotions and in sensitivity to historical passions, the first third suggesting an emotional depth Lewis never really mastered.

The Halliday Brand (1957), more limited in its range than the two preceding Westerns, is accordingly far more successful, a work to place on a par with So Dark the Night, Gun Crazy, and The Big Combo. The most astute of Lewis' films in its use of space, this tale of son Joseph Cotten's revolt against his tyrannical rancher-father (Ward Bond) dramatizes the emotional price conscience can exact. Abusing his role as sheriff, Bond shoots his daughter's chicano husband and later on kills the father of the half-breed girl (Viveca Lindfors) Cotten loves. Cotten is eventually forced to become an outlaw, burning barns and running off cattle, to bring the domineering Halliday brand to heel.

The film conforms to conventional Western patterns: the range baron with a racist streak; one son, inheriting a "soft spot" from his mother, squeamish about violent methods; another, stronger physically but weaker morally, who sympathizes with his brother and plays along with authority; assorted peons and sturdy stoic women. Yet Lewis imparts his personal flair to these familiar elements, his complex visual style emphasizing typical thematic strains. Cotten attempts to moderate the old man throughout, trying desperately not to make a break, until he realizes that he must not compromise—he cannot maintain his family loyalty independent of his moral principles. Forced to extreme action (as Scott was in *A Lawless Street*) to preserve what is most dear to him, Cotten then begins to press his battle too far, prompting Lindfors to plead with him that "there can be no life for anyone until this hate is forgotten." Yet neither Bond nor Cotten will relent. This pattern of implacable adversaries who grow more and more alike until the distinction between the "good" guy and the "bad" guy blurs is reminiscent of *The Big Combo*. Indeed, Cotten's methods eventually generate as much opposition as his father's high-handedness. "You will become like the man you despise," warns Lindfors. In the final scene, Cotten bends, although the father remains intransigent until he falls, dying, into his son's arms, declaring, "You're too much like me."

In the opening shot, Lewis brilliantly summarizes the dramatic situation. A gun in its holster fills the foreground, although it is in slightly soft-focus, facing the Halliday house sharp in the background. The man carrying the gun slowly wheels about, with evident revulsion, from the house. It is Cotten, now facing outward, eyes downcast, still soft in extreme close-up. A yell from the house (Bond's voice) calls Betsy Blair, Cotten's downtrodden sister. The camera rises to pick her up from a high angle as she walks to the house, craning down to a large tree stump that is the symbol of the Halliday clan, which, as the camera descends, fills the frame to cover her figure completely as it approaches the house. In a single didactic shot, Lewis has expressed the essential conflicts of the film.

Inside the house, the characters' movements are not blocked out in conventional theatrical style, with the audience presumed to be viewing them sideways (i.e., arrayed on the same plane as the screen itself). Instead, Lewis stages interior action to place us behind his players. When Blair enters the house, she passes Lindfors, and the two women swerve around in order to avoid facing one another. In many ways, *The Halliday Brand* anticipates Antonioni, not merely in terms of stylistic choices but also in the uses to which the choices are put.

For Lewis, the frame's foreground is where we reach inside his characters, who in turn are tortured by forces reaching out from the hard-focused background, frequently dominated by the looming figure of Bond. Dolly-ins are freely employed as visual gestures indicating some form of internal confrontation. Bond is frequently given a fixed motion that doesn't alter despite the camera's adjustment for another character's entrance or speech. For example, Bond is set pacing back and forth in the foyer, facing forward into the camera, which pans to show Cotten entering the room, interposing Bond's to-and-fro between us and Cotten.

When the members of the family finally confront a raging, defeated Bond, he stands astride the right foreground, his gun thrust forward in center frame, the camera over his shoulder, looking at the grouped family organized against him. When he falls into Cotten's arms, he falls across the front of the frame. Lewis gives the father's dying declaration of defiance and pride the foreground as the old man reveals himself at last. In *The Halliday Brand*, there is a proper place for everything within a shot.

Cotten's moral decisions are persuasively conveyed by Lewis' direction, thankfully, since the badly miscast actor is unable to communicate them very well. His resolve to defy his father stiffens at the funeral of Lindfors' father. This is underlined by a crane shot down to the couple, followed by a defiant exchange of dialogue with Bond, who walks into the shot, and ends with a crane shot up away from the couple, again alone in the frame, unseparated despite the strenuous objections of Bond. Later on, in a very typical Lewis shot, Cotten hides in a darkened barn while an agitated group of people search for him. The camera reveals his hiding place by panning from its interior position looking outward at the search to the concealed Cotten. A dolly-in conveys his change of heart. Its visual impact softens the overall unconvincing motivation supplied by the script and the actor.

With Lewis' last film, *Terror in a Texas Town* (1958), made in ten days for the "ridiculous" sum of about $80,000, we have come nearly full circle back to the desultory inspiration of *The Mad Doctor of Market Street*. Lewis infuses a ludicrous project with enough personal involvement, stylistic verve, and pure zombie audacity to bring off something even Allan Dwan might have scanted. The film isn't exactly good, yet it is marvelous: involving and colorful, personal and awful. On one hand, the story of oil interests attempting to exploit a peaceful town seems made for Lewis, and the arousal of gentle Sterling Hayden to fight a gunfighter with a harpoon is a fitting climax for a career built on the intersection of insane plots with a reasonable man. On the other hand, as Richard Thompson has ingeniously noted, the film underplays like a ". . . mild switch on the avenge-my-father's-death Western, but in reality is the elephant's graveyard of a century's worth of Dumb Swede jokes . . ." It's the kind of picture about which you can say such things.

Lewis notes with pride how he cast blacklisted actor Nedrick Young, who also worked, uncredited, on the screenplay. It was the kind of bold gesture in a crazy context you might expect of the man who made *Gun Crazy* and *Cry of the Hunted* and all the rest. Maybe it's only because he's in the insane asylum of B films, but Joseph H. Lewis, almost unique in his position in Hollywood, seems eminently sane. It couldn't have been easy. But if, as Machiavelli noted, in the land of the blind, the one-eyed is king, then Joseph H. Lewis, his one eye keener than ever, deserves his privileged place as one of America's most fascinating film artists.[1]

[1] I should like to thank Peter Meyer, without whom this article could not have been written. Also Doug Lemza and Fred Camper, who generously assisted me in screening certain titles, and William Simon and Janet Adams, who helped immeasurably with the manuscript. I should also like to recommend the Lewis material in *Cinema* (Fall 1971), which includes an interview by Peter Bogdanovich and some especially insightful work by Richard Thompson, as well as a thorough filmography (with minimal inaccuracies). Finally, the Film Study Collection of the Art Institute of Chicago has an extensive inventory of Lewisiana (stills, notebooks, scripts, sketches, outtakes, and complete prints, including material from his television work) that is eagerly awaiting more assiduous researchers.

Val Lewton

VAL LEWTON: UNORTHODOX ARTISTRY AT RKO* (1951)

MANNY FARBER

The death of Val (Vladimir) Lewton, Hollywood's top producer of B movies, occurred during the final voting on the year's outstanding film contributors. The proximity of these two events underlines the significant fact that Lewton's horror productions (*The Ghost Ship*, 1943; *The Body Snatcher*, 1945; *Isle of the Dead*, 1945), which always conveyed a very visual, unorthodox artistry, were never recognized as "Oscar" worthy. On the other hand, in acclaiming people like Ferrer, Mankiewicz, and Holliday, the industry has indicated its esteem for bombshells who disorganize the proceedings on the screen with their flamboyant eccentricities and relegate the camera to the role of passive bit player.

Lewton always seemed a weirdly misplaced figure in Hollywood. He specialized in gentle, scholarly, well-wrought productions that were as modest in their effects as his estimate of himself. Said he: "Years ago I wrote novels for a living, and when RKO was looking for producers, someone told them I had written horrible novels. They mistook the word *horrible* for *horror* and I got the job." Having taken on the production of low-cost thrillers (budgeted under $500,000) about pretty girls who turn into man-eating cats or believe in zombies, Lewton started proving his odd idea, for a celluloid entertainer, that "a picture can never be too good for the public." This notion did not spring from a desire to turn out original, noncommercial films, for Lewton never possessed that kind of brilliance or ambition; it came instead from a pretty reasonable understanding of his own limitations. Unlike the majority of Hollywood craftsmen, he was so bad at supplying the kind of "punch" familiar to American films that the little mayhem he did manage was crude, poorly motivated, and as incredible as the Music Hall makeup on his Indians in *Apache Drums* (1951)—the last and least of his works. He also seemed to have a psychological fear of creating expensive effects, so that his stock-in-trade became the imparting of much of the story through such low-cost suggestions as frightening shadows. His talents were those of a mild bibliophile whose idea of "good" cinema had too much to do with using quotes from Shakespeare or Donne, bridging scenes with a rare folk song, capturing climate with a description of a West Indian dish, and, in the pensive sequences, making sure a bit player wore a period mouth instead of a modern lipsticky one. Lewton's efforts not infrequently suggested a minor approximation of *Jane Eyre*.

The critics who called Lewton the "Sultan of Shudders" and "Chillmaster" missed the deliberate quality of his insipidly normal characters, who reminded one of the actors used in small-town movie ads for the local grocery or shoe store. Lewton and his scriptwriters collaborated on sincere, adult pulp stories, which gave sound bits of knowledge on subjects like zoanthropy or early English asylums while steering almost clear of formula horror.

The Curse of the Cat People (1944), for instance, was simply for the overconscientious parent of a problem child. The film concerns a child (Ann Carter) who worries or antagonizes the people around her with her daydreaming; the more they caution and reprimand, the more she withdraws to the people of her fantasies for "friends." When she finds an old photograph of her father's deceased, psychopathic first wife (Simone Simon, the cat woman of an earlier film), she sees her as one of her imagined playmates; the father fears his daughter has become mentally ill and is under a curse. His insistence that she stop daydreaming brings about the climax, and the film's conclusion is that he should have more trust and faith in his daughter and her visions. Innocuous plots such as these were fashioned with peculiar ingredients that gave them an air of genteel sensitivity and enchantment; there was the dry documenting of a bookworm, an almost delicate distrust of excitement, economical camera and sound effects, as well as fairy-tale titles and machinations. The chilling factor came from the perverse process of injecting tepid thrills into a respectable story with an eyedropper, a technique Lewton and his favorite scriptwriter, Donald Henderson Clarke, picked up during long careers writing sex shockers for drugstore bookracks. While skittering daintily away from concrete evidences of cat women or brutality, they would concentrate with the fascination of a voyeur on unimportant bric-a-brac, reflections, domestic animals, so that the camera would take on the faintly unhealthy eye of a fetishist. The morbidity came from the obsessive preoccupation with which writers and cameramen brought out the voluptuous reality of things, such as a dangerously swinging ship's hook, which was inconspicuously knocking men overboard like tenpins.

Lewton's most accomplished maneuver was making the audience think much more about his material than it warranted. Some of his devices were the usual ones of hiding information, having his people murdered offstage, or cutting into a murderous moment in a gloomy barn with a shot of a horse whinnying. He, however, hid much more of his story than any other film-maker, and forced his crew to create drama almost abstractly with symbolic sounds, textures, and the like, which made the audience hyperconscious of sensitive craftsmanship. He imperiled his characters in situations that didn't call for outsized melodrama and permitted the use of a journalistic camera —for example, a sailor trying to make himself heard over the din of a heavy chain that is burying him inside a ship's locker. He would use a spray-shot technique that usually consisted of oozing suggestive shadows across a wall, or watching the heroine's terror on a lonely walk, and then add a homey windup of the cat woman trying to clean her conscience in a bathtub decorated with cat paws. This shorthand method allowed Lewton to ditch the laughable aspects of improbable events and give the remaining bits of material the strange authenticity of a daguerreotype.

The Leopard Man (1943) is a cleaner and much less sentimental Lewton, sticking much more to the suspense element and misdirection, using some of his favorite images, people moving in a penitential, sleep-walking manner, episodes threaded together with a dramatic sound. This fairly early peak example of his talent is a nerve-twitching whodunit giving the creepy impression that human beings and "things" are interchangeable and almost synonymous and that both are pawns of a bizarre and terrible destiny. A lot of Surrealists like Cocteau have tried for the same supernatural effects, but, whereas their scenes still seem like portraits in motion, Val Lewton's film shows a way to tell a story about people that isn't dominated by the activity, weight, size, and pace of the human figure. In one segment of the film, a small frightened señorita walks beyond the edge of the border town and then back again, while her feelings and imagination keep shifting with the camera into sagebrush, the darkness of an arroyo, crackling pebbles underfoot, and so on, until you see her thick dark blood oozing under the front door of her house. All the psychological effects, fear and so on, were transformed by Jacques Tourneur into nonhuman components of the picture as the girl waited for some noncorporeal manifestation of nature, culture, or history to gobble her up. But, more important in terms of movie invention, Lewton's use of multiple focus (characters are dropped or picked up as if by chance, while the movie goes off on odd tacks trying to locate a sound or a suspicion) and his lighter-than-air sense of pace created a terrifically plastic camera style. It put the camera eye on a curiously delicate wavelength that responds to scenery as quickly as the mind, and gets inside of people instead of reacting only to surface qualities. This film still seems to be one of Hollywood's original gems—nothing impure in terms of cinema, nothing imitative about its style, and little that misses fire through a lack of craft.

Unfortunately, his directors (he discovered Mark Robson and Robert Wise in the cutting department) become so delirious about scenic camera work that they used little imagination on the acting. But the sterile performances were partly due to Lewton's unexciting idea that characters should always be sweet, "like the people who go to the movies"—a notion that slightly improved such veteran creeps as Karloff, but stopped the more pedantic actors (Kent Smith, Henry Daniell) dead in their tracks. Lewton's distinction always came from his sense of the soundly constructed novel; his $200,000 jobs are so skillfully engineered in pace, action, and atmosphere that they have lost little of the haunting effect they had when released years ago.

Russ Meyer

RUSS MEYER: KING OF THE NUDIES* (1973)

ROGER EBERT

The first time I saw Russ Meyer at work, he was filming an underwater scene in his own swimming pool. He has since moved into a much larger house with a much larger swimming pool, but this would have been in early 1969 when he was living a few blocks down from Sunset Strip in a four-room house with a pool that literally occupied the entire backyard. You walked out onto the back porch and dived in.

Meyer was a millionaire at the time, *Vixen* having opened the previous autumn, but he had settled into this bachelor lair with little thought of luxury. The front bedroom was for storage—sound effects, outtakes, racks of prints of his earlier films. There was a bedroom, a kitchen, and the pool. Meyer lived here for a couple of years with his late cat, Chester, and it was out of these digs that he made *Good Morning—and Goodbye* (1967),

Common Law Cabin (1967), *Finders Keepers, Lovers Weepers* (1968), *Vixen* (1968), and *Cherry, Harry and Raquel* (1969).

The personal nature of his films has been much written about, and everybody who is interested knows that the Meyer independent productions were shot in the wilderness with casts that frequently outnumbered (or doubled for) crews. *Cherry*, with a budget of around $90,000, was Meyer's most expensive independent film. You know this, and yet when you watch Meyer at work the intensely personal nature of his involvement is surprising all the same. If there was an auteur working in American commercial film-making during the 1960s—a man totally in control of every aspect of his work—that had to be Meyer. It wasn't so much that he operated his own camera as that he also *carried* it.

The underwater scene was intended for *Cherry*, and appears near the end of the film when the two nurses are revolving in the swivel chair. Meyer was concerned at this period about private censorship pressures (mostly from the Citizens for Decent Literature) in some of the Midwestern and Southern states that represent his best markets. He wanted the lesbian scene in the swivel chair, but he wanted to take the edge off it somehow. *Vixen* had contained a celebrated lesbian scene, but even there the position of the two girls was face-to-face (a technical detail much questioned by some critics) because of the censorship situation. For *Cherry*, Meyer hit upon the idea of diluting the lesbian encounter by intercutting the two nurses with subjective underwater shots of two girls embracing: "We'll get the effect of subliminal pearl diving," he explained. "We won't have to show it."

The two actresses in *Cherry* had completed their commitments some time ago, and drifted away to wherever it is that Meyer stars go (he rarely uses actresses more than once, although he has a male stock company). So Meyer hired two different actresses to portray the symbolic underwater nurses. One of them, Ushi, can also be seen in *Cherry* as the symbolic figure named Soul, who appears from time to time in Indian headdress, playing a saxophone or leaping through wheat fields. The other actress Meyer hired was black. The original nurses had both been white, but this discrepancy did not concern Meyer. "It's part of the symbolism," he explained.

Is he serious when he talks about his symbolism? Almost never. One of his chief delights on his independent productions were the spoken narrations he used for prologues, epilogues, and the underlining of the morals of stories. He usually composes these right after breakfast in less than half an hour, and they are designed to sound portentous and universally significant, although, in fact, having little logical meaning at all. I was working on the screenplay for *Beyond the Valley of the Dolls* while Meyer was in post-production on *Cherry,* and I was awakened at six one morning by a telephone call: Meyer wanted to read me the epilogue he had just written, and found it so amusing that he could hardly get it out between gasps of laughter. Audiences reacted to it in the same way, and yet (of course) its antimarijuana message is part of the film's socially redeeming content.

But I digress. On the evening of the underwater scene in question, Meyer and an old Army buddy named Fred were the entire crew. An underwater light had been placed in the shallow end of the pool, the girls were treading water in the middle, and the camera was at the deep end. Meyer's idea was to backlight the girls in order to get explicit silhouettes without excessive nude detail. The shooting strategy was simplicity itself. Meyer had an Arriflex camera in an underwater mount. When the actresses were ready, he took a deep breath and went under. Fred stood on his shoulders and called out, "Action, girls." The girls went under, Meyer shot until he ran out of breath, tapped Fred on the ankle, Fred let him up, and Meyer gasped "Cut!" with a big grin. "You don't see Preminger doing this," he said.

All of the Russ Meyer independent films were shot in this direct and informal way, without large crews or costs, and their remarkably high technical quality is due mostly to Meyer's training, experience, and compulsive perfectionism. He was a combat newsreel photographer in World War II (some of the Signal Corps footage of Patton in the movie *Patton* is his). After the war, he failed, like most of the service cinematographers, to find a job inside the Hollywood union system. He moved to San Francisco, shot many industrial films, gained a reputation during the 1950s as a leading pinup photographer, did about half a dozen of *Playboy's* earlier Playmates, and shot an obscure mid-1950s burlesque film in which Tempest Storm had a plaster-of-paris cast of her bust made, for insurance reasons and to offset the publicity generated by Evelyn (Treasure Chest) West.

The first actual Russ Meyer film was, of course, *The Immoral Mr. Teas,* shot in 1959 at a cost of $24,000 and largely improvised during a four-day shooting schedule. *Teas* was partly bankrolled by a San Francisco burlesque theatre owner, and was the first authentic American nudie. Meyer's assignment was to imitate the popular nudist-camp films imported from Europe. Their inevitable strong point was a volleyball game made somewhat awkward by the need for the male actors to keep their backs to the camera. The nudist-camp movies were one of the most pathetic and least significant of the 1950s subgenres, and were of interest largely because of the actors' difficulties in manipulating bath towels and in standing in shrubbery. Their bookings were typically limited to burlesque theatres (as audience chasers) and marginal hardtop operations.

The notion of directing the ultimate nude volleyball game did not much appeal to Meyer. He felt that the success of *Playboy* had prepared the American market for an unabashed, high-quality skin flick. The occupation of his lead character and a great many of his interior locations were suggested when his dentist agreed to let his office be used on a weekend ("The chair was well lighted," Meyer explained). And so Mr. Teas, played by a Meyer Army buddy named Bill Teas, came into life as a bicycle deliveryman for false teeth. The rest of the movie was more or less made up as they went along, Meyer recalls, and the voice-over narration was added later.

The premise of *The Immoral Mr. Teas* is simple: Teas is a harassed city man, cut off from the solace of nature and burdened by the pressures of modern life. He can find no rest, alas, because he has been cursed by a peculiar ability to undress girls mentally. At the most unsettling times (in a soda fountain, in a dentist's office) women suddenly appear nude. What's worse, Teas cannot even control his strange power; it seems to have been invested naturally in him, and doesn't require the magic sunglasses or secret elixirs employed in such *Teas* imitations as *Bachelor Tom Peeping* (c. 1961).

As plots go, *Teas* was not terrifically subtle. It is essentially a silent comedy with counterpoint narration. But the movie's jolly irony overcame any feeling of embarrassment or self-consciousness on the part of audiences who were, for the most part, seeing a nude woman on the screen for the first time. *Teas* caused a moderate sensation on its release in late 1959, and would probably have caused a greater one if more theatres had been available for skin-flick bookings at the time. It played for nearly a year in some college towns. *Teas* was the genesis for the years of increased screen nudity that were to follow; *The Wall Street Journal* claimed in an article that it inspired one hundred and fifty imitations within a year, or more films than the genre had produced in the previous five decades.

Almost all of these films (the most successful early nudies also included *Bachelor Tom Peeping, Goldilocks and the Three Bares, Not Tonight, Henry*, and Meyer's own *Eve and the Handyman*, 1961) have dropped out of release and are not even available for film society rental. It is hard to say how they would look today; Meyer tends to be of the opinion that his pre-synch-sound films have dated, and he doesn't include them in retrospectives such as the one held at Yale. My own memory of *Teas* is that it worked because of its good-natured humor, not its sex, and that it would survive well. There is certainly a place for it in the current cultural renaissance of the 1950s. The other film from this period that deserves attention is Meyer's *Naked Gals of the Golden West* (1962), an ambitious attempt at comedy and satire. It is one of Meyer's personal favorites, but did badly at the box office because, he now believes, he paid too much attention to the humor and not enough to the sex, and was overcautious in assigning pasties to his actresses.

All of Meyer's independent productions (with the exceptions of *Eroticon*, 1961; *Mondo Topless*, 1966; and *Europe in the Raw*, 1963—significantly, among his less successful titles) were to follow in the direction of *Teas* and present characters who had a problem and existed within a narrative situation. This is one of the reasons, I think, that his films found such large audiences and made so much money; the sex occurred in context (whether farcical or dramatic) and was never just trundled on screen.

This was such a novelty in the genre, and yet so easily perceived, that it's astonishing so few of Meyer's competitors seem to have noticed it. One of the most distracting enemies of film eroticism is a lack of context. This is particularly true of the new generation of erotic movies—the gynecological specials, or Frisco beaver flicks—which often reduce themselves to a survey of disembodied sexual apparatus. Although there is apparently a novelty for some audiences in taking a voyage up the vaginal track with gun and camera, the general falling-off of business in the hard-core houses is not surprising.

Meyer has generally avoided full frontal nudity in his films, not because of prudishness, but because he feels that complete explicitness is an enemy of erotic fantasy. He has also avoided, for the most part, films in which nudity for its own sake is the only subject matter. All of his most successful films have placed strongly defined characters in a particular situation, however elementary. And so his films are structured narratives, and the sexual activities in them involve characters with personalities and motives. True eroticism is therefore more possible, Meyer believes, because eroticism is caused by interplay between the imagination and a specific fictional situation, and is not inspired by essentially documentary records of genitalia.

Meyer's independent productions fall into three categories that are more or less chronological, with some overlapping. There were the early voyeuristic comedies, always in color and with voice-over; the middle period of black-and-white, synch-sound Gothic-sadomasochistic melodramas; and the last five color, synch-sound sexual dramas. All three categories were inspired to a large degree by Meyer's reading of the marketplace, and in each case he moved into the new area of filmmaking ahead of his contemporaries. Thus each of his three largest-grossing independent films was the first of its type. *Teas* was the first uninhibited American nudie; *Lorna* was the first fully scripted sex-violence-and-nudity movie to attempt to escape the limited booking situation of the skin-flick genre; and *Vixen* was the first American skin flick intended to appeal to women as well as to men, and aimed at bookings in respectable first-run situations.

Because market considerations dictated his themes as much as, or probably more than, Meyer's personal sexual interests, it is a little tricky to attempt to psychoanalyze Meyer on the basis of his films. This is true despite his own willingness to imply that his films are his fantasies. During a panel discussion at the Meyer retrospective at Yale, he was accused by a feminist of being a breast fetishist. His response was to grin and wag his eyebrows. In discussing the lesbian scene in *Vixen,* he has claimed that the rhythmic camera movement, barely perceptible during the photography of the scene, records his own personal response to it. "I won't do a sex scene unless it personally turns me on," he said in a 1969 interview about *Vixen.* "I get involved in a scene, and I'm down on the floor looking through the viewfinder, shouting instructions to my actors, to my crew, and don't bother me then. We can discuss it tomorrow, but don't hassle me now."

This is part of his image, and it is no doubt true that some of the sexual situations in Meyer films mirror his own fantasies. But he is not the primitive or untutored artist he sometimes likes to appear to be; his method of work on a picture is all business, he is a consummate technical craftsman, he is obsessed by budgets and schedules, and his actors do not remember how "turned on" a scene was, but how many times it was reshot. In a genre overrun by sleazo cheapies, he was the best technician and the only artist.

He was also, perhaps, one of the canniest psychologists. His films found such large audiences because he understood, instinctively or not, why men go to skin flicks. His imitators noticed his use of actresses with unusually large breasts, and either tried to outcast him or derided him, depending on their own taste and preferences. But the big boobs were symptomatic of an overall psychological orientation in Meyer's skin flicks. The girls were overdeveloped not because Meyer was a breast fetishist (although he says he is) but because he wanted them to seem like pornographic fantasies in the flesh. His female characters were often caricatures, broadly drawn, and their common denominator was insatiable sexual hunger.

The typical non-Meyer erotic film of the decade usually featured a male lead as the dominant character. (An exception was the stylish Radley Metzger, whose leads were women and, as often as not, lesbians.) He was a satyr with no capacity for exhaustion, and he rutted his way through his costars whether or not they were willing. In Meyer's films, however, the women were often the dominant characters, initiating the action and, more often than not, getting too little of it. This was a fantasy more suited to skin-flick audiences, who perhaps felt uncomfortable identifying with male characters who would employ coercion or rape, if necessary. The fantasy came to the audience; it did not require identification with aggression.

Meyer's male characters fell into a limited number of categories. At first (memorably in *Teas*) they were voyeurs, primarily because in the very early days of the American skin flick it was legally not prudent to show physical contact. In Meyer's middle period, the men tended to be impotent (the husband in *Lorna*) or aggressors (the convict-rapist in the same film). In his later color films, the men tended to level out somewhat into the delighted partners of such nymphets as Vixen. Another character who often crops up is the middle-aged, hard-as-nails woman hater. Hal Hopper played such a character in *Lorna* and *Mudhoney*, and Franklin Bolger plays him as the bedridden lecher in *Cherry*. The good guys generally got the girls in the end, and poetic justice was an obsession during the last five or ten minutes of most of Meyer's melodramas.

This mix of a variety of men and a single kind of (insatiable) super-woman gave Meyer's films the possibility of a variety of sexual situations, and there was apparently at least one that suited most members of his audience. It is hard to say. The patrons of skin flicks have many and various reasons for patronizing them, but mostly they share one common circumstance: they are without an alternative means of sexual fantasy or release at the moment. They join together in the democracy of the darkened theatre, the middle-aged husbands, the servicemen, the tourists, the horny high-school kids. The audience is almost always all male, and its members are careful to avert their eyes from one another and to choose seats as far as possible from their nearest neighbor. Some of them come to masturbate (Meyer cheerfully calls them "the one-armed viewers"), but most do not. They sit in silence as complete as it is depressing.

There is a difference, however, in the way a skin-flick audience reacts to a Meyer picture. I noticed it as an undergraduate attending *The Immoral Mr. Teas,* and I have seen it consistently during my later days as a film critic. Meyer audiences enjoy themselves more obviously; they laugh. It is such a good thing to hear laughter during a skin flick. Meyer's films never imply, or inspire, the sense of secretiveness or shame present in so many examples of the genre. They are good-hearted, for the most part, and the action scenes are as liberating and exhilarating as the work of a Donald Siegel or a Sergio Leone. What sometimes comes across most strongly in a Meyer film is a burly, barracks-room heartiness, a gusto. What came to be most impressive about Russ Meyer's work, as the 1960s wore on, was that audiences came to see them for other than specifically sexual reasons. Meyer apparently realized this at about the time he made *Lorna,* and perhaps a survey of his independent productions will help to show this development.

After *Teas,* which Leslie Fiedler praised in a celebrated review in *Show* magazine, there was *Eve and the Handyman* (1961), starring his wife and business partner, Eve Meyer. (They have since divorced, but maintain a friendly business relationship; Eve was the associate producer for Meyer's two Twentieth Century-Fox productions, and they are currently coproducing *Blacksnake!,* 1973.) The male lead was once again a shy voyeur, portrayed by another of the large supply of Meyer's old Army buddies, James Ryan. One of the most interesting scenes in the movie has Eve dancing in a low-cut dress while playing a pinball machine: the rhythm and cutting suggest sexual intercourse, and the scene has a nice balance between eroticism and humor. A frequent Meyer turnabout theme—the desirable woman who is rejected by the undesirable man—turns up in *Eve* in a hitchhiking scene. Unable to get a lift, Eve takes off one garment after another, still with no success.

At some point in this early period—the dates are difficult to determine because his films were not always released in the order they were made—came *Eroticon,* advertised as "the footage the producers of *Mr. Teas* had to leave on the cutting-room floor." Most of the movie was new, actually, and some of it is semidocumentary footage showing "America's leading adult filmmaker" hard at work. *Naked Gals of the Golden West* came soon afterward, but was not successful for some of the reasons already noted. It contains scenes satirizing several famous moments in Western classics (and ten years later Meyer was to return to *Duel in the Sun* for the final shoot-out in *Cherry*).

Naked Gals helped convince Meyer that the traditional skin flick had outlived its useful life at the box office, and that his field was crowded with competitors. With *Lorna* (1964) he attempted to open up a new market. He wanted to make a well-acted and well-scripted melodrama with a strong action plot to support the necessary nudity; theatre bookers were supposed to recognize it as a "real" movie and not a nudie, and enough of them did so that *Lorna* eventually became Meyer's fourth most profitable independent production. He used a budget of around $60,000, or nearly three times his previous high, and there was a crude vitality in the production that made it work.

Lorna's plot, summarized, sounds like a morality play, and so were the plots of the next three Meyer productions: *Mudhoney* (1965), *Faster Pussycat, Kill, Kill!* (1966), and *Motor Psycho!* (1965). This group of four black-and-white pictures forms a quartet apart from the rest of Meyer's work, and exhibits (Fred Chappell wrote in *Man and the Movies*) "very odd 'serious attempts' full of big, gloomy archetypes and Gothic puzzlements." Chappell even described *Pussycat* as a "blood brother" to Kyd's *The Spanish Tragedy*, which is perhaps going a bit far to make a point. Meyer himself refers to *Lorna* and *Mudhoney* as his John Steinbeck period, when he went out into the woods and filmed stark (but semi–tongue in cheek) melodramas about demented hillbillies, religious fanatics, oversexed baby dolls, violent woodsmen, and obscene grandmothers.

Lorna has been widely seen, and is still in release as part of a Russ Meyer Film Festival package. But *Mudhoney* is Meyer's neglected masterpiece: his most interesting, most ambitious, most complex, and longest independent production. He describes it as a case of overachievement; it was not necessary, or perhaps even wise, he believes, to expend so much energy on a movie that had so few directly exploitable elements. Nevertheless, it won an enthusiastic response at the Yale retrospective, and one critic described it as looking like a recently rediscovered 1930s Gothic drama in the visual style of King Vidor.

Mudhoney's plot is impossible to synopsize in a limited space (Meyer's plots are either capable of being described in a sentence or impossible to describe at all). But it has to do with a fanatic preacher, a terrorized town that turns to mob violence, and a backwoods family that is apparently deficient in all genes not related directly to chest development. The visual style is unlike Meyer's other work: he opens with a protracted shot of feet walking through the village, and closes with a terrifically effective point-of-view shot of a body toppling into an open grave; in between, there is more mood, more languorous camera movement, and less quick-cutting than we expect from Meyer.

There are three films from this general period that fall outside the categories we've established. They are *Fanny Hill* (1965), *Europe in the Raw,* and *Mondo Topless.* Albert Zugsmith, the independent producer of exploitation pictures, hired Meyer to direct *Fanny Hill* in Berlin. It was Meyer's first experience with a film produced by someone else, and he remembers it unhappily. He found Zugsmith difficult to work with, the German backers of the film unreliable, and the shooting conditions all but impossible. I haven't seen *Fanny Hill,* but Meyer agrees with the general consensus that it isn't representative of his work.

"The only thing that got me through at all," he recalls, "was working with Miriam Hopkins, who was our star. The two of us pulled that picture through somehow. I told her once that it was remarkable how much she knew about making a picture, and she reminded me that, after all, she had once been married to Fritz Lang."[1]

While he was in Europe, Meyer made an independent production, *Europe in the Raw,* which is of interest primarily because of the way he filmed it. He concealed a 16 mm. camera in a suitcase and shot footage in the red-light districts of Paris, Amsterdam, and elsewhere. The trailers for this film explained the shooting method and displayed the concealed equipment, but I recall thinking at the time that the footage must have been conventional and that the "hidden camera" was a fake gimmick. Meyer assures me, however, that he did indeed use a suitcase camera, that it was unhandy and difficult to use, and that he would not recommend making a film in that way again.

Mondo Topless is in some ways quite an interesting film, especially for the light it sheds on Meyer's attitude to his big-busted actresses. It was a color nudie that was made to cash in on the San Francisco topless boom, and has nothing in common with the black-and-white Gothics he was making at the same time. It opens with a voice-over documentary about the topless industry. The cutting is quick, and we see a montage of neon signs,

[1] Actually, Ms. Hopkins was married to director Anatole Litvak. Lang was, however, courting Ms. Hopkins for a while and once found himself with her on a train headed east. Lang persuaded a friend to masquerade as a clergyman and to "marry" him to Ms. Hopkins. Lang and Hopkins then shared a stateroom for the five-day trip. Upon arriving in New York, Lang shared the joke with Ms. Hopkins, who, it is said, took the joke admirably well.

stage performers, topless waitresses, and so on. But Meyer is, of course, not interested in shooting a movie from the orchestra pit. Almost all of the rest of his footage involves topless dancers in incongruous situations. The stripper Babette Bardot, for example, is seen topless while driving a convertible through the city. Another performer, the remarkably endowed model who uses the name Candy Morrison, does a go-go dance in the desert (and in doing so gains a certain immortality as undoubtedly the most voluptuous actress Meyer has *ever* used in a film). Meyer also has topless girls halfway up oil rigs, on top of Cadillacs in the desert, and dancing next to a railroad track (this last includes a nicely timed zoom reaction shot of an engineer on a passing diesel train).

The film's real interest is in its sound track, which consists of tape-recorded interviews with the dancers. They talk about the hazards and advantages of having large bosoms. There seems to be something subtly sadistic going on here; Meyer is simultaneously photographing the girls because of their dimensions, and recording them as they complain about their problems ("I have to have my bras custom-made"). This sets up a kind of psychological Möbius strip, and the encounter between the visuals and the words in *Mondo Topless* creates the kind of documentary tension Larry Rivers was going for in *Tits*.

After these three films and the Gothic quartet, Meyer turned to the more direct color melodramas of his most recent independent period—the films that finally won him a general reputation. Some of his best work can be found in the films of 1967 through 1970, although the dramatic intensity of the Gothic movies is often missing. With the exception of the man-versus-machine desert scene and the final shoot-out in *Cherry*, there is nothing in Meyer's last five films to match the sustained action direction of *Faster Pussycat*. There is one montage of images in *Pussycat*—a woman in a Volvo is attempting to crush the muscular hero against a barn—that is classical in its urgency and impact. The heroines of *Pussycat* and *Motor Psycho* were dominant, castrating, and sadomasochistic, and both of these films contain very little nudity. They were intended for the action-exploitation market, especially in the South.

With *Common Law Cabin, Good Morning—and Goodbye, Finders Keepers, Lovers Weepers, Vixen,* and *Cherry,* however, Meyer returned to heroines that were mostly complaisant; there seems to be some kind of mellowing process going on in these films. Meyer does occasionally use a scene of symbolic castration (the hero in *Finders Keepers* having the hair on his chest shaved off as a prelude to sexual intercourse), but he dilutes his effects with humor. (The same scene ends with intercutting between the bed and a stock-car demolition derby, and then the heroine announces that she wants to go to the symphony: "Erich Leinsdorf is conducting Maxim Gorky's *Prelude in D Major.*")

Neither *Common Law Cabin* (briefly titled, in some situations, *How Much Loving Does a Normal Couple Need?*) nor *Good Morning—and Goodbye* represents Meyer's best later work. The plots are too diffuse to maintain dramatic tension, the acting is indifferent, and there is an uncharacteristic amount of aimless dialogue. In retrospect, however, these films can be seen as Meyer's gradual disengagement from plot. The Gothic quartet was heavily plotted, sometimes (as with *Mudhoney*) dripping with such a wealth of complication and detail that they seemed baroque. *Cabin* and *Good Morning*, however, were essentially soap operas whipped up to display voluptuous actresses, and their plots were not only superfluous but distracting. Meyer seems to have realized this, and with his final three independent productions he makes an almost surrealistic use of plot. Plot is *there*, but somehow just offstage, or buried, or set aside for the moment. He uses the conventions of movie genre fiction—dialogue clichés, music that points, character stereotypes—to give us the impression that a genre story is unfolding. But then he doesn't bother to unfold it. He sort of slips around it, but so deftly that we have the uncanny impression it's all there anyway.

This directorial sleight of hand can be most clearly seen in *Cherry, Harry and Raquel*. It is not generally known, I believe, that Meyer edited this film under a rather considerable handicap, the De Luxe color lab inadvertently destroyed a fourth of his footage. So occupied was De Luxe in rushing through the print of *Hello, Dolly!* (1968) that the error was not discovered until after Meyer had returned from his desert location and disbanded his cast and crew.

The cost of reshooting the missing footage was prohibitive, and so Meyer took what seems to me a brave and inventive course. He hired the actress Ushi to *symbolize* some of the missing scenes. When footage was missing, Meyer simply cut to Ushi doing something that substituted for the lost action or replaced it. He also shot a great many other brief takes of Ushi (who nowhere appears in the story proper) in order to give the film a consistent texture. The result is that audiences don't even realize anything is missing; a close analysis might reveal some cavernous gaps in the plot, and it is a little hard to figure out exactly how (or if) all the characters know each other, but Meyer's subjective scenes are so inventive and his editing so confident that he simply sweeps the audience right along with him. *Cherry, Harry and Raquel* is possibly the only narrative film ever made without a narrative.

Vixen is another film that suggests plot without laboring it. Its story situation is pure simplicity: Vixen and her husband, a wilderness guide, live in the "bush country" of the Canadian Northwest. Rooming with them, for the time being, are Vixen's brother and a black American draft evader who's a friend of his. An American couple come to spend the weekend, a red-bearded Scottish Communist happens down the road, and most of these characters interact sexually and /or politically with each other for about an hour.

At the end of that time, the Communist and the black (who has been instantly radicalized by Vixen's racism and the Scottish Communist's recitation of several pseudopolitical ravings no doubt concocted by Meyer in a fit of hilarity before breakfast that morning) attempt to force Vixen and her husband to fly them to Cuba. The movie ends with a ten-minute sequence in the air, during which the characters discuss Communism, Cuban Marxism, Vietnam, draft evasion, civil rights, and airplane hijacking. This is the socially redeeming content, of course, and it is just possible that Meyer stuck it all in at the end in order to (*a*) avoid interrupting his main story line, and (*b*) chase the audience. It's certainly true that the word got around during *Vixen*'s year-long Chicago run: When everybody gets on the airplane, Meyer audiences told each other, it's OK to go.

The word also got around about *Vixen before* the movie opening in Chicago, and there was the unprecedented phenomenon of a dozen or so patrons who bought tickets every night simply to see the *Vixen* trailer. *Vixen*'s astonishing success may have been because it was the first skin flick really to break into the quality first-run markets; it was the first booking of its kind in many engagements. It may also have appealed because it was good-natured, for the most part, and celebrated the typical Meyer gusto and lack of inhibition. Meyer himself thinks it may have made it because it was the first skin flick designed for couples to attend on dates.

None of these factors by itself seems to account for the movie's $6,000,000-plus gross, however. My own notion is that *Vixen* is the quintessential Russ Meyer film (not the best—*Mudhoney* and *Beyond the Valley of the Dolls* rank ahead of it). The opening sequence clearly establishes the movie's ground: Vixen, wearing a bikini, is pursued through the Canadian Northwest bush country by an unclad man. He pins her to a tree. She struggles . . . to undo her bikini. They make love. Afterward, she gazes up dreamily at him, and the reverse shot shows him putting on his Royal Canadian Mounted Police uniform. Meyer's ability to keep his movies light and farcical took the edge off the sex for people seeing their first skin flick. By the time he made *Vixen,* Meyer had developed a directing style so open, direct, and good-humored that it dominated his material. He was willing to use dialogue so ridiculous ("We decided to stop doing this when we were twelve," *Vixen's* brother protests as she seduces him in a shower), situations so obviously tongue in cheek, characters so incredibly stereotyped and larger than life that even his most torrid scenes usually managed to get outside themselves. *Vixen* was not only a good skin flick, but a merciless satire on the whole genre. It catalogued the basic variations in skin-flick plots, and ticked them off one by one.

Of all the sex scenes in *Vixen,* the only one with genuine erotic impact is the lesbian encounter between Vixen (Erica Gavin) and the wife of the visiting fisherman (Vincene Wallace). And this one works, I believe, because Meyer wanted it to. He doesn't cut into it with asides or embellishments. He stays with the characters. His editing rhythm is deliberately sensuous. And his direction of the actresses (Erica Gavin remembered in an interview several months later) was "exhaustive." The scene was talked over, run through, rehearsed, and finally shot so many times, she recalled, that the thin edge of exhaustion began to look like the thin edge of passion.

That was apparently Meyer's strategy; his actresses, who were not experienced movie professionals and who felt some personal awkwardness about a lesbian scene, naturally tended to be inhibited. The repetition of the scene eventually wore through their reserve until their primary concern was simply to get the scene over with, somehow, as soon as possible. And this essentially grim determination was created, photographed, and edited by Meyer to result in what looks like a totally authentic erotic scene. There is no doubting Erica Gavin's wild magnetism as an untrained but natural actress, and her personality as Vixen was central to the movie's working, but Meyer's effects are almost always brought about through great effort. His willingness (in an *Argosy* interview about *Vixen,* for example) to make it all sound like a good time up in the hills is primarily for public-relations purposes.

Perhaps the most brilliant scene in *Vixen,* cinematically, is the dance Vixen does before the campfire for the benefit of the visiting husband. The scene is comically counterpointed with her own husband's pipe-smoking complacency (his characterization is one of the funniest things in the movie), but there is no doubting her own erotic intentions. She fondles, of all things, a freshly caught fish, finally dropping it down the front of her dress and then leaning forward so that it slides out and creates one of the most inexplicably erotic shots in all of Meyer's films. Inexplicable, because—with apologies to the Marx Brothers—why a fish?

Meyer's ability to find subjective metaphors for his scenes of eroticism and violence is one of the most distinctive characteristics of his cinema. The desert chase scene in *Cherry, Harry and Raquel* is transformed, for example, when Meyer uses camera placement, music, and montage to transform his wounded Mexican into a matador, and a Jeep into a vengeful bull. He also has fun with his cutaways (a wild sexual encounter is likely to be translated into a stock-car demolition derby); his literal cuts among scenes (in *Cherry,* there is three-way cutting between sexual entry, a gynecologist's vaginal examination, and a tire tool plunging into an auto jack); and his musical puns (Z-Man's homosexual advance on an unwilling partner in *Beyond the Valley of the Dolls* is scored with "Stranger in Paradise").

Meyer doesn't mind being obvious with these devices and, indeed, his cheerful willingness to go for an outrageous effect is one of the things that makes his movies endearing. His cuts to subjective substitutes for the same action are so literal, so direct, so basic, that they recall a kind of filmmaking not seen in the commercial cinema since the 1920s. Some of his effects are so old-fashioned that in his hands they seem positively experimental, and audiences react to them with a delight that has nothing to do with the erotic impulse of the movie.

Many critics have wondered in print, however, whether Meyer really knows he's being funny. This might seem like an incredible question to anyone who has seen his films: his sense of humor is so clearly up front. But the question does get asked. One of the New York reviews of *Beyond the Valley of the Dolls,* for example, found it full of stereotypes and clichés: The critic apparently was unwilling to believe that each stereotype and cliché had been put into the movie lovingly, by hand. My own contacts with Meyer, over a period when he was casting, preparing, shooting, and editing three films, left me with the impression that very little gets into one of his films by accident. He is a surprisingly enthusiastic film buff, has seen almost every American sound feature of importance, was a still photographer on location for such directors as George Stevens, and has—I keep getting back to this—an instinctively satirical sense of the ridiculous that comes from something of the same 1950s sensibility that produced Bob and Ray, Lenny Bruce, Stan Freberg, and *Mad* magazine.

This became apparent to me when we began work on the original screenplay for *Beyond the Valley of the Dolls* (1970, which will hereafter be abbreviated to *BVD*, and which I intend to discuss in terms of my memories and experiences—leaving it to others to evaluate it critically). At the time Meyer was approached by Twentieth Century-Fox about the project, it consisted mostly of the title, which had been purchased by Fox for a possible sequel at the time Jacqueline Susann sold them her *Valley of the Dolls*. Miss Susann had worked from time to time with several writers on a series of potential *BVD* scripts, but none of them had succeeded in pleasing the Fox management. The only pre-Meyer *BVD* script I saw was a melodrama set in New York and involving the office politics and sexual intrigues of a group of people in the magazine and fashion photography businesses.

Meyer was brought in on a highly speculative deal. He was given a suite of offices, a sum of money, and six weeks to produce an acceptable treatment for a movie to be called *Beyond the Valley of the Dolls*. No specific subject matter or characters was specified. It was originally intended, however, that the movie be in some way a sequel, and Fox had Barbara Parkins under contract to portray her original *Valley of the Dolls* character, Anne Welles.

Even in the original treatment, however, Meyer suggested that another actress be used instead of Barbara Parkins, whose salary would have stretched the movie's $900,000 budget. Meyer's plan was to pay close to Equity minimum and use the savings to buy extra shooting days. As it happened, a lawsuit by Jacqueline Susann made it necessary to drop all of the names of her original characters from the screenplay; "Anne Welles" became "Susan Lake" and, in the process, *BVD* added a line to its advertising pointing out that it was "NOT a sequel—there has never been anything like it before."

At the time we began work on our screenplay, however, we were under the impression it would be a sequel. This explains certain residual characters in *BVD* who do not seem organic to the story. We were not much concerned with Miss Susann's original novel or film, however. Neither of us ever read the novel, although I attempted to at one time. We did screen Mark Robson's film version of *Valley of the Dolls* (1967) before starting to write, and this gave us the notion of making *BVD* as a parody. We would take the

basic situation (three young and talented girls come to Hollywood, find love
and success, and then are brought low by booze, drugs, and pride) and
attempt to exaggerate it wildly. We would include some of the sensational
elements of the original story—homosexuality, crippling diseases, characters
based on "real" people, events out of recent headlines—but, again, with flat-
out exaggeration. I originally saw the movie as a total parody; Meyer, with
his characteristic unwillingness to stop at the merely total, saw it as a total
parody *and* a total sex-and-violence trip. At one point we described our
project to Fox executive David Brown as "the first exploitation-horror-camp-
musical," and that wasn't far off.

Working with Meyer, I found, was simplicity itself: I only had to
devote nine hours a day, seven days a week, to the actual writing. The
evenings could be spent in story conferences and discussions about the style
of the film. Meyer had determined to give Fox, not a treatment, but an
actual screenplay at the end of the six weeks.

We devised the plot, more or less in collaboration, by creating characters and then working out situations to cover the range of exploitable
content we wanted in the film. Meyer wanted the film to appeal, in some
way, to almost anyone who was under thirty and went to the movies. There
had to be music, mod clothes, black characters, violence, romantic love, soap
opera situations, behind-the-scenes intrigue, fantastic sets, lesbians, orgies,
drugs, and (eventually) an ending that tied everything together.

In the event, it was hard to keep so many characters floating all the
time, and the first hour of *BVD* moves somewhat slowly through all the
setups of character and story. But we did manage to tie everything together
at the end, with a quadruple murder and a triple wedding that effectively
punished all the bad guys and rewarded all the good ones. We knew we
would have the murder orgy (we were working before the Tate case was
solved, and it was one of the exploitable elements we wanted to use), but
we didn't know how we would follow it. Meyer wanted to end the movie
with a happy ending to end all happy endings. Inspiration came one night
during dinner: Harris, the paraplegic rock-group manager, would be jostled
during the final shoot-out, and his wheelchair overturned. As the violence
subsided, we would cut to a close-up of his toe moving. And then we'd pull
the old "I can walk again!" routine and cut to a parody Easter Seal commercial of Harris and his original girl friend, Kelly, walking through a meadow.
A triple wedding would come as an epilogue. This was so totally impossible,
ridiculous, and obvious that we saw it as pure gold inspiration and used it.
There is a scene near the end in which Kelly assists Harris, on crutches, to

cross a log across a little stream. There was some talk of having him fall into the water, but Meyer felt this would sabotage both the emotional uplift of the scene and its function as visual satire. He also saw the epilogue as a parody of old justice-of-the-peace wedding scenes, and shot and scored it in a frothy 1940s style.

The movie itself seemed to take shape quickly after we had our basic premise, which was that nothing could be too outlandish, obvious, stereotyped, clichéd, gaudy, or extreme. We needed a heavy, of course, and created one in the person of Ronnie "Z-Man" Barzell, the Teen-Age Tycoon of Rock (a character meant to *seem* to be based on one of the young rock music producers, although neither Meyer nor myself had ever met one—a neat touch, we thought, after all the guessing games about Susann's characters). Z-Man began his career as a boy, and it only occurred to us to make him a secret transvestite as we were writing the orgy scene. We had done the lesbian encounter between the two girls, and symmetry seemed to dictate a homosexual encounter between Z-Man and the movie's other heavy, Lance Rocke. Meyer was of the opinion that the American mass audience was not ready for an erotic homosexual scene played straight, and we had already written the Z-Man/Lance bedroom scene as it now exists when it occurred to us, offhand actually, to reveal Z-Man as a character who had been female the whole time. This kind of triple twist (girl plays male homosexual) would have audiences coming out of the theatre, Meyer said, "totally confused." He greeted this possibility (as he had greeted the notion of making Harris walk again) with an immensely satisfied chortle.

The basic thrust behind *BVD*, Meyer said more than once, was to leave the audience wondering what had hit it. The movie had to be outrageous, a total put-on; and *still* work as melodrama. Individual scenes were conceived on two levels, usually: at the dramatic level, and then at the level of whatever inside joke was to be conveyed. Sometimes this dualism works quite effectively, I think, as when (*a*) Harris is discovered on the catwalks of a television studio, prepared to commit suicide on the air, and (*b*) the camera movement quotes Welles's famous opera-house shot in *Citizen Kane* (1941). (The shooting script called for the camera to duplicate Welles's effect exactly, but we couldn't do this without spending extra money. We did not know at the time that the middle section of Welles's shot was, in fact, a miniature. We wouldn't have had the money for the miniature either, however, and so a zoom was used.) Another dual scene involves the surgeon, Dr. Scholl, advising the grief-stricken friends that Harris may not walk again. This scene was written and scored as soap opera, as was the chess-game scene between Kelly and Harris.

The movie's transitional montages, intended to symbolize Z-Man's growing influence with the rock trio and Harris' personal disintegration, were conceived as a kind of throwback to 1940s and 1950s musical biographies. We didn't use *Variety* headlines only because we had already used a series of roadside signs superimposed on a map to indicate a journey; we wanted our visual fun to be as eclectic as possible. The movie originally began with a symbolic bedside and coffin-side scene between Kelly and her mother (who had been disowned by her family years before for marrying an Irish-American Catholic, and who only now told Kelly about her rich Aunt Susan and the family inheritance). This scene was cut, and about ninety percent of the scene in Aunt Susan's photography studio (where she first meets Kelly) was also cut: Meyer felt they moved too slowly, although it disappointed him to cut a fashion photography sequence designed as a parody of *Blow Up* (1966).

The supporting characters in the movie were intended as a glossary of Hollywood character and name types. "Porter Hall," the shyster lawyer, was Meyer's contribution, and a bow in the direction of the late character actor. "Randy Black," heavyweight champion of the world, probably needs no identification. "Ashley St. Ives," the superstar of sex movies, has a splendidly Hollywood name, but I liked her better when she was "Ashley Famous." Unfortunately, the Fox front office wasn't sympathetic to our reference to Ted Ashley of Warner Brothers and his former agency.

Our actual writing fell into a pattern fairly easily. We talked out the characters and the plot, making notes on yellow legal pads, and then I wrote the scenes and Meyer embellished them with technical notes and indications of his visual strategy. The final screenplay was not a polished shooting script, however, because Meyer's intention was to work in his usual manner and develop scenes shot-by-shot on the sets. This was a particular challenge at Fox, where he was supporting a large overhead and daily shooting costs and couldn't afford the perfectionism of his independent productions.

He was able to gain shooting time not only by economizing on actors' salaries, but by using existing Fox sets and props where possible, and bringing in associates from his independent days (including composer Stu Phillips) to work at less than Fox's ordinary expense. Z-Man's ornate bedroom was mostly gotten together from old Fox props for historical swashbucklers. The elaborate living room of the Z-Man manor was actually a set for *Myra Breckinridge* (1970), but can be seen only briefly in one shot in *Myra.*

Meyer's personal opinion was that *BVD* was really about Harris, the bedraggled manager who passes through impotence and paralysis and lives again to walk through the valley of the dolls. I was never really sure whether the movie had a focus on one character; in writing it, it felt more like a juggling act, and the problem was to keep all the characters alive. It's possible that there *were* too many characters, but I don't think so. The profusion of cast members gave the movie a nice chaotic feeling, and there are times when I believe *BVD* is the only movie that actually duplicates on the screen the insanely crowded feeling of the Jack Davis cartoon ads for comedies like *It's a Mad, Mad, Mad, Mad World* (1963).

It was also slightly easier to keep the characters in mind because each one was drawn as a caricature and then typecast. Meyer was able to heighten this effect by directing all the actors in an absolutely straight style. This was his intention from the outset: to write a parody and direct it deadpan. If he succeeded, he said, there should never be a moment in the movie when any actor seems to understand the humor of his dialogue or situation. This was true even in a scene of deliberately extreme exaggeration (later cut from the screenplay for reasons of length) in which Casey, the latent lesbian, is pursued around an office by the lecherous Marvin Fruchtman, head of Bellevue Studios. Some of the acting in *BVD* was criticized as inept and amateurish, but in fact the movie must have been terribly difficult for the actors, who were given (deliberately) impossible lines and asked to read them as realistically as they could.

The movie was also linked with *Myra Breckinridge,* attacked for its violence, and seen as the harbinger of various alarming trends. It seemed to me that *Myra Breckinridge* was a chickenhearted movie, timid about its own vulgarity, whereas *BVD* was saved by Meyer's gusto. In writing *BVD*, I tried to keep a classic like *The Producers* (1968) in mind. It was impossible, I thought, to handle bad taste in good taste, but possible for a movie (as Mel Brooks once put it) to "rise below vulgarity."

Beyond the Valley of the Dolls was Meyer's highest-grossing film, taking in an estimated $9,000,000 worldwide (*Myra* grossed $3,000,000 on a cost of $4,000,000). But Meyer's next production at Fox, *The Seven Minutes* (1971), was his first commercial failure. This should probably not be surprising; the project itself was unsuited to Meyer's strongest points, which are eroticism, action, and parody in about equal doses. *The Seven Minutes* was intended as a serious consideration of pornography and censorship and, alas, that is the way Meyer approached it. He got serious about the theme. He had been harassed for years by various amateur and professional vigilantes, and he intended *The Seven Minutes* as his statement against censorship.

The result, whatever it was, was not a Russ Meyer film in the classical vein. There were some nice touches, like making the United States Senator from California into a woman played by Yvonne De Carlo. There were a few flashes of Meyer humor, like a self-important character speaking on a car telephone that turns out to be in a Volkswagen. But Meyer's main thrust seemed to be to bring *The Seven Minutes* to the screen more or less faithfully and seriously, and I think that was a mistake. The courtroom scenes and the philosophical discussions clashed with the melodrama (as they also do in the Irving Wallace novel), and the result was a film of a project that should probably not have been made at all, and certainly not by Russ Meyer.

By this time, however, Meyer was occasionally being seen as an auteur whose gifts consisted of something quite apart from the dynamic, sexy, funny personal style his admirers cherish. An earnest critic for the UCLA *Daily Bruin* perceived that *The Seven Minutes* was shot entirely from stationary camera positions (except for one pan that kept a car in mid-screen, and thus had as its purpose a stationary composition), and described Meyer as the stylistic heir of Eisenstein.

I don't think that says it. He is an original, who developed his own style during a decade of independent productions he totally controlled. He has a direct, vital, literal approach to his material, and the ability to make the same scene fully effective in two different ways for two different audiences. Unlike many contemporary directors, he doesn't seem to have been directly influenced by anyone—his approach to a scene is a visceral and intellectual expression of his personality.

POSTSCRIPT, 1974

Meyer's *Blacksnake!*, released in 1973, was intended as a box-office mixture of violence and blaxploitation, but it failed to do much business under its first title or even after being retitled *Sweet Suzy.*

"I misjudged the market," he says. "People simply didn't *enjoy* the picture. The violence was a downer." And, he might have added, urban black audiences didn't particularly turn on to an hour of a sadistic white woman whipping black slaves—even if they did get to whip her to death at the end.

Meyer then began work on a project called *Viva Foxy*, for which I wrote the screenplay. It was to star his wife, Edy Williams, and was to be about an early 1920s border war between two South American banana republics. The Williams character, Foxy McHugh, was an orphan of missionary parents, who had grown up street-wise to become the power behind both thrones. One throne was occupied by an obese dictator modeled after Peter Ustinov's Nero in *Quo Vadis*, and the other was a sleek proto–Che Guevara character.

The project fell through, partly because of a temporary breakup between Russ and Edy, and partly because of difficulties in putting together a deal (*Penthouse* magazine at one time was interested). Meyer's theory about *Viva Foxy*—and about the two-picture deal he subsequently made at American-International—was that the public expected a certain type of entertainment from him, and his best bet was to supply it. *The Seven Minutes* and *Blacksnake!* were aberrations. With the deal at AIP, he returned to his own tradition with enthusiasm.

The first of the AIP projects, *The Supervixens*, started shooting in February 1974. It was to be followed in August by another original, which (as this book goes to press) I am writing.

Originally entitled *Son of Beyond the Valley of the Dolls* (although not really a sequel) when it was being talked about as a Twentieth Century-Fox production, the project had gone forward under various titles: *Son of Beyond, Beyond Beyond, Escape from the Beyond* and (most recently) *Russ Meyer's Beyond Taste*. Its characters will include thinly disguised versions of famous millionaires and pop singers, as well as Adolf Hitler and a certain Dr. Praetorious who has a scheme for assuring eternal life through regular injections of liquids from the pituitary glands of female beavers.

Joe Solomon

JOE SOLOMON: THE LAST OF THE SCHLOCKMEISTERS* (1971)

ROGER EBERT

. . . movies are so rarely great art, that if we cannot appreciate great *trash*, we have very little reason to be interested in them.—PAULINE KAEL, *Trash, Art and the Movies*

There is a critic's superstition in New York City that a certain kind of exploitation movie needs to be seen in a Forty-second Street grind house. I believe in the superstition myself—or I believe in what it's getting at—but I don't think Forty-second Street is the place to exercise it. The street has the peculiarly New York problem of being *too* typical: all the grind houses in the world have come together there to make their stand. No, you're going to have to look somewhere else for Joe Solomon's audience.

I saw *Hell's Angels on Wheels* (1967) in the Woods Theatre on

Randolph Street in Chicago on the afternoon when Seiji Ozawa conducted the Chicago Symphony across the street in Civic Center plaza and Mayor Daley dedicated the Picasso. I think that was about the right place and time. The audience wasn't so violence-hungry that it grew impatient with the movie's stoned easiness, and civic notions of good taste were close-by. Films of the Picasso dedication, indeed, have the *Hell's Angels* marquee in their background, winking through the great iron bird's orange wings. No matter. Ordinary good taste has nothing to do with *Hell's Angels on Wheels,* nor with that entire class of inspired dreck that settles where the American exploitation film bottoms out.

Dreck, but inspired dreck. *Hell's Angels on Wheels* did for the motor-cycle what *The Endless Summer* did for the surfboard. Laszlo Kovacs went manic with his camera; his photography was so liquid that Roger Corman's *The Wild Angels* of the season before looked like studio setups without the studio. The movie was *fluid.* It moved through the conventions of the bike genre with the same grace Warner Brothers' gangster movies used to have. If a genre movie can manage to wear its conventions well, it picks up the authority to let its actors do all sorts of interesting things and, in *Hell's Angels,* Jack Nicholson, Adam Roarke, and Jack Starrett *did* all sorts of interesting things.

Joe Solomon put just about everything he had into *Hell's Angels on Wheels,* and it came home for him. It was his first really big win, after the black light, the rayon banners, and *Mom and Dad* (1945) with a woman in a nurse's uniform on duty. It cost $200,000, it grossed $2,464,000, and Joe Solomon's time had come, finally.

Joe Solomon, his official Fanfare Films biography explains,

> is the prototype of the Hollywood mogul, typical in the thirties and forties, but almost a lone ranger in the motion-picture industry of the 1970s. To illustrate his vital concern for every detail in which his company may become involved, he often types his own memoranda and letters on a portable electric typewriter at a speed which could potentially shatter the sound barrier or the floor-to-ceiling windows that encircle his high-rise Sunset Strip offices.

"On a clear day," Solomon said, one smoggy morning last spring, "you can see forever." He sat back in his swivel chair and looked down upon the Strip. "This has been a busy day already, and it's only . . . what time is it? Who cares? You know what I found out this morning? A witch is a female, but you can't call a male that. A male is a warlock. We're preparing this picture, *Simon, King of the Warlocks*.[1] Everything is going to be authentic. We have a writer who brought in a witch from Orange County. Hell, we have a whole coven down there if we need it."

I wanted to meet Solomon because he's one of the very last to have done it all himself. He built Fanfare Films (now known as Fanfare Corporation) with one movie, *Hell's Angels on Wheels,* and the movie represented a gamble of all his assets and credit. It was successful, and he gambled again on *Angels from Hell* (1968) and won again, and kept winning until he had a company and a product list and a network of distributors and his own board of directors.

You read about the Hollywood pioneers like Harry Cohn, who wrote checks in the West on a bank account in the East to gain five days on his balance, and who built his studio out of exploitation pictures because he couldn't afford anything else—stars, stories, directors—that would sell, and you wonder if that sort of gambling still goes on.

With Solomon, it does. In March of 1970, a few weeks before the market slump, Solomon went public and sold 220,000 shares. The issue was 20,000 shares oversubscribed, and Solomon was handed a check for $1,200,-000. "Now we can initiate product without waiting for our return on previous productions," he said, and that, more than the fact that he was a millionaire, was what the check represented: a chance to keep on gambling in the exploitation market.

Exploitation pictures used to be the third category of Hollywood studio releases, after A pictures and B pictures. Most of them came from Columbia, M-G-M, Republic, Universal, and RKO, and they fell off sharply after the arrival of television.

Television *was* B pictures, and for a while there simply wasn't a market for anything worse.

Then American-International identified the teen-age market about the time that rock pried pop music away from Percy Faith. AIP's Samuel Arkoff and James Nicholson and the early Joe Levine are the major 1960s figures in the exploitation field, but by the end of the decade, if you thought of a producer out there all by himself on a shoeshine and a dream as it were, financing the next one out of the last one (if the last one came in), you thought of Joe Solomon. Darryl Zanuck is the last tycoon, and Joe Solomon

[1] The distinction was lost when Solomon decided to retitle it *Simon, King of the Witches* (1971).

is the last schlockmeister. I will be sorrier to see Solomon go; he performs the more entertaining function.

"My director brings in a disciple of the devil the other day," Solomon was explaining. "This is a guy who celebrates the Black Mass. He advises us on *Simon, King of the Warlocks.* This picture has got me up to here." He drew a line at his chin. "You know what I think? Seriously? The kids are turning to witchcraft because organized religion has failed us. We're starting a brand-new motion-picture cycle right here in this office."

He was a short, round man dressed in the Strip executive uniform: slacks, an expensive sweater, and an expensive cigar. "If *Simon* hits," he said, "I have another project about a motorcycle gang that goes to a monastery with the idea of raising a little hell, manner of speaking. All the monks have hoods, you can't see who's a monk or who isn't. Anyway, it gets turned around on them and the gang members are turned into werewolves, one by one. It's a fantasy. I have a writer on it. I don't quite understand myself whether they were taken over by demons, or whether the monks are the devil. . . .

"Of course now with *Simon,* everybody is immediately thinking it's a picture about Charlie Manson. The day we ran the ad in *Variety,* CBS put it on the news, which of course it isn't really. *Simon* is about a magician who practices the black arts and lives in a storm sewer under Los Angeles. I never heard of Manson practicing witchcraft. It wasn't his bag, from all my sources. He was into communes. He surrounded all these people around himself. Anytime you do a supernatural murder picture, people will be reminded of Manson. Don't convict anyone on hearsay is all I say."

He studied the end of his cigar. "Referring to us, not to him."

Solomon said the plot of *Simon, King of the Warlocks* would be revolutionary in its impact on horror pictures. "It is a psychedelic trip into the mind, with supernatural undertones," he said. His top director, Bruce Kessler (*Angels from Hell, The Gay Deceivers,* 1969), was on it. Solomon referred me to a Fanfare press release with more details about the revolutionary screenplay:

> A circular plot construction is used causing the greatest impact to come out of the resolution as the tightening spiral swirls to its final conclusion. Within the framework of this construction are such dramatic devices as the Magic Mirror Trip that symbolistically prereveals the ending, causing at the film's conclusion a feeling of déjà vu in the minds of the audience.

"They'll never know what hit 'em," Solomon assured me. "It's our big summer picture. Between Memorial Day and Labor Day, we fight the majors to a standstill. *The Losers* [1970] had a summer playdate in every one of *Variety*'s chart cities. We made a million. We made *more* than a million, that's only an expression. *The Losers* was the first antiwar exploitation film. We shot it on location in the Philippines. I like the realism of locations. The now generation has seen so much TV that they can spot a phony scene a thousand miles away out of their Benjamin Franklin hippie sunglasses.

"You know something? We spent $350,000 and Robert Aldrich used the same crew for *Too Late the Hero* [1969], he spent ten or twenty times as much and did half the business. He did a war picture. We did a war picture. Our picture was about these Hell's Angels who were flown into Vietnam to stage a special raid on Cambodia and rescue some prisoners of war. That was the difference. Our picture was commercial."

"It was also prophetic," I said.

"Yeah, that's right," he said. "You bet it was. It was the first commercial antiwar film. It comes up with a fair statement at the end, which we like to do, after we give out all this crap. We like a message of some sort at the end, and the kids don't resent it. The critics, a lot of them, didn't like it. So screw the critics. We know the market. I'll tell you something. Know the market, screw the critics."

He shrugged. "I opened a picture called *Devil Doll* [1967] here four or five years ago, on a double bill with a picture called *My Baby is Black*. Those are the two worst pictures ever made. I broke every record in town. I understand the market. I don't *want* to hire Richard Burton. I make the exploitation film. The majors have virtually abandoned the field. They've left a hole, and we've crawled right into that hole between the majors. We outgross them drive-in for drive-in.

"These sex pictures, the beavers, you can have them," he said. "We don't want that image. Not that I give a damn about my image. But I went down to Santa Monica Boulevard the other day, and what do they show me? A birth scene. Christ, I did the live childbirth fifteen years ago, in a picture called *Mom and Dad*, when that was the dirtiest thing you could show."

He was on his feet now, moving around the office as if this were a stockholders' meeting, and the stockholders were clamoring for filth. "Who needs it?" he said. "We have a policy and we stay with it. We avoid the X pictures, we want the teen-agers. We've found a market that is more lucrative, more legitimate, and cleaner than that kind of crap. We find a topic on everybody's mind, we stay inside our budget, we stay away from expensive names. We don't *want* Richard Burton."

He paused, staring at a photo the size of a one-sheet, framed on his office wall. It pictured George Hamilton astraddle a motorcycle and wearing leathers. It was signed, with a felt-tip pen: "To Joe: May our association be *long, prosperous,* but most of all a *sincere* and *close* one. George Hamilton."

Solomon turned and stood beside the poster as if posing for a group photo. "An exception is George Hamilton," he said, "but we're staying inside a $450,000 budget. Hamilton did *Evel Knievel* [1969] for us. He produced and starred. It's a motorcycle theme, about the greatest motorcycle dare-devil in history, with George in the kind of costume Evel wears, and Evel doing stunts."

The stockholders' meeting was over. Solomon returned to his desk, selected a cigar from a humidor, lit it. "This guy Evel Knievel," he said at last. "You know when he went over the fountain at Caesar's Palace in Las Vegas? It was in all the papers? He loses control of his bike and cracks up. This guy breaks every bone in his body. He has steel pins holding him together. His goal is to jump over the Grand Canyon. When he jumps over the canyon, that's when he's gonna die. I told him so. I stood right there and I told him so. Even before we started the picture, I told him we've got an agreement and he doesn't jump until we finish it."

Solomon shook his head in sorrow. "But, Christ, I've made enough motorcycle pictures to know this guy ought to be better at it than he is. By now, this guy ought to be able to do a simple jump without falling off his goddamn bike. He was doing a wheelie in Buffalo . . . you know what a wheelie is? That's when you gun it and rear up on your back wheel. We have one in every picture. And he runs into a tree and cracks up. Christ, he ought to be able to do a *wheelie* by now. He's the greatest loser of all time. The kids will love this picture."

"The kids love losers," I said.

"That's the one thing you've *got* to have," he said. "If you sat there and asked me, what is the one indispensable element in an exploitation picture, I would say: it has to have a loser. The word *loser* in a title will sell more tickets than the word *sex*. This picture, *The Losers*, we cleaned up. The perfect title. I only wish I could use it again. Originally it was titled *Nam's Angels*. Never in a million years.

"And Simon, King of the Warlocks, he's the same thing. He's a loser.

He lives in a storm drain in Los Angeles. He meets a young man and takes him back to the storm pipe and performs a number of magical acts. So far, so good. But then he reaches in over his head and gets involved with Molloch, the rain-god. He's trying to take over the world, Simon, and this terrific windstorm blows up. He's washed away down the drainpipe and drowned. *'Don't grieve for me,'* are his last words, *'this is not the end, it's only the beginning!'* "

Solomon beamed. "What a loser," he said. "You feel like a little lunch?"

He had a reservation at Scandia. Over lunch, he told me his life story. Joe Solomon was born in San Francisco, the son of an immigrant printer from Romania, and he kissed a girl for the first time in the back row of what is now the St. Francis Theatre: "I was an usher, my father got me the job." His father was a theatrical printer, specializing in enormous twenty-four-sheet billboards. "I'd be up all night folding the bastards," Solomon said. "We used to have to make our own type; there was no commercial type in San Francisco big enough to suit him. We'd make letters that would run twenty-two by eight inches, and that was only *half* a letter. It used to be my job to rout them out. I'd have to sit there by the hour, digging that crap out. Jesus! Maybe that's where I developed my sense of exploitation, routing out the biggest letters in San Francisco. . . .

"And then, oh, down through the years, I was active in publicity, exploitation, any way you could draw a crowd. In about 1935, I developed a special sign rayon to put across the bottom of a marquee. You see them everywhere today, but I was the guy that developed them. I tried renting them, theatre to theatre, great big flags nine by thirty-five. *It's cool inside,* and that type of thing. And I rented out ushers' uniforms for a while.

"During the war I found myself involved with nightclubs in Los Angeles. Then I went back to San Francisco and in the late forties I developed an idea that I thought was going to make me a millionaire. I introduced a black-light type of poster, where you put the infrared on it and it glowed. I opened a company in Detroit, the Majestic Poster Company, a name my father and I had always been identified with. But I ran out of capital and we couldn't market the goddamned things. National Screen Service stepped in and took it over. It was a debacle."

He sighed, even now. "So by then I wasn't exactly setting the world on fire. I was looking for an avenue to stay in show business. I had a talent for exploitation, I *knew* that, but what was I going to do? I went out East and got involved with a picture called *Mom and Dad,* which broke the New York censorship law. We cracked Pennsylvania and New York. That was our territory, we had the picture under states' rights."

Solomon was the advance man. He'd go into Allentown, say, and book the picture and set up a campaign. The picture itself wasn't much; something about a girl who fell in with the wrong crowd and got pregnant. It was in black and white, but at the end they'd spliced on a live childbirth in full color. "I think they bought it from some educational film company," Solomon recalled. "They just spliced it onto the end of our story, and nobody could tell the difference."

Solomon, as advance man, hit on the idea of having sexually segregated showings. Women in the afternoon, men in the evening, "so as not to offend the delicate." He also advertised that a uniformed nurse would be on duty at all times. Before each screening, a man in a business suit would climb onto the stage and make a speech about the book they were selling on birth control, sex hygiene, venereal disease, and the hazards of promiscuity. Then a woman in a nurse's uniform would peddle the books up and down the aisles.

"Just the campaign alone, we'd have the whole town steamed up," Solomon said.

"And then at the afternoon show, I'd turn off the ventilation in the theatre, or throw some kind of crap into the ventilation, some gas to make them nauseous, and I'd call the local paper to come and get a picture of the people fainting. The women would be pouring out of the theatre holding their heads and moaning. By now we had every guy in town ready to see that picture. They broke down the doors for the evening show. The funny thing was, when the childbirth came on, the men fainted for real. This was the middle fifties. It was a great gag. It was good for two weeks in any town in the country."

Solomon also operated, he said, "at the opposite end of the pale. We had a little picture called *Prince of Peace* [1949], about the sunrise services at Lawton, Oklahoma. Naturally our approach was different. This time we'd peddle books about Christ and Lawton, Oklahoma, and the biography of the guy that played Christ in the play. We'd enlist the ministerial associations. What a beautiful sight, we'd have school buses lined up in front of the theatre at ten o'clock in the morning.

"The gag was, both pictures were in release at the same time. We'd do a town and come back six months later. The only place we had a problem was Newark; they remembered us from *Mom and Dad*."

After a look at the territory in Pennsylvania, Solomon settled in Philadelphia as a distributor for American-International, which had just been formed, and organized his own company on the side to distribute the landmark nudist film, *Nature's Paradise* (c. 1955) It was a success, and he began to import foreign films for the Eastern market.

"I had some good pictures and I lost my shirt," he said. "I had *Big Deal on Madonna Street* [1962], I lost my shirt. I had *Concrete Jungle* [1962] by Joe Losey, I lost my shirt again; it went directly from a flop to a classic, no money for me. I had *La Dolce Vita* [1960] in a few territories. Remember Anita Ekberg laying on the floor with that fur coat? And the scene with the balloons, and the sad little guy with the horn? That little guy, that scene never failed to move me. I always seem to have great losers. And then you can make money with junk and you know it's junk. . . ."

He left Philadelphia in 1965 in possession of his first big idea since the black light. He judged the market was ready for a low-budget motorcycle film, and he would produce one himself. It was, at last, the right big idea, leading eventually to Fanfare Films and beyond. In February 1971, Solomon changed his company's name to Fanfare Corp., and announced diversification plans, including a merger with a company that supplies prizes to quiz shows in return for promotional considerations.

Back in his office, I asked Solomon to grow philosophical for a moment. To take the long view, and talk about where his life was leading. "Well," he said, "the first thing, I'm always looking for a new angle on a motorcycle picture. I hope to do one a year for ten years. But the old style is dead, it's gone, buried. The days of a picture about the Hell's Angels driving down a road and drinking beer have gone by. We probably read ten cycle scripts a month around here, looking for that new angle. . . .

"The thing so many of these writers don't understand is that you have to have the new twist, but it has to stay inside the formula. The formula is simplicity itself: You've got to have this anti-Establishment theme perfectly identified with a loser, but a loser that kids can identify with. He's running free and high and wild . . ."

Solomon threw his hands into the air as if he'd just let loose of the handlebars—"and he's a loser in the end. Life *is* that way. Kids know life is tragic, they're going to be buried in the sand forever.

"Now I am not a scientist, a philosopher, but this I know. During the Depression, you had millions of people leading dull, dreary lives. They went to the movies to see rich men, beautiful girls, exotic homes. Today, the picture has changed. Now millions of people have swimming pools, they drink Scotch, they smoke grass, they drive cars. The teen-agers reject this affluent kind of life. They're looking for new values, they want realism. The exploitation picture of thirty years ago filled one need. Today that picture fills another."

"You take a motorcycle gang. They're putting down cops, smoking grass, laughing at the law," Solomon said. "They're taking women by force! Carnage! Pillory! They've got money, guns. Some guy on a bike grabs a girl and screws her. No consequences, no kids, riding off free . . . kids think, God! I've got a mother, a father, I'm living at home. *God!* If I could have that freedom. . . ."

One of Solomon's assistants knocked on the door and said that Purdy was ready. "Purdy?" Solomon said. He lit a fresh cigar. "*Freedom!* Put that down," he said. "That's what it's about. All right, bring in Purdy." The assistant disappeared. "Purdy is testing to be the love idol in a new film," he explained.

Purdy came into the room. She was a slim but busty girl with straight blonde hair framing her eyes.

"You're Purdy?" Solomon said.

"Yes sir, Mr. Solomon," she said.

"Have a seat, dear," Solomon said. "How old are you?"

"Twenty-one."

"Twenty-one." Solomon meditated. "How much do you weigh?"

"Ninety-eight pounds."

"Wet or dry?"

"Wet." Purdy giggled.

"With or without a brassiere?"

"Without. Always, Mr. Solomon."

Solomon meditated. "You look a little tired," he said finally. "You getting enough rest?"

"I was on this picture they shot in a weekend," Purdy said. "They shot eighteen hours a day. Usually I have unlimited energy, really."

Solomon nodded to his assistant. "All right, dear," the assistant said. "Mr. Solomon would like to see you now."

Purdy stood up and took off her dress. She turned around twice and then stood, looking at Solomon. Solomon meditated. "In the scene we're thinking of, dear," he said, "you'll be a love idol. You'll be laying on your back in a magical, supernatural setting. Can we see you laying on your back now?"

Purdy stretched out on the couch.

"Not very firm," Solomon said.

"They go like that naturally," Purdy said. "I don't have silicone or anything. It's natural."

"All right, dear," Solomon said. "You can put your dress on now."

Purdy put on her dress again. "What's a girl gonna do if she's just . . . natural?" Purdy said.

"No, no, that's all right," Solomon said. "We'll probably be getting in touch with you in a few days. Stop on your way out and talk to Miss Kempton, she's our casting director."

Purdy giggled. "Then I guess I'm firm enough, then?"

"We'll take care of that," Solomon said. "Ice makes them stand up. We'll use some ice before we shoot."

"Ice?" Purdy said.

"Ice," Solomon said. "Don't you worry about a thing." Purdy and the assistant left.

"This sort of thing," Solomon said, waving a hand at the couch, "you're in my position, you can't be too careful. I always have at least one additional person in the room. These broads come in here, they don't get the job, the next thing you know they're screaming about rape. A man in my position, you can't be too careful. You didn't mind, did you, the little interruption?"

"Not at all," I said.

"We'll stick them in a little ice, they'll stand up," Solomon said. "Where were we? Talking about my philosophy. I'll tell you one thing. My goal in life is to see Fanfare grow. I want to see it grow through mergers, through acquisitions; my dream is that the stock I hold will become very valuable. I want to leave an enormous estate when I die. I'm not really doing it for myself, I'm doing it for the *idea*.

"Say I'm worth a million, I want to be worth six million. Or twelve million. The thing that gives me enjoyment is the thought that I started with an idea, and by sheer creativity we were able to go public and we were oversubscribed, from people's confidence in the way I handle Fanfare. It's great for your ego."

There was a picture of Solomon's thirteen-year-old daughter on the wall, and I asked if he were doing it for her.

"One of the joys of my life is my daughter," he said. "But I'm doing it for my ego, for the *knowledge*. How many meals can you eat? Suits can you wear? Money is OK, money is great, but I'm not going to not eat at Scandia today so my daughter can have a couple of more bucks twenty years from now. I couldn't be happy sitting in Palm Springs, having my check mailed to me every Friday. It's not money, it could be beans or rice, it's only a measurement of how successful you've been. I get a physical satisfaction out of declaring a dividend for the stockholders."

Solomon looked at me as if he weren't sure I had understood. He drew on his cigar. A small silence fell. "And another thing, of course," he said. "I get great satisfaction out of finding young, frustrated talent, and giving it a chance. You take that one picture, *Hell's Angels on Wheels*. It starred Jack Nicholson. Jack Starrett, who played the state trooper in any number of motorcycle pictures, is in London right now directing a picture for Twentieth Century-Fox. Richard Rush, who directed *Hell's Angels*, directed *Getting Straight* [1970] for Columbia. Laszlo Kovacs, the photographer, he went on to *Easy Rider* [1969] and *Five Easy Pieces* [1970].

"Now one thing these people had in common, they were starving," Solomon said. "Starrett, when I found him, he was parking cars and starving. He worked for scale, he was glad to have the work. Nicholson the same way. When I met Nicholson, he was grabbing for straws. Richard Rush . . ."

Solomon rotated his cigar in the ashtray. "I ran into Richard Rush just the other day," he said, " 'When you coming back and doing a picture for me,' I say. 'Aw,' he says, 'you probably couldn't afford me,' " Solomon rapped the ash from his cigar. "OK, Mr. Big, I say."

EDGAR G. ULMER: THE PRIMACY OF THE VISUAL* (1972)

MYRON MEISEL

"No matter what you do, no matter where you turn, Fate sticks out its foot to trip you." So cries Tom Neal, condemned to wander the dingy roads of a faceless America, in *Detour,* one of the masterworks of Edgar G. Ulmer who died in October 1972, at the age of sixty-eight.

For many years, scattered cults of film lovers had cherished the impossibility of his demented poetry in such forsaken projects as *The Black Cat* (1934), *Bluebeard* (1944), *Detour* (1946), *Ruthless* (1948), *The Naked Dawn* (1955), and *Beyond the Time Barrier* (1960), to name his best. Such cults thrived on those very titles that were certain to earn the reflex contempt of all "serious" students of film, all of whom could learn a lot from such *films maudits* as *Girls in Chains* (1943), *Babes in Bagdad* (1952, released 1954), *Club Havana* (1946), *St. Benny the Dip* (1951), *Jive*

* Copyright © 1972 by Myron Meisel. Portions of this essay previously appeared in *The Boston Phoenix* (November 1972).

Junction (1943), and even (help us) *My Son, the Hero* (1943). Far more than any other film director, Ulmer represents the primacy of the visual over the narrative, the ineffable ability of the camera to transcend the most trivial foolishness and make images that defy the lame literary content of the dramatic material.

Ulmer worked on the lowest depths of Poverty Row, far beyond the pale of the B film into the seventh circle of the Z picture, shooting his films in dingy studios on makeshift sets, on lightning-swift schedules (*Detour* is rumored to have taken a mere four days). If it is possible that severe limitation of means can stimulate poetry, or that adversity might breed a tenacious reserve of inner feeling, to cite two assumptions common to critics who wouldn't give Ulmer the time of day; then, neither Piet Mondrian nor Alexander Solzhenitsyn have anything on Edgar G. Ulmer. Ulmer transformed his camera into a precise instrument of feeling, and his convulsive abstractions of screen space intensify that feeling by investing it with particular gestures of light, shadow, form, and motion that define his own director's soul, and none other.

As a young man in Germany, Ulmer was part of a group of theatre and film people dedicated to radical conceptions of design and dramatic rhetoric. His first film, *Menschen am Sonntag* (*People on Sunday,* 1929), rested within the tradition of the German street film, although it was shot with an innovative impulse for freedom and fresh air not unlike the contemporaneous work of Jean Vigo in France. His associates on the film all achieved more prestigious success when they and Ulmer came to these shores, among them codirector Robert Siodmak, screenwriter Billy Wilder, cinematographer Eugen Shuftan, and production assistant Fred Zinnemann. Somehow Ulmer would never find fresh air in Hollywood, where his films assumed the somber, pervasive futility that distinguished most of his serious work.

Settling here after Hitler came to power, Ulmer first attracted attention with a film about venereal disease, *Damaged Lives* (1933). Ulmer followed this with the best Karloff-Lugosi vehicle, *The Black Cat. The Black Cat* dealt with the occult, with flourishes more redolent of diabolism than was Universal's wont, and Ulmer's uniquely pessimistic view of Christianity and of the efficacy of any inquiry into the human condition gives the film thematic underpinnings that effectively neutralize the inherent camp tendencies of the genre.

As much a set designer as a director, Ulmer's work on *The Black Cat* is deeply disturbing in its suggestiveness, as much for what is left out as for what has been detailed in. For Ulmer, a few sticks of wood in primary shapes, dressed with a modicum of essential props, when photographed in shadows that respect no natural light, can create a world cognizant of the legitimacy of nightmare, of encompassing despair unable to muffle the cries of profound spiritual pain. His settings for musical numbers, in the absurdly minimalist *Club Havana* or in the perverse cantina number in *The Naked Dawn* or in *Minstrel Man* (1944, as designer for director Joseph H. Lewis), contradict the normal function of such numbers: to entertain and relax, to relate through music the stylized sense of unfettered feeling. Instead, dance sequences in an Ulmer setting become stern denials of relief, oppressive spasms of unsatisfied sex, mysterious rituals to be observed without understanding, hollow soundings in a hopeless vacuum.

Ulmer worked for most of the 1930s as a specialist in ethnic productions, making films in Yiddish, Czech, Slovak, Hungarian, Ukrainian, and German. Most of them were shot on shoestrings for the native-language market, so their success was guaranteed as long as the product could be reliably supplied. Ulmer supplied it. Much of this work is unsigned, most of it lost, little of it catalogued. *Cossacks in Exile*, a 1939 Hungarian-language picture, received some subtitled release, and the Yiddish *The Singing Blacksmith* (1938) became a regularly revived Second Avenue classic.

What is little understood about the Ulmer of the 1940s and 1950s, however, is that he did not make these films as a hack director on salary, on commissioned assignments. Ulmer *chose* to make these films, frequently serving as his own producer when the ubiquitous Leon Fromkess of PRC was elsewhere.

Ulmer employed absurd scripts and monotonal acting to reach the kind of controlled expression he felt compelled to create. Once Ulmer was typed as a cheapie director, it became nearly impossible for him to command any budget whatever, but it was more important to Ulmer to do his work as he wanted it done than to compromise in the attempt to mount more expensive productions. It was hard to reconcile production values with a cinematic world so dubious of value. In many ways a comparison with Ingmar Bergman is apt, in the repeated use of settings, actors, and motifs, and in their shared insistence on a personal and obsessive cinema.

Girls in Chains is a disappointing women's-prison picture, but Ulmer's low ceilings provide an evocative backdrop (shot with a disdain for walls) for the heroine's efforts to reform conditions and maintain her sexual integrity against the cheap advances of hoodlums and the battle-hardened skepticism of the girls. As always with Ulmer, each shot carries its own emotional mileage, although here each shot has pretty much to survive on its own in the face of an appallingly ridiculous script, which actually requires a running drunk joke in order to pull together its badly organized plot strands (including an outrageous use of stock footage that looks audacious when it was probably merely necessary). Like most of Ulmer's films, *Girls in Chains* can be reckoned terrible on any number of ordinary grounds, yet it cannot be dismissed as an ordinary film, full as it is of minor triumphs of indefatigable artistic spirit and extraordinary mise-en-scène, the visual element working overtime to compensate for the sagging plot line. Equally unsatisfactory is the ludicrous *Babes in Bagdad,* featuring Paulette Goddard and Gypsy Rose Lee eluding the wily eunuch of Sebastian Cabot. Still, the spectacle of Paulette winding through the elaborate tunnels beneath Baghdad, while Ulmer's camera placement contains all her rush within a placid, indifferent pan, achieves an emotional honesty in a fraudulent context in a unique way that few would be advised to imitate. Similarly, before they wind up with perfunctory diffidence, *Club Havana* and *Jive Junction* display remarkably fluid camera movements and an ability to bear down on essentials amid the superfluous that is frequently moving in itself.

In the mid-1940s, Ulmer hit his peak with *Detour, Bluebeard,* and *Ruthless,* the last named featuring stars of the magnitude of Zachary Scott and Sidney Greenstreet. A *Citizen Kane* in miniature, *Ruthless* is often as foolish as it is compelling, but the characters are put through their paces with relentless logic until their accumulated gestures comprise a meditation on worldly goals. The first third of the film elaborates on Welles's single bravura shot of the young Kane viewed through the window playing in the snow, and it is as beautiful in its tender prolixity as the Welles was brittle in its compressed taciturnity. *Bluebeard,* an ostensibly straight horror entry, links the artist-figure to repressed passion (John Carradine's Bluebeard is a puppeteer); rather more respectable than most Ulmer projects and therefore perhaps less distinctive, it is nonetheless a major effort that proves Ulmer was capable of sustained achievement when presented with a moderately coherent project.

Detour (with *The Naked Dawn,* his finest work) employs only three sets, plus a car driving interminably in front of an unceasing back-projection machine. The story is beneath trash: a musician is hitchhiking out to California to marry his girl, only to become inextricably entangled in a web of circumstance and fate. *Detour* is an exercise in sustained perversity, a consistent demonstration of the absence of free will. Tom Neal carries his five o'clock shadow with him as he worms his way from nightclub to beanery to barren motel room (Ulmer's Los Angeles consists of a single used-car lot), writhing desperately to free himself, only to ensnare himself still further. It is not even a question of fatalism any longer—the mechanisms of disaster have long overwhelmed any of our own intimations of mortality. Ann Savage gives a performance that defies conventional credibility: ugly, unpleasant, a shrill, unmodulated embodiment of Yeats's dictum that only the unexplained is irresistible.

Detour follows the route of mad poetic tragedy. Its inevitability reminds one of F. W. Murnau's *Tabu* (1931): the lighting and the camera serve as instruments of the inexorable progression to disaster, tracking shots that signal the subtle passage from a state of passion to a state of pain, creating images that exist so strongly on the screen that each subsequent shot literally forces the previous one from its place on the screen. Editing in both Ulmer and Murnau takes the form of usurpation: each new image is a presumptive challenge to the standing validity of the shot before it, only to be toppled by a new pretender to the frame thereafter. Both their images proclaim their integrity by their controlled poetry of shape and shadow, occupying their appointed time on screen and raging against the dying of their light. Only in Ulmer, and in Murnau, can a shot be both definitive and evanescent. *Detour* mercifully lasts little more than an hour, during which it compulsively grasps at the intolerable, only to find it readily within its reach.

François Truffaut has recently acknowledged that *The Naked Dawn* was the inspiration for his *Jules et Jim* (1961). Indeed, the two stories are parallel: two friends in love with the same woman. Shot in lurid color in just ten days, two scenes in *The Naked Dawn* stand out: a flat, underplayed robbery early in the film (the impetus for a chain of events that ultimately entraps the characters), and a bizarre Mexican dance in a seedy café. *The Naked Dawn* is a "semi-Western"; its final shot of Arthur Kennedy riding off on his horse, silhouetted against the sun, is a deliberate visual parody of Fordian cinema. But Ulmer's feeling for the characters and for the project ultimately transcends his apathy toward the genre.

With age, Ulmer's films grow more reflective, until, with *Beyond the Time Barrier*, we have reached a state of near-complete abstraction, with triangles, circles, and squares separating the characters into apportioned-off spaces. By now the story line has passed beyond the bad into the nonexistent, the only action being the postulation of individual emotions as visually perceivable properties, as the artist confronts the prospect of death with its dread implied denial of ever having lived. All we need bring to *Beyond the Time Barrier* is a lugubrious awareness of the exigencies of low-budget filmmaking and we can take away a moving contemplation of survival in which the absence of means has eliminated the ability to conceive of ends. Ulmer's last effort, a coproduction called *The Cavern* (1965), carries on this trend rather less successfully, although the parade of superimposed titles ("56 Days Later" or "842 Days Later") to show the irrelevance of time in a cosmic situation provides a dolorous counterpoint to the opposite use of them by Luis Buñuel in *Un Chien Andalou* (1928). *The Cavern*, for all its admirable timelessness, was shot, like most Ulmer films, almost instantly, and it rambles feverishly, as if it had to burn out its course. Civilization is reduced to an underground room full of *objets d'art;* it avails us not at all.

During his last two years Ulmer was nearly paralyzed by a stroke, sustained by an occasional admiring letter. Few cared that Ulmer had chosen the most impossible of terms and had functioned as a true artist. To disregard Ulmer is to miss the affecting experience of the triumph of the essential over the impossible. For a long time Ulmer cultists like myself enjoyed using him as a club to demonstrate to the unbelieving that art can indeed thrive in even the least fertile soil. But Ulmer's work needs no polemic to defend its glories. Ulmer made no excuses and his work stands as it is—intransigent in its disregard for the normal niceties of conventional aesthetics. So Edgar G. Ulmer lives, and we shall never seek his like again. To quote the last lines of *Ruthless:* "He wasn't just a man. He was a way of life."

FILMS

SIODMAK
(SEE-ODD-MACK)
PRONOUNCED THIS WAY

Robert Siodmak and Barbara Stanwyck

THREE FACES OF FILM NOIR: STRANGER ON THE THIRD FLOOR, PHANTOM LADY, AND CRISS CROSS* (1971)

TOM FLINN

Rather than hazarding a definition of *film noir,* this article contains a descriptive analysis of three films that the author paradoxically considers both typical and distinctive. Together they provide a sample of the *noir* output from the important years of 1940, 1944, and 1949. This in no way attempts to trace the limits of *film noir* since that style continued well into the 1950s and is still subject to periodic revivals. But *film noir,* like shoulder pads, wedgies, and zoot suits, was an essential part of the 1940s outlook, a cinematic style forged in the fires of war, exile, and disillusion, a melodramatic reflection for a world gone mad.

One of the earliest American examples of the *film noir* is *Stranger on the Third Floor,* an ambitious sixty-five-minute B film made in 1940 at RKO. Although not entirely successful, it is extremely audacious in terms of what

* Copyright © 1973 by John Davis and Susan Dalton. Reprinted from *The Velvet Light Trap,* No. 5 (1971).

it seeks to say about American society, and is particularly impressive in view of the way in which it predicts the conventions of the *film noir. Stranger on the Third Floor* was directed by Boris Ingster, and scripted by Frank Partos, who deserves full credit for the thematic content of the film since he adapted it from his own story.

Like most *noir* films, *Stranger on the Third Floor* takes place in an urban milieu, in this case a studio-built New York of sleazy rooming houses and run-down restaurants, populated by hostile strangers and prying neighbors. The protagonist, Michael Ward, is a young journalist who discovers a murder at an all-night beanery. His exclusive story on the crime and the subsequent publicity get him the raise he needs to marry his girl friend, but his testimony implicates a young ex-con (Elisha Cook, Jr.), who is railroaded toward the chair by a conviction-hungry D.A. The trial of the ex-con is a vicious rendering of the American legal system hard at work on an impoverished victim. The film displays a fine sense of caricature that is especially apparent in the figure of the judge, who, when roused from a judicial stupor, reprimands a sleeping juror. A realistic assessment of the gullibility of the average jury and a cynical appraisal of the sinister role of the police and prosecutors in obtaining confessions and convictions were hallmarks of the hard-boiled literature that paralleled and predicted what we call *film noir*. But even in Bay City, Raymond Chandler's outpost of corruption, trials were conducted with more decorum than is evidenced in the legal proceedings in *Stranger on the Third Floor*. In the film, the congenital cynicism of the genre is personified by Ward's elder colleague and mentor on the newspaper—the newspaper reporter being traditionally the most hardened of mortals (*Ace in the Hole*, 1951)—who spends most of his time mixing wisecracks and whiskey at the press-club bar.

Moved by the sincerity of the ex-con's courtroom outbursts, Ward begins to feel pangs of guilt, since it was his testimony that completed the web of circumstantial evidence responsible for the conviction. Back in his grimy room, he suddenly realizes that his obnoxious next-door neighbor Mr. Meng (Charles Halton at his slimiest) is not snoring as usual. When banging on the wall does not bring an answer from the normally sensitive neighbor, Ward flashes back to several "run-ins" he had with Meng involving threats he had made on Meng's life. At this point Ward's paranoia reaches epic proportions and is expressed in a marvelously apt expressionistic dream sequence that is the psychological center of the film. Unlike the neat, modish Freudian dream montages of the fashionable 1940s films of psychoanalysis

(*Spellbound,* 1945), the dream in *Stranger on the Third Floor* is alive with subconscious desires, seething with repressions, awash with pent-up hatred, and constructed from the nightmarish circumstances of the character's real situation.

Ward's paranoia links him to other denizens of the urban jungles of Hollywood's nightmare films of the 1940s, where the dividing line between dream and reality can be merely the whim of a director, as in Fritz Lang's *The Woman in the Window* (dream) and *Scarlet Street* (reality), both from 1945. In *Stranger on the Third Floor* Ward's paranoid fantasy works because the twin motivations of guilt (for participating in the sham trial) and fear (of being caught up in the system himself) are well established; and the climax of the dream in which the "victim," Meng, attends Ward's execution functions perfectly as dream logic expressing Ward's strong subconscious desire that Meng be alive.

The dream sequence itself is so completely expressionistic in style that it resembles an animation of one of Lynd Ward's woodcut novels (*God's Man, Madman's Drum*) with strong contrasts in lighting, angular shadow patterns, and distorted, emblematic architecture; in short, a kind of total stylization that manages to be both extremely evocative and somewhat theatrical. The use of a tilted camera destroys the normal play of horizontals and verticals, creating a forest of oblique angles that recalls the unsettling effects of expressionist painting and cinema. This tilted camera was a favorite device of horror director James Whale (*The Bride of Frankenstein,* 1935), and it later enjoyed a great vogue around 1950 (*The Third Man,* 1950; *Strangers on a Train,* 1951). In *Stranger on the Third Floor* the Germanic influence, so important in the creation of the *film noir* style, is quite obvious, and not confined to the dream sequence. Throughout the film the lighting by Nick Musuraca is very much in the baroque 1940s manner, with numerous shadow patterns on the walls.

Peter Lorre, who appears only briefly in Ward's dream, brings a full expressionistic approach to his brief role as an escaped lunatic, slithering through a door in a manner distinctly reminiscent of Conrad Veidt in *The Cabinet of Dr. Caligari* (1919). In 1940 Lorre was quite thin and much more graceful than he had been in his debut as the pudgy child murderer in *M,* made nine years earlier. Actually his role, although even briefer than in *M,* is quite similar, and in both films he manages to obtain the audience's sympathy in the final moments with just a few lines of dialogue.

Working in a more naturalistic style, Charles Halton portrays a particularly obnoxious specimen of hypocritical busybody, a vicious prude who is totally fascinated by sex; while Elisha Cook, Jr., is suitably intense as the unjustly accused ex-con.

Unfortunately, John McGuire as Ward is stiff and reserved, although he does perform near the top of his limited range (compared with his disastrous role in John Ford's *Steamboat 'Round the Bend*, 1935). On the positive side, McGuire handles a considerable amount of voice-over narration quite well, and his very vapidness is an aid to audience identification.

In comparison Margaret Tallichet (who later became Mrs. William Wyler) gives a remarkably honest and unaffected performance as Ward's fiancée. More sensitive than Ward, she is first to sense the disastrous effects of his involvement with the murder trial on their relationship. Later when Ward is being held for the murder of Meng, she searches for the man with a scarf (Lorre), who actually committed both murders. Thus in its last moments *Stranger on the Third Floor* becomes a girl-detective yarn. This segment of the film clearly prefigures *Phantom Lady* in which another working girl (both are secretaries) searches for the elusive witness that will save her man from the chair.

Thematically, *Phantom Lady* (1944), based on a tepid thriller by Cornell Woolrich, is far less interesting than *Stranger on the Third Floor;* but Robert Siodmak's mise-en-scène is so exciting that other considerations pale in the face of his inventive direction. Like *Stranger on the Third Floor, Phantom Lady* concerns an innocent man convicted of murder, but Siodmak's work lacks the specific social criticism of the earlier film, although it retains the aura of menace in its portrait of the city, a quality that is absolutely *de rigueur* for any *film noir*. *Phantom Lady* was also filmed on studio sets, although in contrast to *Stranger on the Third Floor,* the atmosphere of New York City sweltering in midsummer heat is evoked with extreme veracity. With one or two exceptions, the sets are near-perfect in their simulation of reality, demonstrating a far greater interest in realism than is evident in pre–World War II films. The realistic atmosphere of the decor is aided by Siodmak's sparing use of background music, all the more remarkable in an era of "wall-to-wall" scoring. The suspense sequences, in particular, benefit from an adroit use of naturalistic sound.

With *Phantom Lady*, Siodmak, who had served a tough apprenticeship in America (directing five B pictures followed by "vehicles" for two of Universal's biggest attractions, Lon Chaney, Jr., and Maria Montez), established himself as one of the foremost stylists of *film noir,* creating a somber world of wet streets, dingy offices, low-ceilinged bars, crowded lunch counters, and deserted railway platforms, all unified by an atmosphere of heightened realism in which the expressive quality of the image is due entirely to lighting and composition. Siodmak arrived at this UFA-esque style naturally since he directed in Germany from 1928 to 1933. On *Phantom Lady* he enjoyed the services of legendary *noir* cameraman Elwood Bredell, who, according to George Amy, could "light a football stadium with a single match."

For a film of bravura visual style *Phantom Lady* opens rather unpromisingly on a close-up of Ann Terry (Fay Helm). Wearing one of those improbable creations that only 1940s milliners could envisage, Miss Helm looks very much like a middle-aged neurotic left over from a Val Lewton film. Into Anselmo's Bar comes Scott Henderson, successful civil engineer on the brink of marital disaster. He suggests that they pool their loneliness ("no questions, no names") and take in a show, typically one of those Latin revues so popular in that era of Pan-American solidarity. After the show, he deposits his companion back at Anselmo's and returns to his wife's apartment. Here the nightmare begins. When he turns on the light, he notices the room is already occupied by a formidable triumvirate of police officers (Thomas Gomez, Joseph Crehan, and Regis Toomey). Siodmak stages the confrontation with his usual flair; breaking the rules by deliberately crossing the axis during the interrogation to emphasize Henderson's isolation, framing him with a portrait of his murdered wife in the background, and tracking in slowly on the suspect (Henderson) while the cops deliver a snide, menacing third degree.

Like Ward in *Stranger on the Third Floor*, Scott Henderson is caught in an impenetrable web of circumstantial evidence, although his situation is further complicated since a number of witnesses were bribed by the real murderer in an attempt to destroy Henderson's alibi (already very weak since he could not produce the "Phantom Lady" he took to the "Chica Boom Boom Revue").

In contrast to *Stranger on the Third Floor*, Siodmak handles Henderson's trial obliquely. The camera never shows the accused, the judge, the jury, or any of the lawyers. Only the voice of the prosecutor (Milburn Stone) relates the proceedings, as the camera dwells on the spectators, singling out Henderson's secretary, Kansas (Ella Raines) and Inspector Burgess (Thomas Gomez). The trial sequence serves as a transition. Kansas and Inspector Burgess become, in effect, the new protagonists in the search to prove Henderson's innocence.

Kansas, like Ward's fiancée in *Stranger on the Third Floor,* is a determined innocent who contrasts sharply with the corrupt society she must
search. This juxtaposition was a favorite device in 1940s films, reaching its
climax in *The Seventh Victim* (Val Lewton/Mark Robson, 1943) in which
schoolgirl Kim Hunter ferrets out a colony of Satanists in Greenwich Village. Kansas (the name reeks of Midwestern grit and determination) begins
her quest by dogging the night bartender at Anselmo's (Andrew Toombes).
Seated at the end of the bar, she watches and waits. On the third night of
her vigil she follows the bartender through the wet streets to a deserted El
station where Siodmak emphasizes the vulnerability of his protagonist with
a quick turnaround in which the hunter becomes the hunted. Undaunted,
Kansas follows the bartender downtown through narrow streets, where,
long after midnight, the residents are still lounging on their front stoops and
the atmosphere is charged with latent violence.

The high point of her search (and of the film) is her encounter with
Cliff Milburn (Elisha Cook, Jr.), the trap drummer in the orchestra at the
"Chica Boom Boom Revue." Seated in the front row, dressed in a black satin
sheath, and chewing at least three sticks of gum, Kansas in about as incon-
spicuous as Princess Grace on the Bowery. Naturally she has no trouble
picking up the hapless musician and he takes her to a jam session that ranks
as one of the most effective bits of cinema produced in the 1940s. Siodmak
gives full rein to his expressionistic propensities in a rhythmically cut riot of
angles that "climaxes" in a drum solo that melds sex and music into a viable
metaphor of tension and release.

Unfortunately, the last half of *Phantom Lady* is dominated by Jack
Lombard (Franchot Tone), the real murderer, who is afflicted with delu-
sions of grandeur, migraine headaches, and overly emphatic hand gestures.
Van Gogh's *Self-Portrait with a Bandaged Ear* on Lombard's studio wall
neatly identifies him as the mad artist, but he comes off more like a refried
Howard Roarke (*The Fountainhead*) than like Van Gogh. Though he sounds
vaguely Nietzschean, "When you've got my gifts you can't afford to let them
get away," Lombard generates very little excitement.

Phantom Lady is primarily a work of style, created by the interaction of
considerable intelligence (on the part of the director, producer, and cameraman) with very bland pulp writing (Woolrich's novel). Some of the
dialogue is, as James Agee has pointed out, depressingly banal, but the film
is redeemed by the originality of its mise-en-scène and by its all-pervading
style, which represents a considerable advance over the more overtly expressionistic *Stranger on the Third Floor.*

In the pessimistic postwar years, the *noir* influence grew like an orchid in General Sternwood's overheated greenhouse. Rare indeed was the Hollywood melodrama that did not include some *noir* element or theme. The influence of Italian neorealism combined with already existing domestic tendencies toward location shooting to produce an expressive, increasingly veristic style tinged with violence and sadism. At the same time, plots of bewildering complexity proliferated as Hollywood's affair with the flashback reached the height of absurdity during the period from *Passage to Marseilles* (1944) to *The Locket* (1948). The newsreel reporter of *Citizen Kane* reappeared as the insurance investigator in Siodmak's *The Killers* (1946), while the comedies of Preston Sturges, such as *The Miracle at Morgan's Creek* (1944) and *Mad Wednesday* (1947), have intricate plots worthy of the author of "narratage."

Siodmak's *Criss Cross* (1949) combines complexity of narrative, a realism born of location shooting, and Siodmak's expressive stylizations. The opening aerial shot of Los Angeles sets the tone for what proves to be a fascinating chronicle of lower- and middle-class life in the western metropolis. Much of the action in *Criss Cross* takes place in the shadow of the funicular railway (Angel's Flight) in the Bunker Hill section of Los Angeles, described most eloquently by Raymond Chandler (though none of the films made from his books or scripts can compare with *Criss Cross* in the evocation of this milieu):

> Bunker Hill is old town, lost town, shabby town, crook town. Once, very long ago, it was the choice residential district of the city, and there are still standing a few of the jigsaw Gothic mansions with wide porches and walls covered with round-end shingles and full corner bay windows with spindle turrets. They are all rooming houses now, their parquetry floors are scratched and worn through the once glossy finish and the wide sweeping staircases are dark with time and with cheap varnish laid on over generations of dirt. In the tall rooms haggard landladies bicker with shifty tenants. On the wide cool front porches, reaching their cracked shoes into the sun, and staring at nothing, sit the old men with faces like lost battles . . .[1]

Criss Cross attains a kind of formal excellence, due to the tautness of its complex narrative structure, the uncompromising nature of its resolution,

[1] *The High Window* (New York: Pocket Books, Inc., 1942), p. 48. The passage originally appeared in Raymond Chandler's short story "The King in Yellow," reprinted in *The Simple Art of Murder* (New York: Ballantine Books, 1972).

and the inexorable character of its Germanic fatalism. The film opens *in medias res* with Steve Thompson (Burt Lancaster) and Anna (Yvonne De Carlo) sharing a furtive kiss in the parking lot of the Rondo Club. The reason for their secrecy soon becomes obvious. Anna is married to Slim Dundee (Dan Duryea), a local tough guy who is giving himself a farewell party in a private room at the club. Gradually the audience becomes aware that Steve and Slim, obvious rivals, are connected in a robbery scheme. The action continues the next day as Steve, driving an armored truck, picks up a huge cash payroll at the bank. During the forty-minute run to the plant at San Raphelo, Steve reviews the intricate chain of circumstances that brought him into the robbery. By opening in the middle, the audience is forced to accept the central situation—the robbery—as reality, and the contrived circumstances leading up to it are given additional credence.

The success of *Criss Cross*'s fatalistic mood depends to a large extent on the complex relationship between Steve and Anna. Anna is a creature of dazzling insincerity, another in the seemingly endless succession of 1940s *femmes fatales*. The archetype is, of course, Mary Astor hiding her Machiavellian designs behind a mask of gentility in *The Maltese Falcon* (1941). Barbara Stanwyck in *Double Indemnity* (1943) was of a tougher, less bourgeois breed, which reappeared with subtle variations in Siodmak's *The Killers* (1946, Ava Gardner) and in Jacques Tourneur's *Out of the Past* (1948, Jane Greer). Anna definitely belongs to this second class of fatal women, although her essential coldness and grasping ambition are accompanied by immaturity, a general ineffectualness, and vulnerability. Her hold on her ex-husband Steve depends on his feeling sorry for her. She is, in fact, persecuted by the police (at the instigation of Steve's mother), and tortured by Slim. But she finds it difficult to overcome the specter of divorce, with its overtones of betrayal and failure, that divides her from Steve and reflects the film's central theme of treachery.

Anna is always seen from Steve's point of view, for *Criss Cross*, like a Chandler novel, is set firmly in the first person. Steve narrates his flashbacks, supplying additional motivation and coloring events with his own fatalism. Siodmak complements the first-person nature of the script (by Daniel Fuchs) with a number of subjective shots that make crucial thematic points. Steve's loneliness is expressed in a shot of his brother and future sister-in-law kissing in a corner of the dining room, seen from Steve's point of view on the living room couch. A far more frightening example of the same technique occurs after the robbery goes haywire and Steve ends up in the hospital with his arm and shoulder in traction. Here Siodmak uses numerous subjective shots that force the audience to participate in Steve's nightmare situation: lying helpless in the hospital bed waiting for Slim's vengeance, playing a cat-and-mouse game with a traveling salesman (Adam Williams) who turns out to be one of Slim's hirelings. The "salesman" snatches Steve from the hospital in a scene that can only be described as a paroxysm of pain. The ever-venal Williams is too easily bribed to take Steve to Anna instead of Slim, and the executioner is not far behind.

The role of Steve Thompson is so important to the film that those offended by Lancaster's mannerisms may not enjoy *Criss Cross,* in spite of a number of excellent character portrayals: Percy Helton, the rotund bartender with a voice like wood rasp; Dan Duryea, with or without an icepick, the ideal pimp and small-timer of the decade; Tom Pedi, Slim's henchman Vincent, who delivers his dialogue with a greedy verve ("That's the ticket"); John Doucette, another of the gang, with a dour voice to match his somber personality; and Alan Napier, Finchley, the alcoholic mastermind of the big "heist."

The central importance of the robbery in *Criss Cross* demonstrates an increasing interest in criminal methods and mythology. *Criss Cross* is actually a "caper" film, a subgenre of the gangster film that can be traced back to *High Sierra* (1940), and further. The caper film concentrates all values and expectations on one last crime that, if successful, will put all the participants on easy street. The influence of *Criss Cross* can be seen in subsequent caper films including John Huston's *The Asphalt Jungle* (1950), in which Sam Jaffe's Doc Riedenschneider resembles a Germanized Finchley, and Stanley Kubrick's *The Killing* (1956), which carries the temporal experimentation of *Criss Cross* to the point of absurdity.

Although *Criss Cross* has a more realistic, less decorative look than *Phantom Lady,* both films demonstrate similar photographic stylization. The sharp, fluid, high-contrast photography and low-key lighting in *Criss Cross* are the work of Franz Planer, another old UFA colleague of Siodmak's and another link between Weimar cinema and *film noir.* Siodmak, himself, never lost a taste for the "disguised" symbolism found in German silents. In one symbolic cut he juxtaposes his principals, appropriately clad in black and white, to form a visual pun on "criss cross."

As in *Phantom Lady,* Siodmak displays a real interest in American popular music, including a number by Esy Morales and his band, that, unlike most 1940s musical numbers, is an impressive musical performance, well integrated into the context of the film. Miklos Rozsa, who ranks as the chief composer for *film noir* (*Double Indemnity, The Killers,* ad infinitum), provided an effective score with garish harmonies that mirror the harsh conflicts of the narrative.

By 1949 the battle against that scourge of Hollywood known as the "happy ending" was largely won, and the essential pessimism of the *film noir* could be fulfilled. As a result, *Criss Cross* has a thematic completeness that *Stranger on the Third Floor* and *Phantom Lady* lack. Slim stalks into the doorway of the beachhouse hideout like an avenging angel, awakening memories of other destiny figures: Bernard Goetzke visiting the young couple in Lang's *Der Müde Tod* (1921), or Hitu hounding the lovers in F. W. Murnau's *Tabu* (1931). With its thematic pessimism, realistic mise-en-scène, and aura of ambient fatalism, *Criss Cross* reflects something of the mood of a country about to discover the apocalyptic nature of the coming decade of nuclear stalemate.

Edmund Goulding

NIGHTMARE ALLEY: BEYOND THE Bs* (1974)

CLIVE T. MILLER

Nightmare Alley (1947) is the quintessential B movie spoiled by an A production. If the studio, Twentieth Century-Fox, had left well enough alone, *Nightmare Alley* would have been hard and nasty. Or if they had turned it into a full-fledged A project, it would have become a classic. Instead they went halfway and ruined it, the deprived bastard child of a millionaire. The amazing thing is that they didn't turn it into a mess.

You get a feeling, as you trace the changing facets of its production and view the end result, that everyone concerned with the movie recognized its power, although none could find the source. The entire project seems to have been shot through with bewilderment and a reluctance to follow any one lead to its conclusion.

George Jessel's remarks to the *Herald-Express* during filming suggest how often and how easily the picture must have been sent sailing in wrong directions. They also explain why the self-styled "nation's foremost toast-master" and producer of musicals (*The Dolly Sisters*, 1945; *I Wonder Who's Kissing Her Now,* 1947) was put in charge of probing a world of swindling and debasement:

> I really gave birth to the picture. I read a review of the novel, *Nightmare Alley,* rushed to Zanuck and told him to buy it. When Darryl got around to the book itself, he said: "You so-and-so, you never even read this book, it's full of censorable stuff."
>
> I admitted it, but the censorable stuff was not the picture I wanted to make. I was interested in the story of a carnival barker who found he could hypnotize a few hicks, decided to become a fake spiritualist, mocked the Deity and got punished for his impudence.

Hollywood has always been scorned for turning great novels into lousy, botched-up movies. All you have to do is look at the 1930 version of *Moby Dick* to see why the industry deserved its bad name. But virtually nothing's been said about how Hollywood took the most awful novels and the world's worst prose and transformed them into perfectly dandy movies with brilliant craftsmanship. That was more often the case, and *Peyton Place* (1957) is one of the best examples. For Hollywood, the greatness of the book and the greatness of the movie are usually in inverse proportion.

So perhaps your judgment of *Nightmare Alley* as a novel will affect what you think of it as a movie. But I doubt it. The movie's so good, it's bound to disappoint you. There are infinitely less worthy movies that are more satisfying simply because they are so mediocre that we wind up being grateful for small favors—an actor, a well-played scene, an audacious moment, or maybe merely a clever line.

The trouble here is that, in raising the film level, the front office didn't know which expensive props to use. The irremediable mistake must have been their allowing Tyrone Power to play the lead. He appears quite dapper in his snap-brim hat, navy blue pinstripe suit, boutonniere, and white pocket handkerchief during the day, and in white tie and tails when performing at night; and he does a good acting job with a part he was so perfectly suited for. Philip Scheuer of the Los Angeles *Times* found him "more convinc-ing as a phony spiritualist than he was as the real thing in *The Razor's Edge.* His is a surprisingly incisive performance surrounded by incisive performances. . . ." James Agee wrote that he "steps into a new class as an actor."

The problem was that Tyrone Power had become a star in 1936, when he made *Lloyds of London,* and none of his twenty-four movies since then had lost money for the studio. So cast him in the lead, and from that premise only soft opulence follows. As far as the studio was concerned, they had too much at stake to try something austere.

The most common story is that Power had to beg for the part. It's probably true, although the studio itself spread the story around to build sympathy and interest. If it wasn't going to get high marks for grandeur, it wanted them at least for artistic integrity.

Yet the casting of Power was neither an artistic nor a conciliatory decision. His last appearance had been in *The Razor's Edge,* which unfolded in the early 1920s—in studio terms, a period picture. By Christmas 1946, it had opened in major theatres throughout the country.

Power's next announced role was as the *Captain from Castile,* a costume picture in color, based on Samuel Shellabarger's best seller, set at the time of the Spanish Inquisition and Cortez's conquest of Montezuma's glorious empire. Completed on location in Mexico, *Captain from Castile* was originally scheduled to open around Thanksgiving 1947 on a road-show basis, the special exhibition treatment designed to return most of the production costs within eight or nine weeks. But the studio ran into trouble when it realized that it had no definite commitment from Technicolor to deliver color prints by the release date, and that Technicolor had little thought of making the deadline. The problem was that Technicolor, with numerous commitments to other studios, was spending all of its efforts for Fox on turning out four hundred and fifty prints of *Forever Amber* to be released the end of October.

There was nothing to do but postpone *Captain from Castile's* release date to January 1948. But Fox did not want to keep its star off the screen for that long; and finally someone convinced them it would be a good idea as a change of pace to cast him in a modern role (something Power seldom got even after *Nightmare Alley*).

To minimize the risk, the studio wrote Power into every scene save one, so that in the completed picture he would be off the screen for only two minutes. Included were twenty-eight love scenes divided among his three leading ladies.

Nor did Fox intend to skimp on extravagance just because *Nightmare Alley* was in black and white and set in contemporary times. The studio built a replica of the Spode Room in Chicago's Sherman House, along with ninety other sets, one of them particularly extensive.

For the movie's first segment, the studio hired three veteran carnival men as technical advisors and proceeded to pitch a carnival with one hundred sideshow attractions spread over ten acres. Mike Mazurki, playing the Strong Man, was given a forty-two hundred dollar leopard skin costume to wear. And when the fire-eaters worked, the studio called out the entire fire department to stand by.

According to a press release from Harry Brand, Director of Publicity, the set attracted a continuous flow of celebrated visitors:

> Joan Crawford pitched rings to win a Kewpie doll. Lana Turner brought her daughter, Cheryl, to see the Fat Lady and the Thin Man. Gregory Peck tried out his muscle and rang the bell when he brought the sledgehammer down on the "Test-Your-Strength" machine. Rex Harrison got the Fire-Eater to give him a couple of lessons. Dana Andrews tried his hand at shooting ducks. . . .
>
> Goulding and Jessel, who ran the carnival midway for six weeks straight, complete to hot dogs and taffy, kept the *Nightmare Alley* troupe in high spirits throughout the filming.

Presumably, Jessel told jokes. In any case, he managed to find time during the filming to travel twenty-five thousand miles on personal appearance tours and to finish the screen treatment of his autobiography, *So Help Me*. Who, then, was minding the store?

Edmund Goulding? But why Edmund Goulding, who was primarily excellent as a woman's director? Perhaps no one else was available. More likely, in keeping with the studio's other misinterpretations, the front office decided that what the film needed to become a successful A production was the director of *The Razor's Edge*. Why break up a winning team? The fact that they were two totally different kinds of films seems to have made no impression at all, any more than did Goulding's past record. Is it any wonder that the sharp edges of *Nightmare Alley* got smoothed? Of course they would in an A production! I doubt if people ever debated the point. Goulding: the former British stage actor and discreet romanticist who had directed *Grand Hotel* (1932), *The Constant Nymph* (1943), *Claudia* (1943), plus three of Bette Davis' most tasteful melodramas, *Dark Victory* (1939), *The Old Maid* (1939), and *The Great Lie* (1941), in addition to one of her most maudlin and unbearably tedious films, *That Certain Woman* (1937). The front office added lushness when they should have been sounding for resonance.

One Fox story has it that Goulding—who composed the songs "Love, Your (Magic) Spell Is Everywhere" from *The Trespasser* of 1929; "Oh, Give Me Time for Tenderness" from *Dark Victory* a decade later; and "Mam'-selle," the then-current Art Lund hit, from the French café scene in *The Razor's Edge*—wrote a mood melody every morning to go with his scenes for that day. He would show up at the studio an hour earlier than the schedule called for, in order to compose his daily tune, record it and have it ready to play for his cast when they arrived! If so, fortunately Fox went to the trouble of having Cyril Mockridge compose an additional background score.

Another story claims that Goulding waited until after 11:00 A.M. to film the big love scenes, on the theory that no one could make torrid love right after breakfast.

But if a third story's true, that Goulding finished writing a novel, *One for the Book*, during the filming, who was paying attention to the picture?

And when we finally do look at the picture, it bears little relation to the inane facts of the production. It's as if the film came into existence in spite of the production.

This is how five contemporary reviewers reacted:

Nightmare Alley is the story of a cold young criminal (Tyrone Power) who starts as a carnival "mentalist," moves on to a Chicago nightclub, and is on the verge of the big time (pseudo-religion, with prospects of a personal "temple" and radio station), when two of the women he has used gum up his act. The picture goes careful just short of all that might have made it very interesting. . . . Even so, two or three sharply comic and cynical scenes make it worth seeing. . . . In any mature movie context these scenes would be no better than all right, and an intelligently trashy level of all right, at that; but this kind of wit and meanness is so rare in movies today that I had the added special pleasure of thinking, "Oh, no; they *won't* have the guts to do *that*." But they do; as long as they have any nerve at all, they have quite a lot. The rest of the show is scarcely better than average. . . ."
—JAMES AGEE, *The Nation*

Nightmare Alley is a hair-raising carnival sideshow. At the dead end of the alley lives the Geek, an is-he-man-or-is-he-beast carnival exhibit that tears up and eats live chickens. He is able to stomach this job because he is in the last stages of dipsomania, and is paid a bottle a day and a place to sleep it off.

The ultimate pit of carnival-life degradation fascinates shrewd, up and coming young Stan Carlisle (Tyrone Power), but it takes Stan nearly two hours' playing time to learn that in spite of all his talents he was born to be a Geek. Stan is one of the most wholehearted and resourceful heels yet to leave a print on the U.S. screen. He climbs a ladder made of ladies. Rung Number 1 is Zeena (Joan Blondell), the midway's mentalist. He plays cozy with her just long enough to swipe a pseudo-telepathic formula through which he can graduate to the big time. Number 2 is a luscious, loyal dimwit named Molly (Coleen Gray), whom he marries. Number 3 is Lilith (Helen Walker), a pseudo-psychiatrist who outsmarts him at his own racket.

Nightmare Alley would be unbearably brutal for general audiences if it were played for all the humor, cynicism and malign social observation that are implicit in it. It would be unbearably mawkish if it were played too solemnly. Scripter Jules Furthman and Director Edmund Goulding have steered a middle course, now and then crudely but on the whole with tact, skill and power. They have seldom forgotten that the original novel they were adapting is essentially intelligent trash; and they have never forgotten that on the screen pretty exciting things can be made of trash. . . .—JAMES AGEE, *Time*

Some restraining hand has kept *Nightmare Alley* from realizing its full potentialities, but so long as it remains cynical there's a harsh power in this new film. . . .

Unfortunately the tabernacle sequence—which should have crowned this inspection of rackets—has been deleted. It is described in the synopsis distributed by the theatres, but some pussyfooting instinct must have moved the makers to strike it out. . . .

George Jessel, the producer, deserves congratulations for at least making a film above the average.—VIRGINIA WRIGHT, LOS ANGELES *Daily News*

Nightmare Alley is likely to come as an unpleasant shock to many people, for it is about the "lower depths" of show business—the traveling carnival. However, the novel . . . was a great deal more shocking, and, everything being comparative, 20th Century-Fox has done a skillful job of cleaning it up . . . comparatively.

It is such a story and a milieu as would have delighted Europe's prewar cinema makers. . . . In Tyrone Power . . . one is more conscious of the [magnetic] personality than in the novel's Stan; nor is he the unmitigated cad that the latter was.

Consequently, when the movie lets him off easier, with a 50–50 chance of moral and physical redemption, the spectator is likely to be more glad than sorry. To abandon "our Ty" when—as a wretched "geek" exhibit who is supposed to bite the heads off live chickens—he has tasted the dregs of ignominy would be to outrage the sensibilities of the millions to whom a star can do no lasting wrong. Besides, is it not the love of a good woman that saves him?

At any rate this Molly is—again, comparatively—good. . . . Indeed, the weakest part of the picture, from a standpoint of motivation, is that she cries, "Enough!" before Stan's plot has barely had time to hatch. . . .

Goulding's production, repellent as its theme may be, develops considerable fascination up to the closing reel or so. Jules Furthman wrote the tricky (apparently) censor-proof screenplay and George Jessel—of all past escapists!—produced.—PHILIP K. SCHEUER, LOS ANGELES *Times*

. . . this film traverses distasteful dramatic ground and only rarely does it achieve any substance as entertainment. . . . Like the book, the film is productive of its moments of shock and revulsion.—TOM PRYOR, *The New York Times*

To round out a disappointing week, Twentieth Century-Fox came up with *Nightmare Alley*—at the end of which you can, provided your stomach doesn't revolt, meet the "geek." . . . The irritating deficiency about *Nightmare Alley* is its shocking lack of good taste.—*The Sunday New York Times*

Nightmare Alley still has a good deal of fascination and tense melodrama, but it has lost much that was in the book. . . . We are now gazing upon Tyrone Power . . . who is doing a pretty good job, but who is always Tyrone Power, a nice guy chewing gum to look tough. Actually the fault is not Power's, it is Hollywood's. Censorship being what it is, Fox couldn't have projected the full terror of Gresham's book. They are even, you might say, afraid to try. They have it in the back of their minds that at the very end of all this, there will be a rainbow. . . .—SEYMOUR PECK, *PM* (New York)

Right from the opening sequences, the carnival scenes, the picture is slightly askew. For all their background movement and mixture of sounds, they come across as strangely flat. The fault is partly that the camera hardly moves, but mainly that the director is unable to draw the audience into the atmosphere and milieu. You never lose the sense that scenes are being staged. Later on, when the characters stage scenes intentionally—the night-club act, the apparition—there is a finesse and professionalism to them that the "straight" parts of the movie seldom attain. The actors, particularly Ty

Power, seem most comfortable when their characters are most self-conscious. And they seem most self-conscious when the characters are not
supposed to be.

The dialogue is primarily to blame. Nobody would be comfortable
having to face Zeena and deliver the line: "I give up," twirling his cap, "Yes
sir, I give up." This odd characteristic, of the dialogue and the actors'
readings just missing the mark, pervades the 1940s movies, particularly
dramas. Listen again to *They Drive By Night* (1940), *Gilda* (1946), and
Beyond the Forest (1949). For whatever reasons—the technical advances
within the industry, the wider exposure of foreign films made by serious film
artists, the growing awareness and acceptance by audiences of movies as an
art form, the making of *Citizen Kane* (1941), the war and the changing
social morality—by the 1940s the movies lost all of their sense of fun and
became, instead, conscientious.

They took on a portentousness that, even in the lightest movies, added
intolerably to their length. Consider in Tracy and Hepburn's first movie
together, *Woman of the Year* (1942), not just the slow pace, which can be
attributed to director George Stevens, but the inclusion of the *entire* serious
wedding ceremony, something that never would have been allowed in a
1930s comedy. It was around this time, too—precisely 1943—that Bette
Davis' mannerisms became so pronounced that they started detracting from
her performances. People who haven't seen the Davis performances from
1938 to 1942 hardly consider her our greatest actress! It was in the 1940s
that B movies reached their prime. Small wonder, with such pretentiousness
and self-consciousness smothering whatever honest life and energy there did
exist in A productions.

Even when everything meshed perfectly, as in *The Ox-Bow Incident*
(1943), the audience was acutely aware of it—as if one of the intentions
of 1940s movies was to bury all spontaneity and thereby keep the audience
constantly at a distance (when, of course, the moviemakers intended and
thought they were doing just the opposite). To the moviemakers, planned
spontaneity served for the real thing. It never occurs to television executives,
either, that a canned laugh track might irritate a viewer and keep him on his
guard rather than convince him he's participating in fun.

Nightmare Alley is typical of 1940s movies in other ways, too. Notice,
for instance, how certain gadgets that were new at that time keep popping
up in the films. *Woman of the Year* has a long, silent comic sequence that
takes place in a modern kitchen. Comedy or drama, the characters are

always skeptical about the gadgets, in awe of them, tormented by them, and duped by them. In 1947 and 1948 the home recorder device was strategic to the plots of several films—*The Unsuspected* and *Unfaithfully Yours,* as well as *Nightmare Alley.*

Psychiatry may have been viewed by the studio executives as just another gimmick to hang a plot on or they may have finally come around to recognizing its insights. In any case, they exploited the new field at the same time that they illuminated it for the audience. It was fresher ground when Warner Bros. made *Now, Voyager* in 1942. Now it served as the basis for such movies as *Spellbound* (1945), *The Dark Mirror* (1946), and *The Snake Pit* (1949).

Viewing *Nightmare Alley,* you must bear in mind the puritanical times. Nowadays it's hard to convince us that a town marshal would consider closing a carnival for the amount of Coleen Gray's "indecent exposure," nothing more than a two-piece bathing suit. Not even her navel is showing! (The same stricture, by the way, remained with television until almost 1970.)

Not just the Hollywood factory product but the entire film output of the 1940s is based on fundamental naïveté: political, intellectual, moral, and emotional innocence that is simply appalling. It's as if everything that everyone knew in the 1930s was completely forgotten, all of the gay sophistication that movies had carried to the point of esoteric knowledge. And movies of the *early* 1930s had an even greater sense of worldliness.

Under such conditions, when most movies now were either banal or bathetic, *Nightmare Alley* was extraordinarily audacious. Its fundamental premise, that the handsome hero is a son of a bitch who will wind up in the black abyss of debasement, was not something any studio would deal with outside the gangster genre. Even more unusual and startling is the fact that the most crooked heroine of the piece gets away with her brand of corruption, and presumably goes on soaking the rich, having discovered that consulting psychology can be a very rewarding racket, at least along Lakeshore Chicago. This would not have been new in 1932, but it was new now, fifteen years later. And it was 1960 before movie audiences were shown *Elmer Gantry;* 1972 before they found out about *Marjoe.*

The ending of *Nightmare Alley,* with the hero's rush to disaster, is hurried in the wrong way. I suspect the company used up their allotted time. I mean budget time, not running time; because they could, and should, have cut from the story the instances of extreme naïveté: the pedantic explanations of what a geek is, what tarot cards are, how you can rig a mentalist act; and the tone of surprise implied by the explanations—that there *is* such a thing as a geek, as tarot cards (hadn't anyone seen *Carmen!*), as a *rigged* mentalist act.

In the last reel, Stanton Carlisle crashes too quickly for the denouement to be dramatically convincing. He seems neither far enough down to accept the job of geek nor self-destructive enough to accept it with the line, "Mister, I was made for it."

The line echoes our introduction to him as carnival barker and assistant in Zeena's small-time, simplified mentalist act. "You like this racket, don't you?" she says to him.

"Oh, lady, I was made for it. . . . I *like* it!"

When The Great Stanton finally hits bottom, the line is probably not meant to reveal his self-destructiveness. And I think Power delivers it a little more bitterly than he should, implying a degree of perception the character hasn't shown so far. If the line works at all, it is merely as an ironic comment on the curve of his life—in which case, for it to be effective, he would have to be more down-and-out than he appears. He's not nearly as mashed up as Pete was at this point (even granting that it may be an intentional irony, that we're to recognize how soulless Stanton is in contrast to Pete, who was farther down but not willing to be a geek). On the other hand, the makeup is improved, and Power does look appropriately spaced out the next night when Stanton goes berserk (by then he's had a stomachful of live chicken heads).

At least one scene, the tabernacle sequence, we know was filmed but cut out. There may have been others. Certainly we never see enough of Stanton's warm feelings for his wife Molly to believe that he loves her. In fact, the scene in which he cons her into playing Grindle's dead mistress—by reasserting his love, with the music strategically coming in under his avowal—demands, for its sharpness and irony, that we know he does *not* love her. Otherwise, what's the point of the scene at all? So it comes as quite a shock, after Molly breaks down with moral compunction in the midst of the Grindle swindle and Stan tells her to get out (of his life, we assume, not out *of the area*), then, to find her sitting next to him in the car and him agreeing to take her away with him. Their separation at the train station is quite moving—but now only if we *do* believe he loves her!

Also, it *feels* as if there was more to Grindle than what appears in the available 16 mm. rental print,[1] which had possibly been chopped to fit tele-

[1] From Films, Incorporated, Hollywood, California.

vision time but which had more likely been chopped by the studio itself: Stan's summation of his first confrontation with Grindle, told to Lilith on the motorboat, is very crude exposition. And I do seem to remember, when the film first came out, more scenes elaborating the Stan-Lilith relationship. Did I simply fill it in myself?

What makes the film so admirable for the 1940s, in addition to the artistry of several individual scenes, is the fact that it manages to remain honest for as long as it does. It fearlessly follows the implications of the plot and characterizations, and because it goes so unremittingly where it should, we are constantly surprised. The duping of the religious believers may be the most memorable scenes: the town marshal (James Burke), whose look of sincerity may have gone unmatched but for Lyndon Johnson's repeated proclamation, "We want no wider war!" twenty years later; and the industrialist Grindle (Taylor Holmes), viewing his mistress' apparition, causing in the audience just the perfectly right kind of embarrassment as he cries on his knees, "Oh, Dorry, forgive me; forgive me, Dorry. I believe now, I believe everything. Oh, Dorry, ask God to forgive me. Ask him to give me one more chance. Please, please!" blubbering now, "I'll do anything! What right have I to ask for mercy, when I've never shown mercy to anyone!"

My own favorite scene takes place in the diner, the scene in which Bruno (Mike Mazurki) confronts Stan about making time with his girl Molly, and Zeena backs Bruno up.

Goulding filmed the fight, during which Mazurki hurled Power sixteen feet, by planting three cameras at different angles to give a newsreel effect. Such had been the usual method in the cumbersome early sound days, when cameras had to remain stationary. And such is the method now for movies made for television, with little time to plan shots ahead or to spend shooting retakes.

In preparing us for the confrontation scene, the filmmakers play on the 1940s' morality. So, although we've viewed Stan and Molly only kissing, the ensuing scene convinces us that there's been much more, that the kissing was blatantly used as a symbol acceptable to the Breen censorship office. Stan and Molly's two lovers forcing them to marry each other is one of the most inventive and appealing pieces of perversity that Hollywood ever came up with.

Actually, you might notice that there is an intermediary scene between the kiss and the diner: we see Molly waiting for Stan outside her trailer; when Stan comes round the trailer, he's fixing his tie. An innocent first viewing would suggest that Stan had simply gotten dressed up, changed his clothes to go out with Molly. It may take a second viewing to realize that he's had his clothes *off*. In which event, it's a nice touch that she has managed to get dressed with time to spare before he has completed *his* primping.

Also nice, although not inventive, are those moments when genuine mysticism intrudes: Zeena and her tarot cards in her room, Stan reading Lilith's mind in the nightclub. Agee called Lee Garmes's camera work "lush but vigorous"; and Peck noted the "brooding, moody photography is of enormous help." But marvelous as it is, it is quite typical of the fine, expert, stark black-and-white photography of the 1940s, when virtually every movie seems to take place at night and under railroad bridges or in dark alleys and hallways, in badly lit, squalid hotel and boardinghouse rooms. The sound department, under E. Clayton Ward and Roger Heman, did an especially excellent job.

Perhaps most exciting of all is Cyril Mockridge's outstanding but unobtrusive music score, full of activity and eerie discomfort, with occasional undertones of terror. The music is used sparingly, at strategic points, and then as much ironically as dramatically. Notice the adept intimations of Stan's doom (mixed with the terrifying echo of the geek's screams); the ironic romanticism when Stan resorts to the final words for getting Molly to go along with the Grindle ruse, the attestation of his love for her and utter reliance upon her; the drama and high irony when Grindle views the apparition and proclaims his own abjectness (and the organ, playing beneath his words, swells).

Goulding is at his best handling Joan Blondell and stage actors Taylor Holmes and Ian Keith. Keith, a Shakespearean actor who had also appeared in operettas, gives a fine performance as Zeena's partner, the dipsomaniac. He was a sturdy supporting player in Hollywood from silent days until his death in 1960.

Holmes is quite brilliant. A matinee idol in the silent days and the original Ruggles of Redgap, he had not really been back in Los Angeles since the 1920s, when he had appeared in stage musicals there. During the next twenty years he stayed in the East, acting on Broadway. He returned to movies in 1947 by acting in *Boomerang* and *Kiss of Death,* both shot in New York. After *Nightmare Alley,* he remained in Hollywood, ironically to portray crooked politicians and confidence tricksters, until his death in 1959.

Joan Blondell is probably our least acknowledged great actress. Infectious as a 1930s gold digger, with none of the bitchiness of her Warner

Bros. cohorts, she had recently attained more serious parts in *Cry Havoc* (1944) and *A Tree Grows in Brooklyn* (1945). Unfortunately for *Nightmare Alley*, she drops out of the picture a third of the way through. But to get the measure of her splendid performance, just watch her eyes, her face, in the truck scene, when she rides up front with Ty Power and plays the whole scene over to him. However, because of pieces of business, such as her stubbing out her cigarette on the hood through the missing windshield, and because of the way it's cut, with emphasis on her reacting, the scene remains hers. According to publicity reports, she read minds with such gusto that she knocked her crystal ball on her foot and had to hobble for several days afterward. When she finished the picture, she married producer Mike Todd.

Goulding had less luck with the actresses who carry the film's other two thirds. Coleen Gray has achieved a small reputation as an underrated actress. On the contrary, she seems to me an overrated one in having been given such an important, pivotal role in the first place.

Born Doris Jensen in 1922, she grew up in Hutchinson, Minnesota, where her father ran a farm. After graduating from Hamline University in Saint Paul, she worked her way to Los Angeles by waiting tables. If the publicists are to be believed, in Los Angeles she worked as a USC librarian, a YMCA receptionist, a ceramic painter, and a drugstore cashier. She earned around eighty dollars a month and spent twenty of it on dramatic training. Fox talent scouts saw her in a little-theatre play and signed her. They seem to have been torn about giving her an Irish name. Since she was Danish, they decided to spell Coleen with only one *l*, instead of two. She acted in *State Fair* (1945) and in *Kiss of Death* before *Nightmare Alley*, and in *Red River* (1948) right after. Her first scene in *Nightmare Alley* had to be postponed because her year-old daughter had whooping cough and Goulding did not want to take any chances with his cast.

I should have much preferred the limited talent of Fox's star Linda Darnell, who the following year played a beautiful parody of the model docile wife in Preston Sturges' murderous comedy, *Unfaithfully Yours*.

Although Helen Walker had more experience—playing opposite Alan Ladd in *Lucky Jordan* (1942), in *Brewster's Millions* (1945), *Murder, He Says* (1945), and *Murder in the Music Hall* (1946), among others—Fox decided to give up on her.

She had been born in Worcester, Massachusetts, and gone on to Boston's city hall, where she sold dog licenses before making it in New England summer stock companies and on Broadway in *Jason*. At Fox she was specialized in aristocratic home-wrecker roles. Her best film, Ernst Lubitsch's *Cluny Brown,* with her as the Honourable Betty Cream, was made in 1946. Most recently, in *The Homestretch* (1947), she had tried to come between Cornel Wilde and Maureen O'Hara. But, according to Fox, she felt, "I'm no different from the average girl who thinks pretty highly of marriage and never would make a play for another woman's husband, no matter how attracted I might be to him. I find myself saying, 'Walker, how can you do that even in make believe?' "

Some months before *Nightmare Alley,* the studio gave her her release. Yet, at the same time that her casting in the picture was announced, so was her new long-term contract—"as the result of the present large budget of 20th Century-Fox screenplays containing roles ideally suited to Miss Walker's talents."

In her man's suit with wing collar and bow tie, she comes across as "clean" as Ty Power. Mannish attire for women was familiar in the 1940s (Ingrid Bergman dressed similarly in *Notorious* in 1944). As far as talkies were concerned, Marlene Dietrich and Josef von Sternberg were indulging the style as early as *The Blue Angel* of 1929. In their early 1930s movies they created variations on the androgynous vision, continuing to play on the transvestite sexuality with a wit and sophistication that diminished in the 1940s to mere ugly taste in fashions.

Virginia Wright thought, "Helen Walker makes a striking psychologist, though I doubt if her interpretation will be admired in some quarters." I find it hard to assess her acting ability other than to say that she was adequate in restrained roles. Is the ineffectual emoting—for instance, the look that she gives Ty Power in the nightclub when he reads her mind—the director's fault or her own? The look contains no surprise, no admiration, no mystery, even though, perhaps, all three were intended. The statue look is one of the easiest evasions in picture-making: you let the audience read whatever they want into the look. In point of fact, I don't think that kind of look inspires an audience to read anything into it.

I prefer Mike Mazurki's transparent but forceful expression. Six feet, five inches tall and 238 pounds, of Ukrainian descent and with a B.A. from Manhattan College (class of 1930), Mazurki came to pictures from a successful wrestling career. He made his debut in von Sternberg's *The Shanghai Gesture* (1941) and was appropriately cast as Moose Malloy in *Murder, My Sweet,* the 1944 film version of Raymond Chandler's *Farewell, My Lovely* (with Dick Powell playing Philip Marlowe). A brunet, Mazurki dyed his hair amber blond for *Nightmare Alley,* with the same dye the studio used on Linda Darnell. In addition, whether Hollywood forced him to do it or his own glamorous aspirations, he had recently undergone surgery to remedy a cauliflower ear. Although Mazurki couldn't overcome the usual one-dimensional role of Strong Man, he did well with what he had. Late in the movie, when he and Zeena show up in Stan's room to make amends, Mazurki manages to convey that Bruno has within him something of a decent human being.

Of course, *Nightmare Alley* might have been a great movie had Orson Welles gotten hold of it and transformed it slightly. It wouldn't even have needed transformation, just a shift in balance here, something accentuated there—the sort of thing Welles could have done brilliantly had he been more restrained and adaptable to the system, and had the system been less fearfully anti-intellectual and more accommodating. Imagine the subtlety and depth he could have added to the picture from his own profound knowledge of personal attachments: the constrictions and small cruelties we impose on people we "care" for in order to assert and maintain our dominance over them. At the same time, all of the intellectual pretentiousness, staginess, and phony spontaneity that was soon to ruin *The Lady from Shanghai* (1948) could have been used to coat layer upon layer of irony.

As *Nightmare Alley* ultimately evolved, the irony is so shallow and so are the personal relations, that the veneer of the story becomes its authentic attraction. Unlike *The Sting* (1973) or the awful opening segment of *Butch Cassidy and the Sundance Kid* (1969), *Nightmare Alley* allows the audience to be in on the con game all the way; the film doesn't ever cheat the audience. The complicity between the audience and the swindlers is one of *Nightmare Alley*'s most powerful appeals. But scratch away the veneer and you've scratched away the finished product entirely; you're left only with ideas.

Among all conjectures there's a practical regret. For the studio didn't need to go outside its lot to satisfy us. With a little more nerve and a more appropriate contract director (perhaps Henry Hathaway), they could have turned *Nightmare Alley* into a great, straightforward *Hollywood* movie, less suggestive but not necessarily less daring.

For me, *Nightmare Alley* remains one of the most intriguing projects if I had the power to remake movies. Until then, a friend of mine probably caught its essential success exactly and paid it its highest tribute when she said to me, "*Nightmare Alley*? Oh, that's terrific! It's one of the movies that most affected me growing up. The geek . . . Why, it's one of my *diary* movies!"

NIGHTMARE ALLEY

Completed July 31, 1947; released October 18, 1947, by Twentieth Century-Fox; directed by Edmund Goulding; producer: George Jessel; screenplay: Jules Furthman, based on the 1946 novel by William Lindsay Gresham; art directors: Lyle Wheeler and J. Russell Spencer; set decorations: Thomas Little; assistant: Stuart Reiss; wardrobe director: Charles LaMaire; costumes: Bonnie Cashin ["ghost's" hat: Louise Germaine]; makeup: Ben Nye; photographer: Lee Garmes; special photographic effects: Fred Sersen; editor: Barbara McLean; music: Cyril J. Mockridge; orchestral arrangements: Maurice de Packh [all studio announcements, however, credit Earle Hagen]; musical director: Lionel Newman; sound: E. Clayton Ward and Roger Heman; assistant director: Gaston Glass [technical advisors: Jimmy Woods, owner of the Patterson-Yankee carnival; Mike DeRonda, carnival operator for 40 years; Ed Mundy, who started with a carnie in 1892]; days in production: 59; running time: 110 minutes.

CAST OF CHARACTERS

STAN CARLISLE
    ("The Great Stanton," "Sheik Abracadabra")   *Tyrone Power*
ZEENA   *Joan Blondell*
MOLLY ("Electra")   *Coleen Gray*
LILITH RITTER   *Helen Walker*
EZRA GRINDLE   *Taylor Holmes*
BRUNO, the Strong Man   *Mike Mazurki*
PETE, Zeena's partner   *Ian Keith*
MRS. ADDIE PEABODY   *Julia Dean*
HOATLEY, co-owner of the Hoatley & Henny Carnival   *James Flavin*
MCGRAW, a carnival owner   *Roy Roberts*
FAT LADY, 614 pounds
    "the biggest actress in show business"   *Jollie Nellie B. Lane*
THIN MAN, 7 feet, 10 inches   *Clem Erickson*
FIRE-EATER, who can spit a flame 30 feet   *Maurice Navarro*
DETECTIVE   *Leo Gray*
HEADWAITER   *Harry Hays Morgan*
CAPTAIN   *Albin Robeling*
GEEK   *George Beranger*

MRS. PRESCOTT   *Marjorie Wood*
MR. PRESCOTT   *Harry Cheshire*
FARMER   *Edward Clark*
OLD FARMER   *Eddy Waller*
CHARLIE   *Mike Lally*
WAITER   *George Davis*
DELIVERY BOY   *Hollis Jewell*
BIT WOMAN   *Laura Treadwell*
WORRIED MOTHER   *Nina Gilbert*
MAN IN SPODE ROOM   *Bill Free*
BIT MAN   *Henry Hall*
FRIEND IN SPODE ROOM   *Jerry Miley*
HUSBAND IN SPODE ROOM   *Gilbert Wilson*
MAID IN GRINDLE HOME   *June Bolyn*
MASSEUR   *Gene Stutenroth*
BELLBOY   *Charles Flickinger*
HOUSEKEEPER   *Florence Auer*
CAB DRIVER   *Al Herman*
RADIO ANNOUNCER   *John Wald*
HOBOS   *George Chandler, Oliver Blake, Emmett Lynn,*
George Lloyd, Jack Raymond

CREDITS COMPILED BY CLIVE T. MILLER

Nicholas Ray

THEY LIVE BY NIGHT (NICHOLAS RAY)* (1971)

DOUGLAS GOMERY

Nicholas Ray is the least examined of the major "discoveries" of the auteur theory by critics writing in the English language. No such neglect exists in France, as a quick glance through past issues of *Cahiers du Cinéma* will reveal. Also there are the famous cinematic homages (especially to *Johnny Guitar*) in the work of ex-critics Jean-Luc Godard and François Truffaut. Yet in America, Ray is largely ignored and today, nine years after the release of his last feature, *55 Days at Peking*, almost completely forgotten. He did begin a documentary film (with James Leahy) on the Chicago Seven trial in 1970, but later abandoned it. His most famous (and most personal) film remains *Rebel Without a Cause*.

Ray directed his first film in 1947: *They Live by Night*. He still lists it among his own personal favorites, the others being *Rebel Without a Cause*

(1955) and *Bigger Than Life* (1956).[1] Yet except for short notices in articles on *film noir* or reviews of *Bonnie and Clyde,* American critics have neglected this film, as they have its director. This lack of critical attention is unfortunate, for *They Live by Night* is a fine first effort. French critic François Truchaud has noted that it is "a statement which contains the premises of the themes of his work. It already has the makings of a masterpiece."[2]

They Live by Night came to be made primarily because of two important friendships Ray had cultivated during his professional career on the stage. The first was with Elia Kazan, whom he met in the 1930s, shortly after launching his career as a Broadway actor. In fact in 1935 Ray's first performance on the New York stage was directed by Kazan.[3] Ray and Kazan were associated in many theatrical projects during the next ten years. Thus when Kazan went to Hollywood to make his first film, *A Tree Grows in Brooklyn* (1945), he took Ray along as his assistant director. This was Ray's first contact with Hollywood and film production.

Ray's friendship with producer John Houseman also played a major role in initiating his film career. He first became associated with Houseman in the late 1930s, about the time Houseman and Orson Welles began the Mercury Theatre. After moving to radio in June 1938, the Mercury Theatre's fourth broadcast, "War of the Worlds," caused a national scandal. This and the show's general popularity brought Welles the necessary fame to attract the attention of Hollywood and to secure for him a contract at RKO. Houseman followed Welles to California, where he continued the radio show. After Pearl Harbor Houseman was appointed chief of radio programming for the overseas branch of the U.S. Office of War Information, and named Raymond Nicholas Kienzle, who became Nicholas Ray, his broadcast director. During and just after the war Houseman produced and Ray directed two successful Broadway plays: *Lute Song* (1943) and *Beggar's Holiday* (1946).

Another Ray-Houseman collaboration was their production of *Sorry Wrong Number* for CBS television in 1946. One of the first large television dramas, it was a success and inaugurated television theatre.

Sorry Wrong Number attracted the attention of Dore Schary, who had been hired as executive producer at RKO late in 1946. Schary, in an attempt both to free himself from the burden of large production costs and to vent

[1] Vincent Canby, "Unemployed Director—Nicholas Ray," *The New York Times,* June 8, 1969.
[2] François Truchaud, *Nicholas Ray* (Paris: Éditions Universitaires, 1965), p. 22.
[3] The play was *The Young Go First,* May 28, 1935.

publicly his liberal leanings, instituted an experiment of employing new young directors on what were B budget films, giving these directors virtually a free hand in their work. Among the films resulting from this experiment were Joseph Losey's *The Boy with Green Hair* (1948) and Edward Dmytryk's *Crossfire* (1947). In the early part of 1947 Schary was searching for someone to direct a project entitled *Your Red Wagon*. John Houseman agreed to produce the film, on the condition that Schary hire Nicholas Ray, then thirty-six years old, as its director.

Your Red Wagon was shot in forty-seven days and was completed during the week of August 21, 1947. It was retitled *The Twisted Road* and scheduled for national release in July 1948. In fact it was previewed during the week of June 30, 1948, quite favorably, at the Academy Award theatre in Hollywood before an all-press audience. Writing after this preview, William Weaver of *Motion Picture Herald* labeled it "good" and called Nicholas Ray's direction "outstanding."[4] *Variety* also liked it, despite some reservations about its attempt at social significance. *Variety* wrote: "Nicholas Ray adapted the novel and directed, demonstrating a complete understanding of the characters. It's a first rate job of moody story telling."[5]

The Twisted Road never reached the American audience at this time. In May 1948 Howard Hughes took control of RKO and almost immediately began to quarrel with Schary. In June 1948 Schary left the studio. For his own particular reasons Hughes put *The Twisted Road* in RKO's vaults (along with Robert Wise's *The Set-Up*, 1949), despite its favorable reaction from the press. Late in 1948, retitled *They Live by Night*, it was released in England, premiering at the Academy Cinema. Its critical reception was quite favorable. Gavin Lambert in *Sequence* 7 wrote: "Nicholas Ray's direction is striking: in the first half it is swift, compact, tense, with many expressive and appropriate angles, and always shows an original, very promising talent."[6] By all reports it was just as successful at the box office.

Finally Hughes, using his own magical intuitive formula for making decisions (he was thinking of selling RKO), released *They Live by Night* along with several other features in the United States. It first played in New York during the week of October 26, 1949. RKO tired to sell it as a hot-rod teen-age crime picture. A full page ad in *Variety* was headlined: "Cops or no cops, I'm going through!" The text of the ad explained what the film was

[4] Product Digest, *Motion Picture Herald*, June 30, 1948, p. 37.
[5] *Variety*, June 30, 1948, p. 19.
[6] Gavin Lambert, *"They Live by Night and The Window,"* Sequence, 7 (Spring 1949).

about: "Hot-rod teen-agers . . . living on the razor edge of danger . . . stumbling into crime . . . tumbling into love . . . too mixed up to know what they're doing."[7] Despite this misleading advertising, the few critics who reviewed it liked it. *The New Yorker's* John McCarten is typical: "Essentially a rather thin tale about an escaped convict with whom society eventually catches up, the film is enlivened by an excellent depiction of the bandit's flight, and by . . . Nicholas Ray's sure and unobtrusive direction."[8] Before more "intellectual" audiences Iris Barry championed the film by presenting it at a special showing at The Museum of Modern Art. But after its first release it dropped from sight, its only further exposure coming from repeated television showings throughout the 1950s and the 1960s.

In France its reception was not nearly so warm. It premiered at the Rendez-Vous de Biarritz theatre in 1950 to a hostile audience. André Bazin wrote at the time that the film didn't even remain there a week and that the spectators "left, livid with anger, advising the people who were waiting to see the film, not to see it!"[9] It took the critical interest of *Cahiers du Cinéma* throughout the 1950s to "rediscover" this film. Ray's most ardent supporter, Jean-Luc Godard, sums up the admiration for it best: *They Live by Night* may have had a "B budget, but it deserved A for ambition."[10]

This long discussion of the film's distribution is presented to set the record straight once and for all. It helps to explain the fact that three different release dates are given, depending on the source one consults. The story of how it was held up seems to be based primarily on John Houseman's interview in *Sight and Sound*,[11] but on at least one point his memory is incorrect. *Motion Picture Herald* lists the end of shooting during the week of August 21, 1947, and given a minimum amount of time to edit, assemble prints, etc., it rested in RKO's vaults at most *two* years, not the *three* that Houseman claims and Truchaud echoes.

On the first level *They Live by Night* is a fine example of *film noir*. This cycle of American films, which was to reach its peak in the late 1940s, was first noticed by French critics just after World War II. In viewing the deluge of American films that came to France at the close of the war, they noticed that a new mood had come over them, one of cynicism, pessimism,

[7] *Variety,* October 26, 1949, p. 23.
[8] John McCarten, "Current Cinema," *The New Yorker* (November 12, 1949), p. 83.
[9] Truchaud, *op. cit.*, p. 16.
[10] Jean-Luc Godard, quoted in Truchaud, *op. cit.*, p. 17.
[11] Penelope Houston, "Interview with John Houseman," *Sight and Sound* (Autumn 1962).

and darkness. In the succeeding years this mood became even more fatalistic, daring to examine subjects that had been taboo since the strict enforce-
ment of the production code by the Hays Office had begun. *Film noir,* as
Raymond Durgnat notes,[12] is not so much a genre as a tone or mood,
expressed in the films of many genres. *They Live by Night* embodies many
of the characteristics that identified this tone.

The very name *film noir* implies that most of the scenes in these films
take place at night. *They Live by Night* is not so extreme as some examples
of the *film noir; The Asphalt Jungle* (1950) contains at most three scenes
that could be called day lit. But most of the scenes in *They Live by Night*
do take place at night. More important though is the fact that the *key* scenes
occur at night. When Bowie, the film's central character, first meets Keechie,
their agreement to flee together after Bowie's participation in the Zelton
bank holdup, their marriage, Bowie's decision to take part in one more
holdup, and finally his death, *all* take place at night. This extreme use of
darkness, first detailed in *They Live by Night,* became characteristic of all
Ray's later work, and prompted François Truchaud to call him, "the cinéaste
of the twilight of the soul, of the falling night."[13]

For Ray, in *They Live by Night,* night serves two functions. First, it
liberates his characters. Bowie and Keechie are able to find each other, and
thus some measure of happiness, at night. It is during the daylight hours
that they must flee, and that Bowie commits his robberies. Likewise later in
Ray's career in *Rebel Without a Cause* James Dean is only able to express
his true emotions at night. In both films night is the world in which the
central characters are most free. Its direct counterpart is the daylight world
of respectable, conventional attitudes that restricts Ray's heroes. Second,
night is a symbol of death. Thus in *They Live by Night,* Bowie dies at night,
as does Plato in *Rebel Without a Cause.* In his first film, Nicholas Ray
blends, quite beautifully, these two symbolic uses of night: liberty and
death.

On a visual plane, the oblique lines characteristic of *film noir* recur
frequently in *They Live by Night.* They splinter the screen, and combined
with the ever present shadows help Ray create the film's mood of restlessness and instability. This method of lighting and composition, clearly influenced by German expressionism, was foreign to the American tradition of
clean horizontal lines, then being manifested by John Ford. Its use in *They*

[12] Raymond Durgnat, "The Family Tree of the Film Noir," *Cinema* (U.K.) (August
1970), p. 49.
[13] Truchaud, *op. cit.,* p. 18.

Live by Night is best illustrated in the film's final scene: as Bowie walks to the cabin to see Keechie "one last time," there are jagged lines of light crisscrossing his path from every direction. They are a visual warning to him (and to us) of the presence of too much instability in his universe. His death, only moments later, is the only event that can relieve this tension.

Ray makes excellent use of shadows in defining his characters and the situations in which they live. These shadows are everywhere, many times completely engulfing the actor, thus equating him with the objects that surround him. This creates a powerful sense of suffocation and confinement. It seems as if Bowie and Keechie are never able to break out of their straitjacket into the daylight world. Their few moments of pure joy come only in their car as they flee or in their "honeymoon" bungalow, and these are the only times they escape from the shadows around them.

Thus these shadows serve as the film's antagonist. The usual antagonist in *film noir*, the police, are presented only three times throughout the film, although we are reminded from time to time of their constant pursuit of the couple. When the police do appear, they possess a completely indifferent attitude toward the couple. Their presentation lacks the usual bite of the *film noir*. But in actuality their presence is never needed for the constant shadows serve in their place. Thus it is only proper that in the end the police emerge from the shadows, kill Bowie, and retreat almost as quickly as they came.

Ray combines all these elements of lighting style with an exciting use of the camera. Leaning on his experience in the theatre, he always portrays the actions as moving around his actors rather than having them control the action. This style helps give his films their famous emotional impact. In the Zelton holdup, we are never shown Bowie's partners, T-Dub and Chicamaw, performing the actual robbery. Rather the camera, as in *Gun Crazy*, is placed with Bowie in the getaway car. The jeweler from whom Bowie had purchased a watch for Keechie only days before spots him waiting and walks over to talk. Realizing T-Dub and Chicamaw are about to emerge from the bank, Bowie shoves him away. The two bandits exit from the bank, Bowie drives up, and they escape. Only then, after the trio is safely away, does Ray, like Joseph H. Lewis, change the camera's viewpoint and cut from inside the car to a full shot of the three men.

Decor and physical objects also play an important role in Ray's films. In *They Live by Night* a simple gift, the watch Bowie buys for Keechie, serves Ray as a symbol on a number of different levels. First it is a symbol of the growing love between Bowie and Keechie. This is later reinforced when Keechie returns the favor and gives Bowie a watch for Christmas. When Keechie attempts to set her new watch, both she and Bowie realize they have no idea what time it is, so she sets the watch for the time it happens to read. This symbolizes the couple's innocence and reinforces the film's opening title: "this is a couple who were never properly introduced into the world which we live in." Later, just prior to their marriage, probably the single most important event in either of their young lives, Keechie reads Bowie the time from her new watch: "it's ten minutes to twelve." This links together the symbols of love and innocence. Ray continues the use of this symbol, following it to its logical conclusion. Yet he does not try to press its significance too hard. After Bowie has made what turns out to be his most important moral decision, and is just about to leave to execute what is to be his final bank robbery, Keechie tries to warn him of the danger and at the same time remind him of her love. Thus she simply repeats this key phrase, "It's ten minutes to twelve, Bowie." He turns, realizing what she has said, yet leaves anyway.

One motif of decor in Ray's work, first employed in *They Live by Night,* is what V. F. Perkins has called "the concept of upstairs." Probably the most famous example of this motif comes in *Johnny Guitar* (1954). In that film Vienna (Joan Crawford) lives at the top of a long flight of stairs, away from the gambling tables of her saloon. They represent her isolation. In *They Live by Night* the "stairs" represent the couple's escape from their usual world into one more innocent and pure. Stairs are used only twice in this film. When Bowie and Keechie walk up to Hawkins' marriage parlor in order to be wed, they first climb a short flight of stairs. Later their happiest moments come in a bungalow, away from the other cabins, also up a short flight of stairs. In both these moments—among the happiest they are to share—the couple is escaping from a world of harsh reality into one more private and secluded.

Thematically *They Live by Night* fits into the third section (of eleven) in Raymond Durgnat's classification of *film noir:* On the run.[14] Durgnat's classification system is very broad: he includes both *The Informer* (1935) and *You Only Live Once* (1937) in this category. *They Live by Night*'s closest relatives in what is traditionally accepted as *film noir* are Anthony Mann's *Desperate* (1947) and Joseph H. Lewis' *Gun Crazy* (1949). Its proper historical antecedent in the American cinema is Fritz Lang's *You*

[14] Durgnat, *op. cit.,* p. 53.

Only Live Once. These four movies, along with William Witney's *The Bonnie Parker Story* (1958) and Arthur Penn's *Bonnie and Clyde* (1967), virtually form a separate subcategory, in Durgnat's system, of films loosely or closely based on the legend of Bonnie Parker and Clyde Barrow. All are characterized by a narrative in which a man and a woman attempt to flee from the police, performing robberies for a variety of reasons preceding or during their flight. Only the last two, however, deal directly with the Bonnie and Clyde legend. *Gun Crazy,* for instance, is based on a McKinley Kantor short story for *The Saturday Evening Post,* and *They Live by Night* is derived from a novel by Edward Anderson, *Thieves Like Us,* adapted for the screen by Nicholas Ray.

On the surface the structure of *They Live by Night* seems to contain many elements of tragedy. The tragic form usually involves one man, here Bowie, using all his powers in a struggle with an already determined outcome: his fate. Classically this man possesses a single flaw in his makeup that, as he strives to regain his position in the moral order, eventually leads to his downfall. Thus at the end of *They Live by Night* Bowie must accept his fate, death, since he has failed to gain a place in law-abiding society. He has struggled on his own terms according to his own moral code and failed.

Bowie's single flaw is his innocence. He has only the experience of a teen-age youth, having been in jail since the age of sixteen. He totally relies on T-Dub, Chicamaw, and Hawkins, the marriage broker, for his guidance, and seems to be aware of no other sources of counsel outside this closed universe. It is thus easily understood why in the end he is unable to escape from their world into one of respectability. He has taken on some of the characteristics of the "daylight" world: he is frugal, does not drink, and strives to plan for the future. Yet he can never fit into respectable society, only into a halfway world between crime and normality. Since he is incapable of fitting into the order of either world, he is threatened by both. His only self-realization can be his death.

In the strictest sense *They Live by Night* can never be considered a pure tragedy because Bowie lacks the necessary heroic stature. His fate is determined by his crushing environment: the lack of any family life as a child, and the implied mistreatment by the courts. Bowie is the product of forces beyond his control; he lacks the opportunity to make *any* moral judgment that could significantly alter his position in the universe. In short, he can't be considered a pure tragic figure, because he isn't able to fall. The character of Bowie descends more from the tradition of American naturalism and realism. He is the innocent victim of society's inhuman rules and conventions. It is only when he tries to live beyond his environmental boundaries, beyond the worlds of law and crime, that he achieves a sense of nobility and thus creates the tragic sense of the film.

A current of nineteenth-century romanticism, which was to surface in much of Ray's later work, was first manifested in *They Live by Night*. Here he first established the rebellious youth, with all his purity and love, attempting to discover his own individual sense of order in the face of a corrupt society. The romantic's love of spontaneity and nature is also presented for the first time by Ray in *They Live by Night*.

The couple's spontaneity is beautifully portrayed in the few moments Bowie and Keechie are able to spend alone in their bungalow hideaway. For a few precious days they are free to revel in their mutual love and innocence, to act as naturally and instinctively as they wish. Their natural expressions of love are even more strongly felt because of the constant danger the couple always faces. Jacques Rivette described it best when he spoke of the "taste for paroxysm, where the most restful moments are still marked by something feverish and temporary."[15] Rivette's description also fits James Dean's visit to the planetarium in *Rebel Without a Cause,* and is also characteristic of a number of other moments in Ray's later work.

The emphasis the romantics placed on nature and landscape is beautifully represented by Bowie's casual remarks about his desire to travel. During the couple's trip to New Orleans, they cross the Mississippi River. This reminds Bowie of earlier statements he has made, and he again tells Keechie, "Someday I'd like to see all of this country," motioning with his hand, "its mountains, its rivers." Here Ray becomes most personal; he himself had made such a trip, into the Rockies and around the American West, in the late 1930s. His interest in nature was to play an even stronger role in many of his later films. In *The Savage Innocents* (1961) it is the primitive man, Inuk (Anthony Quinn), who is threatened from the outside civilized world. Nature was also to play an important role in *Johnny Guitar* and *Wind Across the Everglades* (1958).

In this same spirit, happiness can only come to Bowie and Keechie when they are away from civilization and closer to nature. It is in their bungalow, the furthest from the road and civilization of all the cabins, or later in their walk in the park and by the bridle path that they find moments of true happiness. Only when they flee to New Orleans, following Chica-

---

[15] Jacques Rivette, *Cahiers du Cinéma*, No. 5, p. 20.

maw's advice ("it is the best place to get lost in the crowds") are they actually physically threatened. Instead of finding their recreation in the simpler, more natural pleasures of life, they go to the artificial world of a nightclub. Here they must keep on reassuring each other that they are having a "good time," for there is a mood of extreme tension throughout their whole visit. This tension climaxes when a drunk falls on their table, creates a commotion, and draws attention to their presence. As they leave, Bowie stops momentarily in the bathroom, is recognized, and is *told* for the first time that he isn't wanted in respectable society. His life is in danger from forces he can see, and the long arm of fate, first represented by the helicopter shots during and just after the opening credits, is just about to catch up with him.

But it is the romantic's stress on individualism that is central to *They Live by Night* and all of Ray's later work. One only has to examine *Johnny Guitar,* with Vienna the individual against the hysterical mob, or *Rebel Without a Cause,* with James Dean struggling with himself and his family, for examples in the subsequent films. In fact Ray's most successful films always center around a single character, his relations with the opposite sex, and his quest for financial security and spiritual happiness. Usually these individuals are young; if they are not, they are treated in many ways as youths. Notice the proliferation of youthful names, even of middle-aged characters: Jeff in *The Lusty Men* (1952) or Tommy in *Party Girl* (1958). In *They Live by Night* this youthful individual is, of course, Bowie. Despite the misleading title, typical of Ray's work, the narrative centers around his quest for adjustment. His associations, even with Keechie, can never free him from *his* own struggle. Ultimately it is he who must rebel, escape, flee, and die.

Ray's view of romanticism in *They Live by Night* (and his later films) is a very pessimistic one. His individuals are always intruders in a turbulent, indifferent, and chaotic world. Their "friends" and enemies (such as Chicamaw and Mattie) are continually represented as persons who cannot recognize their own irrational desires, a fact that makes it almost impossible for the protagonists to deal with these people or even understand them. This irrationality is most pronounced in Ray's villains, the most famous example being Emma (Mercedes McCambridge) in *Johnny Guitar;* her sexual hysteria almost leads her to lynch Vienna, to burn Vienna's saloon to the ground, and finally to attempt to shoot her. In *They Live by Night* Mattie, the bandit trio's assistant and T-Dub's sister-in-law, is a forerunner of Emma. She is driven by an almost fatalistic desire to free her husband, feeling that that action alone can alter her existence and make her happy. Mattie sees in Bowie a facsimile of her husband. She hates him because she, almost in the role of fate, alone understands what will eventually happen to him. But it is her jealousy of Keechie, who has the potential not to repeat Mattie's mistake of marriage, that torments her the most. She sees in Keechie an image of herself, before her awful marriage, at a time when there was still hope. Thus at the end of the film she is naturally quite willing to exchange the knowledge of Bowie's whereabouts for the immediate release of her husband. This is the only "hope" that she feels is still open to her since she is unable to rewrite the past.

They Live by Night expresses a sense of pessimism in yet another way. A constant feeling of loneliness is conveyed by all the major characters in the film. This also is a theme that will play an important role in Ray's later films. Bowie and Keechie are almost always alone in their flight from the police, meeting few people, and making no real friends. Even prior to their initial meeting they had been very alone in their own respective worlds. Bowie expresses his feeling of solitude best when he tells Keechie about the "crime" he committed, which secured for him his sentence of life in prison. He was not a member of the gang that committed the robbery ("I only went along to see how it was done"). When the man was killed, the others ran; he, alone, did not. Keechie also was friendless as a child. She tells Bowie that she has no idea "what the other girls did." Both find a temporary resolution for their past loneliness in this new relationship.

All these important thematic elements come to bear in what is probably the most important scene in the film, in which Bowie decides to perform one last robbery. This shatters (as Chicamaw does the Christmas bulb) the momentary happiness the couple has known, and eventually will lead to Bowie's death. In this key scene Bowie makes his most important moral decision. Keechie begs him not to perform the robbery, and clearly they have enough money to live on for a while. But Bowie, struggling with himself, *feels* that he must complete one more holdup because of the attachment he has to his cell mates, Chicamaw and T-Dub. They had been his only "friends" in jail and he feels he cannot desert them now. He wants to be honest, and even momentarily attempts to decline participation. But they threaten him physically and he quickly accedes. His naïveté prevents him from realizing that rationally this is a large error in judgment. Yet always the decision is shrouded in a cloud of pessimism; whichever way he turns, he is threatened. His "friends" intimidate him physically and the police still seek him. He is caught in a dilemma from which there is no escape.

Most of Ray's important themes and the beginnings of his singular technical style are evidenced in *They Live by Night*. But with too much analysis one tends to lose sight of what is the essential beauty of his films: the integration of these various themes and technical style. The emotional power of his films, combined with their sensitivity to personal adjustments, first attracted the French critics to his side. As time passes, trends in film criticism change. Today criticism is primarily concerned with the social and political elements of a film, as manifested by a director's style. Thus a study of personal rebellion is analyzed in the context of the various social movements present in the film. Perhaps film criticism will shift course in the near future and concern itself with more romantic, thus individualistic, works, such as those done by Nicholas Ray. If so, then Ray will be "rediscovered," this time by the critics in his own country, and *They Live by Night* will be recognized as the fine film it is.

Note: The author wishes to thank Melissa Kepner for her help with the translations of the French texts.

THE PHENIX CITY STORY: "THIS WILL HAPPEN TO YOUR KIDS, TOO"* (1971)

MARK BERGMAN

In the summer of 1954, in a series of events that sent the writers back to the Chicago of Al Capone for comparison, the apparently somnolent town of Phenix City, Alabama,[1] became nationally famous as "Sin City." Prostitution, gambling, and drugs flourished openly in Phenix City, along with more esoteric rackets like a safecrackers' school and a black market baby ring, but only after the murder of the state's attorney general elect was the citizenry moved to demand a cleanup. All this is the stuff of which grade B thrillers are made, and the very next year, right in Sin City itself, one was: *The Phenix City Story.*

---

* Copyright © 1973 by John Davis and Susan Dalton. Reprinted from *The Velvet Light Trap,* No. 4 (1971).

[1] *Phenix* City, not Phoenix City. Leonard Maltin, Steven Sheuer, Colin McArthur, and Stuart Kaminsky, all of whom should know better, are in error.

I

Officially known as Lively and unofficially as Sodom when it was founded in the early 1800s by runaway blacks and renegade whites, Phenix City was long known for violence and lawlessness. A haven for deserters during the Civil War, the town later attracted pleasure-seeking soldiers from Fort Benning, located across the Chattahoochee River at Columbus, Georgia. During World War II, when Phenix City vice lords ran "mattress vans," canvas-covered pickup trucks containing girls, to the very gates of Fort Benning, Phenix City had the highest venereal disease rate in the nation. General Patton, in command of the base, threatened to clean up Sin City with tanks, and Secretary of War Stimson angrily declared "Phenix City is the wickedest city in the United States."[2] Political pressure was exerted, however, each time Phenix City was placed off limits.

Reform movements arose from time to time as they are wont to do, but each was thwarted by the entrenched criminal element, which in fact had deeper roots in the community than did the reformers. Mostly the average citizen merely ignored the goings-on on notorious Fourteenth Street, and much of it was even regarded as normal:

> As a boy I would spend my leisure time playing the slot machines with no sense of wrongdoing. They would be found not only in the honky-tonks but in the drug and grocery stores and clothing shops, even within two blocks of the high school. They came equipped with wooden stools for those too short to reach the handle.[3]

In 1951 the reform element, made up of a handful of pious businessmen and a semisecret ladies auxiliary and kept small and ineffective by threats of economic reprisal and violence (murders of soldiers were said to be commonplace), found a leader in Albert A. Patterson, a local lawyer and former state legislator, who began to direct the Russell (County) Betterment Association's legal campaign against Phenix City's mob. In 1954, feeling that the only way to get results was to gain statewide power, he ran for attorney general, narrowly winning the Democratic nomination despite a massive

[2] William Slocum, "America's Wickedest City," *Look* XVIII, No. 20 (October 5, 1954), p. 20.
[3] John M. Patterson (as told to Burman Bisher), "I'll Get the Gangs That Killed My Father!," *Saturday Evening Post* CCXXVII, No. 14 (November 27, 1954), p. 20.

criminal attempt to defeat him by voter intimidation, ballot buying, and alteration of returns. Even though the nomination virtually assured election in solid Alabama, Patterson was pessimistic, telling a Phenix City gathering, "I believe I have only one chance out of one hundred of being sworn in."[4] The next day, June 14, 1954, he was gunned down outside his law office.

Reaction was instantaneous. Governor Persons, who had previously dismissed Phenix City's notoriety as "undeserved,"[5] dispatched the National Guard. The less static criminal element, sensing doom, had already fled, while the hard-core homegrown variety, mostly descendants of the riffraff that founded the town, stayed to weather yet another storm.

A new grand jury returned 749 indictments for offenses ranging from gambling to murder; gambling equipment was confiscated and destroyed; a reform ticket was swept into office under the watchful eye of the National Guard. Church leaders, who had been prominent among the intimidated, rose to the occasion by requesting that Billy Graham revive the city, and *The Christian Century* gleefully reported that

> The impotence of the churches to deal with deeply rooted vice was revealed in the satisfaction with which they greeted the state-sponsored cleanup. Ministerial and church groups now are making themselves felt in the selection of new primary candidates and in the purging of voting lists and jury rolls.[6]

II

The Phenix City Story (1955) would be a notable film if only for its extraordinary toughness in an era of consumptive B pictures. Although contemporary audiences might have found the film's headline sensationalism enthralling, most of its power today lies in its uncompromising, documentary-style evocation of violence and evil. Comparison with other exposé-type movies of the time (*The Tijuana Story*, 1957; *Inside Detroit*, 1955) will indicate the possible fate of even the most promising story in less sure hands.

Director Phil Karlson's best films—*Tight Spot* (1955), *Five Against the House* (1955), *The Brothers Rico* (1957), *Hell to Eternity* (1960)—present a consistent theme of betrayal, violence, and revenge and an admirable

---

[4] "The Odds Were Right," *Time* LXIII, No. 26 (June 28, 1954), p. 22.
[5] Slocum, *op. cit.*, p. 36.
[6] "Alabama's Year One of Sorrow," *The Christian Century* LXXI, No. 42 (October 20, 1954), p. 1284.

bluntness of style acquired, probably, in his years at Monogram. More powerful than the King of the B Movie, Fred F. Sears (though lacking Sears's improbable humor and wild energy), more consistent than Joseph H. Lewis, and definitely more self-controlled and "establishment" than Fuller (if Fuller is the *National Enquirer,* Karlson is the *Daily News*), Karlson brings class and intelligence even to the reprehensible Matt Helm films he is subjected to today.

(*The Phenix City Story* is prefaced with a newsreel-style sequence entitled "Report from Phenix City, Alabama," in which reporter Clete Roberts conducts interviews with people prominent in the town's cleanup. Although it lends documentation to the film's horrors, the general effect is that of afterthought and padding. Roberts seems bored, patronizing, and often at a loss for words, and it appears that his close-ups were shot to tie together older interview footage. In contrast, the staged newsreel footage at the end of the film is fast and effective, making questionable Karlson's part in the prologue.)

The Crane Wilbur–Dan Mainwaring screenplay laces the cold hard facts of the Phenix City story with cold hard fiction. Their aim is not documentary but drama and every addition or alteration introduces an element of tension and shapes the film's themes of violence and corruption. Time is compressed, or rather, events are taken from fact and placed into a fictional time span to make a more tenable narrative. New characters are introduced, some obviously based on fact, others merely types, but all under the influence of the mob leaders. The boy-girl subplot has a nice air of inevitability, and John Patterson's hysterical wife and kids give a strident urgency to the removal of the evil. The made-up criminal violence seems a logical extension of established fact.

Karlson emphasizes the sleaziness of the infamous Fourteenth Street even to the extent of punctuating all his forays into it with a raunchy blues riff, but he never loses sight of the cancerous nature of the area and its deadly danger to the larger community. All transitions from the neon block of loan sharks, honky-tonks, and gambling dens to the more conventional parts of town are accomplished with dissolves: Fourteenth Street seems to hover over the entire city, whether the respectable home of Patterson or the shack of Zeke (James Edwards, once again pushing a broom) and his family, inexplicably the only blacks in the movie.

The mob's spies and thugs are everywhere, perched high above the milling crowd in Rhett Tanner's saloon, lurking in alleyways, installed in the police department, and even agitating in the ranks of the reform movement.

As their actions become more blatantly violent the stated comparison of the town's situation with a dictatorship becomes self-evident. Intimidation of the opposition (punching out a dissatisfied cardplayer, beating up reformers in an alley while the police look on, the abduction and murder of Zeke's little girl—she is tossed on Patterson's lawn with a note reading: "This will happen to your kids too," sort of a Phenix City "Stay out of the North Side"), intimidation of the general public (houses are blown up, bricks are thrown through the windows of churches, newsboys are roughed up, voters are bought off with booze and women or advised how to vote by big, mean rednecks), and political assassination follow in rapid succession. It is the central irony of *The Phenix City Story* that John Patterson returns from several years of prosecuting war criminals to encounter a very real totalitarianism at work in the old hometown.

The traditional, hometown nature of Phenix City's vice industry provides a sense of collaboration. The ringleader Tanner (Edward Andrews, the best of a number of fine performances in the movie) strolls affably around town, inquiring about the health of children and expressing regret at missing a fire-and-brimstone sermon on the Sodom and Gomorrah theme. Gambling, he tells Patterson, "was good enough for my father and his father before him—yours too." It's also good enough for Ellie Rhodes (Kathryn Grant), who deals marked cards in Tanner's joint, and, by implication, for Patterson who once defended a gang member from a murder charge and now expresses a "Who am I to try to reform it" attitude that complements Tanner's view that "half the trouble with the people in the world today is they just don't want to let things stay the way they are."

It is only after the mob's "This will happen to your kids too" threat to his own children that Patterson is moved to oppose them, knowing that their fear of him as a political force makes his action doubly dangerous. Now the terrorism, begun with the brutal attack on reformers Gage, Britten, and Bentley, becomes more overt, and a palpable air of paranoia settles over Phenix City. Patterson's determined campaigning has an air of fatality underlined by the constant menacing presence of Tanner and his henchmen. Nevertheless, Patterson's murder, with the same shadowy figures emerging from the same alley as in the previous attack to fire two point-blank shots, is shocking in its suddenness.

Karlson finally allows the heroes an all-too-brief moment of purgative retaliation as John Patterson confronts Tanner, who has just eliminated Ellie, the only witness to the murder. It is an open question whether he will beat Tanner to death or drown him, until Zeke, who has very nearly fallen victim himself, intervenes with the obligatory "This is what we've been fighting against" plea. The picture closes with an earnest promise by John Patterson, now elected attorney general in his father's place, to root out and destroy any remaining corruption in Phenix City.

It is clear, however, that just as the cretinous Clem Wilson (John Larch), the agent of most of *The Phenix City Story*'s violence, is the tool of Tanner, so is Tanner the tool of higher-ups, faceless men referred to throughout and glimpsed as the film ends. This unobtrusive pessimism is just one of the vestigial *film noir* elements that permeate the film: low angles, lights hanging low from ceilinged sets, sleek cars on wet streets, and the all-pervasive paranoia.

It would be easy to equate the Phenix City situation with any of a number of prominent foreign "isms." Mainwaring wrote the screenplay for Don Siegel's hysterial red menace picture *Invasion of the Body Snatchers* (1956) and John Larch's mouth-breathing redneck is as soulless as any commie-cum-space-monster. Nor is *The Phenix City Story* the celebration of American democracy that the prologue would make it. Rather, it is a pointed commentary on postwar America, with the implication that peace and freedom are as far removed as ever, even in the era of Eisenhower.

Arthur Ripley

THUNDER ROAD: MAUDIT—"THE DEVIL GOT HIM FIRST"* (1969)

RICHARD THOMPSON

Let me tell the story,
I can tell it all,
About the mountain boy who ran illegal alcohol.
His Daddy made the whisky,
Son he drove the load,
And when his engine roared they called the highway Thunder Road.

Sometimes into Asheville,
Sometimes Memphis town,
The revennooers chased him but they couldn't run him down.
Each time they thought they had him,
His engine would explode,
And he'd go by like they were standing still on Thunder Road.

Thunder, thunder, over Thunder Road,
Thunder was his engine and white lightnin' was his load.
Moonshine, moonshine, to quench the devil's thirst,
The law they swore they'd get him but the devil got him first.
—ROBERT MITCHUM, "The Ballad of Thunder Road"

Foreign critics have begun applying an important concept to film: the idea of the *maudit*—the damned, the disreputable, the illegitimate—a mode of creation that threatens the respectability of art itself. The idea found its way to film because the movies provide us with more compelling works existing outside the boundaries of traditional Western culture than most other art forms. One interesting implication of *maudit* is that the movie—and so, any medium—can liberate itself from art, and once liberated, no barrier exists between the medium, the audience, and the soul of the work. When this admirable state is reached, the raw texture of the work is rubbed across our minds. Such a work is Robert Mitchum's *Thunder Road*.

Why single out *Thunder Road*? Why burden the precarious progress of the writer's dubious reputation with such an outrageous and easily ridiculed association? Why isn't this article about *Bullitt* (1968) or *Les Yeux Sans Visage* (*Horror Chamber of Dr. Faustus*, 1959) or Stanley Baker? Because I suspect that nourishing the root of every writer's passion for movies is an irrational love for a type of film that drives and informs his examination of all other films. In these other films the critic seeks an objective key to his private obsession. Big-time slick reviewers deal their instincts from the bottom by either patronizing such affections out of existence or rationalizing them into respectability. Either course proves to be a disservice to the works involved. What is called for is some perspective on the alchemical existence of these films.

Thunder Road came out in 1958, designed for ozoners and grind houses, and since then has made the late-show circuit. As a work, it shrinks from art straight toward its own truth. It transcends the limits of art because it is uncompromised by any elevated artistic intent: it exists at the white-hot juncture of fact and legend. The film's being is completely determined by the anti-art genius of Robert Mitchum: star, author of the story, composer and singer of the film's hit song, father of the second romantic lead, and producer. It is the film of Mitchum's in which he is most deeply involved on the most levels—a considerable contrast to his current peekaboo position in films "Starring Dean Martin and Robert Mitchum," with two hours of the former and ten minutes of the latter.

Thunder Road has a long-standing underground reputation among recent films. It has a following as devoted as *One-Eyed Jacks'* (1961), and as intense as *The Wild One's* (1953), before everybody picked up on it. Its reputation is truly underground in the shibbolethic sense, unlike such relatively fashionable films as *Rio Bravo* (1959) and *Shadows* (1961). This following surprises people, much as they are surprised to learn that Don Siegel's *Flaming Star* (1960), an Elvis Presley Western, has an underground reputation in urban black high schools.

Wound up in this curious acclaim is a cultural bond of the devoted, a communion that renders the film's significance immune to standard criticism. *Thunder Road* was tastefully sold down the river by major reviewers, presumably because by any accepted critical standard the film is garbage. It was not made for critics. The film exists for a postwar subculture built on adolescence, cars, roads, night, windows rolled down, sleeves rolled up, and Chuck Berry on the radio. Traditional works of narrative art can be set in locales and circumstances unfamiliar to the audience, but which are still open to vicarious participation that does no damage to the success of the work. Not so *Thunder Road*. It is a work whose charm is open only to those who have firsthand knowledge of the world it depicts. Not moonshine smuggling, which is only the plot pretext, but the ambience of night driving, which convinces us that life is one long four-wheel drift. Audiences must be primed with this experience in order to recognize and respond to Mitchum's vision, a truly *maudit* vision, because by its very form and structure it is damned. A work like this frustrates critics straining to infuse popular art with culture, because it brings them face to face with an audience for whom criticism is irrelevant and *art* a school word. For this group *Thunder Road* is a private myth irradiating the secret corners of a lost existence with the savor of true existentialism.

An instructive comparison for understanding this elusive *maudit* quality is that of Dean Martin and Robert Mitchum. In their screen persona and their recordings, both trade on tailored country and western malaise. Similarities also arise in their casual offscreen characters. The crucial distinction is that Dino is a careful, conscious construction stage-managed by Dean Martin. If Mitchum represents no such sense of self, it is because his divinity allows no separation of action, expression, and reflection.

Thunder Road disciples envy those who saw it exactly right: at a drive-in, sitting in their customed Fords and Chevs, just after leaving the high school dance and just before juking on down to Shakey's Pizza Parlor. The film's base is the mystique of the cheapo, with all its gaudy, vital economy of imagery. Mitchum the moonshine runner and his girl Keely Smith are talking in a roadside cocktail lounge. She wants him to quit; he says after just this one last trip. The scene is filled with wistful pathos. Mitchum asks her to put a nickle in the jukebox, and the camera follows her to the machine; she puts in the nickle, and turns to say something to Mitchum. Then, as we follow her gaze to the empty booth, we hear the double-time twangy guitar and squealing sax record over the roar of Mitchum's car pulling away.

Elements of the film suggest better-known directors, and a cult-hero auteur at the helm would undoubtedly have brought the film greater attention: the attention paid to Don Siegel's loners, their private codes undermined by the vicious order of a disintegrating community; or Phil Karlson's three-way struggle between the individual, the ineffectual federal government, and the nearly allegorical syndicate; or Raoul Walsh's flawed hero, presented with extreme charisma in a setting that hints at his cosmic stature; or Anthony Mann's moral fetishism of cars, roads, tools, and lights. Mitchum chose none of these accomplished underground poets to shape his most personal film. Instead, he put longtime enigma Arthur Ripley in the director's chair. The brilliance of this strategy rests on two phenomena: (a) Ripley's Stone Age flat shooting style; (b) the complete dissipation of Ripley's minor personal style into ecstatic incoherence whenever a profound theme sneaks into his films. *Thunder Road*'s themes push Ripley over this line, leaving Mitchum's conception virtually unaltered. The film looks like a cheap Hollywood imitation of newsreel style. The obviousness of the interior sets confounds one's perception of reality in the film; it seems that Mitchum is so alienated that he is denied even the reality of shacks, garages, and motels. Like most cheapies, *Thunder Road* falls back on location shooting for the road scenes, thus directly rendering the mysterious and appropriate connection between Robert Mitchum and neon honky-tonky mainstreets. The hard actuality of the road sequences playing against the cardboard interiors amplifies the distinction between existence off the road and life on it.

Thunder Road is the saga of Luke Doolin, played by Robert Mitchum. His family has brewed moonshine in their ancestral hollow since before the Revolution, like the other independent distillers. They form a loose co-op, united to protect a man's born right to make and sell anything he wants to, provided it is by the sweat of his brow and the tilling of his soil. This cottage industry buoys up the Appalachian standard of living in the Doolin neighborhood. Doolin himself is the oldest of the area's good old boys, the best backroad lightnin' driver around. He runs superstocks filled with corn whiskey down the mountains and into the cities. His natural antagonists are Revenue Agents and syndicate gangsters. The T-Men are led by Gene Barry, a Northerner regarded with suspicion by the hill people. Though responsible for shutting down illegal liquoring, Barry is most concerned with breaking up the big-city syndicate. The gangsters want to take over the independent stills and their urban markets, by force if necessary, thus depriving honest men of their dignity and the rewards of their industry. Although the factory is the neighbor of cottage industry in technological evolution, the cultural gulf separating the two is enormous.

In the drama, the political relations between these groups are rapidly brought into focus. The sincere but ineffectual federal government seems to defer to each man's right to individualism, while taking away its basis in privacy and free will. The ruthlessness of the syndicate calls into question all impersonal bureaucracies handing down decisions, from the top to flunkies. The fundamental validity of the farmer's co-op is based on each individual's autonomy within his own land and time, and on an equal role in participatory democracy as the mechanism through which they govern their destinies. The film stops short of right-wing diatribe when it demonstrates that competition, division of labor, and specialization are not healthy, but generate violence, degradation, and institutional murder.

Cutting short the implied gloss of separate stages of economic development (rural individualism, syndicate warfare, state control), we step into the garish light of metaphysical aesthetics—*plan français*. These stages have a one-to-one relationship with the thematic past, present, and future of the film. The entrepreneurial figure linking the three states of economic life, Doolin/Mitchum—the one man possessing the social skills to deal with all the forces in the drama—is also an existential pluperfect-subjunctive tense linking the antagonistic conjugations of the film.

The backwoods valley itself is a pocket of the past, guided by a strong heritage of family, land, pious labor, and constitutional privacy. The government is an unwelcome but potentially benevolent intrusion of national organization, a concept alien to the hill people (see also *Sergeant York*, 1941). The government stands for present-tense law, order, cooperation, and guidance, demanding a sacrifice of privacy and independence. The mountain people scrupulously deal more honestly with the government than it deals with them. When Barry crashes a still and offers the proprietor the choice of handcuffs or appearing at a federal court at ten on Monday morning, the local says, "I'll sure-hell be there," and we know he will. The liquor syndicate is the organized destroyer of communities, of individual industry, of a man's pride. It achieves its ends by raw fiscal and physical violence. Its base is the city; its tentacles strangle the country by controlling the roads.

Mitchum stands apart from all these groups. While the hillmen are at home on their farms, while Barry is at home in his righteous crusade, while the gangsters are very much at home in urban corruption, Mitchum has left his birthplace for the world, and now has no home. When his girl, Keely Smith, tells him he might be killed and never see home again, Mitchum talks about ". . . all those dead heroes on their benches in heaven, just heartsick for home. I'd be heartsick for home too, if I knew where it was." It is this American fillip that Godard makes explicit in *Alphaville* (1965): the realization by the hero, the dynamic center of the film, that he has passed from a normal position in the world into the anachronistic godhood of legend— without dying first. Biographical parallel: Mitchum claims to have served time on a Georgia chain gang when he was a kid, to have escaped, and to have been in technical jeopardy when he returned there to shoot *Cape Fear* (1961).

But the dying is to come. Death hangs over the film, always linked with the subthemes of mobility and change. Again the filmmakers bypass inherently conservative attitudes by making it clear that the only escape, the only direction for life, is into the future. Luke's younger brother, played by Jim Mitchum, itches to haul hooch too. But the kid has a natural technical aptitude, he talks about building cars with turbines and ramjets, and Luke's major commitment in the film is to keep his brother bound for engineering school and off the road. It is in this scene that we begin to feel that the road is right only for those who have nothing else.

Mitchum seals his death with the *maudit* classicism of the gangster: he forgoes the loner's code to do something for someone else. Actions that grow from an interior code beyond worldly temptation, unselfish commitments to other persons, are the death warrants of the gangster genre: they always cause his downfall. When his brother decides to run a load of dew into what Luke knows to be a syndicate setup, he cuts off the kid and goes himself. Along the line, he holes up in cabin Number 13 at a motel, runs through the "Please don't go"—"It's my last trip, honest" exchange with Keely Smith (who refers to him as "The only natural man I ever knew"), and tries to reassure her by asking her to hold several hundred dollars for him until he

comes back. He tops it off with a familiar Mitchum gesture: the announce-
ment to his antagonist, the mob chief, that he is coming in to get him right
now. Usually in Mitchum films this is done by telephone, as here, in *Cape
Fear*, and in *The Angry Hills* (1959), but sometimes it's face to face, as in
The Night Fighters (1960).

Why are these familiar images employed? Because they invoke the
proven magic of a tradition. This is, after all, generic rather than experimental art—evolutionary rather than revolutionary—even if the genre is
Mitchum.

Death as an event occurs several times in the film, but always with the
violence so underplayed that *Dragnet* seems an orgy of senseless brutality
by comparison. When Mitchum uses violence, it is first pragmatic, then
expressive. In the well-guarded office of the liquor syndicate *kapo*, the hard-
boys threaten to get Luke's kid brother. With no change of his insolent,
bored expression, Mitchum judo chops the boss, rings the alarm on the desk,
and jumps out a second-story window. Within ten seconds, he is snaking his
Ford onto the road.

Deaths occur only on the road. Mitchum sends two other drivers
hurtling into the pinewoods at top rpm, because in practice they threaten
him while in gesture they dare question his skill by challenging him on his
road: they attempt to disturb an Aristotelian harmony of all the elements
under Mitchum's control. Mitchum dispatches one with a flick of the wrist,
spraying oil from his tailpipe onto the road, the simple gesture dripping
with disdain for a challenger so easily shucked off. The other comes abreast
of Mitchum, trying to run him off the road. Again, Mitchum straineth not.
He flips his cigarette from his right-hand window through the other car's
driver-side window into the face of his opponent. Bingo. In neither case do
we dwell on the victim. The simple fact of leaving the road becomes a
metaphor for death, because the road is a creative life-force in the midst of
living oblivion.

Mitchum's own death is more dramatic, in the high-octane tradition of
Raoul Walsh's *White Heat* (1949). Before the eyes of the protective federal
agents, Mitchum's car is put into a spin by a bed of spikes the gangsters
have laid across the road. His death comes not at the hands of another man,
a bullet, or even his car, but from millions of volts of electricity as he plows
through a TVA substation. Thus, within a context of loner existence and
cultural privacy, Mitchum observes his obligations to his own past while
leading his brother into the future.

Certainly this is Robert Mitchum's vision brought to film. Inextricably trapped in the present, representing it, he catalyzes and focuses all the elements of the film. Sublime as it is here, he does this in other films as well. The unique and subtle charm of this movie, and the source of its lasting underground reputation, lies elsewhere: in the realization of the road as its own poetry.

Road poetry is a common American experience, one in which an aesthetic dimension extends from a functional process. *Thunder Road* is a film made for those among us who have felt the mystery and elation of driving—not being in a car, but driving—a road at night, the blackness interrupted only by the contrapuntal rhythm of passing streetlights and the opposed streams of headlights and taillights as they merge, maneuver, clash, and vanish—marking motion but not progress. French New Wave directors have aped the American road sequence, most eloquently in *Alphaville;* but French roads are never a world unto themselves. Instead, they are logical A-to-B progressions. They fail to capture the sensation of suspension, apartness, and isolation, the timeless floating mystique of American driving.

In *Thunder Road*, the highway suggests, but doesn't really represent, escape, or progress to an exotic outside world. It is the road that took Luke Doolin out of the community, into the Army, to Europe, ultimately to prison and back to the hollows where he became king of the roost as a man of the world. But it wasn't the direction of the road that did this for Mitchum—it was his immersion in and devotion to the road as a way of life.

The road is more than a means, more than a common object binding the lives of all those who live within the culture it dictates. It has a spell when you're driving on it; the spell slips into *Thunder Road*'s off-the-highway sequences at night: two-shots of people talking in which the road appears in the upper background, invisible but for the solitary headlights tracing it slowly across the screen, a motif that informs the entire film. The road need not appear in such shots, but it does, its presence at once a threat and a blessing. In many such images, the film demonstrates that the road is all-possessive once you've been exposed to it. The only honorable liberation is death.

The film's haunting car sequences occur at night; moonlight, headlights, ghostly forms by the shoulders, the road itself fading in front and behind. This tiny microcosm formed by the radius of Mitchum's lights picking out for an instant a tunnel through blackness is the perfect metaphysical conceit for Mitchum's meaning in the film. It is an appropriate central image from which the rest of the film springs. It needs no flashy subjective camera work, because it draws on the experience of initiates who revere it. The film is a specialized, limited artistic experience—much as *Last Year at Marienbad* (1961) is. *Thunder Road,* however, confounds literary intellectuals because they are *not* privy to its values and images. I suspect that few who love *Thunder Road* while recognizing its shortcomings can ever love *Last Year at Marienbad*—although it must be admitted that corridor-gliding freaks are the overcultured *reductio ad absurdum* of road people.

Robert Altman

THE DELINQUENTS (ROBERT ALTMAN) (1974)

TODD McCARTHY

A reasonable number of people must be aware that Robert Altman directed films before *M°A°S°H* (1970), but most would probably be hard pressed to come up with many titles. Some may have seen *That Cold Day in the Park* (1969) and a few watchful airplane passengers and television viewers might have noticed that Altman directed *Countdown* (1968; with some uncalled for assistance from Jack Warner). The elongated *Kraft Suspense Theatre* episode *Nightmare in Chicago* (1963, currently showing as a feature on late-night television), a definitive documentary of the city's Edens Expressway if nothing else, can claim a few partisans on the underground Chicago-Madison critical axis, and if Altman's and George W. George's distinctive and evocative *The James Dean Story* (1957) were rereleased today, the combined Dean and Altman cults might even help Warner Brothers turn a profit on the film (it was a dismal flop when originally released in the summer of 1957, two years after Dean's death).

But the real skeleton in Altman's closet is another film that was released in 1957, but was considerably more successful. It's *The Delinquents*, which Altman, ever the auteur, wrote, produced, and directed in his hometown of Kansas City during the summer of 1955 on a $63,000 budget. As Altman puts it,

> Well, this guy back there said he had the money to make a picture, if I'd make it about delinquents. I said OK and I wrote the thing in five days, cast it, picked the locations, drove the generator truck, got the people together, took no money, and we just did it, that's all. My motives at that time were to make a picture, and if they said I gotta shoot it in green in order to get it done, I'd say, "Well, I can figure out a way to do that.". I would have done anything to get the thing done.

Altman may have been glad to get the thing done, but today he doesn't seem all that glad to have people see the film. At the 1973 San Francisco Film Festival tribute to Altman, an enthusiast asked how *The Delinquents* might be seen today. The director replied that he possessed a print, but that, if he had anything to do with it, the young man would never see the film. Although delivered offhandedly, this is quite a severe judgment on a work that, although by no means a great, undiscovered classic, is certainly nothing to be embarrassed about, even for one of the greatest American filmmakers. Altman: "I'm not embarrassed about it. But nobody knew what they were doing. I don't think it has any meaning to anybody."

He probably didn't know what he was doing, but in those five days that he wrote the script, Altman was unobtrusively laying the groundwork for a vast number of the teen problem (or problem teen) pictures that were to follow. By the time *The Delinquents* was finally released, of course, every-one from Sam Katzman to AIP to Jerry Lewis had jumped on the j.d. band-wagon, but in early 1955, *The Wild One* and *The Blackboard Jungle* had only just been released and *Rebel Without a Cause* was still in the shooting stage. (*The Delinquents* was even pre-rock 'n' roll, and part of its score consists of some smooth Kansas City black jazz, with some on-camera work by the late singer Julia Lee.) The youth exploitation field was untested and uncharted and, if he wanted to, Altman could lay claim to having invented, in one picture, many of the conventions (and, soon afterward, clichés) of this subgenre.

The setting is WASPville, U.S.A., that clean-cut community small enough to get by with only one drive-in and one high school, but big enough to have two sides of the tracks. On right side of tracks, good, straight but troubled boy and sweet, innocent but ripe girl are very much in love but her parents stand between them since she's "not ready to go steady" and he "hangs out with the wrong crowd." Forbidden to see his sweetheart, boy implores hot-rodding pal to pick up his girl for him. Pal gets duded up, leads girl out from under noses of suspicious parents, and whole teen crowd meets for party at abandoned mansion outside town. Filter cigarettes and 3.2 beer cause party to get out of hand, reunited lovers leave to be alone, fuzz mysteriously appear and break up drunken free-for-all. Apprehended toughs suspect boy of snitching, kidnap him next day and force him to gulp down whole bottle of Scotch when he won't admit to being informant. Taking besotted boy for ride, toughs bungle gas station holdup and speed off, leaving boy behind with cash and dead attendant. Boy finally staggers home, learns gang has abducted girl, tracks down and beats up toughest tough, learns girl's whereabouts, saves her from clutches of gang, and walks off to confront police, who will surely clear him of gang's crimes.

The Delinquents is framed with sanctimonious narration about how "This story is about violence and immorality," and how "We are all responsible. Citizens must work against the disease of delinquency by working with church groups, community groups," ad infinitum, ad nauseam. Altman claims that this was added by United Artists when the company picked up the film for release (UA paid $150,000 for the film and grossed nearly $1,000,000 with it), but it is curious that a preachy narrative is also the prime weakness of *The James Dean Story*. Aside from this, however, and an occasional line, delivered by the girl friend to her parents, such as, "Why can't you leave him alone?" (perhaps the definitive line of all 1950s teenpix), the film is relatively passive and undidactic in its attitude toward the spectacle of youth led astray. Even then, Altman seemed drawn toward an improvisational approach, and the casual sound of the dialogue reduces the frequency of overblown melodramatic moments. And although not withdrawn to the extent that it is in *Thieves Like Us* (1974), the camera normally records the violence in *The Delinquents* from a distance, often from a high, overhead angle, thereby implicating neither the viewer nor even society-at-large in the misdeeds of the characters (even so, critics at the time felt that *The Delinquents* was an extremely violent film).

The players, who include Altman's daughter and then-wife, were all found in Kansas City, with three major exceptions. The film gave Richard Bakalyan his first stab at playing the greasy punk who makes life miserable for everyone in town, and he did it so well that he was typed forever. Peter

Miller, fresh from *The Blackboard Jungle,* was also brought in from California. Tom (Billy Jack) Laughlin, who apparently had a considerable James Dean complex, played the troubled young man and the mere mention of his name makes Altman cringe even today:

> Tommy Laughlin was just an unbelievable pain in the ass. Unbelievable. He's a talented guy, but he's insane. Total egomaniac. He was so angry that he wasn't a priest. Big Catholic hangup. I found out that this Laughlin kid was doing all the things he'd heard about James Dean doing. Like he'd run around the block when he was supposed to be exhausted and he'd say, "OK, I'll sit down there on the fireplug and when you hear my whistle, you start rolling your cameras." Otherwise, he wouldn't do it. In fact, he did the last half of the picture under protest. He'd say, "OK, tell me what you want me to do." And I'd say, "Well, I want you to . . ." He'd say, "No, tell me exactly what you want. I'll do it just the way you want it. I'm not going to act in this picture. I'm just here because I have to be." And I said, "OK, I want you to fall out of the car like this," and I'd fall out of the car. "Then I want you to take your right hand and move it up and put it on the gravel. Then I want you to look up a minute . . ." He couldn't remember it, but that served his purpose and he'd do it. And he was as good at doing that as when he was really working in the first part of the picture.

Although extremely mannered (he couldn't keep his eyes fixed in one place for more than two seconds), Laughlin gives an adequate performance and manages to make his relatively thankless character somewhat less bland than it might otherwise be. In movies of this sort, the scenes involving the romantic leads are usually so vacuous that, after initial laughter, one begins counting the minutes until the toughs return to liven things up. In *The Delinquents,* there is at least a modicum of concern generated for the admittedly pasty lovers; even in the campiest of moods, one cannot wish total degradation upon them.

In what so far must sound like a perhaps passable but hardly distinguished film, there are two notable features—its technical excellence and its paradoxical relationship with the director's subsequent work. Altman served his apprenticeship making industrial films and documentaries in Kansas City and his know-how in lighting and in photography is impressively evident in his first dramatic film. The quality of the black-and-white image is brilliantly sharp and rich, far better than any produced in similar fare (under studio conditions) by AIP, Allied Artists, or Columbia, and astonishing in a film made independently for so little money.

One need take little more than a casual look at Altman's recent work to realize that the director is fascinated with the conventions of genres. Today, particularly in *McCabe and Mrs. Miller* (1971) and *The Long Goodbye* (1973), he works within established generic frameworks, but subverts and plays upon the conventions, simultaneously expressing his feelings about his characters and the history of the genres' development. In *The Delinquents*, he plays it straight. Foreshadowing, to a remarkable extent, his attitude toward the hoodlum's violence in *The Long Goodbye*, Altman says of his first film, "My main point was to say that kids like this don't plan anything. They don't say, 'Tomorrow we're gonna go knock off the filling station.' They say, 'Hey, there's a filling station, let's go in there and mess around.' And it happens. It's not a premeditated kind of thing. It's just a restlessness kind of thing, I think."

It's this restlessness, principally expressed through the edgy, nervous performances, as well as a fatalistic ambivalence about the plight of the lovers, and a reluctance to implicate society too heavily in the misguided lives of the characters (see *McCabe* and *Thieves*), that sets *The Delinquents* apart from other examples of its genre and reveals that at least some thought went into its creation. Like much of Nicholas Ray's work, it leaves one unsettled and off-balance emotionally. Decidedly a minor work by a major artist, *The Delinquents* could nonetheless furnish proof to those still skeptical of his abilities that Altman can, if he wants to, tell a straightforward story without stylistic mannerisms. Happily, he's doing a lot more than that today.

THE DELINQUENTS

United Artists. Running time: *71 minutes.*
Released: *March, 1957.*

Producer, director, screenwriter: *Robert Altman.*
Art director: *Chet Allen.*
Cinematographer: *Charles Paddock.*
Editor: *Helene Turner.*
Cast: *Tom Laughlin, Peter Miller, Richard Bakalyan, Rosemary Howard, Helene Hawley, Leonard Belove, Lotus Corelli, James Lantz, Christine Altman, George Kuhn, Pat Stedman, Norman Zands, James Leria, Jet Pinkston, Kermit Echols, Joe Adleman.*

FROM ROCK AROUND THE CLOCK TO THE TRIP: THE TRUTH ABOUT TEEN MOVIES* (1969)

RICHARD STAEHLING

It is unclear what teen-agers did in the very early 1950s. It is hard to believe they were grooving on Patti Page and her doggy in the window, or Frank Lovejoy as he tracked down yet another triple agent working for the Communists, but that is about as relevant as any mass culture ever got for them. Perhaps the Korean War gobbled them up; perhaps they never existed. Whatever the explanation, "youthville" was absolutely nowhere in 1953; kids were to be neither seen nor heard.

Within two years things had changed. American youth were in head-lines uniquely their own: Juvenile Delinquency and Rock 'n' Roll. The origin of either phenomenon may not be as important as the fact that they were supposedly engaged in unholy and incestuous collusion; rock 'n' roll caused juvenile delinquency, and juvenile delinquency naturally caused rock 'n' roll. Both were expediting the downfall of the nation's young and the nation didn't like it one little bit.

In keeping with time-honored tradition, newspapers examined the trouble, politicians condemned it, parents ignored it, clergymen bemoaned it, and the kids laughed at it. However, it remained for Hollywood to take the drastic and truly appropriate measures such a situation called for: they cashed in on it.

In the spring of 1956 *Rock Around the Clock* hit the local neighborhood theatres, and the flood of "exploitation" films aimed at the youth market was under way. True to their genre, these films had one purpose: to gross mucho money, which is exactly what they did, time and time again. Easily recognized by their supersurreal screenplays, amorphous plots, and cut-rate production, such flicks could be literally ground out during the noon hours, tossed together in under thirty days of post-production work, and fanatically promoted in every way, conceivable or inconceivable. Along with horror films, "juve" movies were the quickest money-makers going, being veritable gold mines when double-billed at drive-ins during the summer.

A year earlier, in 1955, the older folks had their say about problem kids in *The Blackboard Jungle* and *Rebel Without a Cause,* the first films to deal with juvenile delinquency. Both efforts were controversial when released, and are damn good period pieces even now. Dealing respectively with "poor kids gone bad" and "middle-class kids gone bad," they make up for their naïve oversimplifications with sheer power and brute force. Soon they turned out to be the only tangible inspiration for the deluge of "quickies" that followed, with James Dean's performance in *Rebel* sending every B-rated actor back to the bathroom mirror for a few more hours practice.

Appropriately enough, since the pictures were serious and intended for adult audiences, all the adults did was bitch. A movie censor in Memphis banned *Jungle* calling it the "vilest picture I've seen in twenty-six years . . . ," and it received even stranger treatment at the hands of none other than Clare Booth (Mrs. Henry) Luce, then the United States Ambassador to France. She insisted that the film be pulled out as an American entry at the Venice Film Festival, the objection being to the portrayal of the New York City school system and the presentation thereof to European audiences. As could be expected, *The Blackboard Jungle* failed to make the scene at Venice, the Europeans were saved from its debilitating effects, and that was Hollywood's last quasi-serious word about kids for some time to come. The blue-jean set were now in the hands of the exploiters, which may not have been such a bad thing after all. At least they never take themselves too seriously.

Exploitation films are nothing new to the film business, nor are the colorful purveyors of the craft. Sam Katzman, who started the whole thing rolling when he grabbed Bill Haley and his Comets for *Rock Around the Clock,* has produced over three hundred and forty films in the last thirty years. This is no mean feat in itself, but what really makes the motion-picture industry take notice is the fact that not one of those films has lost money. Long before switchblades and Les Paul Customs were big business, Mr. K (as he is known in the biz) was treating the world to such gems as *Jack Armstrong, All American Boy,* and *Captain Video.* It is he who turned Johnny Weissmuller into Jungle Jim when he wasn't up to swinging through the trees anymore, and, as if that weren't enough, he also begat the original Batman serial and the first 3-D movie.

His formula has been a simple one: topicality. If there is a trend or fad sweeping the country that looks as if it has a buck in it, Sam Katzman (and, most often, Columbia Pictures) will turn it into a feature film before *Time* magazine can even attempt to explain it. While many exploiters attempt to cash in on trends in movemaking, Katzman zeros in on trends outside the boundaries of film, usually on things that show up in popular music.

The twist is an excellent example. Back in 1961 one Chubby Checker hit the top of the record charts, riding the crest of the twist fad. Twenty-eight days later he was still there, and he was also starring in a full-length motion picture featuring Dion, the Marcels, the twist, and everything else remotely associated with the craze that would make money.

It was a typical Katzman maneuver. In less than one month he had signed Checker for the film, had an entire script written (". . . two or three days to write it, and with luck, the weekend to polish it up and make changes . . ."), shot it, edited it, added sound, promoted it, and released it. In a stroke of creative genius, the picture was called *Twist Around the Clock,* and was in the theatres long before the dance phenomenon began to ebb.

In fact before the bottom *really* fell out, the great cinematic entrepreneur had still another one on the silver screen, *Don't Knock the Twist,* featuring the Dovells, Gene Chandler, and the redoubtable Chubby again. The plots in both films may have been negligible, but the box-office figures were not; and this is what "rush releasing" and Mr. K are all about.

Albert Zugsmith has a different approach to exploitation: "The box-office success of a picture in today's market is in direct ratio to the talk it arouses. It is not enough for the picture to just entertain; the audiences must derive from it a reaction that will cause talk for a week after." Thus, whereas Katzman patterns his films after already existing trends, hoping to cash in on the hysteria, Zugsmith uses a more direct route: he causes his own hysteria, most often with sex, dope, cheap thrills, and Mamie Van Doren. Mamie, who is sort of a third-generation Marilyn Monroe (Monroe to Jayne Mansfield to Van Doren), has spiced up quite a few Zugsmith turgid melodramas, most notably *High School Confidential*. In that particular opus, spiffed out in a white cashmere sweater at least four sizes too small, Mamie tells a superstraight young schoolteacher: "Don't tell me you never rode in a hot rod or had a late date in the balcony." It is one of the finest moments in the history of teen-age flicks, and indicative of Zugsmith's modus operandi.

Dealing in unbelievable double entendres, innuendos, and hip jargon, he has "exposed" just about every skeleton in teendom's closet. During a long and apparently pleasant association with M-G-M,[1] Zugsmith told all in *High School Confidential*, graduating to *College Confidential*, with *Sex Kittens Go to College* not far behind. Somewhere, in between such scholarly endeavors, he found time to cast a glance at *The Beat Generation,* a film that owes a lot more to Krafft-Ebing than to Jack Kerouac. When pressed by a *Life* reporter about just what redeeming values it might have had, Zugsmith opined: "Why, it was a terrific exposé against criminal rape. My pictures are moral essays. I don't make movies without a moral, but you can't make a point for good unless you expose the evil." You can't argue with conviction like that.

If Katzman and Zugsmith were the individual titans of the teen-age film biz, there can be no doubt about the single most important film company: American-International Pictures. Under the guiding influence of James H. Nicholson and Samuel Z. Arkoff, AIP released at least twenty juvenile delinquency films in the 1950s, matching that output with as many in the horror and war genres. The company was and still is a closely knit unit, much like the Stax Records family; a recurring lineup of directors, actors, writers, and producers who know their business and keep prerelease costs to an absolute minimum. The going rate for most of their early teen flicks was $125,000,

[1] For Zugsmith's version of the M-G-M association, see interview, pp. 411–424.

with promotional costs nearly always equaling or passing that figure, and although profits were never staggering, there was always enough bread to get another double feature out and keep the AIP machinery well oiled.

The tactic of saturation promotion for low-budget films is common practice with American-International, and the extent to which some of it goes is astounding. With each new double-feature release the company circulates brochures with marketing options for the theatre owners. In the 1950s it was called the *American News,* with the slogan "dedicated to showmanship" printed directly underneath. Later on it turned into a more stylized press book, but if the packaging changed, the contents did not. A revelatory example is the press book for *Maryjane,* which, under the bold-faced type headline EXPLOITATION, has the following tips for promotion:

> IMPORTANT . . . The subject of *Maryjane* is highly controversial, there-fore the pattern of your exploitation campaign should be slanted accordingly . . . with the approach distinctly different from that given the more "conventional" film story. This is screen fare that people will talk about. The subject of marijuana has now become one of the most written and talked about controversies in years.
>
> *Maryjane* deals with this controversy in an intelligent but provocative manner. Your campaign should adopt the same controversial approach. Expressions from representative groups listed here can give your campaign factual basis and powerful impact:
>
> *The Clergy:* Members of the clergy have a keen interest in their communities and are eager to assist with local problems. Marijuana is a growing problem in most communities, and after your clergyman has attended a screening of *Maryjane,* there is no doubt that he will be forthcoming with favorable comment from the pulpit.
>
> *Psychiatrists:* This group should be included in your special doctors' screening. Favorable comment on *Maryjane* from a recognized head of the psychiatrist group would be a most valuable asset. He may even submit a story to the newspaper on, "What Prompts Youth to Possess Something Which Is Illegal."
>
> *Contest:* Perhaps you can interest your newspaper in a tie-in where they would request readers to write, in 200 words or less "My Most Memorable Experience." No restrictions should be put on subject matter. Together with promoted prizes, include guest tickets.

Also listed are *Students, Police, Women's Clubs, Forum Discussions,* and *Editorials.* For merchandising tie-ins one may choose from the following: Dodge cars, sports clothes, bowling alleys, artists' supplies, fresh milk and, of course, drugstores. The finest stroke was saved for the radio campaign though; a catchphrase that clearly demonstrates AIP's "intelligent but provocative approach": "*Maryjane . . .* not the girl next door, but a trip to hell!"

Absurd as it may seem, it is this very medicine-show type of promotion that has kept the company alive and prolific. It is part of the basic attitude and approach to cinema that stamps their work with unmistakable characteristics. Call it tawdry, slapdash, low-budget, or Z-rate, American-International Pictures nonetheless has a style as distinct and identifiable as that of Orson Welles, Fritz Lang, or Ingmar Bergman. A style, in fact, that has influenced and been influenced by one of America's few interesting younger directors, Roger Corman.

Corman views his long association as producer and director at AIP as an outlet for refining technique *and* for finding some degree of freedom in Hollywood. He has cranked out a frightening number of films at breakneck pace (*The Little Shop of Horrors,* 1960, took one week; *The Terror,* 1963, with Boris Karloff set some kind of record by taking under three days!), and although some are amusing disasters, the majority of them are brilliant in a low-budget way. A good deal of Corman's early work at AIP was in the horror bag (*The House of Usher,* 1960; *The Raven,* 1963) but it was not until he made *The Wild Angels* (1966) with Peter Fonda and Nancy Sinatra that critics and audiences in the States decided they would have to face the unnerving prospect of taking him and AIP seriously.

His most impressive teen flick was made for Allied Artists in 1957 and unfortunately has not received the attention and accolades garnered by *Angels* and his later effort *The Trip.* Slammed in *Film Daily* for its "unnecessary gore and crude surroundings," *Teenage Doll* has all that and more. Sporting a great B-rate lineup of players, including Fay Spain and June Kenney, the picture dealt with gang wars, including an all-girl gang called the Black Widows.

American-International, Albert Zugsmith, and Sam Katzman are not responsible for all the teen flicks since 1955, although they can take credit for nearly half of the output. The rest is divided among a diverse spectrum of companies that tried their hands momentarily at the genre. Allied Artists, Paramount, and Warners all did their thing, along with some ultracheap independent efforts by Fairway International and the Marathon Filmgroup that would make AIP's films look frivolously expensive by comparison. Republic Pictures even got into the scene for a short time.

Never to be forgotten for their serials (*Zorro's Black Whip, Don Dare-*

devil Rides Again, Government Agents-vs.-Phantom Legion), Republic's teen numbers bore the same stamp as everything else they did: plenty of action, zero characterization, and plots that often defy comprehension. Usually the films alternate between an action sequence, and a more static expository scene in which the preceding events are explained, and those to follow are foreshadowed. Then back into the action, back to a respite from the action, then back to the action again, etc. Watching these films is an amazing experience for there is no actual beginning or end, nor is there even a middle; it is merely an assemblage of active and passive scenes. Of course there is always the death or capture of a criminal to signal the impending end of the film, but otherwise it is pure McLuhanesque montage and formula moviemaking at its wildest.

With so many exploitation movies made according to formulas that are instantly repeatable and easily copied, it is no surprise that distinct categories emerge in talking about the films themselves. It is even less surprising that a film that inspires a succession of imitations is almost always the definitive, if not the finest, effort in that genre. A good rule of thumb is that the quality of each genre of teen film decreases from the first film on; any spark of spontaneity and creativity in an original is thoroughly extinguished in a third- or fourth-generation imitation. There are, of course, "sleepers," which emerge after a category has been clearly defined, but they are either mavericks that do not follow the prescribed formula exactly, or pure formula films that become new milestones by assimilating and synthesizing all previous attempts in the genre.

Teen flicks break down into four distinct categories: musicals, wild youth, mild youth, and beach films. Each has unique characteristics that make it as difficult to confuse *Date Bait* with *Juke Box Rhythm,* as it is to confuse Echinodermata with Platyhelminthes.

There are also two types of films that masquerade as "juve" movies but are really nothing more than mainstream Hollywood wearing leather jackets and saddle shoes. One type has been discussed briefly, and will be called the "serious" teen-age movie. Made with top talent (Glenn Ford, Burt Lancaster, James Dean) and costing a great deal more than exploitation films, they were geared for adults and supposedly portrayed (". . . as timely as today's headlines! . . .") the juvenile delinquent in action. The list is short: *The Blackboard Jungle, Rebel Without a Cause, The Young Savages,* and despite their influence on the lower-budget productions, they bear little similarity to them: *The Blackboard Jungle* has a lot more in common with, say, *To Kill a Mockingbird* (1963) than it does with *High School Confidential.*

The other great pretender to "juve" moviedom status is the "personality" film, a particularly disgusting formula that made many pennies by casting popular rock 'n' roll stars in insipid melodramas, letting the marquee do the rest. The first but not worst offender in this category was *Love Me Tender* (1956), starring old Elvis hisself. Set during the Civil War, it is nothing more than a ho-hum, predictable Western with the usual robberies, double crosses, and shoot-outs that allows Presley just enough time to belt out a couple of songs and do a great dying bit at the end. Rank as it may be, Elvis was at the vanguard of his popularity when the flick was released, and it didn't much matter what the story was; there was no denying he was up there on that screen and that's all the teen-age chicks wanted to see.

The apparent theory behind such epics is that a charismatic personality can transcend any cliché, and Elvis sure had his fair share to contend with in *Tender* and in the myriad to follow. In no time at all the Hollywood execs had it figured that if Elvis could do it, there were other lads around with enough top-40 power to do it too, and the talent hunt began. It unearthed several likely candidates, even though their talent was dubious, and almost overnight audiences were witness to such forgettable drivel as: *Hound Dog Man* (1959), with Fabian, *Sing, Boy, Sing*, with Tommy Sands (1958), and *Bernardine* (1957), with Pat Boone. History has proved that these stars may not have been very good singers, and it leaves no doubt that they are fumbling actors, but that is not the worst of it. The plots and screenplays are so moronic as to prohibit utterly their viewing today; it would take a masochist of the first order to sit entirely through something like *State Fair* (1962), with Pat Boone. The general level of such fare rivals the really bad segments of *Gomer Pyle, U.S.M.C.,* or *Family Affair,* and didn't even have the benefit of canned laughter to get the audience over the rough spots.

Before issuing a blanket warning to avoid personality films at all costs, passing mention should be made of two exceptions (both 1957). In *Jailhouse Rock,* with Elvis Presley, the cretin simplicity is still there, but there are also some undeniably cool moments, mainly because the film loosely parallels Elvis' rise to fame and fortune. It may be mythology, but the scene in the recording studio, in which Elvis (after a series of slow ballads) decides to cut an up-tempo jam, is not to be missed. Part of the thrill comes from the musicians backing El in that scene and others—Scotty Moore and Bill Black.

It may not feature a rock 'n' roll star, but *The James Dean Story* certainly falls into the personality bag too. Dean was one of the few really big nonsinging idols (even Tab Hunter had a hit record) in the 1950s and his fiery Porsche accident rattled the teens as much as the Valens/Holly/Big Bopper plane crash. The film (a sort of cinematic equivalent of "Three Stars" by Tommy Dee, Carol Kay, and the Teen-Aires, which eulogized the passing of the singing stars), utilized stills, interviews, home movies, and film clips to recount Dean's life. Admittedly they lay it on a bit thick here and there, but James Dean was a mighty heavy dude, and the film is successful at getting that much across.

FEAR ROCK 'N' ROLL "CLOCK" MAY TIME-FUSE TEEN ANTICS

NEW YORK, April 1956—First major film themed directly to rock 'n' roll craze has run headlong into a storm of trouble which the offbeat music has stirred in several communities . . . Basis of the difficulty is the growing feeling against rock 'n' roll in many quarters, and various communities have already taken steps to halt teen-age hops and other gatherings at which rock 'n' roll is featured. In this connection it is known that theatremen have received warnings from local police, community groups, and newspapers.

LONDON, September 1956—As a sequel to outbursts of hooliganism in various parts of the country during the screening of Rock Around the Clock, a number of local authorities have put a ban on the picture . . . it has now been banned in Wigan, South Shields, Bootle, Gateshead, Brighton, and Birmingham.

With the unabashed success of Rock Around the Clock in both America and England, the rock 'n' roll musical was born. Following a pattern set by musicals with Jeanette MacDonald and Nelson Eddy, and Betty Grable and Don Ameche, the accent was on music at the decided expense of the plot. The recipe for rock musicals is a simple one: Take two or three top rock acts with ten to fifteen songs and add them to a thin plot with romantic interest and passable acting; mix in equal parts of "hep talk" and disc jockey Alan Freed; and serve up apologetically, assuring everyone that rock music is not the work of the devil. If the proper amounts are used, and the concoction served immediately, the teens will eat it up (or so the business thought in the 1950s).

In the case of Rock Around the Clock, the stars were Bill Haley and the

Comets, the Platters, and Freddie Bell and his Bellhops; the cast was studded with Johnny Johnston, Henry Slate, Lisa Gaye, Earl Barton, and Alix Talton. The plot, about as thin as any plot is going to get, went something like this:

> Two dudes who have quit their unpopular dance band (Johnston and Slate) stumble into Strawberry Springs looking for a place to crash for the night. The town is really hopping, for it is Saturday eve and the teen-agers are all heading for the town hall to hear Haley and his Comets. Following the crowd inside, the two are amazed to hear a "new type of music with a different beat," and are even more impressed with the dancing of brother/sister team Earl Barton and Lisa Gaye. "I like your sound," says Johnston. "Thanks," says Haley. In no time at all Johnny also discovers he likes Lisa, and sealing the dealing with a kiss, agrees to manage the band and the dance duo.
>
> Heading for New York, he tries to get the band some gigs through the booking agency of former girl friend Alix Talton, who is still carrying a torch for him, and the trouble begins. Jealous of little Lisa, Talton books the group for the graduation prom at an exclusive girl's school in Hartford, figuring that Haley and Company will be a bit raunchy for the upper crust of Connecticut. Such is not the case, for the band blows many minds and before the night is over Lisa and Earl have everyone out on the dance floor boppin' the blues. Hell hath no fury, etc., and Alix flatly refuses to book the act after this pagan display.
>
> Things look pretty grim for Johnston, Haley and the Comets, and of course for the entire future of rock 'n' roll. Only one man could save the day, and sure enough, deus ex machina, Alan Freed appears on the scene. Freed (who at the time was top disc jockey on WINS, or anywhere else for that matter) books the crew into his own club and they immediately become the talk of all New York. From here on the film follows their meteoric (or perhaps cometic) rise to fame, with Alix Talton still trying unsuccessfully to lay waste to Lisa and Johnny. The finale is in (where else?) Hollywood, with an extravaganza show featuring Haley, the Platters, and the Bellhops. Johnston marries Lisa, Talton falls for some lackey who's been after her all along, and the curtain falls.

To say the curtain falls is partially untrue, for no sooner was it down than up it came again, this time ushering in *Don't Knock the Rock*, with Bill, the Comets, Little Richard, the Treniers, and the ubiquitous Mr. Freed. The plot centered around protagonist Alan Dale's efforts to convince his hometown that rock 'n' roll was clean, healthy fun, and fifteen or so rock numbers later everyone agrees, but only after giving Dale and the audience a lot of grief.

Such stuff can be viewed as pure camp or hard-core surrealism; either way one can't go wrong spending a couple of hours in front of the tube if a rock 'n' roll musical shows up on *The Late, Late Show*. The movies themselves are awfully entertaining, but everything is subordinate to the music, there seldom being fifteen minutes of action and dialogue before someone rips off a tune. In *Rock Around the Clock* alone, there were nine numbers by Haley: "Rudy's Rock," "Mambo Rock," "Rock," "Rock-a-Beatin' Boogie," "Happy Baby," "See You Later, Alligator," "Razzle Dazzle," "ABC Boogie," and the title tune. The Platters sang "Only You" and "The Great Pretender," with Freddie Bell and the Bellhops doing some mighty fine dance steps even though their jams were lame.

Lurking within the reels of fifteen films are classic performances of classic tunes by Bill Haley and his Comets, Gene Vincent and the Bluecaps, Frankie Lymon and the Teenagers, Danny and the Juniors, Fats Domino, Chuck Berry, Little Richard, Johnny Otis, LaVern Baker, the Del-Vikings, the Diamonds, the Cadillacs, Eddie Cochran, Richie Valens, and (what else?) many, many more. The original records will always be an artist's legacy, and hopefully more things like the Richard Perry/Fats Domino LP are forthcoming, but the only place vintage performances can now be seen is in the rock musicals. It's been a long time since musicians writhed on the floor while playing stand-up bass, climbed on top of their pianos, or shouted orders like "bop, Bluecats, bop," to the sidemen; such acts are already history and can be best revived by the screening of rock musicals; hopefully, they will not be allowed to disappear into the movie vaults and never be seen again.

If the musicals are the preservers of music, the wild youth, mild youth films are the preservers of myth, enabling us to view the fantasy-sociology of the 1950s. To the majority of Americans, confronted with news of gang wars, Elvis, and drag racing, there were only two kinds of kids: the good ones and the bad ones. The same stereotypes emerged in films, only in exaggerated form. The wild-youth-kid stereotype was of a bum who rode around in his hot rod, half-crazed from drugs and liquor, looking for a chick to lay, a store to rob, or another car to drag; discourteous, greasy, irresponsible, and mean. In short, he was un-American and nobody's kid.

His mild youth counterpart was everybody's baby: clean, honest, moral, and bright; everything a parent could hope for, incarnate. He was a little mixed up about love, and did silly things like playing the record player too loud and tying up the telephone, but he was all-American nonetheless, another clean-living member of the silent majority. Another handy rule of thumb: (*a*) if you can groove on Paul and Paula ("Hey, Paula") or Shelly Fabares ("Johnny Angel"), and have a liberal sense of humor, you should have no trouble sitting through any mild youth movie; (*b*) if you like or liked the Shangri-Las ("Leader of the Pack") or the Angels ("My Boy-friend's Back"), then you're sure to enjoy most wild youth films. In either case one should not apply preconceived standards to such flicks; it's not in the spirit of the thing, and will undoubtedly result in disappointment and indignation.

"It's sure to be a smash with the youngsters. At a special screening at RKO last week, the audience greeted the film with howls of delighted approval. Oddly enough, the picture, while aiming at the younger set, also has family appeal for it presents an interesting and wholesome glimpse of family life in suburbia."

So went part of the *Film Daily* review of *Rock, Pretty Baby,* the first mild youth movie. Released almost concurrently with *Rock Around the Clock,* it was considered a much more respectable and sympathetic portrayal of teen life than the garish Katzman musical. A quick glance would reveal why, for it is merely a soap opera for the younger set, an unfortunate characteristic of all such films. Filled with the angst of adolescence, and steeped in Americana, many mild youth stories are reminiscent of the absurd family comedies that dominated television at the time: *Father Knows Best, Bachelor Father, Ozzie and Harriet,* etc. The original Universal synopsis of *Rock, Pretty Baby,* tells the tale all too well:`

> The future doesn't look too bright to the hot combo of a group of high school boys led by Jimmy Daley (John Saxon) when they are thrown off their first job, which was playing at a college fraternity dance.
>
> It seems they played too well. The college boys were not so much interested in dancing as in necking and petting, but the hot music of Jimmy's combo made the girls more eager to dance than to neck. Among the girls is Joan Wright (Luana Patten).
>
> When the musicians are told to leave, she leaves too, accepting the invitation of the members of the departing combo to let them drive her home. Joan, the daughter of a musician, has ambitions along musical lines herself, and eventually becomes an arranger for the Daley combo. Their

mutual devotion to music sparks a romance between Jimmy and Joan, though neither realizes it at first.

Jimmy has other worries. His father (Edward Platt) is unsympathetic toward Jimmy's ambition to be a professional musician. His mother (Fay Wray) is on his side but not emphatically enough to do any good. And he has no money for a down payment on a $300 electric guitar, vital to the success of the combo.

Jimmy's father, blind to his emotional needs, refuses to advance the money; Nino Barrato (Sal Mineo), flashy drummer, and real gone on girls, sparks a campaign to collect money for the guitar among Jimmy's friends. Guitar in hand, beautiful arranger by his side, Jimmy is on cloud eight. But when Joan reveals hitherto hidden charms in a bathing suit, they move to cloud nine.

The boys begin to work preparing for the combo contest of DJ Johnny Grant when catastrophe strikes. Joan, afraid of her passion, tries to be sensible by dating others. When she shows up at Jimmy's party with a known wolf, Jimmy flips his teen-age lid. He takes a poke at Joan's escort and starts a free-for-all, leaving the Daley home in a shambles and causing the neighbor's Continental kit to be ripped off. Humiliated, Joan takes off for the San Francisco music school where she was supposed to enroll before meeting Jimmy.

The old man makes the kid pay for the damages by hocking his guitar, and things really get morose around the Daley home until

. . . Joan, full of forgiveness and love, returns from S.F. after Dr. Daley has asked her to come back. A now-understanding father reclaims the guitar and takes Jimmy on a hair-raising ride to Johnny Grant's contest using his doctor's privileges to get motorcycle cops to clear the way. Jimmy arrives in time to meet the combo and play, but they don't win.

They are, however, launched on a professional career when a representative of the Order of Bisons offers them a two-week job at summer camp. Besides Jimmy gains a girl and the understanding of his father.

Not one to miss out on a good thing, Universal followed Jimmy and his combo when they played that gig at summer camp, calling it *Summer Love*. Luana Patten disappeared, to be replaced by Judy Meredith, but the rest of the cast remained the same, as did the plot: much ado about nothing, featuring silly misunderstandings and petty jealousy.

The audiences for this schmaltz were mostly young teen-age chicks who came to see their screen idols fall in love and neck; John Saxon and Sal

Mineo were both getting a lot of space in the movie tabloids, and *Rock, Pretty Baby* and *Summer Love* were the perfect places to show their profiles. One can't help but feel that Hollywood (willfully and in a premeditated manner) produced such flicks as vehicles for introducing their younger talent. The list of mild youth regulars certainly has a familiar ring to it: John Saxon, Sal Mineo, James Darren, Ed "Kookie" Byrnes, Doug McClure, Roberta Shore, Shelly Fabares. Serving time in these soap operas was seen as a springboard to bigger things, a not too crucial proving ground that would/could lead to bigger and more "serious" roles for the juvenile stars. For some the breaks came, usually in the form of a television series (although Mineo has racked up a formidable list of screen credits) and for others it was the end of the line. Little has been heard from people like Bobby Driscoll, Lee Kinsolving, or Mark Damon since their cinematic high school days.

What, one might ask, can these films offer the audience of today, when many teens spotted them as pure corn the first time around? They are certainly the featherweights of "juve" moviedom, with their ridiculous scripts, and unerring ability to turn all they touch into sugar; but this is not where their strength lies. It is the myth they project, that Ann Landers quality of cleanliness/godliness so closely associated with good kids of the 1950s, that makes them such funfests today. The gap between the 1950s and the 1960s is a wide one indeed: movies from the 1930s and 1940s have already passed from cliché to archetype, but the mild youth numbers of the last decade are still out there somewhere in never-never land—where junior asks dad for the keys to the family car, and has to have his date home by eleven o'clock. Pretty terrible stuff; but if your constitution is strong and your nature tolerant, the laughs come fast and furious.

Less than a year after the debut of rock musicals and mild youth melodramas, a third genre appeared, most likely as a backlash reaction to such adolescent fluff. Packed with action, sex, drugs, and parental hypocrisy, the wild youth films were sensationalism with no apologies; the *National Enquirer* of teen movies.

Of the twenty-five to thirty films of this sort, none rises from the depths showing as much class as Albert Zugsmith's *High School Confidential*. Made in 1959, it followed the pattern set by American-International and Allied Artists releases of 1957/1958, surpassing them in every respect. The story concerns the efforts of a young undercover agent (Russ Tamblyn) to crack a high school dope ring. He enrolls in the school as a student and eventually makes a contact for marijuana through John Drew Barrymore, a fellow hipster and student. This is accomplished by building a reputation as a ne'er-do-well, insulting his teacher with jive talk, and smoking a joint in the principal's office.

As part of his front Russ lives in the home of his supposed "aunt," played by Mamie Van Doren. One of the numerous delights in the film is Mamie's earnest attempts to put the make on him ("You looking for excitement?" "I'm a citizen."), even though he's a government agent. The script never attempts to clarify exactly who, or what, Mamie is; no matter though, it makes those scenes even more surreal.

At any rate, Barrymore introduces Russ to the head pusher who is operating out of a combination malt shop/dope den; he gets the evidence he needs and (thanks to the miracles of judo) apprehends the evildoers, sending them off to the pokey with an appropriate speech. Such stories are nothing new to the genre, but Zugsmith has embellished this simple tale with numerous niceties:

An opening that, once seen, will never be forgotten. The film starts with a close-up of a man behind a desk looking directly into the camera; it looks as though he's about to endorse a candidate for office. Instead, we are informed that he is a member of a narcotics control board who wishes to endorse the film. It seems the film we are about to see is "not pleasant," but will bring forth some of the hard-hitting facts about drugs and their use in high schools. The gentleman urges us to study *High School Confidential* closely, and be ever on the alert for such problems in our own schools. Cut to Jerry Lee Lewis (with piano and band) on the back of a flatbed truck that is slowly driving through town. Jerry is pounding out the title tune (a hit for him on Sun Records) and a pack of jumping, jiving teen-agers are following alongside as if he were the Pied Piper. Cut to Russ as he arrives at the high school.

Jive talk that will boggle the mind; the highlight being Barrymore's story of Ferdinand and Isabella rendered fully in jive, after he takes over the history class. Other samples: "You got thirty-two teeth, you wanna try for none?" "Wham, bam, thank you Ma'm."

First-rate acting by the intrepid cast, with Jackie Coogan as the head pusher, looking mighty mean behind them shades, and John Drew Barrymore as the chief reptile and coolest cat in town.

There are other films in the wild youth bag that merit attention, and are almost as sharp as *Confidential*. AIP's *The Cool and the Crazy* has great acting by Scott Marlowe and Richard Bakalyan, and the dubious distinction of having been filmed without any sets, in Kansas City. *Teenage Doll* by Roger Corman for Allied Artists is the grisly gang-war number that bears the foreword: "This is not a pretty story, but is true." For hard-core enthusiasts *Date Bait* and *Wild Youth* come highly recommended; both are low-budget crudities that inhabit a cinematic twilight zone where "nothing is real."

Zugsmith may win the award for quality, but American-International and Allied Artists are the unquestioned champions of quantity, with probably seventy-five percent of all wild youth films to their credit. All of their films show the influence of *The Wild One* (the amazing motorcycle film with Marlon Brando and Lee Marvin) and *Rebel Without a Cause*, although a good deal more attention is paid to style than to content. The content in fact is almost always the old "triangle plot": good guy loves beautiful chick; she loves him, too, but is impressed with virile antics of bad guy; she goads good guy into confrontation with bad guy; tragedy occurs and good guy is blamed; only in second confrontation and last reel of film is bad guy done in, good guy cleared, and chick made to realize what a drag she's been. Insert hot rods, motorcycles, gang wars, drugs, or all of the above, into such a skeletal plot and you have every AA and AIP delinquent flick ever made.

The chicks in such psychodramas are usually Anne Neyland, Fay Spain, June Kenney, or Yvonne Lime; their thespian abilities deriving from their measurements and from watching Mamie Van Doren movies and high school plays, yet they consistently turn in performances that have undeniable gut-level appeal. It is not so much a question of acting prowess as of projecting an aura; they are simply great broads. If the script calls for a good chick, you will get an all-American WASPish blonde with a latent evil streak ("thrill crazy" is AIP's description) that can only be cured with the emotional panacea of true love. When a bad girl is required, everything goes. She smokes a lot (with the cigarette dangling precariously out of one side of her mouth), leans on walls, scuffs her feet, and spends her time perpetuating anguish, cruelty, and misunderstanding.

The dudes are even more amazing. When the male lead is a good guy, his motivation is always the same: a vague sense of ethics and an impulsive nature that will instinctively lead him down the straight and narrow. This makes our hero little more than Gary Cooper in a leather jacket and a pretty square cat, no matter who plays him. Usually that unfortunate task fell to Steve Terrell, with Dick Bakalyan, Scott Marlowe, and John Ashley having all the fun playing the baddies.

Wild youth scripts deal in stereotype and formula and the bad guy is always one hundred percent cliché. Usually there is an attempt in teen flicks to explain the causes of the delinquency—broken homes, hypocritical parents, etc.—but no such protocol is required by AIP and AA. The bad guy doesn't sell reefers to kids in high school or run old men down with his rod because his father doesn't understand him. He does it because he is bad and that is what bad guys are supposed to do; it's as simple as that. Faced with such roles, the actors with Allied and American have wrought miracles. Their basic approach seems to be: "When faced with an oversimplified cliché be sure and overplay it," and the results are notable. What usually emerges from such artless art is grotesque exaggeration and overblown affectation; the ultimate bad-ass.

Unfortunately, after four years of fast-lived, existential antics the bad-ass started to tire. The wild youth formula showed distinct signs of overkill; it had been drubbed to death. The replacement was a Goody Two Shoes who traded in his switchblade and hot rod for a surfboard and beach blanket, an exchange that was to influence the course of teen flicks for some time to come.

William Asher, the director of American-International's first three beach epics (*Beach Party, Muscle Beach Party, Bikini Beach*), was once asked about the company's shift from gang wars to beach bashes: "Our audiences welcome clean sex," said Asher. "They are bored with juvenile delinquency." It was hardly a revelation, but Asher was right. The press had abandoned delinquency as one of its favorite subjects by 1958, and was off covering phone-booth packing and leisure living in California. Delinquency ceased to be a marketable commodity. No one wanted to watch mayhem in the city ghettos when they could watch the same thing at Malibu Beach. It was the time of the Beach Boys, Jan and Dean, and the Four Seasons. Columbia and M-G-M had already shown that the fun-in-the-sun syndrome was a sure money-maker with *Gidget* and *Where the Boys Are,* and it didn't take AIP long to pick up on the good vibrations.

The first one off the American-International assembly line was *Beach Party* with Annette Funicello and Frankie Avalon, a dynamic duo that would see action in nearly every beach bomb to follow. The film was a bold departure for the company, for it featured some famous (and talented) actors and was shot in flaming color. The budget was considerably larger than anything done in the black-and-white, leather jacket days (*Bikini Beach* cost $600,000, a far cry from the $100,000 or so put out for something like *Dragstrip Girl*) and it reaped proportionally larger profits. The plot (perhaps *drift* is a better word) of the film was absolute nonsense, something easily demonstrated by quoting *Time*'s appropriately nonsensical review:

> *Beach Party* is an anthropological documentary with songs. Robert Cummings, in ambush behind a wind-Schwepped beard, is gathering material for a book on teen-age sex play. Just outside his window at Balboa Beach the puberty rites and other coming-of-age-in-California shenanigans of a tribe of overripe adolescents are in full cry, and Cummings' telescope and electronic eavesdropping rig provide him with an eye-opening earful.
>
> The beach resembles Seal Rock in the mating season. Frankie Avalon with his pack of gold-necklaced surf-jockeys, and Annette Funicello with her bevy of busty beach-bunnies are—in the words of one of their tribal hymns—"just a-surfin' all day and swingin' all night." But danger lurks in the dunes: a marauding band of post-Brando wild ones roar up on a midnight raid. Quinquagenarian Cummings with little help from Frankie sends them yelping off with their motorcycles tucked between their legs.
>
> The climax of this primitive business is a custard-pie war in a beatnik beer and poetry parlor . . . Annette goes ape for Frankie, crooning, "I was such a fool/to treat him so crool." As a study of primitive behavior patterns, *Beach Party* is more unoriginal than aboriginal . . .

As could be expected, little changed when AIP's follow-ups hit the screen. Harvey Lembeck stayed on as Eric Von Zipper, the leader of the motorcycle gang; Keenan Wynn replaced Buddy Hackett who had replaced Cummings as the nasty member of the older generation; and Frankie and Annette were still on hand to play imbecilic lovers. The super-up-tight sexual overtones remained—never outside *Playboy* has such sick plastic sex been seen—with the chicks all looking like centerfolds from *Nugget* or *Escapade* and the fellows all straight out of the Hardy Boys. And of course no one smoked, drank, or touched each other (except in volleyball). "They're what I want my son to be at their age," said director Asher. Yikes!

Looking back on the early 1960s, the beach films appear to have been the death knell for teen exploitation films. The musicals and wild/mild youth genres had emerged with the first shock wave of rock 'n' roll and juvenile delinquency and they faded when neither subject could provide new fodder for the scriptwriters. The musical was finished (except for a brief spasm when the twist hit) because rock 'n' roll itself seemed finished; there was no trend, no charismatic star, and very little excitement to rejuvenate the senile formula. The mild/wild youth numbers similarly lost their edge when their subject matter became passé and pedestrian. The perimeters of these genres had not expanded since the early days, and without external inspiration and stimuli the films devoured themselves.

Things must have looked brighter for the Hollywood execs when the surfing craze took hold. One can almost imagine the AIP staff sitting in their offices in anticipation of the next trend or controversy; planning, researching, and waiting for that moment when they could spring into action again. When they finally did, they launched into the beach bit with such overzealous enthusiasm that the genre became a dull stereotype within one year, and a lifeless cadaver in two. The surf scene fell victim to the fastest and most thorough exploitation campaign ever conceived, and although such films were produced well into the mid-1960s, anything made after 1964 is merely an epitaph for an already long-departed genre. No matter really, for even if AIP had been more prudent in exploiting the magic of the West Coast beaches, Frankie and Annette would have still hit the skids in 1964; that was the year the Beatles really arrived.

Perhaps the most revealing thing about post-Beatle exploitation films is that there aren't many. Since *A Hard Day's Night* (1964) the flow of 1950s-style teen movies has been reduced to a tiny trickle. Most of the juve-movie producers bailed out long before the Beatles arrived and, although the "mop-tops from Liverpool" were certainly a new trend, there was little a Hollywood huckster could do to cash in on them; they were simply too unique to be exploited. The task of continuing the tradition of pre-Beatle teen films fell to the most deserving and accomplished company of all— American-International; even today they are perpetuating the bravado and absurdity of the last decade. Since the demise of the beach formula, AIP has managed not only to put out their usual pap, but actually to expand and continue trends in exploitation.

In 1965 they released *The T.A.M.I.* (Teen-age Awards Music International) *Show,* an extravaganza of rock talent shot with videotape and brought to the theatres through the "miracle of *electronovision.*" It featured an all-star cast that included Chuck Berry, James Brown, the Beach Boys, Marvin Gaye, and the Rolling Stones (it is still the Stones's finest appearance on the screen despite their excellent showing on *Shindig* in 1965 and in Godard's *One Plus One,* 1969). 1966 saw the AIP release of Roger Corman's *The Wild Angels,* a film based loosely on the antics of the Hell's Angels and other such clubs, which started a trend that is still going strong today. The latest of their cycle films, *Hell's Angels 69,* hit the screens this summer.

In 1967 they scored with a Sam Katzman production of *Riot on Sunset Strip,* a film based on the shenanigans that took place in Hollywood in the same year. *Riot* clearly demonstrates that neither AIP nor Mr. K have lost their touch for the lurid, the topical, and the sensational. In 1968 it was *Maryjane,* with Fabian; *Wild in the Streets,* a copy of the English film *Privilege,* which had a rock 'n' roll star ruling the country; and *The Trip,* another Roger Corman classic with Peter Fonda sulking away to the strains of the Electric Flag.

It is unclear if any of AIP's recent efforts have appealed to the younger audiences as did their releases in the 1950s. A visit this June to a theatre to see *Hell's Angels on Wheels* and *Run, Angel, Run* would indicate that such stuff is popular with certain folks in their early thirties and a few aspiring young cycle bandidos; the teens are most likely down at the Bijou, stoned out of their minds, catching *Weekend* or *2001.* Whatever the case, the era when cheap and sleazy films sold well with kids is over. One may be able to make films for them, but the days of exploiting them have passed. Today you have to be good to make it; or at least you have to give the impression of being good. Assembly line moviemaking is over, the medium is the message, and so on and so forth.

The present is one thing, the past is another. The Beatles themselves are facing the inescapable problem of being associated with a decade and a generation that no longer represents the young; of acknowledging that in a way *they* are a phenomenon of the past. The years from 1955 to 1964 seem to be light-years away from the world we live in today. Catch a few teen flicks on *The Late Show* and see just how long ago those years really are; they represent a loss of innocence that will not be matched until someone writes about the teen films of the 1960s.

FILMOLOGY

For some odd reason or another most teen films from the 1950s have been made available for television stations. If your local station is either very hip, or very lame, these movies should appear on *The Late, Late Show* or *The Early, Early Show* at one time or another. The star rating system is not so much one of intrinsic quality as it is of entertainment value.

M—musical; P—personality; WY—wild youth; MY—mild youth; MO—motorcycle gang film; B—beach film; S—serious film.

***THREE-STAR CLASSICS

Big Beat (Universal, 1958) (M) William Reynolds, Gogi Grant, Hans Conried, Buddy Bregman, Del-Vikings, the Diamonds, Fats Domino, Four Aces, Harry James, Lancers, Mills Brothers, George Shearing, Cal Tjader.

One of the better musicals, this one has William Reynolds fresh out of college trying to persuade his father to get into releasing rock 'n' roll along with the other lame records he already produces. Dad relents and gives the kid a subsidiary company to be overseen by his A & R man. It's pure non-sense from then on, as Reynolds almost blows the whole gig, saving it at the last minute with a scheme to push his records in supermarkets. Of special interest is Fats Domino with "I'm Walking," and the Diamonds doing an incredible bit on "Little Darling." In color.

Blackboard Jungle, The (M-G-M, 1955) (S) Glenn Ford, Anne Francis, Louis Calhern, Margaret Hayes, John Hoyt, Richard Kiley, Sidney Poitier, Vic Morrow, Rafael Campos; directed by Richard Brooks.

Glenn Ford plays new teacher Richard Dadier (his students call him Mr. Daddy-O), who finds himself in the middle of trouble in a New York vocational school. The story really isn't much as Ford tries to "get through to the kids" and encounters opposition on the way; but there are other things that make this film a must.

(*a*) Top-notch performances by the entire cast, especially Ford, Poitier, and Campos. Vic (*Combat*) Morrow is a gas as the chief student troublemaker—"I don't think you like me, teach." (*b*) Suspenseful moments as the high school guys smash the 78 rpm record collection of a math in-structor, try to rape their homeroom teacher in the library, and beat the shit out of Ford in an alley. (*c*) Any movie that has this foreword on the Euro-pean version can't be all bad: "The scenes and events depicted here are fictional. The U.S. is fortunate in having a school system that is a tribute to its faith in youth."

Cool and the Crazy, The (AIP, 1958) (WY) Scott Marlowe, Gigi Perreau, Dick Bakalyan, Dick Jones.

From *The Hollywood Reporter*: "A few weeks ago a Brooklyn school principal committed suicide because he could not suppress the rape and hoodlumism in his institution. *The Cool and the Crazy* is a badly written, sloppily edited, poorly directed, low-budget film that may well inspire more such tragedies." It's a classic. Just out of reform school, Scott Marlowe starts turning on his classmates at the high school. Eddie the Pusher gives Scott the weed, and when they all "come back for more" they find it costs money.

The hard-hitting truth continues as a kid is killed attempting to hold up a gas station for reefer money, with Marlowe finally killing Eddie for more dope only to get his just deserts in a flaming car crash. All this was filmed on location in Kansas City, where actors Bakalyan and Jones were actually busted when "their ducktails and delinquent appearance attracted the attention of the local police." Don't miss it.

Crime in the Streets (Allied Artists, 1956) (S) John Cassavetes, James Whitmore, Sal Mineo; directed by Don Siegel.

Back on the streets again with this drama originally designed for television. A social worker, who feels the plight of the juvenile delinquent is understandable, tries to make friends with a nasty John Cassavetes, the leader of the pack. Although a lower budget effort than other "serious" films, director Don Siegel creates a fast-moving and convincing story. Siegel is also responsible for *Flaming Star* with Elvis, Fabian's *Hound Dog Man,* and the mind-blowing *Invasion of the Body Snatchers.*

Don't Knock the Rock (Columbia, 1956) (M) Bill Haley and the Comets, Alan Dale, Alan Freed, the Treniers, Little Richard, Dave Appell and the Apple Jacks; produced by Sam Katzman.

This sequel to *Rock Around the Clock* is at least as good as the original, with Dale and Freed engaged in varied high jinks as they try to prove rock 'n' roll is a "harmless outlet for today's youth." Many excellent songs, including "Calling All Comets," and "Don't Knock the Rock," by Haley; "Tutti Frutti," and "Long Tall Sally" by Little Richard.

Girl Can't Help It, The (Fox, 1956) (M) Tom Ewell, Jayne Mansfield, Edmund O'Brien, Fats Domino, Little Richard, the Platters, Gene Vincent and the Blue Caps, the Treniers, the Chuckles, Nino Tempo, Eddie Cochran, Abbey Lincoln; directed by Frank Tashlin.

Jayne Mansfield's first flick and a strange one indeed as the scriptwriters dust off the "gangster who wants his dame to make it in show business" bit. Edmund O'Brien is great as the head hood, with Tom Ewell playing the agent who must find Jayne a gig. The show is equally divided between Mansfield's body and some great jams by Little Richard, Gene Vincent, and Eddie Cochran. Good clean fun, in color.

Go, Johnny, Go (Valiant, 1959) (M) Alan Freed, Jimmy Clanton, Sandy Stewart, Chuck Berry, Eddie Cochran, the Cadillacs, the Flamingoes, Jackie Wilson, Richie Valens; produced by Alan Freed.

Another star-studded musical with Jimmy Clanton starring as Johnny Melody, a poor orphan boy who makes it big through a talent search held by Alan Freed. The hardships, ironies, and humor en route to the big time are supposed to provide the basis for the story, but as usual the music is the only thing that's really worthwhile. Among the standouts are the Flamingoes and the Cadillacs, with rare appearances by the late greats Richie Valens and Eddie Cochran. Freed not only stars but also produced the film and his knack for lining up heavy acts is undeniable.

High School Confidential! (M-G-M, 1958) (WY) Russ Tamblyn, Mamie Van Doren, Jan Sterling, John Drew Barrymore, Michael Landon, Jackie Coogan, Charles Chaplin, Jr., Jerry Lee Lewis; produced by Albert Zugsmith; directed by Jack Arnold.

Not enough can be said to recommend this farfetched tale of high schoolers and the evil weed. A cameo appearance by Jerry Lee Lewis (doing the title tune), a script loaded with jive talk, some great drag racing scenes, and memorable performances by the entire cast, especially Barrymore and Coogan, make the film a classic in the genre. Zugsmith at his exploitative finest.

Jailhouse Rock (M-G-M, 1957) (P) Elvis Presley, Judy Tyler, Dean Jones, Mickey Shaughnessey, Anne Neyland.

Elvis ends up in the cooler for accidentally killing a dude in a bar fight and learns how to play folk music from cellmate Shaughnessey. Upon his release our hero makes the big time (after a few false starts) and even tries to help Mickey achieve the same status. Mick doesn't have the chops to pull it off though and gets mad at Elvis; cheering up only by the end of the flick. The best Presley picture, which boasts some gutsy music—something sadly missing from the majority of his cinematic efforts.

James Dean Story, The (Warners, 1957) (P) Produced, edited, directed by George W. George and Robert Altman; written by Stewart Stern.

Documentary of Dean's life starts with footage of his fatal car wreck; flashes back to his early life in Fairmont, Indiana, through use of stills, home movies, interviews, etc. High spot is the screen test Dean made for *East of Eden*. Engrossing material on a legend of the 1950s.

Rebel Without a Cause (Warners, 1955) (S) James Dean, Natalie Wood, Jim Backus, Ann Doran, Rochelle Hudson, Sal Mineo, Nick Adams, William Hopper, Corey Allen, Jimmy Baird; directed by Nicholas Ray.

Buzz (Corey Allen) and Jim (James Dean) are about to have a "chickie run," which results in Buzz barreling over a cliff to his doom. Buzz (*from car*): "You know, I kind of like you." Jim: "Why do we do this then?" Buzz: "You've got to do something now, don't you." Jim Backus and Mineo are brilliant; ditto Dean and director Nicholas Ray.

Rock Around the Clock (Columbia, 1956) (M) Bill Haley and his Comets, the Platters, Tony Martinez and his Band, Freddie Bell and the Bellhops, Alan Freed; produced by Sam Katzman.

The granddaddy of them all, with nine songs by Haley and his Comets, and Alan Freed playing himself. Highly recommended.

T.A.M.I. Show, The (AIP, 1965) (M) Chuck Berry, the Rolling Stones, James Brown, the Beach Boys, Marvin Gaye, and others; produced by Electronovision.

An incredible lineup of talent makes this one of the best of the post-Beatle movies, and, except for *Monterey Pop*, the finest rock musical. Brown, Berry, and the Stones are all incredible. Recommended.

Teenage Doll (Allied Artists, 1957) (WY) June Kenney, Fay Spain, John Brinkley, Collette Jackson; produced and directed by Roger Corman.

Variety: "This low budgeter is ostensibly directed toward the fight against juvenile delinquency. However only real contribution in this direction is that it offers employment to a corps of juve actors and thus keeps them off the street . . . the characters talk a stylized jargon and engage in continual brutality and violence, their motivations, delinquent or otherwise, bearing only the slightest resemblance to human beings." A magnificent teen film from Roger Corman. Mood and pace are excellent.

Wild Angels, The (AIP, 1966) (MO) Peter Fonda, Nancy Sinatra, Bruce Dern, Gayle Hunnicut, Michael J. Pollard.

One of Roger Corman's best, with great performances from a fine cast. Bruce Dern plays "The Loser" who is shot by the cops, heisted from his hospital bed by his cronies, and honored with a postmortem wake in a church. Peter Fonda sulks profoundly; the bikers are nasty and rotten; and the action sequences are nonpareil.

Wild Guitar (Fairway International, 1962) (WY) Arch Hall, Jr., Cash Flagg, William Walters.

This one boasts two professional actors in the cast . . . the rest are, well, inexperienced. Arch Hall motors into town and ends up in the clutches of promo man Walters, who proceeds to steal him blind. Hall gets hip but is kidnapped, and brainwashed. Honesty and integrity save the day at the last moment, as the laughs come a-mile-a-minute in this supercheapie.

Wild One, The (Columbia, 1954) (MO) Marlon Brando, Lee Marvin, Mary Murphy, Jay C. Flippen.

Johnny and the Black Rebels drink a lot of beer and raise a lot of hell in an unsuspecting small town. When they finally bust him, a local chick clears him and he motors off into the sunset in an unclear state of mind. A really powerful and influential film, with stellar acting by Brando and Marvin.

Wild Youth (Cinema Associates, 1961) (WY) Robert Hutton, John Goddard, Carol Ohmart, Clancy Cooper.

Two guys and a gal escape from an honor farm and, after their car breaks down, get picked up by dope peddler Revis and his drug-crazed moll. There is a battle for the dope, which is hidden in a huge doll, but the border police break things up eventually. A cheapie with lots of engrossing mistakes. ". . . arrange with a scrap dealer to use a badly wrecked car—preferably a sports model—in your foyer with the sign above it reading: Was he a narcotics addict?"

Young Savages, The (United Artists, 1961) (S) Burt Lancaster, Dina Merrill, Shelley Winters; directed by John Frankenheimer.

Director Frankenheimer puts out with some power scenes and moments, although the plot is again questionable. The gang-fight scenes, acting, and camera work are brilliant however, with a particularly flashy bit where a blind man is stabbed to death by young toughs.

* * WORTH WATCHING

Beat Generation, The (M-G-M, 1959) (WY) Steve Cochran, Mamie Van Doren, Fay Spain, Louis Armstrong, Ray Anthony, Jim Mitchum, Charles Chaplin, Jr., Vampira; produced by Albert Zugsmith.

Any similarity between this Al Zugsmith tale and the artists/beatniks of the 1950s is purely coincidental. A psycho case spends his time raping chicks until the cops catch on and track him down. The raunchy sets, lurid plot, and jive talk make the whole thing eminently palatable though, and Mamie is there to keep interest up when all else fails.

College Confidential (Universal, 1960) (WY) Steve Allen, Jayne Meadows, Mamie Van Doren, Mickey Shaughnessey, Conway Twitty, Elisha Cook, Walter Winchell, Earl Wilson; produced and directed by Albert Zugsmith.

Yikes! Al Zugsmith tries to outdo *High School Confidential* with this one and he almost makes it, in spite of Winchell and Wilson. It takes an amazing amount of violence and sex, both overt and covert, before calm is restored to a small-town college campus, but what can one expect when the professor is Steve Allen and the student body, Mamie Van Doren and Conway Twitty. Recommended!

Date Bait (Marathon Filmgroup, 1960) (WY) Gary Clark, Marlo Ryan, Richard Gering.

It's cheaply made, it's lurid, it's great! A young couple who want to get married and find some peace and security can get none, thanks to their parents, gangsters, and the chick's dope-crazed ex-boyfriend. By the last reel justice is done, although the parents deserve more comeuppance than they get, and Clark and Ryan live happily . . . etc.

Dragstrip Riot (AIP, 1958) (WY) Yvonne Lime, Gary Clark, Fay Wray, Connie (*Hawaiian Eye*) Stevens.

"This is the story of teen-age youths who live as fast as their hot rods will carry them. Gary Clark as the newcomer to the gang is running away from his past, his flight being hampered by a gang of motorcyclists who throw a reign of terror over his very existence. Courage is measured as drag races are performed on railroad tracks, the climax building up to a free-for-all between the two gangs. All this is accompanied by rock 'n' roll numbers and actual flat races at Santa Barbara, California." The AIP synopsis sums things up quite well—make sure you catch the "free-for-all."

Life Begins at 17 (Columbia, 1959) (MY) Mark Damon, Ed Byrnes, Ann Doran, Tommy Ivo; produced by Sam Katzman.

Suffice it to say that this "family drama of adolescent love" has some of the worst acting and dialogue ever committed to celluloid. A laugh riot; with Ed "Kookie" Byrnes outdoing himself.

Mister Rock and Roll (Paramount, 1957) (M) Alan Freed, Teddy Randazzo, Lois O'Brien, Lionel Hampton, Frankie Lymon and the Teen-agers, Chuck Berry, LaVern Baker, Clyde McPhatter, Little Richard, Ferlin Husky.

The credits promise more excitement than this one can deliver. Reporter O'Brien is anxious for a story from Freed on rock 'n' roll and is introduced to singer Teddy Randazzo. They fall for each other immediately, but break up in a row over what Lois' editor is doing to slander rock and Alan Freed. Once again, though, Al saves the music and the star-crossed lovers, by explaining the music's origins and putting on a benefit for the editor's favorite charity. Too many of the performers are saddled with pre-rock material, although Chuck Berry (with "Baby Doll") and Little Richard (with "Lucille") are a gas to watch. Uneven.

Motorcycle Gang (AIP, 1957) (WY) Anne Neyland, Steve Terrell, John Ashley, Carl Switzer.

". . . will undoubtedly satisfy those youngsters who find reckless speed exciting and disregard for the law completely understandable."—*Film Daily*. Good jive talk, sex, and lots of action as Anne Neyland is torn between good guy Terrell and bad boy Ashley. Seems John went up the river for a cycle death he and Steve were responsible for; Steve only getting probation. When John gets out of jail, the fun begins.

Riot on Sunset Strip (AIP, 1967) (WY) Aldo Ray, Mimsy Farmer, Michael Evans, Laurie Mock, Tim Rooney; produced by Sam Katzman.

Katzman hasn't lost the old touch; he got this one out into the theatres within six weeks of the Strip riots. Law and order provided by Aldo Ray as a cop trying to clean up the Strip. Sensationalism courtesy of Mimsy Farmer (as Ray's daughter), who gets fed drugs and raped at a party. Music by such favorites as the Standells, Chocolate Watch Band, and the Enemies.

Rock, Pretty Baby (Universal, 1956) (MY) Sal Mineo, John Saxon, Luana Patten, Rod McKuen, Edward Platt, Fay Wray.

The misadventures of Jimmy Daley and his Combo, as they seek fame, fortune, and glory in the music business. The first and scariest of the mild youth type; Rod McKuen plays bass, Sal Mineo plays drums, and John Saxon plays lead sax. What more need be said?

Summer Love (Universal, 1958) (MY) John Saxon, Molly Bee, Rod McKuen, Jill St. John, Judy Meredith, Edward Platt, Fay Wray, Shelly Fabares, Troy Donahue.

The revenge of *Rock, Pretty Baby* as the Daley Combo takes the Order of the Bisons up on their offer to play a two-week gig at a summer camp.

Highlights are "Beatin' On the Bongos," "To Know You Is to Love You," and a happy ending.

Teenage Bad Girl (D.C.A. [English], 1957) (WY) Sylvia Sims, Anna Neagle, Norman Wooland, Kenneth Haigh.

Another British juvenile delinquency drama with excellent acting and direction. Sims plays the poor unfortunate chick who ends up on the wrong side of the law, but all turns out fine in the end.

Teenage Wolfpack (D.C.A. [German], 1957) (WY) Henry Bookholt (known later as Horst Buchholz), Karen Baal, Christian Derner.

The plot is a triangle again but the acting is good for a change. German-made originally, it comes to the states via England, and is a real cultural oddity. Dubbed, but pretty good nonetheless.

Untamed Youth (Warners, 1957) (WY) Mamie Van Doren, Lori Nelson, John Russel, Eddie Cochran, Lurene Tuttle, the Hollywood Rock 'n' Rollers.

Mamie and Lori get busted for vagrancy and put on a reform school farm, run by a naïve old woman judge and a vicious bad guy, who has some nasty watchdogs. Mamie struts the stuff in this one, with John Russel as the horny bad guy. Entertaining.

* FOR THE DEDICATED FAN

Beach Party (AIP, 1963) (B) Bob Cummings, Dorothy Malone, Frankie Avalon, Annette Funicello, Jody McCrea, Morey Amsterdam, Eva Six.

If you've got the stamina to sit through any of American-International's beach films, this might as well be it; the original that started the whole wretched excess in the first place. Bob Cummings valiantly tries to inject talent into the plot, playing an anthropologist who's studying teen-agers, and Harvey Lembeck excels as Eric Von Zipper, cycle-gang leader, but it's downhill from there on.

Beat Girl (English, 1960) (WY) Adam Faith, Noelle Adam, Christopher Lee, Gillian Hills, David Farrar, Shirley Ann Field, Oliver Reed.

English beatniks are apparently nothing more than juvenile delinquents; no matter—whatever they are, a London girl gets mixed up with them (because she hates her stepmother) and finds herself involved in a striptease murder. It's always fun to see what was cooking in the U.K. back then, and horror movie great Christopher Lee offers a little incentive to watch the acting.

Because They're Young (Columbia, 1960) (MY) Dick Clark, Michael Callan, James Darren, Doug McClure, Tuesday Weld, Roberta Shore, Duane Eddy and the Rebels; directed by Paul Wendkos.

Break out the Percy Faith strings and the American flag for this one. Clark plays an ex-football star and new teacher at the high school who meets his share of misguided youth while falling in love with the principal's secretary. For aficionados of the syrupy high school syndrome, this is one of the biggies; others approach with a ten-foot pole.

Bikini Beach (AIP, 1964) (B) Frankie Avalon, Annette Funicello, Martha Hyer, Harvey Lembeck, Don Rickles, Keenan Wynn.

Meanwhile back at the beach . . . ; this time it's Keenan Wynn who wants to (*a*) prove his chimpanzee is as intelligent as teeners, and (*b*) build a retirement home on the kids' beach. Neither idea seems all that outrageous until the "Potato Bug" (a spoof on the Beatles, get it?) shows up to complicate matters. This is the third of AIP's sun-and-fun opuses, and as usual the only hope lies with the old pros: Wynn, Harvey Lembeck, and Don Rickles. Rickles is particularly good as he overplays a role that predates his rise to fame on television, but protracted exposure to the film is discouraged.

Dangerous Youth (Warners [British], 1958) (WY) Frankie Vaughn, Carole Lesley, George Baker.

Frankie Vaughn sets new all-time lows for acting, with the script not far behind. Drafted into the army after just making it big as a singer, he becomes embroiled in more trouble than imaginable. Adding insult to injury, he ends up marrying his singing partner Miss Lesley and becoming a military career man.

Don't Knock the Twist (Columbia, 1962) (M) Chubby Checker, Lang Jeffries, Mari Blanchard, Gene Chandler, Vic Dana, Dovells; produced by Sam Katzman.

Unrequited love threatens the plot of yet another rock musical. This time the suspenseful question is will the romantic triangle spoil an upcoming Twist Spectacular slated for national television? The answer is not worth waiting for, although Chubby, Gene Chandler, and the Dovells (with a cooking version of "Bristol Stomp") are pretty spiffy.

Dragstrip Girl (AIP, 1957) (WY) Fay Spain, Steve Terrell, John Ashley, Frank Gorshin.

Fay Spain loves hot cars but her parents don't. She likes wealthy, existential hot rodder John Ashley but her parents don't. After a lot of bitchin' footage of illegal street drags and even a few legal ones on strips, Fay renounces her evil ways for poor but honest Steve Terrell, whom her parents don't like much either. A typical AIP flick with the old gang mugging their way through yet another outrageous script; may well be Fay Spain's finest performance.

Explosive Generation, The (United Artists, 1961) (MY) William Shatner, Patty McCormick, Lee Kinsolving, Billy Gray; directed by Buzz Kulik.

An excellent example of what happens when Hollywood tries to get serious. William (*Star Trek*) Shatner is a high school teacher with the usual qualifications: dedication, principles, integrity. When he starts talking about zygotes and sperm cells in class, everybody gets uptight; the students don't back him, the administration is spineless, the parents are pissed off, and his job is in jeopardy. Every cornball cliché is paraded across the screen before the viewer is spoon-fed the usual happy ending and moral at the end. Learn about sex elsewhere.

Gidget (Columbia, 1959) (MY) Sandra Dee, James Darren, Cliff Robertson, Doug McClure, Four Preps; cinematography by Burnett Guffey; directed by Paul Wendkos.

Girl plus midget equals Gidget. Get it? Ha, ha, ha. Sandra Dee is pert and perky; James Darren is strong and sensitive; and with a duo like that and another godawful triangle romance, things couldn't get much worse. They do, however, for by some bizarre twist of fate two recent Academy Award winners (Cliff [*Charly*] Robertson and Burnett [*Bonnie and Clyde*] Guffey) are forced to humiliate themselves in the company of talentless beach bums.

Hot Car Girl (Allied Artists, 1958) (WY) Richard Bakalyan, June Kenney, John Brinkley, Robert Knapp; produced by Roger Corman; directed by Bernard Kowalski.

It's good girls gone bad again, as four teens steal cars, selling them back to a junk dealer to make pocket money. When one of the chicks kills a motorcycle cop during a chicken race, the trouble really begins. Such stuff is standard fare for delinquent dramas, but Dick Bakalyan's virtuoso acting job as the baddie really keeps things pumping. Bakalyan is one of the teen flick greats and deserves attention.

Hot Rod Rumble (Allied Artists, 1957) (WY) Leigh Snowden, Richard Hartunian, Wright King, Joey Forman, Brett Halsey.

The scene is a party somewhere in teenland: Big Arny is uncouth and dresses flashy. His chick tells him to clean up, and he tells her to forget it. She does just that, riding home with another club member. On the way a car, which looks suspiciously like Big Arn's, drives them off the road. Did Arny do it? If he didn't, who did? Only on the day of the "big race" is the mystery solved and the ending happy. Another "loose-youth" entry from AA, complete with actual footage of the Pomona drag strip.

Juke Box Rhythm (Columbia, 1959) (M) Jo Morrow, Jack Jones, Brian Donlevy, George Jessel, Hans Conried, Earl Grant Trio, Johnny Otis, the Nitwits; produced by Sam Katzman.

Not up to Katzman's earlier endeavors in rock musicals. Jack Jones manages to bore more than the plot or script, with little music to take the viewer's mind off such problems.

Juvenile Jungle (Republic Pictures, 1958) (WY) Richard Bakalyan, Corey Allen, June Whitfield.

A Republic picture with some unfathomable production work. A smart guy comes up with a plan for the perfect kidnapping but blows it when he falls in love with the victim. Trying to back out brings resistance from his cohorts: getting kicked, slugged, knifed, shot, and all but drawn and quartered. With superstar Richard Bakalyan.

Let's Rock (Columbia, 1958) (M) Julius La Rosa, Phyllis Newman, Paul Anka, Danny and the Juniors, Roy Hamilton, Wink Martindale, Della Reese, the Royal Teens, the Tyrones.

Let's rock with Julius La Rosa (!?) as he plays a lame-ass ballad singer who can't sell records anymore. Phyllis Newman helps him out though; you see she's a newcomer to the business and understands what all the rockin' new sounds are about. With West Coast 1950s disc jockey Wink Martindale, and some 4/4-time music from Danny and the Juniors and the Royal Teens.

Maryjane (AIP, 1968) (WY) Fabian, Diane McBain, Kevin Coughlin, Michael Margotta, Patty McCormack.

This 1968 release clearly indicates AIP has not lost the touch with exploitation pictures. Fabian plays a school teacher who gets framed and busted for possession while trying to stamp out the local dope ring. Bailed out of jail by fellow teacher Diane McBain, he goes through a lot more hard knocks and pot parties before discovering that she is in fact the big pusher. Not the greatest, but it will mellow with age.

Rock Around the World (AIP [English], 1957) (M) Tommy Steele, Tom Littlewood, Chris O'Brien's Carribeans, Humphrey Lyttleton's Band, Charles McDevitt Skiffle Group, Hunter Hancock.

Lousy photography and lots of stock footage, but this one will nonetheless give an excellent impression of what was going on over there when the Beatles were still incubating. With a great introduction to the film by L.A. disc jockey Hunter Hancock, and a jam session at the end of the film where the words to the song appear on the screen.

Teenage Millionaire (United Artists, 1961) (M) Jimmy Clanton, Rocky Graziano, ZaSu Pitts, Chubby Checker, Bill Black's Combo, Dion, Marv Johnson.

Clanton is a young millionaire looked after by ZaSu and Rocky. They let him program records on stations owned by the family trustees; he programs one of his own and it clicks! Before his rise to fame completely engulfs him, he falls for a girl at the local radio station to ensure a happy ending. Some lighter moments with Dion and Marv.

Twist Around the Clock (Columbia, 1961) (M) Chubby Checker, Vicki Spencer, the Marcels, Dion; produced by Sam Katzman.

Take the rock out of *Rock Around the Clock* and replace it with the twist. A simple formula is simply executed, with our hero discovering the new dance craze in a mountain town and importing it, and Chubby, to New York. A romantic triangle provides the necessary dead air between tunes.

INTERVIEWS

Samuel Z. Arkoff

SAMUEL Z. ARKOFF*

Her brother, the monster, came up.—SAMUEL Z. ARKOFF

It's a rather shocking thing to realize, but Samuel Z. Arkoff has the longest tenure of any current Hollywood studio head—by far. Even though it seems as though they were around forever, such moguls as Louis Mayer, Darryl Zanuck, and even Harry Cohn didn't hold the reins at their respective companies for that much more than twenty years. In 1974, American-International Pictures celebrated its twentieth birthday, and Arkoff has been in control every step of the way.

Arkoff was born in Iowa in 1918, was an Air Force cryptographer during World War II, went to law school at Loyola University of Los Angeles, and was involved in television's early days. Arkoff's late

* Interview with Linda May Strawn, February 11, 1974, Beverly Hills, California.

partner, James H. Nicholson, had a background in movie theatre man-
agement on the West Coast and together they founded American Releas-
ing Corporation, which became AIP in 1955. To form such a low-budget
company at that time must have seemed foolhardy to many within the
industry, for it was then that the other, established B studios, such as
Republic and Monogram, were floundering. Arkoff and Nicholson had
their eyes on a different market, however, and their faith in and
apparent knowledge of that market has kept their company almost
constantly in the black.

That market, of course, is the so-called youth market. The manner
in which the company has moved from sci-fi to horror to beach pictures
to motorcycle epics surely constitutes exploitation in its purest sense,
but AIP, as opposed to the larger studios, is able to get these pictures
on the market so quickly that, in the long view, these films become a
part of the culture that produced them, not a stale reflection of some-
thing that has already passed.

AIP went public in the late 1960s, and things have never looked
better for the company than they do today. Budgets are up, but so are
profits, and it has finally become respected, by others in Hollywood, as
a company to take seriously. Mr. Arkoff agreed to be interviewed in his
office in Beverly Hills.

LINDA MAY STRAWN: What is your definition of a B movie, Mr. Arkoff?

SAMUEL Z. ARKOFF: That term has been used, and overused, and misused, and it really has no significance at all today. The term really goes back, I presume, to the days prior to the antitrust ruling and the breakup of the distributor-exhibitor companies, when the companies not only manufactured and distributed the pictures, but owned the theatres, or some of the theatres, where the movie played. There's no need for me to explain all that.[1]

After the antitrust decree, the companies would make inexpensive pictures that would play the middle of the week, or programs, or for lesser prices, which was a continuation of the old B days. But even that pretty well ended a number of years ago . . . when television became a menace and it was found that you couldn't even recover the cost of prints and advertising for B pictures. Let me explain why.

[1] See "The Economic Imperative," pp. 13–43.

As long as they were in black and white, and as long as there were a lot of theatres, those pictures could play as second features in many places.

But the minute that everything became color, and the cost of color prints was approximately two-and-a-half times the cost of black-and-white prints, some smart chap discovered what everybody should have known all along: namely, that you were better off with a second feature that was not a new picture. Today, if you look at the theatres that play double features, which is true of practically all drive-in theatres and most multiple theatres, you will see that they used to want a second feature that was a less expensive *new* picture. In other words, a B picture. A program-type picture. But when these pictures had to be made in color, they discovered—it was really obvious—that the average picture that had played as a top-of-the-bill feature was only seen by a small number of people. Very, very few people ever see a picture theatrically. Look at the *Variety* list of top-grossing pictures, pictures that have grossed over $4,000,000 in film rentals. There aren't many pictures that have made over $4,000,000. Yet—if you figure the net to the distributor is about $.50 a ticket, assuming an average ticket price of $1.50 to $2.00, of which the distributor gets about a third—only 8,000,000 people see a picture that makes $4,000,000 in net rentals. That's less than four percent of the population!

Since so few people see a picture on its first run, the theatres figured you were better off bringing back a picture that had been sold as a so-called top feature as your second feature.

A lot of people would have heard of the picture, but wouldn't have been able to go to the theatre during the few weeks that it played first run. You brought back as your second feature an old top feature! And your now top feature would ultimately be brought back in a few months as the second feature.

Consequently, there is no market anymore for Bs. Particularly true, because now television is where all the Bs are. The TV series are really B picture series. What used to be Bs in the past? Four Hoot Gibsons a year, four Ken Maynards a year, four Gene Autrys a year, two Jones Families, two Doctor Kildares . . . those were the Bs. All of that is now on television. And since that is being given away free, you can't sell that to people.

The situation today is: You must try to give people what they *can't* get on television. That either has to be a difference in subject matter, or the same subject matter, but done more opulently. You can't even give away a B picture!

LMS: Could we backtrack a bit to what the situation was when you first put AIP together?

SZA: Jim Nicholson and I put this company together in 1954 as a distribution company. I had actually been in television first. I went to law school here after the war. A chap named Hank McCuen was making a television show on film, which in those days was very unusual, because it was all live in those days. Those were the days of *Philco Playhouse,* and the like. It was all live; nothing was on film. Hank was a comedian of sorts, with some very good ideas. In 1950, Hank and I had the first film show on the NBC network. That was called the *Hank McCuen Show.* We made that show for $5,500 a week. Hank was under contract, to NBC. We made the film ourselves. Fifty-five hundred dollars for a half-hour TV picture.

LMS: That's incredible . . .

SZA: It can be explained: There were no unions effective in those days. IATSE[2] represented Hollywood films. The networks were doing everything live in those days, so they were dealing with different unions. They were NABET[3] and IBEW.[4] So there was sort of a no-man's-land when film started on TV. We made our TV in 16 mm. They're now talking again about going back to 16 mm. They really should, frankly. It's really ridiculous to make a show in 35 mm. and only show it once. They're moving toward videotape, too.

Jim Nicholson and I started in 1954 as a result of the antitrust decree and the retirement of the old moguls . . . which left only the scared, younger, would-be moguls. Pardon me.

LMS: That was you?

SZA: No. And as a result of television, which started around 1950. That was really the turning point, when it became a household commodity. A lot of the studios became scared. They dropped their star and director and writer lists. The word went out that there would be no more B pictures. So there was, in essence, a shortage of pictures. That's why we started in that particular time.

The first picture we made ourselves really was a B picture. It was a Western in color called *Apache Woman* [directed by Roger Corman, 1955]. Lloyd Bridges was in it, with Joan Taylor. And unfortunately, it played as a second feature. We realized when it went out and played as a second

---

[2] The International Alliance of Theatrical Stage Employees.
[3] The National Association of Broadcast Electronic Technicians.
[4] The International Brotherhood of Electrical Workers.

feature that we would go broke if we continued that way. So we decided to make two comparatively inexpensive pictures, but to book them together as a combination. And not sell them separately. The next picture we made was *The Day the World Ended* [directed by Roger Corman, 1956], a science-fiction picture. About a world atomic debacle, et cetera. Overnight, some people were mutated. One girl wasn't affected. Mike Connors starred in that picture . . . he was in a lot of our pictures. At least a dozen or more. He was called Touch Connors. In those days, they all had names like Touch, Tab, Rock . . . he was called Touch.

The girl's brother was mutated and wound up as a monster. We had a scene where she was bathing. It was nothing by today's standards . . . we didn't show anything. But it was a little titillating. Anyway, her brother, the monster, came up. He only had one eye—one big eye. It was a dormant thing in all people. The monster was some kind of sponge-rubber concoction.

We made the picture. Since we didn't have the money to make the second picture, we contracted with a couple of Hollywood editors to make another picture, which was *The Phantom from 10,000 Leagues* [1956].

We put those two pictures together and sent them out on a percentage basis. We would not sell them separately as second features. So, beginning right after the first picture, we would make two pictures and sell them as a combination.

As far as cost was concerned, these were not costly pictures. *The Day the World Ended,* I think, was somewhere around $100,000. Pictures were cheaper to make in those days. They were black and white. You'd shoot them in two weeks, and those were six-day weeks.

Those were certainly B-picture prices, if you want to look at it from that standpoint. But they didn't play off as B pictures. It was an exploitation combination. That did very well, and we went on to make any number of them. *I Was a Teenage Werewolf* [1957] was part of a combination. With Michael Landon. *The Bonnie Parker Story* [1958], which starred Dorothy Provine, in her first picture, was half of a combination. *Dragstrip Girl* [1957], *Hot Rod Girl* [1956], *She-Creature* [1957], there were all kinds of titles back then. Those played together and they were not expensive pictures. There might have been people who said, "These are B pictures." But that didn't have any significance anymore. They weren't B pictures, unless you think of a B picture as a picture that doesn't cost that much. But to the public, cost has never been of any significance.

We were not going to make program pictures. Because program pictures was a sure way to death. There were still companies making program pictures at that time. Republic went out of business a little later, making program pictures. Yates called Jim and I over, three or four years after we started, and wanted us to go to work for him.

The major companies wound up cannibalizing themselves. Selling off their real estate and backlogs of pictures to TV. Because they insisted on continuing to make "nice" pictures. For an audience that wasn't there anymore.

LMS: So you had a situation where the major studios failed to realize two things: that TV was a major source of competition, and that the audience had shifted to a much younger group. And that's what you built AIP on.

SZA: That's true. Because you have to be needed. It's not easy to start a picture company. Even with the tremendous amounts of capital some people have started with. Look at the millions ABC tossed in. Look at the millions National General tossed in. Look at the millions Cinerama tossed in. CBS! And they were all in the business to start with—or some part of the business. There's always been the snob-appeal factor. Producers have always wanted to make "dignified" pictures. That's not a good word for it. They want to make "nice" pictures. They want to make pictures for their mothers and their wives, and their friends. And, damn it, their mothers and their friends don't go to pictures anymore!

LMS: Are you still making films for the audience you started with in the 1950s?

SZA: To a great extent we are.

LMS: Aren't the young people more sophisticated today?

SZA: Sure. You have to make a more sophisticated picture. Of course, our pictures vary. I think a *Dillinger* [1973] will attract some older people who may remember Dillinger. But the basic audience is still going to be that audience that most frequently goes to the picture show.

I'll tell you something that people just won't recognize. Because they want to be arty-farty. We have so goddamn many arty-farties and pseudo-intellectuals in this business. Not only that, we have so many in the field of printing, publishing, writing, comment, and criticism. Just loaded with arty-farties. Our whole civilization, unfortunately, has become one of half-baked people. It's true when people say it's a more sophisticated civilization. But they're using the word *sophistry* in its original meaning, which means *artificial*. Sure, it's sophistry. It's not genuine. It's artificial. We're a cocktail-party group today. People don't much go to pictures, people don't much read

books. You know what people do? They read reviews! And they talk very
learnedly at cocktail parties.

LMS: What sort of criteria do you use when you're deciding what type
of pictures to make?

SZA: You don't make a picture for everybody and then hope that out of
that group, two or four or six million people will come. Maybe you don't
reason it out—maybe you fly by the seat of your pants—but you aim the
picture to a specific audience.

Some pictures may have a young male audience, as opposed to a young
female audience. *Wuthering Heights* [1971], for example, had a female
audience. Which didn't mean that men didn't go. A lot of young men, of
course, went with young girls. But it was a picture that young women
bought. In the same sense, our motorcycle pictures were pictures that the
young men would buy. But then you have to break it down even further.
When you talk about young males, are you talking about city or country?
The motorcycle pictures never did too well in the big cities. They did the
best, really, in the drive-ins. In, let's say, the Middle West, the South,
smaller towns.

You break these groups down even further. Obviously, *Heavy Traffic*
[1973] was more limited. First because of its X rating. Therefore it played
fewer theatres because there are theatres in many places that will not play X
films. But even with an R rating, it would have been, to some degree, a
specialized picture.

You look for certain elements. And when you're writing a script, you
put in certain elements that you feel will give it appeal.

LMS: Such as sex and violence?

SZA: Such as sex and violence. Or other aspects. It depends on the
particular subject matter.

LMS: How did you arrange distribution of AIP pictures when you were
starting out?

SZA: We started out the way many companies did: states' rights.[5]
Franchise holders. We started out with twenty-nine franchise holders, which
meant we had a subdistribution office wherever the old-line companies had
one. And we came through the same process, to where today, we own
practically all our exchanges. And today, we have more exchanges than most
of the major companies do.

The first couple of years, we made only four or five pictures a year. So

[5] See "The Economic Imperative," p. 18.

our franchise holders handled other pictures, too. Then, gradually, they became more or less exclusive AIP distributors. They had to ask us and get our consent to take on some other producer's pictures. Finally, we took them over.

LMS: How has distribution changed since you started AIP?

SZA: Over time, some of the new methods were really pioneered by us. For example, we were one of the first to play drive-ins together with hard-tops. For a long time, conventional theatres would not play with drive-ins. They would not play the same movie at the same time. Hard-tops wanted an exclusive run on a picture.

In order to have a decent advertising campaign and not lose money the first week, we wanted more theatres. Which would help divide the cost of advertising, in essence.

LMS: Were you concerned with getting back as much money as you could right away?

SZA: Sure. Because most pictures of that general type don't last, don't hang around for a year. They play one, two, three weeks, depending on how big the area is. And how important the picture is.

You go in, you get your money, and you get out. Take a *Dragstrip Girl*. When we opened it in the Los Angeles area, we played thirty or forty theatres. About sixty percent were hard-tops, forty percent were drive-ins. Although very often the greater part of the money would come from the drive-ins.

Every picture, in a sense, is an exploitation picture. But some pictures have more basic, inherent exploitation elements. *The Exorcist* [1973] is an exploitation picture. No question about it. The fact that a picture costs a lot of money does not exclude it from being an exploitation picture.

LMS: What is the most successful picture you've ever had?

SZA: Our top-grossing film is *Three in the Attic* [1968].

LMS: Do you think that was due to exploitation?

SZA: No, I think it was because of the theme of the picture.

LMS: That was the boy in the attic with three girls.

SZA: That's right. Chris Jones, who should have been a big star, but got sidetracked by some . . . nervous problems. Chris had real possibilities.

LMS: What was the biggest flop you've ever had?

SZA: Let's see . . . *De Sade* [1969], probably. Yes, *De Sade*. Even though we had, probably, one thousand dates[6] on it, or more. We really try

---

[6] That is, separate bookings at separate theatres.

with pictures. You take the old-line companies, if they don't like what a picture's doing, it just vanishes.

LMS: You push all of your films . . .

SZA: Yes. Of course. Some of the studios, once a film goes on television, take it out of release. We *never* take a picture out of release. We "cannibalize" the prints. Take print 1, maybe reels 1, 3, and 7 are good.[7] Take print 2, maybe 2, 4, 5, and 6 are good. So you put together a whole print with better reel 1, better reel 2, and so on. You make one good print out of, maybe, three that aren't so good. And we keep playing them. Like the Poe pictures, which are now on television. Although we hold pictures from television longer than anyone else does.

We take three or four of the Poes, and have a "dusk-to-dawn" show. In the drive-ins. People go to them, even if they've seen them before.

Two kinds of people go to those. The intellectuals—there are about three in the whole country—the pseudo-intellectuals, of which there are a lot more, and the arty-farties, who are universal. They go on the basis that they're campy . . . campy fun. And then you get the people who take them seriously. You keep playing to those groups.

LMS: What, to change the subject a little, was the exact gross on *De Sade,* if you recall?

SZA: That grossed $1,250,000. We've had lower grossers than that. But it was our biggest flop, because we had a very big advertising bill on that.

There are pictures today that will not even make back the cost of prints and advertising. That never used to happen. The old-line major companies, especially, make many pictures like that. And, remember, they've got other costs to get back, like the cost of the picture itself.

LMS: To what do you attribute AIP's success?

SZA: A certain measure of luck. Consistency of management. We're one of the few companies in the business where the original owners are still running the company. Until we went public a few years ago, Jim Nicholson and I were personally liable on the notes at the bank. For millions of dollars' worth of notes. When you're urinating your own money, you don't urinate it away quite as quickly. I won't use the vernacular.

Other film companies have another problem. Let's be frank about it. I have to think about what's good for this company next year, too, not just this year. Take a company with salaried management—they only think about this year, because if this year isn't good, they may not be there next year. That

---

[7] Not worn out from excessive scratches and splices.

was the difference with the old Hollywood moguls. Some of them were characters, but at least they had the welfare of this industry at heart. As they saw it. We wouldn't agree with the blacklist today, for example. We wouldn't agree that they were smart in rejecting television. They should have jumped in with both feet. But, according to their own lights, they were looking to the future, for the betterment of their companies.

Today you don't have that. You have conglomerates that own a lot of them. Movies are not an industry today, in the sense that an industry is unified. It's not unified at all. It's a lot of cottage industries, if you want to look at it that way.

LMS: Why did you go public?

SZA: I was the largest stockholder. I didn't want to go public. I didn't need to. Others in the company felt it would make their own stock interests more *meaningful,* to use one of those words that isn't meaningful. It was an internal matter, really.

LMS: What were the major turning points for the company?

SZA: We followed the young people, really. We were making those combinations I told you about, and in 1958 we made twenty-two pictures right here in Hollywood. Eleven combinations. That's quite a few pictures to make. By that time, the other companies started to make combinations, too. Or, started to acquire them from independent producers. Everyone looked and saw what we were doing and started to copy us. By the summer of 1958, we were having lots of competition. By the spring of 1959, we realized that we couldn't go on any longer with those combinations. We had to go into something else. We did a number of different things to change the mill. We haven't really operated with combinations since then.

Jim and I imported a picture from Italy with Anita Ekberg: *Sign of Rome.* That was a pretty dismal title. We decided to change the title to *Sign of the Gladiator* [1959], and we put a hell of a gladiator in our ads. Now, there really was no gladiator in the picture; but in the dubbing, Jacques Sernas, a French actor who played a Roman general, became a gladiator. It worked. We did quite well with the picture.

We bought a Hercules picture from an Italian producer. Since Joe Levine was about to release *Hercules,* we changed the name to *Goliath* [1960]. I think we put down $20,000 for that picture. It grossed about a million eight.

The Italian pictures were a turning point, and then we started the Edgar Allan Poes about that time. Then the beach pictures came along a couple of years later.

You always have to be concerned about competition, any time you start something new. And we have been innovators. Nobody was able to compete with us on the beach pictures. The other companies saw they were successful, that they should make some but they didn't understand the fundamentals. We had no parents or serious adults in any of our beach pictures. The adults were comic: Buddy Hackett, Don Rickles, Keenan Wynn. Once the others started to compete, they used adults. One company made one and called it *For Those Who Think Young* [1964]—the old Pepsi-Cola slogan. That is the most ridiculous, hidebound, stupid concept I can think of. To put a middle-aged slogan on a youth picture. What kid would go to see a picture called *For Those Who Think Young*?

We made those pictures because we sensed a trend. We were not trying to create new areas that young people didn't want to go into or had blocks against or weren't ready for. We were trying to fathom how far and how fast the youth changes were occurring.

American Graffiti [1973] is a beach picture, x years later. Well done. As a consequence of *American Graffiti*, the networks came up with a television series, *Happy Days*. I looked at the first one. It stank; it had the parents again, which the film didn't. But that may not be a mistake in television where you have an older audience. You can do that for television. But if you did that in a theatrical picture, it would die today, just as it would have died in the time of the beach-party pictures.

From the beach pictures, we went to rebellious youth. *The Wild Angels* [1966], *Wild in the Streets* [1968]. Open rebellion. Just as the other companies started to get into that, we got out. Kent State was a tip-off. The kids turned off. When they saw students could get killed, they realized it was serious.

About that time the nostalgia routine came in because nobody wanted to look at the present. Look at *Summer of '42* [1971]. The people who made that picture's success weren't even born in 1942.

We try to figure these things out as they go along. We were the only people who weren't caught by the narcotics pictures. We made *The Trip* [1967], which made a profit. Then we stopped. Everybody else picked it up; and as late as last year they were still coming out with dope pictures! And there isn't one single company that made a buck on dope pictures! The young people had turned off. They want escapism. Not old-fashioned romantic pictures, but the young public doesn't want to look at today.

LMS: What were AIP's production methods like in the 1950s?

SZA: We'd take a title and a theme, and then make the picture based on the title and the theme. We'd write the story based on that. It was a pretty good method. It wouldn't work quite as well today, although we're really not that far from it.

Jim Nicholson was very good at that. We did most things together, but he certainly had more to do with the advertising and the titles and so forth. Jim was a very nice guy . . . you might say that he drove the white car and I drove the black car. If there were ever any problems, I was always the one involved. I enjoyed the part of picture-making that had to do with putting the pieces of the picture together. Getting the picture started. I always felt that once a picture got started, it was the director's picture. And I frankly could never get much enjoyment from just hanging around a set. Jim loved being on the stage. There are a great many people who love it; I don't happen to love it. I don't like being a part of anything where I'm secondary. At the beginning, when you're deciding what to make, dealing with the writer, picking a director, those are things over which you have control.

Once they get on the set, it's really in the hands of the director. I look at the rushes. If there's anything conspicuously wrong, I'll talk to the director. I don't like to hang around a set, but some people love it. But if there are any problems, I'm always the man they call for first.

Once the rough-cut is put together, I come back into the picture.

If there's any trouble, I drive over in my black car. Not literally, but that's what it amounts to. And once I arrive, they know I mean business.

I like the business. I like the people in the business. They're rogues. It's a business of rogues. I say it nicely. But it's a business of rogues.

LMS: And you're a rogue?

SZA: No, I'm the only one who's not!

Steve Broidy

STEVE BROIDY*

Not everybody likes to eat cake. Some people like bread, and even a certain number of people like stale bread rather than fresh bread.—STEVE BROIDY

If anyone knows about B movies, it's Steve Broidy. For twenty of his nearly fifty years of involvement in the film industry, Broidy was president of Monogram/Allied Artists, the longest-lived of the genuine Poverty Row companies.

Unlike many studio heads, Broidy was born in this country in 1908, and was formally educated. Finishing law school but finding himself legally too young, at age twenty, to take the bar examination in Massachusetts, Broidy accepted what he thought would be temporary employment in Warner Brothers' Boston franchise. He became a sales-

* Interview with Linda May Strawn, January 21, 1974, Los Angeles, California.

*man for Monogram in New England in 1933 and, shortly after the
company's reorganization in 1936, was promoted to general sales manager, a position he was to hold until he replaced Ray Johnston as
Monogram's president in 1945.*

*Broidy engineered the transition of Monogram into Allied Artists in
the late 1940s and early 1950s and generally attempted to upgrade his
firm's image. As he points out, however, the small studios were the first
to feel the effects television had upon the movie industry, and finally, in
1964, Broidy began paying off the company's bank debts and soon
departed to pursue independent production. Needless to say, he never
got around to taking his bar exam.*

*As an independent producer, Broidy has been as successful as he
has been unobtrusive. He backed William Friedkin's first film,* Good
Times *(1967), with Sonny and Cher,* The Fox *(1968) and* Midas Run
(1969) and, to a great extent, bankrolled The Poseidon Adventure
*(1972). A recipient of the Academy's Jean Hersholt Humanitarian
Award in 1962, Broidy has been heavily involved in philanthropy
in Los Angeles: he has been president of Cedar Sinai Hospital since
1962, a director of the Union Bank since the late 1950s, and a bene-
factor of such schools as Loyola University of Los Angeles, Marymount,
and Claremont colleges.*

*Steve Broidy consented to be interviewed in his office at the west-
ern end of Sunset Strip.*

LINDA MAY STRAWN: What is your definition of a B film?

STEVE BROIDY: Back at the time I was connected with Monogram originally, a B film was presumed to be a low-budget picture. At that point in
time, the double-feature program was in vogue, and it became vital, in any
number of areas of the country, to use the double feature, to have a second
feature.

LMS: You're talking about the thirties and forties . . .

SB: Thirties, forties, into the fifties. Down South, where they had a
single-feature program, for the most part, they used these B pictures on
Saturdays, Saturday being a very, very big day. Not wanting the distributor
or major to participate in the gross on Saturday, they'd run pictures in two
three-day runs and keep Saturday for themselves. They'd play a Bowery
Boys or a Western or some other picture because they were assured of a
maximum gross that day, irrespective. Not only that, the type of people that
used to gravitate to these small towns in the South were once-a-week visitors

to the theatres. They were farmhands and the poorer element, and they were more interested in an action picture, such as most of these B pictures represented, than in a bedroom farce or a comedy or a sophisticated picture such as Metro made. So it served a dual purpose at that time: it got us some playing time, and it got the exhibitors some additional profits. And the major companies didn't seem to mind it too much, at that point.

As time went on, and the modest success of the companies that were making these B pictures became apparent to the major companies, they started to make a secondary A picture, known in the parlance of the business at that time as a "nervous A." They didn't spend the kind of money on these that they spent on the better quality pictures on the theory that, if the picture did not turn out to be a real big picture—and some of them might have, because budgetary limitations are not necessarily the key to an A or a B—but, in answer to your specific question, without including the exceptions, they used this as a training ground for some of their contract players and contract directors. At that time, they employed these people on a fifty-two-week-a-year basis, so they had to absorb the salaries anyhow.

LMS: Can you give an example of a "nervous A"?

SB: Well, I can't think back . . . there were so many of them. There's any number of them that were made and some of them turned out to be real top-grossing pictures. That's the bonus you'd get. We used to make these B pictures, but every once in a while we'd make a *Where Are Your Children?* [1944]. That turned out to be a big, big-grossing picture, even for us, in competition with the majors for better playing time and better terms. Things like *Dillinger* [1945], which was made for $193,000 and grossed, worldwide, in excess of $4,000,000. Now, these things came up. But with us, it was a premeditated attempt to upgrade our status in the industry. With the other companies, it was an attempt to garner all the market and to have a place to absorb the accumulated overhead that was created by having a contract list of players, directors, etc., etc. Their overhead was the same whether they made these pictures or not, so, to the extent that they absorbed some of this, it helped create a profit motivation.

LMS: *Dillinger*, then, was an attempt on your part to make a better type of film, or was that a fluke?

SB: A better type of film. Prior to that (1945), the most that we had spent on a picture was about $75,000 or 80,000, and at that point we spent $193,000, which for us was a big budget. We normally could have made four pictures. We made pictures as low as $16,000, 17,000. We made a picture with Kim Hunter, Dean Jagger, Robert Mitchum, directed by

William Castle, with musical score by Dmitri Tiomkin, the total cost of which was under $50,000.

LMS: *When Strangers Marry* [1944], yes.

SB: Now, I didn't do that. The King Brothers did that, under our direction and with our empathy for what they were trying to do. I bought the original story from William K. Howard, and I turned it over to the King Brothers and asked them if they'd apply themselves to it, because I felt they had the talent and the know-how to do that type of picture, as evidenced by other pictures that they had made for us.

Now, that kept cropping up every once in a while. We moved, because our ambition was to make a major company out of Monogram. We had some successful years and every once in a while we'd come a cropper. Being a company with small capital, the impact of anything good would show up quickly. Anything that was bad would show up just as quickly, because you're dealing within a narrow range.

LMS: I seem to remember Bill Castle saying that you tried to sell *When Strangers Marry* on a percentage deal, as opposed to a flat rental. Did you succeed, and did you sell many on a percentage basis?

SB: We started percentages with *Dillinger*. That was the first picture that we got a percentage on. And we tried, from time to time, on other pictures, and occasionally we'd get it. If we didn't get it every place, we'd get it some places. We kept making progress in that direction. One of the big things that kept us from making as much progress as we deserved to make, at a time when we were making a fairly good run of product, was the fact that the exhibitor, in those days, bought pictures based on the precedent he had paid for product. So if Monogram's top price to him was $100 per picture, he didn't want to go to $150 for fear that in the succeeding year you'd be looking for $150 for all the pictures. So he didn't differentiate about the quality of the picture—$100 was the price. That's what led to the creation of Allied Artists. It was the same company, same personnel, same everything, but we created a totally different image by calling it Allied Artists. That applied—strange as it may seem, and silly as it seems today—that applied to agents, stars, directors, all of whom would not work for Monogram, but they would work for Allied Artists, which was the selfsame company, selfsame personnel. But there was a facade created that made it conducive to them, not thinking they were being sold down the river to go to Monogram.

LMS: When you became president of Monogram in 1945, I believe, and formed Allied Artists, was it in your mind at that time that, eventually, Allied Artists would phase out Monogram?

sb: Oh, that was premeditated. We had trouble enough trying to run the one arm of the operation without trying to keep the other one going also. And we did. We successfully did that, to a point. We had a bad run of product for awhile. But we did sign Wilder, Wyler, and Huston to contracts with Allied Artists,[1] which we never could have done with Monogram. We went on from one picture to another and phased some of the smaller pictures into the Allied Artists program. We were trying to do the same thing as the major companies were doing, although on a more modified basis because we didn't have the capital structure or the fat.

Let me go back a bit. When we fell on bad times in the 1960s, I predicted that every major company would fall on bad times. I had predicted earlier that this was going to happen. I knew that what we were forced to do, they ultimately were going to be forced to do. We were just a small pea in the pod, but all the ills that were visited on us would be visited on them, the only difference being that they had a lot more fat on the bone, so they could withstand it for a lot longer than we could. We sold pictures to television first, we did a lot of firsts, and the majors kept complaining that this never should be done, and speeches were made, and meetings were held with the exhibitors and everybody else, and I could go on and on. But the position I took was that I would sell anything in the company, including my desk, to keep the company alive. I said, "You fellas may rue the day you didn't review the thing in the light of our experience. You may be Number 5 on the totem pole but there's a number on you, as there was on us." We were Number 1.

lms: What you're saying, then, is that the small studios, such as Monogram, are better barometers of the health and trends of the industry than the majors are, because that's where everything shows up first?

sb: That's right. They were at that time, because the format of the business then was entirely different than it is today. Today, people don't go to the movies, they go to the movie. Companies can't sell movies, they sell *a movie*. So the whole concept of the business is different than it was at that time. Now, the major company can no more force the sale of an indifferent, poor box-office picture today than we could in those days.

[1] Billy Wilder made *Love in the Afternoon* (1957) and William Wyler made *Friendly Persuasion* (1956) for Allied Artists, but John Huston never actually directed a film for the company.

LMS: Are there any B films today?

SB: Well, there are pictures that start out as Bs and wind up as As, and that start as As and wind up as Bs. Any unsuccessful A picture is a B picture. It just falls into that category automatically. Now, Sam Arkoff[2] has done a fantastic job of maintaining a B-picture structure and doing it profitably in these times. It's been done through very astute marketing, through great advertising, and through the timeliness of the subject material that they choose. They deserve a lot of credit. Now, he, too, is finding it more difficult to make that policy work, and he's reaching out for a little better type of product on the same basis as we did. He takes a shot here or there and, if it's successful, moves on to another. If it isn't, he digests it and waits for another opportunity to make that effort.

LMS: Would it be fair to say that television has taken the place of what used to be the B film industry?

SB: Well, fundamentally it has. More so today than even four or five years ago, because what you can do on television today, you never could have done four or five years ago. The treatment of certain material, the opening up of television by the force of the creative talent, the demand to do it that way has made television take a more liberal point of view about what goes on on the screens than was true four or five years ago. If anything, this is what might affect American-International adversely. That's the type of B picture they were making that turned in A-picture grosses, which meant that the public wanted to see that type of product. Television had its own built-in censorship and didn't want to play that type of thing. Whatever the chemistry was that created the change—I'm not fully aware of it nor am I an expert on that—but the change is there on the screens. So, this may have an adverse effect on the so-called B picture with that type of subject matter. It's just natural evolution.

LMS: How important was exploitation and advertising to you?

SB: Well, it was very important. You see, most of our material was original material. We'd start with a title, sometimes, and write a story around the title.

LMS: And this is in contrast to the majors?

SB: That's right. They used to buy material, they had some top-rated screenplay writers who were very creative and who got big money in those days. We had to use ninety-five percent original material, unless it was something in the public domain. We made the Gene Stratton Porter story,

[2] Head of American-International Pictures.

The Girl of the Limberlost [1945], things of that nature. We very rarely ever bought a book. We made *Treasure Island* [1934], *Kidnapped* [1948] . . .

LMS: So, for the most part, you had to do all the selling yourself because your material wasn't presold?

SB: Yes. But the type of theatres that we played were receptive to that type of product. What I'm trying to distinguish is that not everybody likes to eat cake. Some people like bread, and even a certain number of people like stale bread rather than fresh bread. So there was a varied market and we were trying to find a niche in that market, knowing full well we had to start at the bottom. As and if we made progress, we could move ahead because we knew that that market was limited and that we could never really amount to too much catering solely to that market for the rest of our corporate existence.

LMS: Did you own any of the theatres in which you played your product?

SB: No.

LMS: In that case, you weren't affected by the divestiture order . . .

SB: No. We were not any part of the consent decree or anything else, so we could always sell our film in block and we always did.

LMS: Which theatres did you mainly use?

SB: All of them. See, I started as sales manager of the company. I could go on for hours and hours and hours . . . days! . . . giving you examples and experiences about the sale of film and this type of product to major circuits. Of itself, it's a story.

LMS: I'm sure it is. It must rely on a lot more personal contact and gimmicky promotion . . .

SB: And sometimes, the sheer force of logic. Just let me give you one example. When I became sales manager, I reviewed the country and I felt that, if I was going to be successful, I'd have to know something about every market that there was. So I decided that, over a period of a year, I'd make every city in the United States of ten thousand population or more and I'd become acquainted with every top circuit. In a fifty-two-week period, I was away the equivalent of forty-six weeks. I was on the road. I knew nobody was coming in to buy our pictures—we had to go out to sell them. But to try to sell a man pictures without knowing anything about the background of his territory was kind of stupid. The reason I was chosen sales manager was that I had been the franchise holder in New England and I was doing extremely well, while the rest of the country, with the selfsame pictures, was doing rather poorly. That's what made me stand out and gave me the opportunity to become sales manager. I made the simple deduction that all the other franchise holders were in the same basic position as I was in New England, and that why wouldn't the same things I was doing in New England apply in the rest of the country. Either one of two things: either they didn't use the approach or they didn't have the background to project an image that would be meaningful to the exhibitor, so that he would step out and do something extraordinary in giving them playing time that he didn't feel they deserved, and they accepted certain things as a *fait accompli* without trying to offset it.

So I came to California and I started here in the Fox West Coast offices. There were two buyers there, Cullen Espy and Eddie Zabel. I'm in the office of these film buyers, with the franchise holders, trying to sell some pictures. Now, the year previous, Monogram had done $7,900 and some-odd dollars' worth of business, total, with the Fox West Coast circuit. That gave me a good start because I had nothing to lose, so I could say whatever I wanted to say.

LMS: This is the early forties?

SB: Yeah. So I started arguing with these fellows and they said, "What would we want to buy this crap for? What do we want with it?" I said, "Just one minute. I'm not going to argue about what you term as crap, but let me ask you this simple question: is the best picture we make—just the single best picture we make—is it better than the worst picture of all the other companies?" And they all said, "Well, yes." I said, "Well, tell me, are the two best films we make better than the two worst films they make?" And they said, "Well, yes, they probably are." I said, "Well, then, why are you making the public sit through crap when you could get our two best films and give them a better grade of product?" Well, they didn't go for this. They didn't think it was worth it. It so happened that Charles Skouras[3] was outside the office and overheard this. He called everyone into his office. About twenty fellows, everybody with the company, traipsed into his office. He sat me down and he said, "You tell the story." I said, "Well, Mr. Skouras, it's kind of embarrassing." He said, "You tell the story. You want to do business, don't you? Tell the story!" So I went through this routine all over again. Then he turned to everybody and said, "Look. He sells a bunch of junk. Just look at his pictures! But you see how hard this man fights to sell his product? And I give you the best pictures that the market has and you complain that

---

[3] President of National Theaters Corporation and Fox West Coast Theaters Corporation.

this is wrong, that's wrong, something's always wrong. With him, with the worst pictures on the market—nothing wrong!" So he said to his boys, "Give him some business." From that developed a friendship. Two years later, we did $790,000 worth of business with them. A hundred times as much business.

In every part of the country, I went through that type of experience. In one place, Sedalia, Missouri, I sat there and waited until eleven o'clock at night. The woman's husband was running the show someplace else . . . two nights a week he ran a show in some town about eighteen, twenty miles away. I waited for him, and I was sales manager of the company. He said to me, "Are you the sales manager of this company, the general sales manager?" And I said, "Yeah." He said, "You'll sit around here until eleven o'clock at night to see me?" I said, "Yeah." He said, "Oh, I can't be that important!" I said, "Well, you're very, very, very important." He said, "Why?" I said, "The theatres that you think are important won't buy our pictures. They have no use for our product, so they're not important to us. Anybody that can't be a customer—no sense in wasting our time. Now, you can be a customer, so you are important." Well, he started to complain about this and that and to give us a negative sales talk, when his wife stepped up and said, "Look, I want you to buy some pictures from these fellas. They're perfect gentlemen, they've waited here for three and a half hours to see you and I think you ought to buy some pictures!" Well, the contract we got out of him amounted to about $700 or $800, but the thing I was trying to do—I wasn't so interested in selling that $700 or $800 as I was in impressing the man I was with, who ran the office in Kansas City, with the fact that it could be done. That was the thing that I was looking for, because the $700 or $800 wasn't the difference between success and failure. All the way back, driving back to Kansas City, he kept saying, "That's amazing. Utterly amazing. I wouldn't believe it could be done."

All over the country, it was the same thing. Selling circuits like RKO on a total-product basis. It had never been done. There's no sense in boring you with story after story, but these things stand out. There's a sense of satisfaction in having undertaken a thing and having lived with it through thick and thin, through trial and error, and still seeing the thing carry on. Those things are very vivid. Anything dealing with people as individuals is very vivid in my imagination. That's the kind of effort, I presume, that some of the big, successful companies employed in their early days when they started. Then, of course, the force of their product took over, and, having the theatres as well, they had a natural outlet, and they could swap playing time between each other, trade off playing times. But that was an entirely different ball game.

LMS: What kind of guidelines did you set down for production qualities?

SB: That's a difficult question to answer, and answer it truthfully. There were two guidelines. First, it was dictated by the amount of money we could budget, as to what we thought we had and what we thought we could borrow. That was number one—the sum total money available to make product. We tried to divide it down into the series we had. That was a pretty fixed thing, like the Western series, the Bowery Boys, the Charlie Chans, the Mr. Wongs, the things of that nature, as they may have appeared on each year's program. Then we tried to divide it amongst what we thought, in our own minds, were pictures that would get a wide play in the theatres that would normally use our type of product. So if somebody wanted the Bowery Boys or the Chans or the Westerns, we could sell some of these pictures, they were the right type. Then we had a limited amount that we could experiment with, try something different. Make a picture like Bill Castle made, make pictures of that type, which were not necessarily the kind of pictures we were noted for. Not that that one cost so much money, but we had others that cost more money.

LMS: Did you have a certain rule of thumb when it came to cost/profit ratio?

SB: Not that would mean anything to you. When we did well, we did far better than we expected and when we did poorly, we lost a heck of a lot more money than we ever anticipated. The vagaries of the marketplace had a heck of a lot to do with the ultimate success or failure. Sometimes we had a run of product that should have done extremely well, but then something would come out—Metro would make a picture, or somebody would make something, and chew up some of the playing time that normally would have been available to us. And since we were an added starter—we were only called on like a convenience station—"Here, we need some pictures. Get a couple of pictures from Monogram." So, quality of product, unless it was truly outstanding, and we had some of those, was not necessarily the yardstick by which we could gauge our potential success or failure. We had to sit there and take it a heck of a lot of times, and keep from getting a case of apoplexy watching some pictures play when we had pictures that deserved to play.

LMS: Why did Monogram never make serials?

SB: There were several things involved. We sized up the market and there was a sufficient number of serials being played at that time. We were one of the first to understand what television was going to do to the motion-picture business. We kept saying that, and we tried to sell to television. We were the ones that fought the Internal Revenue Service and established the fact that the sale of a negative constituted a capital gain. We got the first ruling on that. I could see very clearly, and I hoped, that television would employ the technique of the serial. I wasn't foresighted enough to think of a *series*. I was thinking of it as a serial. I went to all the networks; I tried to sell them on the idea of serials. Well, they didn't know themselves what they wanted to do, or how they wanted to do it, as best evidenced by the fact that I tried to sell each one of the networks 200 negatives for a total of $1,000,000, $5,000 apiece. There was a company called PRC that had sold 171 negatives for $1,750 apiece. Anyway, they wouldn't buy it. I kept saying to the fellows, "What are you going to run, slides?" He said, "No, we're going to have all live shows, we're not going to fall into the hands of the agents like we did in radio," etc., etc. I said, "Live? There won't be rehearsal halls enough in the United States. Are you kidding?" He said, "We only have to have six to eight hours of product." I said, "You're going to need twenty hours of product before you get through." But you couldn't get anyplace because they had their minds made up. That was it and that's the way it was going to be. You just might as well give up as try to change their plans.

LMS: When you were head of the studio, where did you exercise most of your power? Were you directly concerned more with talent, production, budgeting, policy—I know you were involved with all of them, but, as an individual, which one involved you the most?

SB: I tried to get involved on the creative side only to the extent of deciding what type of material we were making. Once it was determined that a picture was going to be made, I stayed away from it all unless I was invited in by the producer for any comment I might wish to make. But I never went near there, and I do the same thing now when I back a picture. I don't go near the place unless I'm asked, because the die is cast and all you can do is confuse the issue and make it worse. Now, if a fellow was starting to go over budget! We made the picture *Black Gold* [1947] with Tony Quinn—I helped get Tony to do that picture, it was the first starring role he had. Now, this was going on and on and on. Jeffrey Bernerd was the producer. He had made *Women in Bondage* [1943], which title I created. I said, "This thing could break the company, the way you're going on and on. When are you going to finish?" He said, "We're going to finish tomorrow night at seven." I said, "Is that a promise?" He said, "That's a promise." I said, "Jeff, you're not going to shoot one minute past seven. Whatever you need, whatever cover shots there are, you'd better shoot them early and get it all over with, because you're not going to shoot past seven o'clock tomorrow night."

The following day at four o'clock in the afternoon I went out on the stage and I saw them starting to make preparations to change a box that presumably made the set look like Churchill Downs. I knew that was going to take a couple of hours of physical labor by carpenters just to rearrange the box. So I walked up to Jeffrey and I said, "Jeff, I'm just going to tell you this: I'm giving instructions now that the lights go out on this stage at seven o'clock. You're not going to shoot another minute. Whatever you've got, you're going to have to make do with. You're not at Metro and you're not at Paramount. This is it. You've taken advantage of things as far as you're going to be able to take them." That box never meant anything to the picture, he made a darned good picture, it turned out to be an extremely well-accepted picture and it *was* a good picture. A change in that box wouldn't have added one thing to the picture. There's the old cliché that they tell about D. W. Griffith shooting a picture and having an assistant director come to him late in the afternoon and say, "Mr. Griffith, I made a terrible mistake. I'm afraid you're going to have to shoot everything all over. It's all my fault." Griffith said, "What's the trouble?" He said, "That clock over the desk hasn't been moved forward. It says two o'clock and all the action takes place the rest of the afternoon and it still says two o'clock." He said, "Son, don't worry about it. If the people are watching the clock, as against what's taking place in this sequence, it won't make that much difference one way or the other."

LMS: You had many people come in as independent producers at Monogram. You had the King Brothers, Katzman, Corman. What was the degree of independence that these independent producers had, once they had made a deal with you?

SB: They couldn't have any more. They had it all. I mean, we had the final cut if we wanted to make changes, but I never exerted it. I don't know, that's for them to say, not for me to say. But I think our approach to that was rather constructive, irrespective of what the contract might say. We gave them a lot of latitude.

LMS: You had the final cut, though. Were you apt to turn his lights off at seven if he was going over budget?

SB: No, that was the only time in my experience at the studio. I only illustrate that in trying to prove the point that there was no purpose in spending that extra money, because the picture was made. The fact that the box was at this angle, rather than that angle, was of no consequence to the story or to the impact of the picture, or anything else.

LMS: Sometimes directors get very perfectionistic.

SB: Well, don't you see, there's another thing you have to keep in mind. A lot of these fellows that made pictures for us were using us to get a screen test for a major-company opportunity. We were aware of this, because that's where most of them went! So we felt there was a certain price they could pay for the luxury of us giving them a screen test.

LMS: If that's where they went, where did they come from?

SB: They had worked as assistant directors, or some of them had just been promoters, as they are today. Don't forget, working for us provided hard, fast, tried proof. If you could make pictures for Monogram, you could make pictures for anybody. When they moved into that studio, they knew they had people capable of making the pictures.

LMS: Did you ever have people who came from within the studio itself become directors?

SB: Oh, Jerry Thorpe, any number of them. Eddie Dmytryk worked for us as a writer and assistant director and became a director.

LMS: Who do you think were the best directors who worked at Monogram or Allied Artists?

SB: Oh, let me think of who made the most successful pictures . . .

LMS: Which pictures were most successful?

SB: *Friendly Persuasion.*

LMS: Oh, that's a wonderful picture.

SB: Well, that's a case where nobody wanted to make that picture. It was a trick to make it. Of course, Mr. Mirisch was involved in getting that package put together with those three directors. I don't want to do anybody a disfavor by not mentioning their names. There are any number of them. We had Don Siegel. Phil Karlson made some extremely successful pictures. *Hell to Eternity* [1960] was a very, very successful picture that was made by independents, Levin and Mandel. You're talking about 1939 to 1965, that's twenty-six years of exposure. It's very hard to highlight any one, but there are any number of them.

Let me give you a more current case in point. I gave Billy Friedkin his first job as a feature director.[4] I gave Mark Rydell his first job as a feature motion-picture director.[5] I didn't do it by record; these people were called to my attention. I looked at some of the commercials they had made and some of the film they had made. I said, "Yes, let's go." These were far more expensive pictures.

LMS: Was it your idea to form Allied Artists?

SB: Yes. I was the one who was exposed to this problem, running around the country trying to sell film. The people who were then running the company were amenable to anything that could get the job done. I just came up with the crazy idea that, since we were franchise holders, we were *allied*. And we used the word *artists*, so that's where the name came from.

LMS: What was your relationship with Ray Johnston and Trem Carr?

SB: I was a salesman working in the Boston exchange area. The franchise holder was a man named Herman Rifkin, who was a very close friend of both Ray Johnston and Trem Carr. In prior years, they had Rayart Films. Before that, they had something else. They decided to form this unit called Monogram. I was a film salesman and then I was promoted to city salesman. Then, around 1935, Monogram was merged into Republic, and I couldn't see this going anyplace. I went to see Mr. Rifkin, and I said, "I enjoyed working here and it's been fun, but I'm not particularly interested in pursuing this any further because I think this is a monopoly of B pictures and that it isn't going to go anyplace." Now, I wasn't entirely right in my assumption at that time, but that was my assumption. He said, "Don't do anything. Something's going to happen soon." So the next thing I knew, Monogram was re-formed. The time in the contractual relationship between Johnston and Carr and Republic had terminated, and Mr. Yates,[6] in his purchase of Monogram, didn't buy the *name* Monogram. So Johnston quit and re-formed Monogram. Rifkin bought the franchise for New England for Monogram and I became the franchise holder, because, legally, he couldn't own the Republic franchise and own another franchise. His Republic contract prevented it. So I operated the exchange in Boston.

Now, things went from bad to worse with Monogram. They were down to doing about $28,000 a week, national gross. I was averaging about $5,000 out of that $28,000, so they invited me to become a member of the board of directors of the company, figuring I could give them some ideas. Of course, my relationship with Johnston and Carr had expanded during this period.

[4] *Good Times* (1967).
[5] *The Fox* (1968).
[6] Herbert Yates, head of Republic Studios.

They had called me and borrowed money from my banks in Boston. There's a whole long story about that. The bank said, "You mean you're coming in here to borrow money for a third party? Why don't they borrow it themselves?" I said, "They can't get it." The bank said, "Well, how do you expect us to give it to them if they can't get it?" I said, "There's a simple equation: the money's in trust, based on the contracts that we have written, and your share of the money, to the amount I'm asking, is protected in any event, otherwise I wouldn't be in here asking." I got it. They thought I had something to offer and they brought me into New York and elected me to the board of directors. There was a lot of uproar about this but, without bragging or trying to be egotistical, I can say that I made my presence felt because I was the only one who knew anything about the distribution of product, other than Ray Johnston. These people were lawyers, stockbrokers. They didn't know up from down about the picture business. It was ridiculous. Here's a company slowly expiring, that needed a good shot in the arm, and these people couldn't help. They would if they could, but they didn't know enough about the problem to even suggest anything. So, more and more, it became a matter of Trem Carr saying to Ray Johnston, "If you and Steve agree, go ahead. We'll do it." The board was like a rubber stamp. All they wanted to know was if the company would stay in business.

Finally, I got a call from California, and they said, "Look, we want you to be sales manager of the company." I came out here in November of 1939 and I worked out on the range all the time. It wasn't for all that much more money than I was getting before, but I included a profit participation, a percentage of the gross over double what they were doing, which they gladly gave me because they never figured that they could ever do that much. I didn't know that they could ever do it either, but I figured that if I'm going to have an objective, I might as well have some of the benefits that might accrue from any accomplishments that did develop.

The first thing I said when I got out here was, "Stop making pictures." They said, "Why? That's silly." I said, "I'll tell you why. Your product, which you've made for the past year and a half or two, is practically new in every situation in the country. Why not concentrate on trying to sell those pictures and get as much as we can out of that, which will be all one-hundred-cent dollars, before we start expanding and making newer product. This will be dead inventory gone" [i.e. making back the cost of films whose production costs had already been written off as a loss]. They couldn't understand it, so I sat down and took a pad and a pencil and showed them what had happened in New England. I said, "If I can get them to accomplish twenty-five percent of this in the rest of the country, you'll have more money than you could ever have by making ten successful pictures of the type that we're making." They started thinking about it and thinking about it, and they finally said, "Gee, we'll stop for about five or six months and give you a chance. We'll see what happens."

Dealing with the franchise holders, I tried to relate the product to the requirements of each territory. It was a different kind of approach. In some places, where there were no requirements, I tried to relate it as an insurance policy against the major companies, at some point or other, determining to get terms that were not consistent with the theatres showing a proper profit. It was a rather philosophical approach, rather than selling the value of the picture as a picture. How do you come to a man and try to sell him a picture that he passed up a year ago, and have him play it today? The man would say you're out of your cotton-pickin' mind! But if you sold the philosophical side of what this meant, that he was going to help keep a company in business that might turn out to be a very, very valuable source of supply, then this calls for extraordinary action. If all this doesn't make that much difference to him, why should we gamble more money on new product? Now, they bought that, whereas they wouldn't buy the pictures. To a man named Fitzgerald in Milwaukee, I said, "You spend $3,000,000 a year for product. Would it be asking too much for you, in the next six months, to spend $50,000 or $60,000 with Monogram? Don't you think your bookers can find a place to squeeze these pictures in? It might be meaningful to you and a lifesaving operation for us." And that's the way it went.

William Castle

WILLIAM CASTLE*

I say an audience doesn't know what they want to see, but they know what they *don't* want to see.—WILLIAM CASTLE

William Castle could reasonably be called the Last of the Great Showmen. Like Hitchcock, he has gone out of his way to make his name, if not his face, familiar to moviegoers all over the world. Castle can also be thought of as Mr. Gimmick, for a trick device of some sort was invariably the key to the promotional campaigns for his horror films of the late 1950s and early 1960s. There are probably few children of that era who didn't experience Castle's buzzing seats during The Tingler (1959) *or his flying skeletons during* The House on Haunted Hill (1958).

Apparently, Castle cultivated his taste for both terror and clever

* Interview with Linda May Strawn, December 6, 1973, Beverly Hills, California.

exploitation early in life. When barely out of his teens, he directed Bela Lugosi in a Brooklyn stage version of Dracula. *One summer in the mid-1930s, Castle took over the direction of an East Coast regional playhouse from Orson Welles (Castle was later an associate producer on* The Lady from Shanghai, *1948). To boost business for a play featuring an unknown actress recently arrived from Germany, Castle, in the dead of night, threw bricks through his theatre's windows and painted swastikas on the walls. This "Nazi attack" was front-page news the next morning, and business was brisk for the remainder of the engagement.*

Harry Cohn must have got wind of this, for by 1937, Castle was with Columbia in Hollywood. As a director, Castle's major contributions in the 1940s consisted of several installments of The Whistler *series and the B classic,* When Strangers Marry *(1944). The horror cycle established Castle as a major independent producer, and the high point of his career, financially and critically, was* Rosemary's Baby *(1968), which, of course, he did not direct.*

One wall of Castle's comfortable office in downtown Beverly Hills is covered with photographs of him in the company of assorted celebrities. He delights in challenging his visitors to guess the celebrities' identities, and so far, he claims, no one has been able to guess them all. Castle was busy editing his latest film, Shanks *(1974), when he agreed to take time out for the interview.*

LINDA MAY STRAWN: What is your definition of a B film?

WILLIAM CASTLE: It was a category, in the early days of Hollywood, that existed when the audiences insisted on having two features before they'd go to the theatre. No matter how big the picture was, no matter what star it was, they wanted two features; and theatres had to book two features to please the audience. Obviously, the first feature would have a big star of the day, a Gable or a Harlow or a Crawford, and was made for a relatively large amount of money. That film was played on a percentage basis. The distributor would sell the film to the exhibitor on a percentage. In other words, a percentage of the take. It could be a 50/50 split or whatever . . . it could be sold at 60/40, or 30/70, depending on how important the film, but it was on a percentage basis. In order to fill out the bill, outside of the newsreel and the cartoon, they needed another feature. This feature was sold at a flat rental, so the studio, or distributor, knew exactly what that feature would get at the theatres because they knew how many bookings they had. So they could almost tell going in that it would make a small profit. It could only be made at a certain price, usually a very low price, anywhere from $50,000 to $80,000. Possibly the studios on flat bookings would spend, maybe, $100,000 and make about $20,000 or $25,000 profit. Therefore, they insisted that those films be made on schedule and on budget, and, in order to categorize them, they called them As and Bs. The As were the percentage films and the Bs were the flat booking films. It did not mean that the B picture was not a good picture, or that the A picture was better because it had an A. It only meant that there was more money that went into the A, that it had bigger stars. The B picture was really a workshop, and some of the big directors and stars were built out of the B units, and some of the great pictures of the time were made as Bs and released as As. As and Bs mean nothing today. The only thing that makes any difference in today's market is whether a picture makes money or not. Many pictures that were made inexpensively have proven themselves, and many pictures that were terribly expensive were flops, like *Star!* [1968], *Paint Your Wagon* [1969], and *Darling Lili* [1969], which was in the $25,000,000 bracket to make and lost at the box office. Little pictures, like *Marty* [1956], and *Mean Streets* [1973], and *American Graffiti* [1973] of today, made for relatively small money, cannot be called As or Bs. They're just good pictures.

LMS: Could you give an example of a film in the past that was made as a B film and released as an A film?

WC: That goes way back, because the B connotation went out a long time ago except for bad or good films, which is a misnomer. I know Charlie Vidor, the director, the one that did *Gilda* [1946] and all the Rita Hayworth pictures, made a film on a twelve-day schedule, supposedly, on a B unit at Columbia, that went twenty-four days. Usually, you'd be fired if you went one day over schedule. He went twenty-four days—double his schedule. I don't remember the name of it, but Harry Cohn liked the picture so much that he pulled it out of the unit and released it as an A. But I don't remember the name of it. It's very difficult to go back and remember the Bs that were promoted into As, but there were a few that made the A realm and were sold on percentage.

Speaking of today, *American Graffiti* was made at a very low price. Universal *did* know what they had, and it's one of the biggest grossers there is. It's an amazing thing. My films, like *Homicidal* [1961], *The Tingler* [1959], *Strait-Jacket* [1964], were made on very low budgets and played top, top theatres on percentages. So it isn't a question of what you spend on a picture that gives it the connotation A or B, even though they call them

Bs—"King of the Bs: Castle." The pictures played percentages, like any other A picture, and sometimes beat the A pictures.

LMS: The reason in the past, then, that a B film might have been promoted to an A film was simply quality?

WC: Yes. Harry Cohn, for example, would see it and say, "This picture's much too good to give it a flat rental. Let's put it on a percentage and we'll make a great deal of money."

LMS: What, then, were the production qualities you would associate with B films? A low budget, to begin with.

WC: Well, a low budget means that you don't have the time to make the picture you might like to have, and that you can't pay prohibitive prices for the cast. The whole essence of the B movie is that it's done on talent, not on spending money. You don't have to spend a great deal of money on a film. You use the director's talent, the artist's talent, to make the picture. Sometimes a picture becomes better in spite of itself, because maybe too much money spoils a picture. You don't have as big a canvas to work with, so therefore you must . . . I think Polanski's *Knife in the Water* [1963], which is a classic, is far better than some of the films he's made for many millions of dollars. It was made on a shoestring, but, because of his artistry in spite of having to work on a shoestring, he was judged by the merit of his work. I think many, many directors have started that way.

LMS: With the demise of the studio system, what has happened to the B film? Do you think television has taken its place, in any sense, as a proving ground?

WC: As a workshop, yes. But there is no such thing as a B film today, it's no longer in existence, except some people still remember A and B in terms of good or bad, expensive or cheap, which no longer exist. Many people would debate that, but it's true. There is no such thing as a B film or an A film, there's a good film or a bad film. The nearest thing we have to it is the Movie of the Week, which is a workshop. Some of them are magnificent, some of them are very bad, but it's the same thing. They're made on a very low budget, with very small cameras. Very ambitious, some of them, and some of them are brilliant and have been turned into films.

LMS: I understand that you had a certain financial formula all your own that you stuck to, and that this practically guaranteed that you wouldn't lose money.

WC: There's no guarantee that you lose or gain money. It's a crapshoot no matter what you do. You can minimize your losses by, first, knowing why you're making the picture and for whom you're making the picture. I think most producers today just make a picture to satisfy their own ego trip. It's something they want to do, which is fine. But does the audience want to see what they want to do? Everyone asks, "Does the audience know what they want to see?" I say an audience doesn't know what they want to see, but they know what they *don't* want to see. If you take what they don't want to see, that eliminates a great many films. I also feel that an audience wants to be entertained. They don't care what a picture costs. You can say the picture cost $500,000 or $50,000,000—if they don't like the picture, they're not going to see it. It's a chemistry. So if the creative artist will at least think before he goes, and say to himself, "Is there an audience for it, and what audience?" We have very many splits in our society today for motion pictures. There was a time when you put a sign out: Moving Pictures Tonight, and people would line up just to see a movie. But now with the competition of sports, night baseball, boating, outdoor camping, television, all the other things that the public does to entertain themselves, movies are no longer the only mode of entertainment. Where we used to have ninety million people a week in attendance, we have fifteen million today. But, those fifteen million, ironically, are split up in three or four segments, as proven by *Airport* [1970] and *The Poseidon Adventure* [1972], as against *Last Tango in Paris* [1973], as against *Mean Streets,* as against *The Godfather* [1972], as against *Love Story* [1970], as against *American Graffiti.* You've got all different segments, even the *Deep Throat* [1972] segment, of people that want a certain type of entertainment.

LMS: Who were you making your films for?

WC: The maximum is to try to do it for the largest mass. Let's face it, our audience today is comprised of, outside of the children, the group between sixteen and thirty. That's eighty percent of your audience. I would even go as high as eighty-five percent. Our young adults from sixteen to thirty—if you want to stretch it to thirty-five, OK—but within the radius of those years. The rest is a minority group. They're not going to make your picture. So, therefore, you are appealing to a younger element and if you can try to figure out what that younger element wants, you're in business. They don't want to be lied to, that we know. I do think the pendulum is swinging back to the linear story line, with a beginning, middle, and end. I think the day of the *Easy Rider* [1969] is over. I think we've had the pot-smoking . . . I think we were really mixed up in our entertainment. We were trying new things and we went after every phase of what was happening in our society. I do think that that is over with, hopefully for good. Now we're going back to more linear entertainment, and also going back to the nostalgia of the thirties, forties, and fifties. The pictures that have been the most successful, and hopefully *The Great Gatsby* [1974] will prove it, are the nostalgic pictures. *Gatsby* is in the twenties, *American Graffiti* is in the sixties, the Barbra Streisand–Robert Redford picture is in the forties[1] . . . almost every time I pick up the paper today and read what's playing at the movies, there's some nostalgic picture that seems to have caught the fancy of the American public. Schlesinger's doing *The Day of the Locust* [1975], which is the thirties. Just go right down the line.

LMS: Is this audience of sixteen to thirty the same one you were aiming for when you made your horror films?

WC: Oh, yes. It's always been my audience. But I went lower. In other words, I got them, hopefully, from nine and ten. Mostly, my audience was comprised of nine-, ten-, eleven-, twelve-, up to about fifteen-, and sixteen-year-olds. The majority of my audience was the youngsters and young adults. But then, they were a little more sophisticated.

LMS: The youngsters were?

WC: The youngsters were. My films weren't. Of course, they're studying them now. It's an amazing thing that's happening. They've now become important in studies in school, which is a rarity. I spoke at USC last night and talked about my films, which they had seen as children. They're students today, college students. Harvard has called me, Stanford has called me, and Yale has called me to ask what I meant by certain things in films that I had done in the past that they are now studying. It's amazing. I didn't take them seriously myself. I did them for fun. But they're taking them very seriously now. I had a scene in *Strait-Jacket* where Crawford was coming off a train and she was enveloped by the smoke coming from underneath the car, and when she left the railroad station she was completely enveloped in smoke. I was asked by somebody in a workshop at Harvard whether or not what I had in mind was to envelop her in her mother's womb in the fetus position. This is rather ridiculous, and what can you say? It merely was because lunch was late and I had to get off that set. The special effects man pushed the button for too much smoke. I couldn't actually say that it was a question of my being late for lunch, so I said, "Whatever is in your unconscious mind is probably what I had in mind too."

[1] *The Way We Were* (1973).

When I did *The Tingler,* which has the tingler struggling to possess part of a person's body, and when you'd scream you'd release the tingler, I used a deaf-mute, who obviously couldn't scream, and the tingler finally strangled her to death through her back, which is a swell gimmick. I was asked by somebody at Yale whether the tingler was my statement against the establishment and whether it was my plea against war and poverty. Again, I said that maybe it's something in my unconscious mind. I asked Alfred Hitchcock what he said and he thought that would do well. But it's very difficult to answer these questions. Who knows? It might have been in my unconscious mind. But at least I made entertainment.

LMS: That's right. Didn't you develop a basic core of people who worked with you from film to film?

WC: Yes. I had them all under contract, I had my own unit. I had my own cameraman, Hal Stine; I had my scripts from Leonard Poole; I had my associate producer, Dona Holloway; I had my own press man, Lynne Unkifer; Sidney Balkin in charge of my exploitation materials and merchandising; I had three or four secretaries . . . I had a big, big staff. My own cutters . . . it was a movie studio within a movie studio just making the Castle films.

LMS: These were people whom you found . . .

WC: These were people I found along the way. I liked working with them, so I put them under contract.

LMS: What about your work at Monogram Studios?

WC: Well, Monogram Studios was a little studio that nobody paid much attention to. Again, there were A and B studios and, again, that's a false connotation. Monogram, which later became Allied Artists, made inexpensive B pictures, which they tried to book on percentage. They called them small As. I got my start, really, at Columbia but I was on loan-out to Monogram and I did a couple of very fine films there. *Dillinger* [1945], with Lawrence Tierney, was one that I wrote with Phil Yordan. I didn't direct this one, but I directed *When Strangers Marry* there, which is one of the best films I've ever done. It really was great. It had a script by Phil Yordan, music by Dmitri Tiomkin; it was Rhonda Fleming's first film; Bob Mitchum got marvelous reviews, and it was one of his first films; Dean Jagger, Kim Hunter was just starting, and I directed it. It was made on a shoestring and it really got all sorts of awards. It's still playing in Paris.

LMS: Was that a Monogram film that was released on a percentage?

WC: It was released on a percentage and made a great deal of money.

Allied Artists has now grown in proportions and they're just releasing *Papillon* [1973], with Dustin Hoffman and Steve McQueen. So, those days were marvelous days because Allied Artists, or Monogram, as you put it, was a workshop. It was marvelous to work in a small studio, where you were the kingpin.

LMS: Did Monogram take young people in order to develop them or exploit them because it could get them cheaply?

WC: No, they'd try to make deals with stars cheaply, stars who were out of work at the time, or were starting. Yeah, they'd use beginners.

LMS: And directors?

WC: And directors. They'd take newcomers that were under contract to other studios and borrow them. They borrowed me from Harry Cohn at Columbia after seeing one of my pictures.

LMS: I wanted to ask you about your relationship with Harry Cohn . . .

WC: What can I say about my relationship with Harry Cohn? He was my father, my brother, my boss, I feared him, I loved him. It was a hate/love relationship. He was a fantastic man, *the* movie mogul of those days, he ran people's lives. He was very good to me. He really taught me the motion-picture business. He said, when I walked into his office for the first time, that he was going to teach me every facet of it. And he taught me every facet of movies, from cutting to acting to dialogue directing to directing to producing to production manager to assistant director . . . everything! I got the entire bit, which people are learning in film schools today, which they didn't have then, I got it firsthand from the master.

LMS: This was special treatment that he afforded you?

WC: Not special treatment. It was just the school he believed in. He thought that the people like Capra and Stevens were not getting any younger and he wanted to develop new talent. He was way ahead of his time, because we're doing that today. As early as the forties, he wanted to develop young talent to take the place of the masters. He had three or four people that he really liked that he put through this school. I got fifty bucks a week for learning, but I would have paid him if I could have afforded it, because it was a marvelous school. He was a visionary. He got me into every one of those jobs, and finally said, "You're ready to direct," and gave me my first picture. Which, ironically, was called *The Chance of a Lifetime* [1943].

LMS: Could you say a few words about your cost/profit ratio on your horror films, and, also, is such a ratio possible today?

WC: Oh, it's much greater today. The costs are greater and the profits are greater! Look, I got up to bat during the late fifties through the middle sixties, and every time I had a ball I struck a home run. I was a money machine. Now those days are over, because each one is an individual picture on its own. They were booking Castle pictures sight unseen. They wanted to know just when the next one was coming. I had no stars, so my name was above the titles and on the marquees. It was "William Castle Presents," and they booked my pictures a year in advance. All I had to do was deliver and I could do no wrong. Each one made more and more money. Those days are finished, but something else has happened today. The roll of the dice is not as hot, but if you do get hot, i.e., *The Godfather*—$120,000,000, that is unheard of! *Love Story*—$75,000,000 and they think they're going to do $80,000,000. *Rosemary's Baby* in the upper thirties. You know, these were pictures that were made for a fraction of the cost. So if you can make a picture for a half million dollars today and do ten times its negative cost, you've got $1,000,000 profit there. But it's tough to get $5,000,000 today. It's as tough to get 5,000,000 as 120,000,000. But if you hit, you will make unheard-of fortunes. But there are more misses because your audiences today are much more perceptive.

LMS: How did you average out in the past?

WC: I never had a loser. All my pictures made money. Some made a little money and some made great money. Some averaged as high as twenty times the negative cost, if you can believe this. That's unbelievable. Some just broke even and made a couple of bucks. When I say twenty times the negative cost, I might be exaggerating a little bit.

LMS: Which film was this?

WC: Well, I don't want to mention pictures. But just imagine making a picture for $100,000 and pulling in $5,000,000. Or spending 300,000 and earning $6,000,000. That was the ratio. Of course, I spent a great deal of money in exploitation. Sometimes I spent double what I spent on the negative. I might spend $300,000 or two-fifty to make the picture and 500,000 to exploit it.

LMS: You were certainly unique in the field of exploitation.

WC: I was unique.

LMS: And your ideas were all your own?

WC: My ideas were all my own.

LMS: Which you just pulled out of the air?

WC: Which I pulled out of the air, or which I pulled out of my nightmares. Or which I thought of at night, or during the day. Even during the day, I'll be sitting and all of a sudden say, "I've got an idea." Where they come from, you don't know. It's something that you either have or you don't. And I have ideas. I'm an idea man.

LMS: And you stressed personal contact, didn't you, with the actual exhibitors?

WC: And also with the audience.

LMS: You must have been the first to do that—to go out on the road from theatre to theatre?

WC: Shake hands with the customers, sure. Meet the ticket taker, meet the candy girl, meet the audience. Shake hands with them, talk to them, find out what they're all about. One cannot make a picture and know what a public wants, sitting in an ivory tower with a projection room, like some people I know. I think you have to go into theatres and see what the audience wants in order to have contact with them. I think this is why many Hollywood executives miss a great deal of what they're making, because they don't know. All they can do is get figures of what pictures are doing business. But they're not on the level of an audience. They're not ready to stand in line, as I do. I'll go to a theatre and I'll stand in line with the rest of the people, the poor slobs—of which I am one—and I'll stand in line, buy my ticket, buy my popcorn, sit down, and talk to people. I'm a talky guy. I relate to people and, as a result, I get a feel of young people and what they want today. I don't know if I'm going to be able to make successful pictures at the box office, but I'm jolly well going to try.

LMS: Would you say that you couldn't make the films that you made for your nine-to-sixteen audiences today? Do you think kids nine to sixteen are too sophisticated?

WC: Oh, God yes. There are no nine-year-olds anymore! It's amazing, the whole communications field. Communication schools, study centers, everything, how far they've advanced! So, we don't have children anymore, do we? We have mental giants. We are no longer in the Doris Day–Rock Hudson era. They are movie buffs, they are sophisticated. The nines and tens, literally, today have the mentality of the twelves and thirteens. The thirteens are dating and the sixteens—the sixteens are having their first baby. God, where are we going? It's a society that is growing up fast. It's possibly because of what has happened in our country and throughout the world. There's no communications gap. We find out immediately what's happening. And no longer is our president on a great white horse, as you so well know. What you feel politically doesn't matter in this discussion, but communications—television, news media—everything is instantaneous.

Therefore, everybody is growing up fast. And it's a very strange thing that, in this growing-up era, we're going back to a nostalgia for the past, for what it was like when it was a different world. I think our audiences today are a lot more sophisticated. Why they are is because of the times. With the words they use on the screen today . . . I was the first one that brought *shit* to the public . . . I'm talking about the word, not the film! In *Rosemary's Baby,* it was the first time in an American film that word had ever been used. It was very rough to get the thing through, but we finally did.

LMS: The new film, *The Battle of the Amazons* [1973], has been using a bit of the outlandish, old-fashioned, hoopla P.R. gags that you pioneered. Do you see the old gimmicks you used coming back in any way, shape, or form?

WC: It's a very difficult question. I think there's a lack of showmanship in Hollywood today that is very apparent, next to what Mike Todd used to do, and what I did. I really feel that there is no showmanship to speak of in Hollywood today. I think it's an ingredient that is sadly missing from our American scene—the fun of exploitation. Every picture's different and has to be sold on its own merit, but you've got to let people know about it. You can't just let them know about it through newspapers and television and reviews, and I think this has been proven. I was watching television and I saw Billie Jean King and Bobby Riggs in that tennis match. Now this is tennis. It's not a prizefight or a football game, this is tennis. And although people enjoy playing tennis, tennis on an international basis of spectatorship, at a hundred dollars a ticket like a prizefight, my God! And Billie Jean King coming out as Queen of Sheba, in her litter with slaves carrying her, and Bobby Riggs coming out in his regalia, and all the cheering and yelling, and all the showmanship, which is about as cornball as you can get, proved again that this can be an important thing. I do feel, however, that we do have to be more sophisticated on our current level. No longer can I have the insurance policies, or the seat belts, or the tingler buzzing the seats, but I can have a little more sophisticated gimmick and I have used it. Such as, "Pray for Rosemary's Baby," and buttons and streamers that were magnificent. I didn't create "Pray for Rosemary's Baby." It was done by a young advertising man, but I think that was the most fantastic gimmick on a sophisticated level. I still think we have popcorn eaters and candy eaters at movies. I think if we can cater to them, not on a subtle or subliminal level, but a sophisticated level of advertising and promotion—I can't give you a direct example, but it could be a catchphrase, or it could be something at the theatre level to attract the patron on a sophisticated level. Showmanship is there. The guy that gets out and barnstorms with his picture, if he has anything at all, is the guy that's going to make twice as much money. We tested pictures, and the places where we didn't do it, no matter what we spent on the picture, we'd just do an average gross. The places I visited and barnstormed and came up with gimmickry did six and seven times the normal gross. So it proves that the personal care that a producer or creator will give his picture is going to make it do that much more business. Talk shows, of course, help too. You can go on Johnny Carson and Merv Griffin and Dick Cavett, but you do have to go further. You've got to have some little hook, whether it's perfume, whether it's incense, or whether it's a flamethrower. But you've got to have something.

Roger Corman

ROGER CORMAN*

I don't make B movies and nobody makes B movies anymore.—ROGER CORMAN

Roger Corman, businesslike as always, suggested we interview him at his New World Pictures office. The office itself, decorated with posters for Rohmer's L'Amour, l'après-midi *(1972) and the British Film Institute's Corman retrospective, is on the top floor of a Sunset Strip building. One reaches New World by ascending in a glass-enclosed elevator.*

After speaking to an associate who was setting up the East African distribution of The Student Teachers *(1973), Corman turned to the interview.*

Roger Corman rode the crest of just about every major film trend

* Interview with Charles Flynn and Todd McCarthy, September 6, 1973, Los Angeles, California.

301

of the last twenty years: teenpix, sci-fi movies, the Poe cycle, motorcycle movies, and finally, the soft-core, R-rated, sexploitation genre.

After several disappointing experiences with major studios, Corman realized his long-standing dream in 1970 when he formed his own company, New World Pictures. He started by speaking about the firm.

ROGER CORMAN: It's growing a little more than we counted on . . . the company is growing a little faster than we had originally planned. . . .

Anyway, in regard to the B movie, just as Al Zugsmith may say he doesn't make formula movies, I'd say I don't make B movies and nobody makes B movies anymore. The B movie was really the second feature movie in the great days of the major studios when they turned out vast numbers of motion pictures. A certain number were specifically earmarked as A and a certain number were specifically earmarked as B. And the Bs were always the second feature, the supporting picture. Occasionally, of course, one well-made B would come up and become an A, but that was an exception. The changing patterns of distribution, and the cost of color film specifically, has just about eliminated the B movie. The amount of money paid for a second feature is so small that if you're paying for color-release prints, you can't get it back. You can't get your negative costs back distributing your film as a B or supporting feature.

I don't know how this affects your book, but if you stay with the concept of the B movie as such, you're writing about past history.

CHARLES FLYNN and TODD MCCARTHY: Would you call television films today's B movies?

RC: Yes. I think you can now start to expand upon the meaning of the word *B*. And I would say to a large extent they take the place of the B movies, because they're slotted into a certain area the way the B movie was. They know roughly how much money they're going to get for them before they make them, which was one of the hallmarks of the B movie.

For motion pictures, everything is made to *try* for the top half of the bill. The picture that fails then goes to the bottom half. Or, very often, a picture that had previously been top half will be brought back on the bottom half the second time around, as a second feature. A lot of our films do that. We'll play *The Student Nurses* [1972] as a first feature, then we'll come up with our sequel, *Private Duty Nurses* [1972], and we'll bring back *The Student Nurses* as a second feature with *Private Duty Nurses*.

CF and TM: To go way back into history, would you call the films you did in the fifties, your first few films, B movies?

RC: The first one or two. The first picture I made was a science-fiction
picture called *Monster from the Ocean Floor* [1954], and that was probably
somewhere in between a B movie and what is today considered top half.
Because it played in some areas as a second feature, and in some areas,
because of the subject matter, science fiction, it did play top half. Although
the picture cost, as I recall, something like $12,000, cash, and was shot on a
six-day schedule. But it did play top half.

My next picture, *The Fast and the Furious* [1954], which was a road-
racing picture, was probably a little bit closer to the traditional B movie.
Because, again, of the subject matter, it fit more into the second feature
category. Although it occasionally played top feature.

By the time I did the third one, *Five Guns West* [1955], the first
picture I directed, I did that picture in color. And the very fact that it was in
color put it top half through most of the country, although in some major-
city situations, such as the New York circuit break, it became a second
feature. So at that time, we were bridging the two.

CF and TM: We wanted to ask about some of the people you've worked
with over the years, like Daniel Haller and Floyd Crosby, who worked on
all your Poe movies, and, of course, the actors you've used many times. How
did you happen to come across these people? And then, why did you keep
them from film to film?

RC: I kept them because they were good. It's as easy as that. When I
started off, I found that a large percentage of the crew and cast were not
particularly competent at their jobs, but a small percentage were. So when I
did my second feature, I simply hired back the ones I thought were good,
dropped the ones I thought were bad. I repeated that process on the third
and fourth pictures. So by the time I had made four or five pictures, I had
assembled a crew who were the best men I could find. And I worked with
that crew for many years. It got to the point where they worked together
much like an athletic team. One man knew in advance how another man
would function, and they knew how I would function. They were so good
they began to be hired by other producers as a unit. When I wasn't working,
many other producers would simply pick up Floyd Crosby, Dick Rubin, the
whole crew.

With actors, it worked roughly the same way, but of course that had
many more intangibles because it was dependent on the picture. Someone
might be a very good actor I had worked with, but there might be nothing
specifically for him in one picture.

CF and TM: Could you describe some of the releasing companies you went through in those days, like Woolner Brothers, Howco and Filmgroup?

RC: These were primarily small, independent companies. On my first picture, I just raised $12,000 and made the picture. Then I made a deal with Lippert Releasing to release the picture. I took the money from that and made a second picture, and realized that producing independently was a very slow process. You had to wait for the money to come back from one picture to put it in the other. That means that you might do one picture a year. So I made a deal with Jim Nicholson and Sam Arkoff, who were starting a company called American Releasing. On my second picture, *The Fast and the Furious,* I had offers from Republic and Columbia, but they were just straight deals.

I made a proposition to Nicholson and Arkoff: that if they would take my picture and give me an advance, I would make a three-picture deal with them, getting money from the franchise holders (that's kind of a states' rights operation throughout the country) in advance of each picture so that I would have financing. So Jim Nicholson and I flew around the country together, carrying the print of *The Fast and the Furious* with us. He talked about his distribution company and I talked about the three pictures I was going to make. And we signed up all the major franchise holders. I actively started making a series of pictures at that time and American Releasing, which later became American-International, started on the basis of that plan.

The pictures were successful, and I was immediately offered other pictures—but by other little independents. For instance, there would be other independent companies like American Releasing operating through the same franchise holders. My picture, *The Fast and the Furious,* went out and was successful. Other people, such as Howco, which was George Houck's company, or the Woolner Brothers, who were both theatre owners and had connections with the franchise holders, became aware that these little pictures were doing business. So they would come to me with an idea.

CF and TM: Does that states' rights system still exist today?

RC: Yes, it still exists. Now that I have my own distribution company, I am basing it somewhat on my original formula with AIP. I have modified it because we're making bigger pictures, and I'm putting much more of my own money in, with the states' rights operators. Now that we're in our third year of operation, we are starting to open our own New World branch offices. We have our own offices in New York and part of the East Coast and the entire West Coast, but we go states' rights in the rest of the country.

CF and TM: We wanted to ask when you plan to go public. . . .

RC: We have *no* plans to go public! I think Sam Arkoff regrets AIP went public. It's given him additional sources of capital, but has given him additional problems as well.

CF and TM: Was the Filmgroup your own company?

RC: Yes. And it did well. In fact, Filmgroup never had a losing year. One year we made $3,000, another year we made about $1,500! It was too small a company. I was making pictures for $30,000 to $40,000, and getting my money back and making a little, tiny profit. I wasn't much interested in it. It was a sideline, and I was making pictures for other companies that were more expensive, so I finally made an arrangement with American-International to take over the distribution of the Filmgroup pictures. In return, I made some pictures for AIP.

But I've always remembered it as an idea that, had I been more interested or had more capital, could have gone, and that's why I started New World.

CF and TM: What was the average budget for your fifties sci-fi films?

RC: On the ones I was making for American-International and Allied Artists, I would say anywhere from $70,000 to $100,000.

CF and TM: Didn't you once say that *War of the Satellites* [1958] was released within a few weeks after the first Sputnik in 1957?

RC: Yes.

CF and TM: Would you call that the essence of the exploitation film?

RC: Yes . . . it really was! Actually, it was released within a month or two. What happened was this: The Sputnik went up,[1] and the day after it went up I told Steve Broidy, the president of Allied Artists, that I could deliver the picture in eight weeks, I think it was, and that if they would start the ads right away, based upon what I told them the picture was about, and if they would give me the money, I would deliver the picture. He said yes, because I had had a couple of pictures that had been successful with Allied.

We did it exactly on that schedule, and it was one of those rare times when everything meshed. I delivered the picture on the exact date I promised, and they had the advertising campaign ready at the same time. We booked it directly into the theatres, and the picture did very well.

CF and TM: Why did you go to Fox to do *I, Mobster* [1959]?

RC: They came to me; I really didn't go to them. I had done *Machine Gun Kelly* [1958] for American-International, which, again, had done

---

[1] On October 4, 1957.

nicely, so Eddie Alperson, who was actually an independent releasing through Fox, came to me with the script of I, Mobster, and asked if I and my brother[2] would do this picture for him, and we said yes.

CF and TM: But that was your last film for a major as big as Fox for a while?

RC: Yes.

CF and TM: Do you consider yourself a black humorist?

RC: Probably . . . right. If you talk about The Little Shop of Horrors [1960], A Bucket of Blood [1959], Creature from the Haunted Sea [1960], and, more recently, Gas-s-s-s [1970], I would say they're somewhere in that vein. We did the first one before the term black humor was used. But they're probably somewhere within that genre.

CF and TM: What happened to Gas-s-s-s?

RC: AIP became very, very frightened of the picture, and when I was in Europe working on another film [Von Richthofen and Brown, 1971], they completely re-cut it, taking out "God," one of the major characters, and eliminating the entire end of the picture. They took every questionable or controversial point out of the picture; and that was what the picture was all about. So it became an extremely innocuous and slightly meaningless picture. And that's what went out. No one ever saw the picture as it was made—and the picture did not do well.

CF and TM: Would you say that's the most disappointing experience you have had?

RC: Probably that and The Intruder [1962]. Gas-s-s-s I believe was wrecked by AIP; on The Intruder, I can't blame anybody. I made the picture; I got extremely good reviews on it. It was a picture about integration in the South in the mid-1950s, and the public just didn't want to see that picture, at that time.

CF and TM: Does Gas-s-s-s more or less sum up your attitude toward the whole Poe thing, or is there a film in the Poe series that you consider your ultimate statement?

RC: No, no one in particular. I'd say each one was an attempt to deal with the individual short story of Poe. At no time did I try to put it all together in one unit. I let each one speak for itself. And Gas-s-s-s wasn't that closely related to the Poes. It was actually a second thought when we put Poe in it. We just started putting things in. In the original concept, he wasn't

[2] Gene Corman.

in it. And we just decided to put him in on a motorcycle—it seemed appropriate.

CF and TM: Of course, you also poke fun at the Poe films in *The Trip* [1967].

RC: Yes. . . .

CF and TM: In fact, most of the Poe films seem to be somewhat tongue in cheek themselves.

RC: Toward the end, yes; not at the beginning. *The Fall of the House of Usher* [1960], *The Pit and the Pendulum* [1961], *The Masque of the Red Death* [1964]—although that was later—*were* serious films. It was starting with *Tales of Terror* [1962], which was a trilogy, one of the three I played for humor. And then *The Raven* [1963] we played for humor.

CF and TM: About visual style: going back over your career the Poe films seem visually much more elaborate, if you will, than the films that came both before and after . . .

RC: I think that's true, and there are two reasons. One, on the Poe films I had a three-week schedule, which was the longest schedule I had ever had, so I had more time to shoot in an elaborate style. On the earlier pictures, *Little Shop of Horrors* was shot in two days, *Bucket of Blood* in five, and most of the others were shot in five to ten days. So there was simply no time to get into an elaborate camera style. I had to shoot very quickly, and relatively simply, although I tried to get as much interest into them as I could, within the schedule.

With a three-week schedule on the Poe pictures, I had a little more time to work with the camera. And also, I felt the subject matter lent itself to that. On the pictures that came after that, say, *The Wild Angels* [1966], that was also a three-week picture. But I was looking for more of a realistic style, so I deliberately came back to a slightly simpler camera movement.

CF and TM: Why did you shoot the last two Poe films, *The Masque of the Red Death* and *The Tomb of Ligeia* [1965], in England?

RC: Simply economics. We had offers from England, the Eady Plan, which was a heavy subsidy from the English government, and we went there for that reason.

CF and TM: Is it true that you used the leftover sets from *Becket*?

RC: Yes, for *Masque of the Red Death*. And *Ligeia* as well . . . I've forgotten which was which. I don't remember, but I know that in both pictures we used units from major English pictures, and one of them was *Becket* [1964].

CF and TM: *The Secret Invasion* was shot in Yugoslavia, wasn't it?

RC: *The Secret Invasion* [1964] was shot in Dubrovnik. . . .

CF and TM: And some of your New World productions have been shot in the Philippines . . .

RC: Yes, we've shot in the Philippines a great deal.

CF and TM: Do you feel, then, that economics forces you to seek out new locations?

RC: Right. Two things: the look for an interesting, unusual location, and the economics as well. With New World, I'd say the majority of the New World pictures have been shot in the United States. A minority have been shot overseas.

CF and TM: In many of your films, you have a weak central character—someone who is sort of a schlemiel . . .

RC: Of course, in things like *Little Shop of Horrors* and *Bucket of Blood* it was deliberate. In some of the other films, I'm not quite certain . . . I'm not positive. I think anybody who works in a creative way is conscious of what he's doing only to a certain extent. He's working a great deal out of his unconscious. It may be that I, personally, rebel. I've thought a little bit about this and I have no great thoughts on it, other than that I personally may rebel against the concept of the hero. It may be that I dislike the hero. And so I deliberately play up people other than the hero. I figure that if you've gone through school and the halfback is getting all the girls, and you get a chance to make films, and the format of the film is that the halfback gets the girl, you may deliberately undercut him.

CF and TM: Could you describe why you left AIP? Of course, you spent a little time with UA and Fox, and then set up your own company. Why?

RC: There's no particular split as such, because I still have some relations with AIP. I had lunch with Arkoff and Melamed[3] last week, as a matter of fact, talking about a few things. As a matter of fact, I work quite closely with them in certain areas. It was just that I felt their subject matter and their budgets were limiting to me. So I deliberately went to the majors, with the hope of doing bigger and—quote—"more important" pictures. I found there were a great many limitations placed upon what I did from the majors. And I became more interested in doing films my way, and not thinking so much about the budgets.

So once I had come to that conclusion, the logical thing seemed to be to

[3] D. J. Melamed, AIP's treasurer.

start my own company. Work with a low-budget type of operation, but at least have total control.

Certain things with the casting and cutting of my films for the majors, and specifically with the casting, and cutting, and story changes as AIP . . . I finally said, "That's it." *Gas-s-s-s* was the final straw, really. I said, at that point, "I want to do my own films. If they succeed, fine. If they fail, I know who was responsible."

CF and TM: Can we expect to see another film directed by you coming along one of these days?

RC: Eventually. At the moment, I'm really caught up in this whole business of running this company, which is both production and distribution. And it's rather involved. It'll probably take at least another year to get really organized, but at that point, I'll probably start directing again.

CF and TM: What do you think are the key elements in selling a film? Some people might say intelligent distribution patterns, or word of mouth . . .

RC: I think the quality of the film is most important of all. That's probably not the answer you're looking for in relation to exploitation films or B films, but I think it's true, and I always base everything on that. I have always believed that the man who makes the best film will do the best with it commercially, providing the other aspects aren't completely thrown away. Subject matter is important, but the quality, I think, is the most important.

CF and TM: What do you think of the gimmicks people like William Castle use?

RC: I think they're great! I have nothing against them. We've used them a little bit. I don't work quite as flamboyantly as Bill Castle. But I think it's fine. You know the old word *showmanship*. Why not?

CF and TM: How do you maintain the quality of films you produce and distribute, but do not direct?

RC: I pick the best writers, the best directors, and the best actors available under the given circumstances, which, in low-budget films, has very often led us to new directors. On the basis of my theory that if you're dealing with a veteran filmmaker, in general, he should be doing more important work if he's really good. A man who is doing B pictures after thirty years might be very competent, and probably is, otherwise he wouldn't be working at all, but in general, what he will give you will be a competent B picture. And what I've always looked for is the B picture, the exploitation picture, that is better than that, that has some spark that will lift it out of its bracket. And that's why the Kershners, the Coppolas, the Bogdanoviches, and so forth.

CF and TM: We're interested to know if you have a strong sense of being a patron of the arts . . .

RC: A little bit. Because I am conscious that I am doing a little bit more of this than other people I know. In fact, the *Los Angeles Times* had an article on Sunday[4] about the American Film Institute. And they said something in it, that the American Film Institute wasn't doing as much as Roger Corman. The reason is, of course, that I have a distribution company, I am a producer, I have access to capital. And with my own company, I don't have to have someone to second-guess me. I can say, "OK, I think this young director is talented, I'll gamble with him." As I said, the Coppolas and Bogdanoviches and so forth have gone on to great fame and success.

We're working with some young directors now that we think are very, very good. Marty Scorsese is moving up very rapidly. Jonathan Kaplan is on his way. Steve Carver has just finished a picture for us in Rome, and even before he's back—he isn't due back in the United States for two weeks—AIP called me last week and wanted to know when he's due back. And it's his first picture! I told Sam Arkoff last week that I can't develop young directors fast enough to keep the American-International production schedule going. In the past year, they've taken three directors from us, not even counting Marty Scorsese. Kaplan, Eddie Romero, and Jack Hill have all had successes with New World and have gone on to AIP. And, as I say, Carver's just on his first picture. They haven't even seen it! And they're already trying to find out what time he's due back in town!

CF and TM: There must be thousands of new Peter Bogdanoviches calling you on the phone or trying to see you, because they know that's what you do, to some extent.

RC: Yes.

CF and TM: How do they prove to you that they are really talented?

RC: It's very tough. For this reason: Bogdanovich and Coppola had been my assistants before I gave them their first chance at directing. I had great faith in them, and they knew my style of working—and they knew what was required. Some of the other young directors I've worked with, I have not had a chance to work with before giving them a chance at directing. I just talked with them. And it hasn't turned out to be quite that successful. They hadn't had this little, as it were, in-house training. So what

[4] September 2, 1973.

we've been doing recently to make up for that, because I'm a believer to a large extent in the all-around filmmaker, we've been hiring them as cutters. And they'll work on one or two pictures as a cutter; and if I like what they've done as a cutter, I'll give them a chance to move on. For instance, Steve Carver cut for us for eight or ten months before he did his current film.

CF and TM: What do you feel is your most important contribution to film: your own work as a director, your innovations in the business, or, as we were saying, your sponsorship of new talents?

RC: I think it all goes together. I couldn't really pick any one aspect. Just as I think in terms of the all-around filmmaker, a director who is also an editor and who may well be a writer, I'd like to think of myself just as working in film. Francis Coppola used to try to call himself a filmmaker, not a director. I think of myself a little bit that way. It all has to do with the making of films.

Joseph Kane

JOSEPH KANE*

I enjoyed making Westerns. I like the scenery and the outdoors . . . the horses and the cowboys.—JOSEPH KANE

One of the most prolific directors of American Westerns (yet, amazingly, not even mentioned in Raymond Bellour's and Patrick Brion's Le Western*), Joe Kane directed 113 films between 1935 and 1971—109 of them for Republic Pictures.*

Kane, also associate producer on most of his films from 1944 on, directed three Republic serials (in collaboration with B. Reeves Eason) and many television episodes for Bonanza, Laramie, Cheyenne, Rawhide, *and* Whirlybirds. *At Paramount in the early 1930s, he edited Tay Garnett's* Her Man, *among others.*

* Interview with Charles Flynn and Todd McCarthy, September 2, 1973, Pacific Palisades, California.

*We interviewed Joe Kane the day after John Ford died, and Kane
was still visibly moved by Ford's passing.*

*Always Republic's most reliable director, Joe Kane now lives in a
modest frame house in Pacific Palisades. His 1962 Ford Falcon still
wore a "McGovern for President" sticker on the rear bumper.*

JOSEPH KANE: I remember when sound first came in. I was a film editor
over at Culver City, which later became the Selznick Studio, where *Gone
with the Wind* was made. When sound first came in there, boy, they were
king of the hill. The sound men would sit up on top of the sound stage—it
was all made of glass—and look down on the people making the picture
down below. They'd tell everybody what to do. The director was nowhere,
for a while. When it first came in, it was all on records . . . discs. And then
they put it on film. And at first they said you couldn't cut the film. I
remember when Joe Kennedy—that was President Kennedy's father—came
in there. He was head of that studio, that was before the Selznick days. He
was making a picture with Gloria Swanson, Eddie Goulding was directing it
[*The Trespasser*, 1928], and they said you couldn't cut the sound track. So
he built a set with nine rooms—it was supposed to be the office suite of a
great big corporation, or something like that. Everything happened within
this complex of nine rooms. They had microphones all over the place, and
everything went on from room to room. They had nine cameras, all hitched
together with sound, and they were doing it all at once because you couldn't
cut the track. You'd have all these pictures at different angles, and you'd
intercut these pictures . . .

CHARLES FLYNN and TODD MCCARTHY: So you could cut the picture . . .

JK: But you couldn't touch the sound track. And they got away from
that pretty quick. That was terrible.

CF and TM: You started as an editor . . .

JK: Yes, I was. I started in as a writer. That's how I broke into the
business. A long time ago, down in Long Beach. That was the Balboa
studios. Then I became an assistant director, and then I became a film
editor. The director I was working with as an assistant was supposed to
direct and edit his own pictures. So he showed me how to edit, because he
didn't want to work nights. He taught me how to do it, so I did it. That's
how I became a film editor. There's no set way of getting into anything in
this business. You can do it in different ways.

That's how I became a film editor. I went to Pathé and started editing
serials for Spencer Bennet. He was a veteran serial director; he directed a

lot of serials in New York, came out to California, and that's how I met him. Then I went out to the Culver City Studio, and that's when Kennedy took over. He didn't actually run the studio, he owned it and operated it. He had a couple of guys named E. B. Darren and Charlie Sullivan running it. They were picture men who ran it for him. He made these pictures. Erich von Stroheim was directing for him, and Gloria Swanson was out there.

CF and TM: Were these silents?

JK: No, this was sound. The beginning of sound.

CF and TM: Did Kennedy try to dabble in film, say, the way Howard Hughes did?

JK: No, he simply stayed with the financing part of it; but he made a lot of money, of course. He always made a lot of money. And that's when Harry Joe Brown and Charlie Rogers took over. And I stayed on as a film editor, editing for Tay Garnett—who's still active, by the way—he's even older than I am, but he directed a film down in Tennessee a few years ago called *The Delta Factor* [1971]. It was a murder mystery; I didn't see it.

CF and TM: He just wrote his memoirs.

JK: Did he? He's quite a guy; he used to be one of the top directors back in those days. He was a big shot. He directed Anna Harding and Ricardo Cortez and Jimmy Gleason. We had Gregory La Cava out there, and several other directors.

Then I moved to Paramount. I was an editor over there for two or three years. That was with Charlie Rogers. Lots of different directors over there at that time. That was when Mae West was first starting in. I was there when she did that picture *She Done Him Wrong* [1933]. The studio at that time was in financial difficulties. They came and told us that we were going to have to take half salary, or we were going to shut down. So we all took half salary.

CF and TM: Was half salary at Paramount more than it would have been at some place like Pathé?

JK: No. They were all paying about the same. Anyway, Mae West made *She Done Him Wrong* and that put them back in business. It was a smash. She saved Paramount.

Of course, everyone was over there at that time: De Mille, Sternberg, Marlene Dietrich . . .

When I went over there, I was the first editor with a sound Moviola. Everybody else was working with silent Moviolas. They'd have a sort of court reporter on the set, in addition to the script clerk. This reporter would take down every take of every scene in stenotype, word-for-word. Then, it was transcribed. The cutter would receive a sheet of paper with every word of dialogue on it, and he'd run his picture, see an actor read a line, and make his cut.

CF and TM: Reading lips, in other words.

JK: Sort of. You'd go by the sheet of paper. You'd start off with the first speech, and go from there. You'd go right down the speeches.

I got a sound Moviola because I had come over from RKO, which was a subsidiary of RCA, so naturally they were one of the big sound outfits. There was RCA, which had the variable-field sound track, with peaks and valleys, and Western Electric, which was variable density—gradations of light and dark.

I went in my cutting room at Paramount, and they had given me a silent Moviola. So I went down to Charlie Rogers, and said, "I've got to have a sound Moviola." "Well, go ahead and get one," he said.

I got it and the thing started squawking—you know how much noise they make when you run a scene over and over. All the cutters—Eddie Dmytryk had the room next to mine—and De Mille's cutter, especially, heard it and came in to see what it was. De Mille's cutter insisted on one, and she got it. Pretty soon, they all had one.

Paramount turned out a picture a week. Every week, they'd put a picture to bed in the lab. They had fifteen hundred showcases throughout the United States. A picture'd go in the lab every Saturday and that was that. Once a picture came off the stages, they had the cutting, scoring, dubbing, previewing, and re-cutting scheduled. You had to stay with that. There was no deviating from that at all.

CF and TM: A more or less standardized schedule . . .

JK: Standardized for everybody except von Sternberg and De Mille. Their pictures were ready when they said they were. And they would have a special arrangement for the release.

CF and TM: Today that seems to be the way everybody works!

JK: But then it was the same as turning out Chevrolets.

CF and TM: Did Paramount make B movies?

JK: No. Paramount, M-G-M, Fox, and Warners turned out just what would be called A pictures. Columbia used to make Bs, Universal used to make Bs, RKO made Bs. But the big ones were Paramount, M-G-M, Fox, and Warners. United Artists was pretty big, but they were a specialized operation.

CF and TM: Why did you switch from Paramount to Republic in 1935?

JK: That was kind of an odd thing. When I went over to Paramount,

Charlie Rogers had his own setup. He was an independent producer, releasing through Paramount. Harry Joe Brown was his associate producer, and I was the film editor. Of course, I was working for Paramount, but I edited all of Charlie's pictures.

Harry Joe Brown decided to leave and go to Warner Brothers. So I went to Charlie and told him that I wanted to get out of cutting and into production. I wanted to step into Harry's place, and Charlie agreed that I could. I gave up my cutting job, which could have been a lifetime job, and went on vacation.

When I came back, I found that Charlie was no longer an independent producer. He was a company producer, and he'd given his production manager the job he'd promised me. Since I hadn't signed a contract, I was out. I went back to the cutting department and asked for my old job back. But my job had already been filled by my assistant cutter. So that's how I happened to leave Paramount.

So I went over to this independent outfit in the valley—Republic. Cut a picture called *Headline Woman* [1935] for an old director by the name of Bill Nye. I also cut a musical for Joe Santley.

Then, they decided they were going to make Westerns with Gene Autry. They picked me to direct his first picture. So that's how I started directing.

CF and TM: Was that what you had always wanted to do?

JK: Yes, I wanted to direct. But I'd thought I was going to get into it at Paramount. That's why I tried to get into the production end of it. Harry Joe Brown had done it that way. He was the associate producer, but every once in a while, he'd tell Charlie Rogers, "I'll direct this one."

CF and TM: Do you remember your very first day as a director?

JK: I'll never forget it . . . it wasn't too good! We were out in the middle of the desert in the middle of July. It was 135 in the shade, and there wasn't any shade. The producer of the picture was a very nice guy, but on the set he was a terrible second-guesser. He wouldn't leave me alone. He'd interfere all the time. He'd stand behind me and do all these second-guessing routines; it wasn't too good. But he was a nice fellow. He hadn't directed, and I was just starting. I think we were both a little nervous. We were feeling our way a little.

Anyway, we made Autry's first picture, which was called *Tumbling Tumbleweeds* [1935]. I stayed with Autry and made seventeen of them.

Then, Autry wanted more money and he struck them. He called me on the phone one evening, and said, "Don't break your neck getting ready for the next picture, because I won't be there." I said, "Gene, I can't go back to the studio on Monday and work for this producer"—his name was Mandy, by the way, Mandy Schaffer—great producer, but he's gone now—"I couldn't go back and work with Mandy getting all this ready knowing that you're not going to be here now." I said, "I'll have to tell him." "Go ahead," he said. "I'll be long gone." This was Saturday. So, he did. And they chased him all over the South—he was very big in the South. Process servers trying to catch him. He was so popular in these small towns, the people would just surround these process servers and gently walk them out of town. They never did catch him! And in order to prove to him that he ought to come back, they took this kid, whose name to begin with was Leonard Sly, and then changed his name to Dick Weston, and made a picture. To show Autry that they didn't need him. They didn't know it, but Autry had a nice little nest egg. They thought he was broke . . . they weren't paying him very much. But he was far from broke. Autry was never broke; Autry's a great businessman. You know, he's got millions laid away nowadays.

So I made the first picture with Dick Weston. The kid came on the set, looked around, and said, "What's that?" I said, "That's the camera." He didn't know anything about it at all, and he was playing the lead. So he did very well! They were quite simple. Musical Westerns, that's all they were. Mostly action. And he could ride, he was a natural rider.

While we were on location on that picture, they sent word up that he was going to be called Roy Rogers, and they wanted a name for his horse. We were getting ready to shoot a scene with a revolver, so I said, "Why don't we call him Trigger?" They took that name, and he became Trigger.

CF and TM: So you're the source for that!

JK: I'm the source for that.

CF and TM: How many Triggers have there been?

JK: Quite a few. After it got going, he had two or three. One for close-ups and stills, one for riding, and an extra one. So we made the first picture up there, called *Under Western Skies* [1938]. Sol Siegel produced it. Sol and his brother Moe had come out here . . . both very great guys. Moe became manager of Republic. Sol was a producer. He produced at Republic and then went to Fox. He went on and on, and finally became head of M-G-M for a while. Quite a guy. And he produced this first Rogers picture.

We were up in the Sierra Nevadas shooting, and one day Sol came up and wanted to change things. He wanted to reshoot something. But I talked him out of it.

CF and TM: It sounds like the producers were on the set looking over your shoulder all the time . . .

JK: No, they weren't. It just happened at the beginning, with this fellow Mandy Schaffer. He was a "set-" type producer. Sol was entirely different. He'd usually stay in his office. He'd come down to look at the dailies and tell us what he thought. I got pretty well left alone. But I switched from doing Autrys to Rogers because I didn't like having a producer on the set.

CF and TM: At Republic, did you generally work with the same group of technicians—editors, cameramen, and so on?

JK: As often as I could, yes. You'd get certain guys. They had a large crew of people there, and you'd have to take whoever was available. I always tried to get the same cameraman, Jack Marta, who is still active, I believe. Or Bud Thackeray, but he was usually in process work. With the other technicians, you'd take whoever was available when you started shooting. I got to know them all. . . . It didn't make a lot of difference.

I made forty-three of those Rogers pictures. Finally, in 1944, they decided they wanted me to make a feature with John Wayne, called *Flame of the Barbary Coast*, with Ann Dvorak, Joe Schildkraut, and Virginia Grey. That worked out all right, and from then on, I made larger features with featured players. I didn't make any more Rogers pictures.

CF and TM: Was the market for the Rogers pictures about the same as it was for the Autry pictures?

JK: About the same.

CF and TM: How would you define that—was it basically a Southern or Western rural audience?

JK: Yes, more or less. It was a small-town audience. Throughout the country.

CF and TM: Did these films play in Los Angeles and New York also?

JK: Oh, yeah. They used to play in Hollywood right opposite the Pantages Theatre. There was a little theatre right across the street that played nothing but those kinds of Westerns. Called The Horseshoe or something like that, I think.

CF and TM: Those all made money, we take it . . .

JK: Oh, yes. They made a lot of money with those things. They were musical Westerns. It was a vogue. They [Republic] invented that vogue. Because up to that time, all Westerns had been the real, hard, authentic type thing, like William S. Hart and the other action types. But there was no music—either all very dramatic, like William S. Hart, or all action. This was a new thing, a new concept. It made a lot of money for them, and they kept it up for a very long time. It finally died out. But after I quit doing the Rogers, they kept making them. Billy Witney took over, and he did them for quite a long time. Bud Springsteen, Tommy Carr. Different men directed them, because, in the meantime, after Rogers got started, Autry came back and they made both series. They finally had to settle with Autry because he wouldn't come back, except on his terms. They paid him what he wanted because they wanted him back. So they had both series going. I didn't make any more of either.

CF and TM: When you were working with Rogers and Autry, what sort of budgets and schedules were you working with?

JK: You wouldn't believe it! The first Autry was made for $12,500. By the time I got through, in 1944, they were spending between $50,000 and $60,000.

They were shot in a week. A six-day week. I made three pictures on that kind of schedule with John Wayne. They're still running. You can see them on television all the time: *The Lonely Trail, King of the Pecos, The Lawless Nineties* [all 1936].

CF and TM: In those days, you were making quite a few films a year. Did you work on a film in preparation, and, afterwards, in the cutting stage?

JK: Somewhat. When I started with the Rogers pictures, Sol Siegel was the producer. But he got into bigger and better things, so I inherited his job. I became both producer and director of all the Rogers pictures I made. I did eight a year. I would hire the writers, prepare the scripts. Then, I'd bring in the assistant director and the unit manager, and get the thing ready. Then, we'd go out and shoot it.

We'd bring it back in, and then the cutting department would take over. I'd look at it after the first cut and make any suggestions I had. In the meantime, I'd be getting started on another one. Making eight a year, I had to make one completely in somewhere around six weeks. That doesn't give you too much time.

CF and TM: What was Herbert Yates's role at Republic?

JK: He was the financial man. He was mostly in New York. He had a big office in New York, where he did the financing and distributing. He had this big laboratory, across the river in Fort Lee, N.J. After a while, he came out to Hollywood and decided he was going to get into the production end of it. The trouble was, if he had stuck with the financial end of it, he probably would have ended up with the biggest studio in town. You don't know this, but Yates even owned Universal at one time. Really, he actually owned it. He had loaned them so much money on pictures through his laboratory that he owned the controlling interest in it. But he sold it back to somebody, I don't know exactly how.

The man was a very good financier. Then, of course, he got interested . . . you've heard of Vera Ralston, I presume . . . well, she was a skater. This was at the time Sonja Henie was such a big success, so he decided, if Sonja could do it, this girl could. She was a very pretty girl at the time, she was a blonde. Very pretty blonde. Looked a little like Marilyn Monroe, that type of girl. But, of course, she couldn't talk English. That was a problem, but he was going to star her anyway.

So this poor gal goes in and stars in her first picture. And she did it phonetically, not knowing what she was saying. If you can believe it, that's how she did her first picture. It was called *The Green Monster*.[1] Von Stroheim was in it, he was the mad scientist. It was directed by a little guy who used to be my assistant, and who became a very well-known director, George Sherman. He directed it, but he didn't like the idea. He thought he was going to have to make more with this girl who couldn't speak English, so he quit.

After that, Allan Dwan—he was over there at the time—and I directed most of her pictures. She made twenty pictures in all, and I made nine of them. She got so that she understood English. She could talk all right, but she never was a very good actress. She was fair, but her main difficulty was she was often miscast. One picture I made with her, where she *was* properly cast, was called *Jubilee Trail* [1954]. She played opposite Buddy Baer, an enormous man. And she was a rather tall girl, so, naturally, this was good. He was so big, he made her look small.

But they seemed to think she could play anything from giants to children, as we used to say. I don't think you can in movies. Movies get so close to you, you have to be a certain type.

CF and TM: Was Yates handling her career?

JK: Yes, he was. He was more or less deciding what she would do. And she went along and did whatever he suggested. That's why I think she was often miscast. Although she was very good in several of the pictures she did with me. She was very good in *The Plainsman and the Lady* [1946], for instance.

---

1 Released as *The Lady and the Monster* (1944), and remade in 1953 by Felix Feist as *Donovan's Brain*. This film contains Erich von Stroheim's famous request to Ms. Ralston to "get the giggly saw."

She was very nice to work with. She was in the same sort of position with Yates as Marion Davies was with William Randolph Hearst. So, if she'd been that sort of person, she could have made it rough for everybody. Naturally, when you're in that kind of position with the boss, you can do anything you want. She never took advantage of that situation. She was always very cooperative, worked very hard, tried very hard.

But, you know, the public is a very funny thing. The public either accepts you or it doesn't, and there's nothing you can do about it. If they don't go for you, well, that's it.

CF and TM: With very few exceptions, you certainly stuck to Westerns at Republic . . .

JK: I enjoyed them. I enjoy making Westerns more, because I like the scenery and the outdoors . . . the horses and the cowboys.

CF and TM: How many of the people who played cowboys in your films could have hacked it as real cowboys?

JK: Not very many of them! Of course, you have to use actors, but on the other hand, you have to have the cowboys around to do the riding for you. I'm a strict believer in using stuntmen and cowboys to do the riding, because riding is dangerous.

CF and TM: Shooting a Western, you must have spent most of your time on the action scenes . . .

JK: Yes. Action takes quite a lot of time. Unless you have the proper help, the proper people. You can go along pretty fast if you know exactly what you're going to do. You have to know *exactly* what you're going to do. Before you start out in the morning, you have to plan out what you're going to do. So you don't waste any time. As soon as you say, "Cut! Print!" you move to the next setup right away. You don't hesitate. And you don't change your mind.

As soon as you set something up, the whole damn crew leaps at it and starts getting it ready. Halfway through, you change your mind and you lose them. They say, "Oh, boy. We're gonna have one of those!" That's enough for them. They don't want to have one of those guys who changes his mind. They're working hard and they don't want to fool around. So you have to know exactly what you're going to do. And keep going, keep moving.

But, as you said, I don't care how fast you move, it's going to take time. Television is a superb example. Take shows like *Rawhide, Laramie, Bonanza, Cheyenne,* which I did. We had five days to do those one-hour shows. You've got to have forty-eight minutes of story. Twelve minutes of advertising, main title . . . junk. Five days! And that didn't mean you could go nights! You had to start at eight in the morning and be through at six.

So you had forty-five hours. A very tight schedule. You had to knock off around twenty-eight setups a day.[2] Figure it out—you've got to do a setup every fifteen minutes. And you *have* to do it, because the following Monday they start the new one on the same set. They've hired the cast the week you're shooting. The director is getting ready. And you have to get the hell off that set by Friday night. Thursday afternoon, the new scripts arrive on the set, and the crew and the cast are reading the new scripts while you're trying to shoot your show!

Those kind of pictures are mostly action. To answer your question, the dialogue doesn't really call for any great acting. It's more or less standard formula acting. You certainly make pages on the dialogue, because you can get one dialogue setup and knock off two pages. Then you'll come to a page of action that has half a dozen setups.

CF and TM: So you found that the working conditions on a Western TV show were similar to those on a Republic feature . . .

JK: Yes. That training I got at Republic was great for television. All those little pictures . . . it was exactly the same as television. The only difference was that at Republic, we had to come up with fifty-four minutes of picture.

CF and TM: And you had an extra day.

JK: Yes, we got six days.

CF and TM: What do you think is happening to the Western today?

JK: I saw *Little Big Man* [1970], *The Wild Bunch* [1969], *Pat Garrett and Billy the Kid* [1973]. They were pretty bloody. Good Westerns, but a bit too violent. That guy Peckinpah can really shoot Westerns. I liked *Ride the High Country* [1962]. Peckinpah is the John Ford of today.

CF and TM: How did Republic's fortunes change after the war?

JK: They decided they'd start spending some money. The first big one I made with Wayne, *Flame of the Barbary Coast,* ran around $600,000. Now it sounds like nothing, but they thought that was a lot of money. That was big stuff for Republic in those days. Another picture I made, *Fair Wind to Java* [1953], with Fred MacMurray, cost a million and a quarter.

They started spending some money and making some pretty good

---

[2] A setup is a complete change of lighting and camera position. Today's major-studio features shoot an average of five to ten setups a day.

pictures. I had longer schedules. Thirty-nine, forty days on some of those.[3] It was mostly for the photography. I could move faster than that, but the cameraman couldn't. He had bigger sets and he had to do a good job of lighting them. That takes time.

CF and TM: What was it like near the end for Republic, around 1957 and 1958?

JK: Yates had trouble with the Actors Guild. He refused to pay residuals for pictures that were going on television. So they shut him down. The Actors Guild just closed the place and put him out of business.

CF and TM: Yates owned Republic right to the end?

JK: Yes. He was as stubborn as the Rock of Gibraltar, and that's pretty stubborn, I guess. I went over to television. There was nothing else I could do. Republic was completely out of business.[4] There was nothing left of it.

---

[3] See "The Economic Imperative," pp. 31–74, and the accompanying illustrations.
[4] Officially, on July 31, 1959.

Phil Karlson

PHIL KARLSON*

Every successful picture I've made has been based on fact.—PHIL KARLSON

What comes most naturally to Phil Karlson is making tough, violent action melodramas that almost invariably make money, so it is no wonder that most critics have never considered his career worthy of serious evaluation, the recent success of Walking Tall *(1973) notwithstanding. Indeed, many, if not most, of the director's films were well received at the time of their release, but Karlson, as he himself concedes, always remained in the background.*

Karlson, who looks younger than his sixty-six years, was raised in Chicago and studied at the Art Institute there before entering law school at Loyola University. He continued to pursue his law degree at

* Interview with Todd McCarthy and Richard Thompson, November 19, 1973, Los Angeles, California.

*Loyola University of Los Angeles, but to support himself in the early
years of the Depression, he took a part-time job at Universal "washing
toilets and dishes and whatever the hell they gave me." As Karlson
moved up the ladder at Universal (he was, at various times, assistant to
director Stuart Walker and an editor for William Wyler and John
Ford), the film business became increasingly attractive to him. Any
ideas he may still have harbored about taking up law were abandoned
when he sold a story to Will Rogers. Rogers tragically died before the
story (about the head janitor in the White House during the Teapot
Dome scandal) could be filmed, but Karlson was on his way.*

*Phil Karlson lives in a comfortable home in West Los Angeles,
which is almost exactly midway between the M-G-M and the Twentieth
Century-Fox studios. The astonishingly clear skies on the afternoon of
the interview gave us a glimpse of how beautiful Los Angeles must
have been when Karlson first arrived, before the invasion of the
automobiles and the factories. Karlson also marveled at what he
termed, "the clearest day since they invented smog," and began by
explaining how he finally became a director after working up to it for
more than ten years.*

PHIL KARLSON: How I got my first picture to direct is one of the big
miracles of all time, and how I continued directing is another miracle,
because that picture was probably the worst picture ever made. I had been
an assistant director on Abbott and Costello pictures and I had gone to Lou
Costello at times—very gutty to do this, actually, without checking with the
director, writer, or producer—and I would suggest gags to him. He would
go in and tell the director this is what he wants to do, and he would do it
and he would get laughs. Fade-out. I sort of left there, got mixed up at
another studio, and the war came along and I was in the service. After that,
he looked me up. He said, "You know, we've been trying to find you for two
years now. I want you to direct a picture. I'm not going to be in it, but I'm
going to give you the money to make the picture." He said, "What do you
want to make?" I said I don't know. By this time I'm so flabbergasted that I
had no idea what I wanted to do. But he put up the money and we decided
on the crazy story *A Wave, a WAC and a Marine* [1944]. It was a nothing
picture, but I was lucky because it was for Monogram and they didn't
understand how bad it was because they had never made anything that was
any good. Meanwhile, they had given me another story that I flipped over.
Oh, I knew this was surefire. So I got into production as fast as I could with

the second picture and the second picture was a tremendous hit. It was called *G.I. Honeymoon* [1945].

There's one part of my story that is so important, because at one point, out of the blue, I was signed by Sam Goldwyn. He signed me as a director—I had never directed a thing in my life. Oh, I had, some second units as an editor, when they'd let me go out and shoot a few inserts here or there. An agent called me and said, "Sam Goldwyn wants to sign you." I said, "You must have the wrong guy." He said, "No, it's you. He's bringing a young fella out from New York by the name of Garson Kanin and he wants to form a team because he likes your credits. He's talked to John Ford." I still thought this was a dream. But it wasn't. I went over there. He had an office a mile long and it was the last-mile walk . . . you walked all the way over to his desk, so by the time you got there, you didn't know what the hell you were going to say or what was going on. He had an overstuffed chair for whoever his guests would be in the office, and you sat in it, and I swear to God, it went down . . . and he raised! You were way down here looking up at Sam Goldwyn. Of course, he was a god in those days, he made the greatest pictures. In fact, at the time, in 1937, Willy Wyler was shooting *Dead End* and Jack Ford was doing *The Hurricane* for Goldwyn.

Well, I couldn't believe it. They gave me an office that belonged to Darryl Zanuck, with a private projection room, and the man I was sharing the secretaries with—there were two secretaries in a large outer office—was one of the greatest composers that ever lived, Gershwin. I didn't know what the hell I was supposed to do. We signed the contract, I was told I was going to be with Kanin, but I never even saw Kanin, we never got together. I was in the office waiting for calls to tell me what to do and I kept listening to this beautiful music and I became very friendly with the composer. One day I bumped into Kanin by accident and I introduced myself. He said, "Well, we're supposed to be working together." I said, "Has anybody talked to you?" He said no. I said, "Well, I'm going crazy in there. I've got an office that's so fabulous and I'm playing solitaire in there. They won't even give me anything to read." He said, "Well, you think *you've* got something. Come up to my apartment." He had an *apartment* in there, a dressing room, with kitchen facilities and the whole bit, and nobody's talked to him. And one day we both decided we're going to quit, and that's what'll open up their eyes and make them say, "Well look fellas, we got something for you." This is a complete pregnancy, this was nine months later that we walked in. I walked in first, and they were waiting for me, and in a minute I said, "Well look, if you haven't anything for me, I can't sit here any longer. Look, I've got to do things." Well, the vice-president took my contract out of the drawer, and he tore it up and said, "You have no more problems. You can go. You're free." Same thing happened with Gar Kanin. Some of the things that happen in our business . . . it's strange, but true, which is horrible.

TODD MCCARTHY and RICHARD THOMPSON: What were the conditions like at Monogram? Was it noticeably cheaper?

PK: Oh, of course. They had very little money. They knew what they were doing because there was a certain class of picture they were going to make and they weren't going to make anything any different. They had the Charlie Chans, the Bowery Boys, the East Side Kids, and they had the Shadows, and they had Kay Francis over there for some pictures. I made *Wife Wanted* [1946] with her.

Then, of course, I got an opportunity there to make one of the first pictures, I think, in which a social statement was made on the screen. I never knew this fellow and I went to talk to him. He wasn't a star in those days, he was playing Indian parts, and that's Anthony Quinn. So I went to Tony Quinn and I talked him and his wife into playing *Black Gold* [1947]. I made such a strong statement that the Indian nations all picked it up. They realized what we were saying in there. The average guy that would go see a motion picture in those days went to see entertainment. We weren't making statements, we were making cops 'n' robbers and good guys and bad guys. But to look at something and see the truth, for a change, was something that was unusual in those days.

TM and RT: Who shot *Black Gold?* It's a good-looking film.

PK: He passed away. It was Harry Neumann. He did several things with me. He did one picture that I feel very good about, *The Phenix City Story* [1955]. He was an excellent cameraman. He was what we call a lab man. When you get a cameraman who's started out in the lab, not on the set, he understands development and he knows lighting, he knows what you need. He was of that breed.

Black Gold was the changing of the name from Monogram to Allied Artists because it was their first, they thought, important picture. It was the most expensive picture they had ever made, and that might have been $450,000. I made *The Phenix City Story* for them too, which was much later, of course. *Black Gold* was made in 1946.

It shows you what went on at this little company at that time. It took me a year to make *Black Gold*, but I made four pictures while I was making *Black Gold*. I wanted the seasons. I went to Churchill Downs for the Derby and had to do the races here, and I had to get some desert scenes . . . a lot of time lapses in the picture. I made four or five pictures *while* I was shooting that picture. I did Charlie Chans, I did Shadows, I did the Kay Francis picture . . .

TM and RT: A Gale Storm musical . . .

PK: A Gale Storm musical, right. All while I was doing this one picture.

TM and RT: Were you teamed up with one particular producer? Was that the way the system worked?

PK: No, no. They put me under contract. They were paying me $250 a week, and they figured, if I do enough pictures, they'll be paying me nothing, which was true. I think I did eighteen pictures one year. Well, you can't make eighteen half-hour shows in one year anymore. That's how fast we were turning them out. I'd make 'em in four days, five days, six days, seven days, and when I got a chance to do *Black Gold*, well, this was a career.

TM and RT: Did they have interesting ways of cutting their budgets down to the minimum?

PK: One interesting way is what I told you. You pay a director $250 a week and he makes eighteen pictures. If you break that down over eighteen pictures . . . say I was making $15,000 a year, they were getting a picture for nothing. They were probably putting in about $10,000 for the director when borrowing their money from the bank, so they were making money before we started. Some of those pictures cost $20,000 or $25,000.

TM and RT: What kind of outfit was Eagle-Lion?

PK: Eagle-Lion was a little higher in their standards, but Eagle-Lion is United Artists today. It's the same organization. It was Arthur Krim and Seward Benjamin and the Pickers. Those are the people that now run United Artists. Well, Eagle-Lion . . . that picture, *The Big Cat* [1949], was a complete social statement. That was my answer to John Ford's *The Grapes of Wrath* [1940].

I made a picture at Eagle-Lion . . . I made a discovery. Now, he's my kind of people. I don't know whether he's your kind of people or not, but I discovered Steve Allen. I'd listened to this guy on the radio, I'd go to sleep with him. He had a radio show at CBS and he was funny and entertaining to me. I decided to go down to see him and he flipped me, he really was that good, he was that quick a wit. He would walk through the audience and talk to people and come up with fine answers and very funny lines. Somebody at Eagle-Lion had thought of a feature picture that we could make in two days. We'd use all of Mack Sennett's material, and we had Bing Crosby and W. C. Fields, great talents in there. And Steve Allen was a TV

M.C. In other words, he'd sit at a desk and he'd do commercials that were very funny and whatnot, and then he'd put on this show, so you'd see a W. C. Fields comedy and he'd make cracks in between. Then Crosby would come on and we had all the Keystone Kops in there. I shot it in two days. That was Steve Allen's start.

TM and RT: Was there even a script to that?

PK: Oh yes! He and I wrote it. We wrote it and did it like this in two days. Put the picture together.

TM and RT: That's amazing.

PK: Well, I was an editor, as you know, so it was pretty easy for me to get a lot of these things put together.

TM and RT: That's *Down Memory Lane* [1949].

PK: That's what it is. Two days to make that picture.

TM and RT: Almost *cinéma vérité*. Strange idea. Was there much difference between the small studios like Monogram and Eagle-Lion and the B units of bigger studios like Universal and Columbia?

PK: Oh yes, sure.

TM and RT: Was it a lot nicer to work for a big studio, even if you were working on cheaper pictures?

PK: No! It was a lot nicer working for the smaller studio because there wasn't any committee to worry about. When they gave it to you, you were in charge. You did it. Nobody told you what to do. They couldn't afford all these guys to come in and discuss things—"Let's get together, let's discuss it." You work in a big studio, there's an assistant producer, a producer, then there's an executive producer, then all the way up to the head of the studio.

TM and RT: It was my impression, though, that on the cheaper pictures of a big studio, the brass and the committees and whatnot paid more attention to their big, important productions rather than the small ones. That's not true?

PK: That is true, in the A echelon. But in the B echelon, they had the same bunch of guys right down the line. They had the guy, who thought he was the president of the company, who was the head of the B unit. Then he had his assistant right down the line. No, there was actually more freedom—of course, so fast!—in the smaller studios. Really, it was the greatest teacher in the world for me, because I could experiment with so many things doing these pictures. No matter what I did in the smaller studios, they thought it was fantastic, because nobody could make the pictures as fast as I could at that time, and get some quality into it by giving it a little screwier camera angle or something. That was only a fooler. Not that it was much better than the other guy's.

TM and RT: I have a question that asks for the mentality of the other side, the producers. Take, for example, Eagle-Lion, who seemed to have very good taste in directors. They had you, they had Anthony Mann doing very interesting films. How is it that studios or production units choose directors? How do they hire them? What's the currency? Is it success at the box office or credits?

PK: I must tell you that some of our biggest directors today have made the biggest flops, that is, of the older school, not the young ones coming up, because they haven't had a chance yet. But they go on money, box office. We're in a ball game today where that's even more important than it was in the era that we're discussing. At one time, anything went. Now, we're in another ball game altogether. Today, they look at that record. In all the pictures I've ever made, I don't think there's been but two pictures that lost money. And that's phenomenal, I must tell you!

TM and RT: Did Monogram have a financial formula, so that if they made a picture for, say, $80,000, they knew they could get the distribution that would almost guarantee their breaking even or making a profit?

PK: They had their own distribution. They were very liquid, that company. They really were well organized and they knew how much they could spend. They would have their money back before they even started because they got so much money from their exchanges. Right from the exhibitors. And that's where we're going to be again. That's where the whole ball game is coming back to. People say television is what killed our industry. This didn't kill our industry. What killed our industry was divorcement. Studios and theatres, that's what killed us. When they came in with the idea that this was a complete monopoly—the guy that's making the picture owns the theatre it's playing in and whatnot—that's when we got in trouble. We could have gone on, and this business would have prospered. Sure, this had to happen and it had to hurt, because people that were buying their TV sets when TV first came in were the people that couldn't afford to go to the theatre. They paid for the set and they had to enjoy it and they had to live with it. Of course, now we're in another ball game again. We're getting ready for pay TV and cable TV and everything else, with cassettes and whatnot, and our business is, I think, one day, again going to bloom.

TM and RT: I don't know if you saw it, but in *Variety* today there was a little box that told of a poll among citizens that asked how they felt about the value they get for their dollar paid. And there was a rating saying if they thought they were getting their money's worth with a car, or a refrigerator, or a TV, and the thing that was absolute last on the list was movies. They don't feel they're getting their money's worth when they go to the cinema. It was the very last thing on the whole list—the least value for your dollar.

PK: I have to agree with them. I think the prices they're charging are way out of line. I think it's more important to get people into the theatre than to keep them out by saying they're going to charge $4.00 or $3.50, or whatever it is, and your parking, and a little this and a little that. There was a time when people could wait until it got to the neighborhood theatre. Well, the neighborhood theatre isn't that cheap anymore.

TM and RT: Distribution is so spotty now that, very often, if a film doesn't succeed on first run, it doesn't ever get down to the nabes.

PK: That's true. That's what's wrong with exhibition today. That's why we're so proud of what's happening with *Walking Tall,* and so proud of what happened with *Billy Jack* [1972]. That in spite of bad exhibition, in spite of a lot of bad advertising and bad-mouthing . . . in some cases, when that starts, the critics, if they've seen the picture or not, tear it apart. Critics in big cities I don't think can hurt you, because any picture that'll take off today has to be by word of mouth. You have to tell it to somebody else. But in small towns, the critic is important, believe it or not. Where there's only ten thousand, twenty thousand people, they read the paper from the ads down to everything that's in it, and it becomes important there. Here, I don't know if people are even looking at them. There's too many important things to look at than a review by somebody they don't care about.

TM and RT: I'm still extremely interested in all these decision-making processes at a place like Monogram. Were you able to see stories and say, "I want to do that one"? Did you get to pick material and develop it?

PK: It so happened with *Black Gold,* yes, and *The Phenix City Story,* yes, but when I was there, I was like a mechanic that worked on a line. "OK, is Phil finished with this picture? Well, let's give him this one to do." My biggest job was to go home and work this picture out. Forget the story end of it, because if the story was a Charlie Chan, I knew the final denouement would be in a room and we'd sit around and we'd figure out who killed Cock Robin. But as I got through that and made *Black Gold,* they were so impressed that the company stepped into a whole new world—Allied Artists. They got rid of the Monogram tag. Now, they wanted to know what I would like to do next. Now they had some respect for me. Up until then, I was just somebody for whom they pressed a button and said, "C'mon in and do this."

They didn't know how much good they were doing me, though, because I was experimenting with everything I was making, trying to get my little pieces of truth here and there, that I was trying to sneak in these things that they weren't ever conscious of. In fact, they were just the opposite. They were the most conservative, right-wing guys you ever could see. They had no idea what was going on as far as the actual content was concerned. Later on, with Steve Broidy, after Trem Carr had left, and we started getting the Mirisches in there, then I started making these pictures that really said something.

Every successful picture I've made has been based on fact. Sure, plenty of fiction enters into it, but the basic idea is true. The last picture that I did for Allied Artists, thirteen years ago, was *Hell to Eternity* [1960], and *Hell to Eternity* is one of the most important pictures that I may ever make because it was the true story of the Nisei, what happened in this country. But Allied Artists, even at that point, looked at it as a great war story that you could make for a price. They had no idea what I was doing. But when the picture was so successful, they started to see things in it they had never seen before. Forget the fact that I used five thousand Japanese and five thousand Marines that we were getting for nothing. I shot it in Okinawa in Japan for under $800,000. I defy any company to make that picture for $5,000,000 today.

TM and RT: How did you get the *Louisiana* [1947] project?

PK: Now, on that one, strange as it may seem, I'd met him, I'd met Jim Davis. My agent at the time was handling Jim Davis, he was handling him for his songs and personal appearances. He was a governor and he wanted to be in motion pictures! After I got to know him, I said, "There's a story here and Monogram will go for it. I'll make it." We did what you're doing. I sat down with him, not with a recorder but with a secretary, and we just talked, and she took everything down. Well, his story was amazing. This guy had really come from the backwoods. He became a sheriff, then he became a mayor, then he became a law and order man and fought the Long regime. I said, "That's fantastic. I'll do this picture. And I'll do the story just that way." I had guys come in to him, without mentioning their names, offering him a hundred thousand dollar bribe to do this and do that. We made the picture and it reelected him governor of the state, he became so popular. Now, I've elected two governors of states. I elected a governor of Alabama that I thought might turn out to be a wonderful guy . . . not

Wallace! . . . but a man who was actually an attorney at the Nuremberg trials. Well, I thought, this man I've got to like. When I first met him, his father, who was the attorney general, was assassinated. He was the next governor of the state, right after that picture came out.

TM and RT: Like a lot of the directors that came out of that period, you strike one as being an excellent composer. That must be due to your art institute background. Did you think about that when you set a shot up?

PK: Always, always. I'll tell you one of the most fantastic stories that I don't tell, but this is in keeping with what you're talking about. In 1950 or 51 I was in Paris shooting sort of a second unit, although we had some of the people there. It was a picture that I was later fired on and I came back to the States. I'm shooting at night in Montmartre and I'd seen these paintings—there's sort of a set Montmartre painting with the Sacre Coeur in the background—and I want to avoid all this. I'm setting up in different spots and I'm shooting all night. We started shooting almost at midnight . . . people are going to sleep, so we could stage what we want, and we had cooperation. I had three cameras. I had two French camera crews and one American. I didn't pay too much attention to the French camera crews, because I knew my key angle was always the American crew where I could communicate better and get exactly what I wanted. Then we'd sort of half-tell them, "Now you get this and you get this." The first night, I wanted to check all three cameras and, as I got to the third camera, this elderly guy was looking through the camera. I never got a chance to look in the camera because he was always there.

Now this happened three straight nights. The third night, I got mad and I turned to my assistant and said, "I want you to go over and tell that . . . that cameraman that when I come over, if he'd just give me the courtesy of backing off, so I can look through and see what he's getting." He said, "That's not a cameraman. That's Pablo Picasso." And I said, "That's Picasso?!" And I went over there and practically got on my knees. Started talking to him. I said, "Do you like that?" and he said, "Very nice, very nice!" And he followed me for three straight nights. Pablo Picasso. I kept asking him, "Do you like this? Are you happy with this?" We became very close friends. He entertained me and, oh, it was beautiful.

TM and RT: A curious aspect of that period in the late 1940s and early 1950s is that there was a whole cycle of films then, some comedies, but mainly serious versions, based on *Arabian Nights'* fantasies. This genre just seemed to come out of nowhere. The Western's been with us fifty years or so, but just in those eight or ten years Universal cranked out a lot of them. What prompted that?

PK: It's hard to explain that. I must tell you I made some of those too. I don't know why, but all of a sudden, I think they were trying to recapture something that we lost right after the war. That is, to go into a sort of fantasy-type entertainment. You know, the real hero up there, and he can fight anybody and do everything. I think using period for that might have been the thinking and the solution. It was pretty hard, I must tell you, to make some of that junk. That was a real tough period, actually. I got very lucky about that time because I made quite a few melodramas that had a little guts to them, and had something to say. I pulled out of there. I was lucky, actually.

TM and RT: For my money, the group of your films that interests me most is the group of crime melodramas you did in the fifties. Do you see those as a set? How did you come to deal with those themes and images over and over again, so consistently?

PK: I was born in Chicago, and I was raised in Chicago, and I went through the days of the killings and whatnot in Chicago. I remember getting twenty-five cents to stand on a corner, and if the cop was on this side of the street, to whistle real loud, and if he was on that side of the street, just to whistle softly. I was keeping a brewery going by a little whistle. So, I sort of saw all that. When I got a little older, in high school, I actually came out of a theatre, and the man in front of me was gunned down—a car pulled up alongside and gunned him down. They put five bullets in this man and he lived. His name was David Miller and he had a restaurant on the West Side of Chicago, and his brother was a lieutenant of detectives on the police force. The result of this, and I was old enough now to understand what was going on, was the killing of a great mobster by the name of Dion O'Banion.

I'll never forget when Desi Arnaz, who had seen *The Phenix City Story* —they'd rerun it for him—incidentally, he was the brains of the Desilu Studio, it wasn't Lucille Ball. He was actually the man who called the turns, made the decisions and was the real brain. Of course, everybody thinks it was Lucy because Lucy's such a great comedienne. Anyway, he sent for me and gave me this thing to do that all those awards on the wall are for, *The Untouchables*.

TM and RT: Another true story . . .

PK: Another true story. And I wouldn't do it, I said, because, "You'll never make it the way I want to make it because it's going to be made for

TV and they won't allow this on TV." He said, "I'll get it on TV if you make it the way you did *The Phenix City Story*. You give me the realism." Now, this was a result of *Kansas City Confidential* [1952], 99 *River Street* [1953], *The Brothers Rico* [1957], and all these pictures that I'd made in that era. And I did it, because he agreed to give me carte blanche. What I did was not only make a fortune for him but make a multimillionaire out of Quinn Martin, who had very little to do with it.

TM and RT: It started him on a long line of successes, and he's still working.

PK: Oh, how successful he is! And I wouldn't do TV. That wasn't my bag. I was a motion-picture director and it's sort of a comedown to do TV. At that time, I was doing so many pictures. I did a picture I like so much called *Key Witness* [1960] that took a while to catch on because they didn't realize . . . by the time it ran in New York, I was doing *The Young Doctors* [1961] in New York, and *Key Witness* was the highest acclaimed picture in New York, because *Key Witness* was happening on the street at that time. This was thirteen years ago. They were mugging 'em in Central Park then. Now they're mugging 'em on Broadway. That's what that story was all about. People would not get involved.

TM and RT: In the world that you present in your films, especially in the crime films and in *Walking Tall*, you have the sense of an organized evil that is so big that for an individual to go up against it is almost incredible. This seems to recur in a number of your films. Is this something you believe in?

PK: No, I believe that you've got to speak up. It's unfortunate that I have to show it with *a* person. I would love to see a community get up. This goes back to Carl Foreman's and Freddie Zinnemann's *High Noon* [1952], where the entire community walked away from the guy. They did the same thing with Buford Pusser, they walked away from him. Once they elected him sheriff and they saw what he was doing, nobody wanted to back him up. Everybody stayed away from him. It's too bad. One of the most important things he did was appoint the first black deputy sheriff. The first one in the South. That man was murdered. I didn't show that. I didn't want to show that.

TM and RT: Most films like this deal with the idea of individualism. Ford tried to get away from that in *Wagonmaster* [1950]. Remember that Western where he tried to make the whole community the hero, and involve it in a positive action?

PK: Yes, but it's almost impossible. We've tried it so many times. I think that's the only reason that John Wayne has gone on indefinitely is because he's against the world.

TM and RT: And he's big enough to make you believe it.

PK: I tried to show it in *Walking Tall,* in a small community. I didn't want to say this is a man that will take on Nixon next week, because he isn't and he couldn't.

TM and RT: Too honest.

PK: Yeah! That's the way I feel, too.

TM and RT: I'm very curious about your relationship with cameramen. Not just Harry Neumann, but people like Franz Planer, with the kind of textures you got in 99 *River Street.*

PK: Oh yeah, Franz Planer and, of course, Bernie Guffey, with whom I made many pictures. We had a great simpatico. I must tell you, I direct with very little improvisation. Well, I do use improvisation because you must improvise at different times to get what you're really looking for, because the written word can't always be told just the way we put it down. I must do the picture twice in my mind, I mean from start to finish. Just the way I see it, the entire motion picture. When I start shooting the picture, I still have this overall picture in my mind. It's very important to work that way, for me. I've tried, in lectures at USC and UCLA, to try to give our future young directors this kind of thinking, because you never shoot a picture in continuity. I may be doing the last sequence the first week on account of time and actors and whatnot—mostly money. If you have this overall picture in mind, you're not going to go wrong, and you're not going to be out of key by jumping out of continuity. Now, once I start shooting, I want to make it better than what I had in mind, because I had some wonderful tricks in mind, I had an overall idea of what the picture should look like, but now I've got to improve on it. And I must tell you, I never have. I've never been satisfied with anything I've made, but I try to improve on what I've already pictured.

When I do color, I think in terms of black and white, I don't think in terms of color. If I'm going to do a crime story like *Walking Tall,* we know that blood's going to be awfully red and it's going to be pretty disgusting when they see it. Well, you try to get that toned down, but it's impossible. When it gets through Technicolor, it comes out redder than it was on the set. My communication with cameramen has always been great, because we actually have the same goal. I want the cameraman to become a very important part of the picture, like I want the entire crew to be. It takes every one of those guys to make any of these pictures. I may be the best general in the world, but without all the privates, I'm in trouble. This I found out a long time ago when I had to make 'em in four or five days. If I had one guy that had to go to the bathroom, I was in trouble.

TM and RT: One of the things that sticks with me from those crime pictures are a lot of wonderful images and a lot of weird storytelling gimmicks. Things like John Payne watching his defeat on television at the beginning of 99 *River Street*. Is that the kind of thing you came up with?

PK: Yes, that would be my contribution to scripts. In fact, I must work on the script with the writer. It's impossible for me to do a picture unless I work with the writer. I think all directors should do that; there must be a meeting of the minds. It's too bad when you have a falling apart, like happens every once and awhile, and a picture is botched up because the director had a completely different theory on what the writer was trying to say. When that happens, you have a bad picture.

TM and RT: Do you like to work with the writer at the time, rather than take the finished script and revise it the way you want it?

PK: I like to do both. Sometimes, the script is sent to you, and you go in and have a meeting on the script, for example, and I would lay my cards on the table. It becomes a complete rewrite the minute I open up my mouth. I try to break down all the pictures I make in three acts, and if you change something in the first act, that affects the other two acts and you're out of business.

TM and RT: How did you arrive at the three-act notion? Is that just for dramatic flow?

PK: No. I always feel we have weak second acts. That's the weakest part of any story. Your first act is developing characterization; you get to know the people and you either get to like them or dislike them. In the second act you've got to put them to work, and they've got to do something now. But if you've changed something in that first act, that second act isn't going to work at all, unless you really are with these people. In every picture I've ever done, you'll find that setup and that style. And I have a stylized way of shooting that you're not conscious of. I have what I call a "high and low" setup, and this is the way I put it on the screen all the time. I have directors in France that have copied every shot I've made, in pictures that they shouldn't have. They've written to me and said, "We run *The Brothers Rico* before we write our story." They copy it shot for shot and it means nothing to their story. It meant something to *The Brothers Rico*.

TM and RT: You were talking about violence before, and I must say that I think your films of the fifties were at least as violent, if not more violent, as most other films being made at that time. Do you think this was true, and was this noted at the time?

PK: It wasn't noted at the time, because most of them were in black and white. See, in black and white you're not conscious of blood.

TM and RT: I don't mean gore, necessarily.

PK: I don't mean gore either, but gore is what they say is violent. When Sam Peckinpah shoots somebody and all the blood splurts out, they say that's violent. See, I'm not a Peckinpah fan. I think he did some darn nice things, *before* he became violent. Violence for just violence's sake, to me, on the screen is probably the most horrendous thing you can do. But, I think, when it belongs, you should show it and you shouldn't pussyfoot around it. You should put it on there the way it happened. When people are shot, they bleed.

TM and RT: I prize, even more than shooting and bleeding, the kind of violence that brings home the point of how rough and how disorganized violence is, and how much destructive energy is loosed. Like in the fight between John Payne and Jack Lambert in 99 *River Street* in that little apartment. You really got a notion of how destructive two people can be.

PK: That's true. That picture, I must tell you, at the time, caused as much comment as any picture that had ever been made, on account of scenes like the one you're discussing, and a few other scenes. I can get violence without anybody touching anybody. I can set up three men in this room waiting for a man to walk in and go to a girl on the corner someplace, and you know that this man is dead.

TM and RT: You can feel the energy . . .

PK: I'm so sorry I couldn't talk Eddie Small into it, but I wanted to use slow motion. Only in killing scenes, where somebody's being shot or beaten up. I wanted to use that feeling at that time, but he didn't want me to do it. He said, "People won't believe in you." I said, "We need to give them a first, something different." He said, "You know why I like you, Phil, and why you'll always work for me? You believe in a close-up." Any picture I've ever made, you run it on this box and you'll think it was made for TV.

TM and RT: What kind of guy is Small? He produced a lot of good films.

PK: Oh yeah. I did eight pictures for him. Oh, he's a fantastic guy, actually more astute than most people ever gave him credit for. Probably, in his field—and he made some very good films—the most successful producer in our entire industry. Financially, no doubt about it. This man is a multi-multimillionaire.

TM and RT: But he wouldn't even let you do a test of the slow motion, just to see how it looked?

PK: Oh, he knew what slow motion was. But, you see, slow motion, to him, belonged in a Pete Smith comedy, it didn't belong in a feature film. For him, why waste the time to do all this?

TM and RT: A scene in *Kansas City Confidential* that sticks out in my mind as being unusual for the period—now, of course, we have all these pictures about cops and we all know that cops are just hoods with badges—but the scene that brings home the point about the cops holding him illegally overnight, beating him up, and so on . . .

PK: Exactly. I'll tell you, this was so far ahead of itself that I say these pictures have been copied and recopied so many times. Unfortunately, Phil Karlson never got the credit for it because I've never been a publicity hound. I come from the school where what we want to be judged by is up on the screen, not by how well I know so-and-so or so-and-so. I grew up at Columbia when I started making the important films and I worked with Harry Cohn. There was no tougher man in the whole world, and I had the pleasure of seeing this man sit in a projection room, with Freddie Kohlmar and myself, crying at *Gunman's Walk* [1958]. At the end of that picture, he was literally crying. Harry Cohn crying! Freddie Kohlmar got up; he was so embarrassed he walked out. Got outta there real fast. Then I started to get out and he stopped me, Harry Cohn, and he said, "Wait a minute." He now bawled out the projectionist for turning the lights on, because nobody turns any lights on unless he gives the order, presses the button. He was so moved by that picture because he had two sons and this was a story about a father and two sons. He identified completely with that motion picture and he said to me, "You're going to be the biggest director in this business and I'm going to make sure you are." Wouldn't you know, that's the last picture he was ever associated with. He went to Phoenix, Arizona, and died.

TM and RT: You can't win. So I guess you'd call him tough, but you respected him and, dare I say, liked him?

PK: No, I must tell you, it was only in the last year that I got to know him. It took nineteen years before I got to know the man. I did things that should have been in Thomas' book.[1] I told them to Thomas, but Thomas didn't want to write that side of him for some reason.

---

[1] Bob Thomas, *King Cohn: The Life and Times of Harry Cohn* (New York: G. P. Putnam's Sons, 1967).

TM and RT: Another amazing scene is the end of *Five Against the House* [1955]—the elevator scene. Was that another invention of yours?

PK: Yes it was. You know who wrote that script, Stirling Silliphant. Stirling and I went down to Reno . . . we didn't have a sequence like that, we didn't know how the hell to finish it, and getting the Harold's Club and everything was a problem. I saw this thing, and that's the first time I'd ever seen cars parked like that. And I thought, oh my God, this is a natural. *This is a natural!* I don't know whether you know Stirling or not, but if you give him an idea, he can walk out of the room and finish it in five minutes and bring it in to you. He's the most prolific writer I've ever worked with.

TM and RT: He also coproduced that, didn't he?

PK: Yeah. That was Stirling's first picture. Of course, he was on cloud nine—just the idea that it was being made. But he was so good, oh God! I needed certain things at certain times, and I knew I was coming up to it. All I'd have to do was call him on the phone . . . he'd be in a hotel. He said, "I'll have it there." I said, "I won't get to it for three hours." He said, "I'll have it for you in twenty minutes. I think it's great." And he did. He and I should have teamed up quite a few times, but he got so involved with TV, and he was so successful in it.

TM and RT: John Payne is an actor that kind of fascinates me in all those films of the 1950s. He's almost like the John Wayne of those smaller crime films. He made a lot of them with you, I know.

PK: I must tell you, this is a fellow that I literally fell in love with. This is a great human being. He's nobody's fool, to start with. He's got a wonderful creative mind himself. *Kansas City Confidential* was written in here with he and I loaded with a bottle of Scotch. We wrote the entire script and then we turned it over to a writer to put it in screenplay form. I did three pictures with him, and all three we did the same way. I did 99 *River Street* and *Hell's Island* [1955] with him. With *Hell's Island*, we took *The Maltese Falcon* [1941] and we did . . . *The Maltese Falcon!* In our own way.

TM and RT: It's funny, but no one seems to have seen *Hell's Island*. I saw it years ago on TV, but it's the one that doesn't get mentioned as much as the other titles. Good film.

PK: That's too bad, because it *was* a good film; but I have a lot of films like that. I've never understood why they didn't get the recognition they should have. I don't understand why.

TM and RT: There are some obvious similarities between *The Phenix City Story* and *Walking Tall* . . .

PK: There definitely are, because it's practically the same kind of a story.

TM and RT: Given those similarities, were there any differences that you picked up on, or a different way that you approached somewhat the same material?

PK: Well, of course. I'm sure you saw what I did with the black man in *Walking Tall*. I tried to show, to the rest of the rednecks in the South, that it's possible for a redneck to have a change of heart and admit he's wrong. That I knew I did very well and I was very proud of the way this guy comes back to him after the black man has told us, "Come around to my house tomorrow and see the bonfire." And when Joe Don Baker, the last thing, says, "Jesus, what a disappointment. There won't be a bonfire!"

TM and RT: How did you get into the project with Richard Widmark, *The Secret Ways* [1961]? He produced that, didn't he?

PK: Yeah. Well, he saw *The Phenix City Story*. He wanted to try to get realism in it and, would you believe it, I told him I wanted to do it as a James Bond. But he hadn't heard of James Bond. I said, "If we do this tongue in cheek, we'll be the first ones." He said, "No, I don't want to do it that way." We had a big fight and I never finished the picture. The last week I left on account of that. I said we had to finish it that way, that I wanted to go all out with a bigger-than-life idea. Fade out. Fade in. He's at Columbia doing a picture and I've done *The Silencers* [1966] now, and *The Silencers* is one of the biggest hits Columbia's had. Do you know he tried to get me to do three pictures with him after that? After he saw what I tried to tell him to do seven years earlier in a picture. Now, he realized we'd have had, maybe, the first picture that would have taken him out of the role of the guy who kicks the old lady down the steps.

TM and RT: How would you define a B movie?

PK: Well, I think a B movie was an action movie, and an A movie was a characterization of people. That's about the biggest difference we have. You never get to know anybody in a B movie. That's why I tell you I broke everything down in acts. First act, I want to develop characterization, so you get to know the people, then go on with the story. It's a slow way of telling a story, but it's the only honest way to tell it, unless you happen to have that great writing we're talking about where a character can develop in front of your eyes as you go along. Well, that's great writing. That doesn't happen very often.

TM and RT: So you think a B movie would be defined more in terms of content and story than budget or other limitations?

PK: Oh yeah. A B movie is a *plot* story. It's not a story of people. There's a plot involved. An A story is a story about people. I don't think we've ever made an important story, except about people. No important pictures have ever been made on plots. You know, a *The Day of the Jackal* [1973] will come along where you've got something going, a plot picture with great entertainment and great interest. Now, that can happen and that can work, but that's the unusual. I know I'd have given anything to do *Deliverance* [1972], and I wouldn't have done it the way it was made. I think concepts are very important and everybody sees something a little different.

Our friend Shakespeare had the right idea; if the story isn't there, it isn't there. And a director, to me, isn't a director unless he can help a story. I don't care how good it is, he must make it better. When they tell you, "Here's a great script"—I haven't read a great script yet. Maybe other fellows have, I don't know. I've talked this over with Bobby Wise and Freddie Zinnemann and Mark Robson, and we're all very close friends and we all came up together in this business, and none of us has had the great script. The closest thing to a great script . . . it was a toss of the coin whether I would do it, or Mark, and Mark did it. That was *Champion* [1949], that was the closest thing. Actually so well written. Carl Foreman did a fantastic job on it. That was so many years ago, that kind of story wouldn't mean anything today.

Really, I've never read a great script. I've read some great ideas. But you need more than an idea to do a picture.

Herschell Gordon Lewis

HERSCHELL GORDON LEWIS*

Peckinpah's blood is much more watery than ours. . . . Peckinpah shoots people. We *dismember* them!—HERSCHELL GORDON LEWIS

As with many of his predecessors in the horror/low-budget/short-shooting-schedule field, Herschell Gordon Lewis was "discovered" by French critics, such as Jean-Marie Sabatier in his Les Classiques du Cinéma Fantastique *and by* Image et Son *magazine, at a time when no more than one or two American critics had even publicly admitted to seeing one of Lewis' works. If no one has seen films such as* Blood Feast *(1963),* Two Thousand Maniacs! *(1964), and* The Gruesome Twosome *(1967) it's probably because the pictures have only played in rural drive-ins and an occasional skid row grind house, places not normally frequented by representatives of high-brow magazines and film so-*

* Interview with Todd McCarthy and Charles Flynn, May 2, 1973, Chicago, Illinois.

cieties (that Lewis films have been seen by some French critics is remarkable in itself since they are banned in France; connoisseurs must travel to Belgium to see them).

Lewis specializes in gore, or hard-core violence, for which he found a reliable audience throughout the 1960s among the frankly lower class and less educated. Just as patrons of sex films pay their money to see the graphic sequences that pop up every ten or fifteen minutes, Lewis' public comes for the scenes featuring the gouging of eyes, the pulling out of tongues, and the driving of stakes through heads that inevitably punctuate his films. So well known is "the Lewis touch" that he is frequently asked to direct others' films anonymously, thus making it impossible to determine exactly how many films comprise the Lewis canon. Taking him at his word, Lewis has directed at least four dozen films over the last ten years, all on budgets that would have frustrated directors at Monogram thirty years ago.

Getting his start in film as a partner to Dave Friedman, currently president of the Adult Filmmakers Association, Herschell Gordon Lewis is the only remotely significant commercial filmmaker to be based in Chicago since the very earliest days of American film history. A former English professor at the University of Mississippi, author of books on marketing and advertising, owner of several Chicago movie theatres, and head of his own advertising agency, Lewis invited us to his offices in the Wrigley Building for the interview.

TODD MCCARTHY and CHARLES FLYNN: How did you get started in the gore films business?

HERSCHELL GORDON LEWIS: My very first film in this entire genre was *Blood Feast,* which we shot back in 1963. I made *Blood Feast* because I came to the conclusion that the old-time nudies were finished. That's a term that means nothing anymore, but in the early 1960s it was a very daring approach to filmmaking.

Prior to 1963 we had been making films, I made a lot of movies. In fact, the first film that I made was called *The Prime Time.*[1] It was made in 1960, I think, and it was the first film made in Chicago in forty-four years, and there was all this tremendous Chicago chauvinism, which is also lost back in history somewhere.

But the error that I made was the error that many people in the commercial film business make: they equate technical ability with an ability

[1] Produced by Lewis; directed by Gordon Weisenborn.

to entertain people. There is no correlation at all. None. There is no one I know in the commercial film business who doesn't believe that every film producer is a lucky guy who happens, by some accident, to overcome his innate lack of I.Q. and has been able to bilk the public, and one day they're going to get wise because, look at the way *I* make films, look at the way *he* makes films. Here's a film he made, and he released this film—correction: he excreted this film—and here's a ragged pan. Can you imagine releasing a feature with a ragged pan in it? And look over there, there's something in the background. Why, I make commercials, I wouldn't have a shot like that! Quite right, because the focus is entirely different. And what is wrong is that, as the technicians begin to try to entertain, they only entertain their compatriots.

Well, I was in the slough of despond too. I felt that, as a commercial filmmaker, I knew how to load a Mitchell camera, I knew how to cut for opticals, I knew how to mix a multiple sound track. What else is there to making features?

So I formed a company, and lost many friends doing it, called Mid-Continent Films. We made two films. One was called *The Prime Time* [1960] and one was called *Living Venus* [1961]. *Living Venus* still exists, it still gets playdates. Some fourteen years later, it still gets playdates. It's about a man on the order of Hugh Hefner, who starts a magazine like *Playboy,* and his rise and fall.

TM and CF: How thinly disguised is it?

HGL: It's heavily disguised. It really wasn't designed to show anything other than an arrogant personality in the field of publishing, and, for its time, *Living Venus* was relatively biting. That's the reason it still can play today. *The Prime Time* was not that way at all. And the films didn't do badly, but we made an unfortunate distribution deal, and that's what taught me the film business, the realization that anybody can make a film. But the huge gap between a film sitting in a nice, bright, shiny metal can in your basement, and a film sitting in a filthy, rusty can in a projection booth is the difference between living on the planet Mars and living in a luxury apartment in the Bel Air Hotel.

The distributor of these films went bankrupt, owing Mid-Continent Films about $100,000. Anyway, the company was out of business. So I went back to the commercial film business, sadder, wiser, and completely broke, but not necessarily disheartened. Subsequently, somebody came to me and asked if I could shoot what was then called a nudie. I said, "I can shoot anything. I can shoot a garbage pile, I can shoot a man jumping off the

Empire State Building if you can get somebody to do that." And in the course of conversations, we put together a little hand-to-mouth film that we called *Lucky Pierre* [1961].

I had a partner in *Lucky Pierre* named Dave Friedman. He carried the title producer, which meant he ran the sound, and I carried the title director, which meant I ran the camera. In fact, we were the entire crew on *Lucky Pierre*. We had nobody. The actors, on the sync-sound takes, had to work their own slates and then discard the slate and start to act.

Lucky Pierre had two advantages going for it. One was that it was funny. Until *Lucky Pierre* came along, every nudie had been made very much deadpan. The entire category was originated by a man, Walter Bibo— they used to call him The Flying Dutchman—who shot a picture called *Garden of Eden* [1957] down at Tampa, Florida. Made enormous, enormous money from it and wasted it all as the hardy pioneer who paved the way for everybody else. He wasted it in court cases. Because to Walter Bibo, the American Sunbathing Association was on a par with the American Medical Association or the American Bar Association, and he couldn't understand the persecution that was visited upon him by angry city fathers. But remember that this was some fifteen years ago, long before the permissive society had made films like this obsolete.

TM and CF: Was this the nudist camp film?

HGL: This was a nudist *camp* film, correct. *Lucky Pierre* was not a nudist camp film. We shot it in the Chicago area, using seven of the ugliest girls that ever appeared. The reason we did that was it was not respectable in those days for women to disrobe on camera. Today, they can show up for an audition to appear as Ophelia and the first thing they will do is unzip the front of their dress, which is designed for that purpose. But that, again, is the evolution of the art form. In those days, it was difficult to get people. It starred, as Lucky Pierre, a knockdown comedian named Billy Falbo, who's still around. We shot the film in four days. It ran exactly seventy minutes. We didn't have enough outs—we only bought 8,000 feet of film. The finished film runs 6,300 feet.

TM and CF: Was that in 16 mm. or 35 mm.?

HGL: Thirty-five. I've never shot anything in 16 mm., ever. To me, 16 mm. is a false economy if you're going to play a 35 mm. house. I think the arithmetic will bear me out. Anyway, *Lucky Pierre* was an instant smash.

TM and CF: What kind of theatres did it play?

HGL: The first date was played in the Capri Theatre in Chicago, which was owned by a man named Tom Dowd. We played the picture in there for nine weeks and our film rental—not the box-office gross—the film rental was in excess of what the film had cost us to make, so I was back in the film business with both feet. Subsequently, Tom Dowd, who owned that theatre, made a half-dozen pictures of his own, which I shot for him. He began to feel, why should I pay this kind of film rental when I can own the films? In fact, a whole generation of people went into the film business on that basis; some of them are still in there, some of them are still grinding out films that I feel are obsolete.

TM and CF: Did you know about Russ Meyer at the time?

HGL: Yes, Russ Meyer had made a film in 16 mm. called *Not Tonight, Henry*. That was the only film in release of this type prior to *Lucky Pierre*, but it was in 16 mm. and it didn't have the kind of lip-sync in it we had. Russ Meyer always did have a penchant for getting pretty girls. He had us there. Our film, I thought, was funnier than his, but it wasn't a competitive aspect anyway, because we didn't look at it from the viewpoint of he's got A, we'll make B, or he's got A, we'll make A-plus. It wasn't that kind of a circumstance, there was no such industry. Today, there are hundreds and hundreds of theatres that play nothing but sex product, for example. In those days, there was a peripheral group of theatres, about enough to sustain life and that's all.

TM and CF: How did you get into horror films? Or do you prefer to call them gore films?

HGL: I call them gore films for another reason. In 1962, we shot a film called *B-O-I-N-N-N-G!*, and *B-O-I-N-N-N-G!* was the last film of that type I ever made. I thought it was the best nudie film anybody had ever made. It was about two guys who decided to make one of these films. It was a satire. It was well done, it was well acted, it had pretty girls in it, everybody in the film business loved it. But I felt we had no place to go from there, except into hard core, and one can't play Nostradamus. I felt that the industry was moving in that direction—obviously, films were being played that, a few years before, had been *verboten*. On the other hand, I didn't want to be there for that aspect of it. I didn't want to be the Ralph Ginzburg of the film business.

When one makes independent film product, there is only one criterion to be used for the production of films, and this is where so many producers waste so much money and then wonder why no one will play their films. The only film that an independent can make and survive with is a film that the major producers cannot or will not make. I regard that as a physical law, I don't regard it as a theory. It's been proved so many hundreds of times that it's no longer in question. There are occasional freaks, but they are so occasional as to *be* freaks. So, I said to myself, what kind of film is there that the majors are not making? The majors were already beginning to dip their own toes into the area of casual nudity. The time had come to abandon that particular aspect of filmmaking. What kinds of films are there that a *theatre will play* that Metro-Goldwyn-Mayer, Fox, Warners, Paramount, Columbia will not make? And I had in my hands a script somebody had submitted about a maniac with an Egyptian overtone to it. I had come, in those days, to love Miami as a production site. Prior to 1967, there never was a better place to shoot films than Miami. The unions had not yet despoiled the territory, there was an ample supply of talented people who would work for very little money—they loved to make films—the climate was good, there was a good laboratory there . . . all the pieces were there to make films.

The script was a horror story. Anyway, I felt that if we were to make a simple horror story, we would have no chance of getting it played off, just as if we made a drawing-room comedy that somebody else might make with Doris Day and Rock Hudson, we couldn't get it played off, because we go go into a theatre on equal terms. We don't pass out a sheet to the people walking in, saying, "We're sorry, folks, but it was a low-budget film and you'll have to understand that, and it doesn't have the same production values" . . . you can't do that. They're paying the same amount of money they would to see a high-budget film, so if you cannot titillate them with production value, you titillate them with something else.

So we decided to take a shot at a *gore* film, and *Blood Feast* [1963] was the very first gore film. Prior to *Blood Feast,* I don't care what company you will name, Metro-Goldwyn-Mayer, United Artists, anybody, no one had made films in which people die with their eyes open, not shut. No one had made films in which blood and gristle show at the end. People died very neatly. *Blood Feast* I've often referred to as a Walt Whitman poem—it's no good, but it's the first of its type and therefore it deserves a certain position.

TM and CF: You, then, were years ahead of Sam Peckinpah in that respect?

HGL: Oh yes. Sam Peckinpah made *The Wild Bunch* in 1969 and *The Wild Bunch,* I felt, in many ways was deficient compared to *Blood Feast* back in 1963. Peckinpah's blood is much more watery than ours. Yes, he uses exploding devices in the clothing, but that's because Peckinpah shoots people. We *dismember* them! It's elementary that when you dismember somebody, it's a lot more repulsive than simply to shoot them cleanly. We had people dying in ways that are now regarded as very much "in." A slow-motion shot through the forehead? Nonsense! We anticipated that. In fact, in *Two Thousand Maniacs!*, in 1964, we had many of the devices for which *Bonnie and Clyde* was glorified years later, including that banjo music in the background.

So we shot *Blood Feast*, and we shot it in Miami. We paid very little attention to the plot line.

We shot *Blood Feast* almost tongue in cheek. *Blood Feast* was shot in, I believe, nine days, almost all of which was spent on the effects. We went into a cosmetics laboratory in Coral Gables and compounded our own stage blood. It was my opinion that the stage blood that was being sold was too purple. Also, we had to have stage blood that people could swallow and not die from. So we made our own. We worked with this laboratory and it annoyed me, two years later, to have a form mailer come to me from this same laboratory selling me, at $8.50 a gallon, my own blood, with no royalties. But it was an indication that they, at least, found it serviceable. We still use that same blood and I've got a gallon or two of it here.

While we were cutting *Blood Feast*, Dave Friedman, who was still my partner in those days, and I looked at each other and said, "What are we going to do with this picture?" We might show it at a midnight show on Halloween, but how else can we show this picture? But people who were coming into the cutting room, looking at it on the Moviola, couldn't watch it. Not because it was so repulsive pictorially, but because it was repulsive psychologically. And I thought, maybe we do have something here. Sophisticated people can't stand to look at this picture. It is that gory. We decided to open the picture in the Bel Air Theatre in Peoria, feeling if we drop dead in Peoria, no one on earth will ever know—it's a different planet. We opened on a Friday and we went down there on a Saturday in a driving rain, and here was traffic backed up down the highway, and the state police directing traffic, and I knew we had something. In fact, the second feature with *Blood Feast* was *B-O-I-N-N-N-G!*

I went into the drive-in, and it's hard to get an audience reaction in a drive-in, especially in Peoria, where they bring in five people inside the car and three more in the trunk. Here are these fellas sitting on their fenders, laughing and screaming, and we have a scene in *Blood Feast*, which to this day I'm asked for prints of, in which the maniac reaches into the girl's mouth and pulls her tongue out. And here are these people laughing and shouting "Ooaych! Lousy film!" On comes the tongue scene, and all you see is a bunch of white eyeballs, because that did bring 'em up short.

Blood Feast was a runaway winner. I've had no film before or since, with the possible exception of *She-Devils on Wheels* [1968], that did that kind of a business. It started an entire new category of filmmaking. Everyone was surprised at the business this picture did, including myself. There were many people who would not see it. There were a great many who wanted their money back. There were others who saw it five or six times, which also bewilders me, because I'd never call *Blood Feast* a good production job. We settled for take one a lot of times. I didn't want to saw the leg off again—let it go, we'll just cut around it. We don't cut reaction shots into gore anymore. We did then. Now, if someone's going to cut a leg off, the camera sits there, so the audience will wonder, How'd they do that? There is no reaction shot or cutaway where we can substitute pieces, because the industry has now gone past that. That's the problem with sex films. After you've shown all the aberrations, what do you do next? Which is the reason that some of the places on Murderers Row on Santa Monica Boulevard in Los Angeles that were showing 16 mm. loops and porno and getting $5.00 are now showing similar stuff but they're getting $.99. Because whether he accepts it or not, the President's Commission on Pornography was correct, there is a, not a boredom factor . . . there's a satiation factor.

Well, after *Blood Feast* I said to myself, now, what would happen if we made a good one? So, I wrote a script called *Two Thousand Maniacs!* I was, and still am, proud of that story. In fact, I had it published in novel form. I really felt that I should, for once, put my integrity on the line. *Two Thousand Maniacs!* was written with care, and in my opinion it's a good film. It's a gore film, but it's well done, it's well acted, it's well produced, it's *heavily* produced. We shot it in a town called Saint Cloud, which is a suburb of Orlando. Everybody in Saint Cloud is in that picture. There's a lot of production value in that picture. We had a cherry picker for some of the camera shots and the camera goes *way* up, a hundred feet in the air, and this huge mob comes down the center of the town, and there are banners flying and Confederate flags all over the town. It looks for all the world like a $2,000,000 picture. There are some areas where our budget does betray us, but not in the crowd shots.

We cut *Two Thousand Maniacs!* I was very pleased with it. The background music was good. As I say, we used the guitar/banjo/fast-picking combination, which was subsequently, even up through 1973, so popular. I felt that we should literally become millionaires for *Two Thousand Maniacs!* Critically, the public and the newspapers agreed with me. From the viewpoint of box-office return, nobody agreed with me. *Two Thousand Maniacs!*, as good as it was, I would say grossed perhaps a third to one half of what *Blood Feast* had grossed.

TM and CF: Did it make a profit?

HGL: Oh, yes. Oh, it made a profit, but it didn't build my fortune. I was in Paris last week and a fellow I know there dragged out a moldy clipping from *L'Observateur*, the French critical magazine. And there's a story on *Two Thousand Maniacs!* in this French publication. In *Image et Son*, which is the French very august film publication, it is listed among the great terror films, along with *Repulsion* [1965] by Polanski and *Psycho* [1960] by Hitchcock, so it's in good company, but that isn't the way you keep score. You keep score through net film rentals. If the long-distance runner leads the pack, but his mighty heart bursts two yards short of the finish line, he has not won that race.

TM and CF: You didn't stop making gore films.

HGL: I didn't stop making gore films . . . Oh, I didn't mean to say it was unsuccessful.

TM and CF: You've stuck to . . .

HGL: Oh, yes, we still have the old-fashioned Victorian morality in our films. In *The Gore-Gore Girls* [1972], the maniac pulls the eyeball out of a girl's head and *squeezes*. And you see the knuckles tighten, and you see this eyeball all the time. And finally it bursts, and this inky black glop squirts out all over the place. I have seen people faint, vomit, turn green, leave the auditorium, and go to the washroom because of that scene.

In *Two Thousand Maniacs!* I've got a scene in which a man is pushed into a barrel, and the barrel's got spikes knocked through it in all directions, big four- or five-inch spikes. And they roll the barrel down a hill, and the spikes tear him to shreds. That's one effect that we really don't show graphically, because we don't run alongside the barrel watching him get torn apart. There's an area where audience imagination is better than having the camera linger.

TM and CF: Has there been any effect that you've wanted to achieve that you just couldn't figure out how to do?

HGL: Well, there've been effects that I knew I couldn't afford to do. For example, I wanted to explode somebody. I wanted a stick of dynamite inside a human being, and then the human being is literally exploded.

I didn't do it because of the mechanics of it. I can do it, but to pull off that effect would cost me, in special effects, somewhere between thirty and forty thousand dollars, and no effect to me, in my budgetary area, can justify that kind of cost. I could do it another way, but it would look bad, just as we blew the brains out of somebody's head in *This Stuff'll Kill Ya'l* [1971], which is a PG. The reason it's a PG is that the effect didn't really come off well.

TM and CF: How do you achieve some of those effects that you have done, like the tongue and the eye?

HGL: The tongue effect was done in this way. We found a girl in the Miami Playboy Club named Astrid Olson, whom I have not seen before or since, but she had the size mouth that would accommodate a sheep's tongue we had bought for the purpose. And what had happened was that the sheep's tongue was kept in a refrigerator in the Suez Motel down in Miami; and the power went off for about a day and this whole room began to smell pretty gamy because of the tongue. So one of the more daring guys on the crew got a bottle of Pine-Sol, doused the tongue with it so that it wouldn't smell us out of the entire motel. We had our patented stage blood, which we had developed for *Blood Feast,* we had cranberry juice, and we had gelatin. So into this girl's mouth we crammed the tongue, the cranberry juice, the gelatin, and the stage blood. The lunatic pulled out the sheep's tongue, along with all the stuff that hangs out behind it, not just the tongue that you might buy in a butcher's shop. We had to go to Tampa to get this tongue, which is why I didn't replace it instead of simply spraying it with Pine-Sol. She was instructed to fight with him. In fact, during the instructions I said, "Miss Olson, this man may get a little rough with you," and she said, "Oh, I like a man who *is* rough." Oddly enough, she had her boyfriend there to watch the shooting, and he was outraged at what we did. He thought maybe this was some joke audition and then that she was going to have a lot of lines to speak. She had no lines of dialogue. Her job was to have her tongue pulled out.

TM and CF: We know another device you use is driving a stake into someone's head . . .

HGL: Oh, yes, in *A Taste of Blood* [1967] we did that, and it spurted nobly.

TM and CF: Do you do it in an extreme close-up, or do you move the camera back a little bit? How do you generally shoot something like that?

HGL: Normally, a gore effect will be shot on a medium close-up. The disadvantage of the extreme close-up is that you lose your orientation. The disadvantage of a long-shot is that you can't really tell what's happening. The audience, somehow, . . . going along with what Coleridge called a willing suspension of disbelief, is challenging you at all times while they are watching the film. They're looking for the way you did it. So we normally settle on a medium close-up. Sometimes we'll shoot it with two, three cameras. We have a Mitchell, an Arriflex, a Cineflex, and a little, hand-held Eyemo, which gives us whatever number of angles we want. But I would say, in general, for a gore effect the medium close-up is the best shot, although there's no rule.

TM and CF: What is *Zap-In?*

HGL: *Zap-In* [1971] was made three or four years ago. It's a sexy little film based on Rowan and Martin's *Laugh-In*. It's a sexy version of Rowan and Martin's *Laugh-In*. I self-applied an X to this picture, but if it were rated, it would be no worse than an R. There are no nude fronts; there are breasts shown, but that's all. It's one sight gag after another.

TM and CF: Sort of like *Hellzapoppin.*

HGL: Yes, exactly what it is. It's playing everywhere, an indication, by the way, of the backlash. The full title is *Miss Nymphet's Zap-In.* When we first shot that picture, we could not get that picture played. Now, there's no difficulty at all, I can't keep enough prints in. So there's an evolution in reverse.

TM and CF: You're willing to wait a year or two for a film to turn a profit?

HGL: Certainly. As a matter of fact, with *The Gore-Gore Girls,* I have two titles on this film. The second title on *The Gore-Gore Girls* is *Blood Orgy.* The reason for that is, even though we do live in future shock and we do have television, that great leveler of the strata of society, there are geographical pockets that don't know what *The Gore-Gore Girls* means, and for them I have *Blood Orgy,* which means a second entire campaign. Very expensive. But the ultimate criterion is, does anybody come into the theatre? I have seen a great many films, I've been asked to distribute some films that are potential award winners but have no box-office potential.

TM and CF: Is your audience mostly men?

HGL: Oh, no. No, no. It's considered *de rigueur* to bring a date to share the shrieking and screaming. We do very well in heavily concentrated black areas, but that may well be due to a booking policy rather than to any kind of an ethnic conclusion I might draw.

TM and CF: Your films do very well in the South.

HGL: Oh, the South is a gold mine. If I can't get my negative cost back out of the South, I'm in trouble.

TM and CF: What percentage of the theatres are drive-ins?

HGL: Hmmm, half.

TM and CF: So every one of your films made money, up through *This Stuff'll Kill Ya'!?*

HGL: That'll make money too. We've got a long way to go. That picture will be good for years to come. For example, take *Moonshine Mountain* [1965], which I shot in 1964—I have bookings on *Moonshine Mountain* for this week. The prints are almost shredded but I still get bookings on *Lucky Pierre,* and there were never more than eleven prints on *Lucky Pierre,* so you can imagine the kind of condition those prints are in.

TM and CF: Do many people review your films?

HGL: From town to town, yes. Our more serious stuff, like *Two Thousand Maniacs!,* get reviewed regularly—we've had reviews in *Time, Newsweek, Esquire*—but in general, I avoid reviewers like the plague. What do I have to offer a reviewer? I have a peculiar spur, a by-product, an offshoot of the mainstream of filmmaking, which I understand because it happens to be my bread, but I can't expect a critic to understand the laws of economics in films. Furthermore, I can't imagine getting a good review from someone who is looking at it at two in the afternoon, who in the morning has looked at *Last Tango in Paris* [1973] and in the evening will look at *The Last Ten Days of Hitler* [1973], or some picture that cost three or four million dollars to make. His attitude can't be attuned to what I'm doing.

TM and CF: We were told a couple of years ago that, at that point, you had directed forty-six films. Is that an accurate number?

HGL: That's correct, that's an accurate number. As of now, I've directed forty-nine films, on many of which I was also producer. On many of which, frankly, I was cinematographer, and the reason I don't take the credit as cinematographer is that it looks stupid on a screen credit—written, produced, directed . . . on *Blood Feast* I wrote the background music, which is something I won't do again. I got hold of Cecil Forsythe's book on orchestration and I labored . . . it took me longer to do a little piece of theme music, which is repeated fourteen times, than to shoot the picture, but it was an ego point at that moment. I'm not at that point anymore. My ego has been shot off and hasn't grown back. It's not like a starfish that can regenerate itself. But I don't take the credit. What happens is, if I know what I want in a shot, I will say to Alex, my cameraman, who also cuts the films, "Alex, let me make this shot." And then somehow it becomes part of the filmmaking that I'll be on the camera, he'll move over to being assistant cameraman, or second cameraman, and whoever was assistant cameraman will do something else. But it moves much faster that way, because, when you asked the question earlier about being able to finish a film, the trick in finishing a film is staying inside a budget. That's all there is to finishing a film. All you have to do is keep your ego in tight rein . . . you put a holster on it, you put blinders on it.

TM and CF: Do you have any imitators or competitors?

HGL: They are legion! They are legion! There are many people who feel that the road is paved with gold. Just as they followed us into the nudies, they follow us into gore. I read with interest a remark made at the convention of the Adult Filmmakers Association that, to separate themselves from the 16 mm. producers, they were going to go into horror films. Well, they've heard from the distributors—the pictures make money. But it's a more complex business than aiming a camera and firing. Yes, they can go to California and hire special-effects men; most of them are in California. Whereas I deal with my own ragtag legion that I've dealt with for years. What they *cannot* do is recognize what we have done in the past already. I see films every day being ground out. Some of these people come to work on our crew free, to learn how to make horror films. Which is like saying to a golf pro, "Will you teach my friend how to play golf today? I learned yesterday." You can't do it that way. One learns this business from sitting in an audience and watching a public reaction, and what you thought was a great effect, they laugh at. Something you threw away, they are horrified at and you say, "Oh, why didn't I spend more time with that?" But there are many people now who are, if not making gore films, including gore sequences. There are people who are trying to combine gore and sex in the films, and I think that's a tactical error.

TM and CF: How long are your films, as an average?

HGL: They average ninety minutes. *A Taste of Blood,* the one where you were talking about pounding the stake, is two hours. That's a long film. That's a modern-day Dracula story.

TM and CF: Can you tell us what your average budget is?

HGL: Do I dare?

TM and CF: We don't know . . .

HGL: Well, our budgets average between fifty and seventy-five thousand dollars. I guess it's no great secret. I don't want to bruit it about, and yet, people seem to know it whether I say it or not.

TM and CF: You have no ambitions, like Russ Meyer, to make big-studio Hollywood pictures?

HGL: I sure do! I don't want to make a picture like *Beyond the Valley of the Dolls* [1970]. I sure don't want to make a picture like *Blacksnake!* [1973]. But I would like to be in the position where I can choose a property of my own and shoot it with a decent budget, and not be on the camera myself. It would be foolish to say otherwise. Certainly I do. I'm tired of being self-financing, for that matter. I would like to risk, as Clement Stone says, "OPM"—"Other People's Money."

TM and CF: You know, you were also included in the *Cahiers du Cinéma* issue 150, the big issue on the American cinema. You were classified as a subject for further research . . .

HGL: Well, they also say that about cancer.

Arthur Lubin

ARTHUR LUBIN*

At the moment I'm an animal director. Unfortunately.—ARTHUR LUBIN

Arthur Lubin is certainly one of Hollywood's best judges of public taste. His Abbott and Costello comedies, Francis the Talking Mule films, and Mr. Ed television series were immensely successful. Indeed, he told us that of his sixty-nine films, only "eight have been miserable flops," which is a very good record indeed.

Lubin started his career as a director with Monogram and Republic, and gradually moved up to bigger projects, mostly at Universal and RKO.

When we interviewed him, Lubin (who bears a striking resem-

* Interview with Charles Flynn and Todd McCarthy, September 7, 1973, Los Angeles, California.

*blance to actor Dub Taylor) was working on a pilot for a new
Paramount television series, based on his feature* Rhubarb *(1951).*

*Lubin's large home, just off Mulholland Drive in the Hollywood
Hills, is tastefully decorated with Oriental objets d'art. Lubin looked
down at the late-summer smog hanging over Los Angeles as he started
to speak.*

ARTHUR LUBIN: When I got out of college, I became an actor. Every
part that Joseph Schildkraut did in New York, I did here on the Coast.
Liliom, The Firebrand, Desire Under the Elms. I opened the Vine Street
Theater in *An American Tragedy.* I was the guest star at Pasadena for a
long time with Sylvia Sidney, where I did *Liliom.* I also did *Liliom* on the
road with her.

So directing came kind of naturally to me. When I got out of college, I
directed *The Green Bay Tree* out here. And a man who knew my family
said to me, "Why don't you come with us and Trem Carr and direct a
picture?" The picture was called *A Successful Failure* [1934], which was to
be made in five days. When it was reviewed in *The Hollywood Reporter,*
the headline was: "*A Successful Failure:* Aptly Titled." So that was my first
picture. I didn't think I'd ever be able to direct again! But I did *Two Black
Sheep,*[1] *Honeymoon Limited,* and *Great God Gold* [both 1935]. All at
Monogram, all with Trem Carr.

Then Trem Carr was offered a producer's job at M-G-M, but he turned
it down and instead went to Universal. And I went to Republic, where Nat
Levine was the producer. I did what I thought was a charming picture with
Phillips Holmes called *The House of a Thousand Candles* [1936], and two
horrible pictures called *Mickey*[2] and *Yellowstone* [1936]. I would say that
out of the sixty-nine pictures I have directed, eight have been miserable
flops, which is a very good record.

I was the first director that a man by the name of Charlie Rogers hired
at Universal. He bought the studio from Carl Laemmle, after Laemmle
decided to retire and sell out. Possibly one of the reasons I was used so
much at Universal was my very wonderful early training as a director with
Trem Carr. He had John Wayne under contract at Universal for action
pictures. And when I first went to Universal, I did five John Wayne pictures.
Very few people know that. And they were made in six days, each one of

[1] Released as *Two Sinners* after the Monogram-Republic merger in 1935; Republic
distributed the film.
[2] Released in 1939 as *Mickey the Kid.*

them. We had six days to shoot. There was no time schedule, as there is today, where if you go late at night or start early in the morning, you have to pay more. In those days, you could shoot twenty-four hours a day, and nobody could complain to anyone. So I had the reputation of doing pictures quickly and bringing them in on schedule.

The last picture I did with Duke was going to be very extravagant; we were going to shoot it in ten days. It was going to be a big picture. That picture cost $90,000, I think. It was a sea story called *Adventure's End* [1937]. I think the reason they selected that was that there was a boat on the Universal lot, and they could use that. That's the way pictures were made. They said, "Well, what sets are up these days that we can make pictures on that won't cost us much money?" They used the standing sets. In fact, that's what's happening now in television. Particularly in a television studio as gigantic as Universal. They move a door from here to there and paint the set and it costs them nothing.

When Charlie Rogers was let out as the president of Universal, he went over to the General Service Studio,[3] and I did a picture he produced called *Delightfully Dangerous*[4] with Jane Powell.

CHARLES FLYNN and TODD MCCARTHY: How would you compare Monogram and Republic to Universal? Did you consider it a step up to move to Universal?

AL: Oh, yes. Don't forget that Universal had world distribution. Monogram had a very small distribution setup. They would have to take the best playdates they could in those days. But, in fact, I had no choice. Monogram was finished when Trem Carr left.[5] Republic was a step up. It wasn't whether I wanted to. It was the best thing that was offered me. Usually, a director or any creative person has to grab the first thing he can get, because the competition is keen.

Since I was the first director Charlie Rogers had signed at Universal, it was natural for me to be among those selected for Abbott and Costello.

I had seen them in New York after I graduated from Carnegie Tech in Pittsburgh. I thought they were terribly funny and suggested them to Mr. Rogers, I thought they were a very good comedy team. So when Abbott and Costello were at the World's Fair[6] in New York, Mr. Rogers or another

3 Located at 6625 Romaine Street, this rental sound stage, used by various B producers, was a "studio" in name only.
4 Released by United Artists in 1945.
5 To join Republic in 1935; Carr and W. Ray Johnston re-formed Monogram late in 1936.
6 From 1939 to 1940.

representative of Universal saw them, and that's how I was actually assigned to their pictures.

My first picture with them, *Buck Privates* [1941], was very strange to shoot because they didn't go by much of a shooting script. Being burlesque comedians, they just did their old routines. They would say, "This routine is 'Spit in the Bush.' " And I would shake my head and say, "What the hell is 'Shit in the . . . ,' pardon me, I mean 'Spit in the Bush.' " And they would have to act it for me and show me what it was.

The entire first script was a series of titled gags. I would just say, "We'll take a close-up here and a two-shot here." I never interfered. There was nothing I could do, because these were tried and true old burlesque things that they and their forefathers and *their* forefathers, probably since the Greek period, had done.

I notice that even some of our comedians now repeat the same routines. Maybe giving it a little modern this or a different that or a different name.

It was an interesting task. But after the first one, the studio was a little uncertain about how they were going to be accepted. But at the first preview, the audience just died. *Buck Privates* was a very, very funny show. And, actually, I must say it was very little credit to the director. It consisted mainly of fabulous gags that these two wonderful guys knew from years and years of being in burlesque.

It was so successful that the studio called me in and said they would like me to start almost immediately on their second one, which was then called *Oh, Charlie!* It later became *Hold That Ghost* [1941]. Now, that had more of a plot. Their head writer,[7] whom they brought out with them, used to write all their gags in burlesque. They were very close and their wives were very close. Bud and Lou's wives had been stripteasers, and they made no bones about it. It was their profession; they were wonderful, charming women.

So John Grant wrote the second script, with Alex Gottlieb, who was also the producer on that picture. It was more or less a straight comedy. The boys in those days were just wonderful, but when we got around to the fourth and fifth shows,[8] the novelty had worn off for them. When we started, at first, they were on the set at seven in the morning; they couldn't wait to get going. The fourth and fifth show, they were always late. Lou

[7] John Grant.
[8] The third was *In the Navy* (actually released before *Hold That Ghost*), the fourth was *Keep 'Em Flying* (1941), the fifth was *Ride 'Em, Cowboy* (1942).

didn't know his lines. They started to bicker. It's amazing how comedians, when they get so successful, start to fight.

That's what happened to Lou and Bud that fifth year. Lou became a very bad boy. He had never drunk, and he started to drink; but I think there was a reason for it. He loved his adopted son, a little boy. He was just crazy about him, and one day, the little boy dropped into the swimming pool and was drowned. I think that had a very, very big effect on Lou. That plus the fact that they were making tremendous sums of money. If I'm not mistaken, each one was making somewhere around $10,000 a week, plus a percentage of their pictures.

Their pictures were sensational. They pulled Universal out of the hole. And the five pictures I did with them were delightful . . . even with the problems the last year. Bud and Lou were both terribly generous. Whether it was my birthday, or Christmas, or if anybody in the cast or crew had a birthday, they were fabulous boys.

And I don't think there has ever been a finer straight man in the business than Bud Abbott. Lou would go off the script—because he was that clever with lines—and Bud would bring him right back. "What was that you said? Wasn't it something about an automobile, Lou?" And he'd be back.

I think the straight man is more important than the man who has the jokes. Because the man who has the jokes can go on and on and sometimes become awfully stale, and awfully dull, and get away from what a writer has spent hours on. Particularly *their* writer, who knew Lou and Bud. And Bud would so brilliantly bring Lou back on to the line of the least resistance.

I must say that *Buck Privates* was a great picture, only because of a thing that we need so badly now: people wanted to laugh. That came right before the war, and people were dying to laugh.

CF and TM: Was *Buck Privates* the first comedy to be set in wartime?

AL: *Buck Privates* was made in 1941. The war was just beginning. I had tried to get into the Signal Corps, and they said I was more important making documentaries. I was making documentaries with Jean Hersholt and Mary Pickford, on venereal diseases and all that kind of stuff. And that's how I happened to be one of the fortunate directors at the studio when Abbott and Costello arrived.

CF and TM: The Abbott and Costello movies really made your reputation as a director, then . . .

AL: Yes, indeed. It was good for me as a director, because their names became very well known and very popular. I just regret that the accident happened to Lou's personal life and sort of took him off tangent. Bud was never a very well man. He had an unfortunate disease that prevented him from sleeping too well at night; because of that he drank a great deal. But he never came on the set drunk until the last year, when Lou started drinking a bit, too. And they gambled very heavily in Las Vegas. But I think a lot of that was Lou's attempt to rid himself of the horrible sorrow and depression over his little boy.

CF and TM: One of our sources[9] claims that the total budget of *Buck Privates* was $90,000. Is that correct?

AL: I don't even think it was that much!

CF and TM: How could you make a film for that amount of money?

AL: Well, don't forget that in those days, we shot six days a week. There were no big sets, the whole thing was made on the back lot, there were a lot of stock shots in it. Everything was very simple. There were no sets to speak of. And at that time, I don't think Bud and Lou got any money at all. It was after the hit of *Buck Privates*—and this happens all the time in our business—that they started receiving large salaries. That picture was made for peanuts. The same as the first picture I did with Donald O'Connor.[10] That was an Army picture, too. That was right after the war. And that picture cost, I think, about $150,000. Donald got $30,000 at the time, the mule cost nothing. We had three mules then. And we made that picture in fifteen days.

CF and TM: Could you get most of the shots you wanted of Abbott and Costello in one take? Did they just do it or did you let them go on and on?

AL: I let them go on. If it was a tricky thing, we usually had two cameras: a close-up for Lou, because he had such a dollface; and a close two-shot. I usually tried to have the camera on a dolly so I could move with them. You couldn't keep them in one position. Lou was all over the place. He was a darling, chubby little guy. I would rehearse with them and would ask them not to give me everything, but just to give me where they were going to go. No one could direct their routines as well as they. Because, as they went into a routine, something would spark them, and they would add little things here and there.

It was a joy, it really was, to work with them. They were fabulous.

[9] Leonard Maltin, *Movie Comedy Teams* (New York: Signet Books, 1970), p. 267.
[10] *Francis* (1949).

cf and tm: Then, their routines weren't improvised, in the strict sense . . .

al: No, most of their basic routines were very old. But Lou brought a freshness to them. And if the boys couldn't remember something when they were working, their wives would remind them. "Do you remember that thing we did in Cincinnati—where you lost all your clothes and only your underpants were left?" I'd have to say, "Well, boys, I don't think we can do that. The Hays Office mightn't like it, you know."

But they were, for the most part, very clean. The only time they got dirty was when they gave gifts. I remember my last birthday with them. They filled a suitcase with condoms. For the leading lady, who had a birthday the same day, it was full of Kotex. A suitcase! As they opened it, it fell all over the floor!

At Christmastime, they were terribly generous. We all used to go to Lou's home. Lou had a fabulous mother. They were Italian, very Catholic. She used to cook up fabulous dinners for the cast and crew. A real Italian family they were.

cf and tm: Since Abbott and Costello seemed to have their basic routines mapped out in advance, would you say your major contribution was in the matter of comic timing?

al: Oh, yes. After the first one, they had regular scripts. We would always have a reading, as I do now. Lou and Bud, mostly Lou, since he was the creative one, would say, "I don't think this is blown up enough. Remember, Bud, when we did so-and-so?"

Then, on the set, they would start something and I would make suggestions. Lou was on a parallel with Donald O'Connor as far as a fine comedian is concerned. Lou Costello, Donald O'Connor, and Allen Young had one great thing in common, which all comedians must have, and that is timing. They know how to hold back to get the sock laugh; and if they don't, it's up to me as a director to help them out.

But in this case, those three gentlemen are incomparable as far as timing is concerned. And I feel that so many of these new young actors who want to be comedians are so bad because they don't know how to hold back, how to time it, to get their laughs.

cf and tm: As a comedy director, did you always preview your films— if only to determine how long the laughs would last?

al: You have to. You actually re-cut the picture after the first preview. To try to put a breath in so they can hear the dialogue and what's going to happen.

Although nowadays the feeling is: let it roll. If they don't get it, they'll get it the next time; but don't stop for anything. You must have tempo like this: bang-bang-bang.

I don't always agree with that. I feel that if you get a laugh and it's out, you can time it to die out just enough, and then bring in the next one strong enough so there isn't a pause there.

But in the early days, we would bring it back after a preview and say, "My God, they couldn't hear this whole next scene!" Particularly with Abbott and Costello. And the first Donald O'Connor picture, it was a smash hit right off the bat.

CF and TM: There's no way of guessing how long a laugh will last . . .

AL: No. You can't guess about an audience.

CF and TM: Did your work on a film after the previews ever include reshooting?

AL: Very seldom. You usually cover enough with close-ups to get around it. We occasionally had retakes for a better ending; scratches on the film in the developing lab have forced retakes. Even our biggest directors have had to go back for retakes.

On the Abbott and Costellos, I usually only had to go back to take a close-up of Lou to help his laugh, or to stop the laugh, or to get a cute expression on him that I missed in the rush of shooting. Because, unless you're a very big director, you have to bring your pictures in on schedule if you want to work again. I know some young directors say, "Fuck it! If they don't like what I'm doing, I'll never work again." Well, they must have money.

They try to spot a director out here, put him in a category. He's drama, he's this, he's that. And at the moment, I'm an animal director. Unfortunately. Because I wanted to do a picture last year at M-G-M that I thought I was very right for. And they told my agent, "No, no, it's not for Lubin. There are no animals in it."

You see, after having done five Donald O'Connors and six years of *Mr. Ed,* it's natural they would class me that way. Now, I'm going to do a series with a cat, at Paramount. It's based on a feature picture I did called *Rhubarb*—about a cat who inherits $400,000,000 and a baseball team. The cat doesn't talk. He's just a *deus ex machina* to move the plot. But I know, once I start that, they'll say, "There goes Lubin with his animals again." But I always say, "Well, it pays well."

CF and TM: Unlike W. C. Fields, you do like children and animals . . . or animals, at least.

AL: They don't talk back to you.

CF and TM: Did you discover the David Stern novel that the Francis films are based on?

AL: I had a very good lady friend, who was in a literary agency, who told me about the "Francis" book. I thought it would be terribly funny. I had David Stern come out, and we wrote a script together. I gave it to my agent, and he said, "Arthur, if anybody ever buys this script, I'll eat it." I always love to tell that story. He said, "How the hell do you make a mule talk?" I said, "I don't know. I don't think it can be done with animation, because you'll lose the realism of it." So I took it to Universal, and they weren't the least bit interested in it. Fortunately, they had a story editor there, a man who is now assistant to . . . that man who writes all those dirty novels . . .

CF and TM: Harold Robbins?

AL: Harold Robbins! You know all those dirty novels. You'd better not say that! Just say he's now assistant to Harold Robbins. Anyway, he said to me, "I think this would make a very, very good comedy. You know, the studio still owes Donald O'Connor $30,000 on his contract. We have to get something going right away for him, something that can be made very cheap, or we'll lose the money."

So the studio advanced me $10,000 to see if I could make the mule work. If it didn't work, I had to give the $10,000 back. This was for a test.

I started making tests by putting chewing gum in the mule's mouth. I put tobacco in his mouth. We tried all kinds of things. And finally, in the middle of it, there must have been a moment or two where something worked. I had Chill Wills off scene doing the voice. I guess they were getting panicky that they would have to pay Donald, because even before I finished, they said, "Let's take a chance." And all through the picture, they never thought it stood a chance at all.

Working with the mule, we developed the system that was later used on *Mr. Ed,* that was fantastic. The horse was right on cue. His head movement was perfect. People still don't know how our method worked. They say, "How did Francis and Ed talk?" And I say, "A parrot talks, doesn't it?" And that's the only answer you'll ever get from me.

CF and TM: Did the Francis films lead directly to *Mr. Ed?*

AL: No. There's a long story there. During the Francis pictures, I met a young man in a gasoline station, called Clint Eastwood.

CF and TM: We wanted to ask you about him—wasn't *Francis in the Navy* [1955] one of his first films?

AL: It was. He was working in the gasoline station, and I said to my cameraman, "Let's make a test of him in his shorts." Clint had been coaching swimming at Camp Ord during the war. He's very tall, and he had a beautiful slim body. So we made a test of him, and all he had on was just a little skivvy shorts. He was very sunburned at the time. And I was very smart, I said, "I'm going to show this and I'm going to ask the Universal executives to bring their secretaries in with them." So we crowded the screening room with women, and they all cried, "Oh! Oh!" And I suppose they wet their pants they were so thrilled.

They put him under six-month contracts. The first one, I think, he got $75.00 a week; the second six months, he got $100. And they sent him to acting school—he was terrible. He can't act now, he wasn't an actor then, but he had a great personality.

Finally, they were going to fire him. I begged them to let him stay. I put him in *Francis in the Navy*. In every picture I directed, he had a tiny part. Then, they fired him, and they fired me for keeping him. My contract was up and they wouldn't renew it. They said, "This boy will never amount to anything."

I signed with RKO. And I entered a deal with Clint. He probably won't admit this, but I have a contract to prove it. For ten years, I would get ten percent of his salary. I would not act as his agent, I would act as his advisor, and I would put him in as many pictures as I could that I directed. But I didn't have to.[11]

The first thing he did under this deal with me was *The First Traveling Saleslady* [1956], with Ginger Rogers and Carol Channing. It was Carol's first picture. Then, I went to Japan and gave him a part in *Escapade in Japan* [1957].

But after that, things weren't going so well for him, and I was out of work. So he went to New York. When he came back to Los Angeles, a friend of mine, Sonia Chernus, who was a story editor at CBS, recommended him to the producer of *Rawhide*. That's how he got into *Rawhide*. Soon after that, he forgot Arthur Lubin. I haven't heard from him since.

We were such good friends. He'd say, "We'll have our own company someday. To hell with the money! You'll produce and direct and I'll act and

[11] For Eastwood's version of this story, see Arthur Knight's interview with Clint Eastwood in *Playboy* (February 1974), pp. 57–72.

star." They would come up here all the time for dinner, he and his wife. I even loaned him money. Fortunately, he paid it all back!

He was a charming guy. But, like so many people I can mention, many that I have discovered, I haven't heard from him since.

It's very funny. The girl who recommended the *Mr. Ed* stories to me doesn't talk to me anymore, either. Because she went with Clint; she's Clint's secretary. I introduced them to one another. In fact, we used Clint in one of the *Mr. Ed* shows and he was terrible in it.

CF and TM: Universal went through several financial crises while you were there . . .

AL: They say that I saved them twice: once with Abbott and Costello and again with Francis. And *The Phantom of the Opera* [1943] did very big business for them. Today, it's one of my favorite pictures. It was my favorite cast; I thought Nelson Eddy was just the tops.

CF and TM: How did the production system work at Universal?

AL: Eddie Muhl was the executive producer. When Charlie Rogers bought the studio from Carl Laemmle, he had one flop right after the other. And spent money like mad. Then, it was bought by Nate Blumberg. Nate Blumberg put in a series of producers who were actually only theatre managers. They were wonderful men, but they knew nothing about making pictures. They knew . . . well, they thought they knew what the public wanted, but they didn't know too much about how to make a picture. Eddie Muhl was brought in to be the executive producer to help guide them. I don't think he ever made any pictures per se. He was just in charge of production.

CF and TM: Did Muhl decide what would be made?

AL: No, a committee did. Mr. Blumberg, Cliff Work, and a man from London, in the early days, were on the committee that decided on all those things. But it was composed mostly of ex-theatre managers.

CF and TM: How long did that last?

AL: It lasted quite a while. It lasted until International came in.[12] Mr. Blumberg had died. Cliff Work wanted to get out of it, he never did like the job. Mr. Spitz and Mr. Goetz came in as co-owners of Universal. A man named Milton Rackmil was their president. Finally, MCA-Universal had to divorce itself either from producing pictures or from being a talent agency.[13]

Now, there's no doubt about it, Universal has been terribly successful.

[12] In 1947.
[13] In 1962–1964.

Everybody doesn't enjoy working with them as much as with the other studios because they're running it pretty much like a factory. You have to start at such and such a time, and be finished on time. If you're behind, they call you on the carpet.

But, I must say for them, they're creating a tremendous number of jobs for people who need them very badly. And, if you don't mind having a great many overseers and bosses, it's a job. And, God knows, we need them in Hollywood. It's been a real wonderful godsend to many directors, stage-hands, and technicians. They have about fifteen television shows. But they're not too strong on their feature pictures.

It's an up-and-coming studio, God knows. A fantastic studio . . . I wouldn't enjoy working there now. Fortunately, I don't have to.

cf and tm: Would you say that working conditions on B pictures in the 1930s and 1940s were comparable to TV conditions today?

al: No . . . no. They were pleasanter then. It was like a big family in those days. Of course, money was not as tight then. You could make pictures cheaper then.

There wasn't the hysteria: "My God! One hour is gonna cost us $50,000! Come on, Lubin, get finished!" In those days, things were much easier as far as dollars are concerned. Sets didn't cost as much; salaries weren't as much; directors and stars never got as much money as they get now.

The tempo of the times was different in the 1940s. They *needed* pictures then. Badly. After the war, all the studios, Universal, Fox, were turning out hundreds of pictures to fill the crying need for entertainment.

There was a wonderful feeling. "Let's do the best we can!" A picture like the first Francis cost $150,000 then. I don't think you could make it today for less than $750,000. Even the mule's hay would have gone up since we sold wheat to Russia!

Nowadays, to produce a good half-hour show costs between $150,000 and $200,000. The budget on *Mr. Ed* was $50,000 to $75,000 for a half-hour show; and that included a ten-percent cut for the agent, off the top.

Economics and world conditions have brought about a difference of tempo in these times. Living was easier in those days.

To sum up, making pictures today is very, very expensive. You've got to be very sure of your director, your cameraman, and your cast. But more than that, you've got to be very sure of your story. I personally think the writer is the least appreciated person in Hollywood. Because, if you don't have a good story, they don't care in Ketchikoo or Kansas City whether you dolly in or dolly out . . . shoot through wagon wheels, or up a person's ass. They like a good story, simply told, that they can understand.

One of the great problems of the young directors is that they don't tell a straight-line story. They cut and shoot so you say, "What is it all about? What is he trying to say?" Now, I have a feeling that this is gradually going away. And we will come back to the good, old-fashioned idea that "the play's the thing," as Mr. Shakespeare so aptly said. I think we're coming back to real entertainment. I notice that some of the older men are starting to make pictures again. The directors who care more about the script than the camera angles.

I did think there was a *very* young audience, but I think they're getting tired of seeing the same old crap over and over again. Pornography . . . they've seen so much fucking and sucking. I'm very happy to think that we're returning to entertainment. We've already lost the older audience. And we're losing the younger audience. We've got to try to win them all back. So they can say, "It's fun to go to the theatre. You come out feeling happy."

Edgar G. Ulmer

EDGAR G. ULMER*

I really am looking for absolution for all the things I had to do for money's sake.—EDGAR G. ULMER

Nobody ever made good films faster or for less money than Edgar Ulmer. What he could do with nothing—occasionally in the script department as well—remains an object lesson for directors who complain about tight budgets and schedules. That Ulmer could also communicate a strong visual style and personality with the meager means so often available to him is close to miraculous. But he did—and more than once: Detour *(1946),* The Black Cat *(1934),* Ruthless *(1948),*

* Interview with Peter Bogdanovich, February 1970. Copyright © 1974 by Peter Bogdanovich. A longer version of this interview appears in *Film Culture,* Nos. 58–60.

The Naked Dawn (*1955*), Bluebeard (*1944*) *are just the first that come to mind.*

He had been a kind of legendary figure for years when I decided to look him up in early 1970. We met for our first session on February 2. He was recovering from a stroke that had for a while deprived him of speech and of the power in his legs, but he had struggled back and by the time I saw him he had but a slight limp and only minor difficulties with words. His recovery was as much a miracle against heavy odds as some of his best pictures. Though almost seventy, he was also anything but an invalid in mind or body, was involved in several projects, with plenty of time and advice for students, and generous to me with his energy. He had humor and passion and a kind of demonic charm. We had three sessions in February, and then my work on The Last Picture Show *took me away for almost a year. We spoke several times on the telephone but before we could meet again to finish the interview, another stroke paralyzed him. He never walked or spoke again although he could understand everything that was said to him, could nod, or shake his head. That must have only made it worse for such an active man. I never saw him again. He died a year later.*

PETER BOGDANOVICH: You've really been working a long time in pictures.

EDGAR G. ULMER: Oh, yes, a very long time. If I would tell you my start in pictures, you would laugh yourself sick. I was in Berlin with Reinhardt in 1919. I met [F. W.] Murnau's closest friend, Rochus Gliese, a wonderful stage designer and a motion-picture director. He and Paul Wegener were planning to make a picture called *The Golem*—the first one. When summer came it meant no work for us at the theatre because we were laid off for two months. Gliese said, "Why don't you come and work on the picture?" This was the time of unbelievable inflation. So I said, "What kind of a job? You have a designer—Professor Pelitzer." So he said, "Can you cut silhouettes?" I said, "What kind of a question is that?" He said, "Every shot I make I want shot through a cutout. If it's a love scene, I want to shoot through a heart—in silhouette—if it's trees, through a window." So my job was to sit on the set next to the camera and cut silhouettes, mattes, which the director wanted before the lens. Two weeks later I was building sets, because Pelitzer didn't care. But my start was as a silhouette cutter—and we invented some tricks. Remember the sequence where the magic girls dance on the lake? That was a huge problem. How in the Lord's name are you going to make girls dance on the water? I discovered a way of doing it. We drove piles into the bottom of the lake and we put two-by-fours, which we painted black, into the lake. But unfortunately we used the girls from the Prague Opera House—very hefty Czechoslovakian broads—and when they jumped, they broke the goddamn boards! They were sinking. We had to get iron cantilevers to put into the boards; we hadn't figured how heavy these Czechoslovakian broads would be.

It was an unbelievable time to make pictures. France had a wonderful comedian called Max Linder. He was a French Harold Lloyd. His two-reel comedies were at that time German-French coproductions. So I painted on the floor a whole six- or seven-story house he was to climb over. Maurice Stiller came to Berlin and saw that painted house on the floor and hired me to make the *Gösta Berling Saga* with him in Stockholm—that was Garbo's first picture. I also did the sets of *Street of Sin* [1927] for her for G. W. Pabst. It was entirely different then from the way we make pictures today. Then you had to do everything. Everything.

PB: You were saying you worked with Lubitsch when he was an assistant director?

EGU: Yah. In the unit.

PB: What did you do in the theatre before that?

EGU: I was designer and assistant to Professor Reinhardt, just as Preminger was much later.

PB: How long were you with Reinhardt?

EGU: I was with Reinhardt three years.

PB: And what had you done before that?

EGU: Before that I took my schooling at the Burg Theater in Vienna.

PB: And you always wanted to be in the theatre as a child?

EGU: Yes. I was a child actor, too.

PB: And after your schooling you immediately worked with Reinhardt?

EGU: Yes. I was considered quite a kid at that time because Reinhardt should be the *end* of a career—a climax—not for a boy.

PB: According to your biography you became a designer for Decla-Bioscop in 1918 so you must have been an infant in the theatre.

EGU: Sure. I was still in school.

PB: I see, while you were still going to school. And is that where you worked with Lang?

EGU: No, that was later at UFA.

PB: After you finished with Reinhardt?

EGU: No, during Reinhardt, and I worked with Murnau because Murnau and Dieterle were both actors at Reinhardt's. Dieterle we called the

Iron Stove because he was a very tall guy, not talented, but whenever we needed somebody in armor he had to play these parts, so we had a department called the Iron Stoves. We were very vicious kids as you can imagine.

PB: Was Dieterle a good director?

EGU: No, he wore white gloves and his wife was all day on the stage with him . . . saying, "William, it's enough—now you must rest" . . . and she brought him eyeshades so he could sleep on the set.

PB: What did you work with Lang on?

EGU: *Metropolis* [1926], *Die Niebelungen* [1924], and then I worked with him later, in 1929, on a film called *The Spies* (*Spione*), a classic picture. By the way, something very funny: from 1925 till 1927 Lang and Murnau had two American-English speaking people—for the subtitles—one was Joe Mankiewicz, the second one was Hitchcock. Hitchcock learned his trade under Fritz Lang.

PB: Did you get along with Lang?

EGU: Not at all. Because on the set he was the incarnation of the Austrian who became a Prussian general. A sadist of the worst order you can imagine. He was a great picture maker who fortunately married the best scenario writer in Germany, Thea von Harbou. I also worked later with him on *M* [1932] for Seymour Nebenzal.

PB: Were you only working as a designer?

EGU: No, I was really Bild Regisseur. At that time, up to the coming of sound, there were *two* directors in each picture: a director for the dramatic action and for the actors, and then the director for the picture itself who established the camera angles, camera movements, etc.; there had to be teamwork.

PB: And you yourself were in charge of that?

EGU: Yah. With Murnau I invented a new role called "production design," which meant the designing of each and every angle. Our sets were built in perspective with rising or sloping floors. Everything was constructed through the viewfinder. So what happened was you could only take one shot in that set if you had a room. If there were ten shots of it, you built ten sets of that one room. Because the one eye was the point of the perspective, the furniture was built in perspective. That's where the great look of the pictures came from. It gave you, of course, a completely controlled style. When you look at the old UFA pictures today, you're startled how precise each and every shot is.

PB: Because a set was built for each one.

EGU: Yes, Fritz Lang was a designer too, as you know. He designed advertising posters when he came to Berlin. Lang had an unbelievable energy and stick-to-itiveness; you could never stop him. He saw the picture. Nothing could distract him, he would do it fifty times. So did Murnau. When we came in and saw the rushes at night, Murnau used to get up when the light went on again and say, "Now we know how *not* to do it."

PB: And did it all over again?

EGU: Everything over again. We had worked on and off practically two years on Lang's two *Niebelungen* pictures. It was the time of the greatest inflation. We cut the picture, the premiere was set for the UFA Palace, a theatre that seated 3,000 people. At that time the dollar was 700,000 marks. The night when we opened the picture, Lang carried it, reel by reel, to the theatre because he was still cutting. When the second reel was running, he was cutting the third reel. Meanwhile [Frank] Kellogg, the great American diplomat, had worked all day with the German government and that night the gold mark was born. Seven hundred thousand marks were really one gold mark. Result: the picture cost UFA and Mr. Lang not a penny. That was Lang's luck.

PB: And you worked with Murnau on *Faust* [1926] and *The Last Laugh* [1924]?

EGU: *The Last Laugh.* The first picture I made with him was in Yugoslavia . . . *The Finances of the Grand Duke* [1924]. We photographed at Fiume in Spoleto. A very strange picture.

PB: You continued to work with Murnau when he came to America?

EGU: Yes, Junior Laemmle [Carl] loaned me to him.

PB: That was on *Sunrise* [1927], *Four Devils* [1928], and *City Girl* [1930].

EGU: Yes, but the only picture which Murnau himself counted was *Sunrise*.

PB: Was it made with the same kind of sets?

EGU: Yes, that's when we forced Winnie Sheehan to accept the idea and do it in perspective. They had to buy Fox Studios in Westwood because we didn't have enough space down on Western Avenue.

PB: Did you ever use perspective sets on any of your later pictures?

EGU: Yes, yes. I used it at PRC on *The Wife of Monte Cristo* [1946], *St. Benny the Dip* [1951], and *Menschen am Sonntag* (*People on Sunday* [1929]).

PB: You designed *People on Sunday*?

EGU: No, codirected and produced. [Robert] Siodmak was the other director. Fred Zinnemann was the camera assistant [Eugene] Schuftan was the cameraman—the first time that he ever operated the camera—and Billy Wilder wrote the script—on pieces of scratch paper in the Romanische Café—his first script. It was quite an achievement.

PB: How did you all get together on a thing like that?

EGU: I organized it. I had $5,000 that I had brought from America. I saw a picture made by a Russian director, Dziga-Vertov, called *The Man With the Camera* [1929] and was tremendously taken with the thing because it was photographed in Kiev, in streetcars, in actual houses—no sets built—and done not with actors but with real people—the idea De Sica had twenty years later.

PB: Are you still friendly with any of the German directors that you knew then, like Preminger?

EGU: No. Preminger, I could never accept. You must understand that German film and theatre had two groups. One was the romantic, let me say, art-possessed group; the other was the group to whom theatre and film was a business. Now there are very few still alive from the first group, and we have scattered all over. It's a very, very sad life now, because the real people, most of my friends, are in the Eastern Zone of Berlin. [Bertolt] Brecht drew them over there with him. I would not go across the line into East Berlin. The first time I came back after the war, I was warned not to go over. So one night Brecht's two daughters finally cornered me in the West in a park, and we sat and talked about their father, and would I come over? Then he died and I didn't get to go across to his funeral, which I, of course, found pretty horrible.

PB: How would you rate those directors if you were historically looking at each of their work? Do you think Murnau is the greatest?

EGU: Yes. Murnau was the greatest because he had Carl Mayer, the writer. Because Murnau was really a man who had the camera up there, a man who saw pictures and who built pictures in his head. Lang was very powerful too. He had a rotten personality—selfish and egotistical—but a great picture maker. At the same time, Jacques Feyder, who also did most of his work, not in Paris, but in Berlin, was a fantastic picture maker.

PB: Did you actually work with Hitchcock at UFA?

EGU: No.

PB: What was it like coming over here to do *Sunrise?*

EGU: I came in 1924 to finish up my work on *Miracle at Offenberg.* Then I worked for Martin Beck for six months until Carl Laemmle came after me. Stroheim was making *Merry-Go-Round* and wanted me as his art director. So I made a contract with Carl Laemmle and broke my contract with Beck, which I could do because they had made a mistake. I wasn't of age—I was a boy, twenty years old.

PB: You weren't allowed to sign contracts?

EGU: No. You must be twenty-one. So, Mr. Untermeyer, the lawyer, got me out of this, and I got a contract with Laemmle, which was a "catchall" contract—assistant art director and production assistant—to learn how to direct. So I started, then after six months of designing, I became an assistant director with Willy Wyler and that whole bunch out there.

PB: At Universal?

EGU: I stayed with Universal for many years.

PB: But you never directed there?

EGU: Oh, yes, doing Westerns, a whole flock of them. Then I did *The Black Cat*.

PB: Yes, later, but I mean the silent days.

EGU: In the silent days, I directed Westerns.

PB: Were they any good?

EGU: They must have been very strange. In fact, they were very funny. There were two Western streets—on the upper part of one, Willy worked, on the lower part of the street, I worked. When Willy used the horses and the cowboys, I had to do close-ups in my picture. Then when I ran out of close-ups, *I'd* get the horses. We each made twenty-four of those a year. We had the following schedule: Monday and Tuesday you wrote your script and prepared the production; Wednesday and Thursday you shot; Friday you cut; and Saturday you went to Tijuana gambling with the old man.

PB: What was the first of those pictures you directed? Do you remember any titles?

EGU: No, who can? I made so many of them. It was something like *The Border Sheriff*, that's all I recall.

PB: You remember what year it was?

EGU: Yes, 1925.

PB: My God, I didn't know you were directing that early. How many years were you doing those things?

EGU: I did Westerns up until about August '26, when they loaned me to Murnau.

PB: Murnau had come over here and asked for you?

EGU: Yes.

PB: Were you Stroheim's art director on *Merry-Go-Round*?

EGU: Yes, but Stroheim got fired—Rupert Julian finished the picture.

PB: Did you finish the picture with him?

EGU: Yes. I stayed on.

PB: How did you get along with Stroheim?

EGU: Magnificent—I loved Stroheim. The man invented his own characters—everything. He did a tremendous amount of reading. He himself
was a very strange character. In the year 1917 Uncle Carl at Universal was
sold by one of the directors of the time (I don't know who it was) a script,
which Stroheim, who was a costume man at Western Costume, had written.
The title of the script was *The Kaiser—the Beast of Berlin,* an American
propaganda film. Stroheim was the first wardrobe man—he knew the
Austrian-German uniforms, he knew the American uniforms, and at that
moment he decided he wanted to become a director. He also played a
German general in the picture. And the following day he appeared with a
monocle in his eye and stopped Carl Laemmle on the street and told him
what a wonderful director he was. He had directed pictures in Berlin, in
Vienna, and he sold Carl Laemmle on making a picture which would be
something like eighteen hours long called *Foolish Wives* [1922]. He started
to build all of Vienna and Monte Carlo on the back lot at Universal. He
could be nasty and he could be a sadist, but he knew pictures. He could see
a film, could visualize it.

PB: Are the history books correct—that Murnau was the first one who
moved the camera so extensively?

EGU: And built. When you talk about Murnau, you must talk about his
best friend who collaborated with him—a very fine director, Rochus Gliese,
whom he brought to this country on *Sunrise.* Gliese was my partner, a
fantastic designer and camera builder.

PB: Do you remember how the idea came to move the cameras so
extensively?

EGU: Yes. It was just before *The Last Laugh.* We really had one thing
to sell on *Last Laugh,* which was Emil Jannings' face. Now, Carl Mayer
wrote in the script about how the camera was on top of Jannings when he
walked through that lobby and got into the elevator, which should be one
shot. Murnau then added to what Mayer wanted. He said it was important
to be on the face. And Murnau had insisted, "No subtitles." There wasn't
one.

PB: So, before the picture was shot, it was decided not to have titles.

EGU: Of course, *before.* When that decision was made, he said that
there was only one way to tell the story—with his eyes and by staying with
him all the time. At that time we didn't have telescopic cameras or lenses.
We had 50 mm., which was *the* thing—we didn't know about the 75 and

everything up to 1,000 now. So Murnau finally turned to Gliese and to me, and said, "Isn't there a way to do it?" So we huddled with Karl Freund who was the cameraman—not the actual cameraman, but the supervisor of photography—Gunther Rittau was the actual cameraman. And we walked down the Kurfürstendam to have dinner. A woman with twins in a baby buggy was rolling along, and I suddenly stopped and said, "What's going to stop us from putting the camera on the buggy?" We tried and tried, and we built the first dolly. What the dolly couldn't do! We laid things out for it. We didn't have rolls of film long enough. We had to go to AGFA and convince them to *cut* film for us.

PB: They were only four hundred feet long?

EGU: Two hundred feet! And we needed about seven hundred feet. The stopwatches! What went on with that thing! And when we finally saw the shot, we didn't know how we did it. Everybody was so tense. This was the tenacity of Murnau. He actually had a metronome next to him just to set the pace.

PB: *Sunrise* was also done with very long takes?

EGU: Sure. The script of *Sunrise*—I think I have it still in storage—Herman Bing and I translated it from German. Mayer had written it like poetry—one shot on every page. The language—the most unbelievable love went into that thing.

PB: Did you ever work with Lubitsch?

EGU: Oh yes, sure, here at Warner Brothers.

PB: What did you do with him?

EGU: Art director. I did for him *Lady Windermere's Fan* [1925]. I did Heidelberg for his *The Student Prince* [1927]—at Metro.

PB: Did you like him?

EGU: I loved Lubitsch, mainly for his tremendous desire to make something funny with class.

PB: He was a great director.

EGU: He was. It was strange—he really should have been a Frenchman.

PB: He was the least German of any of the directors. What was your first film in Hollywood?

EGU: *Mr. Broadway*. But it was New York, not Hollywood. It was 1932.

PB: How did you get the chance to direct that?

EGU: I worked with De Mille on *The King of Kings* [1927], made huge miniatures of the Crucifixion with a cameraman by the name of Walter Lang. He went back to New York. He owned a tremendous optical house. I was called by him to New York, and he had put the thing together with a laboratory. That's how I got to direct.

PB: Was *Mr. Broadway* a comedy? I never saw it.

EGU: No, it was a very serious picture. Ed Sullivan was in it—he was the big star.

PB: He was "Mr. Broadway"?

EGU: Yeah. That was his column.

PB: And how did you like the picture?

EGU: Didn't like it at all, because Sullivan forced it into one of these moonlight-and-pretzel things. It was a nightmare, a mixture of all kinds of styles.

PB: And you were unable to control the picture?

EGU: Unable. The laboratory controlled the picture.

PB: And how did you make *Damaged Lives* [1933]?

EGU: That was also very strange. Jack Cohn of Columbia got in a fight with his brother, Harry. Jack was in charge of sales in New York and was very angry and very jealous that he couldn't produce like Harry. Mr. Walter Wanger, at that time, was one of the producers at the new Columbia, which had become very rich overnight. The fight between the brothers was over Wanger, and they decided not to talk to each other anymore. And Jack Cohn, whom I knew very well, brought up the subject one night. He had to make pictures himself. He went back to New York and called me. We met the Canadian health minister who needed a picture for Canada. He told me about a play by [Eugène] Brieux called *Damaged Goods,* translated by Bernard Shaw. It was a huge success before the First World War—came out in the period of *Mrs. Warren's Profession*—I knew that play and I said I could make a picture out of it. Jack and Harry had another brother named Nat, the born schlemiel of the family. He was in charge of the shipping room and was kicked out because he couldn't understand why he should be in the shipping room when his two other brothers were the president and vice-president of the studio. So I had to agree to take Nat as my producer. I wrote a script, the Canadian health minister was delighted. He didn't know a thing about pictures. I came back to the Coast and shot it. Harry, because he was fighting with his brother Jack, wouldn't let me on the Columbia lot. I had to go to General Service Studios, and I made the picture there in eight days.

PB: My God! And who released it?

EGU: *Columbia!* And it made a fortune. At that time the picture made

$1,800,000, played ten weeks at the Central Theatre on Broadway. Harry Cohn never forgave me for that. I was the bad boy. I never worked for Harry himself. It's a story against syphilis.

PB: Was it a good film—did you ever see it again?

EGU: Yes. Yes, I saw it again. An excellent film, really very good.

PB: You made it so quickly.

EGU: Most of my PRC pictures were made in six days. Just try to visualize it—eighty setups a day.

PB: Really? I once did forty and almost died. How can you do eighty?

EGU: Ask my wife—she's my script supervisor. I was known all over town. I could have gone anywhere, but I was under exclusive contract. There would come a time around four o'clock in the afternoon when I would say, "Aces wild, we go into a PRC hour now, I'll give the numbers." But I had a perfect technique worked out. No set of mine existed in these pictures where one wall was not without any paintings, without anything, just a plain wall in gray. I shot my master scene, but left for the last day the close-ups. They would play against that one flat, blank wall, and I would say "camera left," "camera right." They would say two sentences, I would hold my hand in front of the lens not to stop the camera, and he would go into the second speech, because I couldn't afford to go through. I had to cut with the camera, because I was only allowed 15,000 feet for a feature. No more. Two to one, nothing more.

PB: So you didn't even bother to slate. You put your hand in.

EGU: Yes. I laughed when I came over to Italy to make my first picture and they bragged about their fast slates. Because in the beginning, when they didn't have the raw stock, they wouldn't spend more than two feet. I laughed. I said, "You think that's fast?" I showed them how to do it.

PB: You must have also shot many things with long master scenes without cutting.

EGU: Of course. The crews used to do something very funny to me. In every studio where I worked in the forties, they put a sign on the camera, on the magazine: Ulmer Short Line.

PB: Because you were moving so much?

EGU: I had to have my own dolly grips, whom I carried from picture to picture with me. And I took the same thing to Italy. When I did The Pirates of Capri [1949] there, I laid a track of four hundred feet for a master scene on the beach, and from that time on there was only one expression: "Una piccola carrella."

PB: A short rail.

EGU: Just a short rail, just a short one.

PB: Anyway, *The Black Cat* was the next film you directed?

EGU: Yeah.

PB: I think it's one of your best.

EGU: Yah. But a lot of credit must be given to Junior Laemmle on that picture.

PB: Why?

EGU: Junior was a very dear friend of mine, and a very young man. Under the influence of [Lewis] Milestone and the so-called intellectual crew with whom Junior palled around, which means his two cousins, the Wylers, William and Bob [Kuhlman] Henickson, and me a little bit, Junior had made, against all advice from his father, *All Quiet on the Western Front* [1930], which became an unbelievable success. I was very much taken by a German writer of the time called Fallada, who was very much like Remarque, only younger. And I sold Junior on an idea to make his book, *Little Man, What Now?* So Junior found himself in the intellectual picture making. So when I came to him with the idea of *The Black Cat,* which would employ Lugosi and Karloff at the same time in the same picture, because each one had been successful, Junior gave me free rein to write a horror picture in the style we had started in Europe with *Caligari* [1919]. And he gave me my head for the first time. He was a very, very strange producer; he didn't have much education, but had great respect for intelligence and for creative spirit.

PB: You didn't have anything to do with directing *Little Man, What Now* [1934]? That was Frank Borzage.

EGU: Very good picture—I built the sets for it.

PB: *The Black Cat* has really very little to do with the Edgar Allan Poe story—just the title.

EGU: Nothing. The Edgar Allan Poe story is not a story you can dramatize.

PB: Why did you supposedly base it on that—for commercial reasons?

EGU: It was Junior's idea.

PB: Just for the title and name?

EGU: Yah.

PB: Where did you get the idea of the castle being built on the graveyard of a battlefield and all that?

EGU: That came out many years before. I had been in Prague, as I told you, and had worked on *The Golem* [1920]. I met at that time Gustav Meyrinck, the man who wrote *Golem* as a novel. Meyrinck was one of these strange Prague Jews, like Kafka, who was very much tied up in the mystic Talmudic background. We had a lot of discussions, and Meyrinck at that time was contemplating a play based upon Doumont, which was a French fortress the Germans had shelled to pieces during the First World War. There were some survivors who didn't come out for years. And the commander was a strange Euripides figure who went crazy three years later when he was brought back to Paris, because he had walked on that mountain of bodies. And I thought it was a subject that was quite important. And that feeling was in the air in the twenties.

PB: Was that the original idea for the picture and you worked backward from there?

EGU: Well, I wanted to write a novel really, because I did not believe the literature after the war and during the war, on both sides. In Germany and in England, it was very much the heroic thing. And where enemies were fiends like you never saw before. I couldn't believe that. Therefore I took two men who knew each other and who fought their private war during the time that capitalism flourished. I thought it was quite a story stylistically. I had a wonderful cameraman, and Junior let me do the sets and everything at the same time.

PB: *The Black Cat* had a remarkable visual strength.

EGU: It was very, very much out of my Bauhaus period.

PB: How did you get along with Karloff and Lugosi?

EGU: Very well. Karloff was a very charming man.

PB: I knew him. Yes, he was.

EGU: Very charming. And he never took himself seriously. My biggest job was to keep him in the part, because he laughed at himself. Not the Hungarian, of course.

PB: Not Lugosi?

EGU: No. You had to cut away from Lugosi continuously, to cut him down. But there was the huge success of *Dracula* [1931] on film, and on stage.

PB: Of course, Karloff had a big success too, but I suppose he was more intelligent.

EGU: Karloff happened to have been English, that's the marvelous thing. After all, I worked with the man after his gigantic success in *Frankenstein* [1931]. One of the nicest scenes I had with him, he lies in bed next to the daughter of Lugosi, and the young couple rings down at the door, and he gets up and you see him the first time in costume, in that modernistic set. I explained the scene to him and he said, "Aren't you ashamed to do a thing like that—that has nothing to do with acting?" So I told him to be nice and do it, and he never took himself seriously—he got into bed, we got ready to shoot, and he got up, he turned to the camera, after he put his shoes on, and said "Boo!" Every time I had him come in by the door, he would open the door and say, "Here comes the heavy . . ." He was a very, very lovely man.

PB: And a good actor.

EGU: Yes, a very fine actor. Five star. As you know, he lisped—but the way he used that lisp—he knew exactly how to overcome the handicap.

PB: What was it that particularly excited you about making that film?

EGU: The stylistic thing, of course.

PB: Was the picture successful?

EGU: Yah. It started a whole cycle. And Universal didn't make a cycle if it wasn't successful.

PB: And then you went from that to a couple of Yiddish films, didn't you?

EGU: Yes. And I had a very favorite script, a play that [Peretz] Hirshbein wrote called *Greene Felde* (*Green Fields* [1937]).

PB: Why was Jacob Ben-Ami your codirector?

EGU: I didn't speak the language. Also, nearly fifteen years before, Ben-Ami played the lead in *Greene Felde*. Hirshbein insisted I couldn't make the picture if Ben-Ami didn't play the lead. The night before I started shooting I got Ben-Ami out by giving him the co-credit.

PB: Who played the lead?

EGU: The leads were played by Helen Beverley and Michael Goldstein, a very fine actor from the Art Theatre.

PB: Believe it or not, I've seen the picture, and it's quite good.

EGU: It's very good! It was one of the nicest comedies I ever made, but with a very strong philosophic background. In Paris in 1938 the picture got the Best Foreign Picture award.

PB: What happened between *The Black Cat* [1934] and *Greene Felde* [1937]—you didn't direct a picture?

EGU: Oh, yes I did.

PB: What did you do?

EGU: *Thunder over Texas*. I had to make Westerns again to live. I used the name of John Warner.

PB: Why did you do that?

EGU: I didn't want the Western credit. I did four.

PB: Four Westerns, and all as John Warner . . . amazing. You remember the titles?

EGU: No. Not anymore. These were jobs where you got $300 for directing a picture.

PB: These were not one-reelers?

EGU: Features! Shot in five days and five nights.

PB: Well, I think I can find out the names by looking up the credits of John Warner, maybe.

EGU: No. There were other names. We all had given names on these things. I didn't know what was going on, only that I was given a script, not even a script—two pages—and I went out.

PB: Incredible. And then *Green Fields* was the first picture you took credit for again as director?

EGU: No, no. *Natalka Poltavka* [1937], the Ukrainian picture.

PB: What's the title in English?

EGU: The same—it's a city in the Ukraine.

PB: Where did you make that?

EGU: In New York.

PB: And *Green Fields* was made in New York, also?

EGU: Yes.

PB: Where did you shoot the exteriors for *Natalka Poltavka*?

EGU: In New Jersey, never in the studio.

PB: Was that very simple in the way you shot it?

EGU: Very simple. Also very pastoral.

PB: And after that you did *The Singing Blacksmith* (*Yankel Dem Schmidt* [1938]) for the Yiddish Theatre with the same company?

EGU: Yah.

PB: With Jacob Ben-Ami?

EGU: No, Ben-Ami was out. I was able to take over everything myself because *Green Fields* was such a huge success. On *The Singing Blacksmith,* we again had to find a location. Now, you must understand, this was when the Bund was riding high in New York and New Jersey. My staff and I had to build a home for the *Blacksmith,* an entire "shtetl," or little Jewish village, a ghetto town. And next to it, of course, I had to build the Ukrainian backgrounds. The problem was how to find a piece of land without telegraph poles and without roads. It was an unbelievable assignment. I started off with my staff in a station wagon in May, because we were supposed to shoot the end of June. Up in Westchester County we found some big estates, but the moment we started to talk about a Yiddish picture and a Ukrainian picture—nix, out. So we had combed all of New York State, and it was so powerful; you must understand the budgets were practically nothing. So I decided we had to go back to Jersey. We couldn't go on the farm because I wouldn't stand for it. They had the Avremkov farm in *Natalka Poltavka* and I wasn't going to repeat myself. I also knew we couldn't afford a generator for the lights, so I worked out a system where I had to stay on the highlines, it had to be on the electric highlines, because all I could afford was to throw a pig—a transformer—into it. I finally made a contact with City Service in New Jersey and traveled with their plans along the highlines to find the place. My big staff consisted of two boys and four old Jews, in a station wagon we had bought for $110, an old woodie, today maybe worth money even. So the first week in June, I was on the way to Newton, New Jersey, and we followed a dirt road because we always had to be on the main line; and we came to a fantastic piece of land with a lake, everything one could wish for, because I had insisted on finding a sloping ground because I needed the perspective. We tried to find the main farm or somebody we could talk to. After driving for about half an hour we came to the main road and the manor house. It was a monastery—so you can imagine how we felt! But now comes the strange thing. This was a Friday. I went up to the main door in the building—the Jews kept sitting in the station wagon, frightened. On the door hung a sign that said: *Clausura*. I had gone to a Jesuit university so I knew what it meant. The Benedictine monks, all monks, have one day in the week that is called *clausura* when they are not allowed to talk and nobody can speak to them. Now I thought, with all that, what the heck is gonna happen? I saw a little chapel; the door was open so I walked in. There was a monk praying on the altar. I decided I had to face it out. When the monk finished, he came out and I saw by his soutane that he was a dignitary in that setup. He had a big red beard. He asked what he could do for me. So I told him my sad story, that I was looking for a motion-picture location, and he became very interested. I noticed he had a heavy German accent. He introduced himself, took me to his office in the main building and told me he was the prior of the whole monastery. Within two minutes we were talking German. He told me he was head of the monastery in Munich five or six years ago. So I sat in his office, and he told me he could talk with me because he was the top there, the big man. And he noticed how nervous I was and he asked me why. I said, "Such a fantastic piece of ground and I will be very disappointed if I can't get it." He said, "Why shouldn't you be able to get it?" I said, "I better tell you the truth. One picture is a Ukrainian picture and the other one is a Yiddish picture." So he said, "What should make you nervous about that?" I told him what I lived through in Westchester. He said, "All right, show me where it is." We got into his car, which was a roadster, and we drove to the land again. Of course, my Jews outside were dying! They saw me come out with this monk and get in his car. So I showed him the ground and when we came back, he said, "If you want, you can build your sets here." I said, "But is the diocese of New Jersey going to approve it?" He says, "We have nothing to do with the diocese, we are completely autonomous, and further-more, the Catholic Church has always sponsored the arts. Furthermore, I assume this thing is played in a Russian or Polish village and the Jews have beards—all our brothers have beards, so you have extras and you save yourself the money for beards."

Then, believe it or not, we found out when we came back with the plans that next to this ground was Camp Siegfried, the camp of the Bund. And on the left side was a nudist camp! So that nothing should happen to the sets as we built them, the academicians and their pupils stood at night with guns, so the Bund couldn't do anything to our construction. This was the time of the *Sitzkrieg Blitzkrieg* when the Germans walked to Belgium and the big scare came, so the Father came to New York to our apartment and offered to build a bungalow so that we could live on Church grounds. One of the newspapers wrote an article about this thing called "Nudists, Holly-wood and the Bund." It was the most unbelievable story. We opened the picture in October in New York in '38. And the entire Catholic clergy of New Jersey arrived in full regalia to see the picture. And that was an unbelievable time in American democracy. I lived through it, or I would never have believed it possible.

PB: And when did you make the Ukrainian picture?

EGU: They were back-to-back. I finished *The Blacksmith* and went right into the Ukrainian picture. It opened in 1939. It was an unbelievable time.

PB: Did you make the Ukrainian picture at the same place and with the same sets as *Green Fields?*

EGU: No. Different.

PB: Well, that's incredible—did you learn to speak Russian?

EGU: Yes. I had a knowledge of Russian. And I had to learn Yiddish from scratch. Then Pare Lorentz gave me the title, "Director of the Minor-ities."

PB: Don't tell me you did some more!

EGU: Yah. I did two more Yiddish pictures. One with David Opatoshu called *Die Klatsche* (*The Light Ahead*)—*Fishe da Krin* was the original name. Then I did a comedy with Leo Fuchs called *Americaner Schadchen* (*The Marriage Broker*).

PB: None of these are listed. What years are these?

EGU: Thirty-eight, thirty-nine.

PB: What locations did you use for those?

EGU: *The Light Ahead* in the location of *Greene Felde* in Jersey, and on the Ukrainian background. You must realize these pictures were made for practically no money. *Greene Felde* was made for $8,000 cash, in five shooting days.

PB: Really?

EGU: But we had six weeks rehearsal. The assistant and I had to sleep in the same bed in a broken-down hotel in Newark. I mean, we were so poor, you have no idea. We had nothing but ambitions. On *Green Fields* I had 15,000 feet of negative to shoot the picture. It was a two-hour picture. The ratio was one and one-fourth to one. But I used the first BNC.[1] Hollywood never had that—I got it.

PB: So, in other words, when you started making pictures for PRC, it was luxury?

EGU: Oh, my God—this was big time. But you have never seen the cooperation we got on *Green Fields*. As I told you there was $8,000 in cash, which we got from Household Finance. Every one of us, the producers, hocked the furniture in his home.

PB: But the pictures made a lot of money, didn't they?

EGU: Afterwards, sure.

PB: I mean, *Green Fields* became quite successful, didn't it?

EGU: Ach, it broke every record in New York. Over $80,000, and a $16,000 negative. It broke the Garbo record up in Bronxville. It was like a fire—that's another story.

PB: Did you have a piece of it?

EGU: No. No, couldn't afford it.

PB: What was the order of the films?

EGU: *Natalka Poltavka* was first, then came *Green Fields*, then came

[1] *Blimped News Camera:* The standard studio film production camera for 35 mm. (The term *blimp* refers to the soundproof cover for the film magazine, which enables sound to be recorded while the camera is running.)—Eds.

The Singing Blacksmith, Zaporosh Sa Dunayem, and then came *The Mar-riage Broker.* I made a Negro picture before that, too.

PB: You mean *Moon over Harlem* [1939]?

EGU: Yah.

PB: How did *Moon over Harlem* come about?

EGU: That came about through a boy who was very friendly with the man who wrote *Porgy,* DuBose Heyward. The boy had a script. I had nothing to do with the organization of the picture, but was hired as the director. As a matter of fact, the picture was cast when I came in. It was nearly completely ready to go. They had a contract from the Negro circuit in the South; at that time there were black theatres and there were white theatres. I had four days to make the picture. We had two days in a studio, an old cigar warehouse, which was rigged up in New Jersey, and the actual locations, like the nightclub up in Harlem, which had to be done after two o'clock in the morning.

PB: When everybody had gone home.

EGU: Yah. So it was quite an experience. It was done for very little money. There couldn't have been $8,000 in cash there. I knew that the singers, we had over fifty of them, were paid 25¢ a day, and they had to travel back to Harlem and over to Jersey. It was one of the most pitiful things I ever did. It was done on nothing. We didn't have full reels—it was all done with short ends.[2] So you can imagine—we had to reload the camera every two minutes, because some of the short ends were only a hundred feet. It was really something, but we made quite a good picture. I tried for the first time what was later on called the Rossellini style. We didn't use actors, we used real people, and they were very natural.

PB: From the streets?

EGU: Yah. I was given two weeks to rehearse up in Harlem.

PB: It was a musical?

EGU: Musical. Yes. Very much on the style of *Three Dark Saints* and *Porgy and Bess,* but really Negro. Donald Hayward did the music. None of the creative people were white.

PB: Except you.

EGU: Except me.

---

[2] *Short ends:* leftover fragments of unexposed film (cut off the end of a roll in reloading the camera). Usually resold to labs, which in turn sell the short ends to low-budget producers.—Eds.

PB: And how were you approached for that?

EGU: I knew Donald Hayward.

PB: And who released that film?

EGU: They released it themselves and had a Southern distributor.

PB: Was it ever shown in the North?

EGU: Yah. I was at the opening at the RKO's Harlem, which is a very big theatre—seats three thousand.

PB: Oh yes. What did you do after that?

EGU: I did *The Light Ahead,* which was my own production. Then I did the Army teaching films. Then I was a year with the Ford Motor Motion Picture Department.

PB: And what did you do for them?

EGU: All their teaching films, all their convention films. The pictures for the Army were on celestial navigation, on the jeep, on the command car. They had to have teaching films about nuts and bolts!

PB: Let me ask you—you made the one picture at Universal, *The Black Cat,* which was for a major studio. Did you have difficulty getting a job for a major studio again after you made these independent films?

EGU: No, I wouldn't go with a major studio. After *Green Fields* Zanuck wanted me to do two pictures with Shirley Temple. I said, "How do you come to me for pictures with Shirley Temple?" So he said, "You made *Green Fields*—it's a pastoral film." So I said, "Don't let's talk about it. I don't want to hear a word about such things." And as a matter of fact, I knew Mayer very well and I prided myself that he could never hire me! I did not want to be ground up in the Hollywood hash machine.

PB: Why did you decide to go back to PRC, were you given freedom there?

EGU: Yes. That happened in a strange way. A friend of mine, maybe the finest producer in Europe at that time, Seymour Nebenzal, came to America. He made *Mayerling* [1936] and *M,* and was what I considered the Selznick of Europe. He was a man of exquisite taste. He came to New York and we wanted to set up an independent picture company. Before we could formulate our plans, Metro hired him. I was working in New York and Detroit. Of course, Seymour could not get along with the powers that be at Metro and decided to become independent. The moment that I knew Seymour needed me out here, I quit everything in New York and Detroit and came back to the Coast. I wrote my first big script after I returned for Seymour.

PB: What was that?

EGU: *Les Otages* (*The Hostages*). He had made the picture in Europe already. Metro found the writer who was writing for Seymour—I was supervising the writer—and bought the script from the writer and sued us to step out. They lost the suit. We could have collected a tremendous amount of money, but I insisted that Nebenzal not do such a thing and we settled by having Mr. L. B. Mayer come to the court and pay me one dollar in front of everybody, because I didn't submit anything to him. This was the script that was used for *Song of Russia* [1943], which was produced by Pan Berman at Metro.

PB: But you didn't receive any credit for that?

EGU: No. We just turned it over.

PB: Then you made *Prisoner of Japan* [1942]?

EGU: First I worked on *Hitler's Madman* [1943]. Seymour Nebenzal came up with an idea about Nietzsche. He hired Emil Ludwig as a writer, and Ludwig wrote a script that couldn't be used. It was horrible. I got my gang from the Yiddish picture to help us. My wife and I worked with Hirshbein and we got a script. On the strength of the script, Nebenzal raised $300,000 and we started the production. [Leon] Fromkess had come out and the whole PRC thing was collapsing. I met Fromkess, who was an accountant then, through my connection with Pathé Lab. Pathé put me in charge of the whole program with Seymour helping me. The first script they gave me was *Prisoner of Japan*, which already had a contract for a director named [Arthur] Ripley. So I had to produce the picture, rewrite the script, and finally shoot the picture the last two days of the six days he shot. Through that I drifted into PRC and couldn't get out. I did so many pictures for them. What helped me at PRC was that number 1: I could use my crew, and I nearly was running the studio from a technical end. The little *Girls in Chains* [1943] was such a gigantic money success that we could have bought the PRC Studio. I wouldn't sign any contract with PRC, but this was my home and I could operate and bring any idea immediately to the top echelon. I suffered, of course, from one thing. I was so tied up that I couldn't take any contracts on the outside. Nebenzal became a huge producer with *Whistle Stop* [1946], where he found Ava Gardner, *Summer Storm* [1944], which made Linda Darnell, and he discovered Lana Turner. We were friendly and I kept going there. At that time I was called "the Capra of PRC." It was a nice family feeling, not too much interference—if there was interference, it was only that we had no money, that was all.

Fromkess became head of the studio; he would listen, and when I would say I want to make a *Bluebeard* [1944], that's what we would make.

PB: *Hitler's Madman* was directed by Douglas Sirk, wasn't it?

EUG: It was his first [American] picture—I hired him for that. It was sold to M-G-M after it was made.

PB: It was a very good picture but you received no credit on that, did you?

EGU: None.

PB: But you worked on the script?

EGU: Script and sets.

PB: I see. Excellent picture. Sirk also did *Summer Storm*. He was a good director, don't you think?

EGU: He was in my background. He came from the German UFA-influenced group. Of course, what he did later on with Universal—no! That was the typical Universal type of picture that he made.

PB: Well, he brought something to those pictures, too. It was better than the Universal product.

EGU: Universal at that time was pretty bad. Yes, Siodmak made *The Killers* [1946], but that was not typical of Universal.

PB: Now, tell me, why did you have to take over from Ripley and shoot the last two days?

EGU: Because Ripley was not very normal.

PB: He was a good director though, wasn't he?

EGU: He was a much better editor. He was Stroheim's editor on *Foolish Wives*. He was a sick man.

PB: Mentally or physically?

EGU: Mentally and physically.

PB: I know he made very few pictures in his career—I often wondered why.

EGU: He was ill. He made a very good one later called *Voice in the Wind* [1944].

PB: Yes. Excellent. I haven't seen too many. I didn't see *Prisoner of Japan*. Is it a good picture?

EGU: Strange picture . . . Yah.

PB: After that you made *Tomorrow We Live* [1942], which you directed and Nebenzal produced?

EGU: Correct. Bart Lytton wrote the screenplay.

PB: I never saw that film—is it a good picture?

EGU: Yes. Strange, very strange. I was very much influenced by that time by Grand Guignol, which took me twenty years to get out of my system. The melodrama and the absolute theatrics was very, very tempting.

PB: And *Tomorrow We Live* was a thriller?

EGU: No. A horror picture in the desert with Ricardo Cortez.

PB: Then you made *My Son, the Hero* [1943]?

EGU: Yah. I was very friendly with Damon Runyon and I started Columbia on a Runyon streak in the early thirties. I felt that I could write something similar to him, and that's what made the picture.

PB: It was an amusing picture. You must have made it very quickly, too.

EGU: It was again six days.

PB: Evidently you worked on the scripts of some pictures at PRC which you didn't direct—like *Corregidor*.

EGU: Correct. *Corregidor, Danger! Women at Work* [both 1943]—there was a whole slew of these things.

PB: For which you sometimes didn't take credit?

EGU: No, I couldn't.

PB: *Girls in Chains* I saw, and you said it was made in five days?

EGU: Yah.

PB: Incredible. Do you remember how the idea for that came about?

EGU: This came from the newspaper. There was some political graft in one of the women's jails. There was a lot of newspaper coverage on it, and I thought up the title. Fromkess and his right-hand man, Martin Mooney, felt that we had a big chance with the thing. The script was written in something like three weeks.

PB: The title is very commercial.

EGU: Of course! That's what made the goddamned thing. At the beginning of the season, Fromkess would sit down with me and [Sig] Neufeld, and we would invent forty-eight titles. We didn't have stories yet; they had to be written to fit the cockeyed titles. I am convinced when I look back that all this was a challenge. I knew that nothing was impossible. When *Double Indemnity* [1944] came out and was a huge success, I wrote a picture for Neufeld that we called *Single Indemnity*. We were able to write that junk in about two weeks.

PB: The picture was not made?

EGU: Oh, yes, it was made, but not with that title. Paramount made us take the title off! I think it was called *Blond Ice,* or something like that.

PB: You didn't direct it?

EGU: No.

PB: *Isle of Forgotten Sins* [1943], what was that?

EGU: That was a hangover I had left from the time I was with Murnau in Bora Bora on *Tabu* [1931].

PB: *Tabu*—did you work on that?

EGU: Yes, of course. And then John Ford made the picture for Sam Goldwyn called *The Hurricane* [1937]. The miniature department had about two hundred palm trees; I knew I could persuade them to borrow the miniatures for a picture—so I wrote *Isle of Forgotten Sins*.

PB: So that you could use the miniatures?!

EGU: Correct.

PB: You were having fun over there, it seems, at PRC. What did you do on *Tabu*?

EGU: I worked on the script with Murnau, got all his equipment down there, and set up the production for him. When he came back, I cut the picture and got it ready for Eisenfeld to score it.

PB: And [Robert] Flaherty did very little on the picture?

EGU: Flaherty was sent back after the first four weeks. They couldn't get along. The drunk Irishman on one side and the German educated at Oxford on the other. Murnau was a very, very difficult man, but a great, great talent.

PB: And then what about *Jive Junction* [1943]? I saw *Jive Junction*—I don't think that's one of your best pictures.

EGU: No. You saw the conflict I brought into that script. I wanted classical music against jive, and you couldn't do it for the little money I had. And, of course, it was propaganda to get the kids in America working on the farms during the war.

PB: I see in the credits that Irving Wallace had something to do with the story—was that the Irving Wallace who became a novelist?

EGU: Yes, sir.

PB: How did you feel, making pictures like these—so quickly and with a subject matter not always of the most distinction?

EGU: I had to compromise to keep PRC in business. Now I admit to myself that I was somehow schizophrenic in making pictures. On one hand, I was absolutely concerned with box office and on the other, I was trying to create art and decency, with a style. I could not completely get out of the commercial though I knew it limited me. There was no reason for me to make a *Jive Junction*, except that the picture had to be made, and had to be done quickly, and we couldn't jeopardize a penny.

PB: Yes. Then I suppose that even things like *Girls in Chains* and *Isle of Forgotten Sins* fall into that commercial category, whereas *Bluebeard* falls into the other.

EGU: Yes. You can tell by the cameraman I had on the picture if I took a picture very seriously or not. For my serious pictures I always had [Eugene] Schuftan.

PB: Was he on *Bluebeard?*

EGU: Yes.

PB: Who is Jockey Feindel?

EGU: Feindel was actually the operative cameraman, because Schuftan never could get into the union.

PB: So he couldn't take credit.

EGU: Of course not. He took the Academy Award as you know for the best photography, on Paul Newman's picture with Jackie Gleason . . . *The Hustler* [1960]. Schuftan still isn't in the union.

PB: Hm. And so he shot *Bluebeard.*

EGU: Yah.

PB: Did he shoot *Detour?*

EGU: No, *Detour* was shot by my old friend Benny Kline. He shot *The Wife of Monte Cristo* for me and *Strange Illusion* [1945].[3]

PB: Now, how did you get the idea for *Bluebeard?* That's one of your best pictures, I think.

EGU: Yes. It was a tremendously challenging picture.

PB: Shot quickly?

EGU: Very quickly—six days.

PB: Amazing. It had a remarkable sense of mood and atmosphere.

EGU: Yah. All my love for Paris came out in the picture.

PB: And you created Paris on the back lot?

EGU: Of course. I did the sets myself as I did in *The Wife of Monte Cristo.* As an art director, from my earliest time on, I adored the Île-de-France, Montparnasse and Montmartre, and whatever I did I always wound up in that. I adore Paris. I spent two years of my youth in the Victorine in Nice. I was there with Rex Ingram.

PB: Yes, you told me. Well, *Bluebeard* has an incredible style. I really think it's one of your best pictures.

---

[3] Official credits list Adolph Edward Kull as cinematographer on *The Wife of Monte Cristo* and Philip Tannura on *Strange Illusion.*—Eds.

EGU: Yah. First of all, John Carradine was a person, like Arthur Kennedy, I could hang onto. He knew what we were trying to do. Yah, it was a very lovely picture. PRC was unhappy with it at first.

PB: Really. But it did finally make some money.

EGU: Of course. It was one of the pictures that earned tremendous money in France.

PB: The title is a very commercial title actually.

EGU: Yah. I had a fight with Chaplin about that title—I beat Chaplin out of it. He was making *Monsieur Verdoux* [1947]. I think my picture was nicer. *Monsieur Verdoux* was a horrible picture.

PB: After *Bluebeard,* you made *Strange Illusion.* How did the idea for that come about?

EGU: [Fritz] Rotter's play in New York, *Letters from Lucerne,* with Gerte Mosheim, was a big flop. I saw it and it was very nice, though not well written—Rotter mostly did musical comedies. I got Fromkess to buy the play; but when we wrote the script I went so far away from Rotter's play that we sold it back to him! I was fascinated at that time with psychoanalysis and this story was about a father-son relationship. The picture was very well received critically. Whether it made money, I do not know. At that time I was already chafing at the bit and wanted *out* of PRC.

PB: But you stayed there for another five or six pictures?

EGU: Oh, yah. Fromkess really locked me in.

PB: There are some very interesting shots in there; I remember one in particular—there's a painting on the wall and you pan around it. Do you remember that shot?

EGU: Yah.

PB: Was it made very quickly also?

EGU: Six days.

PB: Incredible. Now *Club Havana* [1946] . . .

EGU: . . . That I adored making. I loved it. I had no script—I did a Rossellini again. This was a picture I was never going to make; Russell Rouse and Clarence Greene were going to make it. Fromkess had hired a whole staff and everything, and then threw the script out a week before we were to shoot. He called me in and said, "OK, you say you can do things. Shoot it without a script—invent it." So I got myself some actors. I had only one page—an outline. Schuftan did that picture for me, too.[4] I really had fun

4 Officially credited to Benjamin N. Kline.—Eds.

on that one; we shot the whole picture on one set. We had quite a musical success with the cockeyed thing. "Tico Tico" was used in that the first time.

PB: So the challenge was not the subject matter, but just to make something?

EGU: No! To make something special—to be able to do a *Grand Hotel* [1932] in one place.

PB: This was PRC's *Grand Hotel—Club Havana.*

EGU: Yah.

PB: Very funny. Where did the idea come for *Detour,* which is my favorite of your films?

EGU: Now, I'm going to tell you something strange. The brother-in-law of Tony Quinn wrote a very bad book called *Detour.* [Martin] Goldsmith was his name. I took the thing to Martin Mooney and rewrote the script. I was always in love with the idea and with the main character, a boy who plays piano in Greenwich Village and really wants to be a decent pianist. He's so down on his luck that the girl who goes to the Coast is the only person he can exist with sex-wise—the *Blue Angel* thing. And then the idea to get involved on that long road into Fate, where he's an absolute loser, fascinated me. The same thing, of course, with the boy who played the leading character, Tom Neal. He wound up in jail after he killed his own wife. He did practically the same thing he did in the picture.

PB: Surely not with a telephone cord.

EGU: No, that was the only thing he didn't do.

PB: That was one of the most memorable murders because it's a murder by long distance, through the door, and so on. Was that one of your ideas?

EGU: Yah.

PB: A very grisly touch. Ann Savage was an excellent character. How fast did you shoot that?

EGU: Six days.

PB: All these pictures were made in six days—one week?

EGU: Sure. The only one that took two weeks was *The Wife of Monte Cristo—*

PB: Because it was a costume picture?

EGU: Because it was a *big* picture.

PB: Big picture—two weeks! Are you fond of *Detour,* yourself?

EGU: I adore *Detour.*

PB: Which are your favorite pictures?

EGU: *Black Cat, Detour,* and *Naked Dawn.*

PB: *Naked Dawn* is a remarkable film.

EGU: Also shot in ten days.

PB: In color?

EGU: Yes, sir.

PB: Incredible. That was released by U-I but not made for U-I?

EGU: Right.

PB: Now what about *The Wife of Monte Cristo*—how did that come about?

EGU: Fromkess called me in one day and told me that Eddie Small was making a fortune with *The Son of Monte Cristo* [1940], in fact, with all the family of Monte Cristo. He said he wanted to make a Monte Cristo also, so we decided to make the *Wife.*

PB: I see—so it had very little to do with Dumas.

EGU: Actually there is a very bad novel by Dumas, placed in Arabia, called *The Wife of Monte Cristo.*

PB: I've never seen it; how is it?

EGU: It's a nice picture. It's better than the one Eddie Small made.

PB: And was that shot by Schuftan, too?

EGU: Yah.

PB: And who was Adolph Kull, who got the credit?

EGU: He was also one of the operators.

PB: Terrible that Schuftan couldn't get credit. It's awful.

EGU: It's a pity. He has credit on every European print.

PB: Ah, I see. What is *Her Sister's Secret* [1946]? That was really quite a good picture.

EGU: Yes. That was a remake of a German picture. It was the first American job of the cameraman Franz Planer, a Viennese, who had worked with me in 1920.

PB: On what?

EGU: *Sodom and Gomorrah.*

PB: Was that a movie?

EGU: Yes. Directed by Michael Curtiz, at that time he was Mishka Kehrtez. It was done in Vienna, sets by Julius Borsidine and myself.

PB: *The Strange Woman* [1946] is a difficult film to get to see, but Schuftan gets credit as producer on it.

EGU: Schuftan was not on *The Strange Woman* at all. Beautiful picture. It nearly got Hedy Lamarr an Academy nomination. It's the only picture where she ever had to act. A beautiful picture. Very difficult, very beautiful.

PB: That was the first picture away from PRC?

EGU: Yah. *Her Sister's Secret* was the last picture for PRC.

PB: Did you leave them amicably?

EGU: Yes. I was under contract to them. They got the money for *The Strange Woman*—not me. I got $250 a week, and they were collecting $1,500. I made more money for PRC on *The Strange Woman* than they had paid me the whole time I worked there.

PB: How did you get the job?

EGU: Through Hedy Lamarr.

PB: She wanted you for the picture?

EGU: Yah. It was the first film she made away from M-G-M. She was her own producer.

PB: Who was Jack Chertok?

EGU: The great TV producer—*My Favorite Martian*.

PB: Ah, I see. He was the producer of that with Hunt Stromberg?

EGU: Yah.

PB: You had quite a good cast in that: George Sanders, Louis Hayward, Gene Lockhart. And a good novel by Ben Ames Williams.

EGU: Very difficult to handle because it went over seven lifetimes. But I had a good writer, a boy who became quite famous, Herb Meadow. A very difficult boy, too. He was brought out here for *The Robe* [1953].

PB: *Carnegie Hall* [1947] is a classic of a kind. It's one of your longest pictures, I think. I saw the complete version once, and I've seen it cut also. I must say it loses a great deal when it's cut because those musical numbers are very important.

EGU: It has become the classic textbook for TV and everything.

PB: How did *Carnegie Hall* come about?

EGU: They saw some stuff I had done for *The Strange Woman*, and I had quite a reputation for classical music. Stokowski's a very old friend of mine—I supervised the recordings on *Fantasia* [1940] with him. I did all the Toscanini recordings; I did the Philco Program in Philadelphia.

PB: For television?

EGU: No, for radio. Music is one of my great passions.

PB: It's an interesting picture mainly because of the way you handle the musical episodes.

EGU: It was impossible to tell a story after Wagner's *Meistersinger*. I wanted to do a documentary, which they wouldn't let me do. I wanted the

Hall to speak and have the experience of the music. Couldn't put it across—had to have that silly story. What are you going to do after Rubinstein plays Chopin? You're going to have a scene where *actors talk?* It's impossible. It's as impossible as putting Hepburn and Walker into a picture about Schumann. Just can't be done.

PB: Those two films were released through United Artists, but were made by completely independent companies.

EGU: Correct.

PB: *Ruthless* is another one of your best films.

EGU: Yah. You also see it in a cut version. After the main release, they cut it.

PB: Why?

EGU: I don't know . . . Hollywood ideas.

PB: What was cut?

EGU: There were three big sequences between Hayward and the youngster that were cut, and then two big sequences of Greenstreet and Zachary Scott. It was a dangerous script that had to be cut because McCarthy came in. It was written by Alvah Bessie.

PB: He doesn't get credit, though?

EGU: Of course not.

PB: Who are S. K. Lauren and G. Kahn?

EGU: They were names that were made up. It was in the panic time.

PB: Already in 1948?

EGU: Yah.

PB: Burt Glennon was the photographer. He was very good.

EGU: A wonderful man who did the first *Stagecoach* [1939]. He got an Academy Award for that. Cantankerous bastard, but a wonderful cameraman.

PB: What interested you most about *Ruthless?*

EGU: The interesting thing was going back in characterization—the flashback. Furthermore, the complete evilness and ruthlessness about money—that's what I wanted to do. They cut it out. There still is something left in the picture about that. I wanted to do a morality play, a Jesuitic morality film, on three levels—earth, hell, and heaven. That's why I put the house on top. But they fought me every step, because it was a very bad indictment against one hundred percent Americanism, as Upton Sinclair saw it. And I had a very, very weak producer, Arthur Lyons. Ach—the typical agent.

PB: The morality play is something that interested you all the way through your career.

EGU: Yah. You must understand, I'm speaking of the morality play of the Jesuits, not the morality play in the style of *Everyman*, which is the British morality play in the Anglo-Saxon background. I, however, see the morality play in Gothic form, before the Renaissance. I see it in the dark gray of Germany, Holland, more or less of the Breughel period. Musically, I can only point to *Carmina Burana*, which come from the same time. Now in the telling of a story in films, the director is more or less obliged to stylize characters as characters are stylized in artwork in the church of Notre Dame or the Gothic churches of England. You have only a short time to tell a story, and therefore—I'm now going from one theory to another, so don't misunderstand me—you must have two sides, as in the commedia dell'arte, and later seen in our great Western successes as the man with the white hat, the man with black hat. You have the wonderful chance, which no theatre ever had, to create the background against which your characters tell a story, a complete depth by stylizing them in one form. If you take today, for instance, Z [1969], in it there is the highest form of stylization. The director created a Greek chorus with the blue steel helmets of the police, and this becomes a theme in his film. It reminds you of the Eumenides, whatever you have in the great Greek theatre of the classical time in mythology. You sit and you look at that picture, and whenever danger comes and whenever brutality forces you, these blue-helmeted figures take the whole screen. Now look what Schlesinger does in his *Midnight Cowboy* [1969]—something so amazing—and I'm sure he hasn't thought it out. Maybe it is a feeling. He tells the story from the optical viewpoint of that Texas boy who comes into New York and sees a New York I have never seen, though I've lived there maybe thirty or forty years. Here's a road from Texas, the flashing tremendous signs, the light of the signs, and then that poverty-stricken New York one block or half a block away from Fifth Avenue. I thought his greatest morality shot, stronger than when Everyman stands in front of the cathedral of Salzburg all alone, was that one shot of Dustin Hoffman standing on Fifth Avenue when the boy is meeting the girl in the hotel there, and he starts to dream about Florida. That little figure of that man in the tremendous street and the background of Radio City. No theatre, no book, has that which the camera can give you. With the morality play you have to understand one thing—there is a main theme—one theme that says he is bad, therefore he will go to hell and will pay, though the angels up there will try everything to make him rest. He deserves rest. Now if you try to do that in a motion picture, you have simple depth, and the characters move off the screen. No Cinemascope, no Cinerama can do that to you. A character

moves off the screen. For instance, when Dustin Hoffman dies on the bus
after the boy has said to him two minutes before, "You know, when we get
down there, I'm going to get a job and forget all that other stuff," it would
take you fifteen pages to describe what is done by that dead figure laying
there, and the tragedy of the boy going up there and telling the driver that
he's dead. I'm always trying to do that and it's very difficult to do, because
you must have a viewpoint when you tell the story. You have it in *Detour*
when that boy stands in that shower, after he has found that the guy is a
gambler and realizes he should've been killed anyhow, though he didn't kill
him. I'm trying very hard not to achieve something specific but to give it a
viewpoint. Tell it from somebody I can feel for; don't do it from five view-
points. Sam Goldwyn had a very primitive saying: you have to have a
beginning, a middle, and an ending. What he meant is to follow one character and tell the story from that character's view. Never switch from the boy
to the girl, because the screen cannot tell two stories at the same time. It
must be told from one person's viewpoint; and when you do that, you get a
certain style.

    PB: Why does it have to be told from one viewpoint, do you think?

    EGU: We have been looking, to my knowledge, for over forty years, to
identify ourselves with our audience. That's what the director tries to do.
You take a novel or a play written for the Broadway stage or an original
story and you try to put it on the screen. Outside of *Gone with the Wind*
[1939], which is an American disease (it took the place of *Intolerance*
[1916] or *The Birth of a Nation* [1915] in our heritage), all your great
pictures have been originals—written, conceived, felt for the screen. If a
great novelist could write pictures, we never would have died with pictures
as we are dying now. It doesn't happen by accident that every French
director is called in when the first master script is done. The director does
the decoupage with the writer. Here, a month after the script is finished and
somebody gives you the money, you pick up the telephone and say "What
directors can I get?" The schlup reads it, goes onto the set and he knows
how to make the picture. He does?! Schlesinger came from Europe and spent
a *year* covering the waterfront. He saw New York; he saw Texas; he saw
what people do, which a native American couldn't see. That's what Buñuel
does. Every picture he makes is a morality play, only he goes and brings the
gargoyles down from their niches up on Notre Dame. I don't do that. I say:
use the best and the clearest thought-out—which is simplicity—and play
against that background. King Vidor, whom I greatly admired in my youth,

made a picture, *The Big Parade* [1925]. There is a scene where Renée Adorée hugs Gilbert's boot and hangs onto him as the truck pulls out to the front. I was devastated with that scene. These are the moments that make pictures worthwhile. I really am looking for absolution for all the things I had to do for money's sake.

Albert Zugsmith

ALBERT ZUGSMITH*

I was the only one in town they felt could make a decent picture in five days.—ALBERT ZUGSMITH

The films Albert Zugsmith is proudest of are Welles's Touch of Evil, *Douglas Sirk's* Tarnished Angels *and* Written on the Wind, *Jack Arnold's* The Incredible Shrinking Man, *and Arnold Laven's* Slaughter on Tenth Avenue, *all of which Zugsmith produced during his five years at Universal-International.*

*Albert Zugsmith started his movie career producing low-budget films with unique angles (*Invasion U.S.A., Top Banana*). He contributed* The Beat Generation, High School Confidential, *and* College Confidential *to the teenpic phenomenon. More recently, he has been*

* Interview with Todd McCarthy and Charles Flynn, September 3, 1973, Los Angeles, California.

411

producing and directing independent films, including the memorably titled Movie Star, American Style, *or,* LSD, I Hate You!

Like Richard Brooks, Samuel Fuller, Ben Hecht, Mark Hellinger, and Jerry Wald, Zugsmith came to films from a career in journalism. A crack reporter and editor while still in his teens, Zugsmith moved on to ownership and management of newspapers and radio stations. He was a major force in the journalistic world of the 1930s and 1940s.

Indeed, there is still a trace of the clipped dialect of the city room in Zugsmith's speech. His office is in an attractive house in the hills a few blocks above Sunset Strip. It is furnished in a style reminiscent of Universal's sets for the Sirk films: a large fireplace, white carpeting, paintings on every wall.

Albert Zugsmith invited us to try out his sauna after the interview.

TODD MCCARTHY and CHARLES FLYNN: Could we ask how you got started in motion pictures?

ALBERT ZUGSMITH: I got started when I sold out all my newspaper interests in the East and came out here to Southern California to live. I started my own consulting service for all types of communications. Television stations—I sold the first TV station ever sold out here.

And I went into motion pictures. I decided that that was what I wanted to do. I had enough money by then to do what I pleased. All my dear friends who were in high positions saw me coming and thought I wanted to borrow $10.00 or $20.00 from them or something, so I had no choice but to start my own independent company. This was just at the time when independents were daring to come out of the woodwork a little bit. So I made a deal with RKO, which was then owned by Howard Hughes, to make three very low-budget pictures at prices which Howard Hughes was reputed to have said: "It can't be done." They were $100,000 each. Under strictly union conditions, IATSE conditions, and on the old RKO-Pathé lot, now called the Culver City Studios, which were the old Selznick studios. So we made them with our own money, but Hughes reimbursed us, up to $100,000—no more than that!—on each picture.

TM and CF: So you were taking the risk?

AZ: Yes, *we* were taking the risk that we could do them within the budget. I applied the efficiency methods I had developed in newspapers, radio stations, and TV stations to motion-picture making, and studied it from the ground up. I felt I was in the same position I was when they said,

"Hell, you can't be a newspaper publisher," many years ago. I just said, "Why? Do I need a license?"

We made these three pictures for RKO and, of course, we were forced to use people we didn't want to take as actors, so the pictures weren't that great. The first one was a look into the future, which we called 3000 A.D. RKO, possibly on Mr. Hughes's orders, changed the title to *Captive Women* [1952], which was my first big taste of studio interference.

TM and CF: On your very first film . . .

AZ: It was a look at what would happen to places like New York after the atomic bomb fell, and so forth. Something like *Beneath the Planet of the Apes* [1971]. And certainly, under *Captive Women* [1952], it's got to be *déclassé*. So I was determined then to make a picture of my own and I made *Invasion U.S.A.* [1952], which was my first big sleeper. I made that for $127,000 cash and about $60,000 deferred.

TM and CF: So *Invasion U.S.A.* was the first film you really had control over . . .

AZ: Yes, it's the first film I had any semblance of control over. And while it's far from perfect, for $127,000, for a film shot in seven days, I feel it's a good job. Of course, full of heartaches and headaches, but worth it. And I suppose the public responded, because the net profits on the film were close to $1,000,000.

I really learned my trade on *Invasion U.S.A.* From two masters of motion-picture making. First of all, from Ralph Black, who was production manager and assistant director, probably the best filmmaker (the guy who really makes the film is the production manager) around. And Al Green was the director. Al Green really taught me how to direct; he let me really codirect with him. Between those two fellows and Bob Smith, who was the man who acted as my coproducer on it, I really got a tremendous education.

TM and CF: How did you feel about Hughes?

AZ: I like Mr. Hughes very much. I have great respect for Mr. Hughes. I don't know, as a matter of fact, whether Mr. Hughes himself ever interfered. I suspect that he might have, but I have no proof of it. Any dealings I have had with Mr. Hughes, which have always been through third parties, have made me believe that Mr. Hughes is a man of his word. He is relatively grateful to people. He's a human being, he knows it. He makes mistakes, just like you do and I do. But I have nothing but the warmest respect and regard for Howard Hughes. He's not an intimate of mine, but then, I don't think he's an intimate of anybody's.

As studios go, Howard didn't run the worst and he didn't run the best.

But was he really running it? How much of it was him and how much of it was inattention, I don't know. I don't like to live in the past anyway. There's too much to do now.

So I made three films with RKO and then American Pictures Corporation, which I owned together with some other people who had been associated with me in some other endeavors. We went ahead and made *Invasion U.S.A.*

TM and CF: That's what put you on the map . . .

AZ: That really put me on the map. We made it with our own money, without a release, and with all kinds of trials and tribulations—some of the financial people pulled out at the last minute and I had to raise money while we were shooting.

Columbia went into partnership with me on another picture, *Paris Model* [1953], but we had become disenchanted with the distribution of Columbia on *Invasion U.S.A.* We made a deal: they could keep *Paris Model* if we got *Invasion U.S.A.* back. *Paris Model* was, presumably, a mild success. Then I was hit by a group of people who wanted me to make *Top Banana* [1954] for them, for $150,000 in five days, because I was the only one in town they felt could make a decent picture in five days. So we made *Top Banana* and, since this was in the days of 3-D, we shot it in 3-D in five days. Al Green was on one camera and I was on another, and we just kept shooting. We didn't have a script. Phil Silvers had done the play, so we just shot the play, really. We rehearsed the play straight through for one day, so we could see what it was. We had the lights all set up in various ways, so we could just pull a switch and light that particular scene. I went on the big crane, since Al [Green] was getting pretty old by then, and he stayed on the small dolly and we shot it. And it did pretty well.

TM and CF: What was the point of 3-D on a film like that?

AZ: I don't know what the point was! To my knowledge, it was never shown in 3-D.

After this, the people who were in American Pictures wanted to take their profits and go. We'd made six pictures and had some nice profits, mostly from *Invasion U.S.A.*, so we set about dissolving the corporation, because you can get capital gains if you dissolve. Most of the people who were in it with me were people with big incomes, so they needed the capital gains.

TM and CF: Did you do extensive writing or rewriting on most of your films?

AZ: Yes. The writing is the main thing, and no matter how adept you are in the production end, the physical production, or anything else, first came the word, you know. I have been able to seek out that kernel of something different and rescue properties. *Written on the Wind* [1957] had about a quarter or a third of a million invested in a pile of scripts three feet high and was junked, set aside, written off. When I asked to revive the project and be assigned to it, the studio said, "It's no good, no good." After I told them my first ideas on the treatment, they said, "Well, we'll spend $500 on it, but you can't do it, it's impossible." We had a reader there who had aspirations to write, and since I couldn't do it—he was a member of the writers' guild—he wrote a $500 treatment. Eddie Muhl[1] read the treatment and said, "I still don't think you can do it, but I'll give you an inexpensive writer for eight weeks." George Zuckerman, who used to work for me as a reporter, wrote a magnificent script. I wouldn't read any of the old scripts. I read the book, and we decided how we wanted to tackle it. George worked with me very closely. We shot practically the first-draft screenplay, it was that good.

TM and CF: What exactly was your relationship with Universal at that time?

AZ: Good. Mainly because of Ed Muhl and Milt Rackmil. One of the reasons I have been so successful with newspapers and TV stations is that I have an ability not only to judge past performance, but to psych out the future of communications properties. I saw that there would be a helluva lot fewer daily newspapers in the United States, and so forth. My own newspaper isn't there anymore. I felt that I had an idea of what was going to happen in the future. I felt that you had to do *new* things. I thought that you had to get away from Francis and the Mule and the Abbott and Costellos and the Ma and Pa Kettles—"Ma and Pa Kettle Meet Godzilla," or something like that. I wasn't interested in doing that kind of picture. I was only interested in making something new and different. The thing that attracted me to *Written on the Wind*, of course, was the impotence angle, which, of course, we had to play down, down, down, but we had never shown impotence on the screen before. That was what attracted me to it.

I felt there was a future in coproduction. I felt there was a future in independent production. Because we'd just had the divorcement in 1948, which meant that M-G-M and RKO and the rest couldn't just shove out all their crap to all their theatres, and I thought there was going to be an opening for people who could work outside the system. So I started on

1 Head of production at Universal-International.

coproductions. I had one of the first coproductions set up in Spain. I had bought a property from a writer named Bob Hill, called *The Besieged Heart,* and I changed the title of the script—it had been a play originally— to *Female on the Beach* [1955] and had him rewrite it the way I wanted it. I worked with him on the rewrite and never got credit because I wasn't a member of the writers' guild at that time. I was a member of the producers' guild and later joined the writers' guild.

A friend of mine by the name of Milton Rackmil, who was the head of Decca Records, had taken over Universal. He said, "Why don't you go in and talk to my vice-president in charge of production?" So I went in and talked to a man named Ed Muhl. He was the most artistic and creative studio head I've ever encountered in my life. And I liked the guy. And he wanted to do *Female on the Beach*—with Joan Crawford. Because they needed a picture like that. They were specialists in women's pictures. This was a women's picture. He said, "Have your agent get in touch with me." I said, "I don't have an agent." "You don't have an agent?" He was flabber- gasted. He bought the script from me and said he wished he could afford to hire me to produce it. I said, "OK, you've got me." "How do we negoti- ate?" he said. "We start our producers at $75 a week. The top producer here gets $450 a week." I said, "Tell you what. Let's have a week-to-week deal, Mr. Muhl, and at the end of any week, you can bounce me, and at the end of any week, I can quit. And you name the price. The only proviso I want is that if the picture doesn't come out the way I want, I want my name off it." I have had that almost everywhere. So I went to work for Universal for $450 a week. They said I was the first producer they ever had who actually went out into the various departments, because the departments were making the pictures.

Eddie then asked me if I would make another picture for them. "Of course, at more money," he said. "How much do you want?" "You're going to be my agent," I said. "You put me to work here, so you just tell me what it is, and as long as it's a week-to-week deal, as long as I can take my name off anything I want." That's how I got started with Universal. Every three or four months I got a $150 raise, until finally I was making near what Eddie was making.

TM and CF: So your relations with the studio "brass" were really com- patible. It seems like you had no problems at that point . . .

AZ: My relations with Eddie Muhl were about as good as they could be with any head of any studio. And it was only under his leadership that I was able to make pictures like *Written on the Wind, Slaughter on Tenth Avenue*

[1957], *Touch of Evil* [1958], *The Incredible Shrinking Man* [1957], *Tarnished Angels* [1958], and so forth. Because he was a real leader, a sympathetic, artistic guy, but the sales department would zoom in on him very hard, and what happened was that a man who was the general sales manager[2] was given authority over the studio. Eddie Muhl could no longer operate the way he wanted to operate, and that's when I left. I wouldn't have left if Eddie Muhl could have run the show. They were after me to sign a seven-year noncancelable contract, just to produce, and I wanted to direct by then.

By that time things had got so heavy that I had got an agent, Charlie Feldman, who owned Famous Artists, and the next thing I knew, I was over at M-G-M, and they promised me that I could direct one picture a year myself. And Orson [Welles] would direct one a year and Douglas [Sirk] would direct one a year. It was a three-picture-a-year program. The first thing they did was to call Orson on the phone, and Orson doesn't speak on the telephone. Orson said he would go with me as long as he didn't have to have any contact with the studio. You know, he's mortally afraid of the studio brass, and I can't blame him in too many cases, because of the things that have happened to him. He doesn't know how to handle a studio. He knows how to handle me, he knows that I know my dramaturgy; and we have our consultations but we don't have any fights. He doesn't feel threatened by me. But studio: no! So I lost Orson Welles. And then I lost Douglas Sirk.

TM and CF: How did that happen?

AZ: I don't know what it was, but Universal was never able to loan out Douglas Sirk. Maybe M-G-M made it too difficult; maybe they wouldn't pay the price. After telling me that I would have decent budgets, M-G-M never gave me a decent budget the whole time I was there. Of course, I didn't get along very well with Mr. Benny Thau,[3] and I'd holler back at him when he'd holler at me, and I told him I could yell as loud as he could. I never cared for M-G-M. They gave me all kind of curves: bad cameramen that happened to be under contract, and so on. I wasn't one of the "clique." They wouldn't back me up on the set or anything else.

TM and CF: How did you happen to choose Sirk and Welles?

AZ: Story on Orson is: I became sort of a troubleshooter, a script doctor, at Universal, not only a script doctor. They'd throw me all the

[2] Alfred Daff.
[3] Administrative head of M-G-M studios and a vice-president of Loew's, Inc.

properties they were having difficulties with. There were also certain people I could handle, and work with. Jeff Chandler was becoming a bit difficult and he was their second biggest star at that time. I guess one of the reasons he was difficult was that he was the biggest, and then Rock Hudson came along! So they had me make some pictures with Jeff. They also had me make Westerns, which I'd kind of duck and avoid; they even made Ross Hunter make a Western, which was a terrible flop! It was the last picture Ann Sheridan ever made!

Anyway, I was assigned to a picture called *Man in the Shadow* [1958]. Jeff Chandler was in it, and we had $600,000, I think, to make it with. With studio overhead, that means you get about $375,000 on the screen. Jeff Chandler played the sheriff, and we had a new girl under contract, Colleen Miller, a beautiful girl, as the female lead. We were trying to cast the heavy, the girl's father, the rich rancher who oppresses the Mexicans, and so forth. We're pretty much sold on Robert Middleton who did such a great job for me before.[4] So then I got a call from the William Morris office. Evidently they knew this part was open, and Jack Baur[5] asked me, "How would you like Orson Welles to play the heavy?" "You're kidding," I said. He had been out of this country for some time. He was back, he needed $60,000 very badly for taxes, and he'd play the heavy. "Has he read the script?" I said. "I don't think so. But he's gotta pay his taxes, or he'll be in big trouble."

I had never met Orson Welles—didn't know him at all. I knew his work. So I said, "Let's go down and talk to Eddie." We talked to Eddie, Eddie called New York, New York said, "Terrific." They were going to take a lousy little $600,000 Jeff Chandler picture and they were going to make it a big, big picture by paying another $60,000—which they cut out of the budget somewhere else—so let's do it. So I made a deal with the William Morris office for Orson Welles and I gave them a wardrobe call . . . I think it was on a Monday at one o'clock. When I got in my office that Monday morning, there was a message. Orson Welles's secretary had called and notified us that we were to hire a certain makeup man who got double scale by one o'clock, or Mr. Welles would not be in for wardrobe. I took this message over to Eddie Muhl's office and they were worried to death, knowing Welles's past history and background, as reported by the studios.

I never saw Eddie nervous before in my life—a very calm man; but he was nervous, he was shaking. He didn't like this. He was worried about it. Universal, up to that point, hadn't as many big, outside stars as the other

4 In Jack Arnold's *Red Sundown* (1956) and Sirk's *Tarnished Angels*.—Eds.
5 Universal-International's casting director.

studios, and whenever they brought one in, they had trouble. "What are we gonna do? What are we gonna do?" They called New York. They said, "What does Zugsmith say?" "Zugsmith feels that if he gives in to a threat, he can't be responsible for the picture." New York said, "We'll go with Zugsmith."

We sent word to the William Morris office—who didn't know a thing about this—that we'd gotten this note, read them the note, and said that we're sorry, but Zugsmith won't operate with a gun at his back and Universal won't replace Zugsmith as producer.

I think the picture was scheduled to go in about a week. And they said, "We'll try to reach him—we don't know if we can reach him." At five minutes to one, I got a call from wardrobe: "Mr. Welles is here."

I went up there and he was charming, very, very nice; strangely enough, he knew of my films and knew of my work and was very well researched on it. He had some very good suggestions about his clothes and so forth, most of which we adopted. Didn't mention a word about the makeup man. Well, that was that.

Before I went to the office the next day, I got a note. Hand delivered from Orson, written by Orson. In which he explained the reasons for his *request* for the makeup man. His real nose is never shown in a film, he claimed, because it's so "ridiculous looking," in his words, and if he were not so poor and could afford it, *he* would pay for the makeup man himself. The request that we *please* get this makeup man—which we *might* get for less than double scale—I took to Eddie Muhl. "What do we do now?" he said. "We give him his makeup man, you buy him for as little as possible. He's *requested* it, and that's different!" "All our troubles are over," Eddie said. "No, all our troubles aren't over. Gene Coon has never written a script before. Welles is probably the reigning genius of the business and he's won an Academy Award for writing—you know goddamn well he's going to rewrite his part, if not the whole script!"

We hear nothing from Orson until it's his turn to shoot. I'm waiting in Eddie Muhl's office, I get a call from the set, they're in the mobile dressing room there and Mr. Welles has rewritten the scene.

TM and CF: Only his own scene?

AZ: Yes, only his own scene. Of course, it involved others. So I jumped in my car and went down to the location on the lot. When they finished shooting the scene, I said, "Excellent." Welles said, "You did like it?" like a little boy—there's a lot of the little boy in him. I said, "It's very, very good. Great improvement. Of course, you'd be doing the actors and myself a great favor if we could get these rewrites that obviously you're going to do, at least on your own scenes, prior to the day of shooting, because it's quite a burden on some of these actors, who aren't quite as experienced as you are, to learn the new scenes." He said, "What do you suggest we do?" I said, "Why don't you come down to the office. I have some vodka—left over from Joan Crawford, and . . ." "How do you know I like to drink vodka?" he said. "Oh, I've been told," I said. "I have a box of your favorite cigars, and we could do it right now and have it sent out by messenger to the actors. The director likes to look at the script, too, you know." "OK, let's go," he said.

So every night from then on we'd go to my bungalow at the end of the day's shooting, we'd do the rewrite together, and never once did I have an argument with Orson Welles. He was amazed that a producer knew how to write or rewrite with a sense of dramaturgy, and we really built on each other as collaborators can do if they're really collaborating.

On the last day of shooting, I was on the set and he said, "I guess I can't come down tonight?" I said, "My bungalow is always open to you." He came down there and we really tied one on. He said, "Goddamn it, you're the feistiest son of a bitch I've ever met and I love you. I would like to direct a picture for you." I said, "There's nothing I'd like better, Orson." He said, "Have you got anything I can direct?" In those days I had a shelf full of scripts in back of my desk and I said, "You can have any one you want." He said, "Which is the worst one?" I said, "Right here," and pulled out a script Paul Monash had written from a novel in four weeks on a flat deal, called *Badge of Evil*. I threw it over to Orson, and he said, "Can I have two weeks to write it?" I said, "You can have it."

TM and CF: He then wrote an actual screenplay?

AZ: Completely.

TM and CF: In screenplay form, so that it could be read by any producer?

AZ: Sure. We shot his first draft. We spent a whole day cutting it down to proper size, eliminating things. I've never had a fight with the man. He's a genius. Great man. Great talent.

TM and CF: *Touch of Evil* was his first American film in quite a few years. Was there any problem with the studio?

AZ: No. I didn't have any problems with the studio. The studio had problems with Orson after I left. I consulted with Orson about the M-G-M offer and he thought I should take it. So I left for M-G-M. Orson couldn't make up his mind on a lot of different ways in cutting. He cuts himself, you know, and he got into fights with an editor there. I was at M-G-M by then—during the cutting. I saw a version of it that he cut and I thought it was pretty good. Then he re-cut it anyway. I made some suggestions; as I recall, he took some of my suggestions. As director, it was his first cut; his first cut kept going on and going on. Orson kind of takes off, you know, he lacks discipline. He took off to Mexico and was staying in his favorite place, Caesar's. I don't know whether his liver started bothering him, or what, but he got in some beefs with the studio. Of course, the very fact that he had to talk to the studio was scary to him. He gets very nervous at times. They had some disagreements. But I don't know, I wasn't at the studio then.

TM and CF: Would you say the final cut is more or less what he wanted in the first place, or has it been changed?

AZ: They reshot, I think, one scene. They didn't think it was clear enough. They were old-fashioned in that respect. Orson was forward-looking. I think Orson's version of it was possibly a bit ambiguous, but it was not a serious thing. It was not a big weakness. I think Orson's version was very good. They reshot . . . I think Harry Keller directed it, and they showed me the rewrite. The rewrite wasn't bad. And the acting of it wasn't bad. But it wasn't Orson Welles.

TM and CF: Can you identify the scene?

AZ: It was on the road, I believe. I think Chuck [Heston] was in it. I don't remember the exact portion of it. I don't think there's a big, big difference, but some people would say that the style clashes. Harry Keller isn't Orson Welles. The studio attitude—and that's always a group of faceless men—was that it was unclear, at least to the level of audience they thought they were catering to. And the studio did not push the picture.

TM and CF: What is your analysis of why Welles hasn't made another picture in America since *Touch of Evil?*

AZ: I would love to have him as a director.

TM and CF: Why doesn't anyone else?

AZ: I think they're afraid of him: great talent threatens. I have found out that there are certain people in this business, certain talents, that need some sort of help. Many of the talents that I have helped develop or worked with have suffered by not continuing with me. *And I have suffered by not continuing with them.*

TM and CF: You don't think there's anyone in Hollywood now, at any studio, that would even dare to ask Welles to direct a film for them?

AZ: I don't know. I'm not that close to what the studios think today. I think the studios are prepackaged, mostly, and I'm really not playing that sort of game nowadays; but if you ask me to guess, to surmise, I'd say they don't know of any producer who can handle Orson Welles so they can get a commercial product out of him. The studios certainly aren't interested in artistic product. Orson is primarily an artist, a great one.

TM and CF: That's a real tragedy.

AZ: No question about it. The only two directors I would want to work with as a producer are seemingly not available: Welles and Sirk.

TM and CF: So you did start directing yourself . . .

AZ: Yes, I always wanted to direct, when I felt I was capable of doing it. Directing is much more the game than producing—I don't like to fool around with the figures and the negotiations. I don't play the Beverly Hills game, the Bel Air game, or anything else like that. I don't like to kiss ass or any of that bullshit. Life's too short for that.

TM and CF: How did you pick the subject material for your films? These weren't for M-G-M, so apparently you came to a parting of the ways with them . . .

AZ: The first subjects were picked, really, as a matter of what the studio would let me do. In one case, I agreed to a so-called sequel, which I shouldn't have done. But I thought I had a subject and a writer who would give me something so entirely different that it would be a cinch. That was *College Confidential* [1960].

TM and CF: The sequel to *High School Confidential* [1958] . . .

AZ: It really wasn't a sequel. It was a sequel in title only.

TM and CF: I liked the low-key style you did *Dondi* [1961] in. There haven't been too many films based on comic strips. It was an unusual idea.

AZ: There's one basic problem with *Dondi,* and that is, after I finished the picture, the studio just arbitrarily cut the wrong twenty minutes out of it.

TM and CF: Without asking your opinion, of course.

AZ: That's one of the reasons I left Allied Artists. *Dondi* was made as a favor to the exhibitors of the United States, who wanted a "clean" picture for the family. They talked to Allied Artists, and Allied Artists said, "You've got to make this—the future of the business depends on it." So I got a hold of my old friend Gus Edeson, who had this very popular comic strip, went to work on it, and developed this. Put all the ingredients in it. And then— well, the studio was mad at me. I didn't take their bullshit. And Steve Broidy there at Allied Artists, the worst man I know in the whole motion-picture industry, took twenty minutes out of it.

TM and CF: What interested me about *Dondi* was the photographic style, which is very bleak.

AZ: You can't blame Steve for that . . . you must have had a bad print!

Allied Artists was a very depressing period of my life. Maybe it showed in the films I made there. I was very depressed there. I didn't like it; I felt imprisoned; I had to get away. Almost everybody felt it was depressing there. There was almost nobody on the lot who didn't have a bottle in his drawer. Nobody. Everybody would run to get out of there at eleven-thirty to drink their lunches.

TM and CF: Are there any independents you admire for what they've done—Corman, Russ Meyer, anyone like that?

AZ: Admire in which way?

TM and CF: As businessmen.

AZ: I've only been a businessman when I had to. My interest is in creation.

Russ is a shrewd man. He's a technician. He's a lusty man. I tried to get Russ into better things. I think some of his earlier pictures had more imagination and artistry than some of his later ones had, evidently. I don't see Russ Meyer's pictures now. I'm not a keen critic. I did see *The Immoral Mr. Teas* [1959] and, in its time, I thought it was quite charming, quite nice. I don't much care for pornography. I don't care for nudies. I have seen very, very few of them. I went to sleep on *Deep Throat* [1972] and *The Devil in Miss Jones* [1973]. I'm sorry to say so! I don't usually go to sleep in a movie. I thought *The Immoral Mr. Teas* showed great imagination. I thought that the idea he could make it for the kind of money he made it for, and capture the public's imagination . . . at that time, Russ and I seriously considered making pictures together. The one problem seemed to be who was going to direct. And we agreed that we would try it out: he would direct one and I would direct one. *Fanny Hill* [1965] was the first one. I said he could direct it. But after *Fanny Hill*, I didn't want to make any more pictures with Russ.

Now, just because I don't want to make any more pictures with Russ doesn't make him a failure. He's had a tremendous success; been an innovator in pictures. I haven't seen his recent films, so I don't know how good or how bad they are. But Russ has a lusty talent and he'll survive if he finds himself a new career. I think Russ is smart enough and adaptable enough that he will. I think one of Russ's problems was that he wrote most of his own scripts. I think Russ is a helluva good cameraman and he's a good editor and he knows the business inside and out but, unless he changes, I don't think Russ is going to listen to anybody. I don't know if Russ should even make a picture that costs over $50,000.

TM and CF: What do you feel is the key to low-budget filmmaking? Some of the people we've talked to feel distribution is the big problem . . .

AZ: Distribution is a terrible problem. When I came back from West Berlin with *Fanny Hill* under my arm, due possibly to the end result (which didn't please me any more than it pleased the distributors), the distribution deals I had tentatively set up didn't come through. I faced a big loss and I had to distribute it myself.

TM and CF: Successfully?

AZ: We made almost $1,000,000 out of it, net. But I wouldn't want to do that as a steady diet. It's pretty rough.

TM and CF: We've been having some research problems finding titles of your films after, say, the mid-sixties.

AZ: I took some time off. For writing—about two years. I was determined to see if I could exist without the disease of making movies. And I found out I could.

The motion-picture industry is dead, no question about it. It was killed by television, primarily, unless you want to consider television films the motion-picture industry. Secondarily, it was killed by the elimination of block-booking in 1948. Those were crucial times, '48 to '50, and we're still bearing the fruit of it today. Now there's a television habit. But if you consider making motion pictures for television, then the motion-picture business is not dead. The theatrical business is on its way out, but the art of film must, and will, survive. There will always be a hardy breed of people who have become enamored of the motion-picture business and who have caught the disease. There'll always be pictures made. There'll always be some audiences for some, but the audience today is a splintered audience. But when a studio makes a picture for $7,000,000! And they put another $4,000,000 or $5,000,000 in prints and advertising, and they don't even get the cost for prints and advertising back—boy, that's Disasterville!

TM and CF: You are into independent production at this point . . .

AZ: Very independent . . . maybe too independent! It was either get out or go crazy. I couldn't take it. I wouldn't say that I wouldn't go back if I had a picture I wanted to make. But to be a servant again, and wear a necktie, exist in the M-G-M iron lung over there, wear the symbolic socks and shoes, and kiss ass. Not just for the studio—for the stars and everybody else. Thank God, I've paid my dues. I don't have to anymore.

FILM-OGRAPHIES

William Asher

Jack Arnold

Lloyd Bacon

William Beaudine

Herbert Biberman

Tod Browning with the freaks

Harold S. Bucquet,
Laraine Day, and Helen Gilbert

David Butler

Eddie Cline

Irving Cummings

Roy Del Ruth

Andre De Toth and Veronica Lake

Edward Dmytryk

Gordon Douglas

Robert Florey

Louis Gasnier

Michael Gordon

Walter Grauman

Curtis Harrington

Henry Hathaway

Harry Horner

H. Bruce Humberstone (right), with Hedda Hopper

William Keighley and Genevieve Tobin

Henry Levin

Frank Lloyd

Frank McDonald

Daniel Mann

Norman Z. McLeod

Delbert Mann

Archie Mayo

Ralph Nelson

Gerd Oswald and Claire Bloom

Norman Panama (left), Melvin Frank, and Dorothy McGuire

Unidentified actress with Jerry Paris, Ida Lupino, and Don Weis

Robert Parrish

Joseph Pevney

David Lowell Rich

Martin Ritt

Mark Robson

Wesley Ruggles

Sidney Salkow and Claire Trevor

Mark Sandrich

Richard Sarafian

Victor Schertzinger

Ernest B. Schoedsack

William A. Seiter

George B. Seitz

Lesley Selander

A. Edward Sutherland

Norman Taurog

Norman Tokar

Richard Thorpe

Jacques Tourneur

Paul Wendkos

James Whale

325
AMERICAN DIRECTORS

Compiled by TODD McCARTHY

The following are nothing less than complete filmographies for the directors listed. Only the sound period, from 1929 to the present, is covered, but within this range, every filmography is complete for feature films whether made in the United States or elsewhere. Except in cases where the films were either never exhibited in this country or were withheld from distribution altogether, the *release* date in the United States has been used to determine the film's chronological ranking. Within each year, the films are listed in monthly (or weekly or daily, if need be) order, so if in a given year a director had one film released in February and another in May, they are listed in the appropriate order. In short, the order of films, one before another, is exact. In the case of films made and released only in Europe, the best available dates for their release there have been used. No serials or shorts have been listed.

Each film is accompanied by the name of its United States distributor, which in most cases, of course, is the same as the studio that produced it. In the case of films possessing no distributor, the production company has been listed when possible. Where a director has made a significant number of consecutive films at one studio, the studio (distributor) is listed after such a group, not after each film. An effort has also been made to mention the country of production for each film when it is not the United States, although this aspect of the list is undoubtedly incomplete.

Most of the following directors have worked, at one time or another, in the realm of the B movie, although some are included here simply because they have been excluded from all other easily accessible collections of filmographies published to date. Robert Z. Leonard and Mark Sandrich can by no means be considered B directors, but no one has considered them important enough to list previously.

These filmographies have been compiled and refined through the use of the following major sources: the annual (through 1970) *Film Daily Year Book of Motion Pictures*, the seven volumes of the *Filmlexicon degli Autori e delle Opere*, the *Catalog of Copyright Entries: Motion Pictures*, the annual *International Motion Picture Almanac*, *Variety*, the annual *Screen World*, the *Motion Picture Production Encyclopedia*, published in the late 1940s and early 1950s, *Filmfacts*, *The Filmgoer's Companion*, *The British Film Catalogue: 1895-1970*, the records of the library of the Academy of Motion Picture Arts and Sciences, and numerous private sources.

The full names of distributing companies are used within the filmographies with the following exceptions, which are listed here with their abbreviations:

AA	Allied Artists
AIP	American-International Pictures
BI	British International
BV	Buena Vista
CHEST	Chesterfield
COL	Columbia
EL	Eagle-Lion
FN	First National
FOX	Fox
GB	Gaumont-British

GN	Grand National
M-G-M	Metro-Goldwyn-Mayer
MONO	Monogram
PAR	Paramount
PDC	Producers Distributing Corporation
PRC	Producers Releasing Corporation
REP	Republic
RKO	RKO Radio Pictures
20TH	Twentieth Century-Fox
UA	United Artists
U	Universal
U-I	Universal-International
WB	Warner Brothers
WB-7A	Warner Brothers-7 Arts
WW	Sono Art–World Wide

GEORGE ABBOTT (1889–)

1929: *Why Bring That Up?, Half Way to Heaven.* 1930: *Manslaughter, Sea God.* 1931: *Stolen Heaven, Secrets of a Secretary, My Sin, The Cheat* (all PAR). 1940: *Too Many Girls,* RKO. 1957: *The Pajama Game* (with Stanley Donen), WB. 1958: *Damn Yankees* (with Stanley Donen), WB.

JOHN G. ADOLFI (1888–1933)

1929: *Fancy Baggage,* WB; *Evidence,* WB; *Show of Shows,* WB; *In the Headlines,* WB. 1930: *Dumbbells in Ermine,* WB; *Recaptured Love,* WB; *Sinners' Holiday,* WB; *College Lovers,* FN. 1931: *The Millionaire,* WB; *Alexander Hamilton,* WB; *Compromised,* FN. 1932: *The Man Who Played God,* WB; *A Successful Calamity,* WB; *Central Park,* FN. 1933: *The King's Vacation, The Working Man, Voltaire* (all WB).

WILLIAM ALLAND (1916–)

1961: *Look in Any Window,* AA.

IRVING ALLEN (1905–)
1946: *High Conquest*, MONO; *Avalanche*, PRC; *Strange Voyage*, MONO.
1948: *16 Fathoms Deep*, MONO. 1951: *Slaughter Trail*, RKO.

IRWIN ALLEN (1916–)
1956: *The Animal World*, WB. 1957: *The Story of Mankind*, WB. 1960: *The Lost World*, 20TH. 1961: *Voyage to the Bottom of the Sea*, 20TH. 1962: *Five Weeks in a Balloon*, 20TH. 1974: *The Towering Inferno* (with John Guillerman; Allen directed fire sequences), WB-20TH.

LEWIS ALLEN (1905–)
1944: *The Uninvited, Our Hearts Were Young and Gay*. 1945: *The Unseen* (all PAR); *Those Endearing Young Charms*, RKO. 1946: *The Perfect Marriage*. 1947: *The Imperfect Lady, Desert Fury*. 1948: *So Evil My Love, Sealed Verdict*. 1949: *Chicago Deadline* (all PAR). 1951: *Valentino*, COL; *Appointment with Danger*, PAR. 1952: *At Sword's Point*, RKO. 1954: *Suddenly*, UA. 1955: *A Bullet for Joey*, UA; *Illegal*, WB. 1958: *Another Time, Another Place*, PAR. 1959: *Whirlpool* (England), RANK.

ROD (RODNEY) AMATEAU (1923–)
1952: *The Bushwhackers*, REALART. 1953: *Monsoon*, UA. 1969: *Pussycat, Pussycat, I Love You*, UA. 1971: *The Statue*, CINERAMA. 1972: *Where Does It Hurt?*, CINERAMA.

JOSEPH ANTHONY (1912–)
1956: *The Rainmaker*. 1958: *The Matchmaker*. 1959: *Career*. 1961: *All in a Night's Work* (all PAR). 1965: *Conquered City* (Italy), AIP. 1972: *Tomorrow*, FILMGROUP.

GEORGE ARCHAINBAUD (1890–1959)
1929: *Man in Hobbles*, TIFFANY; *Two Men and a Maid*, TIFFANY; *Voice Within*, TIFFANY; *George Washington Cohen*, TIFFANY; *College Coquette, Broadway Scandals*. 1930: *The Broadway Hoofer* (all COL); *Framed, Alias French Gertie, Straight Shooting, The Silver Horde*. 1931: *The Lady Refuses, Three Who Loved*. 1932: *Men of Chance, The Lost Squadron, State's Attorney, Thirteen Women, The Penguin Pool Murder*. 1933: *The Big Brain, After Tonight*. 1934: *Keep 'Em Rolling, Murder on the Blackboard* (all RKO). 1935: *Thunder in the Night*, FOX; *My Marriage*, 20TH. 1936: *The Return of Sophie Lang*. 1937: *Hideaway Girl, Clarence, Hotel Haywire, Blonde Trouble, Thrill of a Lifetime*. 1938: *Boy Trouble*,

Her Jungle Love, Campus Confessions, Thanks for the Memory. 1939: *Some Like It Hot, Night Work.* 1940: *Opened by Mistake, Untamed, Comin' Round the Mountain* (all PAR). 1942: *Flying with Music,* UA. 1943: *Hoppy Serves a Writ, The Kansan, False Colors, The Woman of the Town.* 1944: *Texas Masquerade, Mystery Man* (all UA); *Alaska,* MONO. 1945: *The Big Bonanza,* REP; *Girls of the Big House,* REP. 1946: *The Devil's Playground, Fool's Gold, Unexpected Guest* (all UA). 1947: *Dangerous Venture,* UA; *King of the Wild Horses,* COL; *Hoppy's Holiday,* UA; *The Millerson Case,* COL; *The Marauders.* 1948: *Silent Conflict, The Dead Don't Dream, Strange Gamble, False Paradise* (all UA). 1950: *Border Treasure,* RKO; *Hunt the Man Down,* RKO. 1952: *The Old West, Night Stage to Galveston, Apache Country, The Rough, Tough West; Barbed Wire, Wagon Team, Blue Canadian Rockies.* 1953: *Winning of the West, On Top of Old Smoky, Goldtown Ghost Riders, Pack Train* (all COL); *Saginaw Trail,* REP; *Last of the Pony Riders,* COL.

JACK ARNOLD (1916-)

1953: *Girls in the Night, It Came from Outer Space, The Glass Web.* 1954: *Creature from the Black Lagoon.* 1955: *The Man from Bitter Ridge, Revenge of the Creature, Tarantula.* 1956: *Red Sundown, Outside the Law.* 1957: *The Incredible Shrinking Man, The Tattered Dress, Man in the Shadow.* 1958: *The Lady Takes a Flyer* (all U-I); *High School Confidential,* M-G-M; *The Space Children,* PAR; *Monster on the Campus,* U-I. 1959: *No Name on the Bullet,* U-I; *The Mouse That Roared* (England), COL. 1961: *Bachelor in Paradise,* M-G-M. 1964: *A Global Affair,* M-G-M; *The Lively Set,* U. 1969: *Hello Down There,* PAR. 1974: *Black Eye,* WB. 1975: *Boss Nigger,* DIMENSION.

NEWTON ARNOLD

1962: *Hands of a Stranger,* AA.

DOROTHY ARZNER (1900-)

1929: *The Wild Party.* 1930: *Sarah and Son, Paramount on Parade* (with O. Brower, E. Goulding, V. Heerman, E. H. Knopf, R. V. Lee, E. Lubitsch, L. Mendes, V. Schertzinger, E. Sutherland, F. Tuttle), *Anybody's Woman.* 1931: *Honor Among Lovers, Working Girls.* 1932: *Merrily We Go to Hell* (all PAR). 1933: *Christopher Strong,* RKO. 1934: *Nana,* UA. 1936: *Craig's Wife,* COL. 1937: *The Bride Wore Red,* M-G-M. 1940: *Dance, Girl, Dance,* RKO. 1943: *First Comes Courage,* COL.

WILLIAM ASHER (c. 1919–)
1948: *Leather Gloves* (with Richard Quine). 1957: *The Shadow on the Window, The 27th Day* (all COL). 1963: *Beach Party*, AIP; *Johnny Cool*, UA. 1964: *Muscle Beach Party, Bikini Beach*. 1965: *Beach Blanket Bingo, How to Stuff a Wild Bikini*. 1966: *Fireball 500* (all AIP).

JOHN H. AUER (1909–)
1934: *Su Ultima Cancion* (Mexico), CINEXPORT DISTRIBUTING CORP. 1935: *Frankie and Johnnie*, RKO; *The Crime of Dr. Crespi*. 1937: *A Man Betrayed, Circus Girl, Rhythm in the Clouds*. 1938: *Outside of Paradise, Invisible Enemy, A Desperate Adventure, I Stand Accused, Orphans of the Street*. 1939: *Forged Passport, S.O.S. Tidal Wave, Smuggled Cargo, Calling All Marines*. 1940: *Thou Shalt Not Kill, Women in War, The Hit Parade of 1941*. 1942: *Pardon My Stripes, Moonlight Masquerade, Johnny Doughboy*. 1943: *Tahiti Honey* (all REP); *Gangway for Tomorrow*. 1944: *Seven Days Ashore, Music in Manhattan*. 1945: *Pan-Americana*. 1947: *Beat the Band* (all RKO); *The Flame*. 1948: *I, Jane Doe; Angel on the Amazon*. 1950: *The Avengers, Hit Parade of 1951*. 1952: *Thunderbirds*. 1953: *The City That Never Sleeps*. 1954: *Hell's Half Acre*. 1955: *The Eternal Sea* (all REP). 1957: *Johnny Trouble*, WB.

HY AVERBACK (c. 1925–)
1966: *Chamber of Horrors*, WB. 1968: *Where Were You When the Lights Went Out?*, M-G-M; *I Love You, Alice B. Toklas!*, WB-7A. 1969: *The Great Bank Robbery*, WB-7A. 1970: *Suppose They Gave a War and Nobody Came?*, CINERAMA.

LEW AYRES (1908–)
1936: *Hearts in Bondage*, REP. 1955: *Altars of the East*, WILLIAM MORRIS AGENCY RELEASE.

LLOYD BACON (1890–1955)
1929: *Stark Mad, Honky Tonk, No Defense, Say It with Songs*. 1930: *So Long Lefty, She Couldn't Say No* (all WB); *A Notorious Affair*, FN; *The Other Tomorrow*, FN; *Moby Dick*, WB; *The Office Wife*, WB. 1931: *Kept Husbands*, RKO; *Sit Tight, Fifty Million Frenchmen, Gold Dust Gertie* (all WB); *Honor of the Family*, FN. 1932: *Manhattan Parade*, WB; *Fireman, Save My Child, Alias the Doctor, The Famous Ferguson Case, Miss Pinkerton, Crooner, You Said a Mouthful* (all FN).

1933: *42nd Street, Picture Snatcher, Mary Stevens, M.D.* (all WB); *Son of a Sailor.* 1934: *Wonder Bar, A Very Honorable Guy* (all FN); *He Was Her Man, Here Comes the Navy, Six-Day Bike Rider.* 1935: *Devil Dogs of the Air* (all WB); *In Caliente,* FN; *Broadway Gondolier, The Irish in Us, Frisco Kid.* 1936: *Sons o' Guns, Cain and Mabel* (all WB); *Gold Diggers of 1937,* FN. 1937: *Marked Woman,* WB; *Ever Since Eve,* WB; *San Quentin,* FN; *Submarine D-1.* 1938: *A Slight Case of Murder, Cowboy from Brooklyn, Boy Meets Girl, Racket Busters.* 1939: *Wings of the Navy, The Oklahoma Kid, Indianapolis Speedway, Espionage Agent.* 1940: *A Child Is Born, Invisible Stripes, Three Cheers for the Irish, Brother Orchid, Knute Rockne—All-American.* 1941: *Honeymoon for Three, Footsteps in the Dark, Affectionately Yours, Navy Blues.* 1942: *Larceny, Inc., Wings for the Eagle* (all WB); *Silver Queen,* UA. 1943: *Action in the North Atlantic,* WB. 1944: *The Sullivans, Sunday Dinner for a Soldier.* 1945: *Captain Eddie.* 1946: *Home Sweet Homicide, Wake Up and Dream.* 1947: *I Wonder Who's Kissing Her Now?* 1948: *You Were Meant for Me, Give My Regards to Broadway, Don't Trust Your Husband.* 1949: *Mother Is a Freshman, It Happens Every Spring* (all 20TH); *Miss Grant Takes Richmond.* 1950: *Kill the Umpire, The Good Humor Man, The Fuller Brush Girl* (all COL). 1951: *Call Me Mister, The Golden Girl, The Frogmen.* 1953: *The I Don't Care Girl* (all 20TH); *The Great Sioux Uprising,* U-I; *Walking My Baby Back Home,* U-I. 1954: *The French Line,* RKO; *She Couldn't Say No,* RKO.

LIONEL BARRYMORE (1878–1954)

1929: *Madame X, His Glorious Night, Unholy Night.* 1930: *Rogue Song* (all M-G-M). 1931: *Ten Cents a Dance,* COL.

HALL BARTLETT (1922–)

1955: *Unchained,* WB. 1957: *Drango* (with Jules Bricken), UA; *Zero Hour!,* PAR. 1960: *All the Young Men,* COL. 1963: *The Caretakers,* UA. 1969: *Changes,* CINERAMA. 1971: *The Sandpit Generals (The Wild Pack),* AIP. 1973: *Jonathan Livingston Seagull,* PAR.

CHARLES T. BARTON (1902–)

1934: *Wagon Wheels.* 1935: *Car No. 99, Rocky Mountain Mystery, The Last Outpost* (with Louis J. Gasnier). 1936: *Timothy's Quest, And Sudden Death, Nevada, Rose Bowl, Murder with Pictures.* 1937: *The Crime Nobody Saw, Forlorn River, Thunder Train.* 1938: *Born to the West* (all PAR).

1939: *Behind Prison Gates, Five Little Peppers and How They Grew.* 1940: *My Son Is Guilty, Five Little Peppers at Home, Island of Doomed Men, Babies for Sale, Out West with the Peppers, Five Little Peppers in Trouble, Nobody's Children.* 1941: *The Phantom Submarine, The Big Boss, The Richest Man in Town, Harmon of Michigan, Two Latins from Manhattan, Sing for your Supper, Honolulu Lu.* 1942: *Shut My Big Mouth, Tramp, Tramp, Tramp; Hello, Annapolis; Parachute Nurse, Sweetheart of the Fleet, A Man's World, Lucky Legs, The Spirit of Stanford, Laugh Your Blues Away.* 1943: *Reveille with Beverly, Let's Have Fun, She Has What It Takes, What's Buzzin', Cousin?, Is Everybody Happy?* 1944: *Beautiful but Broke, Hey, Rookie; Jam Session, Louisiana Hayride* (all COL). 1945: *The Beautiful Cheat, Men in Her Diary.* 1946: *White Tie and Tails, The Time of Their Lives, Smooth as Silk* (all U). 1947: *The Wistful Widow of Wagon Gap, Buck Privates Come Home.* 1948: *Mexican Hayride, Abbott and Costello Meet Frankenstein* (all U-I); *The Noose Hangs High,* El. 1949: *Free For All,* U-I; *Africa Screams,* UA; *Abbott and Costello Meet the Killer,* U-I. 1950: *The Milkman,* U-I; *Double Crossbones,* U-I. 1952: *Ma and Pa Kettle at the Fair,* U-I. 1956: *Dance with Me, Henry,* UA. 1959: *The Shaggy Dog,* BV. 1960: *Toby Tyler,* BV. 1962: *Swingin' Along,* 20TH.

WILLIAM BEAUDINE (1890–1970)

1929: *Fugitives,* FOX; *Two Weeks Off, Hard to Get, The Girl from Woolworths.* 1930: *Wedding Rings* (all FN); *Those Who Dance,* WB; *The Road to Paradise, Father's Son.* 1931: *The Lady Who Dared* (all FN); *The Mad Parade,* PAR; *Penrod and Sam,* FN; *Misbehaving Ladies,* FN; *The Men in Her Life,* COL. 1932: *Three Wise Girls,* COL; *Make Me a Star!* 1933: *The Crime of the Century, Her Bodyguard.* 1934: *The Old-Fashioned Way* (all PAR). 1935: *Dandy Dick* (England), BI; *Boys Will Be Boys* (England), GB; *Get Off My Foot* (England), FN; *Two Hearts in Harmony* (England), BI. 1936: *Mr. Cohen Takes a Walk* (England), WB; *Where There's a Will* (England), GB; *It's in the Bag* (England), WB; *Educated Evans* (England), WB; *Windbag the Sailor* (England), GB. 1937: *Feather Your Nest* (England), ATP; *Transatlantic Trouble* (England), FN. 1938: *Sez O'Reilly to McNab* (England; English title—*Said O'Reilly to McNab*), GB; *Torchy Gets Her Man,* WB. 1939: *Torchy Blane in Chinatown,* WB. 1940: *Misbehaving Husbands.* 1941: *Federal Fugitives, Emergency Landing, Mr. Celebrity, Desperate Cargo, The Blonde Comet.* 1942: *Duke of the Navy, The Broadway Big Shot, The Panther's Claw, The Miracle Kid, Men of San*

Quentin, Gallant Lady (all PRC); *One Thrilling Night, Phantom Killer, Foreign Agent, The Living Ghost.* 1943: *Clancy Street Boys, The Ape Man, Ghosts on the Loose, Spotlight Scandals, Here Comes Kelly, The Mystery of the 13th Guest, Mr. Muggs Steps Out.* 1944: *What a Man!, Voodoo Man, Hot Rhythm, Detective Kitty O'Day, Follow the Leader, Leave It to the Irish; Oh, What a Night; Shadow of Suspicion, Bowery Champs* (all MONO); *Mom and Dad,* HYGIENIC PRODUCTIONS; *Crazy Knights.* 1945: *The Adventures of Kitty O'Day, Fashion Model, Come Out Fighting* (all MONO); *Blonde Ransom,* U; *Swingin' on a Rainbow,* REP; *Black Market Babies.* 1946: *The Shadow Returns, The Face of Marble;* (all MONO); *Girl on the Spot,* U; *Don't Gamble with Strangers,* MONO; *One Exciting Week,* REP; *Spook Busters, Below the Deadline, Mr. Hex* (all MONO). 1947: *Philo Vance Returns,* PRC; *Hard Boiled Mahoney,* MONO; *Too Many Winners,* EL; *Killer at Large,* PRC; *News Hounds,* MONO; *Gas House Kids Go West,* PRC; *Bowery Buckaroos, The Chinese Ring (The Red Hornet).* 1948: *Angels' Alley, Jinx Money, The Shanghai Chest, The Golden Eye, Kidnapped, Smugglers' Cove, Jiggs and Maggie in Court* (with Edward F. Cline), *The Feathered Serpent, Incident* (all MONO). 1949: *The Prince of Peace* (with Harold Daniels), HALLMARK PRODUCTIONS; *Tuna Clipper, Forgotten Women, Trail of the Yukon, Jackpot Jitters* (all MONO); *Tough Assignment,* LIPPERT. 1950: *Blue Grass of Kentucky, Blonde Dynamite, Jiggs and Maggie Out West, Lucky. Losers* (all MONO); *Again-Pioneers!,* PROTESTANT FILM COMMISSION; *County Fair,* MONO; *Second Chance,* PROTESTANT FILM COMMISSION; *Blues Busters,* MONO. 1951: *Bowery Battalion,* MONO; *Cuban Fireball,* REP; *Ghost Chasers,* MONO; *Let's Go Navy,* MONO; *Havana Rose,* REP; *Crazy Over Horses.* 1952: *Rodeo, Hold That Line, Jet Job, Here Come the Marines, The Rose Bowl Story, Yukon Gold, Feudin' Fools, No Holds Barred* (all MONO); *Bela Lugosi Meets a Brooklyn Gorilla,* REALART. 1953: *Jalopy, Roar of the Crowd, Murder Without Tears* (all AA); *For Every Child,* PROTESTANT FILM COMMISSION; *The Hidden Heart,* PROTESTANT FILM COMMISSION. 1954: *Yukon Vengeance, Paris Playboys, Pride of the Blue Grass* (all AA); *More for Peace,* PROTESTANT FILM COMMISSION. 1955: *High Society,* AA; *Each According to His Faith,* PROTESTANT FILM COMMISSION; *Jail Busters.* 1957: *In the Money, Up in Smoke* (all AA); *Westward Ho the Wagons!,* BV. 1960: *Ten Who Dared,* BV. 1963: *Lassie's Great Adventure,* 20TH. 1966: *Billy the Kid vs. Dracula,* EMBASSY; *Jesse James Meets Frankenstein's Daughter,* EMBASSY.

FORD BEEBE (1888–)

1932: *The Pride of the Legion*, MASCOT. 1933: *Laughing at Life*, MASCOT. 1935: *Law Beyond the Range*, COL; *The Man from Guntown*, PURITAN. 1936: *Stampede*, COL. 1938: *Trouble at Midnight*. 1939: *Oklahoma Frontier*. 1940: *Son of Roaring Dan*. 1942: *The Night Monster*. 1943: *Frontier Badmen*. 1944: *The Invisible Man's Revenge*, *Enter Arsene Lupin*. 1945: *Easy to Look At* (all U). 1946: *My Dog Shep*, SCREEN GUILD. 1947: *Six Gun Serenade*, MONO. 1948: *Courtin' Trouble*, MONO; *Shep Comes Home*, SCREEN GUILD. 1949: *Bomba, the Jungle Boy*, MONO; *The Dalton Gang*, LIPPERT; *Satan's Cradle*, UA; *Red Desert*, SCREEN GUILD; *Bomba on Panther Island*. 1950: The Lost Volcano, *Bomba and the Hidden City*. 1951: *The Lion Hunters*, *Elephant Stampede*. 1952: *African Treasure*, *Wagons West*, *Bomba and the Jungle Girl* (all MONO). 1953: *Safari Drums*. 1954: *Killer Leopard*. 1956: *Lord of the Jungle* (all AA).

MONTA BELL (1891–1958)

1930: *Young Man of Manhattan*, PAR; *Behind the Makeup*, PAR; *East Is West*. 1931: *Fires of Youth*, *Up for Murder* (all U); *Personal Maid*, PAR. 1932: *Downstairs*, M-G-M. 1933: *The Worst Woman in Paris?*, FOX.

EARL BELLAMY (1917–)

1956: *Blackjack Ketchum, Desperado*, COL. 1958: *Toughest Gun in Tombstone*, UA. 1962: *Stagecoach to Dancer's Rock*, U-I. 1965: *Fluffy*. 1966: *Gunpoint*, *Incident at Phantom Hill*; *Munster, Go Home!* 1968: *Three Guns for Texas* (with David Lowell Rich and Paul Stanley). 1969: *Backtrack*. 1974: *Sidecar Boys* (Australia) (all U).

SPENCER GORDON BENNET (1893–)

1929: *Hawk of the Hills*, PATHÉ. 1930: *Rogue of the Rio Grande*, WW. 1933: *The Midnight Warning*, *Justice Takes a Holiday*. 1934: *Badge of Honor*, *Fighting Rookie*, *The Oil Raider* (all MAYFAIR); *Night Alarm*, MAJESTIC. 1935: *Calling All Cars*, EMPIRE FILM DISTRIBUTORS; *Rescue Squad*, EMPIRE; *Get That Man*, EMPIRE; *Heir to Trouble*, *Western Courage*, *Lawless Riders*. 1936: *Heroes of the Range*, *The Cattle Thief*, *Avenging Waters*, *The Unknown Ranger*, *The Fugitive Sheriff*. 1937: *The Law of the Ranger*, *The Rangers Step In*. 1938: *Rio Grande* (all COL). 1939: *Across the Plains*, *Riders of the Frontier*. 1940: *Westbound Stage*,

Cowboy from Sundown. 1941: *Ridin' the Cherokee Trail, Arizona Bound, Gunman from Bodie* (all MONO). 1942: *They Raid by Night*, PRC. 1943: *Calling Wild Bill Elliott, Canyon City*. 1944: *Mojave Firebrand, California Joe, Beneath Western Skies, Tucson Raiders, Code of the Prairie*. 1945: *Lone Texas Ranger* (all REP). 1952: *Brave Warrior, Voodoo Tiger*. 1953: *Savage Mutiny, Killer Ape*. 1955: *Devil Goddess* (all COL). 1959: *Submarine Seahawk*, AIP. 1960: *The Atomic Submarine*, AA. 1965: *The Bounty Killer*, EMBASSY PICTURES; *Requiem for a Gunfighter*, EMBASSY.

EDWARD BERNDS (1911–)

1948: *Blondie's Secret*. 1949: *Blondie's Big Deal, Blondie Hits the Jackpot, Feudin' Rhythm*. 1950: *Blondie's Hero, Beware of Blondie*. 1951: *Gasoline Alley* (all COL); *Gold Raiders*, UA; *Corky of Gasoline Alley*, COL. 1952: *The Harem Girl*, COL. 1953: *Loose in London, Clipped Wings, Hot News, Private Eyes*. 1954: *The Bowery Boys Meet the Monsters, Jungle Gents*. 1955: *Bowery to Bagdad, Spy Chasers*. 1956: *Dig That Uranium, World Without End, Navy Wife, Calling Homicide* (all AA). 1957: *The Storm Rider*, 20TH; *Reform School Girl*, AIP. 1958: *Escape from Red Rock*, 20TH; *Quantrill's Raiders*, AA; *Space Master X-7*, 20TH; *Queen of Outer Space*, AA; *Joy Ride*, AA. 1959: *Alaska Passage*, 20TH; *High School Hellcats*, AIP; *Return of the Fly*, 20TH. 1961: *Valley of the Dragons*. 1962: *The Three Stooges Meet Hercules, The Three Stooges in Orbit* (all COL).

CURTIS BERNHARDT (1899–)

1930: *L'homme qui assassina* (France). 1931: *Der Mann, der den Mord beging* (Germany), *Three Loves* (Germany; German title—*Die Frau nach der Mann sich seht*), ASSOCIATED CINEMAS; *Thirteen Men and a Girl* (Germany; German title—*Die Letzte Kompagnie*), UFA. 1932: *Der Rebell* (with Luis Trenker; Germany). 1933: *Der Tunnel* (Germany). 1934: *L'or dans la rue* (France). 1937: *The Beloved Vagabond* (England), COL. 1938: *Carrefour* (France), *The Girl in the Taxi*. 1940: *My Love Came Back, Lady with Red Hair*. 1941: *Million Dollar Baby*. 1942: *Juke Girl* (all WB). 1943: *Happy Go Lucky*, PAR. 1945: *Conflict*. 1946: *My Reputation, Devotion, A Stolen Life*. 1947: *Possessed* (all WB); *High Wall*, M-G-M. 1949: *The Doctor and the Girl*, M-G-M. 1951: *Payment on Demand*, RKO; *Sirocco*, COL; *The Blue Veil*, RKO. 1952: *The Merry Widow*, M-G-M. 1953: *Miss Sadie Thompson*, COL. 1954: *Beau Brummel*. 1955: *Interrupted Melody*. 1956: *Gaby*. 1962: *Damon and Pythias* (Italy) (all M-G-M). 1963: *Stephanie in Rio*, CASINO. 1964: *Kisses for My President*, WB.

JOHN BERRY (1917–)
1945: *Miss Susie Slagle's*, PAR. 1946: *From This Day Forward*, RKO; *Cross My Heart*, PAR. 1948: *Casbah*, U. 1949: *Tension*, M-G-M. 1951: *He Ran All the Way*, UA. 1952: *C'est arrivé à Paris* (France; credited to Henri Lavorel). 1955: *Ça va barder* (France). 1956: *Je suis un sentimental* (France). 1957: *Pantaloons* (*Don Juan*), UNITED MOTION PICTURE ORGANIZATION. 1959: *Tamango* (France), VALIANT; *Oh! Que Mambo* (France), BOREAL. 1966: *Maya* (India), M-G-M. 1967: *A tout casser* (France). 1974: *Claudine*, 20TH.

HERBERT J. BIBERMAN (1900–1971)
1935: *One Way Ticket*, COL. 1936: *Meet Nero Wolf*, COL. 1944: *The Master Race*, RKO. 1954: *Salt of the Earth*, INDEPENDENT PRODUCTIONS CORPORATION DISTRIBUTORS, INC. 1969: *Slaves*, CONTINENTAL.

CLAUDE BINYON (1905–)
1948: *The Saxon Charm*, U-I; *Family Honeymoon*, U-I. 1950: *Mother Didn't Tell Me*, 20TH; *Stella*, 20TH. 1951: *Aaron Slick from Punkin' Crick*, PAR. 1952: *Dreamboat*, 20TH. 1953: *Here Come the Girls*, PAR.

RICHARD BOLESLAWSKI (1889–1937)
1930: *Last of the Lone Wolf*, COL. 1931: *Woman Pursued*, RKO; *Gay Diplomat*, RKO. 1932: *Rasputin and the Empress*. 1933: *Storm at Daybreak*, *Beauty for Sale*. 1934: *Fugitive Lovers*, *Men in White*, *Operator 13*, *The Painted Veil* (all M-G-M). 1935: *Clive of India*, UA; *Les Miserables*, UA; *O'Shaughnessy's Boy*, M-G-M; *Metropolitan*, 20TH. 1936: *The Three Godfathers*, M-G-M; *The Garden of Allah*, UA; *Theodora Goes Wild*, COL. 1937: *The Last of Mrs. Cheyney* (completed by George Fitzmaurice), M-G-M.

DAVID BRADLEY
1941: *Treasure Island*, *Peer Gynt*, BRANDON. 1946: *Macbeth*. 1950: *Julius Caesar*, BRANDON. 1952: *Talk About a Stranger*, M-G-M. 1958: *Dragstrip Riot*, AIP. 1960: *Twelve to the Moon*, COL. 1964: *Madmen of Mandoras*, CROWN INTERNATIONAL.

KEEFE BRASSELLE (1923–)
1958: *The Fighting Wildcats* (England), REP.

ROWLAND V. BROWN (1901–1963)

1931: *Quick Millions*, FOX. 1932: *Hell's Highway*, RKO. 1933: *Blood Money*, UA.

TOD BROWNING (1882–1944)

1929: *Where East Is East*, M-G-M; *The Thirteenth Chair*, M-G-M. 1930: *Outside the Law*. 1931: *Dracula, Iron Man* (all U). 1932: *Freaks*. 1933: *Fast Workers*. 1935: *Mark of the Vampire*. 1936: *The Devil-Doll*. 1939: *Miracles for Sale* (all M-G-M).

CLYDE BRUCKMAN (1894–1955)

1930: *Feet First*, PAR. 1931: *Everything's Rosie*, RKO. 1932: *Movie Crazy*, PAR. 1935: *Spring Tonic*, FOX; *The Man on the Flying Trapeze*, PAR.

HAROLD S. BUCQUET (1891–1946)

1938: *Young Dr. Kildare*. 1939: *Calling Dr. Kildare, On Borrowed Time, The Secret of Dr. Kildare*. 1940: *Dr. Kildare's Strange Case, We Who Are Young, Dr. Kildare Goes Home, Dr. Kildare's Crisis*. 1941: *The Penalty, The People vs. Dr. Kildare, Dr. Kildare's Wedding Day, Kathleen*. 1942: *Calling Dr. Gillespie, The War Against Mrs. Hadley*. 1943. *The Adventures of Tartu* (England). 1944: *Dragon Seed* (with Jack Conway). 1945: *Without Love* (all M-G-M).

DAVID BUTLER (1894–)

1929: *Fox Movietone Follies of 1929, Masked Emotions* (with Kenneth Hawks), *Chasing Through Europe* (with Alfred L. Werker), *Salute* (with John Ford), *Sunny Side Up*. 1930: *High Society Blues, Just Imagine*. 1931: *A Connecticut Yankee, Delicious*. 1932: *Business and Pleasure, Down to Earth, Handle with Care*. 1933: *Hold Me Tight, My Weakness*. 1934: *Bottoms Up, Handy Andy* (all FOX); *Have a Heart*, M-G-M; *Bright Eyes*. 1935: *The Little Colonel, Doubting Thomas* (all FOX); *The Littlest Rebel*. 1936: *Captain January, White Fang, Pigskin Parade*. 1937: *Ali Baba Goes to Town* (all 20TH); *You're a Sweetheart*, U. 1938: *Kentucky Moonshine; Straight, Place, and Show; Kentucky* (all 20TH). 1939: *East Side of Heaven*, U; *That's Right—You're Wrong*, RKO. 1940: *If I Had My Way*, U; *You'll Find Out*, RKO. 1941: *Caught in the Draft*, PAR; *Playmates*, RKO. 1942: *Road to Morocco*, PAR. 1943: *They Got Me Covered*, RKO; *Thank Your*

Lucky Stars, WB. 1944: *Shine on Harvest Moon,* WB; *The Princess and the Pirate,* RKO. 1945: *San Antonio.* 1946: *Two Guys from Milwaukee; The Time, the Place, and the Girl.* 1947: *My Wild Irish Rose.* 1948: *Two Guys from Texas.* 1949: *John Loves Mary, Look for the Silver Lining, It's a Great Feeling, The Story of Seabiscuit.* 1950: *The Daughter of Rosie O'Grady, Tea for Two.* 1951: *The Lullaby of Broadway, Painting the Clouds with Sunshine.* 1952: *Where's Charley?, April in Paris.* 1953: *By the Light of the Silvery Moon, Calamity Jane.* 1954: *The Command, King Richard and the Crusaders.* 1955: *Jump into Hell* (all WB). 1956: *Glory,* RKO; *The Girl He Left Behind,* WB. 1961: *The Right Approach,* 20TH. 1967: *C'mon, Let's Live a Little,* PAR.

EDWARD BUZZELL (1897–)
1932: *The Big Timer, Hollywood Speaks, Virtue.* 1933: *Child of Manhattan, Ann Carver's Profession* (all COL); *Love, Honor, and Oh, Baby!* 1934: *Cross Country Cruise, The Human Side* (all U). 1935: *The Girl Friend,* COL. 1936: *Transient Lady,* U; *Three Married Men,* PAR; *The Luckiest Girl in the World,* U. 1937: *As Good As Married,* U. 1938: *Paradise for Three, Fast Company.* 1939: *Honolulu, At the Circus.* 1940: *Go West.* 1941: *The Get-Away, Married Bachelor.* 1942: *Ship Ahoy, The Omaha Trail.* 1943: *The Youngest Profession, Best Foot Forward.* 1945: *Keep Your Powder Dry.* 1946: *Easy to Wed, Three Wise Fools.* 1947: *Song of the Thin Man.* 1949: *Neptune's Daughter* (all M-G-M). 1950: *A Woman of Distinction,* COL; *Emergency Wedding,* COL. 1953: *Confidentially Connie,* M-G-M. 1955: *Ain't Misbehavin',* U-I. 1961: *Mary Had a Little* (England), UA.

WILLIAM CHRISTY CABANNE (1888–1950)
1929: *Restless Youth,* COL. 1930: *Conspiracy,* RKO; *The Dawn Trail,* COL. 1931: *The Sky Raiders,* COL; *Convicted,* ARTCLASS; *Graft,* U. 1932: *Hotel Continental,* TIFFANY; *Midnight Patrol,* MONO; *Hearts of Humanity,* MAJESTIC; *The Western Limited,* MONO; *Red-Haired Alibi,* TOWER; *The Unwritten Law,* MAJESTIC. 1933: *Daring Daughters,* CAPITOL; *The World Gone Mad,* MAJESTIC; *Midshipman Jack,* RKO. 1934: *Money Means Nothing, Jane Eyre, A Girl of the Limberlost* (all MONO); *When Strangers Meet,* LIBERTY. 1935: *Behind the Green Lights,* MASCOT; *Rendezvous at Midnight,* U; *One Frightened Night,* MASCOT; *The Keeper of the Bees,* MONO; *Storm over the Andes,* U; *Another Face.* 1936: *The Last Outlaw, We Who Are About to Die.* 1937: *Criminal Lawyer, Don't Tell the*

Wife, The Outcasts of Poker Flats, You Can't Beat Love, Annapolis Salute (all RKO); *The Westland Case*, U. 1938: *Everybody's Doing It, Night Spot, This Marriage Business* (all RKO). 1939: *Smashing the Spy Ring*, COL; *Mutiny on the Blackhawk, Tropic Fury, Legion of Lost Flyers.* 1940: *Man from Montreal, Danger on Wheels, Alias the Deacon, Hot Steel, Black Diamonds, The Mummy's Hand, The Devil's Pipeline* (all U). 1941: *Scattergood Baines, Scattergood Pulls the Strings, Scattergood Meets Broadway.* 1942: *Scattergood Rides High* (all RKO); *Drums of the Congo, Timber, Top Sergeant* (all U); *Scattergood Survives a Murder*, RKO. 1943: *Keep 'Em Slugging*, U. 1944: *Dixie Jamboree*, PRC. 1945: *The Man Who Walked Alone*, PRC. 1946: *Sensation Hunters*, MONO. 1947: *Scared to Death*, SCREEN GUILD; *Robin Hood of Monterey, King of the Bandits.* 1948: *Back Trail, Silver Trails* (all MONO).

EDWARD L. CAHN (1899–1963)

1931: *The Homicide Squad* (with George Melford). 1932: *Law and Order, Radio Patrol, Afraid to Talk.* 1933: *Laughter in Hell* (all U); *Emergency Call*, RKO. 1935: *Confidential*, MASCOT. 1937: *Bad Guy*, M-G-M. 1941: *Redhead*, MONO. 1944: *Main Street After Dark*, M-G-M. 1945: *Dangerous Partners*, M-G-M. 1947: *Born to Speed*, PRC; *Gas House Kids in Hollywood*, EL. 1948: *The Checkered Coat, Bungalow 13.* 1949: *I Cheated the Law* (all 20TH); *Prejudice*, PROTESTANT FILM COMMISSION/ MOTION PICTURE SALES CORP. 1950: *The Great Plane Robbery*, UA; *Destination Murder*, RKO; *Experiment Alcatraz*, RKO. 1951: *Two Dollar Bettor*, REALART. 1955: *The Creature with the Atom Brain*, COL; *Betrayed Women*, AA. 1956: *Girls in Prison, The She-Creature, Flesh and the Spur, Runaway Daughters, Shake, Rattle, and Rock.* 1957: *Voodoo Woman* (all AIP); *Zombies of Mora-Tau*, COL; *Dragstrip Girl, Invasion of the Saucer Men, Motorcycle Gang.* 1958: *Jet Attack, Suicide Battalion* (all AIP); *It! The Terror from Beyond Space, The Curse of the Faceless Man, Hong Kong Confidential; Guns, Girls, and Gangsters.* 1959: *Riot in Juvenile Prison, Invisible Invaders, The Four Skulls of Jonathan Drake; Pier 5, Havana; Inside the Mafia, Vice Raid.* 1960: *Gunfighters of Abilene, A Dog's Best Friend, Oklahoma Territory, Three Came to Kill* (all UA); *Twelve Hours to Kill*, 20TH; *Noose for a Gunman, The Music Box Kid, Cage of Evil, The Walking Target.* 1961: *The Police Dog Story, Frontier Uprising, Operation Bottleneck, Five Guns to Tombstone, The Gambler Wore a Gun, Gun Fight, When the Clock Strikes; You Have to Run Fast, Secret of Deep*

Harbor, Boy Who Caught a Crook. 1962: *Incident in an Alley, Saintly Sinners, Gun Street, The Clown and the Kid, Beauty and the Beast* (all UA).

THOMAS CARR (1907–)

1944: *The Cherokee Flash.* 1945: *Santa Fe Saddlemates, Oregon Trail, Bandits of the Badlands, Rough Riders of Cheyenne.* 1946: *Days of Buffalo Bill, The Undercover Woman, Alias Billy the Kid, The El Paso Kid, Red River Renegades, Rio Grande Raiders* (all REP). 1947: *Song of the Wasteland,* MONO; *Code of the Saddle,* MONO. 1950: *Hostile Country, Marshal of Heldorado, Crooked River, Colorado Ranger, West of the Brazos, Fast on the Draw* (all LIPPERT); *Outlaws of Texas,* MONO. 1952: *Man from the Black Hills,* MONO; *Wyoming Roundup, The Maverick.* 1953: *The Star of Texas, Rebel City, Topeka* (all AA); *Captain Scarlett,* UA; *The Fighting Lawman.* 1954: *Bitter Creek, The Forty-Niners, The Bowery Boys Meet the Monsters, The Desperado.* 1955: *Bobby Ware Is Missing.* 1956: *Three for Jamie Dawn.* 1957: *Dino, The Tall Stranger.* 1958: *Gunsmoke in Tucson* (all AA). 1959: *Cast a Long Shadow,* UA. 1967: *Sullivan's Empire* (with Harvey Hart), U.

WILLIAM CASTLE (1914–)

1943: *The Chance of a Lifetime, Klondike Kate.* 1944: *The Whistler* (all COL); *When Strangers Marry,* MONO; *She's a Soldier, Too, The Mark of the Whistler.* 1946: *Voice of the Whistler, Just Before Dawn, The Mysterious Intruder, The Return of Rusty, The Crime Doctor's Man Hunt.* 1947: *The Crime Doctor's Gamble* (all COL). 1948: *Texas, Brooklyn, and Heaven,* UA; *The Gentleman from Nowhere,* COL. 1949: *Johnny Stool Pigeon,* U-I; *Undertow,* U-I. 1950: *It's a Small World,* EL. 1951: *The Fat Man, Hollywood Story, Cave of Outlaws* (all U-I). 1953: *Serpent of the Nile, Fort Ti, Conquest of Cochise, Slaves of Babylon.* 1954: *Charge of the Lancers, Drums of Tahiti, Jesse James vs. the Daltons, Battle of Rogue River, The Iron Glove, The Saracen Blade, The Law vs. Billy the Kid, Masterson of Kansas* (all COL). 1955: *The Americano,* RKO; *New Orleans Uncensored, The Gun That Won the West, Duel on the Mississippi.* 1956: *The Houston Story, Uranium Boom* (all COL). 1958: *Macabre,* AA; *The House on Haunted Hill,* AA. 1959: *The Tingler.* 1960: *13 Ghosts.* 1961: *Homicidal, Mr. Sardonicus.* 1962: *Zotz!* 1963: *13 Frightened Girls, The Old Dark House.* 1964: *Strait-Jacket* (all COL); *The Nightwalker.* 1965: *I Saw*

What You Did. 1966: *Let's Kill Uncle* (all U). 1967: *The Busy Body, The Spirit Is Willing.* 1968: *Project X.* 1974: *Shanks* (all PAR).

WILLIAM CLEMENS (1905–)
1936: *Man Hunt,* WB; *The Law in Her Hands, The Case of the Velvet Claws, Down the Stretch, Here Comes Carter!* 1937: *Once a Doctor* (all FN); *The Case of the Stuttering Bishop, Talent Scout, The Footloose Heiress, Missing Witnesses.* 1938: *Torchy Blane in Panama, Accidents Will Happen, Mr. Chump, Nancy Drew—Detective.* 1939: *Nancy Drew—Reporter, Nancy Drew—Trouble Shooter, Nancy Drew and the Hidden Staircase, The Dead End Kids on Dress Parade.* 1940: *Calling Philo Vance, King of the Lumberjacks, Devil's Island.* 1941: *She Couldn't Say No, Knockout* (all WB); *The Night of January 16th.* 1942: *A Night in New Orleans, Sweater Girl.* 1943: *Lady Bodyguard* (all PAR); *The Falcon in Danger, The Falcon and the Co-eds.* 1944: *The Falcon Out West* (all RKO); *Crime by Night,* WB. 1947: *The Thirteenth Hour,* COL.

EDWARD F. CLINE (1892–1961)
1929: *Broadway Fever,* TIFFANY; *His Lucky Day,* U; *The Forward Pass.* 1930: *In the Next Room, Sweet Mama* (all FN); *Leathernecking,* RKO; *Hook, Line, and Sinker,* RKO; *The Widow from Chicago,* FN. 1931: *Cracked Nuts,* RKO; *The Naughty Flirt,* FN; *The Girl Habit,* PAR. 1932: *Million Dollar Legs,* PAR. 1933: *Parole Girl,* COL; *So This Is Africa,* COL. 1934: *Peck's Bad Boy, The Dude Ranger.* 1935: *When a Man's a Man, The Cowboy Millionaire* (all FOX). 1936: *It's a Great Life,* PAR; *F-Man,* PAR. 1937: *On Again, Off Again; Forty Naughty Girls, High Flyers.* 1938: *Hawaii Calls, Go Chase Yourself, Breaking the Ice, Peck's Bad Boy with the Circus* (all RKO). 1940: *My Little Chickadee, The Villain Still Pursued Her, The Bank Dick.* 1941: *Meet the Chump, Hello Sucker, Cracked Nuts, Never Give a Sucker an Even Break* (all U). 1942: *Snuffy Smith, the Yard Bird,* MONO; *What's Cookin'?, Private Buckaroo; Give Out, Sisters; Behind the Eight Ball.* 1943: *He's My Guy, Crazy House.* 1944: *Swingtime Johnny, Slightly Terrific, Ghost Catchers, Moonlight and Cactus, Night Club Girl.* 1945: *See My Lawyer, Penthouse Rhythm* (all U). 1946: *Bringing Up Father.* 1948: *Jiggs and Maggie in Society, Jiggs and Maggie in Court* (with William Beaudine) (all MONO).

STEVE COCHRAN (1917–1965)
1967: *Tell Me in the Sunlight,* MOVIE-RAMA COLOR CORP.

WILLIAM CONRAD (1920–)

1964: *The Man from Galveston*. 1965: *Two on a Guillotine, My Blood Runs Cold, Brainstorm* (all WB).

FIELDER COOK (1923–)

1956: *Patterns*, UA. 1966: *A Big Hand for the Little Lady*, WB. 1968: *How to Save a Marriage—and Ruin Your Life*, COL; *Prudence and the Pill* (England), 20TH. 1971: *Eagle in a Cage* (England), NATIONAL GENERAL. 1973: *From the Mixed-Up Files of Mrs. Basil E. Frankweiler*, CINEMA V.

ROGER (WILLIAM) CORMAN (1926–)

1955: *Five Guns West*, AMERICAN RELEASING CORP.; *Apache Woman*, AMERICAN RELEASING. 1956: *The Day the World Ended*, AMERICAN RELEASING; *Swamp Woman*, WOOLNER BROTHERS; *The Gunslinger, The Oklahoma Woman, It Conquered the World*. 1957: *Naked Paradise* (all AIP); *Attack of the Crab Monsters*, AA; *Not of This Earth*, AA; *The Undead*, AIP; *Rock All Night*, AIP; *Carnival Rock*, HOWCO INTERNATIONAL; *Teenage Doll*, AA; *Sorority Girl*, AIP; *The Viking Women and the Sea Serpent*, AIP. 1958: *War of the Satellites*, AA; *Machine Gun Kelly, Teenage Caveman, The She-Gods of Shark Reef* (all AIP). 1959: *I, Mobster*, 20TH; *The Wasp Woman*, FILMGROUP; *A Bucket of Blood*, AIP. 1960: *Ski Troop Attack*, FILMGROUP; *The House of Usher*, AIP; *The Little Shop of Horrors, The Last Woman on Earth, Creature from the Haunted Sea, Atlas* (all FILMGROUP). 1961: *The Pit and the Pendulum*, AIP. 1962: *Premature Burial*, AIP; *I Hate Your Guts (The Intruder)*, CINEMA DISTRIBUTORS OF AMERICA; *Tales of Terror*, AIP; *Tower of London*, UA. 1963: *The Raven, The Young Racers, The Haunted Palace, The Terror, X—The Man with X-Ray Eyes*. 1964: *The Masque of the Red Death* (England) (all AIP); *The Secret Invasion* (Yugoslavia), UA. 1965: *The Tomb of Ligeia* (England), AIP. 1966: *The Wild Angels*, AIP. 1967: *The St. Valentine's Day Massacre*, 20TH; *The Trip*. 1970: *Bloody Mama, Gas-s-s-s!* (all AIP). 1971: *Von Richthofen and Brown* (England/Ireland), UA.

HUBERT CORNFIELD (1929–)

1955: *Sudden Danger*, AA. 1957: *Lure of the Swamp, Plunder Road*. 1960: *The Third Voice* (all 20TH). 1961: *Angel Baby* (with Paul Wendkos), AA. 1962: *Pressure Point*, UA. 1969: *The Night of the Following Day*, U.

WILL COWAN
1958: *The Big Beat,* U-I, *The Thing That Couldn't Die,* U-I.

WILLIAM J. COWEN (1883–1964)
1932: *Kongo,* M-G-M. 1933: *Oliver Twist,* MONO. 1934: *Woman Unafraid,* GOLDSMITH.

IRVING CUMMINGS (1888–1959)
1929: *In Old Arizona* (with Raoul Walsh), *Behind the Curtain.* 1930: *Cameo Kirby, On the Level, A Devil with Women.* 1931: *A Holy Terror, The Cisco Kid* (all FOX). 1932: *Attorney for the Defense, The Night Club Lady, Man Against Woman* (all COL). 1933: *Man Hunt,* RKO; *The Woman I Stole,* COL; *The Mad Game.* 1934: *I Believed in You, Grand Canary, The White Parade.* 1935: *It's a Small World, Curly Top* (all FOX). 1936: *Nobody's Fool,* U; *The Poor Little Rich Girl, Girls' Dormitory, White Hunter* (all 20TH). 1937: *Vogues of 1938,* UA; *Merry-Go-Round of 1938,* U. 1938: *Little Miss Broadway, Just Around the Corner.* 1939: *The Story of Alexander Graham Bell, Hollywood Cavalcade, Everything Happens at Night.* 1940: *Lillian Russell, Down Argentine Way.* 1941: *That Night in Rio, Belle Starr* (all 20TH); *Louisiana Purchase,* PAR. 1942: *My Gal Sal, Springtime in the Rockies.* 1943: *Sweet Rosie O'Grady* (all 20TH); *What a Woman!,* COL. 1944: *The Impatient Years,* COL. 1945: *The Dolly Sisters,* 20TH. 1951: *Double Dynamite,* RKO.

MORTON DA COSTA (1914–)
1958: *Auntie Mame.* 1962: *The Music Man.* 1963: *Island of Love* (all WB).

HELMUT DANTINE (1918–)
1958: *Thundering Jets,* 20TH.

FREDERICK DE CORDOVA (1910–)
1945: *Too Young to Know.* 1946: *Her Kind of Man.* 1947: *That Way with Women, Love and Learn, Always Together.* 1948: *Wallflower* (all WB); *For the Love of Mary, The Countess of Monte Cristo.* 1949: *Illegal Entry, The Gal Who Took the West.* 1950: *Buccaneer's Girl, Peggy, The Desert Hawk.* 1951: *Bedtime for Bonzo, Katie Did It, Little Egypt, Finders Keepers.* 1952: *Here Come the Nelsons, Bonzo Goes to College, Yankee*

Buccaneer. 1953: *Column South* (all U-I). 1965: *I'll Take Sweden,* UA. 1966: *Frankie and Johnny,* UA.

ROY DEL RUTH (1895–1961)

1929: *Conquest, The Desert Song, The Hottentot, Gold Diggers of Broadway, The Aviator.* 1930: *Hold Everything, The Second Floor Mystery, Three Faces East, The Life of the Party.* 1931: *My Past, Divorce Among Friends, The Maltese Falcon, Side Show, Blonde Crazy.* 1932: *Taxi!, Beauty and the Boss, Winner Take All, Blessed Event* (all WB). 1933: *Employees Entrance, The Mind Reader, The Little Giant* (all FN); *Captured!,* WB; *Bureau of Missing Persons,* FN; *Lady Killer,* WB. 1934: *Bulldog Drummond Strikes Back,* 20TH CENTURY/UA; *Upper World,* WB; *Kid Millions,* UA. 1935: *Follies Bergere,* UA; *Broadway Melody of 1936,* M-G-M; *Thanks a Million!* 1936: *It Had to Happen, Private Number* (all 20TH); *Born to Dance,* M-G-M. 1937: *On the Avenue,* 20TH; *Broadway Melody of 1938,* M-G-M. 1938: *Happy Landing, My Lucky Star.* 1939: *Tail Spin* (all 20TH); *The Star Maker,* PAR; *Here I Am a Stranger,* 20TH. 1940: *He Married His Wife,* 20TH. 1941: *Topper Returns,* UA; *The Chocolate Soldier.* 1942: *Maisie Gets Her Man.* 1943: *DuBarry Was a Lady.* 1944: *Broadway Rhythm, Barbary Coast Gent* (all M-G-M). 1947: *It Happened on Fifth Avenue,* AA. 1948: *The Babe Ruth Story,* AA. 1949: *Red Light,* UA; *Always Leave Them Laughing.* 1950: *The West Point Story.* 1951: *On Moonlight Bay, Starlift.* 1952: *About Face; Stop, You're Killing Me.* 1953: *Three Sailors and a Girl.* 1954: *Phantom of the Rue Morgue* (all WB). 1959: *The Alligator People,* 20TH.

ANDRE DE TOTH (c. 1900–)

1939: *Balalaika* (Hungary), *Toprini Nasz* (Hungary). 1943: *Passport to Suez,* COL. 1944: *None Shall Escape,* COL; *Dark Waters.* 1947: *Ramrod, The Other Love.* 1948: *The Pitfall* (all UA). 1949: *Slattery's Hurricane,* 20TH. 1951: *The Man in the Saddle,* COL. 1952: *Carson City,* WB; *Springfield Rifle,* WB; *Last of the Comanches,* COL. 1953: *House of Wax,* WB; *The Stranger Wore a Gun,* COL; *Thunder over the Plains,* WB. 1954: *Crime Wave,* WB; *Riding Shotgun,* WB; *Tanganyika,* U-I; *The Bounty Hunter,* WB. 1955: *The Indian Fighter.* 1957: *Monkey on My Back, Hidden Fear* (all UA). 1959: *The Two-Headed Spy* (England), COL; *Day of the Outlaw,* UA. 1960: *Man on a String,* COL. 1961: *Morgan the Pirate* (Italy),

M-G-M. 1962: *The Mongols,* COLORAMA FEATURES INC. 1964: *Gold for the Caesars* (Italy), M-G-M. 1969: *Play Dirty,* UA.

MAURY DEXTER (c. 1928–)

1960: *The High-Powered Rifle, Walk Tall.* 1961: *The Purple Hills, Woman-hunt.* 1962: *Air Patrol, The Firebrand, Young Guns of Texas.* 1963: *The Day Mars Invaded Earth, House of the Damned, Police Nurse, Harbor Lights.* 1964: *The Young Swingers, Surf Party.* 1965: *Raiders from Beneath the Sea* (all 20TH); *The Naked Brigade,* U; *Wild on the Beach,* 20TH. 1968: *Maryjane, The Mini-Skirt Mob, The Young Animals, Born Wild.* 1970: *Hell's Belles* (all AIP).

JOHN FRANCIS DILLON (1887–1934)

1929: *Children of the Ritz, Careers, Fast Life, Sally.* 1930: *Bride of the Regiment, Spring Is Here, The Girl of the Golden West, Kismet, One Night at Susie's* (all FN). 1931: *Millie,* RKO; *The Finger Points,* FN; *The Reckless Hour,* FN; *The Pagan Lady,* COL. 1932: *The Cohens and Kellys in Holly-wood,* U; *Behind the Mask,* COL; *Man About Town, Call Her Savage.* 1933: *Humanity* (all FOX). 1934: *The Big Shakedown,* FN.

EDWARD DMYTRYK (1908–)

1935: *The Hawk,* HERMAN WOHL. 1939: *Television Spy.* 1940: *Emergency Squad, Golden Gloves, Mystery Sea Raider* (all PAR); *Her First Romance,* MONO. 1941: *The Devil Commands, Under Age, Sweetheart of the Campus, The Blonde from Singapore, Secrets of the Lone Wolf, Confessions of Boston Blackie.* 1942: *Counter-Espionage* (all COL); *Seven Miles from Alcatraz.* 1943: *Hitler's Children, The Falcon Strikes Back* (all RKO); *Captive Wild Woman,* U; *Behind the Rising Sun, Tender Comrade.* 1944: *Murder, My Sweet.* 1945: *Back to Bataan, Cornered.* 1946: *Till the End of Time.* 1947: *Crossfire, So Well Remembered* (England) (all RKO). 1949: *The Hidden Room* (*Obsession*—England), EL. 1950: *Salt to the Devil* (*Give Us This Day*—England), EL. 1952: *Mutiny,* UA; *The Sniper, Eight Iron Men.* 1953: *The Juggler.* 1954: *The Caine Mutiny* (all COL); *Broken Lance,* 20TH. 1955: *The End of the Affair* (England), COL; *Soldier of Fortune,* 20TH; *The Left Hand of God,* 20TH. 1956: *The Mountain,* PAR. 1957: *Raintree County,* M-G-M. 1958: *The Young Lions, Warlock, The Blue Angel* (all 20TH). 1962: *Walk on the Wild Side,* COL; *The Reluctant Saint* (Italy), DAVIS-ROYAL FILMS. 1964: *The Carpetbaggers,* PAR; *Where Love Has Gone,* PAR. 1965: *Mirage,* U. 1966: *Alvarez Kelly,*

COL. 1968: *Anzio* (Italy), COL; *Shalako* (Spain), CINERAMA. 1972: *Bluebeard* (Hungary), CINERAMA.

GORDON DOUGLAS (1909–)

1936: *General Spanky*, M-G-M. 1939: *Zenobia*. 1940: *Saps at Sea*. 1941: *Road Show* (With Hal Roach and Hal Roach, Jr.), *Niagara Falls*, *Broadway Limited*. 1942: *The Devil with Hitler* (all UA); *The Great Gildersleeve*. 1943: *Gildersleeve's Bad Day*, *Gildersleeve on Broadway*. 1944: *A Night of Adventure*, *Gildersleeve's Ghost*, *Girl Rush*, *The Falcon in Hollywood*. 1945: *Zombies on Broadway*, *First Yank into Tokyo*. 1946: *Dick Tracy vs. Cueball*, *San Quentin*. 1948: *If You Knew Susie* (all RKO); *The Black Arrow*, *Walk a Crooked Mile*. 1949: *The Doolins of Oklahoma*, *Mr. Soft Touch* (with Henry Levin). 1950: *The Nevadan*, *The Fortunes of Captain Blood*, *Rogues of Sherwood Forest* (all COL); *Kiss Tomorrow Goodbye*, WB; *Between Midnight and Dawn*, COL; *The Great Missouri Raid*, PAR. 1951: *Only the Valiant*, *I Was a Communist for the FBI*, *Come Fill the Cup*. 1952: *Mara Maru*, *The Iron Mistress*. 1953: *She's Back on Broadway*, *So This Is Love*, *The Charge at Feather River*. 1954: *Them!*, *Young at Heart*. 1955: *The McConnell Story*, *Sincerely Yours*. 1956: *Santiago*. 1957: *The Big Land*, *Bombers B-52*. 1958: *Fort Dobbs* (all WB); *The Fiend Who Walked the West*, 20TH. 1959: *Up Periscope*, *Yellowstone Kelly*. 1961: *Gold of the Seven Saints*, *The Sins of Rachel Cade*, *Claudelle Inglish* (all WB). 1962: *Follow That Dream*, UA. 1963: *Call Me Bwana*, UA. 1964: *Robin and the Seven Hoods*, WB; *Rio Conchos*, 20TH. 1965: *Sylvia*, PAR; *Harlow*, PAR. 1966: *Stagecoach*, *Way . . . Way Out*. 1967: *In Like Flint* (all 20TH); *Chuka*, PAR; *Tony Rome*. 1968: *The Detective*, *Lady in Cement* (all 20TH). 1970: *Skullduggery*, U; *Barquero*, UA; *They Call Me MISTER Tibbs!*, UA. 1973: *Slaughter's Big Rip-Off*, AIP.

ARTHUR DREIFUSS (1908–)

1940: *Mystery in Swing*, INTERNATIONAL ROADSHOW. 1941: *Reg'lar Fellers*. 1942: *Baby Face Morgan*, *The Boss of Big Town*, *The Pay-Off* (all PRC). 1943: *Sarong Girl*, *Melody Parade*, *Campus Rhythm*, *Nearly Eighteen*, *The Sultan's Daughter* (all MONO). 1944: *Ever Since Venus*. 1945: *Eadie Was a Lady*, *Boston Blackie Booked on Suspicion*, *Boston Blackie's Rendezvous*, *The Gay Senorita*, *Prison Ship* (all COL). 1946: *Junior Prom*, *Freddie Steps Out*, *High School Hero*. 1947: *Vacation Days* (all MONO); *Betty Co-Ed*, *Little Miss Broadway*, *Two Blondes and a Redhead*, *Sweet*

Genevieve. 1948: *Glamour Girl, Mary Lou; I Surrender, Dear* (all COL).
1949: *An Old-Fashioned Girl,* EL; *Manhattan Angel,* COL; *Shamrock Hill,*
EL; *There's a Girl in My Heart,* AA. 1958: *Life Begins at 17, The Last
Blitzkrieg.* 1959: *Juke Box Rhythm* (all COL). 1962: *The Quare Fellow*
(Ireland), ASTOR. 1967: *Riot on Sunset Strip,* AIP; *The Love-Ins,* COL.
1968: *For Singles Only,* COL; *A Time to Sing,* M-G-M; *The Young Runaways,* M-G-M.

E. A. DUPONT (1891–1956)
1930: *Zwei Welten* (Germany), *Menschen im Käfig* (Germany), *Atlantic*
(England), BI. 1931: *Salto Mortale* (Germany). 1933: *Der Läufer von
Marathon* (Germany), *Ladies Must Love,* U. 1935: *The Bishop Misbehaves,*
M-G-M. 1936: *Forgotten Faces, A Son Comes Home.* 1937: *Night of Mystery,
On Such a Night.* 1938: *Love on Toast* (all PAR). 1939: *Hell's Kitchen* (with
Lewis R. Seiler), WB. 1951: *The Scarf,* UA; *Pictura* (with Luciano Emmer),
PICTURA FILMS CORP. 1953: *Problem Girls,* COL; *The Neanderthal
Man, The Steel Lady.* 1954: *Return to Treasure Island* (all UA).

B. REEVES (BREEZY) EASON (1886–1956)
1929: *Lariat Kid,* U; *Winged Horseman* (with Arthur Rosson), U. 1930:
Troopers Three (with Norman Taurog), TIFFANY; *The Roaring Ranch,
Trigger Tricks, Spurs* (all U). 1932: *The Sunset Trail,* TIFFANY; *Honor of
the Press,* MAYFAIR; *The Heart Punch,* MAYFAIR. 1933: *Cornered,* COL;
*Behind Jury Doors, Alimony Madness, Revenge at Monte Carlo, Her Resale
Value, Dance Hall Hostess* (all MAYFAIR). 1936: *Red River Valley,* REP.
1937: *Land Beyond the Law, Empty Holsters, Prairie Thunder.* 1938:
Sergeant Murphy, The Kid Comes Back, The Daredevil Drivers (all WB);
Call of the Yukon (with John T. Coyle). 1939: *Blue Montana Skies, Moun-
tain Rhythm* (all REP). 1940: *Men with Steel Faces* (with Otto Brower),
TIMES PICTURES. 1942: *Murder in the Big House, Spy Ship.* 1943: *Truck
Busters* (all WB). 1949: *Rimfire,* SCREEN GUILD.

RAY (RAYMOND E.) ENRIGHT (1896–1965)
1929: *Little Wildcat, Stolen Kisses, Kid Gloves, Skin Deep.* 1930: *Song of
the West, Golden Dawn, Dancing Sweeties* (all WB); *Scarlet Pages,* FN.
1932: *Play Girl,* WB; *The Tenderfoot,* FN. 1933: *Blondie Johnson,* FN; *The
Silk Express,* WB; *Tomorrow at Seven,* RKO; *Havana Widows,* FN. 1934:
I've Got Your Number, WB; *Twenty Million Sweethearts,* FN; *The Circus
Clown,* FN; *Dames,* WB; *The St. Louis Kid,* WB. 1935: *While the Patient*

Slept, FN; *Traveling Saleslady*, FN; *Alibi Ike, We're in the Money, Miss Pacific Fleet* (all WB); *Sing Me a Love Song*. 1936: *Snowed Under, Earthworm Tractors, China Clipper* (all FN). 1937: *Ready, Willing, and Able; Slim, The Singing Marine, Back in Circulation*. 1938: *Swing Your Lady, Gold Diggers in Paris, Hard to Get, Going Places*. 1939: *Naughty but Nice, Angels Wash Their Faces, On Your Toes*. 1940: *Brother Rat and a Baby, An Angel from Texas, The River's End*. 1941: *The Wagons Roll at Night, Thieves Fall Out, Bad Men of Missouri, Law of the Tropics, Wild Bill Hickok Rides* (all WB). 1942: *The Spoilers, Men of Texas, Sin Town* (all U). 1943: *Good Luck, Mr. Yates*, COL; *The Iron Major*, RKO; *Gung Ho!*, U. 1945: *China Sky*, RKO; *Man Alive*, RKO. 1946: *One Way to Love*, COL. 1947: *Trail Street*, RKO. 1948: *Albuquerque*, PAR; *Return of the Bad Men*, RKO; *Coroner Creek*, COL. 1949: *South of St. Louis*, WB. 1950: *Montana*, WB; *Kansas Raiders*, U-I. 1951: *Flaming Feather*, PAR. 1953: *The Man from Cairo*, LIPPERT.

DOUGLAS FAIRBANKS (1883–1939)
1931: *Around the World in Eighty Minutes with Douglas Fairbanks* (with Victor Fleming), UA.

JOHN VILLIERS FARROW (1904–1963)
1937: *Men in Exile*, FN; *West of Shanghai (War Lord)*, WB; *Fair Warning*, 20TH. 1938: *She Loved a Fireman, Little Miss Thoroughbred, My Bill, Broadway Musketeers*. 1939: *Women in the Wind* (all WB); *The Saint Strikes Back, Sorority House, Five Came Back, Full Confession, Reno*. 1940: *Married and in Love, A Bill of Divorcement* (all RKO). 1942: *Wake Island*, PAR; *Commandos Strike at Dawn*, COL. 1943: *China*. 1944: *The Hitler Gang*. 1945: *You Came Along*. 1946: *Two Years Before the Mast, California*. 1947: *Easy Come, Easy Go; Blaze of Noon, Calcutta*. 1948: *The Big Clock, The Night Has a Thousand Eyes, Beyond Glory*. 1949: *Alias Nick Beal; Red, Hot, and Blue* (all PAR). 1950: *Where Danger Lives*, RKO; *Copper Canyon*, PAR. 1951: *His Kind of Woman*, RKO; *Submarine Command*, PAR. 1953: *Ride, Vaquero*, M-G-M; *Plunder of the Sun*, WB; *Botany Bay*, PAR; *Hondo*, WB. 1954: *A Bullet Is Waiting*, COL. 1955: *The Sea Chase*, WB. 1956: *Back from Eternity*, RKO. 1957: *The Unholy Wife*, RKO. 1959: *John Paul Jones*, WB.

FELIX E. FEIST, JR. (1906–1965)
1932: *Stepping Sisters*. 1933: *The Deluge*, RKO. 1943: *All by Myself; You're a Lucky Fellow, Mr. Smith*. 1944: *This Is the Life, Pardon My Rhythm,*

Reckless Age (all U). 1945: *George White's Scandals*, RKO. 1947: *The Devil Thumbs a Ride*, RKO. 1948: *The Winner's Circle*, 20TH. 1949: *The Threat*, RKO; *Guilty of Treason*, EL. 1950: *The Golden Gloves Story*, EL; *The Man Who Cheated Himself*, 20TH. 1951: *Tomorrow Is Another Day*, WB; *The Basketball Fix*, REALART. 1952: *This Woman Is Dangerous, The Big Trees, The Man Behind the Gun* (all WB). 1953: *Donovan's Brain*, UA. 1955: *Pirates of Tripoli*, COL.

LESLIE FENTON (1902–)
1939: *Tell No Tales, Stronger Than Desire*. 1940: *The Man from Dakota, The Golden Fleecing* (all M-G-M). 1941: *The Saint's Vacation* (England), RKO. 1943: *There's a Future in It* (England), PAR. 1944: *Tomorrow the World!*, UA. 1946: *Pardon My Past*, COL. 1948: *On Our Merry Way* (with King Vidor), UA; *Saigon*, PAR; *Lulu Belle*, COL; *Whispering Smith*. 1949: *Streets of Laredo*. 1950: *The Redhead and the Cowboy* (all PAR).

JOSE FERRER (1912–)
1955: *The Shrike*, U-I. 1956: *The Cockleshell Heroes* (England), COL; *The Great Man*, U-I. 1958: *I Accuse!*, M-G-M; *The High Cost of Loving*, M-G-M. 1961: *Return to Peyton Place*, 20TH. 1962: *State Fair*, 20TH.

MEL FERRER (MELCHIOR G. FERRER) (1917–)
1945: *The Girl of the Limberlost*, COL. 1950: *The Secret Fury*, RKO; *Vendetta* (with Max Ophuls, Preston Sturges, Stuart Heisler, Howard Hughes; signed by Ferrer), RKO. 1959: *Green Mansions*, M-G-M. 1966: *Every Day Is a Holiday* (Spain), COL.

GEORGE FITZMAURICE (1885–1940)
1929: *His Captive Woman*, FN; *Man and the Moment*, FN; *The Locked Door*, UA; *Tiger Rose*, WB. 1930: *The Bad One, One Heavenly Night, The Devil to Pay* (all UA). 1931: *Strangers May Kiss*, M-G-M; *The Unholy Garden*, UA. 1932: *Mata Hari*, M-G-M; *As You Desire Me*, M-G-M; 1934: *All Men Are Enemies*, FOX. 1936: *Petticoat Fever, Suzy*. 1937: *The Last of Mrs. Cheyney* (begun and signed by Richard Boleslawski), *The Emperor's Candlesticks; Live, Love, and Learn*. 1938: *Arsene Lupin Returns, Vacation from Love* (all M-G-M). 1940: *Adventure in Diamonds*, PAR.

RICHARD O. FLEISCHER (1916–)
1946: *Child of Divorce*. 1947: *Banjo*. 1948: *So This Is New York, Bodyguard*. 1949: *The Clay Pigeon* (all RKO); *Trapped*, EL; *Follow Me Quietly*,

Make Mine Laughs. 1950: *Armored Car Robbery.* 1952: *The Narrow Margin* (all RKO); *The Happy Time,* COL. 1953: *Arena,* M-G-M. 1954: *20,000 Leagues Under the Sea,* BV. 1955: *Violent Saturday,* 20TH; *The Girl in the Red Velvet Swing,* 20TH. 1956: *Bandido,* UA; *Between Heaven and Hell,* 20TH. 1958: *The Vikings,* UA. 1959: *These Thousand Hills, Compulsion.* 1960: *Crack in the Mirror.* 1961: *The Big Gamble* (all 20TH). 1962: *Barabbas* (Italy), COL. 1966: *Fantastic Voyage.* 1967: *Doctor Dolittle* (England). 1968: *The Boston Strangler.* 1969: *Che!* 1970: *Tora! Tora! Tora!* (with Toshio Masuda and Kinji Fukusaku) (all 20TH). 1971: *Ten Rillington Place* (England), COL; *The Last Run* (Spain), M-G-M; *See No Evil* (England), COL. 1973: *Soylent Green,* M-G-M; *The Don Is Dead,* U. 1974: *The Spikes Gang* (Spain), UA; *Mr. Majestyk,* UA. 1975: *Mandingo.*

ROBERT FLOREY (1900–)
1929: *The Hole in the Wall, The Coconuts* (with Joseph Santley), *Battle of Paris* (all PAR). 1930: *Le Blanc et le Noir* (France—completed by Marc Allegret). 1932: *Murders in the Rue Morgue,* U; *The Man Called Back,* TIFFANY; *Those We Love,* WORLD WIDE. 1933: *Girl Missing, Ex-Lady, The House on 56th Street* (all WB). 1934: *Bedside,* FN; *Smarty,* WB; *Registered Nurse,* FN; *I Sell Anything,* FN. 1935: *I Am a Thief,* WB; *The Woman in Red,* FN; *The Florentine Dagger, Don't Bet on Blondes, Going Highbrow* (all WB); *Ship Cafe,* PAR; *The Pay-Off,* WB. 1936: *The Preview Murder Mystery, 'Til We Meet Again, Hollywood Boulevard.* 1937: *Outcast, King of Gamblers, Mountain Music, This Way Please, Daughter of Shanghai.* 1938: *Dangerous to Know, King of Alcatraz.* 1939: *Disbarred, Hotel Imperial, The Magnificent Fraud, Death of a Champion.* 1940: *Women Without Names, Parole Fixer* (all PAR). 1941: *The Face Behind the Mask, Meet Boston Blackie, Two in a Taxi* (all COL); *Dangerously They Live.* 1942: *Lady Gangster* (as "Florian Roberts"). 1943: *The Desert Song* (all WB). 1944: *Man from Frisco,* REP; *Roger Touhy, Gangster,* 20TH. 1945: *God Is My Co-Pilot, Danger Signal.* 1946: *The Beast with Five Fingers* (all WB). 1948: *Tarzan and the Mermaids,* RKO; *Rogues Regiment,* U-I. 1949: *Outpost in Morocco,* UA; *The Crooked Way,* UA. 1950: *The Vicious Years,* FILM CLASSICS; *Johnny One-Eye,* UA.

EUGENE J. FORDE (1898–)
1929: *Outlawed,* RKO; *Big Diamond Robbery,* RKO. 1933: *Smoky.* 1934: *Charlie Chan in London.* 1935: *Mystery Woman, The Great Hotel Murder* (all FOX); *Your Uncle Dudley.* 1936: *The Country Beyond, 36 Hours to*

Kill. 1937: *Midnight Taxi; Step Lively, Jeeves!, The Lady Escapes, Charlie Chan on Broadway, Charlie Chan at Monte Carlo.* 1938: *International Settlement, One Wild Night, Meet the Girls.* 1939: *Inspector Hornleigh* (England), *The Honeymoon's Over.* 1940: *Charlie Chan's Murder Cruise, Pier 13; Michael Shayne, Private Detective; Charter Pilot.* 1941: *Sleepers West, Dressed to Kill* (all 20TH); *Buy Me That Town,* PAR; *Man at Large.* 1942: *Right to the Heart, Berlin Correspondent* (all 20TH). 1943: *The Crime Doctor's Strangest Case,* COL. 1944: *Shadows in the Night,* COL. 1947: *Backlash, Jewels of Brandenburg, The Crimson Key, The Invisible Wall* (all 20TH).

HARRY FOSTER (1906–)
1958: *Let's Rock!,* COL.

LEWIS R. FOSTER (1900–1974)
1936: *Love Letters of a Star* (with Milton Carruth). 1937: *She's Dangerous* (with Milton Carruth), *Armored Car, The Man Who Cried Wolf* (all U). 1949: *The Lucky Stiff,* UA; *El Paso, Manhandled, Captain China.* 1950: *The Eagle and the Hawk.* 1951: *The Last Outpost, Passage West, Crosswinds, Hong Kong.* 1953: *Tropic Zone, Jamaica Run, Those Redheads from Seattle* (all PAR). 1955: *Crashout,* FILMAKERS; *Top of the World,* UA. 1956: *The Bold and the Brave,* RKO; *Dakota Incident,* REP. 1958: *Tonka,* BV. 1960: *The Sign of Zorro* (with Norman Foster), BV.

NORMAN FOSTER (1900–)
1936: *I Cover Chinatown,* STEINER. 1937: *Fair Warning; Think Fast, Mr. Moto; Thank You, Mr. Moto.* 1938: *Walking Down Broadway, Mysterious Mr. Moto.* 1939: *Mr. Moto's Last Warning, Charlie Chan in Reno, Mr. Moto Takes a Vacation, Charlie Chan at Treasure Island.* 1940: *Charlie Chan in Panama, Viva Cisco Kid.* 1941: *Ride, Kelly, Ride; Scotland Yard* (all 20TH). 1942: *Journey into Fear* (with Orson Welles), RKO. 1948: *Rachel and the Stranger,* RKO; *Kiss the Blood off My Hands,* U-I. 1949: *Tell It to the Judge,* COL. 1950: *Father Is a Bachelor* (with Abby Berlin), COL; *Woman on the Run,* U-I. 1952: *Navajo* (documentary), LIPPERT; *Sky Full of Moon,* M-G-M. 1953: *Sombrero,* M-G-M. 1955: *Davy Crockett, King of the Wild Frontier,* BV. 1960: *The Sign of Zorro* (with Lewis R. Foster), BV. 1966: *Indian Paint,* EAGLE-INTERNATIONAL. 1967: *Brighty of the Grand Canyon,* FEATURE FILM CORPORATION OF AMERICA.

GENE FOWLER, JR.
1957: *I Was a Teenage Werewolf*, AIP. 1958: *Gang War*, 20TH; *Showdown at Boot Hill*, 20TH; *I Married a Monster from Outer Space*, PAR. 1959: *Here Come the Jets*, 20TH; *The Rebel Set*, AA; *The Oregon Trail*, 20TH.

WALLACE FOX (1895–1958)
1929: *Come and Get It, The Amazing Vagabond, Laughing at Death* (all RKO). 1931: *Partners of the Trail*, MONO. 1932: *The Cannonball Express*, WW; *Devil on Deck*, WW. 1935: *Red Morning, Powdersmoke Range*. 1936: *Yellow Dust* (all RKO); *The Last of the Mohicans* (with George B. Seitz), UA. 1937: *Racing Lady*, RKO. 1938: *The Mexicali Kid*, MONO; *The Gun Packer*, MONO. 1940: *Pride of the Plains*, REP. 1941: *The Lone Star Vigilantes*, COL; *Bowery Blitzkrieg*, MONO. 1942: *Bullets for Bandits*, COL; *The Corpse Vanishes, Let's Get Tough!, Smart Alecks, Bowery at Midnight, 'Neath Brooklyn Bridge*. 1943: *Kid Dynamite, The Ghost Rider, Outlaws of Stampede Pass* (all MONO); *The Girl from Monterey*. 1944: *Men on Her Mind, The Great Mike* (all PRC); *Riders of the Santa Fe*, U. 1945: *Mr. Muggs Rides Again*, MONO; *Bad Men of the Border, Code of the Lawless, Trail to Vengeance, Pillow of Death*. 1946: *Gun Town, Rustler's Round-Up, Wild Beauty, Lawless Breed, Gunman's Code* (all U). 1948: *Docks of New York*, MONO; *The Valiant Hombre*. 1949: *The Gay Amigo, The Daring Caballero* (all UA); *Western Renegades*. 1950: *Fence Riders, West of Wyoming, Over the Border, Gunslingers, Six-Gun Mesa, Arizona Territory, Silver Raiders, Outlaw Gold*. 1951: *Montana Desperado* (all MONO).

MELVIN FRANK (c. 1917–)
In collaboration with Norman Panama: 1950: *The Reformer and the Redhead*. 1951: *Strictly Dishonorable, Callaway Went Thataway*. 1952: *Above and Beyond* (all M-G-M). 1954: *Knock on Wood*. 1956: *The Court Jester, That Certain Feeling* (all PAR). Alone: 1959: *The Jayhawkers*, PAR; *Li'l Abner*, PAR. 1960: *The Facts of Life*, UA. 1964: *Strange Bedfellows*, U. 1968: *Buona Sera, Mrs. Campbell*, UA. 1973: *A Touch of Class* (England/Spain), AVCO-EMBASSY. 1975: *The Prisoner of Second Avenue*, WB.

HUGO FREGONESE (1908–)
1943: *Pampa Barbara* (Argentina; with Lucas Demare). 1946: *Where Words Fail* (Argentina; Argentine title—*Donde Mueren las Palabras*), M-G-M. 1947: *Apena un Delincuente* (Argentina; *Hardly a Criminal*). 1950: *One Way Street, Saddle Tramp*. 1951: *Apache Drums, Mark of the Renegade*

(all U-I). 1952: *My Six Convicts*, COL; *Untamed Frontier*, U-I. 1953: *Blowing Wild*, WB; *Decameron Nights*, RKO. 1954: *The Man in the Attic*, 20TH; *The Raid*, 20TH; *Black Tuesday*, UA. 1956: *I Girovaghi* (Italy). 1958: *Harry Black and the Tiger* (England), 20TH. 1959: *The Beast of Marseilles* (England; *Seven Thunders*), LOPERT. 1962: *Marco Polo* (Italy), AIP. 1967: *Shatterhand!* (Germany), DON KAY ASSOCIATES; *Savage Pampas* (Spain), COMET FILMS.

KARL FREUND (1890–1969)
1932: *The Mummy*. 1933: *Moonlight and Pretzels*. 1934: *Madame Spy, Countess of Monte Cristo, Uncertain Lady, I Give My Love, Gift of Gab* (all U). 1935: *Mad Love*, M-G-M.

ALBERT C. GANNAWAY (1920–)
1956: *Hidden Guns*, REP; *Daniel Boone—Trail Blazer* (with Ismael Rodriguez), REP. 1957: *The Badge of Marshal Brennan*, AA; *Raiders of Old California*. 1958: *Man or Gun, No Place to Land*. 1959: *Plunderers of Painted Flats* (all REP).

OTIS GARRETT (?–1941)
1937: *The Black Doll*. 1938: *The Last Express, Personal Secretary, Danger on the Air, Lady in the Morgue*. 1939: *The Witness Vanishes, Mystery of the White Room* (all U); *Exile Express*, GN. 1940: *Margie*, U. 1941: *Sandy Gets Her Man*, U.

GREG GARRISON
1961: *Hey, Let's Twist!*, PAR. 1962: *Two Tickets to Paris!*, COL.

LOUIS J. GASNIER (1882–1963)
1929: *Darkened Rooms*. 1930: *Slightly Scarlet* (with Edwin H. Knopf), *The Shadow of the Law* (with Max Marcin), *Mysterious Mr. Parkes* (France), *The Virtuous Sin* (with George Cukor). 1931: *The Lawyer's Secret* (with Max Marcin), *Silence* (with Max Marcin). 1932: *The Strange Case of Clara Deane* (with Max Marcin), *Forgotten Commandments* (with William Schorr). 1933: *Gambling Ship* (with Max Marcin), *Melodia de Arrabal* (Spanish-language) (all PAR); *Iris, Perdue et Retrouvée* (France). 1934: *Fedora* (France). 1935: *El Tango en Broadway* (Spanish-language), *Topaze* (France), *The Last Outpost* (with Charles Barton) (all PAR). 1937: *The Gold Racket*, GN; *Bank Alarm*, GN. 1939: *La Inmaculada* (Span-

ish-language), UA. 1940: *The Burning Question* (*Tell Your Children; Reefer Madness*); *Murder on the Yukon*, MONO. 1941: *Stolen Paradise*, MONO. 1942: *Fight On, Marines*, ASTOR.

MARION GERING (1901–)
1931: *I Take This Woman, Twenty-Four Hours.* 1932: *Ladies of the Big House, Devil and the Deep, Madame Butterfly.* 1933: *Pick Up, Jennie Gerhardt.* 1934: *Good Dame, Thirty-Day Princess, Ready for Love.* 1935: *Rumba.* 1936: *Rose of the Rancho* (all PAR); *Lady of Secrets.* 1937: *Thunder in the City* (England). 1938: *She Married an Artist* (all COL). 1950: *Sarumba* (Cuba), EL. 1963: *Violated Paradise* (Japan), VICTORIA FILMS.

BERNARD GIRARD (c. 1929–)
1957: *Ride Out for Revenge*, UA; *The Green-Eyed Blonde*, WB. 1958: *The Party Crashers*, PAR; *As Young As We Are*, PAR. 1966: *Dead Heat on a Merry-Go-Round*, COL. 1969: *The Mad Room*, COL. 1972: *The Happiness Cage*, CINERAMA.

BERT GLENNON (1893–1967)
1929: *Syncopation*, RKO. 1930: *Around the Corner*, COL; *Girl of the Port*, RKO; *Paradise Island*. TIFFANY. 1931: *In Line of Duty*, MONO. 1932: *South of Santa Fe*, WW.

PETER GODFREY (1899–1970)
1939: *The Lone Wolf Spy Hunt*, COL. 1941: *Unexpected Uncle*, RKO. 1942: *Highways by Night*, RKO. 1944: *Make Your Own Bed.* 1945: *Hotel Berlin, Christmas in Connecticut.* 1946: *One More Tomorrow* (*The Animal Kingdom*). 1947: *The Two Mrs. Carrolls, Cry Wolf, That Hagen Girl, Escape Me Never.* 1948: *The Woman in White, The Decision of Christopher Blake.* 1949: *The Girl from Jones Beach, One Last Fling.* 1950: *Barricade, The Great Jewel Robber* (all WB); *He's a Cockeyed Wonder*, COL. 1952: *One Big Affair*, UA. 1956: *Please Murder Me*, DISTRIBUTION CORP. OF AMERICA.

JAMES GOLDSTONE (1931–)
1968: *Jigsaw.* 1969: *A Man Called Gannon, Winning* (all U). 1971: *Brother John*, COL; *Red Sky at Morning*, U; *The Gang That Couldn't Shoot Straight*, M-G-M. 1972: *They Only Kill Their Masters*, M-G-M.

SAMUEL GOLDWYN, JR. (1926-)
1964: *The Young Lovers*, M-G-M.

BERT I. GORDON (1922-)
1955: *King Dinosaur*, LIPPERT. 1957: *Beginning of the End*, REP; *The Cyclops*, AA; *The Amazing Colossal Man*. 1958: *Attack of the Puppet People*, *War of the Colossal Beast*, *The Spider* (all AIP). 1960: *The Boy and the Pirates*, UA; *Tormented*, AA. 1962: *The Magic Sword*, UA. 1965: *Village of the Giants*, EMBASSY. 1966: *Picture Mommy Dead*, EMBASSY. 1970: *How to Succeed with Sex*, MEDFORD FILMS. 1972: *Necromancy*, CINERAMA. 1973: *The Mad Bomber*, CINEMATION.

MICHAEL GORDON (1909-)
1942: *Boston Blackie Goes Hollywood*, *Underground Agent*. 1943: *One Dangerous Night*, *Crime Doctor* (all COL). 1947: *The Web*. 1948: *Another Part of the Forest*, *An Act of Murder*. 1949: *The Lady Gambles*, *Woman in Hiding* (all U-I). 1950: *Cyrano de Bergerac*, UA. 1951: *I Can Get It For You Wholesale*, 20TH; *The Secret of Convict Lake*, 20TH. 1953: *Wherever She Goes* (Australia), MAYER-KINGSLEY. 1959: *Pillow Talk*, U-I. 1960: *Portrait in Black*, U-I. 1962: *Boys' Night Out*, M-G-M. 1963: *For Love or Money*, U-I; *Move Over Darling*, 20TH. 1965: *A Very Special Favor*, U. 1966: *Texas Across the River*, U. 1968: *The Impossible Years*, M-G-M. 1970: *How Do I Love Thee?*, CINERAMA.

TOM GRAEFF (1929-)
1959: *Teenagers from Outer Space*, WB.

WALTER E. GRAUMAN (1922-)
1957: *The Disembodied*, AA. 1964: *Lady in a Cage*, PAR; *633 Squadron*, UA. 1965: *A Rage to Live*, UA. 1966: *I Deal in Danger*, 20TH. 1970: *The Last Escape* (Germany), UA.

GARY GRAVER
1963: *The Great Dream*, YUCCA PRODUCTIONS. 1970: *The Hard Road*, 4-STAR EXCELSIOR; *Erika's Hot Summer*, BOXOFFICE INTERNATIONAL PICTURES; *Sandra—The Making of a Woman*, A MINI PRODUCTION/GRADS. 1973: *There Was a Little Girl*, FREEWAY FILMS.

ALFRED E. GREEN (1889–1960)

1929: *Making the Grade*, FOX; *Disraeli*. 1930: *The Green Goddess, The Man from Blankley's, Old English, Sweet Kitty Bellaire* (all WB). 1931: *Smart Money*, FN; *Men of the Sky*, WB; *The Road to Singapore*, WB. 1932: *Union Depot, It's Tough to Be Famous, The Rich Are Always with Us, The Dark Horse, Silver Dollar* (all FN). 1933: *Parachute Jumper, The Narrow Corner, Baby Face* (all WB); *I Loved a Woman*, FN. 1934: *As the Earth Turns*, WB; *Dark Hazard*, FN; *The Merry Frinks*, FN; *Housewife*, WB; *Side Streets, A Lost Lady, Gentlemen Are Born* (all FN). 1935: *Sweet Music*, WB; *The Girl from 10th Avenue*, WB; *Here's to Romance*, FOX; *The Goose and the Gander, Dangerous*. 1936: *Colleen* (all WB); *The Golden Arrow*, FN; *Two in a Crowd*, U; *They Met in a Taxi*, WB; *More Than a Secretary*. 1937: *Let's Get Married, The League of Frightened Men* (all COL); *Mr. Dodd Takes the Air*, WB; *Thoroughbreds Don't Cry*, M-G-M. 1938: *Ride a Crooked Mile*, PAR; *Duke of West Point*, UA. 1939: *The King of the Turf*, UA; *The Gracie Allen Murder Case*, PAR; *20,000 Men a Year*, 20TH. 1940: *Shooting High*, 20TH; *South of Pago Pago*, UA; *Flowing Gold*, WB; *East of the River*, WB. 1941: *Adventure in Washington*, COL; *Badlands of Dakota*, U. 1942: *The Mayor of Forty-Fourth Street*, RKO; *Meet the Stewarts*. 1943: *Appointment in Berlin, There's Something About a Soldier*. 1944: *Mr. Winkle Goes to War, Strange Affair*. 1945: *A Thousand and One Nights*. 1946: *Tars and Spars, The Jolson Story* (all COL). 1947: *The Fabulous Dorseys, Copacabana*. 1948: *Four Faces West, The Girl from Manhattan*. 1949: *Cover-Up* (all UA). 1950: *Sierra*, U-I; *The Jackie Robinson Story*, EL. 1951: *Two Gals and a Guy*, UA. 1952: *Invasion, U.S.A.*, COL. 1953: *Paris Model*, COL; *The Eddie Cantor Story*, WB. 1954: *Top Banana*, UA.

TOM (THOMAS S.) GRIES (1922–)

1955: *Hell's Horizon*, COL. 1958: *Girl in the Woods*, REP. 1968: *Will Penny*, PAR. 1969: *100 Rifles*, 20TH; *Number One*, UA. 1970: *The Hawaiians*, UA; *Fools*, CINERAMA. 1973: *Lady Ice*, NATIONAL GENERAL. 1975: *Dynamite Man, Breakout* (Spain-France-U.S.), COL.

HUGO GRIMALDI

1959: *Gigantis, the Fire Monster* (Japan), WB. 1965: *The Human Duplicators*, AA; *Mutiny in Outer Space*, AA.

NICK (HARRY A.) GRINDE (1893–)

1929: *Morgan's Last Raid, The Desert Rider.* 1930: *The Bishop Murder Case* (with David Burton), *Good News* (with Edgar J. McGregor), *Remote Control.* 1931: *This Modern Age* (all M-G-M). 1932: *Shopworn,* COL; *Vanity Street,* COL. 1935: *Stone of Silver Creek,* U; *Border Brigands,* U; *Ladies Crave Excitement,* MASCOT. 1936: *Jailbreak, Public Enemy's Wife.* 1937: *Fugitive in the Sky, The Captain's Kid, White Bondage, Public Wedding* (all WB); *Love Is on the Air,* FN; *Exiled to Shanghai.* 1938: *Down in Arkansas.* 1939: *Federal Man-Hunt* (all REP); *King of Chinatown, Sudden Money, Million Dollar Legs* (all PAR); *The Man They Could Not Hang, A Woman Is the Judge.* 1940: *Scandal Sheet, Convicted Woman, The Man with Nine Lives, Men Without Souls, Girls of the Road, Before I Hang* (all COL); *Friendly Neighbors,* REP. 1942: *The Girl from Alaska,* REP. 1943: *Hitler—Dead or Alive,* PRC. 1945: *Road to Alactraz,* REP.

JERRY GROSS

1968: *Teenage Mother,* CINEMATION INDUSTRIES.

CHARLES HAAS

1956: *Star in the Dust,* U-I; *Screaming Eagles,* AA; *Showdown at Abilene.* 1958: *Summer Love, Wild Heritage* (all U-I). 1959: *The Beat Generation, The Big Operator, Girls Town.* 1960: *Platinum High School* (all M-G-M).

HUGO HAAS (1901–1968)

1951: *Pickup, The Girl on the Bridge.* 1952: *Strange Fascination.* 1953: *One Girl's Confession* (all COL); *Thy Neighbor's Wife,* 20TH. 1954: *Bait,* COL; *The Other Woman,* 20TH. 1955: *Hold Back Tomorrow,* U-I. 1956: *Edge of Hell,* U-I. 1957: *Lizzie,* M-G-M; *Hit and Run,* UA. 1959: *Night of the Quarter Moon,* M-G-M; *Born to be Loved,* U-I.

ALEXANDER HALL (1894–1968)

1932: *Sinners in the Sun, Madame Racketeer* (with Harry Wagstaff Gribble). 1933: *The Girl in 419* (with George Somnes), *Midnight Club* (with George Somnes), *Torch Singer* (with George Somnes). 1934: *Miss Fane's Baby Is Stolen, Little Miss Marker, The Pursuit of Happiness, Limehouse Blues.* 1935: *Goin' to Town, Annapolis Farewell.* 1936: *Give Us This Night, Yours for the Asking.* 1937: *Exclusive* (all PAR). 1938: *There's Always a Woman, I Am the Law, There's That Woman Again* (all COL). 1939: *The Lady's From Kentucky,* PAR; *Good Girls Go to Paris, The Amazing Mr. Williams.* 1940: *The Doctor Takes a Wife, He Stayed for*

Breakfast, This Thing Called Love, Here Comes Mr. Jordan, Bedtime Story.
1942: *They All Kissed the Bride, My Sister Eileen* (all COL). 1943: *The Heavenly Body*, M-G-M. 1944: *Once Upon a Time*. 1945: *She Wouldn't Say Yes*. 1947: *Down to Earth* (all COL). 1949: *The Great Lover*, PAR. 1950: *Love That Brute*, 20TH; *Louisa*, U-I. 1951: *Up Front*, U-I. 1952: *Because You're Mine*, M-G-M. 1953: *Let's Do It Again*, COL. 1956: *Forever Darling*, M-G-M.

DANIEL HALLER (1926–)
1965: *Die, Monster, Die!* 1967: *Devil's Angels*. 1968: *The Wild Racers* (all AIP). 1970: *Paddy* (Ireland), AA; *The Dunwich Horror*, AIP; *Pieces of Dreams*, UA.

VICTOR HUGO HALPERIN (1895–)
1930: *Party Girl*, TIFFANY. 1931: *Ex-Flame*, TIFFANY. 1932: *White Zombie*, UA. 1933: *Supernatural*, PAR. 1936: *I Conquer the Sea*, ACADEMY PICTURES; *Revolt of the Zombies*, ACADEMY PICTURES. 1937: *Nation Aflame*, TREASURE PICTURES. 1939: *Torture Ship*, PRODUCERS PICTURES. 1940: *Buried Alive*, PDC. 1942: *Girls Town*, PRC.

CURTIS HARRINGTON (1928–)
1963: *Night Tide*, AIP. 1966: *Queen of Blood*, AIP. 1967: *Games*, U. 1971: *What's the Matter with Helen?*, UA; *Who Slew Auntie Roo?*, AIP. 1973: *The Killing Kind*, MEDIA TREND–GEORGE EDWARDS PRODUCTION.

HARVEY HART (1928–)
1965: *Bus Riley's Back in Town, Dark Intruder*. 1967: *Sullivan's Empire* (with Thomas Carr) (all U). 1968: *The Sweet Ride*, 20TH. 1971: *Fortune and Men's Eyes*, M-G-M. 1973: *The Pyx* (Canada), CINERAMA.

BYRON HASKIN (1899–)
1947: *I Walk Alone*, PAR. 1948: *Man-Eater of Kumaon*, U-I. 1949: *Too Late for Tears*, UA. 1950: *Treasure Island* (England), RKO. 1951: *Tarzan's Peril*, RKO; *Warpath, Silver City*. 1952: *The Denver and Rio Grande*. 1953: *The War of the Worlds* (all PAR); *His Majesty O'Keefe*, WB. 1954: *The Naked Jungle*, PAR. 1955: *Conquest of Space*, PAR; *Long John Silver* (Australia), DISTRIBUTORS CORPORATION OF AMERICA. 1956: *The First Texan*, AA; *The Boss*, UA. 1958: *From the Earth to the Moon*, WB. 1959: *The Little Savage*, 20TH. 1960: *Jet Over the Atlantic*, INTER CONTINENT

RELEASING ORGANIZATION; *September Storm*, 20TH. 1961: *Armored Command*, AA. 1963: *Captain Sinbad*, M-G-M. 1964: *Robinson Crusoe on Mars*, PAR. 1968: *The Power*, M-G-M.

VICTOR HEERMAN (1892–)
1930: *Personality*, COL; *Paramount on Parade* (with O. Brower, E. Goulding, E. H. Knopf, R. V. Lee, E. Lubitsch, L. Mendes, V. Schertzinger, E. Sutherland, F. Tuttle), *Animal Crackers, Sea Legs* (all PAR).

MONTE HELLMAN
1959: *The Beast from Haunted Cave*, FILMGROUP. 1965: *Flight to Fury* (Philippines), *Back Door to Hell* (Philippines), 20TH. 1971: *The Shooting*, JACK H. HARRIS ENTERPRISES; *Ride in the Whirlwind*, JACK H. HARRIS ENTERPRISES; *Two-Lane Blacktop*, U. 1974: *Shatter* (Hong Kong), *Cockfighter*, NEW WORLD.

PAUL HENRIED (1907–)
1952: *For Men Only*, LIPPERT. 1956: *A Woman's Devotion*, REP. 1958: *Girls on the Loose*, U-I; *Live Fast, Die Young*, U-I. 1964: *Dead Ringer*, WB. 1966: *Blues for Lovers* (England), 20TH.

JESSIE HIBBS (1906–)
1953: *The All American*. 1954: *Ride Clear of Diablo, Black Horse Canyon, Rails into Laramie, The Yellow Mountain*. 1955: *To Hell and Back, The Spoilers*. 1956: *World in My Corner, Walk the Proud Land*. 1957: *Joe Butterfly*. 1958: *Ride a Crooked Trail* (all U-I).

GEORGE W. HILL (1895–1934)
1929: *The Flying Fleet*. 1930: *The Big House, Min and Bill*. 1931: *The Secret Six, Hell Divers*. 1933: *Clear All Wires* (all M-G-M).

ARTHUR HILLER (1923–)
1957: *The Careless Years*, UA. 1963: *Miracle of the White Stallions*, BV; *The Wheeler Dealers*, M-G-M. 1964: *The Americanization of Emily*, M-G-M. 1966: *Promise Her Anything* (England), PAR; *Penelope*, M-G-M. 1967: *Tobruk*, U; *The Tiger Makes Out*, COL. 1969: *Popi*, UA. 1970: *The Out-of-Towners*, PAR; *Love Story*, PAR. 1971: *The Hospital*, UA. 1972: *Man of La Mancha* (Italy), UA. 1974: *The Crazy World of Julius Vrooder*, 20TH. 1975: *The Man in the Glass Booth*, AMERICAN FILM THEATRE.

LAMBERT HILLYER (1889–)
1930: *Beau Bandit*, RKO. 1932: *The Deadline, One-Man Law, The Fighting Fool, South of the Rio Grande, White Eagle; Hello, Trouble.* 1933: *The Forbidden Trail, Dangerous Crossroads, The Sundown Rider, The California Trail, Unknown Valley, Police Car 17, Before Midnight, Master of Men.* 1934: *The Fighting Code, Once to Every Woman, One Is Guilty, The Man Trailer, The Defense Rests, Most Precious Thing in Life, Against the Law, Men of the Night.* 1935: *Behind the Evidence, In Spite of Danger, Men of the Hour, Awakening of Jim Burke, Guard That Girl!, Superspeed* (all COL). 1936: *The Invisible Ray, Dangerous Waters, Dracula's Daughter* (all U). 1937: *Speed to Spare, Girls Can Play, Women in Prison* (all COL). 1938: *My Old Kentucky Home*, MONO; *All-American Sweetheart*, COL; *Extortion*, COL. 1939: *Convict's Code, Should a Girl Marry?, Girl from Rio* (all MONO). 1940: *The Durango Kid.* 1941: *The Pinto Kid, North from the Lone Star, The Wildcat of Tucson, The Return of Daniel Boone, Beyond Sacramento, Hands Across the Rockies, The Son of Davy Crockett, The Medico of Painted Springs, King of Dodge City, Prairie Stranger, Thunder Over the Prairie, Roaring Frontiers, The Royal Mounted Patrol.* 1942: *North of the Rockies, The Devil's Trail, Prairie Gunsmoke, Vengeance of the West* (all COL). 1943: *Fighting Frontier*, RKO; *Six-Gun Gospel, The Stranger from Pecos, The Texas Kid.* 1944: *Smart Guy, Partners of the Trail, Law Men, West of the Rio Grande, Land of the Outlaws, Ghost Guns* (all MONO). 1945: *Beyond the Pecos*, U; *Flame of the West, Stranger from Santa Fe, South of the Rio Grande, The Lost Trail, Frontier Feud.* 1946: *Border Bandits, Under Arizona Skies, The Gentleman from Texas, Trigger Fingers, Shadows on the Range, Silver Range.* 1947: *Raiders of the South, Valley of Fear, Trailing Danger, Land of the Lawless, The Law Comes to Gunsight* (all MONO); *The Hat Box Mystery*, SCREEN GUILD; *The Case of the Baby Sitter*, SCREEN GUILD; *Flashing Guns, Prairie Express, Gun Talk.* 1948: *Song of the Drifter, Overland Trails, Oklahoma Blues, Crossed Trails, Partners of the Sunset, Frontier Agent, Range Renegades, The Fighting Ranger, The Sheriff of Medicine Bow, Outlaw Brand.* 1949: *Gun Runner, Gun Law Justice, Trails End, Haunted Trails, Riders of the Dusk, Range Land* (all MONO).

JACK HIVELY
1939: *They Made Her a Spy, Panama Lady, The Spellbinder, Three Sons, Two Thoroughbreds.* 1940: *The Saint's Double Trouble, The Saint Takes Over, Anne of Windy Poplars, Laddie.* 1941: *The Saint in Palm Springs,*

They Met in Argentina (with Leslie Goodwins), *Father Takes a Wife, Four Jacks and a Jill* (all RKO). 1942: *Street of Chance*, PAR. 1948: *Are You With It?*, U-I.

WILLIAM HOLE, JR.

1957: *Hell Bound*, UA. 1959: *Speed Crazy*, AA; *The Ghost of Dragstrip Hollow*, AIP; *Four Fast Guns*, U-I. 1962: *The Devil's Hand*, CROWN INTERNATIONAL; *Twist All Night* (*The Continental Twist*), AIP.

JERRY HOPPER (1907–)

1952: *The Atomic City, Hurricane Smith*. 1953: *Pony Express*. 1954: *Alaska Seas, The Secret of the Incas* (all PAR); *Naked Alibi*. 1955: *Smoke Signal, The Private War of Major Benson, One Desire, The Square Jungle*. 1956: *Never Say Goodbye, The Toy Tiger* (all U-I); *The Sharkfighters*, UA; *Everything but the Truth*, U-I. 1958: *The Missouri Traveler*, BV. 1961: *Blueprint for Robbery*, PAR. 1970: *Madron*, 4-STAR EXCELSIOR.

HARRY HORNER (1910–)

1952: *Red Planet Mars*, UA; *Beware, My Lovely*, RKO. 1953: *Vicki*. 1954: *New Faces*. 1955: *A Life in the Balance* (all 20TH). 1956: *Man from Del Rio*, UA; *The Wild Party*, UA.

H. BRUCE ("LUCKY") HUMBERSTONE (1903–)

1932: *Strangers of the Evening*, TIFFANY; *The Crooked Circle*, WW; *If I Had a Million* (with J. Cruze, E. Lubitsch, N. Z. McLeod, S. Roberts, W. A. Seiter, N. Taurog), PAR. 1933: *King of the Jungle* (with Max Marcin), PAR. 1934: *The Merry Wives of Reno*, WB; *Goodbye Love*, RKO; *The Dragon Murder Case*, FN. 1935: *Ladies Love Danger*, FOX; *Silk Hat Kid*, FOX; *Three Live Ghosts*, M-G-M. 1936: *Charlie Chan at the Race Track, Charlie Chan at the Opera*. 1937: *Charlie Chan at the Olympics, Checkers*. 1938: *In Old Chicago* (with Henry King; Humberstone directed fire sequence), *Rascals, Time Out for Murder, Charlie Chan in Honolulu*. 1939: *Pack up Your Troubles*. 1940: *Lucky Cisco Kid* (all 20TH); *The Quarterback*, PAR. 1941: *Tall, Dark and Handsome, Sun Valley Serenade, I Wake Up Screaming*. 1942: *To the Shores of Tripoli, Iceland*. 1943: *Hello, Frisco, Hello*. 1944: *Pin-Up Girl* (all 20TH). 1945: *Wonder Man*, RKO; *Within These Walls*. 1946: *Three Little Girls in Blue*. 1947: *The Homestretch*. 1948: *Fury at Furnace Creek* (all 20TH). 1950: *South Sea Sinner*, U-I. 1951: *Happy Go Lovely*, RKO. 1952: *She's Working Her Way Through College*, WB. 1953:

The Desert Song, WB. 1955: *Ten Wanted Men*, COL; *The Purple Mask*, U-I. 1957: *Tarzan and the Lost Safari* (England), M-G-M. 1958: *Tarzan's Fight for Life* (England), M-G-M. 1962: *Madison Avenue*, 20TH.

BRIAN G. HUTTON (1935–)
1965: *Wild Seed*, U. 1966: *The Pad (and How to Use It)*, U. 1968: *Sol Madrid*. 1969: *Where Eagles Dare*. 1970: *Kelly's Heroes* (all M-G-M). 1972: *X Y & Zee*, COL. 1973; *Night Watch*, AVCO EMBASSY.

ROBERT HUTTON (1920–)
1962: *The Slime People*, HANSEN ENTERPRISES–STATES' RIGHTS.

LEIGH JASON (JACOBSON) (1904–)
1929: *Wolves of the City, Eyes of the Underworld, Tip Off* (all U). 1933: *High Gear*, KEN GOLDSMITH PRODUCTIONS. 1936: *Love on a Bet, The Bride Walks Out, That Girl from Paris*. 1937: *New Faces of 1937, Wise Girl*. 1938: *The Mad Miss Manton*. 1939: *The Flying Irishman, Career* (all RKO). 1941: *Model Wife*, U; *Three Girls About Town*, COL; *Lady for a Night*, REP. 1943: *Dangerous Blondes*. 1944: *Nine Girls, Carolina Blues*. 1946: *Meet Me on Broadway* (all COL). 1947: *Lost Honeymoon, Out of the Blue, Man from Texas* (all EL). 1952: *Okinawa*, COL.

LAMONT JOHNSON
1967: *A Covenant with Death*, WB. 1968: *Kona Coast*, WB-7A. 1970: *My Sweet Charlie*, U; *The McKenzie Break* (England), UA. 1971: *A Gunfight*, PAR. 1972: *The Groundstar Conspiracy*, U; *You'll Like My Mother*, U. 1973: *The Last American Hero*, 20TH. 1974: *Visit to a Chief's Son*, UA.

NUNNALLY JOHNSON (1897–)
1954: *Night People, Black Widow*. 1955: *How to Be Very, Very Popular*. 1956: *The Man in the Gray Flannel Suit*. 1957: *Oh, Men! Oh, Women!, The Three Faces of Eve*. 1959: *The Man Who Understood Women* (all 20TH). 1960: *The Angel Wore Red* (Italy), M-G-M.

HARMON C. JONES (1911–)
1951: *As Young as You Feel*. 1952: *The Pride of St. Louis, Bloodhounds of Broadway*. 1953: *The Silver Whip, City of Bad Men, The Kid from Left Field*. 1954: *Gorilla at Large, Princess of the Nile* (all 20TH). 1955: *Target Zero*, WB. 1956: *A Day of Fury*, U-I; *Canyon River*. 1958: *The Beast of*

Budapest, Bullwhip, Wolf Larsen (all AA). 1966: *Don't Worry, We'll Think of a Title*, UA.

NATHAN (HERTZ) JURAN (1907–)

1952: *The Black Castle*. 1953: *Gunsmoke, Law and Order, The Golden Blade, Tumbleweed* (all U-I). 1954: *Highway Dragnet*, AA; *Drums Across the River*, U-I. 1955: *The Crooked Web*, COL. 1957: *Le Imprese di una Spada Leggendària* (with Frank McDonald; Italy); *The Deadly Mantis*, U-I; *Hellcats of the Navy, Twenty Million Miles to Earth*. 1958: *The Seventh Voyage of Sinbad, Good Day for a Hanging* (all COL). 1961: *Flight of the Lost Balloon*, WOOLNER BROTHERS. 1962: *Jack the Giant Killer*, UA. 1963: *Siege of the Saxons*. 1964: *First Men In the Moon*. 1965: *East of Sudan* (England). 1970: *Land Raiders* (Spain) (all COL). 1973: *The Boy Who Cried Werewolf*, U.

JOSEPH KANE (1897–)

1935: *Tumbling Tumbleweeds, Melody Trail, The Sagebrush Troubadour*. 1936: *The Lawless Nineties, King of the Pecos, The Lonely Trail, Guns and Guitars, Oh, Susanna!, Ride, Ranger, Ride*. 1937: *Paradise Express, Git Along Little Dogies, Ghost Town Gold, Round-Up Time in Texas, The Old Corral; Come On, Cowboys!, Gunsmoke Ranch, Public Cowboy No. One, Yodelin' Kid from Pine Ridge, Boots and Saddles, Springtime in the Rockies*. 1938: *The Old Barn Dance, Born to Be Wild, Arson Gang Busters, Under Western Skies, Gold Mine in the Sky, Man from Music Mountain, Billy the Kid Returns; Come On, Rangers!, Shine on Harvest Moon*. 1939: *Rough Riders' Round-Up, Frontier Pony Express, Southward Ho!, In Old Caliente, In Old Monterey, Wall Street Cowboy, The Arizona Kid, Days of Jesse James, Saga of Death Valley*. 1940: *Young Buffalo Bill, The Carson City Kid, The Ranger and the Lady, Colorado, Young Bill Hickok, The Border Legion*. 1941: *Robin Hood of the Pecos, In Old Cheyenne, Sheriff of Tombstone, The Great Train Robbery, Nevada City, Rags to Riches, Bad Man of Deadwood, Jesse James at Bay, Red River Valley*. 1942: *The Man from Cheyenne, South of Santa Fe, Sunset on the Desert, Romance of the Range, Sons of the Pioneers, Sunset Serenade, Heart of the Golden West, Ridin' Down the Canyon*. 1943: *Idaho, King of the Cowboys, Song of Texas, Silver Spurs, The Man from Music Mountain, Hands Across the Border*. 1944: *The Cowboy and the Senorita, The Yellow Rose of Texas, Song of Nevada*. 1945: *Flame of the Barbary Coast, The Cheaters, Dakota*. 1946: *In Old Sacramento, The Plainsman and the Lady*. 1947: *Wyoming*. 1948: *Old Los*

Angeles, The Gallant Legion, The Plunderers. 1949: *The Last Bandit, Brimstone.* 1950: *Rock Island Trail, The Savage Horde, California Passage.* 1951: *Oh! Susanna, Fighting Coast Guard, The Sea Hornet.* 1952: *Hoodlum Empire, Woman of the North Country, Ride the Man Down.* 1953: *San Antone, Fair Wind to Java, Sea of Lost Ships.* 1954: *Jubilee Trail.* 1955: *Hell's Outpost, Timberjack, The Road to Denver, The Vanishing American.* 1956: *The Maverick Queen, Thunder Over Arizona, Accused of Murder.* 1957: *Duel at Apache Wells, Spoilers of the Forest, Last Stagecoach West, The Crooked Circle.* 1958: *Gunfire at Indian Gap, The Notorious Mr. Monks, The Lawless Eighties, The Man Who Died Twice* (all REP). 1966: *Here Comes That Nashville Sound (Country Boy)*, AMBASSADOR FILMS. 1967: *Search for the Evil One*, AMBASSADOR FILMS. 1968: *Track of Thunder*, UA. 1971: *Smoke in the Wind* (with, uncredited, Andy Brennan; unreleased).

PHIL KARLSON (KARLSTEIN) (1908–)

1944: *A Wave, a Wac and a Marine.* 1945: *G. I. Honeymoon, There Goes Kelly, The Shanghai Cobra.* 1946: *Swing Parade of 1946, Live Wires, Dark Alibi, Behind the Mask, Bowery Bombshell, The Missing Lady, Wife Wanted* (all MONO). 1947: *Black Gold*, AA; *Kilroy Was Here, Louisiana.* 1948: *Rocky* (all MONO); *Adventure in Silverado, Thunderhoof.* 1949: *Ladies of the Chorus* (all COL); *The Big Cat*, EL; *Down Memory Lane*, EL. 1950: *The Iroquois Trail*, UA. 1951: *Lorna Doone, The Texas Rangers, Mask of the Avenger.* 1952: *Scandal Sheet, The Brigand* (all COL); *Kansas City Confidential*, UA. 1953: *99 River Street*, UA. 1954: *They Rode West*, COL. 1955: *Tight Spot*, COL; *Hell's Island*, PAR; *Five Against the House*, COL; *The Phenix City Story*, AA. 1957: *The Brothers Rico*, COL. 1958: *Gunman's Walk*, COL. 1960: *Hell to Eternity*, AA; *Key Witness*, M-G-M. 1961: *The Secret Ways*, U-I; *The Young Doctors*, UA. 1962: *Kid Galahad*, UA. 1963: *Rampage*, WB. 1966: *The Silencers.* 1967: *A Time for Killing.* 1969: *The Wrecking Crew* (all COL). 1970: *Hornets' Nest* (Italy), UA. 1972: *Ben*, CINERAMA. 1973: *Walking Tall*, CINERAMA. 1975: *Framed*, PAR.

GEORGE S. KAUFMAN (1889–1961)

1947: *The Senator Was Indiscreet*, U-I.

WILLIAM KEIGHLEY (1889–)

1932: *The Match King* (with Howard Bretherton), FN. 1933: *Ladies They Talk About* (with Howard Bretherton), WB. 1934: *Easy to Love*, WB;

Journal of a Crime, FN; *Dr. Monica, Kansas City Princess, Big Hearted Herbert* (all WB); *Babbitt*, FN. 1935: *The Right to Live*, WB; *G-Men*, WB; *Mary Jane's Pa*, FN; *Special Agent*, WB; *Stars Over Broadway*. WB. 1936: *The Singing Kid*, FN; *Bullets or Ballots*, FN; *The Green Pastures* (with Marc Connelly), *God's Country and the Woman*. 1937: *The Prince and the Pauper, Varsity Show*. 1938: *The Adventures of Robin Hood* (with Michael Curtiz), *Brother Rat*. 1939: *Each Dawn I Die*. 1940: *The Fighting 69th, Torrid Zone, No Time for Comedy*. 1941: *Four Mothers, The Bride Came C.O.D., The Man Who Came to Dinner*. 1942: *George Washington Slept Here* (all WB). 1947: *Honeymoon*, RKO. 1948: *The Street with No Name*, 20TH. 1950: *Rocky Mountain*. 1951: *Close to My Heart*. 1953: *The Master of Ballantrae* (all WB).

HARRY KELLER (1913–)

1950: *The Blonde Bandit, Tarnished*. 1951: *Fort Dodge Stampede, Desert of Lost Men* (all REP). 1952: *Rose of Cimarron*, 20TH; *Leadville Gunslinger, Black Hills Ambush, Thundering Caravans*. 1953: *Marshal of Cedar Rock, Savage Frontier, Bandits of the West, El Paso Stampede*. 1954: *Red River Shore, Phantom Stallion* (all REP). 1956: *The Unguarded Moment*. 1957: *Man Afraid, Quantez*. 1958: *The Day of the Bad Man, The Female Animal, Voice in the Mirror, Step Down to Terror*. 1960: *Seven Ways from Sundown*. 1961: *Tammy Tell Me True*. 1962: *Six Black Horses*. 1963: *Tammy and the Doctor* (all U-I). 1964: *The Brass Bottle*, U. 1968: *In Enemy Country*, U.

RAY KELLOGG

1959: *The Giant Gila Monster*, AIP; *The Killer Shrews*, HOLLYWOOD PICTURE CORP. 1960: *My Dog Buddy*, COL. 1968: *The Green Berets* (with John Wayne), WB-7A.

ERLE C. KENTON (1896–)

1929: *Trial Marriage, Father and Son, Song of Love*. 1930: *Mexicali Rose, A Royal Romance*. 1931: *The Last Parade, Lover Come Back* (all COL); *Leftover Ladies*, TIFFANY; *X Marks the Spot*, TIFFANY. 1932: *Stranger in Town*, WB; *Guilty as Hell*. 1933: *Island of Lost Souls, From Hell to Heaven, Disgraced!, Big Executive*. 1934: *Search for Beauty, You're Telling Me* (all PAR). 1935: *The Best Man Wins, Party Wire, The Public Menace, Grand Exit*. 1936: *Devil's Squadron, Counterfeit, End of the Trail*. 1937: *Devil's Playground, Racketeers in Exile* (all COL); *She Asked for It*, PAR. 1938: *The*

Lady Objects, COL; *Little Tough Guys in Society*, U. 1939: *Everything's on Ice, Escape to Paradise.* 1940: *Remedy for Riches* (all RKO). 1941: *Petticoat Politics*, REP; *Melody for Three*, RKO; *Naval Academy*, COL; *They Meet Again*, RKO; *Flying Cadets.* 1942: *Frisco Lil, North to the Klondike, The Ghost of Frankenstein, Pardon My Sarong, Who Done It?* 1943: *How's About It?, It Ain't Hay, Always a Bridesmaid.* 1945: *House of Frankenstein, She Gets Her Man, House of Dracula.* 1946: *The Cat Creeps, Little Miss Big* (all U). 1948: *Bob and Sally*, SOCIAL GUIDANCE ENTERPRISES. 1950: *One Too Many*, HALLMARK.

BRUCE KESSLER

1968: *Angels from Hell*, AIP; *Killers Three*, AIP. 1969: *The Gay Deceivers*, FANFARE. 1971: *Simon, King of the Witches*, FANFARE.

LOUIS KING (1898–1962)

1929: *The Vagabond Cub, The Freckled Rascal, The Little Savage* (all RKO); *Pals of the Prairie.* 1930: *The Lone Rider, Shadow Ranch, Men Without Law.* 1931: *Desert Vengeance, The Fighting Sheriff, Border Law, The Deceiver* (all COL). 1932: *Police Court, The County Fair, Arm of the Law* (all MONO); *Drifting Souls*, TOWER. 1933: *Robbers' Roost, Life in the Raw.* 1934: *La Ciudad de Carton* (Spanish language), *Murder in Trinidad, Pursued, Bachelor of Arts.* 1935: *Julieta Compra un Hijo* (Spanish language), *Charlie Chan in Egypt, Angelita* (Spanish language) (all FOX). 1936: *Road Gang*, WB; *Special Investigator*, RKO; *Song of the Saddle*, FN; *The Bengal Tiger.* 1937: *Melody for Two, That Man's Here Again, Draeger-man Courage* (all WB); *Wild Money*, PAR; *Bulldog Drummond Comes Back*, PAR; *Wine, Women and Horses*, WB; *Bulldog Drummond's Revenge.* 1938: *Tip-Off Girls, Hunted Men, Bulldog Drummond in Africa, Illegal Traffic; Tom Sawyer, Detective.* 1939: *Persons in Hiding, Undercover Doctor.* 1940: *Seventeen, Typhoon, The Way of All Flesh, Moon Over Burma* (all PAR). 1942: *Young America.* 1943: *Chetniks.* 1944: *Ladies of Washington.* 1945: *Thunderhead—Son of Flicka.* 1946: *Smoky.* 1947: *Thunder in the Valley.* 1948: *Green Grass of Wyoming.* 1949: *Sand* (all 20TH); *Mrs. Mike*, UA. 1950: *Frenchie*, U-I. 1952: *The Lion and the Horse*, WB. 1953: *Powder River*, 20TH; *Sabre Jet*, UA. 1954: *Dangerous Mission*, RKO. 1956: *Massacre*, 20TH.

EDWIN H. KNOPF (1899–)

1929: *Fast Company.* 1930: *Slightly Scarlet* (with Louis Gasnier), *The Light of Western Stars* (with Otto Brower), *Paramount on Parade* (with

D. Arzner, O. Brower, E. Goulding, V. Heerman, R. V. Lee, E. Lubitsch, L. Mendes, V. Schertzinger, E. Sutherland, F. Tuttle), *Border Legion* (with O. Brower), *The Santa Fe Trail* (with O. Brower), *Only Saps Work* (with Cyril Gardner) (all PAR). 1932: *Nice Women*, U. 1951: *The Law and the Lady*, M-G-M.

HOWARD W. KOCH (1916–)

1954: *Shield for Murder* (with Edmond O'Brien), UA. 1955: *Big House, U.S.A.*, UA. 1957: *Untamed Youth*, WB; *Bop Girl, Jungle Heat, The Girl in Black Stockings*. 1958: *Fort Bowie* (all UA); *Violent Road*, WB; *Frankenstein–1970*, AA; *Andy Hardy Comes Home*, M-G-M. 1959: *The Last Mile*, UA; *Born Reckless*, WB. 1973: *Badge 373*, PAR.

HENRY KOSTER (HERMANN KOSTERLITZ) (1905–)

1932: *Das Abenteuer der Thea Roland* (Germany). 1933: *Das hässliche Mädchen* (Germany). 1934: *Kleine Mutti* (Germany). 1935: *Peter* (Hungary), U. 1936: *Marie Bashkirtzeff* (Germany). 1937: *Three Smart Girls, One Hundred Men and a Girl*. 1938: *The Rage of Paris*. 1939: *Three Smart Girls Grow Up, First Love*. 1940: *Spring Parade*. 1941: *It Started with Eve*. 1942: *Between Us Girls* (all U). 1944: *Music for Millions*. 1946: *Two Sisters from Boston*. 1947: *The Unfinished Dance* (all M-G-M); *The Bishop's Wife*, RKO. 1948: *The Luck of the Irish*, 20TH. 1949: *Come to the Stable*, 20TH; *The Inspector General*, WB. 1950: *Wabash Avenue*, 20TH; *My Blue Heaven*, 20TH; *Harvey*, U-I. 1951: *No Highway in the Sky, Mr. Belvedere Rings the Bell, Elopement*. 1952: *O. Henry's Full House* (with H. Hathaway, H. Hawks, H. King, J. Negulesco), *Stars and Stripes Forever, My Cousin Rachel*. 1953: *The Robe*. 1954: *Desiree*. 1955: *A Man Called Peter, The Virgin Queen; Good Morning, Miss Dove*. 1956: *D-Day, the Sixth of June* (all 20TH); *The Power and the Prize*, M-G-M. 1957: *My Man Godfrey*, U-I. 1958: *Fraulein*, 20TH. 1959: *The Naked Maja* (Italy), UA. 1960: *The Story of Ruth*, 20TH. 1961: *Flower Drum Song*, U-I. 1962: *Mr. Hobbs Takes a Vacation*. 1963: *Take Her, She's Mine*. 1965: *Dear Brigitte* (all 20TH). 1966: *The Singing Nun*, M-G-M.

BERNARD KOWALSKI (c. 1933–)

1958: *Hot Car Girl*, AA; *Night of the Blood Beast*, AIP. 1959: *Attack of the Giant Leeches*, AIP; *Blood and Steel*, 20TH. 1969: *Krakatoa, East of Java*, CINERAMA; *Stiletto*, AVCO EMBASSY. 1970: *Macho Callahan*, AVCO EMBASSY. 1973: *Sssssss*, U.

DAVID KRAMARKSY
1956: *The Beast with a Million Eyes,* AMERICAN RELEASING CORPORATION.

NORMAN KRASNA (1909–)
1943: *Princess O'Rourke,* WB. 1950: *The Big Hangover,* M-G-M. 1956: *The Ambassador's Daughter,* UA.

HARRY LACHMAN (1886–)
1929: *Week-End Wives* (England), WW; *Under the Greenwood Tree* (England). 1930: *Song of Soho* (England), *The Yellow Mask* (England). 1931: *The Love Habit* (England) (all BI). 1932: *Aren't We All?* (England), *La Couturière de Luneville* (France). 1933: *Mistigri* (France) (all PAR); *The Face in the Sky,* FOX; *The Outsider* (England), M-G-M; *Paddy, the Next Best Thing,* FOX. 1934: *George White's Scandals* (with George White, Thornton Freeland), FOX; *I Like It That Way,* U; *Baby, Take a Bow, Nada Mas Que una Mujer* (Spanish language). 1935: *Dante's Inferno, Dressed to Thrill* (all FOX). 1936: *Charlie Chan at the Circus,* 20TH; *Our Relations,* M-G-M; *The Man Who Lived Twice.* 1937: *The Devil Is Driving, It Happened in Hollywood.* 1938: *No Time to Marry* (all COL). 1940: *They Came by Night* (England), *Murder Over New York.* 1941: *Dead Men Tell, Charlie Chan in Rio.* 1942: *Castle in the Desert, The Loves of Edgar Allan Poe, Dr. Renault's Secret* (all 20TH).

CHARLES FRED LAMONT (1898–)
1934: *The Curtain Falls,* CHEST. 1935: *Tomorrow's Youth,* MONO; *The World Accuses, Son of Steel, False Pretenses* (all CHEST); *Gigolette,* RKO; *A Shot in the Dark, Circumstantial Evidence, The Girl Who Came Back; Happiness, C.O.D.; The Lady in Scarlet.* 1936: *Ring Around the Moon, Little Red Schoolhouse, Below the Deadline, August Week-End, The Dark Hour, Lady Luck* (all CHEST); *Bulldog Edition,* REP. 1937: *Wallaby Jim of the Island.* 1938: *International Crime, Shadows Over Shanghai* (all GN); *Slander House,* PROGRESSIVE PICTURES; *Cipher Bureau,* GN; *The Long Shot,* GN. 1939: *Pride of the Navy,* REP; *Panama Patrol,* GN; *Inside Information, Unexpected Father, Little Accident.* 1940: *Oh, Johnny, How You Can Love!, Sandy Is a Lady; Love, Honor and Oh-Baby!, Give Us Wings.* 1941: *San Antonio Rose, Sing Another Chorus, Moonlight in Hawaii, Melody Lane, Road Agent.* 1942: *Don't Get Personal, You're Telling Me, Almost Married* (all U); *Hi, Neighbor,* REP; *Get Hep to Love, When*

Johnny Comes Marching Home. 1943: *It Comes up Love, Mr. Big, Hit the Ice, Fired Wife, Top Man.* 1944: *Chip off the Old Block, Her Primitive Man, The Merry Monahans, Bowery to Broadway.* 1945: *Salome, Where She Danced; That's the Spirit, Frontier Gal.* 1946: *She Wrote the Book, The Runaround* (all U). 1947: *Slave Girl,* U-I. 1948: *The Untamed Breed,* COL. 1949: *Ma and Pa Kettle, Bagdad.* 1950: *Ma and Pa Kettle Go to Town, I Was a Shoplifter, Curtain Call at Cactus Creek, Abbott and Costello in the Foreign Legion.* 1951: *Abbott and Costello Meet the Invisible Man, Comin' Round the Mountain, Flame of Araby* (all U-I) 1952: *Abbott and Costello Meet Captain Kidd,* WB. 1953: *Abbott and Costello Go to Mars, Ma and Pa Kettle on Vacation, Abbott and Costello Meet Dr. Jekyll and Mr. Hyde.* 1954: *Ma and Pa Kettle at Home* (all U-I); *Untamed Heiress,* REP; *Ricochet Romance,* U-I. 1955: *Carolina Cannonball,* REP; *Abbott and Costello Meet the Keystone Kops,* U-I; *Abbott and Costello Meet the Mummy,* U-I; *Lay That Rifle Down,* REP. 1956: *The Kettles in the Ozarks,* U-I; *Francis in the Haunted House,* U-I.

LEW LANDERS (LOUIS FRIEDLANDER) (1901–1962)

1935: *The Raven, Stormy.* 1936: *Parole!* (all U); *Without Orders, Night Waitress.* 1937: *They Wanted to Marry, The Man Who Found Himself, You Can't Buy Luck, Border Cafe, Flight from Glory, Living on Love, Danger Patrol.* 1938: *Crashing Hollywood, Double Danger, Condemned Women, Law of the Underworld, Blind Alibi, Sky Giant, Smashing the Rackets, Annabel Takes a Tour.* 1939: *Pacific Liner, Twelve Crowded Hours, Fixer Dugan, The Girl and the Gambler, Bad Lands, Conspiracy* (all RKO). 1940: *Honeymoon Deferred, Enemy Agent, La Conga Nights, Ski Patrol* (all U); *Wagons Westward, Sing, Dance, Plenty Hot; Girl from Havana* (all REP); *Slightly Tempted,* U. 1941: *Ridin' on a Rainbow,* REP; *Lucky Devils,* U; *Back in the Saddle,* REP; *The Singing Hill,* REP; *I Was a Prisoner on Devil's Island, Mystery Ship, The Stork Pays Off.* 1942: *The Man Who Returned to Life, Alias Boston Blackie, Canal Zone, Harvard, Here I Come; Not a Ladies' Man, Submarine Raider, Cadets on Parade, Atlantic Convoy, Sabotage Squad, The Boogie Man Will Get You, Smith of Minnesota, Stand by All Networks, Junior Army.* 1943: *After Midnight with Boston Blackie, Redhead from Manhattan, Murder in Times Square, Power of the Press, Doughboys in Ireland* (all COL); *Deerslayer,* REP. 1944: *Cowboy Canteen, The Ghost That Walks Alone, The Return of the Vampire, Two-Man Submarine, Stars on Parade, The Black Parachute, U-Boat Prisoner, Swing in the Saddle* (all COL); *I'm from Arkansas,* PRC. 1945:

Crime, Inc., PRC; *The Power of the Whistler,* COL; *Trouble Chasers,*
MONO; *Follow That Woman,* PAR; *Arson Squad, Shadow of Terror, The
Enchanted Forest* (all PRC); *Tokyo Rose,* PAR. 1946: *The Mask of Dijon,*
PRC; *A Close Call for Boston Blackie,* COL; *The Truth About Murder,*
RKO; *Death Valley,* SCREEN GUILD. 1947: *Danger Street,* PAR; *Seven
Keys to Baldpate, Under the Tonto Rim, Thunder Mountain* (all RKO);
The Son of Rusty, Devil Ship. 1948: *My Dog Rusty* (all COL); *Adventures
of Gallant Bess,* EL; *Inner Sanctum,* FILM CLASSICS. 1949: *Stagecoach
Kid,* RKO; *Law of the Barbary Coast, Air Hostess, Barbary Pirate* (all
COL). 1950: *Davy Crockett, Indian Scout,* UA; *Girls' School,* COL; *Dyna-
mite Pass,* RKO; *Tyrant of the Sea, State Penitentiary, Beauty on Parade,
Chain Gang, Last of the Buccaneers, Revenue Agent* (all COL). 1951: *Blue
Blood,* MONO; *A Yank in Korea, When the Redskins Rode, The Big
Gusher, Hurricane Island, The Magic Carpet, Jungle Manhunt* (all COL).
1952: *Aladdin and His Lamp,* MONO; *Jungle Jim in the Forbidden Land,*
COL; *California Conquest,* COL; *Arctic Flight,* MONO. 1953: *Torpedo
Alley,* AA; *Tangier Incident,* AA; *Man in the Dark,* COL; *Run for the Hills,*
REALART; *Captain John Smith and Pocahontas,* UA. 1954: *Captain Kidd
and the Slave Girl,* UA. 1956: *The Cruel Tower,* AA. 1958: *Hot Rod Gang,*
AIP. 1963: *Terrified,* CROWN INTERNATIONAL.

SIDNEY LANFIELD (1900–)
1930: *Cheer Up and Smile.* 1931: *Three Girls Lost, Hush Money.* 1932:
Dance Team, Society Girl, Hat Check Girl. 1933: *Broadway Bad* (all FOX).
1934: *Moulin Rouge,* UA; *The Last Gentleman,* UA. 1935: *Hold 'Em, Yale,*
PAR; *Red Salute,* UA; *King of Burlesque.* 1936: *Half Angel; Sing, Baby,
Sing; One in a Million.* 1937: *Wake Up and Live, Thin Ice, Love and Hisses.*
1938: *Always Goodbye.* 1939: *The Hound of the Baskervilles, Second
Fiddle, Swanee River* (all 20TH). 1941: *You'll Never Get Rich,* COL. 1942:
The Lady Has Plans, PAR; *My Favorite Blonde,* PAR. 1943: *The Meanest
Man in the World,* 20TH; *Let's Face It.* 1944: *Standing Room Only.* 1945:
Bring on the Girls. 1946: *The Well-Groomed Bride.* 1947: *The Trouble with
Women, Where There's Life* (all PAR). 1948: *Station West,* RKO. 1949:
Sorrowful Jones, PAR. 1951: *The Lemon Drop Kid,* PAR; *Follow the Sun,*
20TH. 1952: *Skirts Ahoy!,* M-G-M.

WALTER LANG (1896–1972)
1929: *Spirit of Youth,* TIFFANY. 1930: *Hello, Sister, Cock o' the Walk*
(with Roy William Neill), *The Big Fight* (all WW); *Brothers,* COL; *The*

Costello Case, WW. 1931: *Command Performance, Hell Bound, Women Go On Forever* (all TIFFANY). 1932: *Meet the Baron*, M-G-M; *No More Orchids*, COL. 1933: *The Warrior's Husband*, FOX. 1934: *Whom the Gods Destroy*, COL; *The Party's Over*, COL; *The Mighty Barnum*, UA. 1935: *Carnival*, COL; *Hooray for Love*, RKO. 1936: *Love Before Breakfast*, U. 1937: *Wife, Doctor and Nurse; Second Honeymoon*. 1938: *The Baroness and the Butler, I'll Give a Million*. 1939: *The Little Princess*. 1940: *The Blue Bird, Star Dust, The Great Profile, Tin Pan Alley*. 1941: *Moon Over Miami, Week-End in Havana*. 1942: *Song of the Islands, The Magnificent Dope*. 1943: *Coney Island*. 1944: *Greenwich Village*. 1945: *State Fair*. 1946: *Sentimental Journey, Claudia and David*. 1947: *Mother Wore Tights*. 1948: *Sitting Pretty, When My Baby Smiles at Me*. 1949: *You're My Everything*. 1950: *Cheaper by the Dozen, The Jackpot*. 1951: *On the Riviera*. 1952: *With a Song in My Heart*. 1953: *Call Me Madam*. 1954: *There's No Business Like Show Business*. 1956: *The King and I*. 1957: *Desk Set* (all 20TH). 1959: *But Not for Me*, PAR. 1960: *Can-Can, The Marriage-Go-Round*. 1961: *Snow White and the Three Stooges* (all 20TH).

ARNOLD LAVEN (1922–)

1952: *Without Warning*. 1953: *Vice Squad*. 1954: *Down Three Dark Streets* (all UA). 1956: *The Rack*, M-G-M. 1957: *The Monster That Challenged the World*, UA; *Slaughter on Tenth Avenue*, U-I. 1958: *Anna Lucasta*. 1962: *Geronimo*. 1965: *The Glory Guys* (all UA). 1967: *Rough Night in Jericho*, U. 1969: *Sam Whiskey*, UA.

REGINALD LE BORG (1902–)

1943: *She's For Me, Calling Dr. Death*. 1944: *Weird Woman, The Mummy's Ghost, Jungle Woman; San Diego, I Love You; Dead Man's Eyes, Destiny* (with Julien Duvivier). 1945: *Honeymoon Ahead* (all U). 1946: *Joe Palooka, Champ*, MONO; *Little Iodine*, UA; *Susie Steps Out*, UA. 1947: *Fall Guy*, MONO; *The Adventures of Don Coyote*, UA; *Philo Vance's Secret Mission*, PRC; *Joe Palooka in the Knockout*, MONO. 1948: *Port Said*, COL; *Joe Palooka in Winner Take All*. 1949: *Fighting Fools, Hold That Baby!, Joe Palooka in the Counterpunch*. 1950: *Young Daniel Boone* (all MONO); *Wyoming Mail*, U-I; *Joe Palooka in the Squared Circle*, MONO. 1951: *G.I. Jane*, LIPPERT; *Joe Palooka in Triple Cross*, MONO. 1952: *Models, Inc.*, MUTUAL PRODUCTIONS. 1953: *Bad Blonde, The Great Jesse James Raid, Sins of Jezebel* (all LIPPERT). 1954: *The White Orchid*. 1956: *The Black Sleep*. 1957: *Voodoo Island, War*

Drums, The Dalton Girls. 1961: *The Flight That Disappeared.* 1962: *Deadly Duo.* 1963: *Diary of a Madman* (all UA). 1964: *The Eyes of Annie Jones* (England), 20TH.

CHARLES LEDERER (c. 1906–)
1942: *Fingers at the Window*, M-G-M. 1951: *On the Loose*, RKO. 1959: *Never Steal Anything Small*, U-I.

D. ROSS LEDERMAN (1895–)
1929: *The Million Dollar Collar*, WB. 1930: *The Man Hunter*, WB. 1931: *The Texas Ranger, Branded, Range Feud.* 1932: *Ridin' for Justice, The Fighting Marshal, High Speed, Riding Tornado, The Texas Cyclone, Daring Danger, Two-Fisted Law, McKenna of the Mounted.* 1933: *Speed Demon, End of the Trail, Whirlwind, The State Trooper, Soldiers of the Storm, Rusty Rides Alone, Silent Men.* 1934: *Hell Bent for Love, The Crime of Helen Stanley, A Man's Game, Beyond the Law, Girl in Danger* (all COL); *Murder in the Clouds*, FN. 1935: *Red Hot Tires*, FN; *Dinky* (with Howard Bretherton), WB; *Moonlight on the Prairie*, WB; *The Case of the Missing Man, Too Tough to Kill.* 1936: *Hell-Ship Morgan, Panic on the Air, Pride of the Marines, The Final Hour, Alibi for Murder; Come Closer, Folks.* 1937: *Counterfeit Lady, I Promise to Pay, Motor Madness, The Frame-Up, The Game That Kills.* 1938: *Juvenile Court, The Little Adventuress, Adventure in Sahara.* 1939: *North of Shanghai* (all COL); *Racketeers of the Range*, RKO. 1940: *Military Academy, Thundering Frontier, Glamour for Sale.* 1941: *Across the Sierras* (all COL); *Father's Son, Strange Alibi, Shadows on the Stairs, Passage from Hongkong.* 1942: *The Body Disappears, Bullet Scars, I Was Framed, Escape from Crime, Busses Roar, The Gorilla Man.* 1943: *Adventure in Iraq, Find the Blackmailer* (all WB). 1944: *The Racket Man.* 1946: *The Phantom Thief, Out of the Depths, The Notorious Lone Wolf, Dangerous Business, Sing While You Dance, Boston Blackie and the Law.* 1947: *The Lone Wolf in Mexico, Key Witness.* 1948: *The Return of the Whistler.* 1950: *Military Academy with That 10th Avenue Gang* (all COL).

ROWLAND V. LEE (1891–)
1929: *Wolf of Wall Street, A Dangerous Woman, Mysterious Dr. Fu Manchu.* 1930: *Paramount on Parade* (with D. Arzner, O. Brower, E. Goulding, V. Heerman, E. Knopf, E. Lubitsch, L. Mendes, V. Schertzinger, E. Sutherland, F. Tuttle), *The Return of Dr. Fu Manchu, Ladies Love Brutes, A Man from Wyoming, Derelict* (all PAR). 1931: *The Ruling Voice,*

FN; *The Guilty Generation*, COL. 1933: *Zoo in Budapest*, FOX. 1934: *I Am Suzanne*, FOX; *The Count of Monte Cristo*, UA; *Over Night* (England; *That Night in London*), MUNDIS; *Gambling*, FOX. 1935: *Cardinal Richelieu*, UA; *The Three Musketeers*, RKO. 1936: *One Rainy Afternoon*, UA. 1937: *Love from a Stranger* (England), UA; *The Toast of New York*, RKO. 1938: *Mother Carey's Chickens*, RKO; *Service De Luxe*, U. 1939: *Son of Frankenstein*, U; *The Sun Never Sets*, PAR; *Tower of London*, U. 1940: *The Son of Monte Cristo*, UA. 1942: *Powder Town*, RKO. 1944: *The Bridge of San Luis Rey*, UA. 1945: *Captain Kidd*, UA.

HERBERT I. LEEDS (?–1954)

1938: *Love on a Budget, Island in the Sky, Keep Smiling, Five of a Kind, Arizona Wildcat*. 1939: *Mr. Moto in Danger Island, The Return of the Cisco Kid, Chicken Wagon Family, Charlie Chan in City in Darkness*. 1940: *Cisco Kid and the Lady, Yesterday's Heroes*. 1941: *Romance of the Rio Grande, Ride on Vaquero; Blue, White and Perfect*. 1942: *The Man Who Wouldn't Die, Just off Broadway, Manila Calling, Time to Kill*. 1946: *It Shouldn't Happen to a Dog*. 1948: *Let's Live Again* (all 20TH). 1950: *Bunco Squad*, RKO; *Father's Wild Game*, MONO.

ROBERT Z. LEONARD (1889–1968)

1929: *Marianne*. 1930: *The Divorcee, In Gay Madrid, Let Us Be Gay*. 1931: *The Bachelor Father, It's a Wise Child, Five and Ten; Susan Lennox, Her Rise and Fall*. 1932: *Lovers Courageous, Strange Interlude*. 1933: *Peg o' My Heart, Dancing Lady*. 1935: *After Office Hours, Escapade*. 1936: *The Great Ziegfeld, Picadilly Jim*. 1937: *Maytime, The Firefly*. 1938: *The Girl of the Golden West*. 1939: *Broadway Serenade*. 1940: *New Moon, Pride and Prejudice; Third Finger, Left Hand*. 1941: *Ziegfeld Girl, When Ladies Meet*. 1942: *We Were Dancing, Stand by for Action*. 1943: *The Man from Down Under*. 1944: *Marriage Is a Private Affair*. 1945: *Weekend at the Waldorf*. 1946: *The Secret Heart*. 1947: *Cynthia*. 1948: *B.F.'s Daughter*. 1949: *The Bribe, In the Good Old Summertime*. 1950: *Nancy Goes to Rio, Duchess of Idaho, Grounds for Marriage*. 1951: *Too Young to Kiss*. 1952: *Everything I Have Is Yours*. 1953: *The Clown, The Great Diamond Robbery*. 1954: *Her Twelve Men*. 1955: *The King's Thief* (all M-G-M). 1957: *Kelly and Me*, U-I. 1958: *Beautiful but Dangerous* (Italy), 20TH.

HENRY LEVIN (1909–)

1944: *Cry of the Werewolf*. 1945: *Dancing in Manhattan, Sergeant Mike, I Love a Mystery*. 1946: *The Fighting Guardsman, The Bandit of Sherwood*

Forest (with George Sherman), *Night Editor, The Unknown, The Devil's Mask, The Return of Monte Cristo.* 1947: *The Guilt of Janet Ames, The Corpse Came C.O.D.* 1948: *The Mating of Millie, The Gallant Blade, The Man from Colorado.* 1949: *Mr. Soft Touch* (with Gordon Douglas), *Jolson Sings Again.* 1950: *And Baby Makes Three, Convicted, The Petty Girl, The Flying Missile.* 1951: *Two of a Kind, The Family Secret* (all COL). 1952: *Belles on Their Toes.* 1953: *The President's Lady, The Farmer Takes a Wife, Mister Scoutmaster.* 1954: *Three Young Texans, The Gambler from Natchez* (all 20TH). 1955: *The Warriors,* AA. 1957: *The Lonely Man,* PAR; *Let's Be Happy* (England), AA; *Bernardine, April Love.* 1958: *A Nice Little Bank That Should Be Robbed.* 1959: *The Remarkable Mr. Pennypacker, Holiday for Lovers, Journey to the Center of the Earth* (all 20TH). 1960: *Where the Boys Are.* 1961: *The Wonders of Aladdin* (Italy). 1962: *The Wonderful World of the Brothers Grimm* (with George Pal; Levin directed narrative sequences) (all M-G-M); *If a Man Answers,* U-I. 1963: *Come Fly with Me,* M-G-M. 1964: *Honeymoon Hotel,* M-G-M. 1965: *Genghis Khan.* 1966: *Murderers' Row.* 1967: *Kiss the Girls and Make Them Die* (Italy), *The Ambushers.* 1969: *The Desperados* (all COL). 1973: *That Man Bolt* (with David Lowell Rich; U.S.–Hong Kong), U.

HERSCHELL GORDON LEWIS (1926–)

1961: *Living Venus, Lucky Pierre.* 1962: *Nature's Playmates, Daughters of the Sun, B-O-I-N-N-N-G!.* 1963: *Scum of the Earth, Goldilocks and the Three Bares, Blood Feast.* 1964: *Bell, Bare, and Beautiful; Two Thousand Maniacs!, Color Me Blood Red.* 1965: *Monster-A-Go-Go!, Alley Tramp, Moonshine Mountain.* 1966: *Jimmy, the Boy Wonder; An Eye for an Eye; Sin, Suffer and Repent; The Magic Land of Mother Goose.* 1967: *Suburban Roulette, The Pill, The Gruesome Twosome, Blast-off Girls, How to Make a Doll, A Taste of Blood.* 1968: *Something Weird, Just for the Hell of It, She-Devils on Wheels.* 1969: *The Ecstasies of Women, Miss Nymphet's Zap-In.* 1970: *The Wizard of Gore.* 1971: *This Stuff'll Kill Ya'!.* 1972: *Year of the Yahoo, The Gore-Gore Girls* (*Blood Orgy*), *Stick It in Your Ear* (all STATES' RIGHTS).

JOSEPH H. LEWIS (1900–)

1937: *Navy Spy* (with Crane Wilbur), GN; *The Singing Outlaw, Courage of the West.* 1938: *The Spy Ring* (*International Spy*), *Border Wolves, The Last Stand* (all U). 1940: *Two-Fisted Rangers, Blazing Six Shooters, Texas Stagecoach, The Man from Tumbleweeds, The Return of Wild Bill* (all

COL); *Boys of the City, That Gang of Mine.* 1941: *Pride of the Bowery, The Invisible Ghost* (all MONO); *Criminals Within,* PRC; *Arizona Cyclone,* U. 1942: *Bombs Over Burma,* PRC; *The Silver Bullet,* U; *Secrets of a Co-ed* (*Silent Witness*), PRC; *The Boss of Hangtown Mesa,* U; *The Mad Doctor of Market Street,* U. 1944: *Minstrel Man,* PRC. 1945: *The Falcon in San Francisco,* RKO; *My Name Is Julia Ross.* 1946: *So Dark the Night, The Jolson Story* (directed musical numbers). 1947: *The Swordsman.* 1948: *The Return of October.* 1949: *The Undercover Man* (all COL); *Gun Crazy* (*Deadly Is the Female*), UA. 1950: *A Lady Without Passport,* M-G-M. 1952: *Retreat, Hell!,* WB; *Desperate Search,* M-G-M. 1953: *Cry of the Hunted,* M-G-M. 1955: *The Big Combo,* AA; *A Lawless Street,* COL. 1956: *The Seventh Cavalry,* COL. 1957: *The Halliday Brand,* UA. 1958: *Terror in a Texas Town,* UA.

ANATOLE LITVAK (MICHAEL ANATOL LITWAK) (1902–1974)
1931: *Dolly Gets Ahead* (Germany; German title—*Dolly macht Karriere*), UFA. 1932: *Nie wieder Liebe* (Germany), UFA; *Coeur de Lilas* (France; *Lilac*), UA. 1933: *Be Mine Tonight* (Germany; German title—*Das Lied einer Nacht*), U; *Sleeping Car* (England), GB. 1935: *Cette Vielle Canaille* (France), KINEMATRADE, INC. 1937: *The Woman I Love,* RKO; *Mayerling* (France), PAX FILM INC.; *Tovarich.* 1938: *The Amazing Dr. Clitterhouse, The Sisters* (all WB); *Flight into Darkness* (France; French title—*L'Équipage*), FRANK KASSLER. 1939: *Castle on the Hudson, Confessions of a Nazi Spy.* 1940: *All This and Heaven Too, City for Conquest.* 1941: *Out of the Fog, Blues in the Night* (all WB). 1942: *This Above All,* 20TH. 1947: *The Long Night,* RKO. 1948: *Sorry, Wrong Number,* PAR; *The Snake Pit,* 20TH. 1952: *Decision Before Dawn,* 20TH. 1953: *Act of Love* (France), UA. 1955: *The Deep Blue Sea* (England), 20TH. 1956: *Anastasia,* 20TH. 1959: *The Journey* (Austria), M-G-M. 1961: *Goodbye Again* (France), UA. 1963: *Five Miles to Midnight* (France), UA. 1967: *The Night of the Generals* (Germany), COL. 1970: *The Lady in the Car with Glasses and a Gun* (France), COL.

FRANK LLOYD (1888–1960)
1929: *Weary River, The Divine Lady, Drag, Young Nowheres, Dark Streets* (all FN). 1930: *Son of the Gods,* WB; *The Way of All Men,* FN. 1931: *The Lash,* FN; *East Lynne,* FOX; *The Right of Way,* FN; *The Age for Love,* UA. 1932: *A Passport to Hell.* 1933: *Cavalcade, Berkeley Square, Hoopla.* 1934: *Servants' Entrance* (all FOX). 1935: *Mutiny on the Bounty,* M-G-M.

1936: *Under Two Flags*, 20TH. 1937: *Maid of Salem, Wells Fargo*. 1938: *If I Were King*. 1939: *Rulers of the Sea* (all PAR). 1940: *The Howards of Virginia*, COL. 1941: *The Lady from Cheyenne*, U; *This Woman Is Mine*, U. 1943: *Forever and a Day* (with R. Clair, E. Goulding, C. Hardwicke, V. Saville, R. Stevenson, H. Wilcox), RKO. 1945: *Blood on the Sun*, UA. 1954: *The Shanghai Story*, REP. 1955: *The Last Command*, REP.

EUGENE LOURIÉ (1905–)

1953: *The Beast from 20,000 Fathoms*, WB; *The Colossus of New York*, PAR. 1959: *The Giant Behemoth* (with Douglas Hickox; England), AA. 1961: *Gorgo* (England), M-G-M.

ARTHUR LUBIN (1901–)

1934: *A Successful Failure*. 1935: *Great God Gold, Honeymoon Limited* (all MONO); *Two Sinners, Frisco Waterfront*. 1936: *The House of a Thousand Candles* (all REP); *Yellowstone*. 1937: *Mysterious Crossing, California Straight Ahead, I Cover the War, Idol of the Crowds, Adventure's End*. 1938: *Midnight Intruder* (all U); *Beloved Brat*, WB; *Prison Break, Secrets of a Nurse*. 1939: *Risky Business, Big Town Czar* (all U); *Mickey the Kid*, REP; *Call a Messenger*. 1940: *The Big Guy, Black Friday* (all U); *Gangs of Chicago*, REP; *I'm Nobody's Sweetheart Now*, U; *Meet the Wildcat*, U; *Who Killed Aunt Maggie?*, REP. 1941: *San Francisco Docks, Where Did You Get That Girl?, Buck Privates, In the Navy, Hold That Ghost, Keep 'Em Flying*. 1942: *Ride 'Em Cowboy, Eagle Squadron*. 1943: *White Savage, The Phantom of the Opera*. 1944: *Ali Baba and the Forty Thieves* (all U). 1945: *Delightfully Dangerous*, UA. 1946: *The Spider Woman Strikes Back*, U; *A Night in Paradise*, U. 1947: *New Orleans*, UA. 1949: *Impact*, UA; *Francis*, U-I. 1951: *Queen for a Day*, UA; *Francis Goes to the Races*, U-I; *Rhubarb*, PAR. 1952: *Francis Goes to West Point*, U-I; *It Grows on Trees*, U-I. 1953: *South Sea Woman*, WB; *Francis Covers the Big Town*. 1954: *Francis Joins the WACS*. 1955: *Francis in the Navy* (all U-I); *Footsteps in the Fog*, COL; *Lady Godiva*, U-I. 1956: *Star of India*, UA; *The First Traveling Saleslady*, RKO. 1957: *Escapade in Japan*, U-I. 1961: *Thief of Baghdad*, M-G-M. 1964: *The Incredible Mr. Limpet*, WB. 1966: *Hold On!*, M-G-M. 1971: *Rain for a Dusty Summer* (Spain), DO-BAR PRODUCTIONS.

EDWARD LUDWIG (c. 1900–)

1932: *Steady Company*, U. 1933: *They Just Had to Get Married*, U. 1934: *A Woman's Man*, MONO; *Let's Be Ritzy*, U; *Friends of Mr. Sweeney*, WB.

1935: *The Man Who Reclaimed His Head*, U; *Age of Indiscretion*, M-G-M; *Old Man Rhythm*, RKO; *Three Kids and a Queen*, U. 1936: *Fatal Lady*, PAR; *Adventure in Manhattan*, COL. 1937: *Her Husband Lies*, PAR; *The Last Gangster*, M-G-M. 1938: *That Certain Age*, U. 1939: *Coast Guard*, COL. 1940: *Swiss Family Robinson*, RKO. 1941: *The Man Who Lost Himself*, U. 1942: *Born to Sing*, M-G-M. 1943: *They Came to Blow Up America*, 20TH. 1944: *The Fighting Seabees*, REP; *Three Is a Family*, UA. 1947: *The Fabulous Texan*, REP. 1948: *Wake of the Red Witch*, REP. 1949: *The Big Wheel*, UA. 1951: *Smuggler's Island*, U-I. 1952: *Caribbean*, PAR; *Big Jim McLain*, WB; *The Blazing Forest*. 1953: *The Vanquished, Sangaree*. 1954: *Jivaro* (all PAR). 1955: *Flame of the Islands*, REP. 1957: *The Black Scorpion*, WB. 1963: *The Gun Hawk*, AA.

IDA LUPINO (1916–)
1950: *Never Fear*, EL; *Outrage*. 1951: *Hard, Fast and Beautiful; On Dangerous Ground* (uncredited, with Nicholas Ray). 1953: *The Hitch-Hiker* (all RKO); *The Bigamist*, FILMAKERS PRODUCTIONS. 1966: *The Trouble with Angels*, COL.

FRANCIS D. LYON (1905–)
1953: *Crazylegs*, REP. 1954: *The Bob Mathias Story*, AA. 1955: *The Cult of the Cobra*, U-I. 1956: *The Great Locomotive Chase*, BV. 1957: *The Oklahoman*, AA; *Bailout at 43,000*, UA; *Gunsight Ridge*, UA. 1958: *South Seas Adventure* (with Walter Thompson, Basil Wrangell, Richard Goldstone, Carl Dudley), STANLEY WARNER-CINERAMA. 1959: *Escort West*, UA. 1961: *Tomboy and the Champ*, U-I. 1963: *The Young and the Brave*, M-G-M. 1966: *Destination Inner Space*, MAGNA. 1967: *Castle of Evil*, UNITED PICTURES. 1968: *The Destructors*, FEATURE FILM CORP. OF AMERICA; *The Money Jungle*, COMMONWEALTH. 1969: *The Girl Who Knew Too Much*, COMMONWEALTH.

FRANK McDONALD (1899–)
1935: *Broadway Hostess*, FN. 1936: *The Murder of Dr. Harrigan*, FN; *Boulder Dam*, WB; *The Big Noise*, WB; *Love Begins at Twenty*, FN; *Treachery Rides the Range*, WB; *Murder by an Aristocrat*, FN; *Smart Blonde, Isle of Fury*. 1937: *Midnight Court, Her Husband's Secretary, Fly-Away Baby; Dance, Charlie, Dance; The Adventurous Blonde*. 1938: *Blondes at Work* (all WB); *Reckless Living*, U; *Over the Wall*, WB; *Freshman Year*, U; *Flirting with Fate*, M-G-M. 1939: *First Offenders*, COL; *They Asked for It*, U; *Jeepers Creepers*. 1940: *Rancho Grande, In Old*

Missouri, Gaucho Serenade, Carolina Moon; Ride, Tenderfoot, Ride; Grand Ole Opry, Barnyard Follies. 1941: *Arkansas Judge, Country Fair* (all REP); *Flying Blind,* PAR; *Under Fiesta Stars,* REP; *Tuxedo Junction,* REP; *No Hands on the Clock,* PAR. 1942: *Shepherd of the Ozarks, The Old Homestead, Mountain Rhythm* (all REP); *Wildcat,* PAR; *Wrecking Crew,* PAR; *The Traitor Within,* REP. 1943: *High Explosive,* PAR; *Swing Your Partner,* REP; *Alaska Highway,* PAR; *Submarine Alert,* PAR; *Hoosier Holiday,* REP; *O, My Darling Clementine,* REP. 1944: *Timber Queen,* PAR; *Take It Big,* PAR; *Sing, Neighbor, Sing,* REP; *One Body Too Many,* PAR; *Lights of Old Santa Fe.* 1945: *Bells of Rosarita, The Chicago Kid, The Man from Oklahoma, Tell It to a Star, Sunset in El Dorado, Along the Navajo Trail.* 1946: *Song of Arizona, Rainbow Over Texas, My Pal Trigger, Sioux City Sue.* 1947: *Hit Parade of 1947, Twilight on the Rio Grande, Under Nevada Skies* (all REP); *Bulldog Drummond Strikes Back,* COL; *When a Girl's Beautiful,* COL; *Linda Be Good,* EL. 1948: *Mr. Reckless,* PAR; *13 Lead Soldiers,* 20TH; *French Leave,* MONO; *Gun Smugglers,* RKO. 1949: *The Big Sombrero,* COL; *Ringside,* LIPPERT; *Apache Chief,* LIPPERT. 1950: *Snow Dog, Call of the Klondike.* 1951: *Sierra Passage* (all MONO); *Texans Never Cry,* COL; *Father Takes the Air, Yukon Manhunt, Yellow Fin, Northwest Territory.* 1952: *Sea Tiger, Yukon Gold* (all MONO). 1953: *Son of Belle Starr,* AA; *Border City Rustlers,* AA. 1954: *Thunder Pass,* LIPPERT. 1955: *The Treasure of Ruby Hills,* AA; *The Big Tip-Off,* AA. 1957: *Le Imprese di una Spada Leggendària* (with Nathan Juran; Italy). 1960: *The Purple Gang,* AA; *Raymie,* AA. 1962: *The Underwater City,* COL. 1963: *Gunfight at Comanche Creek,* AA. 1965: *Mara of the Wilderness,* AA.

RANALD MacDOUGALL (1915–1973)
1955: *Queen Bee,* COL. 1956: *Hot Cars,* UA. 1957: *Man on Fire.* 1959: *The World, the Flesh and the Devil.* 1960: *The Subterraneans.* 1961: *Go Naked in the World* (all M-G-M).

BERNARD McEVEETY
1966: *Ride Beyond Vengeance,* COL. 1971: *The Brotherhood of Satan,* COL. 1972: *Napoleon and Samantha,* BV. 1973: *One Little Indian,* BV. 1974: *The Bears and I,* BV.

VINCENT McEVEETY
1968: *Firecreek,* WB-7A. 1971: *The Million Dollar Duck.* 1972: *The Biscuit Eater.* 1973: *Charley and the Angel.* 1974: *Superdad, The Castaway Cowboy* (all BV).

HAMILTON MacFADDEN (1901–)

1930: *Harmony at Home, Crazy That Way; Oh, for a Man!, Are You There?*
1931: *Charlie Chan Carries On, The Black Camel, Riders of the Purple
Sage, Their Mad Moment* (with Chandler Sprague). 1932: *Cheaters at Play.*
1933: *Second Hand Wife* (all FOX); *The Fourth Horseman,* U; *Trick for
Trick, The Man Who Dared, Charlie Chan's Greatest Case.* 1934: *As Husbands Go, Hold That Girl, Stand Up and Cheer, She Was a Lady.* 1935:
Elinor Norton (all FOX); *Fighting Youth,* U. 1937: *The Three Legion-
naires,* GENERAL FILMS; *It Can't Last Forever,* COL; *Sea Racketeers,*
REP; *Escape by Night,* REP. 1942: *Inside the Law,* PRC.

WILLIAM H. McGANN (1895–?)

1930: *On the Border,* WB. 1931: *I Like Your Nerve,* FN. 1932: *Illegal*
(England), WB. 1934: *La Buenaventura* (Spanish language), WB. 1935:
Maybe It's Love, FN; *A Night at the Ritz, Man of Iron.* 1936: *Freshman
Love* (all WB); *Brides Are Like That,* FN; *Times Square Playboy,* WB;
Two Against the World, FN; *Hot Money,* WB; *Polo Joe,* WB; *The Case of
the Black Cat,* FN. 1937: *Penrod and Sam, Marry the Girl, Sh! The
Octopus.* 1938: *Alcatraz Island, Penrod and His Twin Brother, When Were
You Born?, Girls on Probation.* 1939: *Blackwell's Island, Sweepstakes Win-
ner, Everybody's Hobby, Pride of the Blue Grass* (all WB). 1940: *Wolf of
New York,* REP; *Dr. Christian Meets the Women,* RKO. 1941: *A Shot in the
Dark,* WB; *The Parson of Panamint,* PAR; *Highway West,* WB; *We Go
Fast,* 20TH. 1942: *In Old California,* REP; *Tombstone, the Town Too
Tough to Die,* PAR; *American Empire,* UA. 1943: *Frontier Badman,* U.

ANDREW V. McLAGLEN (1920–)

1956: *Gun the Man Down,* UA; *The Man in the Vault,* RKO. 1957: *The
Abductors.* 1960: *Freckles.* 1961: *The Little Shepherd of Kingdom Come*
(all 20TH). 1963: *McLintock!,* UA. 1965: *Shenandoah,* U. 1966: *The Rare
Breed,* U. 1967: *Monkeys, Go Home!,* BV; *The Way West,* UA. 1968: *The
Ballad of Josie,* U; *Bandolero!,* 20TH; *The Devil's Brigade,* UA. 1969:
Hellfighters, U; *The Undefeated,* 20TH. 1970: *Chisum,* WB. 1971: *One
More Train to Rob,* U; *Fools' Parade,* COL; *Something Big,* CINEMA
CENTER. 1973: *Cahill: U.S. Marshal,* WB.

NORMAN Z. McLEOD (1898–1964)

1929: *Taking a Chance,* FOX. 1931: *Along Came Youth* (with Lloyd

Corrigan), *Finn and Hattie* (with Norman Taurog), *Monkey Business, Touchdown.* 1932: *The Miracle Man, Horse Feathers, If I Had a Million* (with J. Cruze, H. B. Humberstone, S. Roberts, W. A. Seiter, E. Lubitsch, N. Taurog). 1933: *A Lady's Profession, Mama Loves Papa, Alice in Wonderland.* 1934: *Melody in Spring, Many Happy Returns, It's a Gift* (all PAR). 1935: *Redheads on Parade,* FOX; *Here Comes Cookie, Coronado.* 1936: *Early to Bed* (all PAR); *Pennies from Heaven,* COL; *Mind Your Own Business,* PAR. 1937: *Topper,* M-G-M. 1938: *Merrily We Live,* M-G-M; *There Goes My Heart,* UA. 1939: *Topper Takes a Trip,* UA; *Remember?,* M-G-M. 1940: *Little Men,* RKO. 1941: *The Trial of Mary Dugan, Lady Be Good.* 1942: *Jackass Mail, Panama Hattie* (all M-G-M); *The Powers Girl,* UA. 1943: *Swing Shift Maisie,* M-G-M. 1946: *The Kid from Brooklyn,* RKO. 1947: *The Secret Life of Walter Mitty,* RKO; *The Road to Rio.* 1948: *Isn't It Romantic, The Paleface.* 1950: *Let's Dance.* 1951: *My Favorite Spy* (all PAR). 1952: *Never Wave at a WAC,* RKO. 1954: *Casanova's Big Night,* PAR. 1957: *Public Pigeon No. 1,* U-I. 1959: *Alias Jesse James,* UA.

DANIEL MANN (1912–)

1952: *Come Back, Little Sheba.* 1954: *About Mrs. Leslie.* 1955: *The Rose Tattoo* (all PAR); *I'll Cry Tomorrow,* M-G-M. 1956: *The Teahouse of the August Moon,* M-G-M. 1958: *Hot Spell,* PAR. 1959: *The Last Angry Man,* COL. 1960: *The Mountain Road,* COL; *Butterfield 8,* M-G-M. 1961: *Ada,* M-G-M. 1962: *Five Finger Exercise,* COL; *Who's Got the Action?,* PAR. 1963: *Who's Been Sleeping in My Bed?,* PAR. 1966: *Our Man Flint,* 20TH; *Judith,* PAR. 1968: *For Love of Ivy,* CINERAMA. 1969: *A Dream of Kings,* NATIONAL GENERAL. 1971: *Willard,* CINERAMA. 1972: *The Revengers,* NATIONAL GENERAL. 1973: *Interval,* AVCO EMBASSY; *Maurie,* NATIONAL GENERAL. 1974: *Lost in the Stars,* AMERICAN FILM THEATRE.

DELBERT MANN (1920–)

1955: *Marty,* UA. 1957: *The Bachelor Party,* UA. 1958: *Desire Under the Elms,* PAR; *Separate Tables,* UA. 1959: *Middle of the Night,* COL. 1960: *The Dark at the Top of the Stairs,* WB. 1961: *Lover Come Back, The Outsider.* 1962: *That Touch of Mink.* 1963: *A Gathering of Eagles* (all U-I). 1964: *Dear Heart,* WB; *Quick, Before It Melts,* M-G-M. 1966: *Mister Buddwing,* M-G-M. 1967: *Fitzwilly,* UA. 1968: *The Pink Jungle,* U. 1971: *Kidnapped* (England), AIP.

EDWARD MANN

1956: *Scandal Incorporated,* REP. 1966: *Hallucination Generation,* AIP. 1971: *Cauldron of Blood,* CANNON; *Who Says I Can't Ride a Rainbow!,* TRANSVUE PICTURES. 1972: *Hot Pants Holiday,* AVCO EMBASSY.

EDWIN L. MARIN (1901–1951)

1933: *The Death Kiss,* WW; *A Study in Scarlet,* WW; *The Avenger,* MONO; *The Sweetheart of Sigma Chi,* MONO. 1934: *Bombay Mail, The Crosby Case, Affairs of a Gentleman* (all U); *Paris Interlude.* 1935: *The Casino Murder Case, Pursuit.* 1936: *Moonlight Murder, Speed, Sworn Enemy* (all M-G-M); *I'd Give My Life,* PAR; *All American Chump, The Garden Murder Case.* 1937: *Man of the People, Married Before Breakfast.* 1938: *Everybody Sing, Hold That Kiss, The Chaser; Listen, Darling; A Christmas Carol.* 1939: *Fast and Loose, Society Lawyer, Maisie.* 1940: *Henry Goes Arizona, Florian, Gold Rush Maisie, Hullabaloo.* 1941: *Maisie Was a Lady, Ringside Maisie* (all M-G-M); *Paris Calling,* U. 1942: *A Gentleman After Dark,* UA; *Miss Annie Rooney,* UA; *Invisible Agent,* U. 1943: *Two Tickets to London,* U. 1944: *Show Business, Tall in the Saddle.* 1945: *Johnny Angel* (all RKO). 1946: *Abilene Town,* UA; *Young Widow,* UA; *Lady Luck,* RKO; *Mr. Ace,* UA; *Nocturne,* RKO. 1947: *Christmas Eve,* UA; *Intrigue,* UA. 1948: *Race Street,* RKO. 1949: *Canadian Pacific,* 20TH; *The Younger Brothers,* WB; *Fighting Man of the Plains,* 20TH. 1950: *Colt .45,* WB; *The Cariboo Trail,* 20TH. 1951: *Sugarfoot,* WB; *Raton Pass,* WB.

GEORGE MARSHALL (1891–)

1932: *Pack Up Your Troubles* (with Raymond McCarey), M-G-M. 1934: *Ever Since Eve, Wild Gold, She Learned About Sailors, 365 Nights in Hollywood.* 1935: *Life Begins at 40, Ten Dollar Raise, In Old Kentucky* (all FOX); *Music Is Magic, Show Them No Mercy.* 1936: *A Message to Garcia, The Crime of Dr. Forbes, Can This Be Dixie?* 1937: *Nancy Steele Is Missing, Love Under Fire* (all 20TH). 1938: *The Goldwyn Follies,* UA; *The Battle of Broadway,* 20TH; *Hold That Co-ed,* 20TH. 1939: *You Can't Cheat an Honest Man,* U; *Destry Rides Again,* U. 1940: *The Ghost Breakers,* PAR; *When the Daltons Rode,* U. 1941: *Pot o' Gold,* UA; *Texas,* COL. 1942: *Valley of the Sun,* RKO; *The Forest Rangers, Star Spangled Rhythm.* 1943: *True to Life, Riding High.* 1944: *And the Angels Sing.* 1945: *Murder, He Says; Incendiary Blonde, Hold That Blonde.* 1946: *The Blue Dahlia, Monsieur Beaucaire.* 1947: *The Perils of Pauline, Variety Girl.* 1948: *Hazard* (all

PAR); *Tap Roots*, U-I. 1949: *My Friend Irma*, PAR. 1950: *Fancy Pants*, PAR; *Never A Dull Moment*, RKO. 1951: *A Millionaire for Christy*, 20TH. 1952: *The Savage*. 1953: *Off Limits, Scared Stiff, Houdini, Money from Home*. 1954: *Red Garters* (all PAR); *Duel in the Jungle*, WB; *Destry*. 1955: *The Second Greatest Sex*. 1956: *Pillars of the Sky* (all U-I). 1957: *The Guns of Fort Petticoat*, COL; *Beyond Mombasa* (England), COL; *The Sad Sack*, PAR. 1958: *The Sheepman, Imitation General*. 1959: *The Mating Game, It Started with a Kiss, The Gazebo* (all M-G-M). 1961: *Cry for Happy*, COL. 1962: *The Happy Thieves*, UA; *How the West Was Won* (with Henry Hathaway and John Ford), M-G-M. 1963: *Papa's Delicate Condition*, PAR. 1964: *Dark Purpose*, U; *Advance to the Rear*, M-G-M. 1966: *Boy, Did I Get a Wrong Number!* 1967: *Eight on the Lam*. 1968: *The Wicked Dreams of Paula Schultz* (all UA). 1969: *Hook, Line and Sinker*, COL.

LESLIE H. MARTINSON

1954: *The Atomic Kid*, REP. 1956: *Hot Rod Girl*, AIP. 1957: *Hot Rod Rumble*, AA. 1962: *Lad: a Dog* (with Aram Avakian). 1963: *PT-109, Black Gold* (all WB). 1964: *For Those Who Think Young*, UA; *FBI Code 98*, WB. 1966: *Batman*, 20TH. 1967: *Fathom*, 20TH. 1971: *Mrs. Pollifax—Spy*, UA.

ANDREW MARTON (1904–)

1931: *Die Nacht ohne Pause* (with Franz Wenzler; Germany). 1933: *Nordpol-ahoi!* (Germany). 1934: *Der Daemon der Berge* (Switzerland; *The Demon of the Himalayas*). 1935: *Miss President* (Hungary), REFLECKTOR PRODUCTIONS. 1936: *Wolf's Clothing* (England), WORLD. 1939: *School for Husbands* (England), J. H. HOFFBERG. 1940: *A Little Bit of Heaven*, U. 1944: *Gentle Annie*. 1946: *Gallant Bess*. 1950: *King Solomon's Mines* (with Compton Bennett; Africa) (all M-G-M). 1952: *Storm Over Tibet*, COL; *The Wild North, The Devil Makes Three* (Germany and Austria). 1954: *Gypsy Colt, Prisoner of War, Men of the Fighting Lady, Green Fire* (Africa) (all M-G-M). 1956: *Seven Wonders of the World* (with Tay Garnett, Paul Mantz, Ted Tetzlaff, Walter Thompson), STANLEY WARNER-CINERAMA. 1958: *Underwater Warrior*, M-G-M. 1962: *It Happened in Athens* (Greece), 20TH; *The Longest Day* (with Ken Annakin and Bernhard Wicki; France), 20TH. 1964: *The Thin Red Line* (Spain), AA. 1965: *Clarence, the Cross-Eyed Lion*, M-G-M; *Crack in the World*, PAR. 1966: *Around the World Under the Sea*, M-G-M; *Birds Do It*, COL. 1967: *Africa—Texas Style!* (Kenya), PAR.

RUDOLPH MATE (1898–1964)

1947: *It Had to Be You* (with Don Hartman), COL. 1949: *The Dark Past,* COL; *D.O.A.,* UA. 1950: *No Sad Songs For Me,* COL; *Union Station,* PAR; *Branded,* PAR. 1951: *The Prince Who Was a Thief,* U-I; *When Worlds Collide,* PAR. 1952: *The Green Glove,* UA; *Paula,* COL; *Sally and Saint Anne,* U-I. 1953: *The Mississippi Gambler,* U-I; *Second Chance,* RKO; *Forbidden,* U-I. 1954: *The Siege at Red River,* 20TH; *The Black Shield of Falworth,* U-I. 1955: *The Violent Men,* COL; *The Far Horizons,* PAR. 1956: *Miracle in the Rain,* WB; *The Rawhide Years,* U-I; *Port Afrique* (England), COL; *Three Violent People,* PAR. 1958: *The Deep Six,* WB. 1959: *For the First Time* (Italy), M-G-M. 1962: *The 300 Spartans* (Greece), 20TH. 1963: *Aliki—My Love* (Greece), LIONEX FILMS; *Seven Seas to Calais* (Italy), M-G-M.

WALTER MATTHAU (1920–)

1960: *Gangster Story,* RELEASING CORPORATION OF INDEPENDENT PRODUCTIONS.

KEN MAYNARD (1895–1973)

1933: *Fiddlin' Buckaroo,* U.

ARCHIE L. MAYO (1891–1968)

1929: *My Man, Sonny Boy, The Sap, Is Everybody Happy?, The Sacred Flame* (all WB). 1930: *Vengeance,* COL; *Wide Open, Courage; Oh, Sailor, Behave!, The Doorway to Hell.* 1931: *Illicit, Svengali, Bought.* 1932: *Under Eighteen, The Expert, Street of Women, Two Against the World* (all WB); *Night After Night,* PAR. 1933: *The Life of Jimmy Dolan, The Mayor of Hell, Ever in My Heart* (all WB); *Convention City,* FN. 1934: *Gambling Lady,* WB; *The Man with Two Faces,* FN; *Desirable,* WB. 1935: *Bordertown,* WB; *Go into Your Dance,* FN; *The Case of the Lucky Legs,* WB. 1936: *The Petrified Forest,* WB; *I Married a Doctor,* FN; *Give Me Your Heart, Black Legion.* 1937: *Call It a Day* (all WB); *It's Love I'm After,* FN. 1938: *The Adventures of Marco Polo,* UA; *Youth Takes a Fling,* U. 1939: *They Shall Have Music,* UA. 1940: *The House Across the Bay,* UA; *Four Sons.* 1941: *The Great American Broadcast, Charley's Aunt, Confirm or Deny.* 1942: *Moontide, Orchestra Wives.* 1943: *Crash Dive.* 1944: *Sweet and Lowdown* (all 20TH). 1946: *A Night in Casablanca,* UA; *Angel on My Shoulder,* UA.

IB MELCHIOR (1917–)
1959: *The Angry Red Planet,* SINO PRODUCTIONS. 1964: *The Time Travelers,* AIP.

LOTHAR MENDES (1894–1974)
1929: *Interference* (with Roy Pomeroy), *The Four Feathers* (with Merian C. Cooper and E. B. Schoedsack), *Illusion, Marriage Playground.* 1930: *Paramount on Parade* (with D. Arzner, O. Brower, E. Goulding, V. Heerman, E. Knopf, R. V. Lee, E. Lubitsch, V. Schertzinger, E. Sutherland, F. Tuttle). 1931: *Ladies' Man.* 1932: *Strangers in Love* (all PAR); *Payment Deferred,* M-G-M. 1933: *Luxury Liner,* PAR. 1934: *Power* (England; *Jew Süss*), GB. 1937: *The Man Who Could Work Miracles* (England), UA. 1938: *Moonlight Sonata* (England), ENGLISH FILMS, INC. 1941: *International Squadron,* WB. 1943: *Flight for Freedom,* RKO. 1944: *Tampico,* 20TH. 1946: *The Walls Came Tumbling Down,* COL.

WILLIAM CAMERON MENZIES (1896–1957)
1931: *Always Goodbye* (with Kenneth McKenna), *The Spider* (with Kenneth McKenna). 1932: *Almost Married, Chandu the Magician* (with Marcel Varnel) (all FOX). 1934: *Wharf Angel* (with George Somnes), PAR. 1936: *Things to Come* (England), UA. 1944: *Address Unknown,* COL. 1947: *The Green Cockatoo* (England), DEVONSHIRE FILMS. 1951: *Drums in the Deep South,* RKO; *The Whip Hand,* RKO. 1953: *The Maze,* AA. 1954: *Invaders from Mars,* 20TH.

RADLEY H. METZGER (1930–)
1961: *Dark Odyssey* (with William Kyriakys), ERA KM. 1964: *The Dirty Girls.* 1966: *The Alley Cats.* 1967: *Carmen Baby* (Yugoslavia–W. Germany–U.S.). 1968: *Thérèse and Isabelle* (France). 1969: *Camille 2000* (Italy). 1970: *The Lickerish Quartet* (U.S.–Germany–Italy). 1972: *Little Mother* (U.S.–Yugoslavia). 1973: *Score* (U.S.–Yugoslavia) (all AUDUBON).

RUSS MEYER (c. 1924–)
1959: *The Immoral Mr. Teas,* PAD-RAM ENTERPRISES. 1961: *Eroticon, Eve and the Handyman.* 1962: *Naked Gals of the Golden West.* 1963: *Europe in the Raw* (Europe), *Heavenly Bodies.* 1964: *Lorna,* EVE PRODUCTIONS. 1965: *Mudhoney!,* EVE; *Motor Psycho!,* EVE; *Fanny Hill* (West Germany), FAVORITE FILMS. 1966: *Faster Pussycat! Kill! Kill!, Mondo Topless.* 1967: *Good Morning—and Goodbye, Common Law Cabin.*

1968: *Finders Keepers, Lovers Weepers; Russ Meyer's Vixen.* 1969: *Cherry, Harry and Raquel* (all EVE PRODUCTIONS). 1970: *Beyond the Valley of the Dolls,* 20TH. 1971: *The Seven Minutes,* 20TH. 1973: *Blacksnake!* (*Sweet Suzy*), STATES' RIGHTS. 1975: *The Supervixens.*

RAY MILLAND (1905–)
1955: *A Man Alone,* REP. 1956: *Lisbon* (Portugal), REP. 1958: *The Safecracker,* M-G-M. 1962: *Panic in the Year Zero,* AIP. 1968: *Hostile Witness* (England), UA.

GEORGE MONTGOMERY (1916–)
1961: *The Steel Claw,* WB. 1962: *Samar,* WB.

ROBERT MONTGOMERY (1904–)
1946: *Lady in the Lake,* M-G-M. 1947: *Ride the Pink Horse,* U-I. 1949: *Once More My Darling,* U-I. 1950: *Eye Witness* (England), EL. 1960: *The Gallant Hours,* UA.

HOWARD MORRIS (1919–)
1967: *Who's Minding the Mint?,* COL. 1968: *With Six You Get Egg Roll,* NATIONAL GENERAL. 1969: *Don't Drink the Water,* AVCO EMBASSY.

VIC MORROW (1932–)
1967: *Deathwatch,* ALTURA. 1971: *A Man Called Sledge* (Italy), COL.

TERRY O. MORSE (1906–)
1939: *Adventures of Jane Arden, On Trial, Waterfront, Smashing the Money Ring, No Place to Go.* 1940: *British Intelligence, Tear Gas Squad* (all WB). 1945: *Fog Island,* PRC. 1946: *Danny Boy,* PRC; *Shadows Over Chinatown,* MONO; *Dangerous Money,* MONO. 1947: *Bells of San Fernando,* SCREEN GUILD. 1951: *Unknown World,* LIPPERT. 1956: *Godzilla, King of the Monsters* (with Ishiro Honda; Japan), EMBASSY. 1965: *Taffy and the Jungle Hunter,* AA; *Young Dillinger,* AA.

CONRAD NAGEL (1896–)
1937: *Love Takes Flight,* GRAND NATIONAL.

ARTHUR NAPOLEON
1957: *Man on the Prowl,* UA. 1958: *Too Much, Too Soon,* WB. 1969: *The Activist,* REGIONAL.

ROY WILLIAM NEILL (1890–1946)

1929: *Behind Closed Doors, Wall Street.* 1930: *The Melody Man* (all COL); *Cock o' the Walk* (with Walter Lang), WW; *Just Like Heaven,* TIFFANY. 1931: *The Avenger, The Good Bad Girl, Fifty Fathoms Deep.* 1932: *The Menace, That's My Boy.* 1933: *The Circus Queen Murder, The Whirlpool, As the Devil Commands, Above the Clouds.* 1934: *Fury of the Jungle, The Ninth Guest, Black Moon, Blind Date, I'll Fix It, Jealousy.* 1935: *Mills of the Gods, Eight Bells, The Black Room.* 1936: *The Lone Wolf Returns* (all COL). 1937: *Dr. Syn* (England), GB. 1938: *Thank Evans* (England), WB. 1939: *The Good Old Days* (England), WB. 1942: *Madame Spy, Sherlock Holmes and the Secret Weapon.* 1943: *Eyes of the Underworld, Frankenstein Meets the Wolf Man, Rhythm of the Islands, Sherlock Holmes in Washington, Sherlock Holmes Faces Death.* 1944: *Sherlock Holmes and the Spider Woman, The Scarlet Claw, Gypsy Wildcat, The Pearl of Death.* 1945: *The House of Fear, The Woman in Green, Pursuit to Algiers.* 1946: *Black Angel* (all U).

JAMES NEILSON (1918–)

1957: *Night Passage,* U-I. 1962: *Moon Pilot, Bon Voyage!* 1963: *Summer Magic, Dr. Syn* (England; *Alias the Scarecrow*). 1964: *The Moonspinners* (Crete, England) (all BV). 1966: *Return of the Gunfighter,* M-G-M. 1967: *The Adventures of Bullwhip Griffin,* BV; *Gentle Giant,* PAR. 1968: *Where Angels Go—Trouble Follows!,* COL. 1969: *The First Time,* UA; *Flareup,* M-G-M.

GENE NELSON (1920–)

1962: *Hand of Death,* 20TH. 1963: *Hootenanny Hoot.* 1964: *Kissin' Cousins, Your Cheatin' Heart.* 1965: *Harum Scarum* (all M-G-M). 1967: *The Cool Ones,* WB-7A.

OZZIE NELSON (1907–)

1965: *Love and Kisses,* U.

RALPH NELSON (1916–)

1962: *Requiem for a Heavyweight,* COL. 1963: *Lilies of the Field,* UA; *Soldier in the Rain,* AA. 1964: *Fate Is the Hunter,* 20TH; *Father Goose,* U. 1965: *Once a Thief,* M-G-M. 1966: *Duel at Diablo,* UA. 1968: *Counterpoint,* U; *Charly,* CINERAMA. 1970: *Tick . . . tick . . . tick,* M-G-M; *Soldier Blue,* AVCO-EMBASSY. 1971: *Flight of the Doves* (England), COL. 1972: *The Wrath of God,* M-G-M. 1975: *The Wilby Conspiracy* (Kenya), UA.

KURT NEUMANN (1908–1958)

1932: *Fast Companions (Information Kid), My Pal, the King.* 1933: *The Big Cage, The Secret of the Blue Room, King for a Night.* 1934: *Let's Talk It Over, Half a Sinner, Wake Up and Dream.* 1935: *Alias Mary Dow, The Affair of Susan* (all U). 1936: *Let's Sing Again,* RKO; *Rainbow on the River,* RKO. 1937: *Espionage,* M-G-M; *Make a Wish,* RKO; *Hold 'Em Navy,* PAR. 1938: *Wide Open Faces,* COL; *Touchdown, Army.* 1939: *Unmarried, Island of Lost Men.* 1940: *All Women Have Secrets, A Night at Earl Carroll's* (all PAR); *Ellery Queen—Master Detective,* COL. 1942: *Brooklyn Orchid, About Face, The McGuerins from Brooklyn, Fall In.* 1943: *Taxi, Mister; Yanks Ahoy* (all UA); *The Unknown Ghost,* MONO. 1945: *Tarzan and the Amazons.* 1946: *Tarzan and the Leopard Woman.* 1947: *Tarzan and the Huntress* (all RKO). 1948: *The Dude Goes West, Bad Men of Tombstone.* 1949: *Bad Boy* (all AA). 1950: *The Kid From Texas,* U-I; *Rocketship X-M,* LIPPERT. 1951: *Cattle Drive, Reunion in Reno.* 1952: *Son of Ali Baba* (all U-I); *The Ring,* UA; *Hiawatha,* AA. 1953: *Tarzan and the She-Devil,* RKO. 1954: *Carnival Story,* RKO. 1955: *They Were So Young,* LIPPERT. 1956: *Mohawk, The Desperadoes Are in Town.* 1957: *Kronos, She-Devil, The Deerslayer.* 1958: *The Fly* (all 20TH); *Circus of Love* (Germany), DISTRIBUTORS CORP. OF AMERICA; *Machete,* UA. 1959: *Watusi,* M-G-M; *Counterplot* (Puerto Rico), UA.

SAM NEWFIELD (SAMUEL NEUFELD) (1900–1964)

1933: *Reform Girl,* TOWER; *The Important Witness,* TOWER; *Under Secret Orders,* PROGRESSIVE PICTURES. 1934: *Big Time or Bust, Marrying Widows, Beggar's Holiday* (all TOWER). 1935: *Northern Frontier,* AMBASSADOR PICTURES; *Code of the Mounted,* AMBASSADOR; *Racing Luck,* REP; *Trails of the Wild,* AMBASSADOR. 1936: *Timber War,* AMBASSADOR; *Federal Agent,* REP; *Burning Gold,* REP; *Border Caballero, Lightnin' Bill Carson, Roarin' Guns, Aces and Eights, The Lion's Den, Ghost Patrol* (all PURITAN); *Go-Get'-Em Haines,* REP; *The Traitor,* PURITAN; *Stormy Trails,* GN. 1937: *The Gambling Terror,* REP; *Trail of Vengeance,* REP; *Melody of the Plains,* SPECTRUM; *Bar Z Bad Men, Roarin' Lead* (with Mack V. Wright), *Guns in the Dark, Gun Lords of Stirrup Basin, Doomed at Sundown, A Lawman Is Born, Boot Hill Brigade, Arizona Gunfighter, Ridin' the Lone Trail, Colorado Kid.* 1938: *Paroled—To Die* (all REP); *Harlem on the Prairie,* ASSOCIATED FEATURES; *The Rangers Roundup,* SPECTRUM; *The Feud Maker,* REP; *Code of the Rangers,* MONO; *Thunder in the Desert,* REP; *Desert Patrol,* REP; *Two Gun Justice,*

MONO; *Phantom Ranger,* MONO; *The Terror of Tiny Town,* COL; *Durango Valley Raiders,* REP; *Frontier Scout,* GN; *Lightnin' Carson Rides Again,* PRINCIPAL. 1939: *Trigger Pals,* GN; *Six-Gun Rhythm,* GN; *The Invisible Killer* (as Sherman Scott), *Goose Step (Beasts of Berlin)* (as Sherman Scott). 1940: *The Sagebrush Family Trails West* (as Peter Stewart) (all PDC); *Secrets of a Model,* TIMES PICTURES; *I Take This Oath* (as Sherman Scott), PDC; *Frontier Crusader* (as Peter Stewart), *Hold That Woman!* (as Sherman Scott), *Billy the Kid Outlawed* (as Peter Stewart), *Marked Men* (as Sherman Scott), *Billy the Kid in Texas* (as Peter Stewart), *Billy the Kid's Gun Justice* (as Peter Stewart). 1941: *The Lone Rider Rides On, Billy the Kid's Range War* (as Peter Stewart), *The Lone Rider Crosses the Rio, Billy the Kid's Fighting Pals* (as Sherman Scott), *The Lone Rider in Ghost Town, The Texas Marshal* (as Peter Stewart), *Billy the Kid in Santa Fe* (as Sherman Scott), *The Lone Rider in Frontier Fury, Billy the Kid Wanted* (as Sherman Scott), *The Lone Rider Ambushed, Billy the Kid's Round-Up* (as Sherman Scott), *The Lone Rider Fights Back.* 1942: *The Lone Rider and the Bandit, Billy the Kid Trapped* (as Sherman Scott), *The Lone Rider in Cheyenne, The Mad Monster, Billy the Kid's Smoking Guns* (as Sherman Scott), *The Lone Rider in Texas Justice, Jungle Siren, Queen of Broadway.* 1943: *Dead Men Walk, Along the Sundown Trail* (as Peter Stewart), *Law and Order* (as Sherman Scott), *Prairie Pals* (as Peter Stewart), *The Black Raven, Tiger Fangs.* 1944: *Nabonga, Frontier Outlaws, Thundering Gun Slingers, The Monster Maker, Valley of Vengeance, The Contender, Fuzzy Settles Down, Rustler's Hideout, Swing Hostess, I Accuse My Parents.* 1945: *The Lady Confesses, Gangsters' Den, Stagecoach Outlaws, Apology for Murder, Border Badmen, Fighting Bill Carson, White Pongo, Prairie Rustlers.* 1946: *Lightning Raiders, Murder Is My Business, Gentleman with Guns, Ghost of Hidden Valley, Larceny in Her Heart, Prairie Badmen, Queen of Burlesque, Blonde for a Day, Gas House Kids.* 1947: *Three on a Ticket* (all PRC); *Adventure Island* (as Peter Stewart), PAR. 1948: *Money Madness,* FILM CLASSICS; *The Counterfeiters* (as Peter Stewart), 20TH. 1949: *State Department—File 649* (as Peter Stewart), FILM CLASSICS; *Wild Weed,* JEWELL. 1950: *Radar Secret Service, Western Pacific Agent, Motor Patrol, Hi-Jacked.* 1951: *Three Desperate Men, Fingerprints Don't Lie, Mask of the Dragon* (all LIPPERT); *Skipalong Rosenbloom,* UA; *Lost Continent, Leave It to the Marines, Sky High.* 1952: *Outlaw Women* (with Ron Ormond), *Scotland Yard Inspector* (England; English title—*Lady in the Fog*), *Gambler and the Lady* (with Patrick Jenkins; England). 1955: *Thunder Over Sangoland* (all LIPPERT). 1956: *The*

Wild Dakotas (with Sigmund Neufeld), ASSOCIATED FILM RELEAS-
ING CORP.; *Frontier Gambler*, ASSOCIATED FILM; *The Three Outlaws*,
ASSOCIATED FILM. 1958: *Flaming Frontier* (Canada), 20TH; *Wolf Dog*
(Canada), 20TH.

JOSEPH M. NEWMAN (1909–)
1942: *Northwest Rangers*, M-G-M. 1948: *Jungle Patrol*, 20TH. 1949: *The
Great Dan Patch*, UA; *Abandoned*, U-I. 1950: *711 Ocean Drive*, COL. 1951:
Lucky Nick Cain, The Guy Who Came Back, Love Nest. 1952: *Red Skies of
Montana* (*Smoke Jumpers*), *The Outcasts of Poker Flat, Pony Soldier.*
1953: *Dangerous Crossing* (all 20TH). 1954: *The Human Jungle*, AA. 1955:
This Island Earth, U-I; *Kiss of Fire*, U-I. 1956: *Flight to Hong Kong*, UA.
1957: *Death in Small Doses*, AA. 1958: *Fort Massacre*, UA. 1959: *The
Gunfight at Dodge City*, UA; *The Big Circus*, AA; *Tarzan, the Ape Man*,
M-G-M. 1961: *King of the Roaring Twenties—The Story of Arnold Rothstein*,
AA; *A Thunder of Drums*, M-G-M; *Twenty Plus Two*, AA; *The George Raft
Story* (*Spin of a Coin*), AA.

MAX NOSSECK (ALEXANDER M. NORRIS) (1902–)
1930: *Der Tanz ins Glück* (Germany). 1931: *Der Schlemihl* (Germany).
1932: *Einmal möchte ich keine Sorgen haben* (Germany), *Es geht um Alles*
(Germany). 1934: *Gado Bravo* (Portugal), *Alegre Voy!* (Spain). 1935:
Ponderoso Caballero (Spain), *Le roi des Champs-Elysées* (France), PAR.
1940: *Overture to Glory* (Yiddish documentary), G. & L. DISTRIBUTING
CO.; *Girls Under 21*, COL. 1941: *Gambling Daughters*, PRC. 1945: *Dillinger*, MONO; *The Brighton Strangler*, RKO. 1946: *Black Beauty*, 20TH.
1947: *The Return of Rin-Tin-Tin.* 1950: *Kill or Be Killed.* 1951: *Korea Patrol*
(all EL); *The Hoodlum*, UA. 1953: *Body Beautiful*, SAVOY ROADSHOW
PICTURES. 1955: *Der Hauptmann und sein Held* (Germany). 1957: *Garden
of Eden*, EXCELSIOR.

CHRISTIAN NYBY
1951: *The Thing*, RKO. 1957: *Hell on Devil's Island*, 20TH. 1965: *Young
Fury*, PAR; *Operation CIA*, AA. 1967: *First to Fight*, WB-7A.

ARCH OBOLER (1909–)
1945: *Bewitched*, M-G-M. 1946: *Strange Holiday*, PRC. 1947: *The Arnelo
Affair*, M-G-M. 1951: *Five*, COL. 1952: *Bwana Devil*, UA. 1953: *The
Twonky*, UA. 1961: *1 + 1—Exploring the Kinsey Reports* (Canada), SE-
LECTED PICTURES. 1967: *The Bubble*, ARCH OBOLER.

EDMOND O'BRIEN (1915–)
1954: *Shield for Murder* (with Howard W. Koch), UA. 1961: *Man Trap*, PAR.

CLIFFORD ODETS (1903–1963)
1944: *None but the Lonely Heart*, RKO. 1959: *The Story on Page One*, 20TH.

GERD OSWALD (1916–)
1956: *A Kiss Before Dying, The Brass Legend*. 1957: *Crime of Passion, Fury at Showdown, Valeria*. 1958: *Paris Holiday* (France) (all UA); *Screaming Mimi*, COL. 1961: *Brainwashed* (Austria, Yugoslavia), AA. 1966: *Agent for H.A.R.M.*, U. 1969: *Eighty Steps to Jonah*, WB. 1971: *Bunny O'Hare* (*The Bunny O'Hare Mob*), AIP.

GEORGE PAL (1908–)
1958: *Tom Thumb*. 1960: *The Time Machine*. 1961: *Atlantis, the Lost Continent*. 1962: *The Wonderful World of the Brothers Grimm* (with Henry Levin; Pal directed fairy-tale sequences). 1964: *Seven Faces of Dr. Lao* (all M-G-M).

NORMAN PANAMA (1914–)
In collaboration with Melvin Frank: 1950: *The Reformer and the Redhead*. 1951: *Strictly Dishonorable, Callaway Went Thataway*. 1952: *Above and Beyond* (all M-G-M). 1954: *Knock on Wood*. 1956: *The Court Jester, That Certain Feeling* (all PAR). Alone: 1959: *The Trap*, PAR. 1962: *The Road to Hong Kong*, UA. 1966: *Not with My Wife, You Don't!*, WB. 1969: *The Maltese Bippy*, M-G-M; *How to Commit Marriage*, CINERAMA.

JERRY PARIS (1925–)
1968: *Never a Dull Moment*, BV; *Don't Raise the Bridge, Lower the River!*, COL; *How Sweet It Is!*, NATIONAL GENERAL. 1969: *Viva Max!*, COMMONWEALTH UNITED. 1970: *The Grasshopper*, NATIONAL GENERAL. 1971: *The Star-Spangled Girl*, PAR.

ROBERT R. PARRISH (1916–)
1951: *Cry Danger*, RKO; *The Mob*, COL. 1952: *The San Francisco Story*, WB; *Assignment: Paris*, COL; *My Pal Gus*, 20TH. 1953: *Shoot First*

(England), UA. 1955: *The Purple Plain* (England), UA; *Lucy Gallant,* PAR. 1957: *Fire Down Below* (England), COL. 1958: *Saddle the Wind,* M-G-M. 1959: *The Wonderful Country,* UA. 1963: *In the French Style* (France), COL. 1965: *Up from the Beach* (France), 20TH. 1967: *Casino Royale* (with John Huston, Ken Hughes, Val Guest, Joseph McGrath; England), COL; *The Bobo* (England), WB-7A. 1968: *Duffy* (England), COL. 1969: *Journey to the Far Side of the Sun* (England), U. 1971: *A Town Called Hell* (Spain), SCOTIA INTERNATIONAL FILMS. 1974: *The Destructors* (France), AIP.

LARRY PEERCE

1964: *One Potato, Two Potato,* CINEMA V. 1966: *The Big TNT Show,* AIP. 1967: *The Incident,* 20TH. 1969: *Goodbye, Columbus,* PAR. 1971: *The Sporting Club,* AVCO-EMBASSY. 1972: *A Separate Peace,* PAR. 1973: *Ash Wednesday* (Italy), PAR. 1975: *The Other Side of the Mountain,* U.

BROOKE L. PETERS

1954: *The World Dances,* FESTIVAL PICTURES. 1957: *The Unearthly,* REP. 1961: *Anatomy of a Psycho,* UNITEL OF CALIF.

DANIEL PETRIE (1920–)

1960: *The Bramble Bush,* WB. 1961: *A Raisin in the Sun,* COL. 1963: *The Main Attraction,* M-G-M; *Stolen Hours,* UA. 1966: *The Idol,* EMBASSY; *The Spy with a Cold Nose,* EMBASSY. 1973: *The Neptune Factor,* 20TH. 1974: *Buster and Billie,* COL.

JOSEPH PEVNEY (1920–)

1950: *Shakedown, Undercover Girl.* 1951: *Air Cadet, The Iron Man, The Lady from Texas, The Strange Door.* 1952: *Meet Danny Wilson, Flesh and Fury, Just Across the Street, Because of You.* 1953: *Desert Legion, It Happens Every Thursday, Back to God's Country.* 1954: *Yankee Pasha, Playgirl* (all U-I); *Three Ring Circus,* PAR. 1955: *Six Bridges to Cross, Foxfire, Female on the Beach.* 1956: *Away All Boats, Congo Crossing.* 1957: *Istanbul, Tammy and the Bachelor, The Midnight Story, Man of a Thousand Faces.* 1958: *Twilight for the Gods* (all U-I); *Torpedo Run,* M-G-M. 1959: *Cash McCall,* WB. 1960: *The Crowded Sky,* WB; *The Plunderers,* AA. 1961: *Portrait of a Mobster,* WB. 1966: *The Night of the Grizzly,* PAR.

IRVING PICHEL (1891–1954)
1932: *The Most Dangerous Game* (with Ernest B. Schoedsack). 1933: *Before Dawn*. 1935: *She* (with Lansing C. Holden) (all RKO). 1936: *The Gentleman from Louisiana*. 1937: *Beware of Ladies, Larceny of the Air, The Sheik Steps Out, The Duke Comes Back* (all REP). 1939: *The Great Commandment*. 1940: *Earthbound, The Man I Married, Hudson's Bay*. 1941: *Dance Hall*. 1942: *Secret Agent of Japan, The Pied Piper, Life Begins at Eight-Thirty*. 1943: *The Moon Is Down, Happy Land* (all 20TH). 1944: *And Now Tomorrow*, PAR. 1945: *A Medal for Benny*, PAR; *Colonel Effingham's Raid*, 20TH. 1946: *Tomorrow Is Forever*, RKO; *The Bride Wore Boots*, PAR; *OSS*, PAR; *Temptation*, U. 1947: *They Won't Believe Me*, RKO; *Something in the Wind*, U-I. 1948: *The Miracle of the Bells*, RKO; *Mr. Peabody and the Mermaid*, U-I. 1949: *Without Honor*, UA. 1950: *The Great Rupert*, EL; *Quicksand*, UA; *Destination Moon*, EL. 1951: *Santa Fe*, COL. 1953: *Martin Luther* (England, Germany), LOUIS DE ROCHEMONT. 1954: *Day of Triumph*, GEORGE J. SCHAEFER.

SIDNEY PINK (1916–)
1961: *Journey to the Seventh Planet*, AIP. 1962: *Reptilicus* (Denmark), AIP. 1965: *Finger on the Trigger*, AA. 1966: *The Tall Women*, AA.

TED POST (1925–)
1956: *The Peacemaker*, UA. 1959: *The Legend of Tom Dooley*, COL. 1968: *Hang 'Em High*, UA. 1970: *Beneath the Planet of the Apes*, 20TH. 1973: *The Baby*, SCOTIA INTERNATIONAL; *The Harrad Experiment*, CINERAMA; *Magnum Force*, WB. 1975: *Whiffs*, WB.

H. C. (HENRY) POTTER (1904–)
1936: *Beloved Enemy*, UA. 1937: *Wings Over Honolulu*, U. 1938: *Romance in the Dark*, PAR; *Shopworn Angel*, M-G-M; *The Cowboy and the Lady*, UA. 1939: *The Story of Vernon and Irene Castle*, RKO; *Blackmail*, M-G-M. 1940: *Congo Maisie*, M-G-M; *Second Chorus*, PAR. 1941: *Hellzapoppin*, U. 1943: *Mr. Lucky*. 1947: *The Farmer's Daughter, A Likely Story*. 1948: *Mr. Blandings Builds His Dream House* (all RKO); *The Time of Your Life*, UA; *You Gotta Stay Happy*, U-I. 1950: *The Miniver Story*, M-G-M. 1955: *Three for the Show*, COL. 1957: *Top Secret Affair*, WB.

DICK POWELL (1904–1963)
1953: *Split Second*, RKO. 1956: *The Conqueror*, RKO; *You Can't Run Away from It*, COL. 1957: *The Enemy Below*, 20TH. 1958: *The Hunters*, 20TH.

ALAN RAFKIN

1965: *Ski Party*, AIP. 1966: *The Ghost and Mr. Chicken*. 1967: *The Ride to Hangman's Tree*. 1968: *Nobody's Perfect*, *The Shakiest Gun in the West*. 1969: *Angel in My Pocket*. 1971: *How to Frame a Figg* (all U).

JOEL RAPP

1959: *High School Big Shot*, FILMGROUP. 1960: *Battle of Blood Island*, FILMGROUP.

IRVING RAPPER (1898–)

1941: *Shining Victory*, *One Foot in Heaven*. 1942: *The Gay Sisters; Now, Voyager*. 1944: *The Adventures of Mark Twain*. 1945: *The Corn Is Green, Rhapsody in Blue*. 1946: *Deception*. 1947: *The Voice of the Turtle* (all WB). 1949: *Anna Lucasta*, COL. 1950: *The Glass Menagerie*, WB. 1952: *Another Man's Poison* (England), UA. 1953: *Forever Female*, PAR; *Bad for Each Other*, COL. 1956: *Strange Intruder*, AA; *The Brave One*, RKO. 1958: *Marjorie Morningstar*, WB. 1959: *The Miracle*, WB. 1962: *Joseph and His Brethren*, COLORAMA FEATURES. 1970: *The Christine Jorgensen Story*, UA.

GREGORY RATOFF (1897–1961)

1936: *Sins of Man* (with Otto Brower). 1937: *The Lancer Spy*. 1939: *Wife, Husband and Friend; Rose of Washington Square, Hotel for Women* (all 20TH); *Intermezzo*, UA; *Barricade, Daytime Wife*. 1940: *I Was an Adventuress, Public Deb Number One* (all 20TH). 1941: *Adam Had Four Sons*, COL; *The Men in Her Life*, COL; *The Corsican Brothers*, UA. 1942: *Two Yanks in Trinidad*, COL; *Footlight Serenade*, 20TH. 1943: *Something to Shout About*, COL; *The Heat's On*, COL; *Song of Russia*, M-G-M. 1944: *Irish Eyes Are Smiling*, 20TH. 1945: *Where Do We Go from Here?*, 20TH; *Paris Underground*, UA. 1946: *Do You Love Me?*, 20TH. 1947: *Moss Rose*, 20TH. 1949: *Black Magic*, UA. 1950: *If This Be Sin* (England), UA. 1951: *Operation X* (England), COL. 1953: *Taxi*, 20TH. 1956: *Abdullah's Harem* (Egypt), 20TH. 1960: *Oscar Wilde* (England), FILMS-AROUND-THE-WORLD.

JOHN RAWLINS (1902–)

1938: *State Police, Young Fugitives, The Missing Guest, Air Devils*. 1940: *The Leatherpushers*. 1941: *Six Lessons from Madame La Zonga, A Dangerous Game, Mr. Dynamite, Mutiny in the Arctic, Men of the Timberland,*

Raiders of the Desert. 1942: *Bombay Clipper, Unseen Enemy, Mississippi Gambler, Half Way to Shanghai, Sherlock Holmes and the Voice of Terror, The Great Impersonation, Arabian Nights.* 1943: *We've Never Been Licked.* 1944: *Ladies Courageous.* 1945: *Sudan.* 1946: *Strange Conquest, Her Adventurous Night* (all U). 1947: *Dick Tracy's Dilemma, Dick Tracy Meets Gruesome.* 1948: *The Arizona Ranger* (all RKO); *Michael O'Halloran,* MONO. 1949: *Massacre River,* AA. 1950: *Boy from Indiana,* EL; *Rogue River,* EL. 1951: *Fort Defiance.* 1953: *Shark River.* 1958: *Lost Lagoon* (all UA).

IRVING REIS (1906–1953)
1940: *One Crowded Night, I'm Still Alive.* 1941: *Footlight Fever, The Gay Falcon, Weekend for Three, A Date with the Falcon.* 1942: *The Falcon Takes Over, The Big Street.* 1946: *The Crack-Up.* 1947: *The Bachelor and the Bobby-Soxer* (all RKO). 1948: *All My Sons,* U-I; *Enchantment,* RKO. 1949: *Roseanna McCoy,* RKO; *Dancing in the Dark,* 20TH. 1950: *Three Husbands,* UA; *Of Men and Music* (with Alex Hammid), 20TH. 1951: *New Mexico,* UA. 1952: *The Four Poster,* COL.

ALLEN REISNER
1957: *All Mine to Give,* U-I. 1958: *St. Louis Blues,* PAR.

CHARLES F. (CHUCK) REISNER (1887–1962)
1929: *Noisy Neighbors,* PATHÉ; *China Bound, The Hollywood Revue of 1929, Road Show.* 1930: *Chasing Rainbows, Caught Short, Love in the Rough.* 1931: *Reducing, Stepping Out, Politics, Flying High.* 1932: *Divorce in the Family.* 1933: *The Chief.* 1934: *You Can't Buy Everything, The Show-Off, Student Tour.* 1935: *The Winning Ticket, It's in the Air* (all M-G-M). 1936: *Everybody Dance* (England), GB. 1937: *Murder Goes to College,* PAR; *Sophie Lang Goes West,* PAR; *Manhattan Merry-Go-Round,* REP. 1939: *Winter Carnival,* UA. 1941: *The Big Store.* 1942: *This Time for Keeps.* 1943: *Harrigan's Kid.* 1944: *Meet the People, Lost in a Harem* (all M-G-M). 1948: *The Cobra Strikes,* EL; *In This Corner,* EL. 1950: *The Traveling Saleswoman,* COL; *L'ultima cena* (Italy).

DAVID LOWELL RICH (c. 1923–)
1957: *No Time to Be Young.* 1958: *Senior Prom.* 1959: *Hey Boy! Hey Girl!, Have Rocket, Will Travel* (all COL). 1966: *Madame X, The Plainsman.* 1967: *Rosie!* 1968: *Three Guns for Texas* (with Paul Stanley and Earl

Bellamy), *A Lovely Way to Die*. 1969: *Eye of the Cat*. 1973: *That Man Bolt* (with Henry Levin; U.S., Hong Kong) (all U).

JOHN RICH (1925–)
1963: *Wives and Lovers*, PAR. 1964: *The New Interns*, COL; *Roustabout*. 1965: *Boeing Boeing*. 1967: *Easy Come, Easy Go* (all PAR).

ARTHUR RIPLEY (1895–1961)
1938: *I Met My Love Again* (with Joshua Logan), UA. 1942: *Prisoner of Japan*, PRC. 1944: *Voice in the Wind*. 1946: *The Chase*. 1958: *Thunder Road* (all UA).

ROBERT RISKIN (1897–1955)
1937: *When You're in Love*, COL.

MARTIN RITT (1919–)
1957: *Edge of the City*, M-G-M; *No Down Payment*, 20TH. 1958: *The Long, Hot Summer*, 20TH. 1959: *The Black Orchid*, PAR; *The Sound and the Fury*, 20TH. 1960: *Five Branded Women* (Italy), PAR. 1961: *Paris Blues*, UA. 1962: *Hemingway's Adventures of a Young Man*, 20TH. 1963: *Hud*, PAR. 1964: *The Outrage*, M-G-M. 1965: *The Spy Who Came in from the Cold*, PAR. 1967: *Hombre*, 20TH. 1968: *The Brotherhood*, PAR. 1970: *The Molly Maguires*, PAR; *The Great White Hope*, 20TH. 1972: *Sounder*, 20TH; *Pete n' Tillie*, U. 1974: *Conrack*, 20TH.

HAL ROACH (1892–)
1930: *Man of the North*, M-G-M. 1933: *The Devil's Brother* (with Charles Rogers), M-G-M. 1939: *Captain Fury, The Housekeeper's Daughter*. 1940: *One Million B.C.* (with Hal Roach, Jr., and—disputed in some sources—D. W. Griffith), *Turnabout*. 1941: *Road Show* (with Gordon Douglas and Hal Roach, Jr.) (all UA).

STEPHEN ROBERTS (1895–1936)
1932: *Sky Bride, Lady and Gent, The Night of June 13th, If I Had a Million* (with James Cruze, H. Bruce Humberstone, Ernst Lubitsch, Norman Z. McLeod, William A. Seiter, Norman Taurog). 1933: *The Story of Temple Drake, One Sunday Afternoon*. 1934: *The Trumpet Blows* (all PAR); *Romance in Manhattan*, RKO. 1935: *Star of Midnight*, RKO; *The Man Who*

Broke the Bank at Monte Carlo, 20TH. 1936: *The Lady Consents*, RKO; *The Ex-Mrs. Bradford*, RKO.

MARK ROBSON (1913–)

1943: *The Seventh Victim, The Ghost Ship*. 1944: *Youth Runs Wild*. 1945: *Isle of the Dead*. 1946: *Bedlam* (all RKO). 1949: *Champion*, UA; *Home of the Brave*, UA; *Roughshod, My Foolish Heart*. 1950: *Edge of Doom* (all RKO). 1951: *Bright Victory*, U-I; *I Want You*, RKO. 1953: *Return to Paradise*, UA. 1954: *Hell Below Zero* (England), COL; *Phffft*, COL; *The Bridges at Toko-Ri*, PAR. 1955: *A Prize of Gold*, COL; *Trial*, M-G-M. 1956: *The Harder They Fall*, COL. 1957: *The Little Hut*, M-G-M; *Peyton Place*. 1958: *The Inn of the Sixth Happiness*. 1960: *From the Terrace*. 1963: *Nine Hours to Rama* (all 20TH); *The Prize*, M-G-M. 1965: *Von Ryan's Express*, 20TH. 1966: *Lost Command*, COL. 1967: *Valley of the Dolls*, 20TH. 1969: *Daddy's Gone A-Hunting*, NATIONAL GENERAL. 1971: *Happy Birthday, Wanda June*, COL. 1972: *Limbo*, U. 1974: *Earthquake*, U.

ALBERT S. ROGELL (1901–)

1929: *Phantom City*, FN; *Cheyenne*, FN; *Lone Wolf's Daughter*, COL; *California Mail*, FN; *Flying Marine*, COL. 1930: *Painted Faces, Mamba*. 1931: *Aloha* (all TIFFANY); *Sweepstakes, The Tip-Off, The Suicide Fleet*. 1932: *Carnival Boat* (all RKO-PATHÉ); *The Rider of Death Valley*, U. 1933: *Air Hostess, Below the Sea, The Wrecker, East of Fifth Avenue*. 1934: *Fog* (all COL); *No More Women*, PAR; *The Hell Cat, Among the Missing, Name the Woman, Fugitive Lady*. 1935: *Unknown Woman, Air Hawks, Atlantic Adventure, Escape from Devil's Island* (*Song of the Damned*). 1936: *Roaming Lady* (all COL); *Grand Jury*, RKO. 1937: *Murder in Greenwich Village*. 1938: *Start Cheering, The Lone Wolf in Paris, City Streets* (all COL); *The Last Warning*. 1939: *For Love or Money, Hawaiian Nights, Laugh It Off*. 1940: *Private Affairs, I Can't Give You Anything but Love, Baby; Argentine Nights* (all U); *Li'l Abner*, RKO. 1941: *The Black Cat, Tight Shoes, Public Enemies*. 1942: *Jail House Blues* (all U); *Sleepytime Gal*, REP; *True to the Army*, PAR; *Butch Minds the Baby, Priorities on Parade, Youth on Parade*. 1943: *Hit Parade of 1943, In Old Oklahoma*. 1945: *Love, Honor, and Goodbye*. 1946: *Earl Carroll Sketchbook*. 1947: *The Magnificent Rogue* (all REP); *Heaven Only Knows*, UA. 1948: *Northwest Stampede*, EL. 1949: *The Song of India*, COL. 1950: *The Admiral Was a Lady*, UA. 1956: *Shadow of Fear* (England; *Before I Wake*), UA.

EDDIE ROMERO

1963: *The Raiders of Leyte Gulf* (Philippines), MANHATTAN FILMS INTERNATIONAL; *Cavalry Command*, PARADE PICTURES. 1964: *The Walls of Hell* (with Gerardo DeLeon), HEMISPHERE PICTURES; *Moro Witch Doctor*, 20TH. 1965: *The Ravagers*. 1968: *Brides of Blood* (with Gerardo DeLeon). 1969: *Blood Demon, Mad Doctor of Blood Island* (all HEMISPHERE). 1970: *Beast of the Yellow Night* (Philippines), NEW WORLD. 1971: *Beast of Blood*, HEMISPHERE. 1972: *Twilight People*, DIMENSION PICTURES. 1973: *Black Mama, White Mama*, AIP. 1974: *Beyond Atlantis* (Philippines), DIMENSION PICTURES; *Savage Sisters*, AIP.

GEORGE A. ROMERO (c. 1939–)

1968: *Night of the Living Dead*, CONTINENTAL. 1972: *There's Always Vanilla (The Affair)*, CAMBIST FILMS. 1973: *The Crazies*, CAMBIST FILMS; *Jack's Wife (Hungry Wives)*, LATENT IMAGE.

MICKEY ROONEY (1922–)

1951: *My True Story*, COL. 1960: *The Private Lives of Adam and Eve* (with Albert Zugsmith), U-I.

SHERMAN A. ROSE

1955: *Target Earth*, AA. 1956: *Magnificent Roughnecks*, AA. 1958: *Tank Battalion*, AIP.

PHIL ROSEN (1888–1951)

1929: *The Faker*, COL; *Peacock Fan*, CHEST; *The Phantom in the House*, CONTINENTAL. 1930: *The Rampant Age*, CONTINENTAL; *The Lotus Lady*, AUDIBLE PICTURES; *Worldly Goods*, CONTINENTAL; *Extravagance*, TIFFANY. 1931: *Second Honeymoon*, CONTINENTAL; *The Two-Gun Man, Alias the Bad Man, The Arizona Terror, Range Law, Branded Men, The Pocatello Kid* (all TIFFANY). 1932: *The Gay Buckaroo*, HOLLYWOOD PICTURES; *The Texas Gun Fighter, Whistlin' Dan, Lena Rivers* (all TIFFANY); *The Vanishing Frontier*, PAR; *Klondike*, MONO; *A Man's Land*, ALLIED PICTURES. 1933: *Young Blood, Self Defense, The Phantom Broadcast, The Sphinx, Black Beauty, Devil's Mate* (all MONO); *Hold the Press*, COL. 1934: *Beggars in Ermine*, MONO; *Shadows of Sing Sing*, COL; *Picture Brides*, FIRST DIVISION; *Cheaters*, LIBERTY; *Take the Stand*, LIBERTY; *Dangerous Corner*, RKO; *Woman in the Dark*, RKO;

Little Men, MASCOT; *West of the Pecos,* RKO. 1935: *Death Flies East,* COL; *Unwelcome Stranger,* COL; *Born to Gamble,* REP. 1936: *The Calling of Dan Matthews,* COL; *Tango, The Bridge of Sighs, Three of a Kind, Easy Money, It Couldn't Have Happened, Brilliant Marriage* (all INVINC-IBLE); *The President's Mystery,* REP; *Missing Girls,* CHEST; *Ellis Island,* INVINCIBLE. 1937: *Two Wise Maids, Jim Hanvey, Detective, It Could Happen to You* (all REP); *Roaring Timber,* COL; *Youth on Parole,* REP. 1938: *The Marines Are Here,* MONO. 1939: *Ex-Champ, Missing Evidence.* 1940: *Double Alibi* (all U); *Forgotten Girls,* REP; *The Crooked Road,* REP; *Phantom of Chinatown, Queen of the Yukon.* 1941: *The Roar of the Press* (all MONO); *Paper Bullets (Crime, Inc.; Gangs, Inc.),* PRC; *Murder by Invitation, The Deadly Game, Spooks Run Wild, I Killed That Man.* 1942: *Road to Happiness, The Man with Two Lives* (all MONO); *The Mystery of Marie Roget,* U. 1943: *You Can't Beat the Law,* MONO; *A Gentle Gangster,* REP; *Wings Over the Pacific.* 1944: *Charlie Chan in the Secret Service, The Chinese Cat, Return of the Ape Man, Black Magic, Call of the Jungle, The Jade Mask.* 1945: *The Scarlet Clue, The Red Dragon* (all MONO); *Captain Tugboat Annie,* REP. 1946: *The Shadow,* MONO; *The Strange Mr. Gregory,* MONO; *Step by Step,* RKO. 1949: *The Secret of St. Ives,* COL.

ARTHUR ROSSON (1889–1960)
1929: *The Winged Horseman* (with B. Reeves Eason), *Points West, The Long, Long Trail.* 1930: *The Mounted Stranger, Trailing Trouble, The Concentratin' Kid.* 1933: *Hidden Gold, Flaming Guns* (all U). 1937: *Boots of Destiny,* GN; *Trailin' Trouble,* GN.

RICHARD ROSSON (1894–1953)
1929: *The Very Idea* (with William LeBaron), RKO. 1935: *West Point of the Air,* M-G-M. 1937: *Behind the Headlines,* RKO; *Hideaway,* RKO. 1943: *Corvette K-225,* U.

STEPHANIE ROTHMAN
1966: *Blood Bath* (with Jack Hill), AIP. 1967: *It's a Bikini World,* TRANS-AMERICAN. 1970: *The Student Nurses,* NEW WORLD. 1971: *The Velvet Vampire,* NEW WORLD. 1972: *Group Marriage.* 1973: *Terminal Island.* 1974: *The Working Girls* (all DIMENSION PICTURES).

RUSSELL ROUSE (c. 1916–)
1951: *The Well* (with Leo Popkin). 1952: *The Thief.* 1953: *Wicked Woman* (all UA). 1955: *New York Confidential,* WB. 1956: *The Fastest Gun Alive,*

M-G-M. 1957: *House of Numbers*, M-G-M. 1959: *Thunder in the Sun*, PAR. 1964: *A House Is not a Home*. 1966: *The Oscar*. 1967: *The Caper of the Golden Bulls* (all EMBASSY).

ROY ROWLAND (c. 1910–)

1943: *A Stranger in Town*, M-G-M; *Lost Angel*, M-G-M. 1945: *A Song for Miss Julie*, REP; *Our Vines Have Tender Grapes*. 1946: *Boys' Ranch*. 1947: *The Romance of Rosy Ridge, Killer McCoy*. 1948: *Tenth Avenue Angel*. 1949: *Scene of the Crime*. 1950: *The Outriders, Two Weeks with Love*. 1951: *Excuse My Dust* (all M-G-M). 1952: *Bugles in the Afternoon*, WB. 1953: *Affair with a Stranger*, RKO; *The 5,000 Fingers of Dr. T*, COL; *The Moonlighter*, WB. 1954: *Witness to Murder*, UA; *Rogue Cop*. 1955: *Hit the Deck, Many Rivers to Cross*. 1956: *Meet Me in Las Vegas, These Wilder Years, Slander*. 1957: *Gun Glory*. 1958: *The Seven Hills of Rome* (Italy; *Arrivederci Roma*) (all M-G-M). 1963: *The Girl Hunters*, COLORAMA FEATURES. 1965: *Gunfighters of Casa Grande*, M-G-M. 1967: *The Sea Pirate*, PAR.

OSCAR RUDOLPH

1954: *The Rocket Man*, 20TH. 1961: *Twist Around the Clock*. 1962: *Don't Knock the Twist, The Wild Westerners* (all COL).

WESLEY RUGGLES (1889–1972)

1929: *Scandal*, U; *Street Girl*, RKO; *Girl Overboard*, U; *Condemned*, UA. 1930: *Honey*, PAR; *The Sea Bat*, M-G-M. 1931: *Cimarron, Are These Our Children?* 1932: *Roar of the Dragon* (all RKO); *No Man of Her Own*, PAR. 1933: *The Monkey's Paw*, RKO; *College Humor, I'm No Angel*. 1934: *Bolero, Shoot the Works*. 1935: *The Gilded Lily, Accent on Youth, The Bride Comes Home*. 1936: *Valiant Is the Word for Carrie*. 1937: *I Met Him in Paris, True Confession*. 1938: *Sing You Sinners*. 1939: *Invitation to Happiness* (all PAR). 1940: *Too Many Husbands, Arizona*. 1941: *You Belong to Me* (all COL). 1942: *Somewhere I'll Find You*. 1943: *Slightly Dangerous*. 1944: *See Here, Private Hargrove* (all M-G-M). 1953: *My Heart Goes Crazy* (England; *London Town*), UA.

RICHARD RUSH

1960: *Too Soon to Love*, U-I. 1963: *Of Love and Desire*, 20TH. 1967: *Thunder Alley*, AIP; *Hell's Angels on Wheels*, U.S. FILMS/FANFARE; *The Fickle Finger of Fate*, PRODUCERS RELEASING ORGANIZATION; *A*

Man Called Dagger, M-G-M. 1968: *Psych-Out*, AIP; *The Savage Seven*, AIP. 1970: *Getting Straight*, COL. 1974: *Freebie and the Bean*, WB.

WILLIAM D. RUSSELL (1908–1968)

1946: *Our Hearts Were Growing Up.* 1947: *Ladies' Man, Dear Ruth.* 1948: *The Sainted Sisters* (all PAR). 1949: *The Green Promise, Bride for Sale.* 1951: *Best of the Badmen* (all RKO).

BORIS SAGAL (1923–)

1963: *Dime with a Halo, Twilight of Honor.* 1965: *Girl Happy.* 1966: *Made in Paris* (all M-G-M). 1969: *The Thousand Plane Raid*, UA. 1970: *Mosquito Squadron* (England), UA. 1971: *The Omega Man*, WB.

SIDNEY SALKOW (1909–)

1937: *Four Days' Wonder, Girl Overboard, Behind the Mike.* 1938: *That's My Story* (all U); *The Night Hawk, Storm Over Bengal.* 1939: *Fighting Thoroughbreds, Woman Doctor, Street of Missing Men, The Zero Hour, She Married a Cop, Flight at Midnight* (all REP). 1940: *Cafe Hostess, The Lone Wolf Strikes, The Lone Wolf Meets a Lady* (all COL); *Girl from God's Country*, REP. 1941: *The Lone Wolf Keeps a Date, The Lone Wolf Takes a Chance, Time Out for Rhythm, Tillie the Toiler.* 1942: *The Adventures of Martin Eden, Flight Lieutenant.* 1943: *City Without Men, The Boy from Stalingrad* (all COL). 1946: *Faithful in My Fashion*, M-G-M. 1947: *Millie's Daughter*, COL; *Bulldog Drummond at Bay*, COL. 1948: *Sword of the Avenger*, EL. 1949: *La Strada Buia* (with Marino Girolami; Italy). 1950: *La Rivale dell'imperatrice* (with Jacopo Comin; Italy). 1952: *Scarlet Angel*, U-I; *The Golden Hawk, The Pathfinder.* 1953: *Prince of Pirates; Jack McCall, Desperado* (all COL); *Raiders of the Seven Seas.* 1954: *Sitting Bull.* 1955: *Robber's Roost* (all UA); *Las Vegas Shakedown*, AA; *Shadow of the Eagle* (England), UA; *Toughest Man Alive*, AA. 1956: *Gun Brothers.* 1957: *The Iron Sheriff, Gun Duel in Durango, Chicago Confidential* (all UA). 1960: *The Big Night*, PAR. 1963: *Twice Told Tales*, UA. 1964: *The Quick Gun*, COL; *The Last Man on Earth* (Italy), AIP; *Blood on the Arrow*, AA. 1965: *The Great Sioux Massacre*, COL. 1966: *The Murder Game*, 20TH.

DENIS SANDERS (1929–)

1959: *Crime and Punishment, U.S.A.*, AA. 1962: *War Hunt*, UA. 1964: *One Man's Way*, UA; *Shock Treatment*, 20TH. 1970: *Elvis—That's the Way It Is* (documentary), M-G-M. 1971: *Soul to Soul* (Ghana; documentary), CINERAMA. 1973: *Invasion of the Bee Girls*, DIMENSION PICTURES.

MARK SANDRICH (1900–1945)

1930: *The Talk of Hollywood*, WW. 1933: *Melody Cruise; Aggie Appleby, Maker of Men*. 1934: *Hips, Hips, Hooray; Cockeyed Cavaliers, The Gay Divorcee*. 1935: *Top Hat*. 1936: *Follow the Fleet, A Woman Rebels*. 1937: *Shall We Dance*. 1938: *Carefree* (all RKO). 1939: *Man About Town*. 1940: *Buck Benny Rides Again, Love Thy Neighbor*. 1941: *Skylark*. 1942: *Holiday Inn*. 1943: *So Proudly We Hail!* 1944: *I Love a Soldier, Here Come the Waves* (all PAR).

ALFRED SANTELL (1895–)

1930: *The Arizona Kid, The Sea Wolf*. 1931: *Body and Soul, Daddy Long Legs, Sob Sister* (all FOX). 1932: *Polly of the Circus*, M-G-M; *Rebecca of Sunnybrook Farm, Tess of the Storm Country*. 1933: *Bondage* (all FOX); *The Right to Romance*, RKO. 1934: *The Life of Vergie Winters*, RKO. 1935: *The Dictator* (with Victor Saville; England), GB; *People Will Talk*, PAR; *A Feather in Her Hat*, COL. 1936: *Winterset*, RKO. 1937: *Interns Can't Take Money*, PAR; *Breakfast for Two*, RKO. 1938: *Cocoanut Grove*, PAR; *Having a Wonderful Time*, RKO; *The Arkansas Traveler*. 1939: *Our Leading Citizen*. 1941: *Aloma of the South Seas*. 1942: *Beyond the Blue Horizon* (all PAR). 1943: *Jack London*, UA. 1944: *The Hairy Ape*, UA. 1945: *Mexicana*, REP. 1946: *That Brennan Girl*, REP.

JOSEPH SANTLEY (1889–1971)

1929: *The Cocoanuts* (with Robert Florey), PAR. 1930: *Swing High*, PATHÉ. 1934: *The Loud Speaker*, MONO; *Young and Beautiful*, MASCOT. 1935: *Million Dollar Baby*, MONO; *Harmony Lane*, MASCOT; *Waterfront Lady*, MASCOT. 1936: *Dancing Feet*, REP; *Her Master's Voice*, PAR; *Laughing Irish Eyes*, REP; *The Harvester*, REP; *We Went to College*, M-G-M; *Walking on Air, The Smartest Girl in Town*. 1937: *Meet the Missus, There Goes the Groom*. 1938: *She's Got Everything, Blonde Cheat* (all RKO); *Always in Trouble*, 20TH; *Swing, Sister, Swing*. 1939: *Spirit of Culver, The Family Next Door, Two Bright Boys* (all U). 1940: *Music in My Heart*, COL; *Melody and Moonlight, Melody Ranch, Behind the News* (all REP). 1941: *Dancing on a Dime*, PAR; *Sis Hopkins, Rookies on Parade, Puddin'head, Ice-Capades, Down Mexico Way*. 1942: *A Tragedy at Midnight, Yokel Boy, Remember Pearl Harbor, Joan of Ozark, Call of the*

Canyon. 1943: *Chatterbox, Shantytown, Thumbs Up, Sleepy Lagoon, Here Comes Elmer.* 1944: *Rosie, the Riveter, Jamboree, Goodnight Sweetheart, Three Little Sisters, Brazil.* 1945: *Earl Carroll Vanities, Hitchhike to Happiness* (all REP). 1946: *Shadow of a Woman,* WB. 1949: *Make Believe Ballroom,* COL. 1950: *When You're Smiling,* COL.

RICHARD C. SARAFIAN (c. 1927–)

1965: *Andy,* U. 1969: *Run Wild, Run Free,* COL. 1971: *Vanishing Point,* 20TH; *Fragment of Fear* (England), COL; *Man in the Wilderness,* WB. 1973: *Lolly Madonna, XXX,* M-G-M; *The Man Who Loved Cat Dancing,* M-G-M.

JOSEPH SARGENT

1966: *One Spy Too Many,* M-G-M. 1968: *The Hell with Heroes,* U. 1970: *Colossus—The Forbin Project,* U. 1972: *The Man,* PAR. 1973: *White Lightning,* UA. 1974: *The Taking of Pelham One Two Three,* UA.

GEORGE SCHAEFER (1920–)

1963: *Macbeth,* PROMINENT FILMS. 1969: *Pendulum,* COL; *Generation,* AVCO-EMBASSY. 1971: *Doctors' Wives,* COL. 1973: *Once Upon a Scoundrel,* CARLYLE FILMS.

VICTOR SCHERTZINGER (1880–1941)

1929: *Redskin, Nothing but the Truth, The Wheel of Life, Fashions in Love.* 1930: *The Laughing Lady, Paramount on Parade* (with D. Arzner, O. Brower, E. Goulding, V. Heerman, E. Knopf, R. V. Lee, E. Lubitsch, L. Mendes, E. Sutherland, F. Tuttle), *Safety in Numbers, Heads Up* (all PAR). 1931: *The Woman Between, Friends and Lovers.* 1932: *Strange Justice* (all RKO); *Uptown New York,* WW. 1933: *The Constant Woman,* WW; *The Cocktail Hour,* COL; *My Woman,* COL. 1934: *Beloved,* U; *One Night of Love.* 1935: *Let's Live Tonight, Love Me Forever.* 1936: *The Music Goes 'Round* (all COL). 1937: *Something to Sing About,* GN. 1939: *The Mikado* (England), U. 1940: *Road to Singapore, Rhythm on the River.* 1941: *Road to Zanzibar, Kiss the Boys Goodbye, Birth of the Blues.* 1942: *The Fleet's In* (all PAR).

ERNEST B. SCHOEDSACK (1893–)

1929: *Four Feathers* (with Merian C. Cooper, Lothar Mendes), PAR. 1931: *Rango,* PAR. 1932: *The Most Dangerous Game* (with Irving Pichel). 1933:

King Kong (with Merian C. Cooper), *Blind Adventure, Son of Kong.* 1934:
Long Lost Father. 1935: *The Last Days of Pompeii* (all RKO). 1937:
Trouble in Morocco, COL; *Outlaws of the Orient,* COL. 1940: *Dr. Cyclops,*
PAR. 1949: *Mighty Joe Young,* RKO.

FRED F. SEARS (1913–1957)
1949: *Desert Vigilante, Horsemen of the Sierras.* 1950: *Across the Badlands,
Raiders of Tomahawk Creek, Lightning Guns.* 1951: *Prairie Roundup,
Ridin' the Outlaw Trail, Snake River Desperadoes, Bonanza Town, Pecos
River.* 1952: *Smokey Canyon, The Hawk of Wild River, The Kid from
Broken Gun, Last Train from Bombay, Target Hong Kong.* 1953: *Ambush
at Tomahawk Gap, The 49th Man, Mission Over Korea, Sky Commando,
The Nebraskan, El Alamein* (all COL). 1954: *Overland Pacific,* UA; *The
Miami Story, Massacre Canyon, The Outlaw Stallion.* 1955: *Wyoming
Renegades; Cell 2455, Death Row; Chicago Syndicate, Apache Ambush,
Teen-Age Crime Wave, Inside Detroit.* 1956: *Fury at Gunsight Pass, Rock
Around the Clock, Earth vs. the Flying Saucers, The Werewolf, Miami
Expose, Cha-Cha-Cha Boom!, Rumble on the Docks, Don't Knock the Rock.*
1957: *Utah Blaine, Calypso Heat Wave, The Night the World Exploded,
The Giant Claw, Escape from San Quentin.* 1958: *The World Was His Jury,
Going Steady, Crash Landing* (all COL); *Badman's Country,* WB; *Ghost of
the China Sea,* COL.

EDWARD SEDGWICK (1893–1953)
1929: *Spite Marriage.* 1930: *Free and Easy, Dough Boys.* 1931: *Parlor,
Bedroom and Bath* (all M-G-M); *A Dangerous Affair,* COL; *Maker of Men,*
COL. 1932: *The Passionate Plumber, Speak Easily.* 1933: *What! No Beer?*
(all M-G-M); *Saturday's Millions, Horseplay.* 1934: *The Poor Rich, I'll Tell
the World* (all U); *Here Comes the Groom,* PAR; *Death on the Diamond,*
M-G-M. 1935: *Father Brown, Detective,* PAR; *Murder in the Fleet,* M-G-M;
The Virginia Judge, PAR. 1936: *Mister Cinderella,* M-G-M. 1937: *Pick
a Star,* M-G-M; *Riding on Air,* RKO; *Fit for a King,* RKO. 1938: *The
Gladiator,* COL. 1939: *Burn 'Em Up O'Connor,* M-G-M; *Beware, Spooks!,*
COL. 1940: *So You Won't Talk?,* COL. 1943: *Air Raid Wardens,* M-G-M.
1948: *A Southern Yankee,* M-G-M. 1951: *Ma and Pa Kettle Back on the
Farm,* U-I.

ALEX SEGAL (1915–)
1956: *Ransom,* M-G-M. 1963: *All the Way Home,* PAR. 1965: *Joy in the
Morning,* M-G-M; *Harlow,* MAGNA PICTURES.

LEWIS R. SEILER (1891–1964)
1929: *The Ghost Talks, Girls Gone Wild, A Song of Kentucky* (all FOX).
1932: *No Greater Love,* COL. 1933: *Deception,* COL. 1934: *Frontier Marshal.* 1935: *Charlie Chan in Paris, Asegure a su Mujer* (Spanish language), *Ginger* (all FOX); *Paddy O'Day.* 1936: *Here Comes Trouble, The First Baby, Star for a Night, Career Woman* (all 20TH). 1937: *Turn off the Moon,* PAR. 1938: *He Couldn't Say No, Crime School, Penrod's Double Trouble, Heart of the North.* 1939: *King of the Underworld, You Can't Get Away with Murder, The Kid from Kokomo, Hell's Kitchen* (with E. A. Dupont), *Dust Be My Destiny.* 1940: *It All Came True, Flight Angels, Murder in the Air, Tugboat Annie Sails Again, South of Suez.* 1941: *Kisses for Breakfast, The Smiling Ghost, You're in the Army Now.* 1942: *The Big Shot* (all WB); *Pittsburgh,* U. 1943: *Guadalcanal Diary.* 1944: *Something for the Boys.* 1945: *Molly and Me, Doll Face.* 1946: *If I'm Lucky* (all 20TH). 1948: *Whiplash.* 1950: *Breakthrough.* 1951: *The Tanks Are Coming.* 1952: *The Winning Team, Operation Secret.* 1953: *The System* (all WB). 1954: *The Bamboo Prison.* 1955: *Women's Prison.* 1956: *Battle Stations, Over-Exposed.* 1958: *The True Story of Lynn Stuart* (all COL).

WILLIAM A. SEITER (1891–1964)
1929: *Synthetic Sin, Why Be Good?, Smiling Irish Eyes, Prisoners, Footlights and Fools.* 1930: *Strictly Modern, Back Pay, The Flirting Widow, The Love Racket, The Truth About Youth, Sunny.* 1931: *Kiss Me Again* (all FN); *Going Wild,* WB; *Big Business Girl,* FN; *Too Many Crooks, Caught Plastered, Peach O'Reno.* 1932: *Way Back Home, Girl Crazy, Young Bride, Is My Face Red?* (all RKO); *Hot Saturday, If I Had a Million* (with J. Cruze, H. B. Humberstone, E. Lubitsch, Norman Z. McLeod, S. Roberts, N. Taurog). 1933: *Hello, Everybody!* (all PAR); *Diplomaniacs, Professional Sweetheart, Chance at Heaven* (all RKO). 1934: *Sons of the Desert,* M-G-M; *Rafter Romance,* RKO; *Sing and Like It,* RKO; *Love Birds,* U; *We're Rich Again, The Richest Girl in the World.* 1935: *Roberta* (all RKO); *The Daring Young Man,* FOX; *Orchids to You,* FOX; *In Person,* RKO; *If You Could Only Cook,* COL. 1936: *The Moon's Our Home,* PAR; *The Case Against Mrs. Ames,* PAR; *Dimples, Stowaway.* 1937: *This Is My Affair* (all 20TH); *The Life of the Party,* RKO; *Life Begins in College.* 1938: *Sally, Irene and Mary; Three Blind Mice* (all 20TH); *Room Service,* RKO; *Thanks for Everything,* 20TH. 1939: *Susannah of the Mounties,* 20TH; *Allegheny Uprising,* RKO. 1940: *It's a Date, Hired Wife.* 1941: *Nice Girl?, Appointment for Love.* 1942: *Broadway* (all U); *You Were Never Lovelier,* COL.

1943: *Four Jills in a Jeep*, 20TH; *Destroyer*, COL; *A Lady Takes a Chance*. 1944: *Belle of the Yukon*. 1945: *It's a Pleasure* (all RKO); *The Affairs of Susan*, PAR; *That Night with You*. 1946: *Little Giant, Lover Come Back*. 1947: *I'll Be Yours* (all U). 1948: *Up in Central Park, One Touch of Venus*. 1950: *Borderline* (all U-I). 1951: *Dear Brat*, PAR. 1953: *The Lady Wants Mink, Champ for a Day*. 1954: *Make Haste to Live* (all REP).

GEORGE B. SEITZ (1888–1944)

1929: *Black Magic*, FOX. 1930: *The Murder on the Roof*, COL; *Guilty*, COL; *Midnight Mystery*, RKO; *Danger Lights*, RKO. 1931: *Drums of Jeopardy*, TIFFANY; *The Lion and the Lamb, Arizona, Shanghaied Love* (all COL); *The Night Beat*, ACTION PICTURES. 1932: *Docks of San Francisco, Sally of the Subway, Sin's Pay Day, Passport to Paradise, The Widow in Scarlet* (all MAYFAIR). 1933: *Treason*, COL; *The Thrill Hunter*, COL; *The Women in His Life*, M-G-M. 1934: *Lazy River*, M-G-M; *The Fighting Rangers*, COL. 1935: *Only Eight Hours, Society Doctor, Shadow of Doubt, Times Square Lady, Calm Yourself, Woman Wanted, Kind Lady*. 1936: *Exclusive Story, Absolute Quiet, The Three Wise Guys* (all M-G-M); *The Last of the Mohicans* (with Wallace Fox), UA; *Mad Holiday*. 1937: *Under Cover of Night, A Family Affair, The Thirteenth Chair, Mama Steps Out, Between Two Women, My Dear Miss Aldrich*. 1938: *You're Only Young Once, Judge Hardy's Children, Yellow Jack, Love Finds Andy Hardy, Out West with the Hardy's*. 1939: *The Hardy's Ride High, Six Thousand Enemies, Thunder Afloat, Judge Hardy and Son*. 1940: *Andy Hardy Meets Debutante* (all M-G-M); *Kit Carson*, UA; *Sky Murder, Gallant Sons*. 1941: *Andy Hardy's Private Secretary, Life Begins for Andy Hardy*. 1942: *A Yank on the Burma Road, The Courtship of Andy Hardy, Pierre of the Plains, Andy Hardy's Double Life*. 1944: *Andy Hardy's Blonde Trouble* (all M-G-M).

STEVE SEKELY (ISTVAN SZEKELY) (1899–)

1929: *Rhapsodie der Liebe* (Germany). 1930: *Seitensprunge* (Germany). 1931: *Die grosse Sehnsucht* (Germany), TOBIS FOREN FILMS; *Hyppolit a lakaj* (Hungary), *Er und sein Diener* (Germany). 1932: *Ein steinreicher Mann* (Germany), *Repülo arany* (Hungary). 1933: *Piri Mindont Tud* (Hungary), ARKAY FILM EXCHANGE; *Skandal in Budapest/Pardon tévedtem* (with Geza von Bolvary; simultaneous German and Hungarian versions), *Rakoczy Marsch/Rakoczi induló* (simultaneous German and Hungarian versions), DANUBIA PICTURES; *Iza neni* (Hungary). 1934: *Ida regenye* (Hungary), *Lila akác* (Hungary), *Ball im Savoy/Bal a Savoyban* (simultaneous German and Hungarian versions), *Emmy* (Hungary). 1935: *Buzavirag* (Hungary), DANUBIA PICTURES; *Huszarserelem* (Hungary), DANUBIA PICTURES; *Cimzett ismeretlen* (Hungary). 1936: *Légy jó mindhalalig* (Hungary), *Naszut félaron* (Hungary), *Café Moszka* (Hungary). 1937: *Szenzacio* (with Ladislaw Vajda; Hungary), *Segitseg örököltem* (Hungary), DANUBIA PICTURES; *A lll-es* (Hungary). 1938: *Pusztai Szel* (Hungary), DANUBIA PICTURES; *A Noszthy fiv esete Toth Marival* (Hungary), DANUBIA PICTURES. 1939: *Két fogoly* (Hungary), HUNGARIAN PICTURES. 1940: *A Miracle on Main Street*, COL. 1943: *Behind Prison Walls*, PRC; *Revenge of the Zombies*, MONO; *Women in Bondage*, MONO. 1944: *Lady in the Death House*, PRC; *Waterfront*, PRC; *My Buddy, Lake Placid Serenade*. 1946: *The Fabulous Suzanne* (all REP). 1947: *Blonde Savage*, EL. 1948: *Hollow Triumph* (*The Scar*), EL. 1949: *Amazon Quest*, FILM CLASSICS. 1952: *Stronghold*, LIPPERT. 1957: *Cartouche* (Italy), RKO. 1959: *Desert Desperadoes* (Italy; *The Sinner*), RKO. 1963: *The Day of the Triffids* (England), AA. 1969: *Kenner*, M-G-M. 1973: *The Girl Who Liked Purple Flowers* (Hungary), HUNGAROFILM.

LESLEY SELANDER (1900–)

1936: *Sandflow, Ride 'Em Cowboy, Empty Saddles, Boss Rider of Gun Creek*. 1937: *Left-Handed Law, Smoke Tree Range* (all U); *Hopalong Rides Again*, PAR; *Black Aces*, U; *The Barrier, Partners of the Plains*. 1938: *Cassidy of Bar 20, The Heart of Arizona, Bar 20 Justice, Pride of the West, The Mysterious Rider, Sunset Trail, The Frontiersmen*. 1939: *Silver on the Sage, Heritage of the Desert, Renegade Trail, Range War*. 1940: *Santa Fe Marshal, Knights of the Range, The Light of Western Stars, Hidden Gold, Stagecoach War, Three Men from Texas, Cherokee Strip*. 1941: *Doomed Caravan, The Round Up, Pirates on Horseback, Wide Open Town, Riders of the Timberline, Stick to Your Guns* (all PAR); *Thundering Hoofs*, RKO. 1942: *Undercover Man*, UA; *Bandit Ranger*, RKO; *Red River Robin Hood*, RKO. 1943: *Lost Canyon, Buckskin Frontier, Border Patrol, Colt Comrades, Bar 20, Riders of the Deadline*. 1944: *Lumberjack* (all UA); *Call of the Rockies*, REP; *Forty Thieves*, UA; *Bordertown Trail, Sheriff of Sundown, Firebrands of Arizona, Sheriff of Las Vegas*. 1945: *The Great Stagecoach Robbery, The Vampire's Ghost, The Trail of Kit Carson, Three's a Crowd, The Fatal Witness, Cheyenne Wildcat*. 1946: *The Catman of Paris, Passkey to Danger, Traffic in Crime, Night Train to Memphis, Out California Way*. 1947: *The Pilgrim Lady, The Last Frontier Uprising, Saddle Pals, Robin*

Hood of Texas (all REP); *The Red Stallion,* EL; *Blackmail,* REP. 1948:
Panhandle, AA; *Guns of Hate,* RKO; *Belle Starr's Daughter,* 20TH; *Indian
Agent,* RKO; *Strike It Rich,* AA. 1949: *Brothers in the Saddle,* RKO; *Rustlers,* RKO; *Stampede,* AA; *Sky Dragon,* MONO; *The Mysterious Desperado, Masked Raiders, Riders of the Range* (all RKO). 1950: *Dakota Lil,*
20TH; *Storm Over Wyoming,* RKO; *Rider from Tucson,* RKO; *The Kanga-
roo Kid* (Australia), EL; *Rio Grande Patrol,* RKO; *Short Grass,* AA; *Law of
the Badlands,* RKO. 1951: *Saddle Legion,* RKO; *I Was an American Spy,*
AA; *Gunplay,* RKO; *Cavalry Scout,* MONO; *Pistol Harvest,* RKO; *The
Highwayman,* AA; *Flight to Mars,* MONO; *Overland Telegraph,* RKO.
1952: *Fort Osage,* MONO; *Trail Guide, Road Agent, Desert Passage* (all
RKO); *The Raiders,* U-I; *Battle Zone,* AA; *Flat Top,* MONO. 1953: *Fort
Vengeance,* AA; *Cow Country,* AA; *War Paint,* UA; *Fort Algiers,* UA; *The
Royal African Rifles, Fighter Attack.* 1954: *Shotgun* (all AA); *Tall Man
Riding,* WB; *Desert Sands, Fort Yuma.* 1956: *Tomahawk Trail, Revolt at
Fort Laramie, Outlaw's Son* (all UA); *Taming Sutton's Gal,* REP; *The
Wayward Girl,* REP. 1958: *The Lone Ranger and the Lost City of Gold,*
UA. 1965: *War Party, Fort Courageous, Convict Stage* (all 20TH); *Town
Tamer,* PAR. 1966: *The Texican,* COL. 1967: *Fort Utah,* PAR. 1968: *Arizona
Bushwackers,* PAR.

MELVILLE SHAVELSON (1917–)
1955: *The Seven Little Foys.* 1957: *Beau James.* 1958: *Houseboat.* 1959:
The Five Pennies. 1960: *It Started in Naples* (Italy). 1961: *On the Double.*
1962: *The Pigeon That Took Rome* (Italy). 1963: *A New Kind of Love*
(France) (all PAR). 1966: *Cast a Giant Shadow,* UA. 1968: *Yours, Mine
and Ours,* UA. 1972: *The War Between Men and Women,* NATIONAL
GENERAL. 1974: *Mixed Company,* UA.

BARRY SHEAR
1968: *Wild in the Streets,* AIP. 1971: *The Todd Killings,* NATIONAL
GENERAL. 1972: *Across 110th Street,* UA. 1973: *The Deadly Trackers*
(Spain), WB.

GEORGE SHERMAN (1908–)
1938: *The Purple Vigilantes, Wild Horse Rodeo, Outlaws of Sonora, Riders
of the Black Hills, Heroes of the Hills, Pals of the Saddle, Overland Stage
Raiders, Rhythm of the Saddle, Santa Fe Stampede, Red River Range.* 1939:
Mexicali Rose, The Night Riders, Three Texas Steers, Wyoming Outlaw,

Colorado Sunset, New Frontier, The Kansas Terrors, Rovin' Tumbleweeds, Cowboys from Texas, South of the Border. 1940: *Ghost Valley Raiders, Covered Wagon Days, Rocky Mountain Rangers, One Man's Law, The Tulsa Kid, Under Texas Skies, The Trail Blazers, Texas Terrors, Lone Star Raiders.* 1941: *Wyoming Wildcat, The Phantom Cowboy, Two-Gun Sheriff, Desert Bandit, Kansas Cyclone, Citadel of Crime, The Apache Kid, Death Valley Outlaws, A Missouri Outlaw.* 1942: *Arizona Terrors, Stagecoach Express, Jesse James, Jr., The Cyclone Kid, The Sombrero Kid, X Marks the Spot, London Blackout Murders.* 1943: *The Purple V, The Mantrap, False Faces, The West Side Kid, A Scream in the Dark, Mystery Broadcast.* 1944: *The Lady and the Monster, Storm Over Lisbon* (all REP). 1945: *The Crime Doctor's Courage.* 1946: *The Bandit of Sherwood Forest* (with Henry Levin), *Talk About a Lady, Renegades, The Gentleman Misbehaves, Personality Kid, Secret of the Whistler.* 1947: *Last of the Redmen.* 1948: *Relentless* (all COL); *Black Bart, River Lady; Feudin', Fussin' and A-Fightin'; Larceny.* 1949: *Red Canyon, Calamity Jane and Sam Bass; Yes Sir, That's My Baby; Sword in the Desert.* 1950: *Comanche Territory, Spy Hunt, The Sleeping City.* 1951: *Tomahawk, Target Unknown, The Golden Horde, The Raging Tide.* 1952: *Steel Town, The Battle at Apache Pass, Back at the Front, Against All Flags.* 1953: *The Lone Hand, The Veils of Bagdad, War Arrow.* 1954: *Border River, Johnny Dark, Dawn at Socorro.* 1955: *Chief Crazy Horse* (all U-I); *The Treasure of Pancho Villa, RKO; Count Three and Pray, COL.* 1956: *Comanche, UA; Reprisal!, COL.* 1957: *The Hard Man, COL.* 1958: *The Last of the Fast Guns, U-I; Ten Days to Tulara, UA.* 1959: *The Son of Robin Hood* (England), 20TH; *The Flying Fontaines,* COL. 1960: *Hell Bent for Leather, U-I; For the Love of Mike,* 20TH; *The Enemy General, COL; The Wizard of Baghdad,* 20TH. 1961: *The Fiercest Heart,* 20TH. 1964: *Panic Button* (Italy), GORTON ASSOCIATES. 1965: *Murieta* (Spain), WB. 1966: *Smoky,* 20TH. 1971: *Big Jake,* NATIONAL GENERAL.

VINCENT SHERMAN (1906–)

1939: *The Return of Dr. X.* 1940: *Saturday's Children, The Man Who Talked Too Much.* 1941: *Flight from Destiny, Underground.* 1942: *All Through the Night, The Hard Way.* 1943: *Old Acquaintance.* 1944: *In Our Time, Mr. Skeffington.* 1945: *Pillow to Post.* 1946: *Janie Gets Married.* 1947: *Nora Prentiss, The Unfaithful.* 1948: *The Adventures of Don Juan.* 1949: *The Hasty Heart* (England). 1950: *The Damned Don't Cry, Backfire* (all WB); *Harriet Craig,* COL. 1951: *Goodbye, My Fancy,* WB. 1952: *Lone Star,*

M-G-M; *Affair in Trinidad,* COL. 1957: *The Garment Jungle,* COL. 1958: *Naked Earth* (Africa), 20TH. 1959: *The Young Philadelphians.* 1960: *Ice Palace.* 1961: *A Fever in the Blood* (all WB); *The Second Time Around,* 20TH. 1968: *Cervantes* (Spain), AIP.

S. SYLVAN SIMON (1910–1951)

1937: *A Girl with Ideas, A Prescription for Romance.* 1938: *The Crime of Dr. Hallet, Nurse from Brooklyn, The Road to Reno* (all U); *Spring Madness.* 1939: *Four Girls in White, The Kid from Texas, These Glamour Girls, Dancing Co-Ed.* 1940: *Two Girls on Broadway, Sporting Blood, Dulcy.* 1941: *Keeping Company, Washington Melodrama, Whistling in the Dark, The Bugle Sounds.* 1942: *Rio Rita, Grand Central Murder, Tish, Whistling in Dixie.* 1943: *Salute to the Marines, Whistling in Brooklyn* (all M-G-M). 1944: *Song of the Open Road,* UA. 1945: *Son of Lassie, Abbott and Costello in Hollywood.* 1946: *Bad Bascomb, The Cockeyed Miracle* (all M-G-M); *The Thrill of Brazil.* 1947: *Her Husband's Affairs.* 1948: *I Love Trouble, The Fuller Brush Man.* 1949: *Lust for Gold* (all COL).

CURT SIODMAK (1902–)

1951: *Bride of the Gorilla,* REALART. 1952: *The Magnetic Monster,* UA. 1957: *Love Slaves of the Amazon,* U-I. 1969: *Ski Fever* (Czechoslovakia/ U.S./Austria/W. Germany/Poland), AA.

ROBERT SIODMAK (1900–1973)

1929: *Menschen am Sonntag* (Germany; *People on Sunday;* with Edgar G. Ulmer), FILMSTUDIO. 1930: *Abschied* (Germany). 1931: *Der Mann, der seinen Mörder sucht* (Germany), *Voruntersuchung/Autour d'une enquête* (simultaneous German and French versions). 1932: *Stürme der Leidenschaft/Tumultes* (*The Tempest;* simultaneous German and French versions). 1933: *Quick, Koenig der Clowns* (Germany), *Brennendes Geheimnis* (Germany; *The Burning Secret*) (all UFA). 1934: *Le sexe faible* (France). 1935: *La crise est finie* (France), *La vie Parisienne* (France). 1936: *Mister Flow* (France). 1937: *Cargaison blanche* (France). 1938: *Mollenard* (France). 1939: *Pièges* (France). 1940: *Ultimatum* (with Robert Wiene; France), HOFFBERG. 1941: *West Point Widow,* PAR. 1942: *Fly by Night,* PAR; *The Night Before the Divorce,* 20TH; *My Heart Belongs to Daddy,* PAR. 1943: *Someone to Remember,* REP; *Son of Dracula.* 1944: *Phantom Lady, Cobra Woman* (all U); *Christmas Holiday,* PAR; *The Suspect,* U. 1945: *Uncle Harry,* U. 1946: *The Spiral Staircase,* RKO; *The Killers,*

U; *The Dark Mirror*, U. 1947: *Time Out of Mind*, U-I. 1948: *Cry of the City*, 20TH. 1949: *Criss Cross*, U-I; *The Great Sinner*, M-G-M; *Thelma Jordan*, PAR. 1950: *Deported*, U-I. 1951: *The Whistle at Eaton Falls*, COL. 1952: *The Crimson Pirate*, WB. 1955: *Die Ratten* (West Germany; *The Rats*), CCC. 1956: *Mein Vater, der Schauspieler* (West Germany). 1957: *Nachts, wenn der Teufel kam* (West Germany), DIVINA. 1958: *Flesh and the Woman* (France; *Le grand jeu*), DOMINANT PICTURES. 1960: *Mein Schulefreund* (West Germany), DIVINA. 1961: *Dorothea Angermann* (West Germany), RING FILM; *Portrait of a Sinner* (England; *The Rough and the Smooth*), AIP; *L'Affaire Nina B* (France), CINE-ALLIANCE-FILMSONOR. 1962: *Escape from East Berlin* (West Germany; *Tunnel 28*), M-G-M. 1963: *The Magnificent Sinner* (France; *Katia*), FILM-MART. 1964: *Der Schut* (West Germany), *Der Schatz der Azteken* (West Germany/Spain/Italy). 1965: *Die Pyramide des Sonnengottes* (West Germany/Spain/Italy). 1968: *Custer of the West* (Spain/U.S.), CINERAMA. 1968–69: *Der Kampf um Rom* (West Germany/Italy).

NOEL SMITH (known as **NOEL MASON** until 1935)
1929: *Bachelor's Club*, PARTHENON PICTURES; *Back from Shanghai*, PARTHENON. 1930: *Heroic Lover*, GENERAL PICTURES. 1931: *Yankee Don*, CAPITOL FILM EXCHANGE; *Dancing Dynamite*, CAPITOL; *Scareheads*, CAPITOL. 1935: *Fighting Pilot*, AJAX PICTURES. 1936: *Trailin' West*, FN; *King of Hockey*, WB. 1937: *California Mail*, FN; *Guns of the Pecos*, FN; *Blazing Sixes*, *The Cherokee Strip*, *Over the Goal*. 1938: *Mystery House*. 1939: *Secret Service of the Air*, *Code of the Secret Service*, *Torchy Plays with Dynamite*, *Cowboy Quarterback*. 1940: *Ladies Must Live*, *Calling All Husbands*, *Always a Bride*, *Father Is a Prince*. 1941: *The Case of the Black Parrot*, *The Nurse's Secret* (all WB); *Burma Convoy*, U. 1952: *Cattle Town*, WB.

R. G. (BUD) SPRINGSTEEN (1904–)
1945: *Marshal of Laredo*, *Colorado Pioneers*, *Wagon Wheels Westward*. 1946: *California Gold Rush*, *Sheriff of Redwood Valley*, *Home on the Range*, *Sun Valley Cyclone*, *Man from Rainbow Valley*, *Conquest of Cheyenne*, *Santa Fe Uprising*, *Stagecoach to Denver*. 1947: *Vigilantes of Boomtown*, *Homesteaders of Paradise Valley*, *Oregon Trail Scouts*, *Rustlers of Devil's Canyon*, *Marshal of Cripple Creek*, *Along the Oregon Trail*, *Under Colorado Skies*. 1948: *The Main Street Kid*, *Heart of Virginia*, *Secret Service Investigator*, *Out of the Storm*, *Son of God's Country*, *Sundown in*

Santa Fe, Renegades of Sonora. 1949: *Sheriff of Wichita, Death Valley Gunfighter, The Red Menace, Hellfire, Flame of Youth, Navajo Trail Raiders.* 1950: *Belle of Old Mexico, Singing Guns, Harbor of Missing Men, The Arizona Cowboy, Hills of Oklahoma, Covered Wagon Raid, Frisco Tornado.* 1951: *Million Dollar Pursuit, Honeychile, Street Bandits.* 1952: *The Fabulous Senorita, Oklahoma Annie, Gobs and Gals, Tropical Heat Wave, Toughest Man in Arizona.* 1953: *A Perilous Journey, Geraldine.* 1955: *I Cover the Underworld, Double Jeopardy, Cross Channel* (England), *Secret Venture* (England). 1956: *Track the Man Down* (England), *Come Next Spring, When Gangland Strikes.* 1957: *Affair in Reno* (all REP). 1958: *Cole Younger, Gunfighter; Revolt in the Big House.* 1959: *Battle Flame, King of the Wild Stallions.* 1961: *Operation Eichmann* (all AA). 1963: *Showdown,* U-I. 1964: *He Rides Tall, Bullet for a Badman, Taggart* (all U). 1965: *Black Spurs.* 1966: *Apache Uprising, Johnny Reno, Waco.* 1967: *Red Tomahawk, Hostile Guns* (all PAR). 1968: *Tiger by the Tail,* COMMON-WEALTH UNITED.

RAY DENNIS STECKLER (1939–)
1961: *Wild Guitar,* ARCH HALL, SR. 1963: *Rat Fink a Boo Boo,* MIKE RIPPS. 1965: *The Thrill Killers,* HOLLYWOOD STAR PICTURES; *The Incredibly-Strange Creatures Who Stopped Living and Became Mixed-Up Zombies,* HOLLYWOOD STAR PICTURES. 1974: *The Chickenhawks,* STECKLER ENTERPRISES.

ROBERT STEVENS (c. 1925–)
1957: *The Big Caper,* UA. 1958: *Never Love a Stranger,* AA. 1962: *I Thank a Fool,* M-G-M. 1963: *In the Cool of the Day,* M-G-M. 1969: *Change of Mind,* CINERAMA.

ROBERT STEVENSON (1905–)
1936: *Nine Days a Queen* (English title—*Tudor Rose*), *The Man Who Lived Again* (English title—*The Man Who Changed His Mind*). 1937: *The Two of Us* (with Jack Hulbert; English title—*Jack of All Trades*), *King Solomon's Mines, Non-Stop New York.* 1938: *To the Victor* (English title—*Owd Bob*) (all GB). 1939: *The Ware Case,* 20TH (all in England). 1940: *Tom Brown's School Days,* RKO. 1941: *Back Street,* U. 1942: *Joan of Paris,* RKO. 1943: *Forever and a Day* (with R. Clair, E. Goulding, C. Hardwicke, F. Lloyd, V. Saville, H. Wilcox), RKO. 1944: *Jane Eyre,* 20TH; *Young Man's Fancy* (England), EALING. 1947: *Dishonored Lady,* UA. 1948: *To the Ends of*

the Earth, COL. 1949: *I Married a Communist.* 1950: *The Woman on Pier 13; Walk Softly, Stranger.* 1951: *My Forbidden Past.* 1952: *The Las Vegas Story* (all RKO). 1957: *Johnny Tremain, Old Yeller.* 1959: *Darby O'Gill and the Little People.* 1960: *Kidnapped.* 1961: *The Absent-Minded Professor.* 1962: *In Search of the Castaways.* 1963: *Son of Flubber.* 1964: *The Misadventures of Merlin Jones, Mary Poppins.* 1965: *The Monkey's Uncle, That Darn Cat.* 1967: *The Gnome-Mobile.* 1968: *Blackbeard's Ghost.* 1969: *The Love Bug.* 1971: *Bedknobs and Broomsticks.* 1974: *Herbie Rides Again, The Island at the Top of the World* (all BV).

MEL STUART

1964: *Four Days in November* (documentary), UA. 1969: *If It's Tuesday, This Must Be Belgium,* UA. 1970: *I Love My Wife,* U. 1971: *Willy Wonka and the Chocolate Factory* (England), PAR. 1972: *One Is a Lonely Number,* M-G-M. 1973: *Wattstax* (documentary), COL; *Visions of Eight* (Germany; documentary; Stuart directed connecting footage), CINEMA V.

DAVID SWIFT (1919–)

1960: *Pollyanna,* BV. 1961: *The Parent Trap,* BV. 1962: *The Interns,* COL. 1963: *Love Is a Ball,* UA; *Under the Yum Yum Tree,* COL. 1964: *Good Neighbor Sam,* COL. 1967: *How to Succeed in Business Without Really Trying,* UA.

NORMAN TAUROG (1899–)

1929: *Lucky Boy* (with Charles C. Wilson). 1930: *Troopers Three* (with B. Reaves Eason), *Sunny Skies, Hot Curves* (all TIFFANY); *Follow the Leader.* 1931: *Finn and Hattie* (with Norman Z. McLeod), *Skippy, Newly Rich (Forbidden Adventure), Huckleberry Finn, Sooky* (all PAR). 1932: *Hold 'Em Jail!,* RKO; *The Phantom President, If I Had a Million* (with J. Cruze, H. B. Humberstone, E. Lubitsch, Norman Z. McLeod, S. Roberts, W. A. Seiter). 1933: *A Bedtime Story, The Way to Love.* 1934: *We're Not Dressing, Mrs. Wiggs of the Cabbage Patch, College Rhythm.* 1935: *The Big Broadcast of 1936* (all PAR). 1936: *Strike Me Pink,* UA; *Rhythm on the Range,* PAR; *Reunion.* 1937: *Fifty Roads to Town, You Can't Have Everything* (all 20TH). 1938: *The Adventures of Tom Sawyer,* UA; *Mad About Music,* U; *Boys Town.* 1939: *The Girl Downstairs, Lucky Night.* 1940: *Young Tom Edison, Broadway Melody of 1940, Little Nellie Kelly.* 1941: *Men of Boys Town, Design for Scandal* (all M-G-M). 1942: *Are Husbands Necessary?,* PAR; *A Yank at Eton.* 1943: *Presenting Lily Mars, Girl Crazy.*

1946: *The Hoodlum Saint*. 1947: *The Beginning or the End*. 1948: *The Bride Goes Wild, The Big City, Words and Music*. 1949: *That Midnight Kiss*. 1950: *Please Believe Me, The Toast of New Orleans, Mrs. O'Malley and Mr. Malone*. 1951: *Rich, Young and Pretty* (all M-G-M). 1952: *Room for One More*, WB; *Jumping Jacks, The Stooge*. 1953: *The Stars Are Singing, The Caddy*. 1954: *Living It Up*. 1955: *You're Never Too Young*. 1956: *The Birds and the Bees, Pardners* (all PAR); *Bundle of Joy*, RKO. 1957: *The Fuzzy Pink Nightgown*, UA. 1958: *Onionhead*, WB. 1959: *Don't Give Up the Ship*. 1960: *Visit to a Small Planet, G.I. Blues* (all PAR). 1961: *All Hands on Deck*, 20TH; *Blue Hawaii*, PAR. 1962: *Girls! Girls! Girls!*, PAR. 1963: *It Happened at the World's Fair*, M-G-M; *Palm Springs Weekend*, WB. 1965: *Tickle Me*, AA; *Sergeant Deadhead*, AIP; *Dr. Goldfoot and the Bikini Machine*, AIP. 1966: *Spinout*. 1967: *Double Trouble*. 1968: *Speedway; Live a Little, Love a Little* (all M-G-M).

DON TAYLOR (1920–)

1961: *Everything's Ducky*, COL. 1964: *Ride the Wild Surf*, COL. 1967: *Jack of Diamonds*, M-G-M; *The Five Man Army* (Italy and Spain), M-G-M. 1971: *Escape from the Planet of the Apes*, 20TH. 1973: *Tom Sawyer*, UA.

TED TETZLAFF (1903–)

1941: *World Premiere*, PAR. 1947: *Riffraff*. 1948: *Fighting Father Dunne*. 1949: *The Window* (all RKO); *Johnny Allegro*, COL; *A Dangerous Profession*, RKO. 1950: *The White Tower*, RKO; *Under the Gun*, U-I; *Gambling House*, RKO. 1952: *The Treasure of Lost Canyon*, U-I. 1953: *Terror on a Train*, M-G-M. 1955: *Son of Sinbad*, RKO. 1956: *Seven Wonders of the World* (with Tay Garnett, Paul Mantz, Andrew Marton, Walter Thompson), STANLEY WARNER-CINERAMA. 1959: *The Young Land*, COL.

ROBERT THOM

1969: *Angel, Angel, Down We Go* (*Cult of the Damned*), AIP.

JERRY THORPE

1967: *The Venetian Affair*, M-G-M. 1968: *Day of the Evil Gun*, M-G-M. 1972: *Company of Killers*, U.

RICHARD THORPE (1896–)

1929: *The Bachelor Girl*, COL. 1930: *Border Romance*, TIFFANY; *The Dude Wrangler*, WW; *Wings of Adventure, The Thoroughbred, Under*

Montana Skies, The Utah Kid (all TIFFANY). 1931: *The Lawless Woman,* CHEST; *The Lady from Nowhere,* CHEST; *Wild Horse* (with Sidney Algier), M. H. HOFFMAN; *The Sky Spider,* ACTION PICTURES; *Grief Street,* CHEST; *Neck and Neck,* WW; *The Devil Plays,* CHEST. 1932: *Cross Examination,* ARTCLASS; *Forgotten Women,* MONO; *Murder at Dawn,* BIG 4 FILM CORP.; *Probation,* CHEST; *Midnight Lady,* CHEST; *Escapade,* INVINCIBLE; *Forbidden Company,* INVINCIBLE; *The Beauty Parlor,* CHEST; *The King Murder,* CHEST; *Thrill of Youth,* INVINCIBLE; *Slightly Married.* 1933: *Women Won't Tell, The Secrets of Wu Sin, Love Is Dangerous* (all CHEST); *Forgotten,* INVINCIBLE; *Strange People, I Have Lived, Notorious but Nice, Man of Sentiment, Rainbow Over Broadway.* 1934: *Murder on the Campus, The Quitter, City Park, Stolen Sweets, Green Eyes* (all CHEST); *Cheating Cheaters.* 1935: *Secret of the Chateau, Strange Wives* (all U); *Last of the Pagans.* 1936: *The Voice of Bugle Ann, Tarzan Escapes.* 1937: *Dangerous Number, Night Must Fall, Double Wedding.* 1938: *Man-Proof, Love Is a Headache, The First Hundred Years, The Toy Wife, The Crowd Roars, Three Loves Has Nancy.* 1939: *The Adventures of Huckleberry Finn, Tarzan Finds a Son!* 1940: *The Earl of Chicago, Twenty-Mule Team, Wyoming.* 1941: *The Bad Man, Barnacle Bill, Tarzan's Secret Treasure.* 1942: *Joe Smith, American; Tarzan's New York Adventure, Apache Trail, White Cargo.* 1943: *Three Hearts for Julia, Above Suspicion, Cry Havoc.* 1944: *Two Girls and a Sailor, The Thin Man Goes Home.* 1945: *Thrill of a Romance, Her Highness and the Bellboy; What Next, Corporal Hargrove?* 1947: *Fiesta, This Time for Keeps.* 1948: *On an Island with You, A Date with Judy.* 1949: *The Sun Comes Up, Big Jack, Challenge to Lassie, Malaya.* 1950: *The Black Hand, Three Little Words.* 1951: *Vengeance Valley, The Great Caruso, The Unknown Man, It's a Big Country* (with C. Brown, D. Hartman, J. Sturges, C. Vidor, D. Weis, W. Wellman). 1952: *Carbine Williams, Ivanhoe, The Prisoner of Zenda.* 1953: *The Girl Who Had Everything, All the Brothers Were Valiant, Knights of the Round Table.* 1954: *The Flame and the Flesh, The Student Prince, Athena.* 1955: *The Prodigal, Quentin Durward.* 1957: *Ten Thousand Bedrooms, Tip on a Dead Jockey, Jailhouse Rock.* 1959: *The House of the Seven Hawks* (all M-G-M). 1960: *Killers of Kilimanjaro,* COL. 1961: *The Honeymoon Machine.* 1962: *The Horizontal Lieutenant, The Tartars* (Italy). 1963: *Follow the Boys* (all M-G-M); *Fun in Acapulco,* PAR. 1965: *The Truth About Spring,* U; *That Funny Feeling,* U; *The Golden Head* (Hungary–U.S.), CINERAMA-HUNGAROFILMS. 1967: *The Last Challenge,* M-G-M; *The Scorpio Letters,* M-G-M.

JAMES TINLING (1889–c. 1955)

1929: *True Heaven, The Exalted Flapper, Words & Music* (all FOX). 1930: *For the Love o' Lil*, COL. 1931: *The Flood*, COL. 1933: *Arizona to Broadway, The Last Trail, Jimmy and Sally*. 1934: *Three on a Honeymoon, Call It Luck, Love Time*. 1935: *Senora Casada Necesita Marido* (Spanish language), *Under the Pampas Moon, Welcome Home, Charlie Chan in Shanghai* (all FOX). 1936: *Every Saturday Night, Champagne Charlie, Educating Father, Pepper, Back to Nature*. 1937: *The Holy Terror, Angel's Holiday, Sing and Be Happy, The Great Hospital Mystery, 45 Fathers*. 1938: *Change of Heart, Mr. Moto's Gamble, Passport Husband, Sharpshooters*. 1939: *Boy Friend*. 1941: *Last of the Duanes, Riders of the Purple Sage*. 1942: *Sundown Jim, The Lone Star Ranger* (all 20TH). 1943: *Cosmo Jones—Crime Smasher*, MONO. 1946: *Rendezvous 24, Deadline for Murder, Strange Journey, Dangerous Millions*. 1947: *Second Chance, Roses Are Red*. 1948: *Night Wind, Trouble Preferred* (all 20TH). 1951: *Tales of Robin Hood*, LIPPERT.

NORMAN TOKAR (1920–)

1962: *Big Red*. 1963: *Savage Sam*. 1964: *A Tiger Walks, Those Calloways*. 1966: *The Ugly Dachshund, Follow Me, Boys!* 1967: *The Happiest Millionaire*. 1968: *The Horse in the Gray Flannel Suit*. 1969: *Rascal*. 1970: *The Boatniks*. 1972: *Snowball Express* (all BV). 1974: *Where the Red Fern Grows*, DOTY-DAYTON. 1975: *Apple Dumpling Gang*, BV.

BURT TOPPER

1958: *Hell Squad*. 1959: *Tank Commandos, The Diary of a High School Bride* (all AIP). 1964: *War Is Hell*, AA; *The Strangler*, AA. 1969: *The Devil's 8*, AIP. 1971: *The Hard Ride*, AIP.

JACQUES TOURNEUR (1904–)

1931: *Tout ça ne vaut pas l'amour*. 1933: *Toto; Pour être aimé*. 1934: *Les filles de la concierge* (all France). 1939: *They All Come Out; Nick Carter, Master Detective*. 1940: *Phantom Raiders* (all M-G-M). 1941: *Doctors Don't Tell*, REP. 1942: *Cat People*. 1943: *I Walked with a Zombie, The Leopard Man*. 1944: *Days of Glory, Experiment Perilous* (all RKO). 1946: *Canyon Passage*, U. 1947: *Out of the Past*. 1948: *Berlin Express*. 1949: *Easy Living* (all RKO). 1950: *Stars in My Crown*, M-G-M; *The Flame and the Arrow*, WB. 1951: *Circle of Danger*, UA; *Anne of the Indies*, 20TH. 1952: *Way of a Gaucho*, 20TH. 1953: *Appointment in Honduras*, RKO. 1955: *Stranger on*

Horseback, RKO; *Wichita,* AA. 1956: *Great Day in the Morning,* RKO; *Nightfall,* COL. 1958: *Curse of the Demon* (England), COL; *The Fear-makers,* UA. 1959: *Timbuktu,* UA. 1960: *The Giant of Marathon* (Italy), M-G-M. 1963: *The Comedy of Terrors,* AIP. 1965: *War Gods of the Deep* (England, English title—*The City Under the Sea*), AIP.

FRANK TUTTLE (1892–1963)
1929: *Marquis Preferred, The Studio Murder Mystery, The Greene Murder Case, Sweetie, Men Are Like That.* 1930: *Only the Brave, The Benson Murder Case, Paramount on Parade* (with D. Arzner, O. Brower, E. Gould-ing, V. Heerman, E. Knopf, R. V. Lee, E. Lubitsch, L. Mendes, V. Scher-tzinger, E. Sutherland), *True to the Navy, Love Among the Million-aires, Her Wedding Night.* 1931: *No Limit, It Pays to Advertise, Dude Ranch.* 1932: *This Reckless Age, This Is the Night, The Big Broadcast* (all PAR). 1933: *Dangerously Yours,* FOX; *Pleasure Cruise,* FOX; *Roman Scandals,* UA. 1934: *Ladies Should Listen,* PAR; *Springtime for Henry,* FOX; *Here Is My Heart.* 1935: *All the King's Horses, The Glass Key, Two for Tonight.* 1936: *College Holiday.* 1937: *Waikiki Wedding.* 1938: *Doctor Rhythm.* 1939: *Paris Honeymoon* (all PAR); *I Stole a Million,* U; *Charlie McCarthy, Detective,* U. 1942: *This Gun for Hire, Lucky Jordan.* 1943: *Hostages.* 1944: *The Hour Before the Dawn* (all PAR). 1945: *The Great John L,* UA; *Don Juan Quilligan,* 20TH. 1946: *Suspense,* MONO; *Swell Guy,* U-I. 1950: *Le traqué* (with Boris Lewin; France). 1951: *The Magic Face,* COL. 1955: *Hell on Frisco Bay.* 1956: *A Cry in the Night.* 1959: *Island of Lost Women* (all WB).

EDGAR GEORGE ULMER (1904–1972)
1929: *People on Sunday* (with Robert Siodmak; *Menschen am Sonntag;* Germany), FILMSTUDIO. 1933: *Mister Broadway,* BROADWAY-HOLLYWOOD PRODUCTIONS; *Damaged Lives,* WELDON PIC-TURES. 1934: *The Black Cat,* U; *Thunder Over Texas* (as John Warner), U. 1935: *From Nine to Nine* (as John Warner), U. 1937: *Natalka Poltavka* (Ukrainian), *Green Fields* (with Jacob Ben-Ami; *Greene Felde;* Yiddish), COLLECTIVE FILM PRODUCERS. 1938: *The Singing Blacksmith* (*Yankel Dem Schmidt;* Yiddish), NEW STAR FILMS. 1939: *Cossacks Across the Danube* (*Zaporosh Sa Dunayem;* Ukrainian), AVRAMENKO; *The Light Ahead* (*Die Klatsche;* Yiddish), COLLECTIVE FILMS; *The Marriage Broker* (*Americaner Schadchen;* Yiddish), COLLECTIVE FILMS; *Moon over Harlem,* METEOR PRODUCTIONS. 1942: *Tomorrow We Live.*

1943: *My Son, the Hero, Girls in Chains, Isle of Forgotten Sins, Jive Junction.* 1944: *Bluebeard.* 1945: *Strange Illusion* (*Out of the Night*). 1946: *Club Havana, Detour, The Wife of Monte Cristo, Her Sister's Secret* (all PRC); *The Strange Woman,* UA. 1947: *Carnegie Hall,* UA. 1948: *Ruthless,* EL. 1949: *The Pirates of Capri* (Italy; *Captain Sirocco*), FILM CLASSICS. 1951: *The Man from Planet X, St. Benny the Dip.* 1952: *Babes in Bagdad* (all UA). 1955: *Murder Is My Beat,* AA; *The Naked Dawn,* U-I. 1957: *Daughter of Dr. Jekyll,* AA; *The Perjurer* (Germany), GLORIA FILMS. 1960: *Hannibal* (Italy), WB; *The Amazing Transparent Man,* AIP; *Beyond the Time Barrier,* AIP. 1961: *L'Atlantide* (Italy; Italian title—*Antinea, l'amante della citta sepolta;* released in England in 1964 under the title—*The Lost Kingdom;* released in U.S. in 1965 by EMBASSY under the title—*Journey Beneath the Desert*). 1965: *The Cavern* (Italy), 20TH.

CHARLES VIDOR (1900–1959)

1934: *Sensation Hunters,* MONO; *Double Door,* PAR. 1935: *Strangers All, The Arizonian, His Family Tree.* 1936: *Muss 'Em Up* (all RKO). 1937: *A Doctor's Diary, The Great Gambini, She's No Lady* (all PAR). 1939: *Romance of the Redwoods, Blind Alley, Those High Grey Walls* (all COL). 1941: *New York Town,* PAR; *Ladies in Retirement,* COL. 1942: *The Tuttles of Tahiti,* RKO. 1943: *The Desperadoes.* 1944: *Cover Girl, Together Again.* 1945: *A Song to Remember, Over 21.* 1946: *Gilda.* 1948: *The Loves of Carmen* (all COL). 1951: *It's a Big Country* (with C. Brown, D. Hartman, J. Sturges, R. Thorpe, D. Weis, W. Wellman), M-G-M. 1952: *Hans Christian Andersen,* RKO. 1953: *Thunder in the East,* PAR. 1954: *Rhapsody.* 1955: *Love Me or Leave Me.* 1956: *The Swan* (all M-G-M). 1957: *The Joker Is Wild,* PAR; *A Farewell to Arms* (Italy), 20TH. 1960: *Song Without End* (finished by George Cukor; Austria), COL.

GEORGE WAGGNER (1894–)

1938: *Western Trails, Outlaw Express, Guilty Trails, Prairie Justice, Black Bandit, Ghost Town Riders* (all U). 1939: *The Mystery Plane, Wolf Call, Stunt Pilot.* 1940: *Drums of the Desert* (all MONO). 1941: *Man-Made Monster, Horror Island, South of Tahiti, Sealed Lips, The Wolf Man.* 1943: *Frankenstein Meets the Wolf Man.* 1944: *The Climax.* 1945: *Frisco Sal, Shady Lady.* 1946: *Tangier* (all U). 1947: *The Gunfighters,* COL. 1949: *The Fighting Kentuckian,* REP. 1951: *Operation Pacific,* WB. 1957: *Destination 60,000,* AA; *Pawnee,* REP.

HAL WALKER (1896–1972)

1945: *Out of This World, Duffy's Tavern, Stork Club, Road to Utopia.* 1950: *My Friend Irma Goes West, At War with the Army.* 1951: *That's My Boy, Sailor Beware.* 1952: *Road to Bali* (all PAR).

STUART WALKER (1887–1941)

1931: *The Secret Call.* 1932: *The False Madonna, The Misleading Lady, Evenings for Sale.* 1933: *Tonight Is Ours, The Eagle and the Hawk, White Woman* (all PAR). 1934: *Romance in the Rain, Great Expectations.* 1935: *The Mystery of Edwin Drood, The Werewolf of London, Manhattan Moon* (all U).

RICHARD WALLACE (1894–1951)

1929: *Shopworn Angel, Innocents of Paris, River of Romance.* 1930: *Seven Days' Leave* (with John Cromwell), *Anybody's War, The Right to Love.* 1931: *Man of the World, Kick In, The Road to Reno.* 1932: *Tomorrow and Tomorrow, Thunder Below* (all PAR). 1933: *The Masquerader,* UA. 1934: *Eight Girls in a Boat,* PAR; *The Little Minister,* RKO. 1936: *Wedding Present.* 1937: *John Meade's Woman, Blossoms on Broadway* (all PAR). 1938: *The Young in Heart,* UA. 1939: *The Under-Pup,* U. 1940: *Captain Caution,* UA. 1941: *A Girl, A Guy and a Gob,* RKO; *She Knew All the Answers,* COL; *Obliging Young Lady,* RKO. 1942: *The Wife Takes A Flyer,* COL. 1943: *A Night to Remember,* COL; *The Fallen Sparrow,* RKO; *My Kingdom for a Cook,* COL. 1944: *Bride by Mistake,* RKO. 1945: *It's in the Bag,* UA; *Kiss and Tell,* COL. 1946: *Because of Him,* U. 1947: *Sinbad the Sailor,* RKO; *Framed,* COL; *Tycoon,* RKO. 1948: *Let's Live a Little,* EL. 1949: *Adventure in Baltimore,* RKO; *A Kiss for Corliss,* UA.

JACK WARNER, JR. (1916–)

1962: *Brushfire!,* PAR.

CHARLES MARQUIS WARREN (1912–)

1951: *Little Big Horn,* LIPPERT. 1952: *Hellgate,* LIPPERT. 1953: *Arrowhead,* PAR; *Flight to Tangier,* PAR. 1955: *Seven Angry Men,* AA. 1956: *Tension at Table Rock,* RKO. 1957: *The Black Whip,* 20TH; *Trooper Hook,* UA; *Back from the Dead, The Unknown Terror, Copper Sky, Ride a Violent Mile.* 1958: *Cattle Empire, Blood Arrow, Desert Hell* (all 20TH). 1969: *Charro!,* NATIONAL GENERAL.

ROBERT D. WEBB (1903-)
1945: *The Caribbean Mystery, The Spider.* 1953: *The Glory Brigade, Beneath the 12-Mile Reef.* 1955: *White Feather, Seven Cities of Gold.* 1956: *On the Threshold of Space, The Proud Ones, Love Me Tender.* 1957: *The Way to the Gold* (all 20TH). 1960: *Guns of the Timberland,* WB. 1961: *Pirates of Tortuga,* 20TH; *Seven Women from Hell,* 20TH. 1967: *The Capetown Affair.*

DON WEIS (1922-)
1951: *Bannerline, It's a Big Country* (with C. Brown, D. Hartman, J. Sturges, R. Thorpe, C. Vidor, W. Wellman). 1952: *Just This Once, You For Me.* 1953: *I Love Melvin, Remains to Be Seen, A Slight Case of Larceny, The Affairs of Dobie Gillis, Half a Hero* (all M-G-M). 1954: *The Adventures of Hajji Baba,* 20TH. 1956: *Ride the High Iron,* COL. 1959: *The Gene Krupa Story,* COL. 1963: *Critic's Choice,* WB. 1964: *Looking for Love,* M-G-M; *Pajama Party,* AIP. 1965: *Billie,* UA. 1966: *The Ghost in the Invisible Bikini,* AIP. 1967: *The King's Pirate,* U. 1968: *Did You Hear the One About the Traveling Saleslady?,* U.

PAUL WENDKOS (1922-)
1957: *The Burglar.* 1958: *The Case Against Brooklyn, Tarawa Beachhead.* 1959: *Gidget, Face of a Fugitive, Battle of the Coral Sea.* 1960: *Because They're Young* (all COL). 1961: *Angel Baby* (with Hubert Cornfield), AA; *Gidget Goes Hawaiian,* COL. 1963: *Gidget Goes to Rome,* COL. 1966: *Johnny Tiger,* U. 1968: *Attack on the Iron Coast* (England). 1969: *Guns of the Magnificent Seven.* 1970: *Cannon for Cordoba* (Spain). 1971: *Hellboats* (all UA); *The Mephisto Waltz,* 20TH.

ALFRED (LOUIS) WERKER (1896-)
1929: *The Blue Skies, Chasing Through Europe* (with David Butler). 1930: *Double Cross Roads* (with George Middleton), *The Last of the Duanes.* 1931: *Fair Warning, Annabelle's Affairs, Heartbreak.* 1932: *The Gay Caballero, Bachelor's Affairs, Rackety Rax.* 1933: *It's Great to Be Alive* (all FOX); *Advice to the Lovelorn,* UA. 1934: *The House of Rothschild,* UA; *You Belong to Me,* PAR. 1935: *Stolen Harmony,* PAR. 1936: *Love in Exile* (England), CAPITOL; *Big Town Girl,* 20TH. 1937: *We Have Our Moments,* U; *Wild and Woolly, City Girl.* 1938: *Kidnapped, Gateway, Up the River.* 1939: *It Could Happen to You, News Is Made at Night, The Adventures of Sherlock Holmes* (all 20TH). 1940: *South of Pago Pago,* UA. 1941:

Moon Over Her Shoulder, 20TH; *The Reluctant Dragon,* RKO. 1942: *Whispering Ghosts, The Mad Martindales, A-Haunting We Will Go;* (all 20TH). 1944: *My Pal Wolf,* RKO. 1946: *Shock,* 20TH. 1947: *Repeat Performance,* EL; *Pirates of Monterey,* U-I. 1948: *He Walked by Night,* EL. 1949: *Lost Boundaries,* FILM CLASSICS. 1951: *Sealed Cargo,* RKO. 1952: *Walk East on Beacon,* COL. 1953: *The Last Posse,* COL; *Devil's Canyon,* RKO. 1954: *Three Hours to Kill,* COL. 1955: *Canyon Crossroads,* UA; *At Gunpoint,* AA. 1956: *Rebel in Town,* UA. 1957: *The Young Don't Cry,* COL.

JAMES WHALE (1896–1957)

1930: *Journey's End,* TIFFANY. 1931: *Waterloo Bridge, Frankenstein.* 1932: *Impatient Maiden, The Old Dark House.* 1933: *The Kiss Before the Mirror, The Invisible Man.* 1934: *By Candlelight, One More River.* 1935: *The Bride of Frankenstein, Remember Last Night?* 1936: *Showboat.* 1937: *The Road Back* (all U); *The Great Garrick.* 1938: *Sinners in Paradise,* U; *Wives Under Suspicion,* U; *Port of Seven Seas,* M-G-M. 1939: *The Man in the Iron Mask,* UA. 1940: *Green Hell,* U. 1941: *They Dare Not Love,* COL. 1952: *Hello Out There* (unreleased), HUNTINGTON HARTFORD.

TIM WHELAN (1893–1957)

1934: *It's a Boy* (England), *Along Came Sally* (England). 1935: *The Camels Are Coming* (England) (all GB); *The Murder Man,* M-G-M; *The Perfect Gentleman,* M-G-M. 1937: *Farewell Again* (England), UA; *Smash and Grab* (England), JACK BUCHANAN. 1938: *The Divorce of Lady X* (England), UA; *Action for Slander* (England), UA. 1939: *Clouds Over Europe* (England; English title—*Q Planes*), COL; *The Mill on the Floss* (England), STANDARD PICTURES; *Two's Company* (England), TIMES PICTURES. 1940: *The Thief of Baghdad* (England, with Michael Powell and Ludwig Berger), UA; *Sidewalks of London* (England; English title— *St. Martin's Lane*), PAR. 1941: *The Mad Doctor,* PAR; *Missing Ten Days* (England; English title—*Ten Days in Paris*), COL; *International Lady,* UA. 1942: *Twin Beds,* UA; *Nightmare,* U; *Seven Days' Leave,* RKO. 1943: *Swing Fever,* M-G-M; *Higher and Higher.* 1944: *Step Lively.* 1946: *Badman's Territory* (all RKO). 1949: *This Was a Woman* (England), 20TH. 1955: *Rage at Dawn,* RKO; *Texas Lady,* RKO.

RICHARD WHORF (1906–1966)

1944: *Blonde Fever.* 1945: *The Hidden Eye, The Sailor Takes a Wife.* 1946: *Till the Clouds Roll By.* 1947: *It Happened in Brooklyn* (all M-G-M); *Love from a Stranger*, EL. 1948: *Luxury Liner*, M-G-M. 1950: *Champagne for Caesar*, UA. 1951: *The Groom Wore Spurs*, U-I.

FRED McLEOD WILCOX (c. 1905–1964)

1943: *Lassie Come Home*. 1946: *Blue Sierra, Courage of Lassie*. 1948: *Hills of Home, Three Daring Daughters*. 1949: *The Secret Garden*. 1951: *Shadow in the Sky*. 1953: *Code Two*. 1954: *Tennessee Champ*. 1956: *Forbidden Planet* (all M-G-M). 1960: *I Passed for White*, AA.

RICHARD WILSON (1915–)

1955: *Man with the Gun*, UA. 1957: *The Big Boodle*, UA. 1958: *Raw Wind in Eden*, U-I. 1959: *Al Capone*, AA. 1960: *Pay or Die*, AA. 1963: *Wall of Noise*, WB. 1964: *Invitation to a Gunfighter*, UA. 1968: *Three in the Attic*, AIP.

BRETAIGNE WINDUST (1906–1960)

1948: *Winter Meeting, June Bride*. 1950: *Perfect Strangers, Pretty Baby*. 1951: *The Enforcer* (completed by Raoul Walsh) (all WB). 1952: *Face to Face* (with John Brahm; Windust directed "The Bride Comes to Yellow Sky" segment), RKO.

WILLIAM WITNEY (1900–)

1937: *The Trigger Trio*. 1940: *Heroes of the Saddle, Hi-Yo Silver!* (with John English). 1942: *Outlaws of Pine Ridge*. 1946: *Roll on Texas Moon, Home in Oklahoma*. 1947: *Helldorado, Apache Rose, Bells of San Angelo, Springtime in the Sierras, On the Old Spanish Trail*. 1948: *The Gay Ranchero, Under California Stars, Eyes of Texas, Nighttime in Nevada, Grand Canyon Trail*. 1949: *The Far Frontier, Susanna Pass, Down Dakota Way, The Golden Stallion*. 1950: *Bells of Coronado, Twilight in the Sierras, Trigger, Jr., Sunset in the West, North of the Great Divide, Trail of Robin Hood*. 1951: *Spoilers of the Plains, Night Riders of Montana, Heart of the Rockies, In Old Amarillo, South of Caliente, Pals of the Golden West*. 1952: *Colorado Sundown, The Last Musketeer, Iron Mountain Trail, Border Saddlemates, Old Oklahoma Plains, The WAC from Walla Walla, South Pacific Trail*. 1953: *Old Overland Trail, Down Laredo Way, Shadows of Tombstone*. 1954: *The Outcast*. 1955: *Santa Fe Passage, City of Shadows, Headline Hunters, The Fighting Chance*. 1956: *Stranger at My Door, A Strange Adventure*. 1957: *Panama Sal*. 1958: *Juvenile Jungle* (all REP); *The Cool and the Crazy*, AIP; *The Bonnie Parker Story*, AIP; *Young and Wild*,

REP. 1959: *Paratroop Command*, AIP. 1960: *Valley of the Redwoods, The Secret of the Purple Reef*. 1961: *The Long Rope* (all 20TH); *Master of the World*, AIP; *The Cat Burglar*, UA. 1964: *Apache Rifles*, 20TH. 1965: *The Girls on the Beach*, PAR; *Arizona Raiders*, COL. 1967: *Forty Guns to Apache Pass*, COL. 1973: *I Escaped from Devil's Island*, UA.

JEAN YARBROUGH (1900–)

1941: *The Devil Bat, Caught in the Act, South of Panama* (all PRC); *King of the Zombies, The Gang's All Here, Father Steps Out, Let's Go Collegiate, Top Sergeant Mulligan*. 1942: *Freckles Comes Home, Man from Headquarters, Law of the Jungle, So's Your Aunt Emma!, She's in the Army, Police Bullets, Criminal Investigator, Lure of the Islands, Silent Witness* (all MONO). 1943: *Follow the Band; Good Morning, Judge; Get Going; Hi' Ya, Sailor; So's Your Uncle*. 1944: *Weekend Pass, Moon Over Las Vegas, South of Dixie, In Society, Twilight on the Prairie*. 1945: *Under Western Skies, Here Come the Co-Eds, The Naughty Nineties, On Stage Everybody*. 1946: *She Wolf of London, House of Horrors, Inside Job, Cuban Pete* (all U); *The Brute Man*, PRC. 1948: *The Challenge*, 20TH; *Shed No Tears*, EL; *The Creeper*, 20TH; *Triple Threat*, COL. 1949: *Henry, the Rainmaker*, MONO; *The Mutineers*, COL; *Leave It to Henry*, MONO; *Angels in Disguise*, MONO; *Holiday in Havana*, COL; *Master Minds*. 1950: *Joe Palooka Meets Humphrey, Square Dance Katy, Father Makes Good, Joe Palooka in Humphrey Takes a Chance, Sideshow, Triple Trouble, Big Timber*. 1951: *Casa Manana* (all MONO). 1952: *Jack and the Beanstalk*, WB; *Lost in Alaska*, U-I. 1955: *Night Freight*. 1956: *Crashing Las Vegas, Yaqui Drums* (all AA); *The Women of Pitcairn Island*, 20TH; *Hot Shots*, AA. 1957: *Footsteps in the Night*, AA. 1962: *Saintly Sinners*, UA. 1967: *Hillbillys in a Haunted House*, WOOLNER BROTHERS.

BUD YORKIN (1926–)

1963: *Come Blow Your Horn*, PAR. 1965: *Never Too Late*, WB. 1967: *Divorce American Style*, COL. 1968: *Inspector Clouseau*, UA. 1970: *Start the Revolution Without Me*, WB. 1973: *The Thief Who Came to Dinner*, WB.

VERNON ZIMMERMAN (c. 1940–)

1963: *The College*, NATIONAL FILM BOARD OF CANADA. 1972: *Deadhead Miles* (unreleased), PAR; *The Unholy Rollers*, AIP.

ALBERT ZUGSMITH (1910–)

1960: *College Confidential,* U-I; *Sex Kittens Go to College,* AA; *The Private Lives of Adam and Eve* (with Mickey Rooney), U-I. 1961: *Dondi,* AA. 1962: *Confessions of an Opium Eater,* AA. 1966: *On Her Bed of Roses,* FAMOUS PLAYERS. 1967: *Movie Star, American Style, Or, LSD, I Hate You!,* FAMOUS PLAYERS.

THE CONTRIBUTORS

MARK BERGMAN is a contributor to *The Velvet Light Trap*.

PETER BOGDANOVICH has directed *Targets, Directed by John Ford, The Last Picture Show, What's Up, Doc?, Paper Moon, Daisy Miller,* and *At Long Last Love*. He has written monographs on Howard Hawks, Alfred Hitchcock, and Orson Welles and has conducted book-length interviews with John Ford, Fritz Lang, Allan Dwan, and Welles. In 1973 he published *Pieces of Time*, a collection of his articles on the cinema.

ROGER EBERT has been film critic of the *Chicago Sun-Times* since 1967 and has also been published in *The New York Times* and *Esquire*. He has written the original screenplays for Russ Meyer's *Beyond the Valley of the Dolls* and *Up the Valley of the Beyond*.

545

MANNY FARBER is a noted painter and art critic. His film criticism has appeared in *The New Republic, Film Culture, The Nation,* and *Artforum* and has been collected in the book, *Negative Space* (1971). He is currently teaching film at the University of California, San Diego.

TOM FLINN is a contributor to *The Velvet Light Trap.*

DOUGLAS GOMERY is a contributor to *The Velvet Light Trap.*

MYRON MEISEL, a former editor of *Focus!* magazine, has published many articles on film for various periodicals. A contributing editor of the *Chicago Reader,* he also writes regularly for *The Boston Phoenix.* He collaborated on the feature-length documentary, *I'm a Stranger Here Myself: A Portrait of Nicholas Ray.* A graduate of the University of Chicago, he is currently a student at Harvard Law School.

CLIVE T. MILLER'S first novel, *This Passing Night,* was published in 1962. "Where They Burn the Dead," an excerpt from his second novel, appears in the anthology *The Single Voice.* He wrote *The Goldwyn Years,* a television documentary, for Kaiser Broadcasting and Samuel Goldwyn Productions, and has appeared as film critic on San Francisco's KQED. After teaching at Stanford for several years, Mr. Miller now teaches creative writing, film, and literature courses at Scripps College, Claremont, California.

CHRIS MORRIS has published film, literary, and music criticism in various campus and underground publications. Actor, poet, disc jockey, free-lance sportswriter, and publicist, he is currently studying entropy in Chicago.

ANDREW SARRIS is film critic of *The Village Voice,* associate professor of cinema at Columbia University, and author of *The Films of Josef von Sternberg, The American Cinema, Confessions of a Cultist,* and *The Primal Screen.* He has recently completed a book on the films of John Ford.

RICHARD STAEHLING is a free-lance artist.

LINDA MAY STRAWN has contributed articles to numerous magazines and newspapers, including film-related pieces to the *Los Angeles Times,* the *Los Angeles Free Press,* the *Chicago Daily News,* the *San Francisco Chronicle,* the *Denver Post, Town and Country, Glamour,* and *Action.* She was associate producer of the Academy Award–winning documentary, *The Hell-strom Chronicle.*

RICHARD THOMPSON, a University of Chicago graduate, is former Research Officer of the American Film Institute, where he supervised the AFI's Oral History program. He currently teaches film at the University of California, Riverside.

INDEX